Black Metal

EVOLUTION OF THE CULT
DAYAL PATTERSON

FERAL HOUSE

ISBN: 978-1936239757

© 2013 Dayal Patterson

Feral House
1240 W. Sims Way Suite 124
Port Townsend, WA 98368

www.FeralHouse.com

Design by Sean Tejaratchi

10 9 8 7 6 5 4 3

CONTENTS

INTRODUCTION

EVER SINCE ITS BIRTH in the early eighties—and *especially* after its rebirth in the early nineties—black metal has proven itself to be the most consistently thought-provoking, exhilarating, and vital of all the many offshoots of heavy metal. Truly enduring, it is a multifaceted beast, at once fiercely conservative yet fearlessly groundbreaking, undeniably visceral yet at times thoroughly cerebral. Its combination of primal, philosophical, spiritual, cultural, and artistic qualities have allowed it to transcend even its own fascinating controversies to become one of the most important forms of modern music. If you don't already agree with that statement, there's even more reason for you to read this book.

I first stumbled upon black metal while still at school, thanks to one of the now-infamous—and, as we shall see, influential—exposés that *Kerrang!* magazine ran in the early nineties. By this point extreme metal already dominated my listening tastes thanks to bands such as Sepultura, Carcass, Bolt Thrower, and Entombed, but this (apparently) new genre appeared almost disturbingly radical and alien—in fact, I distinctly remember one of the most vocal of my metal contemporaries warning me not to listen to it. By the time I left school he had cut his hair and sold his metal collection, which probably says it all.

All the same, at the time further investigation was surprisingly difficult; listening to music via the Internet was still a science fiction fantasy, record stores stocked little or nothing from the genre, and actually meeting people who listened to this music was a rarity, at least in a small town. But about a year later—as my attendance at school became somewhat less frequent and I began spending time with some slightly older metal fans from the local college—I was given several dubbed cassettes that would have a profound impact on my listening habits and, I suppose, my life.

During the years that followed, my friends and I—like many others—not only sought out as much black metal music as possible but also the rare interviews with the mysterious, seemingly wraith-like characters who created it. In that sense, while this tome was officially begun in 2009, in many ways its true genesis dates back almost a decade and a half earlier. From 2004 onwards I was interviewing bands on a fairly regular basis, first for a fanzine I put together called *Crypt*, and later for magazines including *Terrorizer* and then *Metal Hammer*, all of which allowed me to speak to a number of the genre's key protagonists. Even so, I've realized that a major part of my motivation for writing this book was to satisfy my own curiosity and get a more rounded understanding of a phenomenon that has entranced me since my early teens.

However, another catalyst was—like black metal itself—considerably more reactionary. As time passed and black metal grew beyond the confines of the underground, I noticed that more and more people were covering it in various forms of media, with varying degrees of care or accuracy. At one time it seemed to me that it was better not to have black metal discussed beyond its own perimeters, but by the end of the nineties, it was clear that horse had bolted. The problem was that many of the writers and filmmakers who covered black metal were either misinformed, or focused solely upon a few strong bands and personalities to the extent that they ultimately distorted the bigger picture.

I'm not suggesting that my perspective was the only right one—indeed, on some issues my opinions only formed as the book progressed—but I knew that if I attempted to cover the genre's history I would at least be thorough and keep going until I felt I'd captured the story. And while the publishers thought it would be helpful to begin the book with a few words about myself, most of all I hope I've allowed some of the individuals who shaped the genre a voice to finally tell their story about the evolution of this remarkable movement.

1
ROOTS of EVIL

WHEN BLACK METAL first began to really make an impact within the wider metal scene in the early nineties—thanks to a combination of new bands, groundbreaking recordings, and the headline-grabbing "Satanic terrorism" taking place in Norway—it appeared from the outside to be a very new phenomenon. And in many ways it was. Almost overnight musicians had converted to the cause, with bands such as Mayhem, Darkthrone, and Burzum presenting a seemingly unified and self-contained movement with a refreshing new take on extreme metal, as well a genre-defining ideology and aesthetic.

Sure, the phrase "black metal" was nothing new to metal fans—England's Venom had given birth to the term with their 1982 album of the same name, simultaneously placing themselves within, and separating themselves from, the general canon of "heavy metal," a phrase used by the rock press since the late sixties. Yet this emerging "second wave" of black metal (as it would later be known) appeared to have taken the term and given it an entirely new meaning. The gulf between this and the "first wave" seemed immense, both in terms of sound and the years that had passed between the two.

So where was black metal really born? While many have found it tempting to delve back into the history of music in order to isolate examples of Satanic or occult references, the attempts to tie such references into a neat timeline of the genre are generally tenuous at best. Did it all begin with Wagner's *Twilight of the Gods*? Or with blues legend Robert Johnson selling his soul at the crossroads?

Well, perhaps. But in more concrete terms, black metal's birth can be directly traced to the birth of metal itself. While heavy, blues-influenced rock bands such as Deep Purple and Led Zeppelin undoubtedly played an important role in this, the general consensus, and rightly so, is that metal as we know it today began largely with Black Sabbath, and in particular their self-titled debut album, recorded in 1969 and released on the auspicious date of Friday the 13th, February 1970.

Like Purple and Zeppelin, Sabbath was heavily rooted in blues rock—indeed, the debut album contains two covers of blues rock numbers—but all the same, the release was a clear move toward darker and heavier territories. Whether this album marks an absolute year zero

**It's not hard to see why the aesthetics of heavy metal godfathers Black Sabbath—
not least their 1970 self-titled debut album—did much to inspire the supernatural
and Satanic obsessions of later metal bands.**

for the birth of heavy metal is naturally debatable, but there's little doubt that it was a mile-stone recording, effectively kick-starting both the heavy metal genre as a whole and arguably black metal itself.

Setting the scene with an eerie church-bells-and-stormy-weather introduction (a com-bination that would become a very familiar part of extreme metal scene-setting), the opening, eponymous number, based around the tritone—or "The Devil's Interval"—immediately led the listener further into the dark. Despite some lighter moments, the record reveled in the macabre and foreboding, with minor-key-dominated compositions coupled with occult-fixat-ed lyrics, the devil himself explicitly mentioned in both the song "N.I.B." and the title track. As if that wasn't enough, the original record sleeve came emblazoned with a large inverted cross—not a subtle move to be sure, but a fairly effective one.

To what extent such interests stemmed from personal involvement, as opposed to lyrical playfulness or even opportunism, is still not entirely clear. An often-reported story tells that a major turning point for the band came when bassist Geezer Butler witnessed a crowd lining up to watch the Boris Karloff horror flick *Black Sabbath*, and realized that people would happily pay money to be frightened out of their wits. However, by his own admission Butler was also studying subjects such as Satanism, black magic, and occultism. And he was in good company—as the sixties ended and the seventies began, the occult was widely celebrated within rock circles, whether by stadium acts such as Led Zeppelin or more under-ground cult bands such as Black Widow and Coven.

In fact, American psychedelic rockers Coven were actually some way ahead of Black Sabbath, releasing their impressively titled debut *Witchcraft Destroys Minds and Reaps Souls* in

**Judas Priest's *Sad Wings Of Destiny*, 1976. Along with Motörhead and Black Sabbath,
Judas Priest helped cement heavy metal's identity during the seventies.**

1969 and staking their claim to many elements of the metal archetype in the process. Among
these were the use of the inverted cross and the "throwing of the horns" hand gesture, seemingly the first recorded example of either within rock culture. Now seemingly ubiquitous,
both in metal and the wider world, the latter gesture remains a sign of heavy metal devotion,
having been popularized by Black Sabbath vocalist Ronnie James Dio, who replaced original
singer Ozzy Osbourne. In another curious Coven/Sabbath twist, Coven actually boasted a
bass player named Oz Osbourne, and the album *Witchcraft Destroys Minds* opens with a
number entitled… "Black Sabbath."

   Still, though fascinating acts, Coven and Black Widow had at most a marginal influence
on black metal, which stemmed more from the heart of heavy metal itself, despite the myriad

Inverted crosses and devil horns: The sleeve for Coven's *Witchcraft Destroys Minds and Reaps Souls*, 1969, presented many now-familiar elements for the first time.

influences it would eventually draw upon. In turn, the seeds of heavy metal and extreme metal were undoubtedly sown primarily during the seventies by an unholy triumvirate of Sabbath, Judas Priest, and Motörhead.

Coming from a heavy blues rock background that was similar to Sabbath's, Judas Priest would do much to refine metal during the seventies, releasing five studio albums during that decade, all of which saw a gradual decline in blues influence while simultaneously upping the pace and aggression. Priest were also responsible for adding the now-familiar dual guitar set-up adopted by many bands that followed, perhaps the most notable being Iron Maiden. Furthermore, Priest helped refine the heavy metal aesthetic through their introduction of leather clothes, studs, and chains, elements still frequently seen in black metal bands today.

Unlike Priest, Motörhead have tended to shy away from and even explicitly reject the metal label, and to be fair, their sound is often just as close to rock 'n' roll or even punk. Nevertheless, the group would also have a huge impact on the genre, introducing a fast-paced, rough-and-ready approach that would pave the way for many of metal's more aggressive acts. As with Priest, the band are hailed directly by many within the black metal scene.

An additional and often overlooked ingredient in the birth of black metal was punk rock, specifically the British scene that exploded from 1976 onwards. Raucous, aggressive, and violent, it's arguable that until the early eighties, punk was the heaviest form of rock music available, at least equal to the aural severity of the heavy metal bands of the time. The

Sabbath Bloody Sabbath, 1973. While not necessarily taking a Satanic position in their songs—occasionally the opposite in fact—Black Sabbath were neck-deep in matters of heaven and hell during the seventies.

crossover appeal of Motörhead had helped trigger the hardcore and crust punk movements, these genres evolving hand in hand with early extreme metal. It's therefore unsurprising that many pioneers of thrash and proto-black metal would draw heavily from this source.

A final mention must go to glam metal stars Kiss, as strange as that may seem, if only for the fact that almost every Scandinavian musician interviewed here discovered heavy metal as a direct result of the group's highly successful merchandising campaign. The fact that so many bands have adopted an appearance similar to the demonically face-painted and blood-spitting Gene Simmons suggests at least an *underlying* influence, even if it's simply a trickle-down consequence of eighties groups such as Mercyful Fate.

While the seeds of black metal were sown during the seventies, it wouldn't be until the eighties that the first wave of black metal would really take form, though it's important to bear in mind that the phrase "first wave black metal," and in some cases even the term "black metal," have only been applied in retrospect. Essentially, this first wave was a very small collection of bands who pushed metal toward harsher territories in both sound and imagery, and for that reason they are frequently hailed by fans and practitioners of *all* forms of extreme metal, including thrash and death metal. Nonetheless, while it's a mistake to consider these bands *exclusively* part of the black metal genre, the work of these pioneers undoubtedly laid the foundations for the cult, and none more so than the originators of the term "black metal" itself: Venom.

2

VENOM

"Above everybody must stand Venom, who really were the first of all these bands. Hellhammer, Mercyful Fate, and especially Bathory were hugely inspired by them. I have no connection to their later catalogue but those early records, especially the first album, is the prototype for all black metal albums."

—Tom G. Warrior (Hellhammer/Celtic Frost)

"I was into Motörhead … in the beginning of the eighties and a friend of mine said that he had picked up an album that he thought would be right up my alley, and that was Black Metal by Venom. And of course it was the best thing I'd ever heard; the rawest, the toughest, the coolest, everything—the music, the lyrics—was cooler than anything else at that time."

—Necrobutcher (Mayhem)

"Venom were a big influence, probably not musically, but as a whole concept, they really went further than anyone had before. Of course Black Sabbath were doing dark music long before Venom, but they had more knowledge about it. It was maybe not just a gimmick, but maybe a little bit more than that … not for them actually, but for those who received their music, it was pointing the way for something."

—Vorph (Samael)

LOUD, AGGRESSIVE, and not afraid to offend, Venom were not only pivotal in the creation and development of "extreme metal," they were also arguably the first band for whom such a description could be considered accurate. In that context the music may seem relatively tame by today's standards, but for a time, Venom were arguably the heaviest, noisiest and most unpleasant metal band on the planet. The iconic trio did much to push the boundaries, not only with their chaotic music, but also their explicitly blasphemous approach, something that would have a massive impact on the metal scene in the years that followed.

Formed in Newcastle in 1979, the group rose from the ashes of a number of ear-

Raise the dead: Abaddon, Cronos and Mantas, the unholy trinity of Venom, up to no good in the cemetery. Photo courtesy of Spinefarm.

lier bands, most notably the short-lived five-piece Guillotine. It was at a 1978 Judas Priest concert that the wheels were put in motion for Venom's creation, when Guillotine guitarist Jeffrey Dunn, waiting at the bar for a drink, found himself chatting to a member of Oberon, another local band who were struggling with lineup difficulties. Recollections differ as to whether the Oberon member in question was guitarist Anthony Bray or vocalist Clive Archer, but either way, the meeting was highly fortuitous for all concerned. Before long, both Bray and Archer had joined the Guillotine ranks and the band name had changed to Venom, following a suggestion from a roadie. Two more lineup changes saw the addition of bassist Alan Winston and, more significantly, guitarist Conrad Lant, who had been playing in a band called Dwarfstar and was working as a tape operator at the nearby Impulse Studios.

The transition from this incarnation to the one that would become famous was relatively swift. The group first stripped down to four members when Alan Winston departed, a move that forced second guitarist Conrad onto bass, a fateful change that would see the band stumbling upon a dirty, rumbling sound that became a staple of their style and influenced many who followed.

"We had a concert in Wallsend, just outside Newcastle," recalls Conrad, better known by his stage name Cronos, "and three or four days before the concert I heard from a friend that the bass player didn't want to do it and was gonna leave the band. So I went to the studio and asked one of the guys if they could lend us the bass. We didn't have time to get another guy in and learn the songs, so I said that I'd basically just play all the root notes, and after the concert we'd get a proper bass player. But all I had to play my bass through was my guitar stack—a Marshall 4x12 plus effects pedals—and when I played the bass into the guitar stack … fucking hell, it was like, *woooooorghbwwwrooooaaaaw*, and that's how the bulldozer bass was born. After the show the other guys were like, 'Keep that, that sounds great,' so I was like, 'Okay, I'm now the bass player.'"

Two months later the band went into Impulse Studios, where Cronos had managed to sweet-talk his way into a free half-day session, and the band's first recordings were made. Revealing a noticeable influence from earlier rock and heavy metal bands, as well as from the British punk scene (now rapidly evolving into the heavier "hardcore/crust punk," a genre whose Motörhead-inspired sounds actually closely paralleled Venom's), the result was an aggressive sound that combined recognizable metal traits with a less polished approach to musicianship.

"We grew up with the rock bands of the seventies," Cronos explains, "from T. Rex to Status Quo to Led Zeppelin to Deep Purple to Judas Priest to AC/DC. But I was also a big punk fan, I loved the Sex Pistols, The Damned, The Clash, Sham 69, all that. I loved the imagery, the youth of it all. It was very much where we were mentally at that time. Living up in the northeast of England, punk was the voice for our frustration, because we were all leaving school and there was no work. But punk was over so quickly—like boom, a total flash in the pan—and the bands that I heard coming out of the back end of the seventies, the Saxons and Samsons and Def Leppards … I mean to me rock music is the devil's music, and it was like, 'Wow, this is pop music, this is *not* rock 'n' roll.' And I thought if we put the *punk* back into metal then we have a winning formula, 'cos it's about the youth, how you felt, how angry you are, and that's something we wanted to put into the music 'cos we weren't hearing it anywhere else."

Cronos' determination to make Venom stand apart from everything else happening at the time stemmed in no small part from his day job at the studio, where he was witness to an endless conveyer belt of metal musicians trying to ape other successful bands.

"Bands would come in and say, 'Can you make my guitar like Tony Iommi?' or 'Can you make my vocals like Rob Halford?' and I thought '*What the fuck…!* These are all club bands, this is karaoke,' so Venom's goal was always to be different, to create something new, and that's exactly what we did. We thought if we took all the best parts of all the greatest bands we could make the ultimate band. So we took the heaviness of Motörhead, the doomy, Satanic side of Black Sabbath, the leather and studs of Judas Priest, the pyrotechnic side of Kiss and combined it all."

While the "Satanic side" would come to the fore as time went on, it's interesting to note that despite their 1980 demo tape being called *Demon*, of the three tracks included, only one—"Raise the Dead"—dealt with anything approaching the supernatural or diabolical. The remaining songs, "Angel Dust" and "Red Light Fever," both draw inspiration from rock's staples of drugs and sex. All the same, the four members shared a taste for macabre and demonic subject matter, and the demo sleeve revealed that the group had now adopted unearthly pseudonyms. Conrad became Cronos, Tony Bray became Abaddon, Jeff Dunn be-came Mantas, and vocalist Clive Archer—perhaps most outlandishly—adopted the stage name Jesus Christ.

"I said, 'Wouldn't it be good if we weren't just called Conrad, Jeff, Clive, and Tony," Cronos laughs, "'wouldn't it be cool if we put this band together with wild fucking stage names?' and told them that David Bowie and Elton John's names weren't theirs. Mantas and Abaddon got theirs from *The Satanic Bible* [the most famous tome of Anton LaVey, founder of the Church of Satan] but I wanted something more personal. Me birthday's in January, I'm a Capricorn, my star's Saturn, and the god of Saturn is Cronos. So you see I wanted something that was mine, something relevant to me, my birthday, all that sort of crap. I thought the Father of Time would be… apt."

With this move the band inadvertently kick-started a tradition that would become almost mandatory within black metal, that of the Black Metal Persona—though Venom were perhaps more mindful to separate this from their offstage personalities than others have been.

"They are more than stage names. They are states of mind. It's sort of possession," Cronos told Gary Bushell in UK magazine *Sounds* a couple of years later. "We actually feel possessed before a gig. We start getting really angry and mad. We have to have a fight before we go on stage… it's the only way we can play."

Further adding to the increasingly theatrical nature of the band, vocalist Clive Archer began wearing face paint, something else that would become common within black metal years down the line. As it turned out, however, the *Demon* demo was not only the first recording featuring Clive, but also the last. Some months after *Demon* was issued the band returned to the studio to record six more tracks, and Jeff—or Mantas as he was now known—having heard Cronos "messing around" with vocals for a new song entitled "Live Like An Angel" during rehearsal, suggested he might also try recording them. Very quickly it was decided that Cronos' vocals were the most suitable for the job, and Clive departed amicably, leaving the band as a trio.

"The reason there was two guitars and a separate singer in the first place was that Mantas, being such a big Judas Priest fan, thought it was the best formula for the band," Cro-nos considers. "But the three-piece worked, and we said 'look at Motörhead, look at Rush—fuck it, we're a three-piece.' And the chemistry was there *immediately*. The first rehearsal, me and Mantas were jumping round like grasshoppers—there was so much room on stage not having the other two guys. We were running round striking a pose like nobody's business. There was no way that lineup was gonna change, there was so much freedom and it sounded so fucking heavy with one guitar and one bass."

The *Demon* demo wasn't exactly released in a blaze of publicity, but was fortunate enough to be picked up and championed by Geoff Barton of *Sounds*, who included the three tracks in his weekly playlist (highly unusual, as the normal form was to include songs by three different bands) for three consecutive weeks. Combined with Cronos agreeing to work extra hours at the studio, this persuaded the head of Impulse Studios, David Wood, to bring the band in to record more demos, and before long Wood had signed the band to his label Neat Records.

In 1981 the band released their first single, a double A-side comprising the songs "In League With Satan" and "Live Like An Angel." Sales proved to be surprisingly good, and Neat—seeing that they were on to a good thing—asked the band if they had any more songs to offer. Replying in the affirmative, Cronos agreed to record all the songs written so far and soon provided Neat with a collection of roughly recorded demo tracks.

To the band's surprise, those same demo recordings were released later that year as their debut album *Welcome To Hell*. By far and away the most blasphemous metal album released up to that point, it was an opus fixated on Satanic themes, its iconic cover emblazoned with Cronos' adaptation of the Sigil of Baphomet, an occult symbol dating back to the eighteenth century but made famous by LaVey's Church of Satan. If any doubt were still in place as to the band's intent, the album opened with "Sons of Satan," while other notable numbers included "Witching Hour" and "In League With Satan," whose lyrics clearly went some way further than anything that had come before in metal.

"I'm a big Sabbath fan and I sing along to Ozzy's lyrics, but it's very obvious to me that he is the tortured soul," the vocalist explains. "He's singing, 'Oh God help me!' and 'The witch is coming for me, the demons are gonna come and get me,' and I thought, 'Well, I want to *be* that witch, *be* that demon,' you know, '*I'm* coming to get you!' and that's where we came from immediately, you know, '*I'm* in league with Satan / *I* was raised in hell / *I* walked the streets of Salem / Amongst the living dead.' I'm not gonna sing about Satanism in the third party, I'm going to fucking speak about it as if I'm the demon, or I'm Satan."

Despite the sinister lyrics, the musicians involved were a far cry from the bloodthirsty devil worshippers they playfully portrayed in their songs. That's not to say that they didn't share an interest in Satanism and the occult—Cronos had been interested in the neo-pagan religion known as Wicca since going out with a girl who was interested in the subject, and the pseudonyms and cover art found within Venom's work reveal at least a passing knowledge of and admiration for LaVey's writings. All the same, Cronos chose not to draw on these subjects directly and instead wrote far more melodramatic, horror-style lyrics that drew on people's *fear* of the dark side, rather than exploring the actual beliefs and activities of genuine practitioners.

"People hear about witchcraft and Satanism and they automatically assume murders and child molesters, and it's like, *wow*. It's incredible really, since the church has such a black mark against it with priests interfering with children and so on, yet in the communities of Wiccans, druids, Satanists, there's no sign of that at all. They teach love to those who *deserve* it, so it's a real shame that people aren't educated. But since people assume all sorts of bad things when you mention Satanism, we were hell-bent on using that against them, to create something that would shock people, the same as punk shocked people or Sabbath shocked

The first black metal album? *Welcome To Hell*, 1981, with Cronos' take on the Sigil of Baphomet.

people. What we do lyrically is anti-Christian, what we sing about is the opposite of what the church says. We're not really preaching Satanism, we're just writing fantastic rock 'n' roll lyrics about anti-Christianism, lyrics that would scare the ignorant deliberately."

Even putting aside the Christian-baiting imagery, the album was an undoubtedly groundbreaking affair, the primitivism and the raw barbarity of the eleven songs making it instantly memorable. With unfussy, crashing percussion, chainsaw guitars, *that* bass sound, and vocals that were more growled than sung, the songs on *Welcome To Hell* were some of the heaviest yet encountered, a point highlighted at the time by Geoff Barton in his five-star review in *Sounds*, in which he described the album as "An epic of ugliness, a riotous noise, an appalling racket and… possibly the heaviest record ever allowed in the shops for public consumption."

Despite their trace elements of blues rock, what most obviously separated Venom from the majority of the bands that had inspired them—and in turn placed them closer to artists from the punk scene—was the chaotic nature of both the playing and the production. Geoff Barton mentioned the latter in his review when he described the album as "having the hi-fi dynamics of a fifty-year-old pizza" and "not so much laid down in a recording studio as slung together from pieces of scrap vinyl at the back of a disused gasometer."

"I was always a massive Sex Pistols fan," says Cronos. "I loved Johnny Rotten's arrogance and that the music was so 'off the cuff,' which is why when we did the recording we weren't really paranoid about the guitars being perfectly in tune, or everything being perfectly in time, it was more about the *feel*. When I was working in the studio I saw so many band arguments over timing, the slight movement of a snare drum, the slight coming in late of a bass guitar, and that's got nothing to do with Venom. Venom's all about feel and compulsion— never mind if it works on a scale or a graph. I don't want [Stephen] Hawkins [*sic*] or someone to analyze the music, I want some kid to drop to his knees with an air guitar and say, 'Yeah, this is amazing.' When we put the first album out and people were hearing glitches, errors, time fluctuations and even tuning issues, it was like, 'Oh, these guys can't play, blah blah…' and we were like, 'For fuck's sake!'"

Despite criticisms of the band's unorthodox approach, Venom were also starting to make a significant name for themselves, earning rave reviews and solid sales, something that came as a surprise not only to the label but to the band themselves.

"It was totally unexpected, as it was really an album for *us*. We weren't really in the clique of bands in Newcastle—and I know we weren't really accepted by those bands, 'cos of the mess we'd make on stage with our pyros in rehearsals. But we were having fun. We were in what we'd have probably thought of as a 'pretend rock band,' you know, writing some songs, setting off some pyros, working on stage gear, coming up with crazy names. But to find out that people were *into* what we were doing… I mean it changed the whole ball game."

Spurred on by the positive feedback they were receiving, the trio set about building upon the foundations they had laid with *Welcome To Hell*, and a year later issued their second album, *Black Metal*, a milestone that managed to give a name to an entire genre while also contributing immensely to its development. To say that the band had "matured" would probably be stretching a point, but while the gloriously anarchic feel of the debut album was relatively intact, the band had certainly refined things considerably. *Kerrang!*'s Malcolm Dome described the album as "altogether more structured than its predecessor" and Gary Bushell commented in *Sounds* that "compared to the DOA disaster area of their debut this is almost considered."

The difference in the two records stemmed largely from the fact that whereas *Black Metal* had been written and recorded as an album, *Welcome to Hell* was simply the demo tracks that the band had provided Neat following the release of their debut single. When Neat had suggested releasing the tracks as an album, the band were more than happy, but assumed

Promo photos from *Black Metal*, the timeless opus that gave its name to an entire movement.

they would be rerecording the numbers. Instead, the label issued them exactly as they were. In contrast, by the time *Black Metal* was recorded, the band had earned enough goodwill with the label to record in a way that suited them, and the increased budget produced a tighter, and far more powerful, recording.

This additional clout with the record label resulted in the band being given a week in the studio as opposed to the three days they spent on *Welcome To Hell*. The extra time allowed them to build on the theatrical elements of their music, perhaps most notably with the memorable "Buried Alive." An atmospheric, mid-paced, and surprisingly considered song, it was described by Malcolm Dome in his *Kerrang!* review as "undoubtedly the most frighteningly effective horror/rock song since the original 'Black Sabbath' number."

"Doing 'Buried Alive,' we were able to push the boat out even further and get the engineer to do mad things. When we wanted to do the burial scene I brought in a big bucket full of mud and some spades in cardboard boxes and said, 'We want to recreate this burial scene, so if we put the microphones inside the cardboard box and shovel the mud into the box then as the mud gets deeper and deeper, you'll hear the thud of the mud getting further away as the muck's coming on top of the coffin.' And this guy was like, 'Hell, yeah, fucking great!'... The people in the studio were like, 'What the fuck's going on here, you're turning the whole place upside down,' but everybody was psyched, it was like, 'This album's going to be amazing.'"

And indeed it was. Improved songwriting and musicianship along with a less noisy

Studs, bullet belts, long hair, devil horns, inverted crosses and weaponry: Venom's imagery has proved enduring—sneakers and spandex notwithstanding. Photo courtesy of Spinefarm.

production resulted in a tighter sound that allowed the songs to shine, while also exchanging some of the violence of the debut for a more foreboding atmosphere. Classic cuts such as the title track, "Leave Me In Hell," "Don't Burn The Witch," and the irresistible and much-covered "Countess Bathory" provided killer riffs, memorable choruses, and spirited performances, even if the inspiration for the tunes turns out not to always have been quite as unholy as the fans might liked to have imagined.

"Years later when I met Dave Grohl [of Nirvana, Foo Fighters, and later Probot, for whom Cronos provided guest vocals] I asked him, 'Have you ever heard of *The Magic Roundabout*, the animated children's program?' 'Cos we wrote this song called 'Countess Bathory,' which is a deadly serious Venom song and the riff is the theme for *The Magic Roundabout*. You know, 'da nana na na, da nana naa.' And I asked, is this where you pinched the [riff for] Spirit of Fucking Whatever? 'Cos it's exactly the same as the Countess Bathory riff, only backwards. He totally didn't get what I was talking about—must be an English thing!"

One *distinctly* English moment that sticks out like a sore thumb on the album even today is "Teacher's Pet," a bluesy number whose crass, tongue-in-cheek lyrics (which see the protagonist caught masturbating under the desk by his teacher) and chant of "get your tits out for the lads" showed how the group's approach differed from many bands that would claim them as an inspiration.

"We came up with a serious band with serious titles, but at the end of the day we're human beings, you know? We're entertainers. This *isn't* Anton LaVey's Church of Satan, this *is* a rock band, so having something like 'Teacher's Pet'—it was the 'wink,' you know, to show we were human. Like on the back of the first album where we had the message 'If this album is warped, scratched or defaced please throw it away and buy a new one.'"

The band's next album, *At War With Satan*, released in early 1984, would complete what most fans now regard as the classic Venom trilogy. It did so in a somewhat unexpected fashion, with a concept album based on a story Cronos had originally intended to release in book format. Given what had gone before, this somewhat more thoughtful approach turned more than a few heads, as did the fact that an entire side of the record was devoted to the opening title track.

"That again was Venom being controversial," Cronos explains. "Everyone expected another *Black Metal* or *Welcome to Hell*, another eleven songs, and I said, 'No, fuck it, let's freak them out and make one song that takes up the whole album 'cos it'll be what they don't expect,' 'cos remember," he adopts a mock-whiny tone, "'Venom can't play, they're crap.' So to be able to create a twenty-minute song was just Venom sticking a massive middle finger up!"

While the move did little to make the band a more respected entity within the mainstream, the album was once again well received by fans, and in many cases the critics too. In *Sounds*, Bushell enthused that "[Venom] top everything they've spewed forth before with a truly terrifying twenty-minute concept-epic, a real fifteen-rounder. It will definitely go down in heavy metal history as the ultimate headbang." Neil Jeffries of *Melody Maker* was similarly positive, declaring the album "the absolute, no-holds-barred, complete and utter last word in total noise/heavy metal… proof positive that Venom are the most awful/best heavy metal band in the world."

When not releasing milestone albums, the band were busy establishing themselves as one of the most over-the-top and entertaining live bands in the business, apparently regularly spending a thousand dollars per show on pyrotechnics. Unusually, the group had never known any different since—aside from a few early gigs in church halls—they had achieved enough success in their early days to avoid ever having to "sweat it in a van." While the band played perhaps their most famous shows in the Seven Dates of Hell tour, taking with them an up-and-coming Los Angeles band called Metallica, the lifestyle that accompanied this tour started causing cracks in the once-close unit, with Mantas eventually departing the band altogether.

"It wasn't really a shock," said Cronos. "The year and a half leading up to it I could smell it coming. If you ever watch [the Metallica documentary] *Some Kind of Monster* and [see] James Hetfield—that was Mantas. He just turned off. He wasn't interested anymore. All demure, all attitude. 'Have you got any ideas?' Nah. 'Any stage gear?' Nah. It was like talking to a different bloke. Speaking to him years later I asked him what happened, and he said he felt under pressure to join in with everyone and didn't want to. And I said, 'For fuck's sake, of all people, you could have had anything you'd wanted, if you'd wanted to go back to the hotel room you could have, you didn't have to fuck that chick or whatever.' I mean me and Abaddon were just drinking the Jack and getting stuck in, but that wasn't for him, because of doing all the fitness and the martial arts. In a way, it made me go the other way—I partied even harder as if to say 'Look how great this is, this life we're having, look how fantastic and happy I am.' But I think that pushed him even further. I think if I'd straightened up, been a bit more sensible and not been *off my fucking tits*, I might have been able to communicate with him better."

While Venom has since developed a reputation as a band whose members couldn't stand each other, Cronos is keen to explain that it was only around this period that things began to fall apart on a personal level.

"I thought we got on very well. From the very early days we *had to*, there was that much animosity around us and we weren't part of the Newcastle clique, so we stuck together like glue, we did everything together, it was always Venom, Venom, Venom, to do with the band. So I felt we got on well and had good communication skills, but as the career went on we went into different directions. I remember Mantas turning round and saying, 'We're all trying to get to Newcastle, it's just we're taking different routes.' We all deeply believed in Venom, we just had a different idea of what Venom was."

The band recorded one final album with the Cronos/Mantas/Abaddon lineup, entitled *Possessed*, but it was a relatively disappointing effort, perhaps inevitable given that when the band reached the studio they had no songs rehearsed. Cronos explains that Mantas was relatively disinterested by this point, and as Abaddon had never contributed much in terms of songwriting, it essentially fell to the singer to teach the other members the songs. Perhaps as a result, there's a definite chemistry missing from the album.

While Venom would release a wealth of material in the years that followed, with a variety of members—even reuniting the classic lineup for 1997's *Cast In Stone*—there's no doubt that it was their early career that really helped create the black metal movement. And of course, Venom will always be the band responsible for the term itself (alongside several others), even if the later bands that appropriated the phrase would interpret it somewhat differently.

"When we started to see people like Eddie Van Halen doing guitar solos for Michael Jackson on the song 'Beat It'—and then that song got into the *Sounds* 'heavy metal chart'— we were just disgusted to tell you the truth," concludes Cronos. "I mean I've got nothing against Jackson, but he's not heavy metal. At that point it was like we are *not* heavy metal, if Jackson's there we do not want to be in that chart... we are *black metal, death metal, power metal, thrash metal*, all of this, but *not* heavy metal. Coming up with a term like black metal or thrash metal, it was great when bands came along and used those titles. The Norwegians used the term black metal ten years later 'cos they knew they would automatically be put into a category they wanted to be in. They were like, 'This is dirty, this is nasty, this is Satanic, we're gonna put fucking corpsepaint on, sing about Satan'... they knew the black metal tag would give them an identity."

3
MERCYFUL FATE

"Mercyful Fate was really important. When I was listening to it I knew instinctively that it wasn't normal heavy metal like Queensryche you know? You can't really compare it, it had something extra, and that was the black metal extract."

—Fenriz (Darkthrone)

"Mercyful Fate do not sound very much like a black metal band as most people define black metal today, but they were very early to incorporate the occult/Satanic aspects as an important part of their artistic expression. Just listen to Don't Break the Oath, *the entire sound and production reeks of the occult! Truly a pioneering band and quite incomparable to anybody else."*

—Dolgar (Gehenna)

OF ALL THE BANDS of the first wave, Danish veterans Mercyful Fate are the furthest away, musically speaking, from what most people now think of as "black metal." First appearing in 1981, the group were fronted by vocalist Kim Bendix Petersen, who had been using the King Diamond moniker since playing guitar in a heavy rock band called Brainstorm, a move prompted by a concern that fans would have trouble pronouncing the group's Danish birth names. When Brainstorm split, Diamond had begun to search for a new band and, finding an ad for a band looking for a singer, made the bold move of attempting to "sneak in as a singer-slash-guitarist," despite having never sung before. That band was Black Rose, an outfit that allowed Diamond to not only make his vocal debut, but also to start to experimenting with the horror themes and stage show that he would become famous for in later years.

"We played several shows and got quite a reputation for the show effects we used, which were very homemade," explains the singer in his soft-spoken and eloquent tones. "An old friend was a butcher at a large butcher's factory, so we used pig's blood and guts and stuffed them into a doll, and then stabbed the doll and pulled out the pig's guts and threw them into the audience. I used to work as a lab technician, and I—you can say in a nice way—'*borrowed*' materials and made our own homemade bombs. It was stupid, it was dangerous, and it was also a lot of fun, that's how we got a reputation for having a wild show even back then."

**Desecration of Souls: Mercyful Fate live at the L'Amour venue in New York, November 1984.
Photo: Frank White.**

The inception of Black Rose came courtesy of guitarist Hank Shermann (Rene Krolmark, then known as Hank De Wank), who was playing in a band called Brats, a punk/hard rock act that had already released one album on the CBS label, aptly (if not imaginatively) titled *1980* and released that very year. The record had received mixed reviews, mainly due to the vocals, which had been performed by the bassist Yenz, and the group were now looking for a lead singer.

"Their musical style," explains Diamond, "some of it was heavy metal, some of it was punk, but when I joined we made an agreement that this was going to be heavy metal, not punk, we were gonna write new stuff and only concentrate on that. We played a few shows and recorded demos for CBS for a new Brats album and when they heard our stuff they freaked out, they told us there was *no way* they were going to release that sort of stuff, that we had to go back to this more pop-oriented heavy metal, more accessible stuff in the style of the first album. That's when me and Hank split and started looking for musicians to make our own band."

The final Brats recording, a rehearsal tape with Diamond on vocals, saw the band already heading in a notably darker heavy metal direction, with many of the songs later becoming Mercyful Fate numbers, albeit under different names. The predominant inspiration at this point was clearly Judas Priest, something Sherman himself confirmed in later interviews. Not only did the music echo that band's galloping pace, progressive blues rock leanings, intricate songwriting, and ferocious hooks, but King Diamond proved more than capable of matching Priest vocalist Rob Halford's impressive range, taking falsettos in metal to new extremes.

"Deep Purple had influenced me to try to sing like Ian Gillan," Diamond explains. "At one of our shows I remember one of our fans saying, 'You should really work on your falsetto, 'cos it sounds really cool those few times you used it.' I had no idea what the word meant, he had to explain to me what it really was. So then I started to work harder on it until I had better control of it and could hold the note and sing more relaxed, so I didn't come home without a voice every time."

While the last days of Brats may have hinted at the musical future of Mercyful Fate, it didn't prepare the world for the important change of image that would occur in the few short months between the two bands. With the need for compromise gone, the group were able to concentrate on their more occult- and horror-based interests. Diamond began using a microphone stand constructed of human femur bones, and sporting ghoulish black-and-white face paint that frequently included an inverted cross, doing much to encourage the use of black metal corpsepaint as we know it today.

Far from the first musician to utilize such stage makeup, Diamond followed in the footsteps of seventies acts such as Alice Cooper, The Misfits, The Damned, and Kiss, all of whom in turn followed the inimitable Arthur Brown, the eccentric and theatrical English rocker who sported a remarkable corpsepaint-like look around the time of his 1968 debut, *The Crazy World of Arthur Brown*.

"I used makeup [even in] the Brainstorm days," Diamond recalls. "I remember seeing Alice Cooper on the *Welcome To My Nightmare* tour, and I thought, 'If I ever get in a band, I'm going to use makeup,' not *like* him, but use makeup, because it had such an impact on me and I thought it must have such an impact on anyone who looks at a stage and sees this. To me he looked like he was not a real person, he looked like something totally out of this world, and it felt like if I could reach up on stage to touch his boot, he would probably disappear into thin air."

So it was that Fate became the first band to pioneer this aesthetic within a resolutely metal (rather than rock) context, and the group continued to break new ground, not merely using Satanic themes in their metal, but extending that interest into reality—King Diamond declaring himself to be a Satanist (probably metal's first musician to do so), and specifically a follower of the form of Satanism espoused in Anton LaVey's *The Satanic Bible*. In fact, Diamond would become one of the few rock musicians LaVey would ever have direct contact with, the High Priest even inviting Diamond to visit him.

"I was so fortunate to be invited to the Church of Satan in San Francisco and spend the whole night there with Anton LaVey… [I] spent two hours in the Ritual Chamber with him at a time when it had not been open to anyone but him. It was reenergizing energy and I think I was the only one who had been there in the last year and a half at that time. It was very interesting and we became… I can't say *close* friends, but friends that had a high respect for each other, and he reflected that in some of his autobiographies… those experiences I will never forget, seeing how serious he was about what he wrote and at the same time the aura he had, and the *humor* he was in possession of, in particular."

As with Venom, there was a significant and clear divide between the band's fantastical lyrics and genuine Satanic belief. While LaVey's philosophy was explicitly *not* based around the belief, much less *worship*, of a personified Christian devil figure, Diamond's lyrics tended to feature Satan in a very traditional role. Songs such as "Satan's Fall" depict Lucifer as an embodiment of evil, complete with glowing eyes and horns, receiving the sacrifice of a newborn child with glee, a far cry from Diamond's own philosophies.

"Journalists would always ask, 'Are you really a Satanist?'" explains the singer, "And I would answer, and I still do, 'Well, first I must know from you, what you consider a Satanist, because otherwise I can't answer truthfully.' If you think a Satanist is what is often described by Christians, sacrificing animals and you'd like to get your hands on a little baby and taste the blood then, no, no, that's insanity to me, complete insanity. That's not treating others with the respect you want to be treated with, so no I'm definitely not a Satanist. But if you're referring to the philosophy that LaVey has in his book, yes, I lived by that philosophy even before I read that book, if that makes me a Satanist, then yes I am."

While it's clear that Diamond distinguished between his own beliefs and the more traditional, horror-styled Christian concept of Satanism featured in Mercyful Fate songs, it's likely that such subtleties escaped many fans at the time. The existence of a band that could claim a link to the unholy subjects they dealt with in their music added a sense of authenticity to the genre, and undoubtedly fueled the attitudes of many bands that would follow. A line had been drawn in the sand; there were now bands who believed and practiced in Satanism and those who merely sang about it.

With all this in mind, it's curious to note that Mercyful Fate actually got their break via BBC's premier music channel, Radio One. Having shuffled ranks over a series of demos and self-releases, the band settled on a lineup that saw King and Hank joined by drummer Kim Ruzz, ex-Brats guitarist Michael Denner, and bassist Timi "Grabber" Hansen (who had played in Denner's post-Brats band Danger Zone, a band Sherman and Diamond had also participated in). The band were invited to play the Friday Night Rock Show thanks to a friend who was helping to distribute their demo, and were given eight hours in the studio to record three songs, namely "Evil," "Curse Of The Pharaohs," and "Satan's Fall."

The broadcast caught the eye of a small label in Holland called Rave-On, who invited the band to travel over and record what would become their self-titled four-song EP, often referred to as the "Nuns Have No Fun EP" after the title of the record's second song and the similarly themed cover art. The four tracks (completed by "A Corpse Without Soul," "Doomed By The Living Dead," and "Devil Eyes") find the wild solos and exuberant vocals for which the band would become known already firmly in place. Compared to later material, however, the riffs reveal a greater hard rock influence, coupled with a definite NWOBHM (New Wave of British Heavy Metal) vibe. The recording is also notably rougher round the edges than later albums, a result, the vocalist explains, of a simple lack of time.

"We did the whole thing in two days. We had so many things prepared, like backing

Melissa, 1983. Thomas Holm's haunting sleeve art perfectly complements the eerie, yet epic, nature of the music within.

vocals, solo overdubs and harmonies, but when we got there we had no time for that. Backing vocals, okay, [they said] you can have one extra vocal—well, that's not what I intended, but there was no time [for anything else]. Hank when he recorded the long intro solo for 'A Corpse Without Soul,' he gave it a couple of shots and didn't quite get it right, then the producer said, 'Okay, we don't have time for this shit, do it now and whatever you make that's what's going on, I'm sorry,' and he did the one that's on there now!"

Despite its limitations, the record met with a good reception and led to Roadrunner picking up the band for a two-record deal, the first half of which was fulfilled by 1983's magnificent *Melissa*. Infinitely slicker than the EP, yet still steeped in a unique atmosphere, the album again demonstrates a pronounced influence from Judas Priest, particularly their early albums, with both dual lead guitars and progressive overtones present. However, *Melissa* also replaces the melancholy found on albums such as *Sad Wings of Destiny* with a creepy malevolence that mirrors the album's lyrics, the frequent use of the word "Satan" still standing out today, especially due to the clarity of Diamond's vocals. From the beginning the focus is on the cruel and the macabre, the album's opening song "Evil" telling the story of a mercenary raised from the cemetery—via hell itself—to murder and torment the living.

"I learnt to write songs better down the road, to express myself better," explains Diamond. "I would get questions like, 'The song "Evil," what is that, do you stand for that, you'd like to be as evil as the character in the song?' No, no. The reason for writing 'Evil' was to have the conversation we're having right now."

Whatever the exact motives for the lyrics, the epic qualities of songs such as the title track and the eleven-minute-long "Satan's Fall" remain undeniable, and further depth is added by the classical influences that frequently come to the fore in the guitars, with long instrumental passages common even in catchier numbers such as the irresistible "Curse Of The Pharaohs," famously covered by Metallica. The album cover is also something of an understated classic, with its almost abstract, black-and-red depiction of what appears to be demonic, skeletal creature.

Interestingly, the title *Melissa* actually came from the name Diamond had attached to a human skull that was given to him, an artifact used as inspiration for the title song. Initially kneeling in front of a Satanic altar, lamenting the death of what appears to be a lover killed for witchcraft, the song sees the protagonist swearing vengeance on a priest who presumably was responsible for her death.

"That was a skull I got the same time as I got the crossbones I used as a microphone," Diamond explains. "It was actually from my brother who is three years younger than me. One of his fellow students' fathers was a doctor who was teaching medical students to operate on donated bodies, and when they finished they would strip the skin off the bones and put them in bags, and he brought some home for his son. The skull though is from an old burial ground. It was over by some cliffs which were eroding and there were churches there—actually we filmed the video for the song 'Uninvited Guest' on those cliffs—and this chalk was slowly eroding away and he found it down where the beach ends and the cliff starts, some of those graves had eroded away and just…" [Diamond makes an uncannily accurate sound of bones rattling on rocks] "… dropped down. But that skull was really odd, you could see this person had had a very heavy blow on the forehead as there was a hole, a part that had come off about the size of a quarter had grown back, so this person had not died [from the wound] and I wondered what had happened to this person. And of course it was not a witch, but I started thinking, 'Wow, imagine if this was a witch,' and then this name Melissa came up out of the blue."

With another memorable album cover (a second skull-faced and horned devil, this time depicted rather more clearly, pointing out at the viewer from the flames), the band returned in 1984 with a follow-up entitled *Don't Break The Oath*. Toning down the progressive blues rock overtones somewhat, the album, despite the addition of infrequent keyboards, proved a heavier and more aggressive listen than its predecessor, frequently entering thrash metal territory, while retaining the Judas Priest/Iron Maiden dual guitar attack. A fuller

No ambiguities: King Diamond's overtly Satanic lyrics are echoed in the cover art (once again by Thomas Holms) for the band's second album, *Don't Break The Oath*, released late 1984.

production—the result of eighteen days in the studio, as opposed to the twelve used for *Melissa*—undoubtedly gives an additional punch to the already meaty riffs, and Diamond's vocals remain hugely dramatic, his range as impressive as ever.

"I think the biggest difference is that *Don't Break The Oath* is a little bit more technical, there were more things recorded, simply because we had more time, so we could realize more ideas. There are more intricate choir parts and guitar pieces, we had a keyboard player in and that was added to a couple of songs, and a harpsichord was added to 'Come to the Sabbath,' so there were more things like that. We had bigger arrangements—it became harder to deal with mixing all this stuff—but it felt like a natural progression. Another thing that is different is that me and Michael Denner got some of our songs on the album. Together with Michael I [wrote] 'Gypsy' and 'To One Far Away,' so we got a little more involved in the songwriting."

Despite the commercial and critical success of the two albums, however, Mercyful Fate turned out to be a fairly short-lived act, at least in its original incarnation. Following *Don't Break The Oath*, Diamond departed (along with Michael Denner and Timi Hansen) to concentrate on a self-titled solo career, which continues to this day, utilizing a horror concept album formula to produce such classics as *Abigail* and "*Them*." Hank, meanwhile, formed Fate, a hard rock band that continues today, though Hank himself departed after the band's second album.

"It was simply musical differences," explains Diamond. "It was Hank, and then Mercyful Fate, the rest of us. We had completely different musical tastes suddenly. It was Hank who changed his tastes a lot and I'm not putting him down, 'cos we're the best of friends and he knows what happened. He was hanging with a certain crowd and there was a lot of disco stuff and watching funk bands, and he wanted to incorporate some Mother's Finest-style funk into what we were doing and also make it a little poppy. We had a meeting and were presenting demos to each other and that was when we got a shock. Because Hank was a prankster—a few of us liked to play pranks on each other—and we thought it was a prank, like, 'Okay, play the real stuff now, this is kinda funny, but come on now.' And he was dead serious. And it was like, 'You're kidding? What the hell are you thinking of?' Well, his intention was that maybe me and Michael Denner could write the music for one side—the 'Mercy side'—and he would write the music for the other side, the Fate side. Like two different bands. *Are you kidding?* I would never do that, that would be like pissing on myself and my fans, I'm never going do something I couldn't believe in. And it was the same from his side. So we parted on good terms. It would be no good if any of us were prostituting ourselves."

The band would eventually reform in 1992, with all of the original lineup save for drummer Ruzz appearing on 1993's *In The Shadows*, an album that also saw Metallica's Lars Ulrich (a longtime fan and fellow Dane) handling the drums on a rerecording of the demo-era song "Return Of The Vampire." Two more albums, *Time* and *Into The Unknown* (1994 and 1996), were recorded minus bassist Hansen, and two more, *Dead Again* and *9* (1998 and 1999) following the departure of Denner, before the band finished activities once again. More recently, the popularity of the hugely successful video game franchise *Guitar Hero* caused a resurrection of the "classic lineup" (again minus drummer Ruzz) to rerecord tracks "Evil" and "Curse of the Pharaohs" for *Guitar Hero: Metallica* since the original masters had been lost. Still, while the later output is well worth further investigation, there is no doubt that it was primarily the band's first three official releases that really changed the metal world, and contributed to the slowly emerging black metal scene.

4
BATHORY

"Bathory had a unique sound to them, totally. They always got the worst marks in the reviews, but they were maybe the most important band for the second wave of black metal. They were obscure, Satanic, they had a shit sound, a very cold production and the vocals were different to what everyone else was doing."

—Apollyon (Aura Noir, Dødheimsgard)

"I'd say it was Venom who created black metal [but] the prototype of today's black metal was created by Bathory."

—Mirai (Sigh)

"If anyone says they are into black metal, but do not know or like Bathory, they do not know what black metal is or where it came from. Sure Venom and Hellhammer were important as well, but Bathory defined the sound of black metal as it is known today."

—Dolgar (Gehenna)

THE IMMENSE SIGNIFICANCE of Swedish legends Bathory within the black metal scene cannot be overstated. Of all the bands in the first wave it was Bathory who had the biggest part to play in creating a template both musically and aesthetically, and for a time they took Venom's position as the heaviest, darkest metal band in existence.

Whether or not the band were *inspired* by Venom is a question that has been floating around almost since their inception, even though such influence was passionately denied by the band's creative force Tomas Forsberg—better known to the metal world by his nom-de-plume Quorthon—right until his untimely death in June 2004. Given the similar qualities of the band's early recordings, such a claim may seem difficult to believe, although it's also worth noting that the two bands were painting from a very similar palette of influences, namely Motörhead, British punk, and of course, Black Sabbath.

It was in 1983 (1 p.m. on March 16 in fact, according to the official Bathory website) when the three founding members—Quorthon, Jonas "Vans McBurger" Åkerlund, and Fredrick "Freddan" Hanoi—first met. Jonas and Frederick were cousins who had played together for some time (most notably in a band called Die Cast), whilst Quorthon also had some previous experience, having played in two other bands, Agnosticum and Stridskuk. The three young men met via an ad for local musicians placed inside a music store in Stockholm, and wasted no time in getting down to work, rehearsing for the first time on the very day of their meeting.

"It was very popular at the time to form bands, it was just what everybody did," begins Jonas, who was eighteen at the time. "We would change names every week, we tried all combinations and styles. It was me and the bass player, who was my cousin, we were looking for a guitarist, to be a three-piece. We had the idea to play really, really fast metal and, like everybody else back then, we put our little advert in the record store where you had all the instruments. [Quorthon] called us and our rehearsal studio was not too far away, so we went straight there to try it out."

Right from the start, Quorthon adopted a commanding role within the band, supplying all the material, much of which he had written before meeting his new bandmates. Years later on the official Bathory website, Quorthon would describe Bathory as an attempt to "amalgamate the gloom of Black Sabbath, sound of Motörhead and the newly found frenzy of GBH," the latter being one of a number of pioneering English hardcore punk bands active at the time whose efforts were pushing into similarly "extreme" territories.

"The bass player was very much into Motörhead," explains Jonas, "I was very much into Sabbath and we were all impressed by the punk rock scene and playing fast, but it felt like [Quorthon] always had the vision anyway, his ideas came forward from the first time that we played. The thing with Quorthon was that he wrote all the music and had been writing songs for *forever*, so he came with a catalogue of stuff. He was already banging it, on the very first day we started playing those songs. He brought so much to the table, because he was a genius musician. We really weren't used to playing with someone like him, so he brought up the level to a higher scale than we were used to. He was a very different kind of guy, his creativity didn't come from listening to other people. His creativity came from inside in a weird way."

"He was kind of an isolated guy, and had this music within him, which just poured out," he continues, "and he was a very good guitarist—he played very, very fast and he had his own style and his own sound. There were a lot of things I never found out about him. We never really talked about other music, because once we started it was all about us, and where we wanted to go with it. It slowly became darker and darker and faster and faster. It felt like it was a completely different era; the combination of the punk rock and the dark bands like Sabbath and Quorthon's guitar playing, it kinda fell into place in a way. But it wasn't really the kind of music anyone else played at the time, especially in Sweden, there was a completely different scene going on."

The band played a few shows in Stockholm—something that was easy to do, as Jonas explains, because of the strong live scene in the city at the time—but their unique material failed to find much of a following. Fortunately for them, they had a personal connection that would aid them immensely in their attempts to reach a wider audience, namely one Borje "Boss" Forsberg, who was working at the time for the record label Tyfon Grammofon. While Quorthon maintained vehemently throughout his life that Boss was in no way related to him, it is generally believed that he was, in fact, Quorthon's father. Certainly it cannot be denied that it was Boss who was responsible for giving Bathory their big break, allowing the then-unknown group to contribute two tracks to the 1984 compilation album *Scandinavian Metal Attack*, alongside more melodic and commercial Swedish heavy metal acts such as Oz and Trash.

"We had an 'in,' 'cos a relative of Quorthon had a connection," explains Jonas, "It wasn't like we were shopping round for a record deal. Boss was involved in some other bands that were way bigger than us at the time, so we were like the little 'sideshow' really, but he was involved with Bathory from the beginning. That [recording for the compilation] was the real deal though, a proper studio, the whole thing. We were all pretty young, we had recorded a lot before, but not like that. I don't remember paying for it… the other bands that were recording—the bigger bands—we went in [the studio] on their spare hours. When they were finished for the evening we would go in and record."

A combination of the unrelenting raw brutality of hardcore punk bands such as Discharge and GBH, and the dark atmosphere and sinister lyrics that had been touched upon by Venom and Mercyful Fate, the two tracks Bathory contributed ("Sacrifice," and "The Return of Darkness and Evil") were instantly recognized as something new. Arguably a step beyond what any metal band had recorded at that point, they thus took the underground (or at least those who heard the compilation) by storm.

"A friend of mine bought *Scandinavian Metal Attack* and the first time I heard it I couldn't believe my ears," explains Necrobutcher of Norway legends Mayhem. "We hadn't heard the techniques that he was using, singing through the guitar microphone to create this effect on his voice, how fast the music was, what the lyrics were about… we were just blown away."

Listening to the recordings today, there's no doubt that the material has a undeniable Motörhead/Venom swagger about it, but also that it was taking things a stage further than anything those bands had done at the time, thanks in no small part to the notably harsher, more guttural vocals. While Satanism, according to Jonas, was not initially a big part of the concept of the band, by the time these two songs were recorded it had become a dominating theme, as evidenced in the lyrics to "Sacrifice," which describe the raping of the mother of Christ, the spreading of darkness on earth, and the sacrifice of angels to the Lord of Hell.

Not long after the release of the compilation, Jonas and his cousin began to drift away from Bathory, moving from Sweden to stay in London for a while. Jonas also discovered a career in film, one that would eventually lead him to create full-length features, advertisements, and also music videos for the likes of Madonna, Metallica, and even Norwegian black metal act Satyricon. Coincidentally, one of his first efforts was a video for Swedish doom metal band Candlemass, and featured a young Per Ohlin—future singer of Mayhem—as a zombie extra. Despite his work in film, Jonas maintained contact with Quorthon, and still speaks of him with admiration today.

"I knew he [Quorthon] was going to keep going, then slowly my film interests grew and that felt way more natural to me. I wasn't that good of a drummer but I realized early that I was pretty good at editing film, so I never regretted that [decision]. He didn't really *need* any other musicians, because he was so talented he could do it all himself. I mean the one thing that we knew was that Quorthon had tremendous star quality, and that he was a very gifted musician. That was very, very clear… It was a good ten years before I realized what Bathory had become though. I see people with the goat head tattooed on them now—we had that very, very early, I think I had that on my bass drum, I don't remember, but I think I did—and I mean, who would have thought that would happen back then?"

Though the first lineup of the band was dissolving, *Scandinavian Metal Attack* had earned the band rave reviews and Quorthon decided to build on the buzz by recording a debut album. He hired Rickard "Ribban" Bergman, who had played in Stridskuk, as well a new drummer called Stefan Larsson whom he'd heard playing on a tape by a band called Obsklass. The result of the three young men's hard work was a self-titled album that would ignite the metal underground. Released via Black Mark Productions—a sub-label of Tyfon Grammofon set up especially for the release (with a "666-1" serial number no less)—the album's cover was emblazoned with the now-familiar goat's head design. Though Quorthon is credited on the Bathory homepage, the image was in fact taken from a drawing by American illustrator Joseph Smith, and has become one of the most iconic images within black metal today. The reverse of the record was illustrated by a large pentagram.

Aesthetically speaking, the sleeve had much in common with the early Venom releases, with one important difference: a complete absence of band photos. This, coupled with the fact that only Quorthon and Boss were mentioned on the sleeve, meant that the element of mystery and anonymity had now well and truly been added to the black metal formula, a mystery made easier to retain due to the decision to keep the band as a studio-only project. While Bathory *wasn't* a one-man band, due to the use of session musicians, it was largely assumed that this was the case. Quorthon later explained on his website that both he and the record label believed it would confuse matters to include the names of "hired guns" in the credits and indeed, even *Kerrang!* stated: "So who is Bathory? No-one knows for sure, but its pretty well ascertained that this… is the work of a fellow called Quorthon. He wrote and played all the instruments on all the songs, as well as co-producing."

Prior to Bathory, one-man bands were pretty much unheard of within metal and there can be little doubt that the common perception of Bathory as a one-man outfit hugely le- gitimized the concept of the solo-driven, studio-only black metal band. It's interesting to

Bathory's self-titled debut, featuring one of the most iconic designs in the genre's history.

note just how many later bands in the movement, from Norway's Burzum and Isengard to America's Xasthur and Leviathan, would adopt this setup, something still largely unheard of in the thrash and death metal scenes.

Of course, if the actual music hadn't delivered, such innovations would have been largely ignored. Thankfully, the eight songs on the album—bookended by two ambient pieces, including a *three-minute-long* Sabbath-esque storm and bells introduction—more than impressed fans. Continuing in a similar vein to the *Scandinavian Metal Attack* recordings, but increasing in both speed and aggression—a point highlighted by the rerecorded version of "Sacrifice," which clocked in at a minute shorter than the original—the songs were aided by a more distorted and punchier sound, the combination of buzz saw guitars, pounding drums, and growled vocals proving a breathtaking formula.

Reviews in the press were, predictably, somewhat mixed. UK magazine *Metal Forces*

Quorthon interviewed in *Kick Ass* fanzine in 1985. "I'm not a fan of Venom at all, though I love the 'Black Metal' album...I thank them for what they have done for the Satanic-based metal movement of today."

gave the album a glowing review, with Dave Constable describing it as "the ultimate in total death," and a mix of the "total raw sound of hardcore punk re DISCHARGE etc with metallic riffs at high speed, such as SLAYER at full throttle… so intense that even the most ardent San Fransiscan [sic] thrasher would have problems keeping up." *Kerrang!* was less enthusiastic, complaining that "the worse this Satanic rubbish sounds, the faster it is and the more out of tune it is, the better it sells—this is obviously going to sell like crazy," and concluding that "Satan should have a word with these boys, they're giving him a real bad name."

One thing the press did agree on were the startling similarities to Venom, a feeling that had no doubt been emphasized by the fact that one of the Newcastle trio's more popular songs was entitled "Countess Bathory." The accusations clearly aggravated Quorthon, who claimed that it was only *after* the release of the debut album that he picked up on Venom and other new acts such as Hellhammer. He argued on the Bathory website that the only impact this exposure had was to "deepen" the Satanic aspect of the band to make it more sincere and less in the style of horror comics or vampire fiction.

If Quorthon *didn't* hear the *Black Metal* album before recording the debut, one might have to assume some higher power was at work as not only do both albums have songs entitled "Sacrifice," but the lyrics to Bathory's "Raise The Dead" and the third song from Venom's *Black*

'Second album *The Return*, 1985, introduced what is probably the very first example of the black metal sound as we know it today. This particular copy belongs to one of the band's most significant fans, Fenriz of Darkthrone.'

Metal, "Buried Alive" (which actually bleeds straight into a track entitled "Raise The Dead"), are startlingly similar, both describing being buried alive and explicitly including mention of a "gasp for air," a "tear at the lid," and the promise that the victim will arise again from the dead.

Certainly there *is* some evidence that Quorthon was a fan of the band's second album. In a 1985 interview in U.S. magazine *Kick Ass*, he commented, "I'm not a fan of Venom at all, though I love the *Black Metal* album," before going on to explain, "I must have been the first maniac to know about Venom in Sweden. Cronos has done a lot for this evil thing and I thank him for that, but he didn't inspire me to sing this way as some think."

Whether "deepening the Satanic aspect" was the only impact Venom had on the band, we shall never know for sure. Either way, the 1985 follow up, *The Return...*, was indeed a darker, heavier, and more Satanic album than its predecessor, and one that had much less in common with Venom. Songs such as "Total Destruction," "Possessed," and "Born For Burning" (dedicated to one Marrigje Ariens, burned as a witch in the sixteenth century) were markedly ahead of the debut in terms of production, performance, and sheer power. Well-received by critics, underground metal fanzines, and fans, the release generated impressive sales, especially considering its more extreme nature.

Indeed, aside from one track—"Bestial Lust"—the album had reduced the rock 'n' roll overtones present in the debut, making the Venom and Motörhead comparisons less relevant and leaving a collection of nastier and more punishing songs that some consider to be the first "true" black metal album. And if *The Return…* didn't create the black metal sound as we know it today, the album that followed it two years later undoubtedly did.

In 1987, Bathory issued the masterful recording that would finally make the frequent comparisons to their contemporaries utterly irrelevant. It was an opus that would show little or no traces of the rock 'n' roll influences originally present within the band, instead pioneering a darker and *colder* direction, one that presented many hallmarks now common within black metal music, including lightning-fast tempos, primitive-sounding production, raspy vocals, Satanic lyrics, hypnotic song structures, and even the occasional use of keyboards.

"*Under The Sign Of The Black Mark* had such a cold atmosphere, so fucking, freezing cold," explains ex-Mayhem vocalist Maniac. "Of course you had the Satanic lyrics, but there was something within the *music* that was really capturing me, it was really cold, sometimes even scary, and it just nailed something there with the whole sound of it. It's always very hard to talk about how music influences you, but it set off an avalanche of emotions, it was like Quorthon actually managed to give sound to something that was inside of you, in a very appropriate way. There was an eerie gloom there that was overwhelming."

By the time this third album was released, the metal world had become a very different place from the one in existence when the band formed, and the thrash metal scene was officially big news. Having begun as a resolutely underground movement, bands such as Metallica were now achieving strong sales, and the previous year had seen the release of the famous *Master of Puppets* album, as well as the equally iconic *Reign In Blood* by California hell-raisers Slayer. Fast, aggressive metal was now becoming relatively commonplace, a total contrast to the situation only three or four years before.

Nonetheless, with *Under the Sign of the Black Mark*, Bathory offered a musical creation of then-unparalleled darkness. Sure, there were other albums that contained unrelenting percussive bombardments, rabid vocals, and malevolent riffing, but where the album differed from the majority of similarly violent metal records of the time was in its hellish, unearthly atmosphere. Unlike the frantic guitar work of, say, Slayer, whose frequent riff changes would be adopted by the death metal movement in the years to come, for the most part the songs on *Under The Sign* utilized repetition and minimalism as their primary weapons, building tension with a mesmerizing effect.

"The eighties was a decade in the metal [scene] where everything was compact, there

1987's *Under the Sign of the Black Mark*: the final chapter in Bathory's Satanic/black metal trilogy.

was no monotony," comments Fenriz of Norway's Darkthrone. "If you played a riff four times, that was it, you move onto the next riff. Ninety-nine percent of the albums were like that. Then came Bathory, with *Under the Sign of the Black Mark*."

The gloomy, cavernous sound and restrained musicianship remain key factors in the album's appeal, the pounding and unfussy drums beating their way into the listener's consciousness in almost ritualistic fashion, nearly threatening to drown out the malevolent guitar lines and the screamed, demonic-sounding vocals. The finishing touch is the eerie synths that are used sparingly, but effectively, perhaps most notably on "Woman Of Dark Desires," an ode to the murderous Countess who inspired the band's name.

"I remember listening to [*Under the Sign*] every morning on my way to the high school," explains Mirai of Japanese black metal act Sigh. "Personally the use of keyboard was a huge factor. Of course there were several thrash metal records with keyboards, but the way Quorthon used it was totally different from others. Back then nobody came up with the idea to use the keyboard to sound eerie or sinister."

Vorph of Switzerland's Samael is another musician who was significantly inspired by the use of keys on the album. "It was an incredible experience to listen to *Under the Sign*, as he was using some synthesizer, which was not common in that sort of music at the time and certainly that influenced [Samael] to have a keyboard later … it showed that you can have a lot of different ambiences and still keep the heaviness."

"Eerie and heavy" aptly summarizes this diabolical opus, yet despite its creative and commercial success, the record would turn out to be the final part of what is frequently described as Bathory's "Satanic trilogy." For Quorthon the interest in Satanism appears to have been predominantly related to thematic inspirations for Bathory (and perhaps as an expression of anti-Christian sentiments and rebellion), as opposed to any kind of personal faith, as the man himself explained on the Bathory website:

"We were just three shit kids aged seventeen/eighteen. We didn't know a shit about life or death, let alone the stuff that metal and rock lyrics seemed to be made from. We'd never get to fuck bombshell bimbos, we'd never get to party all night long … We really couldn't relate to those lyrics. We'd certainly listen to those NWOBHM albums, but when it came to write lyrics for our own material, we just picked up from the sources we thought seemed most graphic or effective … picking up the dark and evil themes was not a stand taken, a point of view made official, or a personal ideology expressed… It was quite simply… to irritate and to annoy those above-all know-all Christians, the church itself and the dictatorial Christian faith on a whole."

After the completion of *Under the Sign*, Quorthon decided to steer the band into a completely new era, and in doing so helped to create another metal subgenre, Viking metal. Building upon the epic riffs that had appeared here and there on *Under the Sign*, and combining these with classical musical influences, Bathory's fourth album, 1988's *Blood Fire Death*, began a second trilogy, an era Quorthon described as the "pre-Christian Swedish Viking era."

Such a description seems to underline his motives for the shift; by incorporating Scandinavian folklore and religion Quorthon was able to integrate his interest in national history while also continuing to voice his opposition to Christianity. If any doubt remained about the latter, eagle-eyed fans were able to locate "hidden" messages in two of the songs, "The Golden Walls of Heaven" and "Dies Irae," by taking the first letter of each line of lyrics, thus spelling out the words "Satan" and "Christ the bastard son of heaven" respectively.

Ideologies aside, this lyrical shift sat well with the increased interest in classical music that Quorthon had picked up thanks to Paul "Pålle" Lundberg, the drummer on *Under the Sign*, who was more interested in the great symphonies, Kiss, and Bowie than he was extreme metal. This, along with the good reception that the classic mid-paced number "Call From The Grave" received, had persuaded Quorthon to move toward rather more bombastic, epic territories. And what better subject matter for such music—especially given the apparent musical influence of Wagner, a composer who based much of his work on the Norse sagas—than these equally epic tales from Northern Europe?

As it turned out, *Blood Fire Death* was only a gentle evolution from its predecessor, maintaining the high pace and ferocious vocals despite introducing emotive acoustic guitars and clean, almost chanted, vocals. It was *Hammerheart*, released two years later in 1990, that *really* created the blueprint for what became the Viking metal genre, with numbers such as "One Rode To Asa Bay" featuring strong melodies, a heroic atmosphere, predominantly clean vocals, and pounding, mid-paced rhythm. The album directly inspired the sound, concept, and aesthetic of many later bands of the genre, such as Germany's impressive Falkenbach.

Though Bathory had departed black metal territory to some extent, the Viking trilogy would still have a marked impact on much of the scene, both with its heroic overtones and its use of pre-Christian spirituality and culture. Bathory would also have the dubious honor of becoming the first in a long line of bands from the black metal scene to be accused of Nazi sympathies. *Hammerheart* raised eyebrows with its use of the sun-cross, while *Twilight of the Gods* fell into considerable hot water upon its release, due to the song "Under The Runes," which partly related to Germany's SS, the SS insignia utilizing two "Sig" runes, hence the titular reference. This, coupled with the sleeve art's use of a sun wheel, an ancient symbol appropriated by right-wing groups since the Second World War, led many to question and reassess the band's use of Scandinavian themes.

While clearly not too concerned with the accusations, Quorthon nonetheless maintained that he was by no means a Nazi. For the rest of his career the only controversies that followed him were down to his musical decisions, with later albums such as *Octagon* departing from both the black metal and Viking styles, much to the horror of many fans.

Of Bathory's twelve albums, there's little doubt that it was only the first six that had significant relevance within black metal. It is therefore testimony to the lasting power of Quorthon's vision that his premature death in 2004 was almost universally lamented within the scene, with fanzines, magazines, and bands paying tribute to the departed legend.

"I never bought any of his music after *Hammerheart*," concludes Mayhem's Necrobutcher. "But when he passed away, it was like something was missing, so I think Bathory was more important to me than I had remembered. … It *showed us the way*, more than inspired us musically, it was a new boundary broken with that band."

5
HELLHAMMER

"The demos were just so raw... I was like, 'Yeah, this is what I've been searching for.'"
—Black Winds (Blasphemy)

"Hellhammer were one of my favorite bands due to the really dark atmosphere they were creating, an unfamiliar gloomy atmosphere that maybe they were the first to do and which spoke straight to your heart."
—Sakis (Rotting Christ)

"A band that did very little, but did it so good. Their approach to raw metal was so stripped down to the basic elements, very few managed to match it. I feel that with many of the riffs that they and Celtic Frost delivered ... you can't really make as heavy [a] riff without simply stealing."
—Mikko Aspa (Clandestine Blaze)

HAILING FROM the somewhat unlikely location of Birchwil, Switzerland, the short-lived but utterly incendiary Hellhammer—along with Celtic Frost, the band who would later rise from their ashes—complete the handful of essential first-wave black metal pioneers. As early progenitors of extreme metal, they have, like Venom and Bathory, inspired numerous metal subgenres, yet it is black metal to which they are most closely aligned and their influence on the movement still resonates clearly today.

The story of Hellhammer is, without a doubt, inseparable from that of its founder, vocalist, and guitarist Tom Gabriel Fischer, better known to the world as Tom G. Warrior. To him the band owes not only its existence, but also its dark and uncompromising nature, which reflects his musical technique and then-limited level of ability, as well as a personality shaped by the severe conditions of his youth.

"I had a regular childhood until I was six years old," Tom explains in his faultless and carefully measured English. "My parents then decided to divorce, and my mother took from the divorce a fantastic record collection. We moved to a tiny farm village of 1,500 inhabitants and my mother put the key around my neck and said, 'You're on your own now, I'm going to smuggle diamonds and watches over the world and you're going to be alone for weeks on end.' So that little six- or seven-year old kid was left at home with no relatives, no friends, no nothing, in a village he didn't know. The only thing I had was this record collection, so basically music became my best friend, that's how it all started. I totally turned to music, I found my sanctuary there, it became my universe.

"Later my mother gradually drifted into insanity and the living conditions in my home became unbearable. I became trapped. There was no family and because I was an outcast and the village was so small, everybody knew about my background and the other young people decided I was going to be the perfect punching bag, being all alone with no brothers or sisters, no father. So I encountered drastic violence every day in that village in my teenage years. Nobody gave a shit. Nowadays in a politically correct society everybody jumps at the chance to help somebody and you read about cases like this in the newspaper, but at that time— mid-1970s, tiny farm town—nobody really gave a shit. The teachers actually sided with the young people who put the violence on me and the farmers made me even more outcast with their comments and their reactions toward me. At home my mother acquired ninety cats that lived in a confined space, the same space I inhabited. I grew up in feces, urine, cockroaches, tapeworms, and maggots for years and when I stepped outside I was beaten violently—that was my youth and this is the direct link [to] why Hellhammer even existed. I'm not telling this to tell a tear-jerking story, it's simply the background to why my music became so dark. Why a little kid from Switzerland—not really a rock 'n' roll country—plays music that barely even exists yet. That music was a reflection of my life at the time."

As Tom matured, his musical tastes moved toward the heavier end of the spectrum, and after following bands such as British heavy metal act UFO, he became a huge fan of the emerging NWOBHM movement. Given a financial reward for finishing high school by a distant relative ("I think it was some sort of token of guilt," he explains, "because they had not taken me out of the indescribable situation of my youth"), Tom visited England, the source of so much of the music that fascinated him. Making a pilgrimage to HMV in London's Oxford Street, he discovered an entire wall of NWOBHM records, including *In League With Satan*, the debut single from Venom. It would prove to be an epiphany.

"I had no idea what they sounded like, but I saw the photo on the back and felt this was the most extreme photo I had ever seen of a band," he recalls. "So I bought it and took it home to Switzerland and was like, 'I have found my revelation.' It literally changed my life, these two tracks on this single completely changed my life."

Along with two other UK bands, Motörhead and Discharge, Venom would have a huge impression on the youth, directly inspiring him to start making music himself, initially as a bass player. "I understood then that it was possible to play the music that was inside of me, and I knew at that point I needed to get an instrument and try myself. It wasn't so much a conscious decision as an *obsession*, an *addiction*. And I'm not saying that to appear like some mythical figure here, I simply began involving myself in music so much that I guess it was inevitable that I would try to start to play music myself. I had so many emotions inside of me, I *wanted* to write music, I *wanted* to write lyrics. The only happiness, fulfillment, recognition, the only *identity* I felt, was in music.

"It was very difficult to get a proper instrument in Switzerland at that time and everything is very expensive here. I was in an apprenticeship as a mechanic and made hardly any money so I had to sign a installment plan for I don't know how many years, to get the rate low. I was into Rush and Motörhead and so I wanted to have a Rickenbacker bass—at that point I didn't think I would ever play a guitar, so I bought that and started paying it off. Having that instrument in my hands was magic beyond any description... I would be sitting in front of that instrument for hours, smelling the scent, touching it, looking at it. It was like some magical thing I had seen in record sleeves and magazines, and even though I didn't know how to *play* it, the power that instrument had over me was amazing."

Hungry to work with other musicians, Tom went to try out with a hard rock group from his school called The Fox Tails. Almost as soon he met them, however, it became clear to the young musician that this was not the band for him, so he instead asked the drummer if he wanted to form a NWOBHM band. "For some reason, which is beyond me, he said yes," explains Tom today, "and with our limited English knowledge we called the band Grave Hill."

Grave Hill proved to be a fairly amateurish affair, with all members having only a rudimentary ability on their chosen instruments and rehearsals taking place in Tom's cramped bedroom. In fact, so difficult was it to find a guitarist who would take them seriously that the band were even forced to recruit a second bass player and then put Tom's bass through a distortion pedal (à la Venom) to make it sound more like a guitar. Ultimately the band was to be short-lived, but it did finally provide Tom—albeit indirectly—with a like-minded character named Urs Sprenger, soon to become the co-founder of Hellhammer.

"Of course my whole life story is that I'm always too radical for the others in the band," Tom sighs. "I wanted to become heavier and heavier. I'd heard Venom's *In League With Satan*, but it wasn't heavy enough for me. The single was on 45 rpm and I played it at 33 rpm to make it heavier and we had some sort of a roadie—even though we never played any concerts, we had a hanger-on—and he was the only one who said, 'Yeah, that sounds much better on 33 rpm.' He listened to punk and listened to Venom, he was like me, so I asked if he wanted to join the band and at that point everyone left the band. They said, 'Hey, these guys are crazy, that's no longer music.' So we felt we might as well form a new band and be dedicated in trying to be as extreme as possible, and that was the birth of Hellhammer in May 1982."

Sprenger took up the role of bass in the newly formed band, with Tom moving on to guitar and vocals. Inspired by a fellow apprentice whose surname was "Krieger," German for warrior, the pair adopted the pseudonyms Tom Warrior and Steve Warrior. "It sounded cool," explains Tom, "and we liked that a lot of the bands in England were brothers—like Raven, with the Gallagher brothers." All that now remained was to find a drummer, a role they initially filled with an individual called Peter Stratton.

"He was a million miles from us," smiles Fischer. "Me and Steve were fanatics and he just wanted to be in a band—and to top it all off his parents were radical Catholics! As you can imagine that only lasted a few months, but it did give us a rehearsal space. The Catholic Church had some nuclear-hardened bunkers at their disposal for youth activities, and they didn't really know what sort of band we were, so they gave us an affordable bunker which was only [the equivalent of] fifty euros a year, which is of course sensational. For us it was hard even to find *that* money, but at least we had a rehearsal room. We lost that drummer after a short while, but Steve and I went to a tiny heavy metal festival in a gym hall in the next city and there was a band, Moorhead, whose drummer was really good. So I went up to the guitarist and said, 'Can you give me the number of your drummer?' and the guy was stupid enough to do it. So I called the drummer and said, 'Hello, my name is Tom Warrior, I'm here with the heaviest band in the world *ever*, do you want to be our drummer?' and it worked. That was Bruce Day."

The stage name "Bruce Day" (his real name being Jörg Neubart) was apparently inspired by another pair of NWOBHM brothers, namely Paul and Brian Day of London-based outfit More. While other musicians also briefly played in the band, it was the core trio made up of Satanic Slaughter (Tom Warrior), Savage Damage (Steve Warrior), and Bruce Day (also known as Bloodhunter and Denial Fiend) who first achieved a real impact with Hellhammer. Together the three young men forged a furious and stripped-down sound, juxtaposing slow, foreboding passages with fast-paced, aggressive parts, while making use of a distinctive guitar sound and Tom's inimitable vocals, which were characterized by unique pronunciations, a gravelly tone, and occasional screams. A fresh and insanely raw experience, the music revealed an obvious debt to the unholy British trinity of Motörhead and their two most influential disciples, Venom and Discharge, while also drawing on more obscure reference points.

"If you look for the key ingredient in Hellhammer it *was* Discharge and Venom," Tom explains, "but there were a whole number of bands that were very crucial to my songwriting at the time, and because of the very nature of NWOBHM at the time, sometimes a single song could have a huge impact that would last for years—sometimes until this very day. For example I picked up the *Metal for Muthas* compilation which had Angel Witch's 'Baphomet,' and that song became an icon for me. To this very day I'm trying to recreate something like that. So completely strange to think a single song might change my life, but it has done so several times."

In a situation that would become depressingly familiar to the band, the newly formed Hellhammer were largely met with disinterest and even outright disgust. Not to be deterred, the group began working even harder, not only on their music, but on the creation of an all-encompassing package that included visual and thematic elements. An important aspect of this was the use of a stark, high-contrast, monochromatic aesthetic, one that drew obvious influence from both hardcore/crust punk and NWOBHM, genres that frequently used similar imagery out of sheer necessity.

1983: A young Thomas Fischer, then known as Satanic Slaughter, poses at the Grave Hill bunker with a Hellhammer setlist in shot. Photo: Martin Kyburz.

"There was absolutely no support, no encouragement, no nothing," Tom sighs. "In spite of that we tried to be as professional as possible, in fact all the bands that had a *name* in Switzerland were actually far lazier than us. We said, 'We need to have an image, a concept, a logo, a symbol,' and since we had no support *whatsoever*, we did everything ourselves. We wrote the lyrics—at first blatant copies of Venom lyrics, then later we tried to make them more original—and worked extremely hard, without having a chance to really achieve anything. Steve Warrior was a massive punk fan and brought in a lot of punk aesthetic, but what shouldn't be forgotten is that NWOBHM was such an underground movement that a lot of the singles were done in an almost pathetic manner, black-and-white, hand-drawn, and I think we took some of our aesthetic from there."

Eventually the band decided it was time to make their first professional recording—the word *professional* being used in its broadest possible sense.

"We couldn't wait to hear a recording of our music—we were so eager even though we knew it was *way* too early to record anything—but we didn't have any money. But my father told me that one of his friends was a sound engineer. I would see my father a few days a year because of a court order; they had told him that he had to see me every month, of course he didn't do that, but I would see him a few times a year. A friend of his was a sound engineer, so I called that guy and said, 'I'm Mr. Fischer's kid, we have no money, could you do us a cheap recording?' The guy said yes and came with a mobile recording unit, which was basically just a tiny tape machine, a four-track tape. Us being completely unprofessional, having never been into a studio, instead of using four tracks, we used sixteen tracks, we were like, 'let's record everything!' The sound engineer was sitting there wide-eyed and said, 'Look, what you're playing is absolutely terrible, it's not music, has nothing to *do* with music, this is a waste of tape, it's awful.' But we insisted. We said, 'You have to mix it and give it to us, we're dying to have it.' So we waited while the tape was just languishing at his place. He waited for weeks until he said he had mixed it—even though he probably didn't do anything to it—then he sent us a cassette. For years after I would hear from my father that he was still talking at the motorcycle magazine where they both were working as journalists, the guy would badmouth my music for years afterwards, saying, 'This guy cannot play and his band is a joke.' But at least we had our first demo."

1983's *Triumph of Death* second demo cassette was the first to be distributed properly. It was released by the band's own label, Prowlin' Death Records.

In fact, the session ultimately resulted in not one, but *two* demos. The first was *Death Fiend*, a tape spread only to a few close contacts with instructions not to copy, and the second was *Triumph of Death*, released by the band's own label, Prowlin' Death Records.

"We were going to [release] two demos originally, the first, *Death Fiend*, with the older songs, and *Triumph of Death*, which was going to be the newer songs. But when we listened to *Death Fiend* we realized ourselves that this was awful. By now it was 1983 and American bands were coming out like Metallica, we had heard the first Slayer demos and the Metal Church demos, and even the English bands had progressed massively. The trend was to go more commercial and get clean productions that sounded fantastic. Most of the singers tried to sing like Ronnie James Dio, they sang very high and had multiple-octave voices, and here we were with our shoddy little tape that sounded just like a bulldozer. So we felt really ashamed initially and we knew this wouldn't go anywhere and everyone that heard it, they were laughing their asses off, nobody took it seriously."

"Back then people approached Hellhammer with ridicule and hatred," he sighs, "they couldn't believe what kind of music we were playing. [These demos were] recorded with a

By Prowlin' Death Records

HELLHAMMER, P.O. Box 12,
CH-8309, Nurensdorf,
Switzerland

Limited edition: 200 copies

PDR
003

Including: **Messiah. Eurynomos . . .**

Side one
-Messiah *
-The third of the storms
 (Evoked damnation)
-Buried and forgotten
-Maniac *
-Eurynomos
Side two
-Triumph of death
-Revelations of doom *
-Reaper
-Satanic rites
-Crucifixion

All songs by T.Warrior,
except * by T.Warrior &
M.Ain.
Produced by T.Warrior &
M.Ain,engineered by Med
Demiral.
Recorded at Sound Concept
Studio,northeast Switzer-
land,2./3./4. Dec.1983.

Satanic Rites **demo, finished on the 31st December 1983.**

mobile recording unit in the rehearsal room bunker, which was barely padded, so the sound was crappy, we couldn't play, we had shitty equipment, it was awful. Of course many years later it would be a *habit* to have bad productions—many of the Norwegian bands purposely wanted to have a production like that and it makes you get *used* to it after hearing this for almost twenty years. When you listen to Hellhammer production now it's very fashionable, but if you see it in the context of the early eighties—when all the bands tried to improve and bands like Venom and even Motörhead were accused of not being musicians—it was extremely anachronistic. We were picking up a lot of reviews and I'm not exaggerating when I say that ninety-nine percent of them were devastatingly bad. We were ridiculed up and down and the most important new magazine, *Metal Forces*… completely ripped us apart repeatedly and rendered any chance of being taken seriously moot."

It was against such a background and following the release of *Triumph of Death* that Hellhammer fell apart for a time, with Steve Warrior departing the group. "I realized that even though Steve and I were as radical as one another, many other things between us didn't match—Steve Warrior enjoyed certain drugs and lots of alcohol and he had problems progressing on his instrument," Fischer states, "and we all knew that we needed to progress on our instruments." Finding a replacement proved to be problematic and time-consuming but eventually the group resurfaced with a new bass player, Martin Stricker, known to fans as Martin Ain or Slayed Necros. It was around this time that Hellhammer experienced its first ray of hope.

"There was a brand new German label, Noise, that had arisen from a punk label [Aggressive Rock Produktionen] and they were looking for the most extreme band in the world," explains Tom. "A fanzine writer in Germany had told them there was a band in Switzerland that would probably qualify for that title, so they sent me a letter. All I had at that time was the *Triumph of Death* demo so I assembled what I believed were the best songs from that demo and sent them a letter saying that we were trying to improve and become more professional. They listened to it, looked at the photos—which were radical at the time—and based on the photos they said, 'If you can come up with a better demo by the end of the year then you get your record deal.' Of course that was something I never expected and it gave us immense energy in the few remaining months of the year, to come up with a better demo, and on the 31st December we had the demo finished and sent it to Germany."

The demo in question, *Satanic Rites*, saw Tom handling vocals, guitars and also bass since Martin—in a move Tom puts down partly to cold feet—fired himself from the band prior to recording, claiming he did not have sufficient ability to participate. The forty-six-minute demo, which featured revamped numbers such as "Messiah" and "Triumph of Death" alongside new material, was enough to convince Noise, who promptly signed the band.

"When I got that letter... well, can you imagine? Here was this complete outcast kid who hadn't been given any chances in life so far, who had just one dream, music, and I get this letter... I was beside myself with happiness. Like, 'Wow, someone actually takes me seriously.' Of course the record deal was ridiculous—they gave us the chance to be on a compilation and *maybe* do an EP—but for me that was the biggest thing in the world. So we worked like maniacs day and night on this music. In my apprenticeship I started failing really badly, because I wasn't doing any homework. I would come home stinking from cooling liquor from the tool machines and go straight to the rehearsal room, play until midnight, walk back home from village to village through the forest, listen to the music at home, then try to get three or four hours sleep, then start again. I failed at school, the CEO of the company where I did the apprenticeship ordered my parents to come and try to forbid me to play music. My whole life became disorganized and catastrophic just because of this musical dream."

While it might have been detrimental to his formal career prospects, this union with Noise soon gave fruit—initially in the shape of a 1984 compilation called *Death Metal*, which featured two rerecorded songs from the *Satanic Rites* demo ("Revelations of Doom" and "Messiah") alongside contributions from fellow Noise Records bands Running Wild, Dark Avenger, and Helloween.

More importantly, the same year also saw the release of the EP *Apocalyptic Raids*, which featured four songs recorded at the same session as the *Death Metal* tracks, including new numbers "Horus/Aggressor" and "Massacra," a song that would end up being revisited by a wealth of black metal bands including Emperor, The Abyss, and Merrimack. Murky and primal in sound, the EP revealed its hardcore punk inspirations on fast-paced songs such as "Massacra"—particularly in the drumming, which featured a more primitive and idiosyncratic take on Discharge's famous "D-beat"—while elsewhere featuring torturously slow and lingering passages, complete with pained screams, such as on the ten-minute-long "Triumph of Death."

Hellhammer's *Apocalyptic Raids* EP, released 1984.

"It was amazing to have an EP in our hands," explains Tom. "Going to Berlin, into a real international recording studio, I mean none of us had any experience of that, it was totally mind-blowing. We came there as the mighty Hellhammer, this radical extreme metal band and pretended we knew everything... and we didn't. We said, '*We're* going to produce this EP blah, blah, blah,' and of course it sounded horrible at the time. And even though it was great to have this in our hands, to have the test pressing, we got a phone call from the record label saying, 'This sounds so terrible, we're thinking of not releasing it.' The subsequent reaction [after it was released] from the rock press was absolutely devastating, there was hardly anybody who loved it. So the EP was a huge step back for our credibility, even though for us it was the realization of a dream."

Despite being utterly demoralized by this blow, Tom and Martin refused to let the opportunity they'd worked so hard for fall through their fingers and instead took desperate measures in order to keep their ambitions alive.

"Martin and I have always been very honest, we never tried to trick ourselves to believe something that wasn't true. At the time Hellhammer was completely beside the sound that everyone was looking for. Martin and I realized that, and we became afraid that we would lose the record deal that was such a dream for us. We were thinking of how to avoid this and realized we needed to completely overhaul what we were doing. By now the first Slayer album had come out and the first Exciter album had come out and Metallica were much bigger, Megadeth and Metal Church were coming out and here we were with this EP, a million miles from the standards being set in America. Radical as we were, we said, 'Instead of trying to reinvent the band a million times, let's start from scratch,' and on the night of May 31, 1984, Martin and I sat together in my room and spent the entire night drawing up the concept for the band, making it as detailed as possible. We designed three albums; we said what the covers would be, the song titles, what the lyrics would be about, we said what kind of photos we would choose for each album, we said how these could be promoted... everything. We put this in a handmade book—this was well before desktop publishing, so we wrote it all down with a typewriter and sketches—then sent it by snail mail to Berlin and said, 'Hellhammer no longer exists, this is Celtic Frost and we'd like to take over the record deal with this new band.' And we thought they would never go for it. But to my huge surprise, once they got our little presentation they called me and said, 'You

Seeing in the new year with leather, bullet belts and big sunglasses: Hellhammer, January 1st, 1983.
Steve Warrior, Bruce Day and Tom Warrior. Photo: Andreas Schwarber.

don't have to do a demo, let's go for a mini-album. The whole thing sounds convincing.' So on June 1, essentially—and retroactively—Celtic Frost was born."

And as of that night, after two short years of existence, Hellhammer was dead. Not only did all activities cease, but for many, many years the band's ex-members did all they could to distance themselves from the project, frequently dismissing it as little more than youthful folly.

"For me, Hellhammer would always inevitably be connected to the circumstances of my private life as a youth," Fischer explains. "I had finally freed myself from the world my mother had created where I was completely helpless, and I really did not want to be reminded of that for many years. For *decades* I pushed that era aside. I did not want to have anything to do with Hellhammer, even in a lighter sense. I was very glad to leave this behind and be in Celtic Frost and be a contemporary and not have to think about why Hellhammer really existed. It was only as I approached my forties that I began to be able to assess that time realistically."

Eventually Tom, and his ex-Hellhammer bandmates, learned to not only accept Hellhammer but even celebrate it, and in 2009 the band's complete discography was released in a collection entitled *Demon Entrails*. The following year saw a lavish book about the band released, entitled *Only Death Is Real*. Having now come to terms with the work and events of his past, Tom acknowledges just how significant those years were in shaping the man and musician he is today.

"I'm a self-confident, grown-up musician now, who's been in the music industry for quarter of a century, and I think there's a point where you have to stop making excuses, be an adult and take responsibility for your own actions. On the other hand, I cannot deny that the background I experienced as a kid has completely affected every detail of my life, my entire outlook, my infinite hatred for mankind, my radically violent reactions nowadays when someone looks at me even slightly the wrong way. Every time that happens a movie plays in my head… back then I was a little kid who wasn't able to defend himself and as soon as I became an adult that turned completely and I would punish the person who exerted this on me by putting all the anger that had accumulated over all these years on that one person."

"It is not an act, my lyrics are not an act, unlike so many who adopt a certain image to look evil. My music has never been that, it's always been very honest, and is a reflection of my background. So I'm very torn between the intellectual who thinks it's time to be different and the radical metal musician who almost *enjoys* that side of me. That's the world I've created for myself, that's the sanctuary I found. I once was *pushed* into that world, and I was pushed so radically that I eventually started loving this world. I found myself in there and that world was darkness, it's become my life, my personality and vice versa."

6
CELTIC FROST

"To me this band is out of this world, the way Tom G. Warrior makes the riffs and puts the notes together is totally unlike other people. I'm lost for words, let's just say that on every album we did there has been something of Celtic Frost there."

—Fenriz (Darkthrone)

"They were a great influence because that was a hard rock/metal band that did things a different way, that created a unique style and aesthetics. And it's wicked, and it's bad, and moody, and dark and all that."

—Snorre Ruch (Stigma Diabolicum/Thorns)

IF HELLHAMMER was the direct result of restrictions placed upon the musicians within it at the time, then Celtic Frost (which is pronounced, contrary to popular opinion, with a hard "c") was a band that actively avoided limitations wherever possible. In fact, as a direct result of the negative experiences with their previous band, Tom and Martin worked actively from the very beginning to avoid being pigeonholed or cornered creatively, a stance that directly influenced the choice of band name.

"This was the time of the Metallicas and Megadeths," smiles Tom, "and we wanted a name that wasn't so 'cliché-metal.' Hellhammer had a name that *completely* defined our music, so we wanted a name that gave us total artistic freedom, that didn't sound metal, that didn't sound *anything,* so we could incorporate whatever we wanted into our music, from jazz to opera. We wanted the name to represent our lyrics—basically the apocalypse—and chose a civilization, the Celts, as we ourselves had Celtic backgrounds, and 'frost' which symbolized the end of the year, the end of a civilization, the end of a cycle. But a new cycle arises after the winter, just as with all civilizations. It was a very symbolic name."

The band's first effort was the groundbreaking mini-album *Morbid Tales,* recorded as a trio with Tom, Martin, and session drummer Steven Priestly, and released midway through 1984. While the band might have been doing their utmost to distance themselves from their past, this collection of songs suggested that Frost still had much in common with the band

The newly formed Celtic Frost in June 1984: Original drummer Isaac Darso, Tom G. Warrior and Martin Eric Ain. Photo: Martin Kyburz.

from whose ashes they had risen. Tracks such as "Into the Crypt of Rays" and "Procreation (of the Wicked)" might have boasted a far tighter, chunkier and more professional sound than anything recorded by Hellhammer, even introducing a hint of groove to the mix, but they were nonetheless clearly cut from the same cloth.

All the same, Celtic Frost were clearly also utilizing a much wider spectrum of influence, including that of gothic rock acts such as Bauhaus and Christian Death, and were already beginning to demonstrate the decidedly innovative approach to songwriting (evident in the restrained but notable use of violin and female vocals) that would increasingly earn them the "avant-garde metal" tag. The record was followed in early 1985 by *Emperor's Return*, an EP that continued where its predecessor left off and saw the introduction of a permanent drummer Reed St. Mark, real name Reid Cruickshank.

"It was still very difficult to find a studio drummer in Switzerland who would believe in our music and there were only so many drummers in the country to begin with," Tom recalls. "We heard all these great drummers coming out of America, and even though we didn't know how to *pay* for an American drummer—his flight and accommodation—we were like, 'Maybe we *need* an American drummer, we won't find a drummer in Switzerland who will match these guys, and these guys are our competition.' Our record label knew of a drummer who was staying in the country, who had played briefly in another Swiss band and was about to head back to America. They met him in a record store and said, 'If you're looking for a new gig, there's a band called Celtic Frost who are looking for a drummer.' In February or March of 1985 we finally hooked up and heard him play. We were in *awe*, he played like all these drummers we'd heard on American albums and we knew we had to have this guy, whereas he was quite bewildered by our appearance and by our music. But he needed a new gig, so he decided to give it a chance against his better judgment."

Vocally, Tom's wonderfully distinct, almost *alien* handling of words continued to define the group's sound, and as in Hellhammer he peppered his vocals with unexpected bursts of enthusiasm, often throwing in a "hey," or, more famously, an "uuuuuurgh!" The latter would become something of a trademark, and in metal circles has become fondly known as the "death grunt," appearing innumerable times in later metal and black metal recordings, a sign of the band's profound influence.

"I never personally said that I created the death grunt, it was I think Xavier Russell of *Kerrang!* who said that, but of course it's not true," smiles Tom. "I first heard the 'death grunt' when I was a child, when I heard James Brown in the early seventies. During the seventies a lot of hard rock bands would do that as well, then NWOBHM bands like Diamond Head, Iron Maiden, and even Motörhead, I simply picked up on that. On the first Iron Maiden single there was a death grunt and we thought that was so unbelievably cool. Maybe I took it to a different level, maybe that's the credit I deserve."

Just as Celtic Frost's music was evolving from the Hellhammer template, so the lyrics and imagery expanded on earlier preoccupations, most notably the dominant occult and anti-religious themes.

"Everything I do in music basically comes from my private life—my life and my music are one, you cannot separate the two," says Tom earnestly. "I carried with me a tremendous hatred for organized religion ever since I was a child. I found it at best ridiculous, and at worst very dangerous and short-sighted. The older I got and the more I read about it and experienced it firsthand, the more the hatred I had for that mechanism increased. That includes all organized religion, not just the Catholic church, but even including Satanism. I'm an extremely unreligious person and Martin and I would spend hours, days, weeks, *months*, discussing certain topics in infinite detail and trying to pick up occult or religious or historic literature that would answer our questions.

"Occultism had always interested me and at times in Hellhammer and Celtic Frost we got a lot of first-hand experience of all that because our extreme music and lyrical topics attracted a lot of very serious people from both sides of the line: Catholic religious fanatics, national socialist Satanists, and everything in between. Some of those would want to literally kill us and some would try to turn us to their direction, it was a very weird time and it frequently still happens actually. At one point we had problems with a local grotto of Satanists that tried to infiltrate Hellhammer to convey their message. Since they also had National Socialist tendencies Martin and I completely blocked them off, which infuriated them no end, and they made very serious death threats. I'm actually friends with these people nowadays, and even though I disagree [with their ideas] I have to really deeply respect them. I respect a lot of radical people simply because they didn't wimp out and cut their hair and become normal citizens, what can I say?"

Adorned in an iconic H.R. Giger painting entitled *Satan I*, featuring a multi-headed devil using a crucifix as a slingshot, the band's 1985 debut full-length is certainly saturated in such occult and irreligious concerns. Entitled *To Mega Therion*, it was an opus that would prove to be a true milestone in the development of both black metal and extreme metal as a whole. Crushingly heavy, it retains an aggressive and muscular sound as well as the familiarly choppy, rhythmic approach to riff writing, but compliments the metal content with apocalyptically grandiose—even pompous—orchestral touches, in particular the eerie use of French horn courtesy of the memorably named Wolf Bender. Careful use of female vocals adds a further level of drama and only helps to increase the overall effect of eclecticism, something which owed much to the band members' musical upbringing.

"It was part of the music we grew up with," Tom replies simply. "The record collection of my parents was very eclectic—classical, jazz, The Beatles—and Martin had a background with a lot of new wave and a lot of church music. We were never a 'small town-minded' heavy metal band, we were always fascinated by *music*. We didn't want to adhere to some invisible border that heavy metal bands had set for themselves, like, 'You can't have a keyboard on an album,' and all the crap that was being said back then. We always felt it was about the music, and we thought it was much more courageous to be a musician and try to make an eclectic album, rather than adhere to a list of things you cannot do. We had a violin and female vocalist already on *Morbid Tales*, and the bigger the budgets became and the more experienced we became as musicians, the more we incorporated that."

Curiously, Martin was not present on the album due to another brief hiatus, and was temporarily replaced on bass duties by one Dominic Steiner, who had previously played in a glam outfit called Junk Food. In something of a nod to the past, *To Mega Therion* also includes an appearance by Hellhammer co-founder Steve Warrior, on the instrumental number "Tears in a Prophet's Dream."

"Steve did a very short-lived musical project after Hellhammer, a fake Icelandic band called Køtzen," Tom explains. "It was more of a joke than a real band but there was one track on the demo which we all felt was fantastic and we asked him if we could use it as a basic track and then build lots of stuff on top of it. Steve actually stayed on with Celtic Frost as a member of the road crew, but he had changed massively and moved in different circles by that time and there was a very unfortunate incident where the rest of the road crew didn't want to work with him anymore and we had to let him go. He used to be one of my best friends but we simply moved into completely different directions."

Translating as "The Great Beast," the title "To Mega Therion" was a biblical phrase adopted by occultist Aleister Crowley, an individual whose influence would surface throughout

Never understated: An advert/promo sheet for Celtic Frost's 1984 debut *Morbid Tales*. During this period Prowlin' Death Promotion/Management represented bands such as Hirax and Drifter, as well as Celtic Frost.

the band's career. All the same, Tom is quick to point out that the man once dubbed "the most wicked man in England" wasn't the only inspiration for the album's title.

"I had discovered his work through Martin, and Martin had discovered his work through the grotto of Satanists in Switzerland. Martin was briefly involved with a female member of that grotto, she was his first girlfriend, and he picked up a lot of things that inspired him from that period, that being one of them. I had known about Crowley but didn't involve myself really until Martin brought it closer to me. But though certain references are obvious within Celtic Frost, in song titles or album titles, you often have to read between the lines. We often liked to play with associations and a lot of things had a completely different meaning to us. *To Mega Therion* is 'the great beast' of course, and for us that had many other meanings both from our own small universe, like the record company, to more global social issues, like our watching of the social system on the planet and human behavior, which often frustrated us."

Frustration was sadly an emotion that largely defined this period of Celtic Frost, and though the band were undoubtedly more warmly received than Hellhammer, they still frequently met with prejudice.

"Hellhammer was such a hated band in the early eighties it made it extremely difficult for Celtic Frost to be given a chance," he sighs. "For the first two albums we had this huge rock tied to our ankles—whenever we went to an interview or a record label or promoter, everyone would say, 'Oh, it's the Hellhammer guys, they can't play and it's crap,' and it was an extremely difficult start for Celtic Frost. Our recipe to avoid this was to distance ourselves radically from Hellhammer; if you read period interviews, Martin and I are very often distancing ourselves just to get a chance with Celtic Frost, so people would recognize that we wanted to do something better. It took many years for Celtic Frost to be taken seriously. It began when we released *Into the Pandemonium* in 1987—that was basically our breakthrough album and the one where we started to get respect."

A revolutionary and highly influential effort, *Into the Pandemonium* would prove to be an even more bold and diverse effort than *To Mega Therion*. Taking the experimental streak even further, the album rarely stands still stylistically, shifting from upbeat hard-rock-tinged thrash (for example "I Won't Dance" or the Wall of Voodoo cover "Mexican Radio") to industrial/electronic efforts ("One in Their Pride") to deeply melancholy metal numbers such as "Mesmerized" and even, perhaps most provocatively, a classical piece with French female vocals, "Tristesses de la Lune." Deeply haunting and epic in tone for the most part, the album also upped the orchestral ante thanks to a legion of session musicians, an addition that wasn't without its challenges.

"Hardly any [metal] bands had ever used classical musicians," says Fischer. "None of us could write scores, so we had to enlist an arranger and he arranged a mini orchestra for the studio. These guys came in and said the same old story: 'What you guys are playing, it's noise, not music.' They were very reluctant to even *try* it, especially when they learnt that none of us could conduct, none of us could write scores and that we were mediocre musicians. They laughed at us, they didn't realize they were taking part in something that was a pioneering album. And neither did we of course."

There was, of course, no way the band could have foreseen the profound influence this album would have on the metal scene, introducing a heavy use of both orchestration and female vocals into the metal template at a time when both were largely unheard of. Nonetheless, the fact that the band were taking a considerable risk with the recording was impossible to ignore.

"I *knew* it was a very dangerous album. It was a time when female vocals and classical instruments were very foreign to heavy metal and no other extreme metal band of the time would have touched it. Metallica, Slayer, all that, they would never have touched it and we did, and I'm very proud of that. I think if you are a musician, an *artist*, you have to have a certain courage. Repeating yourself or photocopying other's art… it's cowardice. If you actually risk your career to do something new, even if it's in a very small way, then it's art. Especially heavy metal musicians who pose like they're big, bad men in their leathers …a lot of those bands are so conservative and scared to ever deviate from their track. …to me heavy metal itself is a powerful, energetic, courageous music. It's a revolutionary music, or at least it was when it arose in the seventies and I cannot believe so many people are scared to go anywhere with that. So this was the music we wanted to make, and surprisingly it turned out to be our breakthrough album."

Unfortunately this achievement came with a heavy price. While the album was warmly received (although inevitably it would prove too challenging for some of the band's more conservative listeners), and earned the band both new fans and critical acclaim, its creation would also directly help to destroy the band.

"We completely overstretched ourselves," Tom reflects. "We were still very limited as musicians, we hardly had a budget and we had a record label that fought every day against this album. They wanted us to do a sure-shot album, they told us literally, 'Make an album like Slayer or Exodus.' They didn't want to have an experimental album and they tried everything; they threatened to put us on ice, to

Celtic Frost's most experimental work,
Into the Pandemonium, **1987**

throw us out of the studio, they paid the engineer behind our backs to sabotage our album, every day was bad news. And in addition we could hardly make the album because we simply were not good enough musicians, so everyday was a gargantuan undertaking for us.

"The record company, when we persisted with this album, turned toward open confrontation. They cancelled our video, they cancelled the tour support that they were contractually obligated to provide and they changed the album round in an attempt to make it a more traditional heavy metal album, which resulted in an exchange of attorney for fourteen months and burdened us with a huge legal bill to regain our artistic freedom. These legal wranglings were one of the reasons the band split up. We were young at the time and didn't have the legal backing, a proper management, the connections or the experience to withstand such an assault from a corporation, and even though we persisted with our principles and got rid of the contract and were free at the end, the free band was a band that no longer existed. It was our breakthrough album but the result was that Celtic Frost was over and done with ... *Into the Pandemonium* is basically the epitaph of the original Celtic Frost."

The band did indeed fall apart after the album, only to be resurrected six months later by Tom, together with a new lineup that included Steven Priestly, the session drummer from *Morbid Tales* who had previously turned down the offer to become a full-time member of the band. The resulting album, *Cold Lake*, is not only Celtic Frost's worst album, but has established a reputation—perhaps slightly unrealistically—as the worst album in metal's history. Indeed, even today the phrase "Cold Lake" is occasionally used by the metal press for "an irredeemable album by a once great band," and although in retrospect its glam rock/melodic thrash crossover attempt doesn't quite live up to its terrible reputation, it's fair to say that it was deeply flawed and a great disappointment compared to what had come before.

"We were completely drained and the consensus was to record a much straighter, more melodic album, with much less experimentation with the lineup of Reed, Martin and myself," Tom explains. "But because the band fell apart I was panicking. My castle, my sanctuary, my harbor had been music ever since I was a kid and I had not faced a single day without a band since Grave Hill. The prospect of there being no Celtic Frost drove me to do something I should have never done, which was to continue with a bunch of idiots. I had also freshly fallen in love with the woman who would later be my wife and the end of that litigation and this never-ending hell and me being in love just conspired in me wanting to be happy, and wanting to do something colorful, something positive. And that's all nice and dandy, but that's not Celtic Frost. I should have done a solo album or whatever, but it should never have been a Celtic Frost album. It also made me relinquish control, I was way too much involved in my new relationship and left the studio for great periods of time and let the people do whatever they wanted to do.

"Of course the whole thing turned out to be a piece of fucking circus play, an album which no one can take seriously including me, it was a hugest mistake of my entire life. There is no other misstep—and I've done a few in my life, believe me—but there is no other misstep that rates so drastically highly in my life as this album. The only redeeming feature is that I swore to myself to never be so careless again, to never relinquish control over an album so much, to never fail on such a gargantuan scale as an artist again. …I am not a coward and I don't run away from this—if I take responsibility for the grandiosity of certain things of Hellhammer and Celtic Frost then I also have to be man enough to take responsibility for this epic failure."

The follow-up, *Vanity/Nemesis*, released in 1990 and featuring the return of Martin Ain, was a far stronger effort musically speaking, closer to the melodic but heavy thrash metal album that the band had originally envisioned for *Cold Lake*. It was not enough to fully rejuvenate the band, however; a compilation featuring unreleased and rerecorded material, *Parched With Thirst Am I and Dying*, was issued in 1992 and the band split for the second time the following year.

Two of metal's most influential bands, Hellhammer and Celtic Frost are rightly hailed as vital catalysts in the creation of various metal genres, including gothic metal, doom metal, orchestral metal, thrash metal, and also the death metal scene to whom they were closely linked at one time. Yet it is unquestionably the black metal scene that they have become primarily linked to as the years have passed.

"That's probably because death metal has become very technical over the years," Tom ponders. "We actually named ourselves death metal in an attempt to get away from the black metal tag, we also called ourselves doom metal, we felt very trapped by the tag 'black metal.' We were also involved I think in the thrash metal scene, that was music we loved and music we played, but you're right, a lot of people focus on our connections to black metal and so be it.

"We were tagged black metal [from the start], and that's not a surprise because particularly during the early days of Hellhammer we copied Venom, or Venom's *lyrics*, to such an extent that, of course, people placed us as black metal. It became very annoying because we didn't just want to write occult lyrics and especially after Martin joined the range of the lyrical themes became even broader."

By the time Frost split up, the second wave of black metal was in full swing and both Hellhammer and Celtic Frost were being discovered by a new generation of fanatics, with numerous covers and tributes to both bands visible. One only need look at the pseudonyms used by Norway's Mayhem, one of the second wave's most important bands, to see this influence: a member named Hellhammer, not to mention Messiah, Euronymous, and Maniac—all Hellhammer song titles. Similarly, where Celtic Frost had boasted the songs "Dethroned Emperor" and "Circle of the Tyrants," now there was a leading Norwegian band called Emperor with a release called *Wrath of the Tyrant*. Both bands are among the legion who have covered Hellhammer/Celtic Frost songs at some stage in their career.

"I found out about all of this much later," Tom explains. "When the black metal wave happened I was living in Texas and it wasn't a big topic there, but Martin was in Europe and he watched all of this first-hand. I found out about it basically from interviews, when the press would interview me they would always ask about it and so I decided to look into this. At first I was extremely skeptical. Number one, I didn't like all the black metal bands—I thought a lot of that music was repetitive and copyist, and very few bands seemed to me to do something original. Number two, I had a lot of problems with a lot of the things going on that were tied to the black metal scene and to [Hellhammer and Celtic Frost]. When the murders happened for example, all the journalists came up to me and said, 'Well the band Hellhammer has been mentioned in conjunction to Norway and the murders.' It became extremely uncomfortable. So I avoided the black metal scene for a long time, it was absolutely impossible for me to listen to this with an open mind, there was too much personal baggage."

All this would eventually change. Of all the early pioneers it would be Celtic Frost, and Tom in particular, who would be most closely involved in the next generation of black metal, particularly the Scandinavian exponents of the genre. This would be evident following Frost's return in 2001, specifically on the 2006 comeback album *Monotheist*. Featuring Tom and Martin, along with guitarist Erol Inala and drummer Franco Sesa, the record perhaps leaned more toward doom than black musically, but was produced by premier second-wave black metal producer Peter Tägtgren, and featured several appearances by vocalists from the Norwegian scene, such as Satyr of Satyricon and Ravn of 1349.

"The radicalness and darkness of certain black metal is what attracts me," says Tom. "I have a hard time accepting modern death metal, it sounds very similar to me, every song uses the same guitar solo and so on, and that annoys me as an artist. Even though these guys can outplay me by a thousand times, it's very one-dimensional music to me. Thrash music … it's like NWOBHM, it was a product of its time and thrash metal as I define it no longer

**Continuing where Hellhammer and Celtic Frost left off, Triptykon now forge ahead
with Thomas Fischer at the helm. Photo: Peter Beste.**

really exists. Black metal on the other hand has developed in very interesting directions. Who
would have thought black metal and ambient could be merged and so on?"

Indeed, the diverse philosophies of the musicians involved interests Tom just as much
as the genre's multifaceted musical identity, even if he initially found himself disappointed
that they were not all the fundamental devil worshippers they initially appeared to be.

"The radicalness of some of the people—not all of them because some are of course
are just projecting an image—but some of them are so radical, so determined, that it attracts
me deeply, because I'm like that and I feel that common ground. The definition of Satanism is
very individual and I've been told of personal philosophies of many of the protagonists and at
first I was almost disappointed that they weren't practicing Satanists. The one thing I noticed
when I started to really involve myself in the black metal story is that so many protagonists

have their own way to define what they mean by Satanism or black metal. When the black metal wave first came into recognition in the late eighties and early nineties, they all basically believed in Satan. But in the years since I've been exposed to so many explanations of what Satanism and black metal really is, that I find it extremely interesting.

"To me, below the line, it is really infinite hatred for mankind and the right to do whatever you want to do regardless of anyone else's opinion or attempts to stop you. For me that defines a large amount of black metal and Satanism without going into religious topics. The misanthropic angle is very legitimate to me. In fact, I can't help but wonder; most of my life Martin and I have fought the black metal association with Hellhammer and Celtic Frost and always made the point that our lyrics go much further than that … But at the end of the day when I listen to several of the explanations of the protagonists it comes down to nihilism and hatred against human beings, or rather the conduct of human beings, sometimes I think I'm just like them."

Though *Monotheist* was hugely acclaimed, making the number two slot on *Terrorizer*'s top albums of the decade and leading to a number of highly successful international tours, the band's resurrection was sadly not permanent. Following significant problems between Tom and drummer Franco, the frontman demanded a lineup change, a point that Martin was unwilling to accept, and in April 2008 Tom left the group, effectively bringing it to an end. It is a situation that seems unlikely to change anytime soon.

"Martin has told me several times since I left the band that we will work together again and I've told him, 'No, that's not going to happen.' I feel betrayed—so much work, so much money went into bringing Celtic Frost back, it was such a gargantuan undertaking to work on this album for five and a half years, it was a risk at every level. I invested so much and in the end Martin lets it slip away, lets me stand there alone. How could I ever trust him again?"

Thankfully, the spirit of Frost continues in the shape of Triptykon, a band whose first album contains material written as a direct follow-up to *Monotheist* and which features Tom along with a number of musicians, including V Santora (Victor Bullok) of contemporary black metal act Dark Fortress, who had previously performed as a live guitarist in Celtic Frost.

"I formed the band with the specific aim of continuing the music of Celtic Frost," concludes Tom, "both to play the old songs which I love to perform and to write new songs in the same vein. It's the same equipment—I bought all the equipment from Celtic Frost—it's the same road crew, it's the same two record labels, Prowling Death and Century Media, it's the same management, it's the same graphic designers, it's exactly Celtic Frost… The only thing that's different is the rhythm section and the lack of ego problems."

7
THE FIRST WAVE
of BLACK THRASH

"It's about extraction; you almost have to search for the black metal in the albums. That was when it was interesting, it was not labeled, you had to find it for yourself, and some of that magic was maybe lost in the nineties when you could get a sticker on the album saying 'This is black metal.'"

—Fenriz (Darkthrone)

"When we started the second wave of black metal it was that feeling we were after. Kreator, Mercyful Fate, Bathory, Celtic Frost, Venom… obviously it was not black metal, but to us it was."
—Apollyon (Aura Noir, Immortal, Cadaver, Dødheimsgard)

THE TRADITIONAL DIVISION of the black metal movement into the first and second "waves" has long been a convenient way to distinguish between the bands from the eighties and the seemingly new movement that exploded in the early nineties—indeed, for reasons of clarity, this division is even used when appropriate within this book. However, this practice can also be somewhat misleading. Far from being two entirely separate entities, the "first wave" gently bled into the "second wave" as the eighties ended, and it was simply the sudden success, notoriety, and proliferation of bands in the early nineties that created the appearance of an entirely new scene. Norway's Mayhem—the band at the center of much of this explosion—formed in the mid-eighties, a fact highlighting some of the confusion at work.

While Venom, Mercyful Fate, Bathory, and Hellhammer/Celtic Frost are generally considered the most pivotal in kick-starting the black metal genre, the bands in this chapter also played a significant hand in its development. Again it should be emphasized that in many cases the band's "black metal" qualities remain a matter of *interpretation*, since the extreme metal scene at the time was simply too small for the sort of intense sub-genre labeling that goes on today. Back then most of these bands were simply considered acts from the darker, heavier side of thrash and indeed, as the years went on, many would evolve into a purer, less "evil"-sounding take on that genre.

The German trio of Sodom, Kreator, and Destruction, as well as the American act Slayer, are a perfect case in point. Formed in the early eighties, these three bands would increasingly be hailed as thrash icons as the decade continued, and are all still going strong today. Nevertheless, the early works of these three acts helped to inspire an entirely different movement, a fact attested to by Fenriz and Apollyon, two important figures in nineties Norwegian black metal who helped resurrect the early primal spirit of these Teutonic acts at a time when it had been all but forgotten, not least by the bands themselves. Still, it was perhaps Mayhem's Euronymous who was most vocal in his admiration for those bands' formative days (indeed, his label was named after Sodom's "Deathlike Silence" song), as well as in his determination not to lose the black metal essence the way those bands had. As his interview in the fourth issue of *Kill Yourself Zine* explains:

"It's quite weird that everybody talks about VENOM, BATHORY and HELLHAMMER as the old Evil bands, but nobody mentions SODOM and DESTRUCTION. They came at the same time as BATHORY and HELLHAMMER and their first albums are masterpieces of black stinking metal! Nobody manages to make music like that now."

SODOM

Formed in 1982 in the West German town of Gelsenkirchen by one Tom Angelripper (born Thomas Such), Sodom were heavily inspired by both Motörhead and Venom. They adopted a similar setup, working as a trio with Angelripper handling vocals and bass, Aggressor (Frank Testegen) on guitar, and one Bloody Monster (Rainer Focke) handling drums. Later that same year Monster departed, to be replaced by Chris Witchhunter (real name Dudek), and the band recorded and released a four-track demo entitled *Witching Metal*. One of the noisiest and most chaotic-sounding metal releases in existence at that time, the tape presents Sodom as perhaps Bathory's only real competition in terms of early metal extremity—and bear in mind, this was two years before the *Scandinavian Metal Attack* compilation was released.

Undoubtedly, part of what makes the tape so brutal is its highly amateurish production, but songs such as the title track and "Devil's Attack" also bore considerable promise, and the hellish subject matter certainly made an impact. Another demo, *Victims of Death*, this time featuring eight songs, followed in 1984, before the iconic *In the Sign of Evil* EP was issued later that year. Featuring a slightly clearer sound than the demos—but only just—the release remains an aggressive, rabid-sounding piece of work. There's a definite Venom influence, not only in the vocals, but also in the somewhat chaotic and primitive approach, which recalls *Welcome To Hell*, albeit with a more extreme and less melodic twist.

Sodom's *Obsessed By Cruelty*, **1986. "Black stinking metal," to quote Mayhem's Euronymous, who named his Deathlike Silence record label after the second song on the album.**

"The attitude, the riffs, it just sounded very violent and evil," explains Apollyon. "'Evil' is a silly word in a way, but you know what I mean. I mean, you're allowed to have fun and care about the environment and so on in private, but there's no need to sing about it. So I still prefer really simple stuff, primitive, Sodom-like lyrics. And Sodom really have the best lyrics ever. Like that 'Blasphemer' song [from *In the Sign of Evil*], 'Spit at the church, Evil I get' ….yeah I'm all for that sort of stuff. You can hear they really want to play as fast as they can and as vicious as possible and it really has a punk attitude, so I prefer the first albums when it doesn't sound technically brilliant, it doesn't sound too controlled or well produced."

Sodom's first full-length, *Obsessed With Cruelty*, was issued in 1986, following in a similarly violent vein while refining the band's sound and including a lengthy atmospheric introduction. The opus impressed many fans, some of whom would go on to form their own bands.

**Kreator's *Endless Pain*, 1985. The band's debut album, it features several songs originally
recorded and released when the band was known as Tormentor.**

"*Obsessed by Cruelty* is a very important black metal album for me," ponders Fenriz of
Darkthrone, "but when I bought it as a kid I was thinking, 'Hmmm, this is strange thrash,' I
didn't understand the *blackness* in it."

Fenriz wasn't alone in his appreciation. The record was also, according to Necrobutcher
of Mayhem, both his and bandmate Euronymous' favorite release of that year. Despite this
positive reception from the underground hordes, it wasn't long before the band started experimenting with catchier, more upbeat territories with their releases, the lyrics moving away
from Satanic subjects and instead drawing on the fear of nuclear war that was making its way
into the public consciousness at the time.

"It used to be spikes, chains, leather and black clothes..." bemoaned Mayhem's Euronymous in 1991.
As photos like this prove, the German black thrash bands of the early eighties were as influential in
their appearance as they were their music.

KREATOR

Based in Essen, West Germany, Kreator formed in 1982 under the name of Tormentor, and featured the talents of vocalist/guitarist Miland "Mille" Petrozza, bassist Roberto Florettie, and drummer/vocalist Jürgen "Ventor" Reil. The trio drew their influence from black metal pioneers such as Mercyful Fate, Bathory, and Venom, hardcore punk music including The Exploited, and American speed metal/thrash bands such as Metallica, who had been steadily releasing demos since the start of that year. Tormentor would release two demo tapes themselves, one in 1983 and the other in 1984, the latter being *End of the World*, a suitably apocalyptic collection of songs.

Changing their name to Kreator the same year—a wise move given that there are a host of metal bands, past and present, called Tormentor—the group released *Endless Pain* in 1985. The album would prove an important milestone, its power and ferocity allowing it to sit comfortably alongside the efforts of Sodom and Destruction, the vocals sounding particularly harsh and demonic for the time.

Refining their sound somewhat while keeping the essence intact, the band issued their second album *Pleasure To Kill* in 1986, as well as a three-track EP called *Flag of Hate*, both of which honed the band's brutal and cruel sound. From that point the group began to undergo something of a stylistic shift, illustrated by 1987's *Terrible Certainty* album as well as the releases that followed. Of the three German black thrash bands at the time, Kreator are perhaps the least frequently credited within contemporary black metal circles, possibly for the simple reason that Mayhem's Euronymous didn't credit them in interviews in the same way that he did Sodom and Destruction. All the same they are an important part of black metal's history, as Apollyon confirms:

"Of the three bands, I was mainly into Kreator originally. *Pleasure to Kill* is maybe the most complete album and I think the *Flag of Hate* EP is also very defining. Along with Destruction, Sodom, and Bathory they set the standards of how this music was supposed to sound."

DESTRUCTION

Another three-piece—consisting of bassist/vocalist Marcel "Schmier" Schirmer, drummer Tommy Sandmann, and guitarist Mike Sifringer—Destruction originated from the southwest of Germany and originally bore the slightly odd name Knight of Demon. Though they formed in 1982—the same year as their Teutonic compatriots Sodom and Kreator—Destruction were the last of the three to issue a release, namely the EP *Sentence of Death*, which saw the light of day in 1984.

With a surprisingly competent production and some notably accomplished musicianship, *Sentence of Death* nonetheless contains its fair share of barbarity and diabolic intent, just as one would expect from a release whose cover photograph featured the members in a uniform of tight black jeans, leather jackets, inverted crosses, studs, chains, and bullet belts, an image that not only spoke volumes about the intent of its subjects but also did much to provide a visual starting point for the scene.

Infernal Overkill, the band's debut full-length, followed in 1985 and was embraced by fans, the punchy, lightning-fast assaults such as "Bestial Invasion" and "Invincible Force" proving violently satisfying yet memorable enough to leave their mark on many of the bands that followed.

Like Kreator and Sodom, Destruction took an unashamed Satanic/anti-Christian position in their early days.

**Slayer's debut album *Show No Mercy*, 1983. An early milestone recording in extreme metal,
it has unsurprisingly been rereleased and licensed countless times over the years.**

"I know six, seven, maybe *ten* versions of that 'Bestial Invasion' riff," laughs Apollyon.
"I think even Darkthrone have something similar on their *Under A Funeral Moon* album, so for
us [in the second wave] that was, and still, is a major inspiration."

In a now-familiar story, the band gradually moved away from the proto-black territories
of their original releases as the years went by, although *Eternal Devastation*, their second album
in 1986, had enough unholy traits to please many fans of their earlier material. In fact, when
Fenriz came to issue his excellent compilation, *Fenriz Presents… The Best of Old School Black
Metal*, he included the song "Curse the Gods" from that very album. From his liner notes:

"I remember Euronymous (Mayhem) and me listening to this intro and wonder[ing]
how the hell they made the guitar sound like that… This is more of a thrash metal number,
but Destruction, Sodom and Kreator's three first releases always had a black metal aura."

SLAYER

Within the metal scene—and perhaps even beyond—Slayer have earned a uniquely iconic status, and they remain arguably the most successful extreme metal band of all time. With humble beginnings as a cover band that celebrated the likes of Iron Maiden, the group got their initial break thanks to a compilation, Metal Blade Records' 1983 *Metal Massacre Vol. 3*, which they opened with the song "Aggressor Perfector."

Both band and label were encouraged by the good feedback the song received, and later that year their debut album *Show No Mercy* was released on Metal Blade. Though the record was somewhat slower, less aggressive, and more melodic when compared to both their later recordings and the early-eighties efforts of, say, Sodom or Bathory, the spirit was surely there, and the group emphasized a "Satanic" image from the start, wearing leather, face paint, spikes, and inverted crosses. *Show No Mercy* itself features numerous Satanic references in classic songs such as "Evil Has No Boundaries" and "The Antichrist," and its cover depicts a large inverted "pentagram" composed of four swords, the one "missing" sword wielded by a slightly comic-book-style goat-headed warrior.

1984 saw the release of both the *Haunting the Chapel* EP and a live album entitled *Live Undead*, and the following year the band released their second album, the much-loved *Hell Awaits*, a record whose title and infernal cover art demonstrated that the group were sticking to their guns with their unholy fascinations. The point was further highlighted with the backward recordings of the words "join us" and "welcome back" in the intro. In 1986 the band released *Reign In Blood*, an album that most metal fans view as both their finest effort and one of the most important albums in metal's history.

Due to the numerous extreme and blasphemous bands beginning to emerge at this point, it's probably fair to say that Slayer's influence on the black metal movement began to wane around this time, though songs such as "Altar of Sacrifice" and "Jesus Saves" remained in a suitably blasphemous vein. Interestingly, unlike most of their contemporaries, the band have never entirely abandoned the Satanic/anti-Christian themes of their early works. Though their lyrics have expanded to embrace other subjects, albums such as 2001's *God Hates Us All* (released, strangely, on September 11th and featuring a blood-splattered, nail-embedded Bible on its cover) and 2006's *Christ Illusion* (whose cover depicted a mutilated Jesus in a sea of blood and severed heads) have continued to cause much controversy—especially since vocalist Tom Araya now claims to be a Catholic.

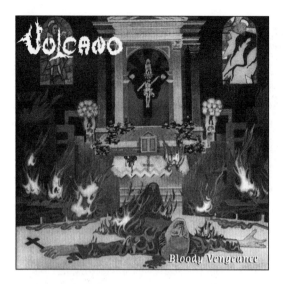

Vulcano: *Bloody Vengeance*. Released in 1986, it is almost certainly South America's first black metal album, and is still one of the most potent.

VULCANO

While North America and Germany certainly dominated the early thrash movement, South America would also prove something of a hotbed, particularly Brazil, the first country in the region to significantly embrace the genre. One of the earliest names was Vulcano, which started life as a hard rock band before reinventing itself a few years later.

"I joined Carli Cooper (bass) and Paulo Magrão (guitar) in '78 and together we created Astoroth," explains bassist/guitarist and co-founder Zhema Rodero. "One year after we resolved to change the name to Vulcano, and in the following year I moved to Santos [São Paulo]. There I reformed the band and we started to play in high schools, college, major events, etc. In 1983 we recorded our first single."

Despite Cooper's absence from the new lineup, the single, *Om Pushne Namah*, would feature hard rock-styled songs he had written way back in 1974. Employing a new vocalist named Angel one year later, the band shifted style considerably, aiming to blend "the lyrics of Black Sabbath with the songs of Motörhead." Recording a demo in 1984 and a live album the following year, the band finally unleashed their debut album *Bloody Vengeance* in 1986. Featuring a cover illustration of a dead priest in a burning church as well as explicitly Satanic lyrics, the album showcased a raw and distinctly sinister proto-black/thrash sound, alternating between a possessed battery and a more crawling pace, the guitar assault topped off by Angel's inhuman bellows. Musical influence had clearly seeped in from the likes of Venom, Celtic Frost, and Sodom, these inspirations also being more than evident in the band's attire.

"*Bloody Vengeance* was recorded during a weekend and we had to use the same amplifier for all instruments so the sound is not so good," says Zhema. "The album was rebellion against the system—laws, moral, ethics and any kind of religion. My biggest influence came from an alchemist and occultist belief. I always made a continuous search for anything that could explain the contradictions of the human being and its destiny, but I never believed in religions, sects, or dogmas. We do not dislike just Christian belief: we always disagreed with all the revealed religions, be it Christian, Islamic, Jewish, etc."

Like their German peers, Vulcano soon made a shift toward a more refined and less infernal thrash sound, partly because the famously corrupt police began hassling the band

Sarcófago: *Rotting*, 1989. While cover artist Kelson Frost apparently refused to include a crown of thorns so as not to identify the figure as Christ, it made the final image no less controversial.

after drummer Laudir Piloni was photographed bringing human bones to a show. This change was noticeable from the *Anthropophagy* album, released just one year later, and a further two albums would follow before the group split in 1990. Happily, they would reform in 2004, and while Zhema is now the sole founding member, the group have kept in touch with their dark roots and have been embraced by new generations of fans thanks to members of significant second-wave bands such as Darkthrone and Mayhem quite literally wearing their influence on their sleeves. Sweden's legendary Nifelheim even released a split with them, describing Vulcano as "one of the only remaining great and real 'black metal' bands."

"In the early 2000s I began to realize [the band's influence]," says Zhema. "It was a big surprise for me because I could not know that our music, rough, raw and brutal, might be a reference. I'm really proud of that."

SARCÓFAGO

Still Brazil's most famous black metal practitioners, the infamous Sarcófago was co-founded by Wagner "Antichrist" Lamounier back in 1985. The previous year had seen him installed as vocalist for the now hugely popular Sepultura (whose *Bestial Devastation* EP and *Morbid Visions* album, released 1985 and 1986 respectively, also demonstrated an influential proto black/thrash sound), but he had fallen out with the other members and left to begin his own project. Warming up with three demo cassettes (*Satanic Lust* and *The Black Vomit* from 1986 and *Sepultado* from 1987), the band would put themselves squarely on the map with 1987's *I.N.R.I.* A genuinely classic opus, the album drew influences from international acts vsuch as Sodom, Bathory, and Hellhammer, putting a distinctive spin on them while maintaining the chaotic violence (the frantic blastbeats of drummer D.D. Crazy being of particular note) and boasting a slightly tighter sound than their contemporaries.

Just as influential was the iconic cover—featuring the band posing in a cemetery clad in an impressive array of spikes, bullet belts, studs and inverted crosses and with black paint around their eyes—which presented an even more extreme aesthetic than that of earlier bands and thus had a huge impact on future acts. It would, in particular, inspire Norway's Mayhem, with Euronymous once famously stating "I'd like to see a scene … where the people in the scene all look like Hellhammer or old Sarcófago, spikes and chains."

1989's *Rotting* maintained the blasphemous intent, its cover painting depicting the grim reaper licking Christ's face, but saw the band moving in a more technical direction, with longer songs and more complexity in the songwriting. By 1991's *The Laws of Scourge* the band had undergone a fairly dramatic—if not unprecedented—reinvention, Wagner and co-founder Geraldo Minelli utilizing new members to create a more technical death/thrash sound, the lyrics covering more earthly subjects as opposed to the infernal topic of old. The band would find greater success with the formula, even getting some love from MTV, but ultimately split in 2000. The legacy of their early days would live on, though, this brief snapshot providing enough ammunition for decades to come.

While the bands that follow in this book did much to connect the first and second generations of black metal, there's no doubt that the groups in this chapter played a vital and often overlooked role, even if only in their more formative years. Black thrash, meanwhile, has had several resurgences in popularity over the years and maintains a dedicated fan base, with bands such as Bestial Mockery and Nifelheim (Sweden), Aura Noir and Vulture Lord (Norway), Destroyer 666 and Gospel of the Horns (Australia), and Sabbat and Abigail (Japan), among others (hell, at a push even the later output—and indeed the demeanor—of the iconic Immortal could be considered pretty black thrash/first-wave black metal in nature), keeping the crazed spirit of the early eighties alive.

8
BLASPHEMY

"Gerry was probably not the most productive guy of the early nineties in tape trading, but it was always the top quality recordings and good contacts he sent me. I thank Black Winds, Blasphemy, and Michelle Remembers *for being a such great inspiration on my journey. I believe Blasphemy."*
— Nuclear Holocausto (Beherit)

BY THE MID- TO LATE EIGHTIES, several key acts had helped push black metal to the raw, chaotic, and violent extremes that were its logical conclusion. Yet in most cases the emphasis on brutality proved to be only a temporary stance, and by the close of the decade legends such as Bathory, Destruction, and Sarcófago had all moved some way from their primitive beginnings and expanded into less primal and aggressive territories as their musical abilities and songwriting evolved. The black flame they had lit could not be extinguished, however, and a new generation of bands soon appeared to take their place, wielding occult brutality not as a temporary weapon to be dropped when one's musicianship had sufficiently improved, but as a permanent medium of expression.

Canadian fanatics Blasphemy first made their mark upon the international black metal scene in 1989, courtesy of demo tape *Blood Upon The Altar*. But they began life as far back as 1984, when the band was formed by vocalist and bassist Gerry Joseph Buhl (otherwise known by the lengthy pseudonym "Nocturnal Grave Desecrator and Black Winds") and drummer Sean Stone ("Three Black Hearts of Damnation and Impurity"). Both were British Columbian teenagers who were rapidly engrossing themselves in both the music and lifestyle of extreme metal.

"We'd known each other since we were ten-year-old kids," explains Black Winds, a man who despite his formidable appearance and reputation (he famously once punched through a car window to get his hands on a fleeing adversary) proves to be a surprisingly laid-back and down-to-earth interviewee.

"We had a beer stash, we had a weed stash, and we would walk up to this record store that was maybe a mile away from us and buy maybe four cassettes or records and then take them back to his place. School wasn't really a big thing by the time we hit about fourteen, the girls were always good but, you know, we had many other ways to hook up with them other than school. So we'd listen to Iron Maiden, Motörhead, Kiss was one of them, all that old stuff and we'd kick back in his yard, blast the tunes, drink our beer, smoke our weed, and just fucking have a good time. We were always in search of something heavier though… "

Soon discovering the likes of Sodom, Hellhammer, and Bathory, the two fans formed their own band with the aim of playing similarly rampaging, malevolent metal, recruiting neighbor and friend Geoff Drakes—better known by his "ritual name" of "Caller of the Storms"—as a guitarist. Trying out a number of band names, including Antichrist, Desaster, and Thrash Hammer, the group finally settled on Blasphemy, picking up a fourth member along the way in the form of Blake "Snake" Cromwell ("Black Priest of the Seven Satanic Blood Rituals"), a close friend of Icelandic origin who was "a pretty serious Satanist and demonologist." Indeed, as the band name suggests, Satanism and demonology were interests held by all members of the group, whose "ritual names" were more than grandiose-sounding pseudonyms, but rather the outcome of secret initiation rituals, many specific to Victoria's notorious Ross Bay Cemetery, a location the band would help bring to international fame.

"You'll feel the vibes when you go to that place," says Black Winds about the iconic graveyard, "you know you're in a very evil place. It's very old—at least as far as Canada goes—and has catacombs and stuff, masses of sarcophaguses that have been cracked open and pushed aside. But it's well-maintained too, it's got hundreds of trees and bushes and so on. But if you get down in any of those catacombs, I mean that's where we used to practice our stuff. We always kept [the exact nature of the rituals] private so I can't say too much, but [each member's ritual] would be something out of a book along with something we created."

Heavily wooded and facing out onto the Pacific Ocean and the Ross Bay from which it takes its name, the historic cemetery has become well known for the occult activities that have taken place within it, having even featured in the notorious "Satanic ritual abuse" book *Michelle Remembers*. It has also gained considerable fame thanks to Blasphemy themselves and interviews such as the one below, taken from *Gallery of the Grotesque* zine and featuring later guitarist Marco "The Traditional Sodomizer Of The Goddess Of Perversity" Banco.

"Watching naked girls rolling around on the freshly cut grass was always amusing at Ross Bay. Years earlier a massive storm had tore [*sic*] the front of the cemetery to pieces, sending coffins and bodies floating everywhere, some hundreds of years dead. There is a hidden tombstone of a buried witch there that is under some bushes, quite odd, the writing is hieroglyphic and places the time of death from the early 1900s: when I found this the fellow that had lived near the place his whole life was astonished that he'd never seen it before. This place points to the gates of Hell, Satanists have known this for two hundred years, that explains the fantastic beauty of the area. When I stand at the front of Ross Bay in the time before dawn facing the ocean and close my eyes and listen to the wind you will hear distinctly the sound of the dead."

"Victoria is one of the Satanic capitals of the world," explains Black Winds today.

"There was this club in this really hard-to-find, back-alley type place, and you'd walk in there and they'd usually be drinking from chalices what would look like blood, but was probably red wine for most. I remember they had their faces painted green, then they had the black war paint. There were also the Satanists we met at Ross Bay itself of course."

The cemetery would be mentioned by name on *Blood Upon the Altar*, thanks to the song "Ritual," which opened with the lines "Ross Bay grave/Black Mass begins." While one might expect these Satanic activities to be responsible for the delay between the group's formation and their first recorded output, the reality was somewhat more problematic, as Black Winds explained: "I got seven months I had to go do in jail ....soon as I got out, our guitarist got six months, so that kinda fucked up time for us, all that in between finding places to practice."

Indeed, in the years prior to their demo—and after that for that matter—the band built something of a reputation for trouble due to their taste for alcohol, drugs, bodybuilding, and fighting. As Black Winds remembers it, however, the band members themselves were never interested in initiating conflict with anyone, even if they weren't ones for backing down once it occurred.

"Say we go to a gig, a party, anything like that, you always get idiots who get in your face and they give you a problem," he sighs. "They want to get tough with you, and it's like, maybe a couple of our bandmates look at each other and go, 'We gotta fire these guys through the fucking wall, what the fuck?' You know, shit like that right? We were pretty much always like that. We don't go looking for trouble, it's just that trouble tends to follow and when the trouble follows we're pretty good at dealing with it."

These conflicts also tended to follow the band to their own notorious live performances, which involved heavy use of barbed wire, candles, bullets, fire-breathing, blood-spitting, war paint, and even stolen tombstones. Blasphemy's shows were not only chaotic on stage, but also saw frequent violence from the audience, a situation that ultimately led to the band being banned from many local venues.

"Yeah, shit like that would happen," laughs Black Winds, "The crowd would go a little *too* crazy, you know, a lot of shit would happen and the cops would show up 'cos bouncers started getting bounced around, windows getting smashed, that kinda thing."

As well as pulling in fans at their shows, the band's demo also found a warm reception, its aggressive and exhilarating sound straddling the worlds of death metal and black metal. Ultimately the tape would sell thousands of copies worldwide, and its success convinced the now infamous Wild Rags, a label run out of the Californian record store and clothes shop of the same name, to sign the band. Though they would release their 1990 debut album *Fallen Angel of Doom*, it was not to be a rewarding relationship from the band's point of view, due to the label's notoriously haphazard financial dealings—which saw the company closed down by the authorities some years later.

"Those guys really fucked up, I mean they could fuck up a cup of coffee, those guys,"

1990's barbaric debut album
Fallen Angel of Doom....

Black Winds spits, the anger evident in his tone. "I don't know how they had bands sign, 'cos they were a bunch of lowlife degenerates. The guy was supposed to pay us a dollar per album he sold, per CD, per cassette, per shirt. Money was never a big thing for me, but when he calls up and says, 'Black Winds, you'll never believe this, we just sold 4,500 copies of the CD alone just in Europe, imagine how much we've sold—especially in other countries!' And I was like, 'Yeah must be fucking over hundreds of thousands.' And he was like, 'Yeah for sure!' I'm like, 'Well that's cool,' you know, 'That's nice,' so I said, 'You making lots of money on it?' and he goes, 'Oh yeah' and I'm like, 'So you think we're gonna see our share?' 'Oh well, well, we're gonna have to fucking reinvest er' …. You mean you're not making enough money off of it to reinvest? You know, sure we've seen a few checks over the years, but nothing too large, I don't think we've seen more than 4,500 dollars and when he says he sold that in less than a month in CDs alone … I mean he's kinda *telling* me. … And whenever we called to say, 'Fire us up some dollars,' he would just ramble on. He was such a fucking fast-talking guy that we couldn't … you know, you just couldn't get a question in with the fucking guy. It's a good thing he wasn't based up here. We'd have had to go in and break some bones and shit like that."

While it might not have made them a great deal of money, *Fallen Angel of Doom* did earn the band an enviable reputation, establishing them as heirs to a throne that had long been vacated by the early-eighties pioneers that inspired them. Primal and aggressive, the album's short songs are almost unrelenting bombardments that focus on a ferocious percussive blitzkrieg and deep reverberating vocals, the lightning-fast atonal riffs buried somewhere within the primitive production. Interestingly, despite its timeless quality the band were actually somewhat disappointed with the finished opus, due to a shift in sound that occurred— for reasons unknown—between the recording (which took part at Fiasco Bros. Studio, the same location used for the demo) and the mastering.

"When we did the mixdown in the studio it sounded awesome," sighs Black Winds, "we could hear the bass, the guitar, the lead guitar, the drums, the vocals—everything was perfect. Then when we get it all pressed it was a complete different sound and you couldn't hear the guitars very well. We were maybe *eighty percent* happy, I know we could have done a lot better. It's a fucking really nice studio, I really don't know how it fucked up. But when boxes of albums are ending up on the doorstep and distributed over the world, it's a bit late to change anything."

Though its sound remains about as flat as the records it's pressed on, the album is none-theless a genre milestone. It also exposed the band to an even wider audience, introduc-ing the Ross Bay Cult to an in-ternational fan base. Another tagline included on the sleeve was "Black Metal Skinheads," a concept that was new to many, but reflected the culture that the band were a part of in Brit-ish Columbia.

"The black metal skin-heads, it really was a big thing," Black Winds remembers. "A lot of black metal skinheads from the other side of Canada, like Toronto and Montreal, would bounce over here. I remember one guy having Venom's 'Black Metal' tattooed on his head and there was another guy called Dale who had 'Black Metal Skins'

" FUCK CHRIST TOUR "

15 Dec.Barbue.Copenhagen.DANMARK.
16 Dec.Aktivitetshuset.Esbjerg.DANMARK.
17 Dec.Kiehool.Bergum.HOLLAND.
18 Dec.Baroeg.Rotterdam.HOLLAND.
19 Dec.Blackcat.Wertheim.GERMANY.
20 Dec.Knaack club.Berlin.GERMANY.
21 Dec.Rohre.Stuttgart.GERMANY.
22 Dec.Rose club.Koln.GERMANY.
23 Dec.Crash.Freiburg.GERMANY.
24 Dec.Batcave.Tilburg.HOLLAND.
25 Dec.Kassablanca.Jena.GERMANY.
26 Dec.Circus.Gammelsdorf.GERMANY.
27 Dec.P.M.R.C.St Niklaas.BELGIUM.
28 Dec.Gibus.Paris.FRANCE.
29 Dec.Rockline.Lille.FRANCE.

Info : call **OSMOSE** at (33)21810374 or **METALLYSEE** at (32)53665926.

A flyer for 1993's legendary *Fuck Christ* tour. The first tour of black metal's 'second wave,' it saw the Canadians appearing alongside Norway's Immortal and Greece's Rotting Christ.

tattooed on his forehead. You could go to a party just about seven days a week. We didn't hang out with white power skinheads, but there were some Oi! skinheads who wanted to hang out with us, and we would let them as long as they didn't get into any political bullshit. We always tried to steer away from that. Politics just ain't our bag."

Despite that, in a scene predominantly consisting of Caucasians, the very fact that Blasphemy featured a black member was something of a political point in itself. While people of color are fairly rare in metal generally, in black metal bands they are still almost all but completely absent (with notable exceptions including the Brazilian pioneers Mystifier). This drew attention to Blasphemy, particularly since racial concerns had begun to creep into some quarters of the scene.

"I know it was very different, since there are only a couple of black dudes in metal bands. For me ....you know, skin color just doesn't matter to me, it's the personality, and one thing I can say about Geoff, our black guitarist, is he's fucking cooler than ninety-five percent of the white people I meet. He is as black metal as they come, the guy plays gui-

Blasphemy's second album *Gods of War*.
Released in 1993, it's been re-released times
with a variety of different covers, all of which
seem to have failed to capture the band's
intended concept.

tar better than anybody I know, he can blast away on the drums better than just about anybody I know, he's got stacks and stacks of black metal photos, he's got every black metal T-shirt you can imagine, that dude just *is* black metal. Nobody would ever give him problems though" …he pauses before laughing at the thought. "That guy would bounce heads off walls, down stairs, everything. He's a pretty big guy."

It would be three years before the next Blasphemy recordings were released in the shape of *Gods of War*, a slightly less chaotic but similarly possessed-sounding release that also includes the *Blood Upon the Altar* demo due to its short twenty-minute running time. By this point Traditional Sodomizer had departed, leaving all guitars to Caller of the Storms. The album also featured a new bass player, the memorably named "Ace Gestapo Necrosleezer and Vaginal Commands." Released by French label Osmose (of whom the band still have good things to say) and benefiting from a less murky sound, the album was an improvement in some respects, though Black Winds maintains its predecessor was closer to the band's vision.

"As far as I'm concerned it just wasn't as good as *Fallen Angel of Doom*. It wasn't as crushing, it wasn't as Satanic … I'm kind of upset at it. You can hear the guitars better, the sound was better but I was kind of disappointed. Someone also fucked up the cover—it was supposed to be four goats pulling what looks like a woman, but it was like a *skull-faced* woman on the original picture we had, and the only colors were supposed to be black, red and white, so things kinda got changed on us here and there along the way."

Nevertheless, fan response was positive and the same year saw the band embarking on the legendary Fuck Christ tour—often described as the first second-wave black metal tour—with Osmose labelmates Rotting Christ and Immortal. While the jaunt enabled European fans to finally see the group, it would also result in drummer and co-founder Three Black Hearts being thrown into jail after "flipping out" on the plane back from Europe and then assaulting several police. By this point the band was in some disarray generally and Black Winds himself was no longer a part of the band due to an earlier tour-related disagreement involving Ace Gustapo.

"I didn't even go on [the Fuck Christ] tour," he explains, "I was really pissed off about the first tour, how I let this bass player play for us … and I must have said to him ten times, 'You got the box with all the bullets, all the hardware for the stage?' 'Yeah, yeah, I got it all,

A more modern incarnation of Blasphemy. Even their official photoshoots encapsulate the unpolished and chaotic nature of this timeless band.

don't worry,' and while we're flying over the Atlantic to Europe, sure enough he didn't have them. And you know when I'm playing on stage without that stuff I feel like I'm fucking naked, I felt I couldn't carry on with it. The look was as important as the music, so it was like, 'I'm just fucking ending this for myself, if you want to go on and embarrass yourselves carry on,' that was the end for me."

Eventually Ace and the band would go their separate ways, with Blasphemy receiving what Black Winds describes as a "rebirth" at the beginning of the millennium. Since then the band have maintained their presence within the scene, headlining events such as Nuclear War Now festival with the aid of guitarist Ryan "Deathlord Of Abomination and War Apocalypse" Foster, also known for his work with fellow Ross Bay Cultists Conqueror. This, along with the proliferation of bands playing a similarly barbaric form of black metal—for example Spain's Proclamation, who stay true to the band's sound and aesthetic and are signed to the Ross Bay Cult label—keep the band from being forgotten, something that Black Winds has been kept acutely aware of, sometimes in surprising circumstances.

"My daughter just graduated from high school, like maybe three years ago, and everybody at her school, they couldn't believe I was her dad. I mean she's not into black metal, but all the older kids at the school had Blasphemy T-shirts and listened to Blasphemy—and of course other black metal bands—so when she would come over to my place and tell me stuff like this of course I was pretty surprised. And then I'd go to the gigs and they'd recognize me. And I'm like, 'Holy fuck, these guys are seventeen, eighteen years old.' I'm just happy black metal didn't die out or nothing, in fact if anything I think it's gotten a lot bigger."

For his part, Black Winds has kept true to the cause, and musically—aside from the perhaps surprising inclusion of English sixties outfit The Animals—his listening habits tend to lean toward the bands who inspired Blasphemy and the bands who were, in turn, inspired by Blasphemy.

"Black Witchery from Florida, Archgoat, Proclamation, Revenge, Order From Chaos," he explains when asked the acts he most favors, "still listen to a lot of Destruction, Hellhammer, Vulcano, Sarcófago, Adorior, Abominator, Venom's *Black Metal* album, Sodom—*old* Sodom that is, Sadistik Execution and Gospel of the Horns, Mortuary Drape, Discharge, and Warfare from England."

Having helped put the wheels in motion for the rebirth of barbaric black metal, Blasphemy's place in the genre's history is assured and it seems only fitting to let the formidable front man end this chapter in the same manner he ended the interview:

"As I always say, keep up the spirits with the black metal, bitches, barbed wire, bullets, and beer!"

9

SAMAEL

"Samael were one of the bands that were feeding the black metal flame in a period when almost no one else did. Samael had a more occult feeling to it and definitely weren't in any black thrash tradition and didn't really have lot of death metal either. I think it's strange, people took the May-hem/Darkthrone/Burzum road, I wonder why didn't more bands take the Samael road, because that was definitely interesting."

—Fenriz (Darkthrone)

"When I read the lyric[s] of the Samael song 'Worship Him,' I felt [sic] on knees over the ground and gave servitude to Satan. This song is a true pray [sic] to the Evil, one can see that it was written… not only with feeling, but faith too!"

—Tomasz Krajewski, later of Pagan Records,
writing passionately in the early nineties in his zine *Holocaust*

"Euronymous was like, 'Oh you gotta listen to this album, it's fucking great,' and gave me the Samael album Worship Him. *That was a musical revelation to me."*

—Silenoz (Dimmu Borgir)

HAVING ALREADY GIVEN the world Hellhammer and Celtic Frost, Switzerland had one more highly significant contribution to make before the eighties came to a close. Formed in 1987 by Michael Locher, otherwise known as Vorphalack and later simply Vorph, Samael drew upon the primal magnificence of the early eighties black metal bands, who were by that point largely forgotten thanks to both the increasingly technical thrash scene promi-nent at the time and the burgeoning death metal scene that was fast emerging.

"Basically when we started up in 1987 we were mainly influenced by what is called the first wave of black metal, the originators; Venom, Celtic Frost, Bathory, stuff like that," begins Vorph. "I had been listening to metal for years, but the darker side of metal was always a little bit more thrilling, a bit more interesting to me. It's probably when I heard *Apocalyptic Raids* from Hellhammer that I thought, 'Wow, this is something that I can do, that I can dig and

that I can do my own way,' because most of the metal bands at the time were very technical, they had a wide range of possibility, whereas we were more limited. So instead of trying
to show off how good you were at whatever instrument you were playing or impress people
with your skills, we were trying to create a mood, an atmosphere. That's how it started really.
I used to say it back in the day, it was more about *feelings* than melody or technique, I was
just trying to create something that [would cause people to] find themselves in a different
dimension or world somehow."

In the early days, Vorph took the leading role in the band, handling everything other
than the drums, which were played by one Pat Charvet. Two rehearsal/demo tapes were issued, entitled *Into The Infernal Storm of Evil* and *Macabre Operetta*, before Pat was replaced by
Vorph's brother Alexandre, who was known as Xytraguptor, later shortening his pseudonym
to the more pronounceable Xy.

"Pat was my best friend at the time and I just convinced him to take up the drums, 'cos
this was something I wanted to do for a long time," Vorph explains. "With him I recorded
two demos, but it wasn't really his thing and he kind of lost interest, which is when Xy took
his place. He wanted to do a band of his own, in fact he had his own band with two other
friends where he was actually playing guitar, but there were a couple of times when Pat didn't
want to come to the rehearsal and Xy was able to learn the songs in one week or so, so we
soon had two songs that were perfect. We were not hanging out and it was probably only
when my father died that we got closer and actually that's when we started to play together."

In 1988 the duo recorded a three-track EP entitled *Medieval Prophecy*, released at the
end of that year, initially as a tape and then as a seven-inch vinyl. This well-received release
contained two original compositions, namely "Into The Pentagram" and "The Dark," as well
as a cover of "Third of the Storms" by Hellhammer, a band from whom Samael had clearly
taken much inspiration. Drawing upon the slow, despairing, yet *aggressive* approach of their
countrymen, Samael pushed things a stage further, not least through Vorph's vocals: slow,
unearthly screams that hinted at the likes of Quorthon (who Vorph explains was "one of my
biggest influences for my vocals") but entered into even more tortured realms.

"We recorded [*Medieval Prophecy*] in a home studio of a guy who didn't have much
clue about metal at all, but at least he had a *place*, so we tried to do best we could. Of course,
it was pretty pathetic, if you listen to it today, he had no knowledge about how to do things
and neither did we, so we had to find ways to make our music as close as we could to what
we expected. I think we recorded for two days and did the mix together at the same time. A
few months later we had the copies of the seven-inch and nine months after we received the
first thousand copies we sold out, so we printed two hundred more with different covers."

It is testament to the strength of the underground (as well the strength of the material) that the band were able to sell out of *Medieval Prophecy* in such a short amount of time,
especially given that they were not yet playing live and were pretty much on their own, both
stylistically and geographically. Though Samael had corresponded with Norway's Mayhem

Pure cult: *Medieval Prophecy*, 1988. Originally released on tape, it was soon pressed onto vinyl in 1000 copies (shown here). It was repressed with a new design after selling out.

since their early days (Euronymous was a great fan, and even suggested that he regretted not having them on his label), at this point there was nothing approaching a "black metal scene." Instead it was a case of engaging with the small but varied collection of bands that inhabited the international metal underground.

"There was no Internet, which is like talking about the Middle Ages somehow," laughs Vorph, "but we were in contact with other bands, trading tapes, and trading tapes against fanzines, so we had a lot of contacts. Once we had the EP out we sent ten or twenty copies to the biggest fanzines we knew and they made reviews and that's how it spread. You spread flyers all over the place, and would get orders from South America, Japan, anywhere in the world. The flyers thing was the best way to have your own name somewhere else, you would spread your own flyers along with those of other bands that you got, everybody helped each other somehow. A lot of those bands don't exist anymore, I don't even remember all the names, but I remember trading with Nick [Holmes] of Paradise Lost, Lee [Dorrian] from Cathedral, Chris [Reifert] from Autopsy, Immolation, Nocturnus, Blasphemy, Beherit, and Carcass.

**A flyer for Samael's 1991 debut *Worship Him*,
featuring a notably youthful-looking lineup.**

Carcass were a fine example, because they already had an album out and it wasn't a rule, but most bands when they had an album out, they would not waste time to trade stuff with people from the underground. But Carcass were one of the only bands who were signed but would take time out to check out what was coming onto the scene or happening in the underground."

Recognizing promising new talent, the newly formed Osmose Productions—a label which, a few years down the line, would gather one of the most impressive rosters in the black metal scene—quickly signed the band. Released on the auspicious date of April 1, 1991, *Worship Him* was not only the first album for the Swiss group, but also, in fact, the first full-length album released on the Osmose label. By now the band had become a trio, having been joined by Christophe "Masmiseim" Mermod, a bassist who had previously played in black metal outfit Alastis and still remains with Samael today, some two decades later.

Vorph—who had contributed vocals to Alastis' demo the previous year—continued with guitars and vocals, his lyrics remaining suitably hellish, the title track being "a prayer to the lord of the dark side's glory" and other songs exploring black magic and occult practices. For his part, Xy was now contributing keyboards as well as drums to the band, a fairly minimal addition at this stage, but one that would increase dramatically in the years that followed. For now, however, the band continued in a vein similar to the "Into The Pentagram" track on their debut EP, playing primitive Hellhammer-inspired black metal, a sound still largely unheard of at the time, not least by Claude Lander, the next producer to work with the group.

"That guy didn't have much idea about metal either," Vorph sighs. "I think he'd recorded two metal bands, but they were more like hard rock. He'd never heard someone screaming their lungs out in the studio, so for him it was kinda weird and he probably didn't consider it to be music, but at least he tried to do his best with the knowledge he had. The charisma of that first record is of working with a guy that doesn't know what he's doing, while you have a precise idea of what you want to do, so there's that confrontation."

After the release of *Worship Him*, the band moved to Germany's Century Media, another relatively small label that would grow massively in stature as the decade progressed. Vorph

Picking up the pace: *Ceremony of Opposites*, 1994, helped break the band internationally.

explains that the band were keen to join the label as they had noticed that bands already on the roster were touring heavily, something Samael were desperate to do, if only to counter the drawbacks of their geographical isolation. The decision paid off, and the band did indeed embark on their first European tour (with labelmates Unleashed and Tiamat) following the release of their second album, 1992's *Blood Ritual*. Adorned with a stunning cover painting that positively oozed atmosphere, it was a record that saw the band finally working with a like-minded individual in the studio, namely Waldemar Sorychta, who produced almost every Samael album that followed.

    Blood Ritual certainly features remnants of the sinister Hellhammer-inspired primitivism found on *Worship Him*, but is a somewhat more sophisticated-sounding effort, the production being notably less raw and the songs being a tad more technical, utilizing instruments such as acoustic guitars and keyboard to powerful effect. Just as the debut album reworked songs from the first demo, the follow-up reworked two songs from *Macabre Operetta*, namely "Blood Ritual" and the title track itself, a song that retained its drawn-out and ritualistic vibe, neatly complementing the similarly inclined lyrics.

A far bigger leap in style, however, would come with 1994's *Ceremony of Opposites*, an album that once again came in a striking sleeve, this time featuring a red-bordered mono- chrome depiction of an eyeless Christ-like face with nails hammered into his head. A notably slicker effort musically, it boasted a significantly more polished production, as well as a fourth member, Rodolphe H., who handled keyboards and sampler. The album picked up the pace considerably, with driving and surprisingly catchy compositions that moved away from the cavernous primitivism of old in favor of a less archaic atmosphere, with orchestral flourishes used to great effect on numbers such as "Baphomet's Throne." It was a record that would surprise and even alienate many of those who had followed the band previously, but one that would also win the band many new fans. This shift in direction reflected a significant change within the workings of the band itself, and from this album onward Xy took over the writing of the music, as a surprisingly modest Vorph explains.

"On that album I let him do what he wanted to, I wrote one song and that was enough," he explains. "I felt a little bit relieved and that things were falling into place. When you learn to interact with other people, you learn to let something go. I mean, I had less control, but I felt better because I agreed that he was better than I am to write the songs. When Xy started to do the music it became more technical, because he's a better guitarist than I am—still today in fact. I had to learn how to play the stuff he was composing, so I had to work a bit more but it also gave me more time to work on my lyrics and go deeper into the subject matter."

Samael's lyrics had already drawn attention from fans and the underground press due to their heavily occult subject matter, and while the third album continued in a similar vein, it also saw Vorph begin to expand his horizons thematically. No longer responsible for the compositions, he began to pour more time into researching the lyrics and to this day the conceptual foundations of the group remain a focal point, with Vorph putting a great deal of emphasis on the subjects of spirituality, philosophy, and self-discovery.

"It was the first time I didn't compose the music so I spent more time on the subjects I wanted to deal with. On the first two albums I would write about things I'd read some- where—occultism, secret societies, stuff like that, that was the main inspiration I had. I never considered myself as a Satanist—of course I had an interest in it, it was one of the things that was around, so I wanted to know what it was all about. Probably already on *Ceremony*, I started to write about things I felt and experienced myself 'cos I started to have a life."

"To me spirituality is not bound to religion," he continues, elaborating on the approach that has defined the content of later records, "it's how you build yourself inside. Part of it is a response to the environment and the education you have, and the rest you're doing your- self, you're building yourself the way you want to be. That's how I look at spirituality, it's

how you work out your 'inside universe.'
And that's why we've used references to
space. A lot of people have thought that
we are about space travel, which wasn't
the case for me; it was more about putting images to this 'inside space,' which
is one of the central themes in our lyrics and concepts. I'm interested in Daniel
Dennett, who wrote a lot about how you
build yourself, about what is predeter-
mined and what is your margin of choice."

If *Ceremony* opened the gates of
self-discovery lyrically, then so did it musically. But while that album showed a
massive leap stylistically, it was nothing
compared to its 1996 follow-up, *Passage*,

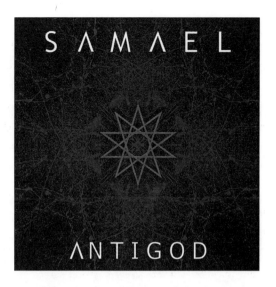

**Over twenty years later and the band's anti-
religious position remains: 2010's *Antigod* EP.**

the first album, incidentally, to boast any galactic imagery. While Xy remained the main songwriter, he removed himself from his drum kit, seemingly permanently, taking over keyboard
duties and handling all percussion on the album via drum programming. It was a bold move
and one that had a massive impact on the band's sound. Retaining the groove present in its
predecessor, *Passage* was an intense and stomping listen that married industrial elements
with then-contemporary black metal overtones in a highly rhythmic fashion. Needless to say,
the shift was another controversial one.

"We never really cared about that," laughs Vorph. "*Passage* was our fourth album and
we had some experience of how things worked. When you released your first album a lot
of people would turn their back on you, 'cos your album was available in the shops, so you
would no longer be part of the underground family. That was the never-ending talk—being
'real,' being 'underground'—so in that sense we'd already betrayed something in the eyes of
some people. Then we did *Blood Ritual*, which had a good sound, which again wasn't good
for some people. *Ceremony*, even though it was sounding good, it was sounding different
to anything else. Then *Passage* had the drum machine—there is always something for some
people to complain about. As long as you're comfortable with what you're doing, it's the
most important thing. That's the reason we're doing this, we're not really a band that's there
to please people."

This disregard for outside opinion stretched as far as the band's record label and, despite protests, the members decided to commit fully to electronic percussion from the *Passage* album onward.

"The label was quite scared by the decision we made and did everything they could
to get us to have a real drummer. In the studio they thought it would be okay, but live

Despite struggling to get out of Switzerland in their early years, Samael are now a regular touring band, headlining venues around the world.

they thought it would be a total mess, which wasn't the case. That *was* probably the biggest change in the band's history though. It opened doors for us, to do different things and play with different sounds. We didn't have to have a drum sound on every song, we could use different samples. We did a mini-album between *Ceremony* and *Passage* called *Rebellion* and there was one song which was *only* programming, an experimental song. We had no idea [then] that on the next album we would use the drum machine, but if you look back, it could be the link. Some of the early industrial bands like Ministry, Godflesh, Pitchshifter, they had an influence on us at that time, definitely. Those were bands who were playing with the drum machine and trying different sounds.

"But I think the way Xy programs the drum is very different," he continues thoughtfully. "It's more like he *plays* the drums, it's not repetitive or about using loops, it's just programming it the way they're played and that makes us more metal than industrial probably. Today there are still people who want the real thing, for us to have a drummer like every other band does, but that's one of the things that makes us different and I don't think we will go back to the original formula. We will stick to our guns."

Samael have certainly done that, continuing with a successful career until the present day. However, *Passage*—rather aptly given its name—was arguably the point when the band really moved away from the black metal movement. Though it shared traits with the then-modern black metal sound (perhaps by coincidence as much as intention) it left behind the early black metal sound the band had worked with so successfully. Later albums would move more squarely into industrial/electronic metal territories and away, therefore, from the central focus of this book.

10
ROTTING CHRIST
AND
GREEK BLACK METAL

"While the Norwegians were good at making headlines and making sure their faces snuck into the frames of magazines, black and extreme metal was actually being shaped from the outside inwards, toward Norway. One of the major Southern European influences was Rotting Christ, with their unique brand of mid-tempo Bathory-esque mystique and eerie atmospheres. Totally unique and magical! And the fact that one of metal's biggest disgraces, Dave Mustaine (eek!), stays away from festivals if they're playing (because of the name), should award them some kind of honorary award."

—Ivar (Enslaved)

"At one time Thy Mighty Contract *was the only black metal album that I was really into. The atmosphere of that album is really unique and it had an aura around it that was very different to the Norwegian cold sound."*

—Blasphemer (Mayhem/Aura Noir)

"If you want to listen to bands that are really original, then listen to Rotting Christ! Their music is so Dark, so BRUTAL! ARGH!!"

—Euronymous, *Slayer Magazine*

DESPITE HAILING FROM GREECE as opposed to Switzerland—and thus avoiding the isolation of coming from a country without an emerging metal movement—Rotting Christ's story bears many parallels to that of Samael. Both are hugely influential bands that formed in 1987, have a lineup based around a pair of brothers, and have exhibited a notable evolution between each and every record.

Rotting Christ's first sticker, provided by Sakis himself, features the band's classic logo.

Unlike Samael, however, the path Rotting Christ walked in their early days had very little to do with black metal at all. Instead the band leaned toward grindcore, a point under-lined by their demo *Decline's Return* and the rehearsal tape *Leprosy of Death*, as well as their 1989 split seven-inch, which saw Sakis "Necromayhem" Tolis (vocals and guitars), Themis "Necrosauron" Tolis (drums), and Jim "Mutilator" Patsouris (bass) cramming in nine songs in less than six minutes. The other side of the record saw a similar display by fellow Greek death/grinders Sound Pollution, a short-lived project that also featured Sakis on vocals.

"We didn't expect big things back then, we were so poor that we were forced even to steal our instruments in order to start playing!" remembers Sakis. "I was feeling like a junkie that couldn't get his smack, so I was forced to do that, something that I only recovered from years after [by] giving the money to the store and apologizing, because I have never ripped anyone off in my life. We were fans of grindcore back then, though not the grindcore sound you hear nowadays, but instead something really primitive with lots of noise. Maybe this is a result of being fans of the punk attitude back then."

Alongside these interests in punk and grind, the band's members also bore a passion for metal, something that actually far preceded the creation of Rotting Christ. Unsurprisingly then, the trio soon decided that they wanted to draw on their original musical inspirations within their own band.

"I will be a liar if I don't mention Iron Maiden, right?" smiles Sakis, "also bands like Motörhead, but we were *really* fascinated with the first-era black metal bands such as Venom, Bathory, Possessed, Hellhammer, and Celtic Frost, and we were really influenced by them in our first steps. I remember when I listened to Hellhammer for the first time, I was actually scared. I couldn't understand how music could sound so gloomy. Every night before I slept I was listening to it on my walkman—cassette of course—in order to have a really weird sleep. The same happened when I first listened to Bathory's song 'Possessed'... I suddenly discovered my dark side and since then I have been following its path. We were basically a company of guys that brought this extreme metal music back to our land in the late eighties and we really wanted to create a horde that would sound like our idols."

The *Satanas Tedeum* demo, released in mid-1989, clearly demonstrated this intent, not only in the title and cover art (which featured a new, more sinister logo and the inclusion of a pentagram) but also in sound. Boasting longer and darker songs, it has a primitive and cavernous sound, and a black thrash/old-school death metal vibe despite the use of keyboards—an inclusion still unusual at that time. The band then described their music as "Abyssic Death Metal," though they explain quite rightly that this was "only because the term black metal was not yet established in the underground, and death and black metal were more or less interchangeable in those days." In fact, when it came to Greece, extreme metal in general was still a pretty new phenomenon and the band found themselves climbing a pretty steep learning curve.

"You can't imagine how hard it was back then for a band that came from Greece, especially during the late eighties when everyone considered Greece an exotic country that was a good place for a vacation and nothing more. But on the other hand, it was a challenge and challenges always make you work harder than normal. You know what created the biggest problem? There were no other Greek bands that had experience of the central European attitude [to releasing music and touring], so we were forced to learn everything from zero and that took a lot of time."

1990 turned out to be a quiet time for the band, but the following year saw them continuing in a similar musical vein on a single entitled *Dawn of the Iconoclast* and a mini-album, *Passage To Arcturo*, that saw the addition of synth player George Zaharopoulos, alternately known as Morbid, Magus Wampyr Daoloth, and now simply The Magus. *Passage* would be the first release to really carve an identity for the group and impress an international audience. Finland native Mikko Aspa (best known for his work in Clandestine Blaze and Deathspell Omega) recalls its impact:

"It presented black metal in the way that I prefer it," he comments. "Unique, untrendy, free of formulas typical of the era, and free of 'scenester' influence. It would be as dark as black metal can get, without sounding like anyone in Sweden, Finland, USA, or Norway. While trendies would jump into popular sounds and gain popularity, the sound of Rotting Christ would remain untainted by false copycats. This is the nature of true black metal, when it is an uncontrolled, spontaneous dark force in both music and lyrics/artwork."

While the quality of the material on the mini-album would certainly play its part in breaking the band to a larger audience, it also undoubtedly helped matters that the group—like many others at the time—had been busily trading with the underground for some time.

"Back then I was in contact with almost all the bands that were around," explains

Sakis. "That was a really important matter of my life, I became a freak and totally addicted to that. A new demo, a new fanzine, a new letter… I was expecting the postman everyday as if he were Santa Claus. He was bringing to me food for my soul. If he was bringing some demos then it was my day, if not I was falling into depression."

The combination of underground trading and impressive recordings began to bring the band to the attention of extreme metal fans worldwide and soon the group was signed by Osmose, who released their debut full-length *Thy Mighty Contract*, a genuine milestone recording. Demonstrating a noticeably more considered approach than their earlier output, the album put both Rotting Christ and Greece into the consciousness of the black metal scene, providing an early showcase of what would became known as the "Greek black metal sound."

This new approach to the genre was defined by surprisingly melodic heavy metal riffs, the use of guitar harmonies, prominent bass, and a far less caustic and treble-heavy production than the one generally coming out of Northern Europe. Moreover, though the record featured a drum machine, it was a take on the genre that was noticeably "warm" in tone— something frequently attributed to the sweltering region from whence it came and a trait that has become fairly traditional among the Greek bands that followed.

"It is in fact true that the Scandinavians have a colder, more 'reverbed' sound, whilst the South Europeans have a more heavy and warm sound in their guitars," opines Alexandros Antoniou of second-generation Greek acts Macabre Omen and The One. "Do not forget that music is art and art always gets inspired by something. The cold is very accessible in the Northern lands, hence the freezing sound and vice versa."

"I wouldn't say it was the climate exactly, but I can say more the mentality of the southern people," Sakis ponders when asked for the reasons behind these distinctive aural traits. "We were always expressing an alternative way on how black metal could sound, even if we were never as extreme as other bands. I think it was a good thing that almost all the bands were recording in the same studio back then, that was a time when we created a unique sound and the relations between the local bands were really strong. It was a place where you could exchange ideas and so on, a meeting point. I am proud that we had created a strong and influential scene back then."

Indeed, a major catalyst for the creation of this "Greek template" was the use of the band's own Storm Studios, a location that would soon be used by many other bands in the local scene, many of whom would share members with Rotting Christ at one time or another.

"It was the time that every band wanted to create its own sound," explains The Magus, keyboard player and second vocalist on *Thy Mighty Contract*. While he would not begin engineering Rotting Christ until the band's second album, he had already engineered works by a number of other bands at Storm and would produce or engineer for bands such as Septic Flesh, Kawir, Astarte, and Varathron as well as his own groups Necromantia and Thou Art Lord.

"When I started working on production I always wanted to underline the lyrical part of the music, which was the melody and the atmosphere, the unique characteristic of the Greek

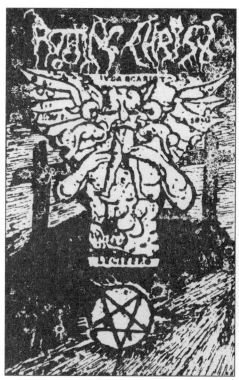

Left: Rotting Christ: *Satanas Tedeum* demo, 1989.
Right: Flyer for *The Black Arts / The Everlasting Sins*, the 1992 split release of Necromantia and Varathron, two of Greece's most seminal bands.

bands," he explains. "You see, in Greece the music was always more emotionally charged than the other scenes. It is in the Greek soul. Furthermore I come from a strong heavy metal background and it was kind of natural to go for the feeling, rather than a brutal ton-of-bricks sound. The funny thing is that the equipment we used was pretty cheap since there was not enough money and we were trying a lot of recipes and experiments until we got a decent sound. Combinations of various amplifiers, expensive microphones, cheap microphones, both combined and a lot more. We had to be inventive and creative!"

Based in Athens, Storm Studios became a focal point for the country's growing black metal movement, bringing together like-minded individuals for various musical and non-musical endeavors. Their recordings soon spread worldwide, with records released by European labels such as Osmose and Holy Records as well as the Athens-based Unisound Records.

"Most of the bands knew each other," explains The Magus. "We were not that many back then so we hung around at the same places and everybody was trying to add their own sound and record an album. The most important bands besides Necromantia and Rotting Christ were: Varathron, Septicemia, Septic Flesh, Horrified, and Death Courier and later on Kawir, Zemial, and Nergal emerged with a strong impact. Like everywhere, only a few had serious interest in the dark side. Few were (and are still) involved in it. I proudly consider myself one of them. My quest through the Abyss has never stopped… For the wide majority it was the 'heavy metal Satanism' which attracted them. You know, a little bit of rebellion, sex, diversity… the usual. But still even this attitude is okay since it creates less sheep!"

Of all the Greek bands, however, it was Rotting Christ who had the biggest international presence and it's notable that one interested party at the time was Deathlike Silence, the Norwegian label owned by Euronymous of Mayhem, with only the latter's death ending the union between the two parties.

"We were so close to doing a split LP with Burzum but Euronymous' death meant this couldn't be done. I was really good friends with Euronymous—in fact, the first-ever Mayhem show outside of Norway was actually supposed to take part in Greece. We had booked the show and we were waiting for the band in the train station to come from Norway, but due to the wrong understanding [sic] of a letter that was received by a relative of Euronymous' when the band was on the road—we didn't have mobiles or e-mails back then—the band was informed by mistake that they cannot play in Greece but in Turkey. I still can't understand how this happened, but that's why the first band's show outside of Norway was in Turkey."

One can only speculate about how a split with Norway's Burzum—and a release on Deathlike Silence—might have affected the band's career, but it's fair to say that their relationship with Osmose certainly didn't do them any harm, and quickly led to an increased international profile. This was further bolstered when the band set off—along with Canadians Blasphemy and Norwegians Immortal—on the legendary Fuck Christ tour.

"It was a great experience for us, though I only remember blurry things. We were not the band that drank alcohol a lot, we were more into smoking pot the whole day. We were stoned all the time and were also inexperienced kids facing first-time experiences. I remember shows were cancelled because of death threats from Christians, people [in the audience] were cutting their veins… every day was a new experience with strange things happening, a really primitive black metal era!"

Recording again in Storm Studios and retaining the drum machine, 1994's *Non Serviam* continued—to some extent at least—where *Thy Mighty Contract* left off. Engineered by The Magus and produced by the band, it undoubtedly offered a far grander and more majestic sound, heavier use of synth, and a greater sense of dynamics than its predecessor.

"You can hear that *Non Serviam* has a heavier, fuller sound than *Thy Mighty Contract*," comments The Magus. "It was the successor of a highly successful album and it had to be better! We recorded a lot more guitars and we tried a variation of guitar amplifiers—back then downtuning was not known so we had to record six guitars in order to choose the ones we wanted and mix them together. We also tried to make the cheap drum triggering sound a little bit better! We were really satisfied because we got the atmosphere we wanted and Sakis' songwriting has started to shape and mature, thus creating more solid songs. I think that *Non Serviam* was the album which shaped Rotting Christ's sound for the years that followed."

Rotting Christ today, the Tolis brothers still at the helm decades later. Courtesy of Century Media.

Powerful and dramatic, it remains one of the band's finest records, yet was also indirectly responsible for one of the most trying periods of the band's existence. Sakis explains:

"Like *Thy Mighty Contract*, *Non Serviam* was created under the influence of holy smoke and I still consider this album to be the one with the most Rotting Christ riffs ever. It was not, however, accepted as that hot by the underground community back then because its distribution was *more* than shitty. It was released by Unisound which was a label only on paper… they had nothing to do with any promotion outside of Greek territories, so this album suffered from a really bad distribution. We actually had thoughts to split up the band back then."

Indeed, in a pre-Internet age, there were many outside Greece who thought that the band *had* split up, simply because they never saw the appearance of the *Non Serviam* album, or at least not until many, many years later. The group's reaction to such trials, however, should remain both an inspiration and a lesson for any band facing hard times.

"A soldier never abandons the battlefield!" says Sakis. "We got a car and drove the whole *continent* in order to give our recordings to labels *by hand*. Of course it was really hard, because we had no money for this travel and I remember we were sleeping in the car with the danger of losing our lives, especially when we were crossing the Alps. Our sleep there could easily have been our last, and an eternal one, because we almost froze."

Fortunately the hard work paid off and the group were soon signed by Century Media, who released 1996's *Triarchy of the Lost Lovers*. As well as losing keyboard player The Magus (who found the band's new direction too melodic and gothic in nature) and the drum machine—Necrosauron returning to the drum kit from this point on—the band also departed Storm, recording in Germany with Andy Classen of Teutonic thrashers Holy Moses. The result was a shift away from the black metal sound of old, toward a more traditional heavy metal-oriented approach, yet with the vocal aggression and much of the heaviness present on earlier recordings. The 1997 follow-up, *A Dead Poem*, would move even further away from the black metal scene, building upon the heavy metal dimension and combining it with gothic overtones, a fusion that saw the band reaching their biggest audiences to date.

The Magus meanwhile would concentrate on Necromantia, arguably Greece's second biggest name in black metal and one that famously used two bass guitars (one eight-stringed) in place of any rhythm guitar, a trait they maintain even today. He would also continue to make music with Sakis in Thou Art Lord, creating what he describes as "pure thrash/death/black metal the old way," and would also find an unlikely creative partner in Mika Luttinen of Finnish outfit Impaled Nazarene, with whom he would work on two industrial metal projects, Raism and Diabolos Rising.

Over the years, Rotting Christ would gradually return to heavier and more blackened territories, their 2007 album *Theogonia* even being hailed by some as their best work yet, introducing ethnic Greek elements that have remained in the records that have followed, the band making heavy use of traditional Greek choirs to impressive effect.

All in all, Rotting Christ have proved to be an ever-shifting entity musically, yet even now they remain defined, and even restricted, by their provocative band name, which over the years has offended many overzealous religious types. These include American politician and one-time Republican candidate Gary Bauer—a man with ties to evangelical Christian groups who famously criticized rap metal act Rage Against The Machine for being "anti-family and pro-terrorist"—as well as Megadeth frontman and born-again Christian Dave Mustaine, who demonstrated his own intolerance by having the band thrown off the bill of two large Greek festivals in 2005. Having braved the cold of the Alps in the name of his art, Sakis has little time for such individuals.

"He thought that our name is offensive on his beliefs," concludes Sakis, "but he didn't think that we live in the twenty-first century and that these ideas belong to other centuries. Originally living in a fundamentalist religious country—as Greece was when we formed—we wanted to show our resistance to this sort of conservative attitude. Black metal is a punch of resistance—or at least was back then—so what better than to choose a name that expressed our opinion about religion? Religions *are* rotting worldwide in our philosophy. Okay, it sounds extreme for many people and it closes doors, but our goal was never to be Metallica. Despite the many shows that were, and still are, cancelled, and the problems that occur with the distribution of our CDs, we kept this name. We are still proud of it. I do consider myself as a spiritual individual that has searched his personality in so many ideologies, including Satanism. I do consider myself more as anti-religion than a Satanist, but still believe that Satanism influences me in my everyday life. Back then we were rebels without reason. But nowadays we are with reason, and this name still represents our band philosophy."

TORMENTOR

"Tormentor made me think, 'Holy shit! This is darkness. Why didn't I understand this when I was listening to Destruction and the likes?' And I got out my Destruction albums again and I didn't hear what I heard as a kid. Then I heard mainly thrash, but now I heard lots of darkness in that thrash, I heard a super distinction between that kind of thrash and stuff like Testament."

—Fenriz (Darkthrone)

"Tormentor was such a unique band and some of the attraction was that they were from Hungary. Not that Hungary is the most obscure place on earth but at that time it was. Kinda like the Brazilian bands—the right influences but still making everything their own."

—Metalion, *Slayer Magazine*

"I always thought Tormentor offered something different. They were somehow exotic coming from Hungary and I found them very inspiring. Their sound was rather unique… a mix of black and heavy metal I guess you could say, but it also had some of that true dark Eastern European feel to it. The musicianship and production was also good. I think to this day Anno Domini is a true classic and I'm proud to have released it through Nocturnal Art Productions."

—Samoth (Emperor)

FOR REASONS UNKNOWN, the name "Tormentor" has been adopted by an unbelievable number of bands (at least twenty to date) throughout metal's history, including, as we've seen, the trio that would eventually become Kreator. Of all the many bands calling themselves Tormentor, however, it is the Hungarian outfit that most black metal fans associate with the name, due in part to their charismatic frontman and vocalist Attila Csihar, who would later become the singer for Norway's Mayhem.

Of course, there is a reason that Mayhem's main man Euronymous thought to offer Attila the position of vocalist in the first place. Tormentor had earned the respect of not only that band, but much of the Norwegian scene, who had discovered the group via the humble format of dubbed cassette. That these cassettes were able to make it into Scandinavia in the

Tormentor's *The Seventh Day of Doom*. Recorded in Budapest, it was originally released in 1987 as a demo cassette, before later being granted a re-release.

first place was no small achievement: Based in Hungary—a country then behind the Iron Curtain and thus under the control of the Soviet Union—the members of Tormentor faced restrictions that resulted in an almost total isolation from the global music scene. That said, Hungary was relatively liberal compared to many other countries in the Eastern Bloc, with music less heavily clamped down upon than in some neighboring states.

"I got into music with AC/DC, Kiss and Motörhead," begins Attila. "However Kiss was just one song, and I still don't know *what* song, 'cos my brother-in-law just recorded it from the radio. Hungary was separated back then, but he lived close to the western border so could get Austrian radio. Like most of us [black metal musicians] I was the kind of person looking for more and more extreme stuff, so I got into Iron Maiden, then the punk stuff like GBH and The Exploited, whatever I could find in Hungary back then. I remember I went to the store—Hungary was a little bit more open than the other countries and there was a private record store—and I said to the guy, "What's the most extreme thing here? I have this hardcore music already, do you have anything else?' And one guy was like, 'Okay, give him the *Venom* record,' and he put it on and within ten seconds I was like 'Okay, I like that!'"

Meeting like-minded young musicians at his school, Attila and his new bandmates were soon playing regular live shows as Tormentor, drawing on the likes of Venom, Celtic Frost, Destruction, and Kreator, and making a name for themselves with a blend of covers and original material. With local audiences hungry for any live music they could get their hands on, the

The *Anno Domini* album, originally released on cassette in 1989. Pictured is the 1995 re-release on Nocturnal Art Productions.

band soon built a strong following, their shows attracting a wide collection of individuals including punks, skinheads, metal fans, and other miscellaneous troublemakers, a volatile combination that often resulted in bloodshed.

"There was no way to think about touring the West—though we played one show in Slovakia and one show in Vienna—so we played a lot in Hungary," Attila explains. "We were a 'trouble' band originally, almost like the Sex Pistols. People who liked trouble came to our show, so it was not just a metal audience, it was a '*wrong people*' audience. There was no security back then either, but somehow it shaped out and of course we got famous. We had a lot of fans in Hungary actually, our crowd was always five hundred people *and up* in the eighties."

In 1987 the band headed into a garage with a homemade mixer and recorded what was technically a demo tape, though one that boasted a surprisingly lengthy collection of material (nine songs over fifty-one minutes). Entitled *The Seventh Day of Doom*, it proved well-received by listeners, blending elements of thrash bands such as Slayer and Metallica with the more heavy metal leanings of Mercyful Fate and even Iron Maiden. Soon the band began work on a "proper" album, investing a year in the writing and recording of their debut, *Anno Domini*, which benefited massively from being recorded in a professional studio.

A remarkably powerful and forward-thinking recording given the youth of the band, and the musicians within it, *Anno Domini* was a heavier and more direct assault than the previous year's efforts, combining frantic and malevolent thrash riffs and violently precise percussive assaults with slower, icier melodies and a taste for eerie, majestic atmospheres. The short, keyboard-dominated intro drew liberally from the horror film *Phantasm* (complementing the *Evil Dead* samples present later on the album) but the track that most embodied the group's

An ad for the Nocturnal Art Productions re-release of
***Anno Domini*, a cause of no small amount of excitement**
at the time given the rarity of the cassette.

more grandiose leanings was the fourth song, "Elisabeth Bathory," based around one of Hungary's most famous historical figures. One in a long line of black metal tributes to the serial killer countess (following in the tradition of Venom and Bathory), the song is a melodic and mid-paced number, rich in dark feeling and deliciously epic thanks largely to a simple three-chord, synth-accentuated, verse and a sinister, yet highly memorable chorus. Elsewhere songs such as "Heaven" and "Damned Grave" demonstrated the angrier, rawer, more chaotic side of the band.

Hailed as a classic by the underground, the record would provide no small amount of inspiration for the nineties black metal explosion that was only a few years away. Tragically, however, the album never saw official release—or at least not before the band split up. For reasons unknown, the head of the record label that was set to release the album vanished, taking the master tapes for *Anno Domini* with him. The band were left with nothing more than copies of the original recordings, which were issued on cassette tape as a self-release. In fact, it wouldn't be until some seven years later that the album would finally receive an official release courtesy of Norway's Nocturnal Art Productions. Understandably disillusioned, the band split as the eighties came to a close, unaware that their work was picking up a legion of fans in other countries.

"We didn't know we had a following abroad at all, it felt like it was going down for us if anything," sighs Attila. "We were very young, I was fifteen when we started and maybe nineteen when we stopped, and all the other members were the same age, so we were just going with the flow. Now I would say it was a mistake to stop of course, but back then we felt it was over; we saw bands change in the West, Celtic Frost changed and became strange, Bathory had changed... even Destruction, and then all this glam metal and white metal was coming up. It was maybe two years after we split that I heard from Euronymous—in '91—

Attila Csihar, pictured shortly after the millennium. Something of a revered figure these days,
his numerous appearances and collaborations stand in contrast to the obscurity and isolation
of Tormentor's early years.

and also this friend of mine sent me stuff from Mexico, [I thought] 'What is this? Someone
from Mexico writes about us?' So we realized then there was something in the air, but the
problem was the guitarist had to go to the military, so in the end we just fell apart."

Attila would go on to work with countless other acts, both within the black metal
scene, such as Norway's Keep of Kallesin and Italy's Aborym, and outside of it, such as
American drone kings Sunn O))) and singer/pianist Jarboe. He would also reform Tormentor
some ten years after they first split, Csihar once again working alongside original guitarist Attila Szigeti and two new members. However, the material on 2001's comeback album *Recipe
Ferrumi 777* proved to have very little in common musically with the earlier recordings, instead taking a decidedly experimental approach. The appreciation of their earlier works would
only grow as the years went on, however, and in 2008 *Anno Domini* even received a re-release
via Csihar's own Saturnus Productions, featuring noticeably improved sound compared to
the earlier release—supposedly due to the sound being taken from the original master tapes,
which were finally located by Attila after many years missing.

12
MASTER'S HAMMER

"When the Ritual album came out we were all rejoicing. The vocals are of course fantastic and a lot of the music was very inspiring, especially for bands like Enslaved. I often say—more like a joke, but it's true—the first Norwegian Black Metal album is Ritual. It is in that style; the atmosphere, the types of riffs, a bit of the way to handle vocals … "

—Fenriz (Darkthrone)

"A fantastic band, Master's Hammer were without any doubt innovators and way ahead of most of the underground back in the day. Franta Štorm has one of the most—if not the most—insane vocals in all of extreme metal, extremely expressive and raw. Anyone interested in something unique should check out Master's Hammer, there is nobody else quite like them."

—Dolgar (Gehenna)

HAILING FROM PRAGUE—then the capital of Czechoslovakia and now of the Czech Republic—Master's Hammer never once toured or appeared live outside of their home country. Despite this, they would become immensely respected within the international scene thanks to their forward-thinking and hugely influential take on black metal. Indeed, as the quote by Fenriz above suggests, in many ways Master's Hammer can be considered the first band in what is now seen as black metal's second generation.

Originally formed in 1987, the group was created by František "Franz" Štorm and Milan "Bathory" Fibiger, school friends who were attending the Academy of Applied Arts in Prague, Štorm studying typography and graphic design, and Milan studying illustration, fields the two men still work in today. With Štorm handling guitar and vocals and Milan taking care of bass, the duo were joined by drummer Franta Fečo, an individual Milan knew from their mutual home city, Mladá Boleslav, located some fifty kilometers north of Prague, where the band would rehearse in their early days.

"We never learned to play any instruments before," admits Štorm, "I don't know about notes [even] now. We fell in love in Bathory about 1986, King Diamond and Motörhead, and in our childhood we used to listen to ABBA and Kiss. But later on, we wanted to be the most

The Master's Hammer logo/coat of arms. It was designed in 1987 by founding member František "Franz" Štorm, who is still a designer by trade.

radical of all bands, I'm not sure for what reason, perhaps as a subconscious reaction to a then-formed—and already glorified—underground scene. Here I don't mean strictly the metal one, but [more] rock and folk. We [also] liked dark things in general."

"Radical" is certainly an apt adjective for the band's first demo, *The Ritual Murder*, which appeared soon after the band's formation and was recorded by the aforementioned trio—though confusingly the cover features *six* individuals ("just our friends," explains Štorm, "mostly Fečo's brothers who wanted to have a photo"). A demented and frantic half-hour effort, it remains a challenging listen, frequently threatening to overwhelm even the seasoned extreme metal fan with its fuzzy sound, thrashy riffing, and sporadic, eccentric vocals.

While the music on the tape might not always sound much like it by today's stan-dards, it's interesting to note that the band had already begun using the term "black metal," a decision inspired, Štorm explains, predominantly by Bathory. Czechoslovakia had at that time contributed only one band to the genre, Törr—with another, Root, forming later that year—making Master's Hammer one of the first within Eastern Europe to really fly the flag for the movement. Not only does the demo include a number entitled "Blak Métl," but the tape's sleeve features a burning cross and the first appearance of the iconic and almost regal Master's Hammer logo, complete with horned skull, inverted crucifixes, and pentagram. "It

An eccentric bunch to be sure: Master's Hammer circa 1988. Note the King Diamond makeup on the left.

represents the essence of my idea of [a] brutal band logo," Štorm explains of the design, "quite naive after so many years, but naturally we'll keep it forever."

For the 1988 follow-up—another half-hour tape entitled *Finished*—the band would go one stage further, inverting an entire *church* for the cover design, hammering the point home with a woodcut image of Lucifer on the inner sleeve, a song of the same name, a "Satan Records" logo (which was there purely for design reasons, this being another self-release) and a backwards recording of the Lord's Prayer.

"The inspiration was quite simple," explains Štorm, "there was no true Satanic band in our country, and we made an effort to fill the gap. Except for some beer drinking with Root members, I haven't noticed any Satanic circles and I'm in doubts if there even were any in my country. But [Root founder] Big Boss soon became a local head of The Church of Satan and I've illustrated LaVey's *Satanic Bible* for my diploma work at the Academy in Prague. In my personal point of view, Satanism is a cultural and literary phenomenon featured in works of many authors like [French poet] Baudelaire or [Czech writer and artist] Josef Váchal, who all referred in a certain manner to those supernatural moods. It never had typical features of a social movement in Czech lands. Books and films are full of descriptions of rites, but I've never seen one for real."

The *Finished* demo, 1988, the first (and probably last) cassette inlay to invert an entire church in its design. In this case it was the one located next door to Milan's grandmother's cottage, which in turn was used as a recording studio by the band.

Musically speaking the *Finished* demo was a far less bizarre listen than the first effort, and also a notably darker one. Kicking off affairs with a winds-and-church-bells introduction (by now a familiar formula within the genre), while adding some disturbing vocals for good measure, the opus was a move toward more cavernous, Bathory-esque territory and somewhat more traditional metal vocals, though a certain degree of eccentricity was preserved thanks to a number of odd, almost random-sounding guitar leads.

Another self-recorded effort, the demo was actually created next door to the very church used for the cover photograph, in the home studio of a cottage belonging to Milan's grandmother. Beneath the church, the cover featured five musicians, all of whom this time actually appear on the recording, the band having expanded to include second guitarist Míla Krovina and "Ulric For" (Olda Liška, a schoolmate of Milan and Franta) who handled timpani, an instrument that would play a regular role within the band.

Soon after *Finished* was released, Ulric was replaced by Charles R. Apron, real name Karel Zástěra, and it was with this lineup that the band played their very first live show, on May 18, 1989. Taking place not long before the peaceful revolutions that overthrew the country's communist government and eventually led to democratic elections, the show was organized without permission from the authorities, and resulted in the band being summoned to explain themselves soon after.

"That was rather funny," Štorm recalls, "the secret police took me for some three hours' interrogation before letting me go. The asshole behind the table was rather interested in the students' movement, and sideways he showed me a huge collection of underground metal fanzines; today, he could have a very valuable, rare collection. I don't believe that black metal ever really attracted the attention of authorities in our country though, this is not Norway."

MASTER'S HAMMER
— "THE MASS" — demo 1989

1. Zapálili jsme Onen svět   4:37
2. Signum Diabolis (instrumental) 3:55
3. Černá svatozář   6:33
4. Skryté síly   3:22
5. Věčný návrat   3:35
6. The Mass   2:58
7. Vykoupení   5:35
8. Kolem kotle . . .   10:04

M. H. are:
F. J. B. Storm — Guitar bewitched by Evil,
                Deathspreading Vocal
Milan B. Fibiger — Brutalo tank bass
Thomas Necrocock — Allmassacring guitar
Carles R. Apron — Fearfull drums,
                Heaven's Choirs
Mr. Silenthell — Tympani War signals
Intro keyboards — T. Necrocock

Recorded 7.–10. 12. 1989 at Dark Cerem-
onies Studio, Prague.
Produced by Master's Hammer.
Mixed by Z. Šitíř.

MEGATHANX TO: Monsieur Dapony,
King Salomon, prof. V. Vondráček, K.
Weinfurter, Camille Flammarion, Black
Dragon and all magic Grimoires, Kryptor,
Ivan, Storm's grandmother (I know very
well that you are still here).
BIG HELLO: "Big Boss", Ferenc Fečo, Ulric Fox, Jim "Mutilator" and the Genital
necrosis' zine, Pípa and Kryptor, Quorthon
(you are the best), and all black metal bangers who love our occult massacre.

Master's Hammer

The Mass demo, 1989. The thanks list includes Štorm's grandmother ("I know very well that you are still here") along with "...all the black metal bangers who love our occult massacre."

In December the same year, the band made their first professional studio recording, heading to a studio in Prague to forge a forty-minute epic entitled *The Mass*, undoubtedly a more focused, potent, and effective effort than any previous recordings. Designed as a fictitious mass ("not Christian, not black, but totally occult") the demo did not attempt to represent one coherent ideology but instead drew on various left-hand-path ideologies such as Satanism and witchcraft, as Štorm explains.

"Occult junk was another thing apart from Satanism and other toys [we used]. Imagine a painter with a number of colors on his palette and various sizes of brushes. We took our tools whenever it suited best. It's the same even now. In the nineties I wrote in one song 'God is our servant and Satan as well,' and I earned bad reactions from so-called Satanists. I'm tired of explaining that Satanism is not a goal by any means, it's just a path. One of tens of thousands of possible paths."

In terms of sound, *The Mass* was the group's most convincing and accomplished effort so far, having done away with some of the quirkier elements of the early days and instead taking on a more epic atmosphere, retaining a Bathory overtone—but this time from their Viking era—thanks to the use of choral voices over the riffs. Another significant lineup shift had taken place prior to the recording, the band losing Fečo, which forced Apron (Karel) to take over the role of drummer. The band also took on two new members at this time—the alarmingly named Necrocock (Tomáš Kohout) on guitar, and Silenthell (Honza Pribyl), who took over the timpani playing from Apron—both of whom would end up being long-term members. While Necrocock had contacted the band seeking to join, Silenthell was simply a regular face at the band's local pub that was approached purely because of his appearance. Asked if he had ever played timpani before, he answered no, and—in a fine example of Master's Hammer logic—was immediately inducted into the group.

"Necrocock sent us an application letter signed by his own blood, which impressed us a lot, [though] we were laughing a lot as the letter was full of language mistakes," Štorm recalls. "Silenthell was chosen for his tall figure, moustache, and hair. We didn't test them for musical skills, that was always ancillary in this band. Karel used to play drums in the period of *The Mass* demo, when Franta Fečo didn't come to rehearsals. Milan and Karel were busy with General Lee—a southern-rock revival band—but we [also] quarreled about record production issues, and the atmosphere was exhausting. Karel left soon with Milan for General Lee and I took a break for a couple of months and Monster appeared suddenly on Necrocock's choice."

Monster (born Tomáš Vendl) was not the only new addition to the band following Milan and Karel's departure, and two new members entered the fray in the shape of drummer Mirek Valenta and keyboard player Vlasta Voral, the first member of the band with any sort of background in music theory. The combination of new members, combined with the departure of Milan, who had co-written most of the material with Štorm, clearly had a big impact on the band's sound. In late November 1990, they issued another half-hour demo entitled *The Fall of Idol*, an opus that demonstrated a sound both powerful and way ahead of its time. As Štorm comments, "*The Fall* was, to me, a step toward a new, very distinctive and original Master's Hammer face, with almost no audible similarities to any other band."

The demo was only available for a short time before a debut album entitled *Ritual* was recorded and released in 1991, the band signing to Monitor, which Štorm explains was the first independent label set up following the country's Velvet Revolution. Featuring superior rerecordings of the six tracks on *The Fall*, as well as fairly significant reworkings of four songs from *The Mass* and one from *Finished*, *Ritual* largely pre-empted the Scandinavian second-wave explosion. The same earnest sense of purpose and sinister grandeur surrounds the epic compositions, the demonic vocals combining the sung and the screeched in a similarly otherworldly manner as those later used in Mayhem by fellow Eastern European Attila Csihar.

Ritual undoubtedly had a major impact on the sound of the albums that flowed from the North in the years that followed, and while it's impossible to say exactly to what degree, there's no doubt that many respected Norwegian bands such as Gehenna and Enslaved were inspired by the band's mysterious compositions, and Mayhem's Euronymous even mentioned in interviews his plans to release the band's work on his label Deathlike Silence. Equally, many would be introduced to Master's Hammer in the mid/late nineties as a direct result of first discovering the Norwegian scene. All the same, the Czech pioneers remained somewhat unknown outside of their home country until that time, even if they were well celebrated within it.

"In 1990 there were just a few metal albums on the Czech market, so Monitor reached the sale of several thousand *Ritual* LPs," explains Štorm. "Hence you must regard this incredible number groundless on real fans' acceptance—musically it [only] became popular in the late nineties. I have a deep feeling that our songs must mature by aging, like wine."

Interestingly, such was the prominence of the band at home that two songs on the *Ritual* album, namely "Černá Svatozář" and "Géniové," were provided with promo videos. Wonderfully hammy and Venom-esque in nature, both are somewhat at odds with the mystical ambience of the album, though hugely entertaining. "Both videos were [made] by dull directors in official TV studios without understanding our music," Štorm comments. "They are just funny."

Keeping the momentum going, this lineup of Master's Hammer made a swift return in 1992, previewing two new songs (under different titles) on a seven-inch entitled *Klavierstuck*, before releasing a follow-up album entitled *The Jilemnice Occultist*, this time on France's Osmose Records.

"Monitor's approach to show business," replies Štorm simply, when asked about the reasons for the move. "They became a part of EMI very soon and we hated the kind of music they released, whereas Osmose seemed to us a distinctive heavy underground company."

An ambitious work, *The Jilemnice Occultist* was a conceptual piece constructed as a "black metal operetta," with Štorm's lyrics giving voice to the various characters in the band's native Czech language. Essentially based around a young character named Altrament, the story follows the protagonist as he arrives in the small town of Jilemnice and meets a fellow occultist, Kalamária, as well as Poebeldorf, a man masquerading as the captain of the town who throws the drunken Altrament in jail and attempts to make off with the local treasure.

Musically, *The Jilemnice Occultist* moved away somewhat from the sinister atmosphere of its predecessor, the songs being less straightforward, emphasizing the more orchestral side of the band, with more prominent use of synths and timpani complimenting the black thrash riffs.

"We love operettas, with [their] lascivious verse-mongering," explains Štorm. "My great-grandfather was a Jilemnice district officer back in 1915 or so. This album has a fully epic story of poor occultist Atrament coming to Jilemnice to rescue beautiful Kalamária and the treasury. Definitely it was hard writing, it [needed] a logical concept."

Three years would pass before the band returned with their third album *Šlágry*. Featuring only Štorm and Voral, the record was, to say the least, a shock to the band's fanbase. With the exception of the final song, the group had now moved away from black metal—indeed, any kind of metal—altogether. Instead, listeners were presented with a collection of irreverent and highly experimental covers of pre-existing compositions (among them Aram Khachaturian's "Sabre Dance" and Chuck Berry's "Rock & Roll Music") along with one other new composition, "Indiánská Píseò Hrùzy," actually one of the stronger tracks on the album. A highly bizarre collection of music, the album has often been viewed as a prank of sorts, and indeed from Štorm's words it does seem that the motivation was, at the very least, somewhat reactionary.

"We needed to move outside a black metal cliché after rumors that we were a 'living legend' and similar nonsense," Štorm replies. "That album also captured the attention of non-metalists in our country, whereas orthodox fans were disgusted about the fall of their idols—that's exactly what we wanted to achieve. The message was clear: don't ever trust us, not one word, always go your own way. If this remains as the sole asset of *Šlágry*, I'm happy."

Perhaps the least likely looking band to make it into black metal's history books: a more candid photo from the archives, courtesy of František Štorm.

To this day rumors persist of a "lost" black metal album recorded by the band between *The Jilemnice Occultist* and *Šlágry*, entitled *Zaschla Krev*. In interviews even Hervé Herbaut, owner of Osmose, has claimed that such a thing exists, though admits he has not heard it, and bootlegs have even been released featuring material purporting to be tracks from the very same work. On this subject Štorm is terse, stating simply:

"I will not comment on unauthorized leaked material, [but] *Zaschla Krev* has nothing to do with Master's Hammer. My computer is crowded by unused music which will never be released." On this subject, the band's official website adds only that "*Zaschla Krev* was not intended for release, someone just picked a tape from trash bin in a studio and misused [it]. We've never signed it, so most probably it's not Master's Hammer on it."

Following *Šlágry*, the band undertook a long, seemingly permanent, hiatus. Some members would begin to appear in their own side projects, most notably Necrocock, who would pursue a truly surreal death- and sex-drenched solo career in his eponymous outfit and the project Kaviar Kavalier. Utilizing laidback beats and seemingly tongue-in-cheek lyrics, he has penned numerous bizarre songs, such as "Saigon Lady" ("*suck me baby*") and "Hong Kong," apparent odes to sex tourism that are complimented by somewhat voyeuristic music videos largely comprised of home videos of his holidays in the Far East and bemused local women in various states of undress.

In 2009, however, to the surprise of many, the band not only returned with a new album, *Mantras: Venkovska*, but did so with all of the members of the *Ritual/Jilemnice Occultist* lineup, save for Valenta, the percussion being handled by Štorm using live and programmed drums.

"We've been in touch since about [2005], for not just musical reasons, and suddenly found that we can do something together again. We were aware of rumors that Master's Hammer were going to the studio, so we did. I don't remember who triggered it, most probably those bootlegs took a part also. That was not a 'return,' because we never really split. Let's call it rather awake [*sic*]."

The work was typically eccentric, but more surprisingly featured (some) music not entirely dissimilar from their first two albums, frequently touching on black metal territories alongside *Šlágry*-esque experimentation and electronics.

"I think you'll safely recognize a true black metal band only by its lyrics, don't trust just what you hear sound-wise," warns Štorm. "There are many miscarried—indeed in good faith—and shallow projects. We don't seem a black metal band anymore, because our lyrics are mostly about fun, but we still use black metal properties occasionally, including Satanic subjects."

Likewise, while 2012's *Vracejte Konve na Místo* (an album whose title is taken from Czech cemeteries and translates as "put watering cans back in their place" and whose wonderfully idiosyncratic cover features said garden implement alongside an angel) showed lyrical playfulness, musically it was essentially a piece of avant-garde/progressive black metal, and indeed improved upon the sound of its predecessor in many respects.

What the future holds for Master's Hammer is all but impossible to say. Though sadly the band have stated publicly that they will never play live again, the fact that they are active at all is surely cause for celebration. Furthermore, their back catalogue remains essential listening, both for those interested in the development of the black metal genre and for fans of pioneering and radical music in general.

VON

"I didn't know about VON until Varg and that 'name thing'... I'd heard them at his apartment but didn't pay attention. Then after some years I started to listen to some tracks and thought, 'Fuck, this is like 'Nitzer Ebb black metal!' Simplistic, toneless.... it's anti-music, it tries to do things you shouldn't do in music and break some of the rules, maybe make it so simple, or 'bad' that it's not necessarily very easy to listen to. I hope someone sees that in my music."

—Snorre Ruch (Stigma Diabolicum/Thorns)

"Metal in the eighties was hectic, often complex and intense. Monotony was seldom heard, but one black metal album had just that—Bathory's Under the Sign of the Black Mark. *However, it was well ahead of its time, and didn't 'take' as much as it could in 1986. The decade wasn't ready for repetitive coldness. Five more years of hectic metal and the world was ready for it, we could feel it in the tiny Norwegian scene when VON's demo hit our shores, and it cemented our belief that this could be elaborated upon. I think Burzum, Mayhem and Darkthrone all did it, and many that followed."*

—Fenriz (Darkthrone)

THERE CAN BE FEW BANDS in the world of metal with a history as convoluted and confusing as VON. Formed around 1987, the group were arguably the first black metal act in North America and proved both revolutionary and uncompromising, illuminating some listeners while simultaneously alienating many more, their truly barbaric primitivism proving unpalatable to the majority of heavy metal fans at that time. But despite that fact—or indeed because of it—in the years that followed their three-letter, one-syllable name would be spoken in the hushed tones of utmost respect. VON would take on an almost mythical status, not least because there was so much confusion about the people behind the band.

For almost two decades the only evidence of the outfit's existence was a handful of live photos and a single demo entitled *Satanic Blood*. A twenty-minute assault upon the senses, its short songs boast a level of barbarity that is still all but unheard of, even within black metal circles. Unrelenting, save for short snippets of strange spoken word poetry, the simplistic pounding of its backbeat provides the foundation for a combination of hypnotic riffing and possessed, guttural vocals, drenched in reverb. Needless to say, it has become mandatory listening in black metal circles.

While the band was ultimately short-lived, splitting—seemingly forever—in 1992, *Satanic Blood* would have a profound impact on generations to come. Though its release a few months before the band's demise was limited to a few hundred cassettes, the eight songs would nonetheless feature heavily on the tape-trading scene in the years that followed and would impact the emerging international black metal scene significantly, including that of Norway. Indeed, there's no doubt that many people's introduction to the band came courtesy Burzum's Varg Vikernes, who not only mentioned the band in a now-infamous interview with *Kerrang!* (where he famously spelled out the name of the band for his interviewer as 'V for Victory, O for Orgasm, N for Nazi,' causing some readers to mistakenly believe this was what the band's moniker stood for) but later wore a VON shirt during his well-publicized trial for murder and church-burning.

From the mid-nineties onward the opus would be released in a number of seemingly official CD pressings, perhaps most famously as a split with Dark Funeral. The popularity of this mysterious group slowly grew, resulting in literally hundreds of cover versions including recordings by such high-profile names as Abigail, Nachtmystium, Dark Funeral, Urgehal, and Taake, not to mention Swedish outfit Watain, whose very name was taken from a VON song title. Hard facts regarding the group or the recording itself were all but nonexistent, but the musicians detailed on the minimal sleeve art—namely Goat (guitar and vocals), Snake (drums), and Kill (bass)—naturally came to be considered the core members of VON, the sleeve's brief text also revealing the band to be based in California. In fact, Kill would for a time become the only tangible element of the group since it was later revealed that he was none other than Joe Allen, bassist of death metal act Abscess/Autopsy.

But as it was revealed some two decades later when the band made a most unexpected return, the group's genesis had taken place not in California, but in Oahu, Hawaii. It was here in the unlikely setting of a deli and bagel joint that the three founding members were brought together; "Snake" (originally "Vennt," first name Brent, surname currently lost to the sands of time) worked as a manager, and "Goat" (originally "Von," real name Shawn Calizo) was employed alongside his longtime friend, a bassist known as "Venien" and born Jason Ventura. Shawn and Jason were both aspiring musicians who had met at school when Jason moved to Hawaii from San Francisco, and had played together in a short-lived band called Mesmeric, fueled by metal inspirations such as Venom, Slayer, and Sodom and hardcore punk bands, most notably Idaho's Septic Death.

Shawn and Jason—who were interviewed for this book at the band's controversial one-off show in London, as well as before and after that event—both turned out to be likeable and eccentric characters, but appeared to be an unlikely partnership, the nervous, twitchy and often cryptic Shawn contrasting with the considerably laid-back and notably more straight-talking Jason, apparently something of a reversal of their personalities at the time of the original VON incarnation.

"Shawn and I had been kicked out of rehearsal spots in town for being too loud and the times we had played in our homes, the neighbors did not take kindly to the sounds," explains Jason. "Brent told us we could jam upstairs in the factory after work and after many failed attempts, I convinced Brent to grab a five-gallon dough bucket and my drumsticks and bang on it as hard and fast as possible. We plugged in our amps and jammed to it. VON was born. But we had discussed everything, even playing the entire set in its entirety, no blabbering about, continuous with no pauses except drumsticks clicking for tempo and song changes. We both played active roles in the development, direction and tone of the band... We both wrote the music together, then Brent came into the picture."

As Jason explains, it was the band's vocalist who came up with the name VON for the group and the almost identical pseudonym "Von" as an alternative for the similar-sounding Shawn, suggesting related stage names for his bandmates also based upon their birth names, thus turning Brent into "Vennt" and Ventura into "Venien." While Shawn naturally came to the fore and became the frontman, it was Jason who determined that the trio should return to his birthplace of San Francisco in order to become part of the famous Bay Area scene, a far cry from the beautiful but isolated existence that the island of Hawaii offered.

"Jason was a big influence in me coming to San Francisco," explains Shawn, "I don't think I would have come if it wasn't for him. We all had these pipe dreams, 'Let's rock out and do this band shit.' We were working together in a job, going to fucking school, it was kind of a far-fetched dream. Slowly we came to some decisions and went for it."

Upping stakes in 1988, the trio soon discovered the hard way that they would have to balance the development of their band with simply struggling to make ends meet. Brent, always the more practical and professional of the three, was a Californian-born surf enthusiast who adapted back to life in the city with reasonable ease, but Shawn and Jason often struggled to keep afloat, with drugs and young families proving awkward bedfellows.

"There was a very big struggle personally to keep fucking food on our tables and do the right thing," explains Shawn. "We were slumming, man, working shit jobs, trying to pay the rent."

"[It was] terrible, to be honest," Jason admits. "I am not proud of my earlier dealings with drugs and the people that I ran with during that time and the hyper-violent attitude that I inflicted on friends and family, but the times and the city brought that out of me during that stage of my life. We argued constantly and bills and being broke was also a constant. Shawn had a small new family starting out at the time, so it was tough on him now that I think of it, and I tried to help, but I always felt guilty bringing him to the city and see[ing] them suffer in poverty. Brent was alone so he was good, he kept snakes as children and he was good to go I guess. My first son was born during that time and it was getting harder with that and the band, so extra money from drugs was my path and it was not all good. Drugs had taken its

Live in 1991 with Kill, Snake and Goat, the only lineup known to the world until almost twenty years later.

part within the fabric of each of us in different ways, but for myself it was more drawn toward violence—the others were really laid back, so there was tension for sure."

These desperate conditions provided the backdrop for the band, who practiced every other day in the cold, dark, damp confines of a basement storage space beneath a tailor shop. Painted black and lit with red bulbs, it was here the band recorded a demo/rehearsal tape for themselves in 1990 entitled simply *Satanic*, which contained many of the songs that would find their way onto *Satanic Blood*.

"*Satanic* I personally recorded because we were so lazy before that, and I wanted some of the songs on tape," sighs Jason. "We didn't even record all the songs we made, but I made each of us a copy."

Recorded with a single microphone hanging down between the band members from a pipe, it is a somewhat less cold and caustic listen than its better-known follow up, with guitars more audible and less distortion overall, most noticeably on the vocals. It is no less primitive or intense, however, its drug-fueled, hardcore punk-influenced black fuzz a far cry from the increasingly technical death and thrash metal of the time.

"I was violent and darkness was in my blood at all times, I wanted to be harder, faster, darker than all those on the scene, but with that punk mentality ... raw!" Venien explains. "Metallica and technical metal was popular, still is, but we wanted to be raw and simple ... and not like anyone else if at all possible. Metal music was a crucial and important form of expression, as was the urban/punk and even tribal sounds that played in my head. The influence for me was the pit, the mosh pit, [but] the raw human condition, the brutal and psychotic mentality within us was what really drove me. I can only speak on what I feel I brought to

VON, which was the raw, brutal, and overpoweringly loud aspect of bands like Septic Death, DRI, Black Flag, Christ on Parade, Cro-Mags, Venom, Sodom, Kreator, Slayer, Samhain, Misfits, and my personal favorite, Diamanda Galás, and more specifically her album *Litanies of Satan* … Tribal expressions have also been extremely dominant in terms of my life and music … due to [their] core, basic, and raw structure. Anything outside of that is over-indulgency; that might be why it was so stripped down in terms of VON."

Indeed, if VON was characterized by one thing, it was utter minimalism and—as Jason suggests—an almost tribal primitivism that lay at its heart. Combining unrelentingly simplistic, hypnotic percussion and stripped-down riffing with an unearthly vocal style, VON's music seemed to be driven by a ritualistic and almost religious fervor.

"You just know something just ain't right, but the feeling behind metal is perfect," explains Shawn of the forces that drove him to create such possessed sounds. "Isolation. Finding things in common with the undercurrent of mysticism. Everything around tells you otherwise but inside, you believe the truth is shrouded. Slowly, through the 'trust' of mysticism you see the hypocrisy of all you are surrounded by. This will germinate in you over time and, in my result, created under extreme circumstances 'this person.' It's just something you're born into. The music was a product of those conditions."

"I was into many things in my development years, and Satan was a pure constant indeed," ponders Jason. "The band was into making dark things and keeping it simple and bloody pure. But organized religions, cults, and things of that flock, no. I am not a follower of any, I am a freethinker and always have been, just having the realization of being able to dictate your own existence is comforting. But Satan and all things good and bad are interjected into the music, even more so in the new writings."

The trio played live at a few bars and gatherings but the reception was far from overwhelming; entirely at odds with the technical thrash and death metal prevalent at the time, VON, as with so many early black metal bands, found their efforts largely unappreciated.

"We played a handful of performances through the years as the original lineup, but nothing to go into detail about," admits Jason. "The response? Negative! Plain old shock. I think even metalheads had issues wrapping their senses around what they heard. It just goes back to the simple fact that there are millions of closed-minded sheep out there in the world."

"The music got poor conditions like us," confirms Shawn grimly, "and was left to fend for itself like us. VON didn't deserve special treatment that I [also] wasn't getting in my own personal life. Nothing here was privilege."

As unhappy as the band's situation was, worse was to come in late 1990/early 1991 when Jason's mother was told by doctors that she had only a few months to live, forcing the bassist to return home to Hawaii. His bandmates were far from happy; having been persuaded to head out to California, they were already struggling to get shows and would now have to deal with losing a band member. The solution came from Joe Allen—whom Jason describes as his then-best friend who would later be the best man at his wedding—whom

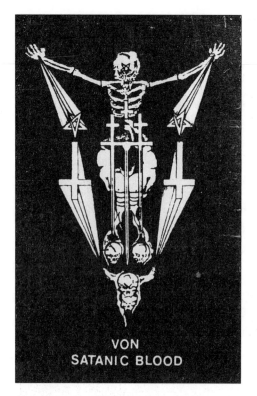

VON
SATANIC BLOOD

*1992's primitive, uncompromisingly
barbaric and highly influential
Satanic Blood demo.*

the bassist introduced as his temporary replacement while he sorted out the family situation back in Oahu. Some resentment over the situation clearly arose and VON sought to distance themselves from their departed bassist, with Shawn/Von becoming "Goat," Brent/Vennt becoming "Snake" (after his taste in pets) and Joe adopting the "Kill" moniker. Furthermore the song that had been named after the bassist (something of a tradition, since Vennt and Von would also have songs named after them) was renamed from "Venien" (as listed on *Satanic*) to "Veinen" (as it appears on *Satanic Blood*). Venien himself was later described unflatteringly in interviews as "an unnamed bass player."

While this was all somewhat messy, it was undoubtedly this new incarnation that put VON on the map, recording the second demo and capturing the imagination of fans with iconic live shows that featured two seven-foot inverted crosses, red candles, and both guitarists stripped to their waist and covered in blood. Even these efforts weren't enough to keep the band going, however, and the group collapsed before Jason had a chance to return. Before their demise the group would record one more demo, *Blood Angel*, but this would go unreleased until many years later.

In the intervening years the band was left largely untouched by its founding members, who kept little contact between themselves, to the extent that the whereabouts of Snake have been a mystery almost since the band dissolved. Jason would go on to work as an illustrator and designer in Arizona, while also working in the urban music scene, and Shawn would lead something of a colorful life, continuing with a variety of musical projects (including death rock project Sixx and moderately successful funk-tinged pop act 10¢) while also appearing as an extra and actor in music videos and films, including *Dead Man on Campus* in which he, rather aptly, plays a guitarist in a death rock band.

Meanwhile, a new generation of black and extreme metal fans and musicians stumbled upon the band's demo recordings, these unique, even avant-garde, efforts providing one of the links between the eighties pioneers and the rebirth of black metal in the early nineties.

"I feel like we kind of contributed to a particular guitar style that [in turn] kind of helped to contribute to the black metal sound," reflects Shawn, "and that came purely from a musi-

**Released almost two decades after the demo tape, The *Satanic Blood* album
was finally recorded in the studio and released in 2012.**

cal standpoint, a guitar standpoint. I sort of gravitated toward the single strumming notes as
opposed to the bigger chord progressions, the heavier, crunchier chord stuff. Something more
like a 'beckoning' or 'calling,' that kind of style, which was influenced by the early Slayer and
Sodom guitar styles. I think what made it interesting was that we brought in the more Satanic
imagery as opposed to the death thing, we brought more of a darker, evil Satanic element to
it. I think that came from the frustration, the anger, the fucking abandonment of family and
displacement of being an outsider."

Despite the many bands inspired by VON's efforts, it was only in the late 2000s that Jason and Shawn really became aware of the amount of interest that their old band had amassed.
2003 had seen a compilation featuring the second and third demos and live material, but this
had apparently only been approved by Kill, and its official status is therefore still disputed to-

day, at least by Jason. Nonetheless, the release indirectly triggered the band's return.

"The return was based on old friends reaching out to me telling me they [had] seen my album," explains Jason. "I thought that was odd when we never *released* an album. I looked into it and to our surprise there had been releases of the old demo material. There were also many bands and other CDs out there with the material. Since all the copyrights are under myself and Shawn, it felt awkward to see something released outside of us. I had already started a company to release new material and rerecorded demo stuff, but once I started it up things got weird."

Indeed, Jason's next move would prove confusing to many black metal fans. Forming a company to release new material, he issued a slew of publicity announcing the launch of "VON Music Group/VON Properties LLC" and its possible distribution by Warners, the rather corporate presentation perhaps reflective of his two-decade absence from the scene and underground sensibilities. He also stated that earlier releases of VON material, including the most recent by the respected Nuclear War Now! were "bootlegs." Given that most black metal fans had not yet learned of Jason's role in the VON story, or even heard his name before, skepticism was rife, with many believing the entire thing to be a hoax.

"VON Properties was only to start the business side of things, to release music to the world and deal with others that need it to be a business," Jason explains. "If people think a guy doing everything DIY, his own cash, his own hands, recording, mixing, planning, and even illustrating every image for every album is corporate, they are misled and need to learn the basics of starting a record label."

While confusion reigned during this time, Jason had also managed to re-establish contact with Shawn and persuaded him to reform the band to record an EP and play a one-off reunion show at the Armageddon festival, a two-day London event where Watain were launching their new album, *Lawless Darkness*. With VON Music Group making the *Satanic* demo available as a free download, and the scheduled appearance of "Venien" (Jason) alongside "Goat" (Shawn), the once-doubted story now proved increasingly legitimate.

"Erik of Watain reached out to me a year before the London show through MySpace and we started talking about VON," Jason explains. "With Erik asking if we would like to perform a set with him in Sweden, it got the ball rolling for us to pick up a few other guys to start the band again. Shawn initially had just been getting ready to get married again, and he was really not into it, he actually said he was done with metal and VON. So I just phoned him up every other day to talk about things and at some point he changed his mind. He wanted to do the show and record a little vinyl for the show for the fans as well. We could not find Brent, so I sought out a local drummer who went by the name of Blood, he was a VON fan and wanted to get involved as well. We rehearsed the old songs a couple times, and also recorded, mixed, and mastered the vinyl in one weekend. We did London a month or so later."

Unfortunately, though the London show would at least prove that the whole affair had not been a hoax, it was not well received. While the playing was certainly not as tight as it

Trouble brewing: Goat and Venien, pictured in London in 2010, prior to their live performance together and consequent estrangement. Photo: Dayal Patterson.

could have been, much of the resentment from fans seemed to focus on the slower renditions of the songs and the lack of stage gear, the band simply playing in their street clothes without the blood or crosses. When I asked about this Shawn replied, "I think we grew as people, it's been twenty years and you have to sort of fucking grow up ... people grow up in different ways, different things take on more meaning and it boiled down more to the music I think."

A scheduled performance at Norway's Hole in the Sky festival was quickly cancelled and Shawn soon decided to leave the band, making the 2010 *Satanic Blood* EP the only non-demo release to feature both Shawn and Jason (alongside J. Giblete Cuervo and Diego "Blood" Arredondo). The two men would later follow their own musical projects, Shawn issuing new full-length albums with the aid of drummer Blood, guitarist J. Giblete Cuervo, Bone Awl bassist He Who Gnashes Teeth, and even session drummer Wrest of contemporary USBM heroes Leviathan/Lurker of Chalice. These slabs of intriguing psychedelic black metal would be issued via Nuclear War Now!, the label making peace with Shawn if not Jason.

For his part, the latter would take on a huge amount of work. Initially going under the name "Von Venien," his solo project would revert to the more straightforward "Venien" and craft an ambitious double album entitled *Tribal Blood*, featuring himself on vocals and bass, Giblete on guitars, and Anthony "Dirty FvKn! Pistols" Mainiero, drummer of sludge metaller The Atlas Moth.

Seven Billion Slaves, **the first part of the Dark Gods trilogy, released in 2013.**

VON itself would continue, meanwhile, under Jason's leadership, initially recruiting Giblete and drummer Charlie Fell (Nachtmystium) to create the album *Satanic Blood* (that title again), a searing and impressively authentic opus featuring studio rerecordings of the demo material alongside unheard songs from the era.

Charlie would then be replaced by Dirty FvKn! Pistols and several new guitarists, with whom VON would record another ambitious project, a trilogy of albums entitled *Dark Gods*, works that would wander quite far stylistically from the early compositions.

Quite how the legacy of VON will be perceived following the band's comeback remains to be seen. For his part, Jason is untroubled by whatever reactions may arise and continues upon a very determined and unusual creative path.

"Respectfully, I never officially got into the scene per se, VON or myself never made it that far. As all things evolve there is a certain amount of backlash and dissent, but it's supposed to be that way in all forms and things, so I take reactions, opinions, and those nasty and positive things and listen, but I do not dwell on them. My current state of mind harbors no ill will toward 'kvlt' VON fans and Goat-worshippers and those that might react to *Satanic Blood* and *Dark Gods* as blasphemy. Those new to it who listen to the screams of those holding on for dear life to a demo, well it's up to them to think for themselves. I respectfully feel the albums will be received, in both camps, good and bad, it is the VON way. I have been in an uphill battle to get this out since the gatekeepers of the metal scene in the eighties told me it's not really what's going on right now, well, let's see if its time is now."

14

BEHERIT

"Beherit were one of the bands who had a real mystique. Their sound was never really popularized so they've remained 'cult,' but their atmosphere of claustrophobic and pernicious ritual had a big impact on a generation of black metal. They represent a whole era when black metal felt vital, and even dangerous, in a way that was swiftly lost."

—V.I.T.R.I.O.L. (Anaal Nathrakh)

"To be a Finnish person that started to listen to black metal in the early nineties, there is no other name that could be as influential as Beherit."

—Mikko Aspa (Clandestine Blaze/owner of record label Northern Heritage)

FORMED BACK IN 1989, Finland's Beherit was another act that preceded, instigated, and then finally became a part of the second wave explosion. Even today their name carries enough cultish clout to rival almost any act in the extreme metal universe, thanks to the band's fierce individualism, underground spirit, and refusal to follow prevalent trends. Consequently they have found themselves both revered and despised, which some might say is a true seal of black metal authenticity.

Originally called Horny Malformity, and then Pseudochrist, the band finally settled on the name Beherit—meaning "Satan" in Syriac, a dialect of the Middle Aramaic language—having found it within the pages of LaVey's *Satanic Bible*. The group itself came into existence thanks to Marko "Nuclear Holocausto Vengeance" Laiho (guitars and vocals) and Jari "Daemon Fornication" Vaarala (bass), with drummer Jari "Sodomatic Slaughter" Pirinen joining the group soon after. All three musicians hailed from Rovaniemi, the capital of Finland's northernmost province, Lapland.

"It was in the summer of 1989 when I met Daemon the first time," Holocausto recalls. "That was at a midsummer festival at the Arctic Circle, we were seventeen years old. We were both playing in our friend's speed/thrash metal bands, but looking for a more extreme and brutal expression. Before that I was playing guitar in a band called Frost, [playing] mostly Celtic Frost and Slayer covers. Beherit was the most northern band in the known scene—Rovaniemi, the most violent city in Finland."

The country's first black metal band, Beherit drew inspiration from acts such as Venom, Slayer, Sodom, Possessed, Rotting Christ, Samael, Sarcófago, Bathory, and also Blasphemy, whose song "War Command" the group covered and who influenced both the band's sound and their lengthy pseudonyms. Given such a musical diet, it was unsurprising that the trio favored a primitive and hellish black metal sound, and during 1990 they proved prolific, issuing no less than four releases demonstrating this primal approach.

First released was the *Seventh Blasphemy* demo, followed by *Morbid Rehearsals* (indeed a recorded rehearsal, though three of the four tracks remain exclusive to the release), and the *Demonomancy* demo. The latter effort was a somewhat more sophisticated affair than its predecessor, though that isn't saying a great deal; indeed, while the near twenty-minute opus did have something approaching a production, its crude and almost unrelenting Sarcófago/ Blasphemy-inspired assault was still chaotic in the extreme. The end of the year saw the fourth and final release of 1990, a four-song seven-inch entitled *Dawn of Satan's Millennium*, released on Turbo Music. Aside from a few seconds of synth that bookmarked the title track, *Dawn* followed a similarly unpolished and unholy blueprint.

Released the following year, the band's debut full-length, *The Oath of Black Blood*, bore a fair few similarities to the two releases that preceded it—more than a few in fact, since it *was* the two previous releases, crudely welded together by Turbo and packaged with new sleeve art. Somewhat disappointing for fans, the release appears to have been even more of a letdown for the band themselves.

"We here think that it's [a] ninety-nine percent shit release," Holocausto told *Bloodshed* zine in 1992, elaborating somewhat in an interview with Robert Müller of *Metal Hammer Germany* early the same year. "I hate the album!" he had complained then. "It's so bad, we never wanted to release it. The songs are from our demo and our label Turbo Music just used a regular cassette for the album pressing. Honestly, I never sent them the master tape."

Quite why Turbo chose such a course of action remains unclear, though a long-running rumor states that the band were presented with the funds to record an album but, in true rock 'n' roll fashion, blew this advance on alcohol and drugs. On this subject Holocausto's recollections are somewhat hazy, the frontman simply stating, "I cannot say where those dollars—which were sent by postal mail in a seven-inch box—were spent, or how much it was in total, but definitely it was not enough to record a whole album in the studio."

Interestingly, in 2012 an album entitled *At the Devil's Studio 1990* was released and marketed as the "official Beherit debut album." Featuring a number of rerecorded demo tracks and two new numbers, the sessions feature only Holocausto and Sodomatic Slaughter in Ala Ky Studio in Rovaniemi, and were apparently rediscovered by the drummer after being lost for two decades. To what extent it represents a lost album, however, is debatable; it seems unlikely, to say the least, that the debut would have opened with a track simply called "Rehearsal" for example.

Despite the continuing confusion, *The Oath of Black Blood* did manage to raise the pro-

Demonomancy, 1990, later repackaged and released without the band's consent as part of 1991's
The Oath of Black Blood.

file of the band considerably. This was all the more impressive considering that Beherit was essentially swimming against the tide of metal fashion, combining eighties-inspired sounds with a similarly old-school aesthetic comprised of spikes, inverted crosses, pentagrams, fire-breathing, and heavy black face paint. ("Perhaps Sarcófago," comments Holocausto when asked the inspiration for the latter, "It just felt a natural thing to do. Fire-breathing came from Black Winds [vocalist] of Blasphemy.")

Beherit was now one of only a handful of bands scattered around the globe who, in an age dominated by commercial death metal and thrash, were doing their best to resurrect the spirit of "black metal," though the band themselves don't appear to have settled on this term until a couple of years after their inception. The aforementioned article from *German Metal Hammer* highlights the parallels between Beherit's own struggle and that of like-minded bands in Norway such as Darkthrone, and also rightly predicts the success of such efforts, as the excerpt below reveals.

"As his musical influences he quotes the early classics of the genre: Venom, the Death demos, early Slayer and, rather exotically, Brazilian bands like Sarcófago, Vulcano and early Sepultura albums," Robert Müller wrote. "In 1992, Beherit seem almost like an anachronism. Either that, or you'd have to admit that Black Metal is not dead after all but is slowly and painfully raising its head again. The new Darkthrone album *A Blaze in the Northern Sky* can be seen as an indication: pure Black Metal. So would I be right in saying that classic Black Metal is coming back? The Finnish view on the matter: 'Black Metal was never dead! Unfortunately there's a lot of bands who start playing Death Metal because it happens to be trendy.'"

In the same article, Holocausto's ambitions seem strikingly similar to those professed by Norway's Mayhem, with whom he maintained strong contact throughout the period:

"We try to get across as much of an evil mood as possible..." Beherit founder Nuclear Holocausto Vengeance.

"We try to get across as much of an evil mood as possible ... There are always some people who are shocked when we appear on stage with our faces painted black, heavy studs and chains; we confront them with the things they're scared of. At a recent show I drank some blood on stage ... It's our aim to put on a show like Venom, maybe even more extreme with lots of pyros and fire effects."

The same article comments that *"The Oath Of Black Blood* met with disastrous reviews, but despite that fact—or maybe because of it—sold remarkably well. In other words a cult band pure and simple." Indeed, Beherit were doing their best to divide opinion among listeners and critics just as earlier pioneers such as Hellhammer and Bathory had done before them.

"People [generally] did hate us and our Satanic image," recalls Holocausto today, "but we hated 'em and their weak bands. We were busy putting together the international network with people in Scandinavia, North America, Brazil, Australia, Greece and all over the world. It was a very fascinating time ... to create something so new, dark, and brutal."

Beherit's imagery and lyrics in this period were indeed just as over-the-top and primitive as their music, especially in the early days. Yet while the lyrics of songs such as "Grave Desecration" ("We'll cause your death / We'll kill Jesus / Rape the dead / We'll spread evil") and "Sadomatic Rites" ("Black-haired witches / Bitches with their goats / Black robes and candles / Rituals can begin") were almost a caricature of the occult—echoing the efforts of early Bathory among others—the band's own interests were notably more serious.

"I applied for enrollment as a student to Collegium Satanas, a correspondence course in Satanism founded by New Zealand Satanist organization Order of the Left Hand Path," Daemon told *Sepulchral Voice*, a Norwegian zine (produced, incidentally, by Stian "Occultus" Johansen, later of Mayhem, in 1991). "I should be qualified as a Satanist priest about in one month."

"I have studied beliefs and cults," confirms Holocausto today. "I have practiced several maneuvers, mostly based on Aleister Crowley's. In the early nineties, we ordered a lot from a place called The Occult Emporium. Earlier, the most effective rites were of course to conjure demons, we [did it] a lot in early days of Beherit, later taking LSD and psychedelic mushrooms to alter the consciousness. Now lately, I am more toward the Vipassana and Tibetan death rituals. I'm all occultist. Ninety percent of songs of Beherit are occult."

Holocausto's interests in spirituality and the occult have clearly evolved as the years have passed but remain as strong as ever, and his interest in Vipassana meditation and Tibetan rituals has led him to travel the Far East quite extensively as part of a greater spiritual journey, one whose outcome may surprise many longtime fans.

"Since I was a teenager, I've been interested in the deeper side of life, searching for answers of our existence, a spiritual meaning," he explains. "After my Satanist youth and years in Odinism, I went to experience various hippie new age movements, paranormal lectures, channeling, and read all possible esoteric

Beherit's debut album-*cum*-compilation
The Oath of Black Blood, 1991.

books. They had valid points but were too often based on superstitious belief. In the late nineties I finally went to the East and found Tao and Buddhism and the Tibetan Book of The Dead, which was quite remarkable reading.

"I started to practice meditation and went to retreats in forest monasteries—a superb experience. I thought 'Fucking hell, this dude who lived 500 B.C. had every single answer and logic in his teachings.' I couldn't do much else than become a Buddhist myself. Not a monk or that active in religion, but as a philosophy. The body is just a short-time container, at least before transhumanists manage to strengthen our parts and extend our lifetime to hundreds of years. But after all, it's still just a temporary state, as is everything on Earth, heaven and hell. There's a lot of beauty in this world, but one should understand that it's not there forever. What was once young and sexy becomes weak and ugly. I would recommend people to study your self, the causality of life and dying."

These days Holocausto's beliefs are complex, but despite his passion for Buddhist ideas, he also describes himself as "more Satanic than ever." In the early nineties, however, things were somewhat more black and white, and Beherit—like fellow Finns Impaled Nazarene—were primarily expounding the ideas of LaVey's Church of Satan, even going as far as to include quotes from the *Satanic Bible* in their music. This position would eventually invite anger from the "pro-evil" Norwegian scene, who were increasingly attacking LaVey for his emphasis on humanistic values and self-empowerment, rather than literal devil worship.

"I believe in [a] horned devil, a personified Satan. In my opinion all the other forms of Satanism are bullshit," Euronymous told *Kill Yourself* zine. Likewise, Varg Vikernes commented in Bård "Faust" Eithun's *Orcustus* zine that "So-called Church of Satan is not in my views a church of Satan … It's rather a humanistic individualistic organization who worship[s] happiness and life … I worship death, evil and all darkness." The same Varg Vikernes would later claim within the pages of *Kill Yourself* that "the only true bands are from Norway," deriding Finnish bands as "stupid clowns."

A feud soon spread between the two scenes, which became known in black metal circles as the "Dark War." This has undoubtedly become somewhat bigger in legend than in reality, being relatively short-lived (partly thanks to Euronymous of Mayhem and Mika Luttinen of Impaled Nazarene sorting out their differences in 1993) and today the only real lasting sign of this conflict is an amusing note on the reverse art of Impaled Nazarene's 1992 debut album, *Tol Compt Norz Norz Norz*, stating "NO ORDERS FROM NORWAY ACCEPTED!!!!!!!!!!"

"I used to have many pen pals in Norway," Holocausto explains, "but it evolved into a situation where you had to be on 'their side' or you become their enemy. I had my own interests, so couldn't care less to belong to any 'Norwegian mafia.' There were a couple of anonymous death threats, I remember some guys from Enslaved threw shit over me and Varg was kind of pissed. I lost a couple of trades, but overall, I didn't see Beherit as a major player of that war, if there was any."

A bizarre project called Fuck Beherit is frequently cited as further evidence of the hatred Beherit had earned in Norway, although the fact that the band covered Beherit material, and had a song entitled "Beherit Are Gods," casts some doubt about the intentions of the group. Equally bizarrely, Holocausto was later accused in *Isten* zine of stirring up paranoia and sparking the Norwegian/Finnish feud by making late-night drunken prank calls to Samoth of Emperor and Mika of Impaled Nazarene, something he strongly denies, stating, "That prank calls story is bullshit, written by liars of *Isten* magazine. Now a long time later, some dude perhaps saw that speculation important enough to add into such a reliable source as Wikipedia."

Such amusing trivialities thankfully didn't affect the band's creative flow, and in mid-1992 they released a four-song demo that would showcase an entirely new musical approach, both for them and the movement. It would also win over a legion of new devotees. "For me personally, their old style wasn't what made a big impact," comments Mikko Aspo, "but *Promo 1992* was something phenomenal and I kept listening to it over and over again for months, even years."

The following year, through new label Spinefarm, Beherit issued *Drawing Down The Moon*, a truly groundbreaking masterpiece that featured rerecorded versions of the four songs on the demo, alongside nine entirely new numbers. Fittingly for an album named after an occult ceremony—in this case one from the Wiccan tradition (the band practiced witchcraft during this period)—*Drawing* was utterly ritualistic in nature, dripping with the atmosphere and primeval violence of the early recordings, while accentuating slower, more minimal songwriting and introducing synths and electronics to the mix, something all but unheard of at the time. Fulfilling—nay, exceeding—the promise of the 1992 tape, this release took rawness and primitiveness into almost avant-garde territories, showing contempt for traditional ideas of musicianship and production and in doing so crafting a truly powerful work.

"We had no budget at all back then," reveals Holocausto. "We had no time to remake or tweak the final mix—that's pretty much how metal albums were done before the money came in. I remember [drummer] Necroperversor was quite worried when we were listening to it the next day. I told him that perhaps he was right, but at least the spirit was there and that was more important."

Certainly this was an album that prioritized spirit and atmosphere. Slow, hypnotic invocations such as "The Gate Of Nanna" (a reference from H.P. Lovecraft's *Necronomicon*) took the concept of a "stripped-down sound'" to new extremes, its ridiculously simple percussion and two-riff structure making it a challenging listen for many. No less challenging were the spacey instrumentals such as "Nuclear Girl," which were also scattered among the more tradition-

"People [generally] did hate us and our Satanic image, but we hated 'em and their weak bands."

ally barbaric assaults such as "Nocturnal Evil" or the memorably titled "Werewolf, Semen and Blood." The result was a varied and immersive listening experience, unlike anything else available then or now, and is still greatly admired by fans and black metal musicians alike.

"I didn't hear Beherit until some years ago," admitted Darkthrone's Fenriz in an interview I conducted with him for *Metal Hammer* in 2009. "But *Drawing Down The Moon* must, for me, in hindsight, be one of the nineties' ten most important black metal albums. Too bad when 'black metal' first had to take some distinct direction in the worthless nineties [no bands] went that way. "

"I remember the old Norsk bands doing interviews shitting on these guys," recalled Blake Judd of USBM act Nachtmystium in the same article, "yet I don't think a single one of those bands ever made something as nightmare-inducing as *Drawing Down The Moon*."

LaVeyan Satanism had a heavy presence in the band's influences at the time. All the same, Holocausto was clearly already painting from a pretty eclectic palette thematically as his cryptic run-through of tracks in Holland's *Masters of Brutality* zine demonstrates:

"'Intro'—The seventh satanic statement (Dr. LaVey). 'Solomon's Gate'—A trip to Israel's history, Solomon's occultism. 'Nocturnal Evil'—Old song by the lord Diabolus, ritualistic vibrations by the black magic witches somewhere near Acheron, Hecate also featured here. 'Sadomatic Rites'—lyrics included: black metal heathens, pagan sex. 'Black Arts'—lyrics included. Nothing special, just old black metal spirit. 'The Gate of Nanna'—lyrics included, based on the texts of *Necronomicon*, the moon calls us to sin. 'Nuclear Girls'—no lyrics but the house 418. 'Unholy Pagan Fire'—so-called unholy lifestyle is very holy for some people, dance with the wolves. 'Down There ... '—lyrics included, old black metal spirit. 'Summerlands'—the land where's eternal summer, after death, medium datum. 'Werewolf, Semen And Blood'—black metal heathens, very old lyric ... blood! 'Thou Angel Of The Gods'—Angelos ton Theon, Crowley-influenced lyrics, pagan texts, a black rose beyond the mirror. 'Lord Of Shadows & Goldenwood'—horned god Bran ... based on the texts of pagan rituals."

Unfortunately, while the musicians had achieved something of a creative breakthrough, the album coincided with the collapse of the band due to both personal—and *personnel*—problems. Drummer Necroperversor and the more improbably named Black Jesus, who had joined the band in 1991 when Holocausto moved to the city of Kuopio, both departed the band shortly after the recording of *Drawing Down the Moon*. To add further stress, Holocausto actually had to sell many of his possessions, including his car, simply to fund the album and was eventually left homeless by the turbulence of the period.

"I even asked Turbo to pay our studio bill, but they told me that they didn't trust us!" he reveals. "Beherit are the most trustworthy group in the scene! Let those shithouse brothers suffer in Hell! I had to pay the studios myself and wait six months to get signed on Spinefarm Records [whom Holocausto would also soon begin working for]. I had less than five friends in Kuopio city and there I even got ripped off by my (ex) best friend. I paid him the advance rent for a small wooden house on an island near the city area, but then wasn't able to move there. That was a week after my (ex) girlfriend left me. Fuck, how much that time made me hate this life. Same things have happened again [with the recording of 2009's *Engram*], it seems that every fucking time we record a Beherit album, all social life is simply destroyed. Fuck, it's [such an] intense time [making] an album in the studio!"

Working alone, Holocausto followed the album with a seven-inch entitled *Messe Des Morts*—later released as a split with Archgoat—at the tail end of 1993, blending primitive black metal, demented vocals, and programmed drums. It would be the last black metal recording released under the name Beherit for over fifteen years. Unable to find suitable musicians to join him and increasingly enthralled by electronic music and its "crossover" possibilities with guitar music, Holocausto created two electronic albums under the Beherit name in 1994 and 1995. The first was the primitive *H418ov21.C* (the strange title taken, Holocausto explains, from Aleister Crowley) and the second was the better-received *Electric Doom Synthesis*, which reintroduced guitars into the Beherit formula while remaining brooding and predominantly non-metal in nature.

"The studio for *H418* was booked just a couple of weeks before [recording]. I had some material written, but the final form was yet to be decided, like [whether] to produce tracks with real instruments or [with] which lineup. That time, we had just opened the first Spinefarm record store in Helsinki, so overall it was a very hectic time. Then doing drugs and

Nuclear Holocausto Vengeance pictured in 2009, around the time of comeback release *Engram*.

studying occultism, [I could] give a fuck about that current metal scene. I was really anti-everything. Tracks for *Electric Doom Synthesis* I spent much longer on, several months with many variations of every track ... it was very fascinating, to have such a freedom from noisy rehearsal rooms. It's a paradox, 'cos now after fifteen years that's the spirit I am looking for again. I found, there's not that much inspiration sitting in front of a computer monitor."

After *Electric Doom Synthesis*, Laiho abandoned both the Beherit and Holocausto monikers altogether, continuing the electronic themes with a "metamusic" project called Suuri Shamaani and creating hardcore techno under the name DJ Gamma G. It would not be until

2009 that Beherit would return, with an album entitled *Engram*, which saw the band boasting a full lineup again, Laiho (as Holocausto again) working with original drummer Sodomatic Slaughter and two newcomers, guitarist Sami "Ancient Corpse Desekrator" Tenetz (founder of Thy Serpent) and bassist Pasi "Abyss, Twisted Baptizer" Kolehmainen.

"I wanted to play with real musicians after years of making music in my home studio," he explains. "Things just evolved into Beherit. I wanted to concentrate on the music itself, so kept the project top secret, because I think it's vital to get some distance to the 'scene' and close your eyes from the forum rants when writing music. I wanted to have a form of music with not too much candy on it, something that would be easy to play live with some basic trigger pedal. I am not a skilled guitar hero, I just love to play guitar, loud and distorted."

Interestingly, *Engram* drew inspiration from a short-lived project called The Lord Diabolus, something that Holocausto and Slaughter had worked on together prior to the recording of *Drawing Down the Moon*, a time when they felt it was unsafe to use the Beherit name due to issues with Turbo. Stylistically the record was very much a return to black metal territories, though it made use of a far more powerful production than might have been expected from the band's previous works. The result was cold, aggressive, and satisfying, but also hinted at the band's minimalist and hypnotic past, as well as carrying an air of Bathory about it. The unexpected return was warmly received by fans, though the recording process itself proved to be a typically testing time for Holocausto, as summed up by the words that open the album: "Because … I just fucking hate this world," an apparently candid recording of the man himself.

"That line was not written before we went to studio," he explains, "that's a hate I felt during the session. We were drinking for three weeks heavily with almost no sleep, very chaotic and disturbing in every sense. The perfect setup for a band like Beherit. I think the Earth itself is a beautiful place and with Internet technology, it's so easy for people to study occultism, learn and enlighten their souls. But it makes me feel sad, when people are not taking their precious time more seriously. Fucking homosapien monkey shit, always with some latest trendy nonsense. I hate their modern lifestyle, their capitalistic dream, political corruption, and headless Western values. I hate blind people acting happily in utter ignorance."

Despite the many trials that have faced the group, and more specifically Holocausto himself, Beherit has survived to tell the tale. Even their surprise return is typical of their frontman's strong determination and refusal to do things by anyone's terms but his own. As he confirms, the future for the band is impossible for anyone to predict.

"I think we are lucky to have such a diverse discography," he concludes. "Beherit is not a prisoner of any particular music style. We have a freedom to do whatever we want in the future and it would still fit the sound of Beherit."

15
MAYHEM
PART I

"Pioneers are always important and barely anything was going on in Norway before Mayhem as far as extreme metal goes. They put out the Deathcrush *vinyl themselves (with the help of a handful of friends), they gained a lot of contacts through the underground network of that time… And then the black metal thing with Dead. No one had really done that before in Norway, and the way people could communicate with Euronymous was very inspiring for younger black metallers. Besides that, the studio tracks they recorded with Dead and the* De Mysteriis Dom Sathanas *album is among the best black metal to come out of Norway."*

—Metalion (editor of seminal Norwegian publication *Slayer*
and co-funder of the aforementioned *Deathcrush* vinyl)

"I was first introduced to Mayhem in a local record shop here in Bergen around 1987. Back then metal was almost unknown in Bergen and to explore a brutal metal band from Norway was awesome. Metal is, in my eyes and ears, meant to be provoking and extreme, and the band is one of a kind, and has inspired me from day one. They were, and still are, revolutionary and artists on a high level, and their history is like the most exciting story you can wish for. Salute!"

—Jørn Inge Tunsber (Hades/Hades Almighty)

EVEN AFTER CLEARING AWAY the cobwebs of myth and rumor, it's hard not to conclude that Mayhem remains the most important and influential band in black metal history. Their name has become synonymous with groundbreaking music, strong personalities, Satanism, church burnings, suicide, murder, and perhaps most importantly, the unification and rebirth of the black metal movement in the early nineties. In fact, thanks to a combination of their art and their extracurricular activities, Mayhem have achieved a genuinely legendary status within the genre.

While the band would make their greatest impact during the nineties, their initial

**Manheim, Necrobutcher and Euronymous, the
three founding members of Mayhem,
in an early studio shoot, 1986.**

formation took place much earlier, specifically 1984, a time when the group consisted of three musicians: bassist Jørn Stubberud, better known as Necrobutcher, drummer Kjetil Manheim, then known simply as Manheim, and guitarist Øystein Aarseth, whose stagename Euronymous would become immortalized within black metal history and culture after his premature death in 1993.

So much gossip and speculation surrounds the band, even today, that it seemed critical for the story of their early days to come directly from the two surviving founding members: Manheim and Necrobutcher. Though separate interviews were conducted later, the initial discussion took place in person with both men. No longer in regular contact—Manheim left the band in 1987—it had been some time since the two had spoken. Nonetheless, a meeting between them and your author was eventually arranged in a bar close to the centre of Oslo, an establishment whose bizarre taxidermy-heavy décor proved to be a suitably macabre setting for the tale.

We began our conversation right at the beginning of the band's story, at the point when the two musicians—who were both living outside Oslo in the village of Langhus and were twelve years old at the time—decided to start a band.

"It felt very natural for me at least," begins Necrobutcher. "It wasn't like a plan, it was what we *were*, what we did, what our interest was: playing music, listening to music, *everything* about music. We were big fans of bands and were looking up to them I guess, wanting to do the same thing as them—releasing albums, touring…"

"We were probably not different from other kids at that time," points out Manheim. "If you were into punk and hard rock at that time, that was a part of it, wanting to play."

"I started out with friends who were in the same block of flats that I was living in," continues Necrobutcher. "I wanted to start a band, bought some instruments and said, 'Hey, wait a minute, we have to have someone who has some clue about notes and things like that.' And Manheim, we were schoolmates, so I brought him into the band. Also his dad was a principal in a school—though not *our* school—so we could arrange rooms for rehearsals."

"It was a small school," Manheim explains, "we met in second grade when we were eight years old. I played in the school band, a brass band, I joined that to learn how to play drums and that was really the start of it. My first record was [British prog/symphonic rock band] Procol Harum, I got it from my uncle and loved it. I never got into Kiss, which was big then, so my approach to it was more diverse. I liked a lot of different music, still do. But heavy metal, it was something that as soon as you heard it, you liked it, it was the energy around it."

"Bands like Iron Maiden, AC/DC, and Motörhead started showing up," Necrobutcher continues. "We were already playing in the band when we discovered these bands. I think that we all had this 'bad boy' attitude, we wanted to play something aggressive, mix it maybe with what we were into and what was around at the time; punk, metal, also rhythm and blues and funk, everything that had some aggressiveness to it. Basically everything that nobody liked, we were kind of interested in. It could be the electronic music coming out of Germany like Kraftwerk, or on the other side Motörhead or the Sex Pistols."

"I think people have a tendency to think that if you are into metal that's all that you are into," Manheim adds. "But that's a fan thing, if you talk to musicians, they have all kinds of influences behind them. ... "

"The third guy was Øystein, Euronymous," explains Necrobutcher. "He was in an elementary school in the next town, Ski, like five kilometers from us. If he were living a couple more kilometers toward us, he would have been in our class, he would have been in the band for sure, it was just the fact that we'd never met...."

"I met [Euronymous] at a station. He was going to show me the way to a friend's house, 'cos I was auditioning for a band, though I was still in this band we had at the time [with Manheim] called Musta and a side project [without Manheim] called &co. When we met up we were like, 'Wow, we have similar interests'—that we didn't know about each other was a shock—and in the fifteen-minute walk to his friend's house we decided to form a band. So I told him that we already have a band, a good drummer, we have a rehearsal place and it turned out he knew a couple of cover songs we were already rehearsing; a Venom track, a Black Sabbath track and a Judas Priest track, that was our first rehearsal. We were very excited."

"Love at first sight," laughs Manheim.

The three became Mayhem almost immediately, the pair explain.

"We started in '84," recalls Necrobutcher, "the first months we were rehearsing cover tracks, and first song we wrote—'Ghoul'—I think was the beginning of '85. We just finished elementary school. [Manheim] and Euronymous went to high school and I went to a school that taught a craft, bricklaying, that sort of stuff. That year I dropped out of school, and the year after Euronymous more or less dropped out of school."

"He was quite good at school actually," Manheim adds, "he quit the last year with top grades, but he didn't finish his exams, he decided to go for the band."

Looking to the recently emerged pioneers of extreme metal, the band's name was directly inspired by a Venom song, namely a fifty-eight-second instrumental from *Welcome To Hell*.

"'Mayhem with Mercy,'" Necrobutcher confirms. "The name [came from] Euronymous.

He had played the graduation day with a couple of friends at school, put together a band and played a song or two and called it Mayhem. We also had a second guitarist, Per Nilsen, who was member for half a year in '84."

"He was a good guitarist," adds Manheim, "but it wasn't *raw*. It was more [virtuoso] Yngwie Malmsteen-style."

"We had a show in April 1985," continues Necrobutcher, "one year after we started the band, we did a Celtic Frost cover and two Venom covers. We hadn't got that far yet to write our own songs, actually that came straight after that, we started to rehearse our own shit."

Though a tight unit, the three musicians had somewhat different ambitions at this point.

"I think we had different goals," Manheim ponders. "I can only speak for myself. First of all, my thing was to play. It was fun to create things to record and it was fun that people recognized it, talked about it, wrote about it and liked what we did. I think Øystein had a much bigger ambition."

"I think I knew that I was going to be in a band and that that was going to be my thing," states Necrobutcher. "Øystein wasn't that guy who sat at home practicing his guitar, he was creating this 'world network,' even at that point."

"We decided this was going to be something totally different," Manheim elaborates. "Even before we'd released or even *recorded* anything, magazines were writing about Mayhem. Which turned out to be a good thing."

"The magazines wrote that this was a fresh breath," Necrobutcher remembers, "some guys doing new shit, coming from Norway. Some of them had been in the rehearsal space."

"Like Metalion [Jon Kristiansen] of *Slayer* zine, he wrote a lot about it," adds Manheim. "You can decide to look at it in terms of brand strategy, which was *not* the case at the time, but looking back, what we did was brag about how special this was going to be. We had journalists and magazine writers who visited us in the rehearsal, and that confirmed that this was something that was completely different and very *wrong*, and *hard*, and *aggressive*. So the rumors started to go round and people were waiting to hear what we were going to release. That's the way to build a brand and I think this is what was happening, Mayhem became a 'name' before people even knew the concept, they just knew the stories. And these stories were blended with Satanism and a lot of dark things. That made it more interesting I guess, for people in the communities."

The obvious question, therefore, is whether any members of the band were actually Satanists.

"No," Manheim replies simply.

"Not even Øystein," adds Necrobutcher. "We were looking at the Satanic thing to see if there was any possibility to write some good lyrics. We bought [LaVey's] *Satanic Bible* and some other books to see if we could get inspiration. So we were interested in that,

Featuring this issue:

Peace and love? Manheim, Necrobutcher and Euronymous appear on the cover of newly acquired vocalist Maniac's *Damage Inc.* fanzine in 1986.

started to investigate, but found out that it was nothing for us. [It was] anti-society yes, but not Satanic. Anti-*social*, but here in Norway, the constitution is based on Christian values. Everything, the government, school system ... "

"The establishment actually," interjects Manheim, "the morals, the state, religion ... "

"So how to rebel against society? To rebel against the laws they build up?"

"Everything that was extreme, [was] good," Manheim smiles. "Everything that could upset a Christian was good. Behind it was rebellion, which was nothing new to youth culture. But at the time, that was our expression and it turned into what you write about [in this book]: the emerging of the black metal genre, and the influence that Norwegian black metal has had around the world. And it's not like we say it was all bullshit, it *is* something real there, but it's not based on Satanism and rituals and religion. On the contrary, it was more in opposition to people in power and people who don't believe that you are a free man who should be able to have free will. Of course we used Christianity as an enemy in the expression, but if you lived in Norway you would understand why."

PURE FUCKING ARMAGEDDON

In 1986 the three members of Mayhem recorded and released the band's first demo, the extremely noisy eight-song tape *Pure Fucking Armageddon*. With its murky sound, there's long been speculation as to who did the vocals on the tape, an issue the pair quickly clear up.

"Me," explains Necrobutcher before continuing. "It was [recorded on] a Portastudio, four tracks, but we never got it to work, that's why only the first side is with vocals! The quality of the sound got very much lower than without vocals, so we printed the b-side without vocals. It felt like, fuck, people wouldn't be able to hear the *songs*."

Perhaps unsurprisingly given its raw lo-fi barbarity, the reception to the demo was not entirely positive. "I thought it was terrible," laughs Necrobutcher, "but that was the good thing. I remember one article—I can't remember if it was *Kerrang!* or *Metal Forces*—but it said 'This tape has no vocals at all, the bass sounds like [Celtic Frost's] Tom Gabriel Warrior's balls in a lawnmower' and what they were talking about was actually the vocals! But it was [next to] a review of [Thin Lizzy guitarist] Snowy White and the review was just 'zzzzzzzzzzzzzzz' repeating itself. I thought this review about Tom's balls was better than this other shitty one, so we felt like we had won."

"I've seen later," Manheim adds, "a lot of times when people write about black metal or death metal recordings, they refer to something that is hard to define, they refer to the early ages where they could feel the *truth* behind something. And that was the point. You were very close to the real thing and I guess that is one of the marks of the early black metal recordings. Darkthrone is the same, it's poorly produced, but it's genuine."

"The same with the Venom albums," states Necrobutcher, "the lack of production is the great thing about it. On the sleeve it would say, 'this was recorded in twenty-two hours blah blah,' to kind of make an *excuse* for themselves, and I was thinking to myself that it should go the *other* way, say, 'We are *proud* not to have used any producers or high-end studios.' And of course these two [Venom] albums are the foundations of extreme metal today."

"Actually I met one of my heroes on our last tour, Jello Biafra [singer of the Dead Kennedys], he came backstage and said that ... they found it very pure, as it was not touched by anyone else. It was *us*, it was *them* and they were proud of the product, which is why [Dead Kennedys' debut] *Fresh Fruit For Rotting Vegetables* has this special feeling, the bad production adds to the whole thing. He's actually a collector and has all our records, he bought the box set."

"He was a hero to us in the eighties," adds Manheim, "the Dead Kennedys."

DEATHCRUSH

Deathrehearsal, the 1987 rehearsal tape for the band's official debut, *Deathcrush*, supports Manheim's assertion, featuring as it does two versions of the Dead Kennedys' song "California Über Alles" from the aforementioned *Fresh Fruit* album. When asked about the Dead Kennedys in a 1986 interview with *Damage Inc.* fanzine, Euronymous explained, "They play some pretty good music, but we couldn't give a shit about what they stand for." In an interesting twist, the unusually professional-looking *Damage Inc.* was produced by one Sven-Erik Kristiansen, better known as Maniac, who would soon appear as a session vocalist on *Deathcrush*, along with a second individual, Eirik "Billy" Nordheim, who went under the stage-name Messiah.

The original *Deathcrush* tape, released in early 1987, before the somewhat-delayed vinyl edition was issued.

"Billy we met, I think, at a Dio concert," recalls Necrobutcher. "It must have been '84, 'cos he was singing at our first concert in '85. Basically we saw a guy with a Venom backpatch so we went straight over and said, 'Hey man, you have Venom on your back,' and we were immediately friends. He told me after Maniac left [in 2004], 'I'm ready! [to sing for Mayhem].' I sent a message back saying, 'Twenty years too late'. Because we were *begging* him to be in the band [back in the eighties], as he was super talented musically."

"Billy also had strange priorities," sighs Manheim. "He had his girlfriend and lots of other shit."

"He grew up on the other side of Oslo and was in a band called Black Spite with the friends he grew up with," Necrobutcher explains, "so he felt he owed them to continue, so he dropped out immediately after the [first] live performance. But we called him as Maniac was not able to sing all the tracks—he was not musically experienced enough to be able to listen to what's going on and then sing on top of it, he was just singing. We were like, 'Come in... now!' Because he was completely out of it, he was just going: 'Waaaaaaaaaaraaaaaaaaagh!'"

"It was effective though," Manheim smiles.

"It *was* effective," Necrobutcher agrees before continuing the tale. "Maniac had written a letter to us after we released the *Pure Fucking Armageddon* demo. He had read about us in *Slayer Magazine* and sent a tape of himself, a one-man band [Septic Cunts]. We had an album and we wanted someone to sing, and we sent him the lyrics. All the music was rehearsed. So Maniac came, did his songs and left, it was too far away from where he lived and everything."

"He was a crazy guy back then," laughs Manheim, "he *was* a maniac. I remember the first sessions, it was quite remarkable when he started to scream. That was the first time I'd met him."

"He had a magazine, so he was into the metal scene," says Necrobutcher, "and it was a very small metal scene, and he was the only person we knew who sung."

In a later interview, Maniac recalled his entrance into Norway's emerging underground metal scene: "Mayhem and Necrophagia inspired me to record the Septic Cunts tape, which consisted of my vocals and my extremely limited guitar skills. When I recorded that tape my mother was sure I had lost any last remaining fragment of sanity I possessed. It was a horrible piece of noise but the voice was to Euronymous' liking and very soon he asked me to join Mayhem. I lived a long away from Langhus so rehearsals were quite infrequent. We rehearsed in an old pigpen and I had to sing through a Peavey Bandit amp with a very lousy microphone, but it sounded so good back then. I still remember when Necro's bass sound hit me in the guts like a wrecking ball and Euronymous' guitar was more like the sound you get when you cut sheet metal. Electrifying. It was like entering a different plane of existence. When we went into the studio I was primed for the three newest tracks but Messiah helped me out with 'Pure Fucking Armageddon' and 'Witching Hour' and I just sang chorus on those tracks. The most amusing thing was that the studio technician was ready to record a reggae band if my memory serves me right. Necro had written most of the gory murderous lyrics and I only made small adjustments to them. It was quite an experience."

Despite the record's artistic merits and groundbreaking nature, reception was once again underwhelming.

"You must remember this," says Manheim seriously, "everybody around us, musicians, told us—"

Necrobutcher interrupts bluntly, "—they laughed at us."

"Yeah, they were laughing at us," says Manheim, "saying that we were spoiling our talents, that this wasn't going anywhere, so why didn't we play new wave like everybody else?"

"They didn't say, 'Don't spoil your talent,'" Necrobutcher spits incredulously, "'Cos they didn't think we *had* any talent. To give you an example, our first performance was at a rock competition—there were eight bands, and we came in last. The judges put us in *last*. There were seven other bands and, you know, they never went anywhere, so that gives you an example of what was going on."

Though *Deathcrush* would be more likely to confirm the opinions of the band's detractors than change them, this exhilarating record was, nonetheless, a definite milestone.

Though still unbelievably raw, the chainsaw guitars, distorted bass, steady drumming, and utterly demented vocals were freed from the mire of the demo's muddy sound to showcase the true barbarity of the compositions.

Though the first studio release by a Norwegian black metal band, *Deathcrush* itself is not generally considered a black metal recording, due partly to both the bloodthirsty gore-obsessed lyrics found on songs such as "Chainsaw Gutsfuck," but also the music itself, which combines many thrash, death, and punk overtones into what was then a decidedly avant-garde sound.

Opening with an introduction track by Conrad Schnitzler of German electronic group Tangerine Dream (a coup achieved after Euronymous found Conrad's home address and sat outside his house until his wife eventually invited him in) and featuring a stripped-down cover of Venom's "Witching Hour," *Deathcrush* is a surprisingly eclectic listen, especially considering that it clocks in at not much more than a quarter of an hour. However, the combination of visceral brutality, experimental moments, tormented vocals, primitive violence, and ridiculously catchy riffs still divides as many fans and critics today as it did when it was released.

Despite this fact and its limited print run, the mini-album would appear in the top twenty on album charts within *Kerrang!* magazine. This was somewhat misleading, however, since the magazine took their sales information from one store in particular—the legendary Shades shop in Soho London, a favorite haunt of the band and one of the few stores that stocked the album. In fact, sales at the time were far from overwhelming and it was some years before the initial print run of one thousand copies had sold out.

Deathcrush was undoubtedly far more abrasive in sound than most people were used to hearing or prepared to accept, even in the wake of the success of thrash metal albums such as Slayer's *Reign In Blood*, released late the previous year. That included those involved in the music industry. Indeed, while recording in a studio was a step up for the band, they soon discovered that they were somewhat on their own in terms of actually capturing the songs.

"When we arrived at the studio, they said, 'Where is your snare drum, you're a reggae band right?'" Necrobutcher recalls with a shake of the head. "We said, 'No, we're *not* a reggae band.' They said, 'Well what sort of music do you play?' We said, 'Well it's better if we just rig up and you hear it.' Because there was no definition for that sort of music at that time. I think the guy was used to pop rock."

"He even told us," laughs Manheim, "this was something he didn't know how to record."

"Yeah, he had no clue," sighs the bassist, continuing the story, "so he just set the settings and we recorded. That was it—no mix, before or after. That's why people can *feel* it nowadays, it's not been tampered with. There were no overdubs—bass, drums, and guitar are live and then we recorded the vocals after. Maniac was originally supposed to do everything but there were two songs he couldn't do, so we called Billy. But I had forgotten the lyrics I wrote back home, so he just sat down and wrote new lyrics for 'Pure Fucking Arma-geddon' in the studio. And then of course it became a bit political, with Maggie Thatcher and Ronald Reagan, so I rewrote it afterwards back to what it was before."

Despite this the punk overtones continued, since by accident or design, the sleeves for the initial run of records were printed in a lurid bright pink, rather than the intended dark red. The sleeve also had text missing, which meant that Euronymous had to ink the back of the sleeves personally with his name under his picture. Whether in pink or red, the record sleeve remains striking, with over half the cover dominated by the then-new Mayhem logo, a truly iconic design that came courtesy Maniac's friend Nella (designer at *Damage Inc.*), and whose sinister and symmetrical qualities would be hugely influential on many of the band logos that followed. Sitting beneath this was a black-and-white documentary photograph of two severed hands hanging on ropes, the overall aesthetic proving similar to the one used by punk bands such as Dead Kennedys—albeit with perhaps a different effect in mind.

"We had set the color codes and everything, so I think they did it on purpose, to make it pink instead of blood red," opines Necrobutcher. "When I opened the first box, it was like, '*What?!*' Then we were thinking they did us a *favor*, this is even *worse* now, so we accepted, rather than sending back. Also we had been waiting for this moment for many, many years, to hear the stylus come down on the vinyl, your own product, we'd never experienced that before. We just wanted to grab it and put it on. We sent everything through a Norwegian company. They had a printing company in Holland and first they didn't want to print it 'cos [they thought the cover] was 'racist,' 'cos it was two black hands hanging. It was two hands hanging in a marketplace in Mauritania on the Ivory Coast of Africa, as a warning to thieves to say, 'okay, here you don't steal.' We actually never thought about it, we were like, 'Racist? What the fuck? It's just two hands.' We didn't think about what color the hands were, it was just so fucking cool."

"It's a press photo," explains Manheim, "we went to the Norwegian Telegraph Company."

"We had an idea to find a picture that could define the music," continues Necro-butcher. "First I went to the torture archive to see if there were any cool torture pictures. I didn't find that, so I went into some other places, then that picture popped out. We thought it was a humorous thing as well, bizarre things going on, this defines the music pretty well."

At this time the band were still known for their humorous undercurrents, and in fact Necrobutcher and Euronymous had recently recorded a cassette called *Metalion in the Park with Checker Patrol*, a one-off joke project they created with members of Assassin and Sodom during a visit to Germany the previous year. Some of this humor was evident in *Deathcrush*: as well as the cow adorning the central sticker on the record itself, there were the ads that appeared in *Slayer Magazine* featuring Necrobutcher playing the piano surrounded by images of the cartoon cat Garfield. Then there was the minute-long unlisted final track—unsur-prisingly removed from later pressings—which captured the band repeating the lyrics to a

The *Deathcrush* EP, released in 1987. A milestone in Scandinavian metal, and a release that led many of Norway's young metal fans and musicians to begin making contact with the band.

composition entitled "(All the Little Flowers are) Happy" in an increasingly demented fashion.

"That [ad] had nothing to do with us," clarifies Necrobutcher, "that was to do with Metalion's bizarre form of humor. I think that all this just adds to bad taste though. The song was spontaneous in the studio, I don't know exactly why. Bizarre humor at the time. You play with stuff that's going on at the time and that was the joke that week."

"It was actually a Young Ones and Cliff Richards thing," adds Manheim, "they had a single out ['Living Doll'] with that song on the b-side and we thought it was ridiculous and funny. And it still is. We're all singing on that song. Even Metalion."

"We were all into Monty Python as well," smiles Necrobutcher.

"We liked English humor, it's sarcastic and dry," Manheim continues. "But all that disappeared. [At that time] it wasn't that serious. It was *ambitious*, but it wasn't that *serious*.

In the early nineties I must say it was kind of scary to see a lot of people going into that and how serious they were about it. What Øystein was talking about; sitting together with him and hearing this extreme thinking and everything was so serious, you know—where's the humor?"

Just as Maniac and Messiah became estranged from the Mayhem camp before *Death-crush* was released, so too did Manheim, who decided to move on from Mayhem shortly after the recording was completed. He would later return to making music, focusing on projects with electronic and experimental elements, most interestingly working with the aforementioned Conrad Schnitzler in an outfit called Big Robot.

"I was together with a girlfriend then and was eager to get out of my parents' house," recalls Manheim, "so I was eager to get a job and get my own place and I didn't have an ambition to follow through with a tour. So I think that was just a pragmatic decision."

"We put more hard pressure and said, 'Now we are going to tour,'" Necrobutcher states, "He was on the way out and that was our way of saying, 'Okay, either you are in or you are out.' *Deathcrush* was recorded in February and released in August but after the studio Manheim was out."

"What I *do* remember is that Øystein was really mad at me," says Manheim, "'cos it meant that leaving the band was destroying the tour plans, as they had to replace me and that sets a band back, and he was probably right about that. But it was a shift in life, that's how things are. My uncle is a musician and he told me, 'If you are going to be a musician, be prepared to eat flatbread *a lot*. If you're prepared to eat flatbread, and do all that, then go ahead. If you're not, do something else.' And that was a turning point, I knew that I was good at other things."

"And yes, we *were* broke for many, *many* years," Necrobutcher sighs. "I had to turn to crime, selling drugs and shit for many years to support myself. I couldn't take a job 'cos it would take away the focus."

"I think all bands will confirm," Manheim concludes, "unless it's a very corporate band, everybody's got to be in it one hundred percent. And I didn't have that. I think it was correct and the right decision to make, though Øystein really was pissed and said a couple of things to magazines. But that's fair enough."

16
MAYHEM
PART II

WITH MANHEIM, Messiah, and Maniac departing from Mayhem even before the band's official debut was released, Euronymous and Necrobutcher were forced to set about the task of replacing them. They began by looking to a local extreme metal band called Vomit, and recruited two of its members: drummer Torben Grue (now an opera singer) and vocalist Kittil Kittilsen (now a devout Christian and retired from music). However, the lineup they formed would end up lasting only until the end of the year.

It wasn't that the two were without merit. Indeed, in 1997 Necrobutcher and the latter two musicians regrouped under the name Kvikksølvguttene ("Quicksilver Boys," a pun on Sølvguttene or "Silverboys," a prepubescent Norwegian choir), an outfit Necrobutcher describes simply as "Mayhem, but under a different name." Going so far as to tackle a "cover" of the first Mayhem song written, "Ghoul," the project would prove just as provocative, making use of artwork featuring the band's stash of drugs and illegal live weapons (Necrobutcher would later serve time for possession of both) and a photo of a deceased woman in a mortuary taken by a trespassing friend of the group.

However, in 1988 two notably more suitable musicians had entered the scene, namely drummer Jan Axel Blomberg, better known by his apt pseudonym Hellhammer, and vocalist Per Yngve "Pelle" Ohlin, otherwise known as Dead. Hellhammer's entry into the group proved fairly straightforward. Impressed with *Deathcrush*, he learned that the band were looking for a drummer and managed to arrange a meeting through mutual friends, bringing with him a tape of his recordings. So obvious were his talents that he received a call the very next day to tell him that he had been accepted as a member of Mayhem, a situation that still stands over two decades later.

Amusingly, his hell-raising antics appear to have caused Euronymous some concern in the early years. In a letter to Morgan "Evil" Håkansson of Marduk, he complains that the drummer "has disappeared again … he's hanging out with glamrockers (!) he seems to find

Euronymous, Dead, Hellhammer and Necrobutcher. Despite the small recorded output, for many this is the definitive lineup of Mayhem. Photo courtesy of Nihil Archives.

it more important to drink with them than rehearse." The letter ends with a note explaining that if the recipient is to organize a concert for the band in Sweden, he "MUST take care of one thing: Hellhammer is only thinking about getting drunk, and then he can't play. So there must be NO access to any alcohol for him before a gig, preferably not even twenty-four hours before a gig." No doubt Euronymous put up with such concerns because of Hellhammer's incredible speed and proficiency, which have led him to become a cornerstone of the Norwegian black metal scene and a contributor to countless other big-name acts, including Dimmu Borgir, Thorns, and Arcturus.

Dead was—to put it mildly—a rather more complicated character. Hailing from Sweden, the eighteen-year-old (a year younger than Euronymous and Necrobutcher and a year older than Hellhammer) had already provided vocals for the Stockholm-based band Morbid, which also featured in its ranks Uffe Cederlund and L-G "Drutten" Petrov, who would later appear in the pioneering death metal bands Nihilist and Entombed. As it turned out, "morbid" was a pretty good description of Pelle himself, something that was obvious even from his unusual method of application, as Necrobutcher explains.

"Metalion told Dead we were looking for a singer," he says shaking his head, "and he sent a tape—the *December Moon* demo by Morbid—with a letter to our mailbox. I was the one who opened the letter that day and inside was the tape, the letter, and a *crucified mouse*. The mouse was starting to disintegrate, it was really rotten and stunk. I had a pickup truck at the time so I put the letter on the back and the tape in the cassette player. Now, of course, this letter flew off the back of the truck. This was the first time he had approached us, so I called Metalion and said, 'Shit, this letter flew away, give me his address.' Then Dead came to Oslo and it turned out he didn't understand what we were saying... people who are Swedish don't always understand the Norwegians and people from Stockholm are the worst. So he didn't understand *shit*, and *we* didn't understand shit that he was saying, so we had to speak English for the first week."

Manheim: "He was a pretty depressing guy. The first time I met him I started being polite, and ended up being really angry. But later I got to know him. I didn't spend too much time with him but he was a

Per Yngve "Pelle" Ohlin, otherwise known as Dead, performing live with Mayhem.

nice guy, but he had this strange, depressive way to look at things, so you just got annoyed."

Necrobutcher: "Normally if you talk to someone, they will reply [to] you, but he was like, if he didn't know you, why the fuck should he even care that you were talking? And of course people like us who are normal... I mean that's why [Manheim] got pissed off, 'cos you couldn't communicate with the guy. I knew how to get into his frame of thinking and after that we were best friends. He was into horror movies, we found the stuff we had common interests in and found each other in that and then he could open up. [He was a] really fucking great guy, loads of black humor, the smile on his face... he was smiling more than anything else, big, fucking, happy smile."

Manheim: "But he had issues."

That is something of an understatement. As well as his impressive vocals (which were equally demonic but notably clearer, more aggressive, and less tormented than Maniac's contributions), the deathly pale Swede brought to Mayhem a new level of grimness, plunging the band into even blacker depths. Though some of it was theatrics, there's little doubt that he was a genuinely melancholic, introverted and, in all probability, clinically depressed individual—something that became even more apparent when the band moved into a shared accommodation.

Previously, the members had lived in their parents' homes, although Dead lived in a variety of places, including the band's rehearsal space, a cabin, and supposedly even some woods on occasion. But in 1988 the group began renting a deserted house in a forest near Kråkstad,

Ski, far from civilization. The dwelling soon acquired such a dubious reputation among locals that children were warned not to go nearby, and residents in the nearest town began to avoid the band members, perhaps not surprisingly given their strange attire and behavior.

"People there were very superstitious," Hellhammer explained in an early 1996 issue of *Spin*. "When we went into a shop, all the old ladies would run out. In Sunday school they told the children that our house belonged to the devil."

Of course, living in close proximity with an eccentric like Dead was a challenge even to his bandmates, especially Euronymous. The two would sometimes come to blows, their fights even including knives. In one instance Dead stormed outside to sleep in the woods because Euronymous' music was keeping him awake, only to find the guitarist further disturbing his peace by coming outside and firing his shotgun, a situation Dead reacted to by hurling a large rock at the guitarist, causing minor wounds to his chest. Much of the time, however, Dead would simply stay in his room, drawing or writing lyrics and generally keeping to himself. He shared very little information about his life, though he did speak frequently about his feelings of not being human, and recalled a near-death experience that had occurred after he fell in freezing water as a child.

Necrobutcher: "He heard music and saw colors, and when he discovered some other people also had a similar thing and wrote books on it, he became super fascinated: read all the books, saw all the films, got in touch with people who had similar experiences, and based on that, came to the understanding that there was something *more*, a three-dimensional thing. I mean he really believed that."

"He was very obsessed with this," explains Snorre "Blackthorn" Ruch, a later Mayhem member, "he felt he 'belonged' to the other side. I was there when Dead came over for the first time from Sweden. We had the same references and we got along, we both liked to draw, we made perverted drawings together. I noticed he was very out there with his depression and stuff. Euronymous lived with him and I can really say that he did not give any positive contribution, so it was a downward spiral."

Dead claimed to have been obsessed with death and dying since his preschool years, but by the time he moved to Norway his behavior was bizarre to say the least as Necrobutcher recalls:

"He used to collect dead animals that he found on the roadside—birds or squirrels that were hit by cars—and took them home because of this fascination with decomposition, the smell… everything to do with death, that was his interest. He kept this picnic basket under his bed and when something happened, like studio or live work, he would bring some of these animals in bags and inhale them between every song, to get this feeling of death. He was getting into the character of 'Dead.' He'd also bury his clothes in the soil several days before the gig so that they were smelling of decomposition. I felt it was a little bit weird, but he had this black sense of humor around it and that made it all right. We were all laughing a little bit about it, but we didn't mind, you know?"

Dead, undoubtedly one of the most iconic figures in black metal history and the man
generally accepted to have created, named and popularized corpsepaint.

Manheim: "[Necrobutcher] knew him much better than me but I remember I was at a party and he was there hammering spikes into his skull."

Dead's frequent self-mutilation was something he brought to the stage, combining the desecration of his own flesh with that of animal parts, most notably pig heads, which would become something of a trademark for the band.

"We haven't had a real gig yet," he explained in *Slayer* zine in 1989. "Three shows in Norway, but only one with parts of our stage show. We had some impaled pig heads, and I cut my arms with a weird knife and a crushed Coke bottle. We meant to have a chainsaw, but the guy who owned it had left when we came to go get it. That wasn't brutal enough! Most of the people in there were wimps and I don't want them to watch our gigs! Before we began to play there was a crowd of about three hundred in there, but in the second song 'Necro Lust' we began to throw around those pig heads. Only fifty were left, I liked that!"

"Something I study is how people react when my blood is streaming everywhere but that's not why I do it," he told *Battery Zine* the following year. "I like to cut, in others preferably, but it's mostly in myself. That I can't do too often which makes me a bit mourning [*sic*] … "

"At New Year's Eve he almost cut up his artery, but he don't remember anything himself," Euronymous once wrote in a letter. "I do. We had to put handcuffs on him."

It seems slightly odd to say that Dead "introduced" self-mutilation to the scene—the theme being explored extensively by later bands such as France's Antaeus and Sweden's Shining—but he was certainly the first black metal musician to visibly indulge in it. One thing he certainly did introduce that had a phenomenal impact on the black metal aesthetic was the use of face paint. As we've seen, face paint had already been used by earlier black metal bands such as Mercyful Fate, Hellhammer/Celtic Frost, Master's Hammer, and Sarcófago, as well as older groups such as Kiss, and these were all undoubtedly an influence upon Dead.

Nonetheless, it was surely Dead's use of what he described as corpsepaint (combined with the influence that Euronymous was beginning to have over the scene) that caused the technique to be adopted so widely. In fact corpsepaint has probably become the most identifiable aspect of the black metal aesthetic, even if the approach has evolved.

"Corpsepaint we invented," Necrobutcher states unequivocally. "That term, Dead actually came up with that from the days when he was in Morbid. The name corpsepaint was *never* used by the bands who used paint like Celtic Frost, King Diamond, Alice Cooper, Kiss or any other bands that used this sort of makeup. They weren't painting themselves to look like they were dead, just to look evil or cool. With corpsepaint today, I don't see any *corpse* … it's to look cool or evil … [With Dead] it wasn't like dark, it was green, decomposition colors, snot coming from the nose… "

Sadly, in his three years with Mayhem, Dead recorded only two tracks in the studio: "Freezing Moon" and "Carnage." Originally recorded for the compilation album *Projections of a Stained Mind* and later released separately, they have earned an iconic status among fans and even some ex-Mayhem members.

"I was in the studio when Dead recorded his only studio vocals for Mayhem and I will *never* forget it," recalls Maniac. "His dedication was something that was very hard to come by even then, let alone these days. I had to hold a bag of dead crows for him when he was singing so he could sniff it for the right atmosphere. These crows had been in the ground for quite some time when he dug them up. His voice was really of another world. Those two are still my favorite Mayhem tracks."

Despite a limited recorded output—later bolstered by the release of the *Live in Leipzig* album—there's no doubt that Dead had a huge impact on the band and the movement as a whole. While it's still hard to say if Pelle felt the need to live up to the "Dead" character, or whether the band gave him an outlet for his extreme tendencies, it does appear that his unbalanced outlook helped shape the direction Mayhem was taking, with the extremity of his behavior certainly appreciated by the rest of the band.

A late 1990 flyer for Mayhem's show at the Eiskeller ('Ice House') club in Leipzig, Germany. The recording of this show would be released a few years later as the legendary *Live In Leipzig* album. The flyer also highlights just how long the debut album title (and even its intended font) existed prior to it actually being recorded and released.

"Weird is not the right word," Euronymous explained in an interview with *Morbid* zine. "I honestly think DEAD is mentally insane. (He knows I am writing this!) Which other way can you describe a guy who does not eat in order to get [a] starving wound? Or have a T-shirt with funeral announcements on it? I've always wanted to have a guy like that in the band."

Thanks largely to Dead and Euronymous, who appear to have spurred each other on, the humor apparent in the band's early days was quickly disappearing, and the tongue-in-cheek approach to over-the-top gore subjects was replaced by a more straight-faced exploration of evil and Satanism, along with more nihilistic offerings.

Unfortunately it wouldn't be long until Pelle actually *was* dead, consumed by the depression that had plagued him for so long. His fragile state of mind was probably not helped by the fact that the band he had moved to Norway to participate in was continuing to struggle. Euronymous had been discussing a forthcoming album entitled *De Mysteriis Dom Sathanas* for some time, but things were progressing extremely slowly, gigs were rare, and without other work the group often found themselves going without food, due to a lack of finances.

Live in Leipzig **would be the only official album to include Dead and features the vocalist on its cover.**

Increasingly isolated from the world, Dead committed suicide on April 8, 1991, first slitting his wrists and wandering around the house before shooting himself in the head with a shotgun Euronymous owned—ironically the same one that had kept him from slipping into unconsciousness previously. Euronymous discovered the body after returning to the house to find the front door locked and climbing in through Dead's bedroom window, where he found the vocalist lying dead on his bed, his head blown open and his brain lying beside his body.

In an episode that has become part of black metal folklore, Euronymous delayed contacting the police, instead heading back into town to purchase a disposable camera before returning to the scene to photograph the body, even apparently rearranging the knife so that it lay on top of the shotgun—an obvious impossibility in the normal chain of events—for dramatic effect. Unsurprisingly, when the police *were* eventually informed, the rest of the band fell under instant suspicion. They were eventually able to satisfy the authorities that the death was a suicide, although it was widely believed for some time within the metal world that Euronymous had a hand in Dead's demise.

These days it's generally accepted that the death was indeed a suicide, and Hellhammer has been quoted as saying that he thought at the time that such a thing was likely to happen eventually. Dead had made "open insinuations" about killing himself, and the last time he saw Hellhammer, he told him that he had just bought "a very sharp knife." Hellhammer had gone to stay with family at the time of Pelle's death, and Euronymous was also away, pointing to the possibility that Euronymous might, at the very least, have been *aware* of Dead's imminent demise.

Manheim says, "The weekend Pelle killed himself Øystein was spending the weekend at my place, we were good friends at that time. When he left my house, he went home and found Pelle dead. He was calm that weekend but they *had* talked about Pelle killing himself, so I guess we will never know what happened before he came to my place … whether they had planned it at all."

Whatever the truth is, the event would prove cataclysmic to the emerging black metal scene, both in Norway and eventually beyond.

17
(RE)BIRTH
OF A MOVEMENT
NORWAY PART I

IF MAYHEM VOCALIST Pelle "Dead" Ohlin had been influential in life, then so was he in death, and many active participants have commented that his premature death provided a turning point for the Norwegian scene, which from then on moved toward even greater extremity. Black metal was now becoming a matter of life and death—or at least was being portrayed as such by Euronymous. Far from grieving, Euronymous appeared to be actively capitalizing on Dead's death, something that disgusted Necrobutcher, the only member who traveled to Sweden for the funeral.

Infamously, Euronymous considered eating parts of Dead's brain, but claimed that he changed his mind due to its condition. As he stated in *The Sepulchral Voice* zine, "I have never tried human flesh. We were going to try it when Dead died but he had been lying a little too long." Instead he and Hellhammer fashioned fragments ofv Dead's skull into necklaces, with further pieces sent to other friends and contacts of the band, including Morgan of Marduk and Christophe "Masmiseim" Mermod of Samael. More controversially, the pair developed the images of Dead's body that had been taken by Euronymous, who openly planned to use these for Mayhem artwork.

"I must add that it was interesting to be able to study (half) a human brain and rigor mortis," he explained in one letter. "The pictures will be used on the Mayhem album."

"I think the way people took it was absolutely wrong," recalls Metalion. "No one really had an idea what was going on, so it was hard for people to deal with this in a proper way. [There was] a lot of stupid stuff, like Euronymous and Hellhammer wearing those necklaces of his brain. I think that people put on a tough mask and really went with the black metal lifestyle."

A gathering in the basement of the legendary Helvete store including Euronymous
and members of Darkthrone"

"It's like the whole black metal scene was traumatized with Mayhem and Dead and all that," considers Snorre Ruch, the pioneering founder of Stigma Diabolicum/Thorns who also became the second guitarist in Mayhem. "There were a lot of unfortunate things happening to a group of people who were already on the sideline. Øystein was a key figure in the scene [and] he handled it by sending skull fragments to his friends. I received a skull fragment with a letter saying, 'Now Dead has gone home,' writing it like it's something positive, something to take advantage of and he was trying to sell the story to the tabloid press, it was really dragging him down I think."

The disrespect Euronymous showed toward Dead proved to be the final straw for Nec-robutcher, who cut all ties with the guitarist.

"First of all I grieved like hell 'cos I loved the guy, he was my brother, one of my best friends. But the reaction from Øystein was not treating him like a friend, but as a piece of shit. He wanted to portray him as a crap idiot motherfucker. Didn't want to go to the funeral, wanted to exploit the photos, all shit like that, so we were very divided in that way. Dead wasn't just a fucking idiot, he was a really good friend, a really good guy, a lot of people loved him, so it devastated a lot of people. Pelle's brother called me recently for the first time—he had plucked up the courage to call me eighteen years later—and the whole family is still completely traumatized."

Euronymous arguably did represent Dead in a particularly cynical and callous manner, treating his death as a sort of statement of intent against the rest of the metal scene, and one that appeared to fit in and promote Euronymous' own ideals. He even told *The Sepulchral Voice*, "When Dead blew his brains off it was the greatest act of promotion he ever did for us… It's always great when someone dies—it doesn't matter who."

"We have declared WAR," he also told *Orcustus* zine. "Dead died because the trend people have destroyed everything from the old black metal/death metal scene, today 'death' metal is something normal, accepted and FUNNY (argh) and we HATE it. It used to be spikes, chains, leather and black clothes, and this was the only thing Dead lived for as he hated this world and everything which lives on it."

"I'm not into this business for FUN, so of course I wasn't scared," he explained to *Kill Yourself* the following year, supposedly only a week before his own death. "It's not every day you get the chance to see and touch the real corpse. And it's important to learn one thing when you are dealing with the dark side: There is NOTHING which is too sick, evil or perverted… Dead wanted to make evil music for evil people, but the only people he saw were walking around in jogging suits, caps, baseball shoes, and being into peace and love. He hated them so much, and saw no longer any reason to waste his time on them."

For his part, Necrobutcher explained to Euronymous that he didn't wish to communicate with him as long as he was planning to use the photos of Dead's corpse. In fact, these photos were never used on any official artwork, but did appear on the notorious live bootleg *Dawn of the Black Hearts*, released originally in limited-edition vinyl by Columbian label Warmaster Records—a label owned by the now-deceased Mauricio "Bull Metal" Montoya, drummer of Columbian death metallers Masacre and a contact of Euronymous'.

The fact that Necrobutcher was gone merely seems to have accelerated Euronymous' process of reinvention. In seeking to redefine *himself*, he also began to lay down his philosophy and beliefs about what metal—and black metal—should be, a move that, thanks to his influence, allowed him to both redefine and relaunch the black metal movement and the so-called second wave. This was new: in the eighties Mayhem had not claimed the black metal tag, and nor had Euronymous, who actually described the band as "brutal, extreme death metal" in an interview with a South American contact.

"Black metal was something Venom came up with so we couldn't steal that." explains Necrobutcher, "we just called our music 'aggressive metal,' 'brutal metal,' 'total death music,' words like that. The only band who could legitimately say they played black metal were Venom."

"There was no black metal scene in 1991 when Darkthrone and Burzum revolted against the death metal trend and did something else instead," Burzum's Varg Vikernes explained to me in an interview for *Metal Hammer* in 2010. "Euronymous called it black metal, because he—unlike me—was a Venom fan and they had used that as an album title, and that name has been used ever since."

"Soon as all the Mayhems and Burzums started coming out, I was like, 'Yeah this is fucking great, another load of young mad kids," recalls Venom frontman Conrad "Cronos" Lant. "It was off-the-wall, dirty, nasty, out-of-tune, out-of-time, exactly where *we* were coming from. [But] I just kept thinking, 'Why have these guys not come up with their *own* title for something they created themselves?' I don't believe they sound like Venom—they were influenced by Venom, but I was influenced by Bowie and Jethro Tull and I don't *sound* like them—so I just thought those guys should take more credit for what they've done. It's great to hear you've influenced someone's career, especially if they're doing well, but at the same time I thought they could have had a title like 'Norse Metal' or something, that would have given them the respect I think they deserved for creating their own style.

"I think those bands are very unique and amazing, heavy as fuck, [but] when some of the Norwegian bands called themselves black metal I thought, 'Well, you're not.' Because for us it was sex, drugs, rock 'n' roll, Satanism, and it was *death metal, power metal, thrash metal; all* these qualities make black metal. What I don't hear in any of these bands is songs like 'Teacher's Pet' or 'Poison' or 'Buried Alive,' it's having that diversity within the style that makes it black metal. In my opinion that's what I created when I called something black metal, it's because it has all those other styles in it. When I hear a death metal band calling themselves black metal I feel like, well, that's death metal, it's all one speed more or less, where's the tongue-in-cheek that we had?"

As Conrad points out, Venom had used plenty of other phrases—perhaps most notably power metal, a term which has a *very* different meaning these days—but the eighties were a time when extreme metal subcategories weren't as well developed. In the early nineties, however, thrash and death metal had broken into the rock and metal mainstream (a fact highlighted by the rise of bands such as Sepultura and Morbid Angel and major label Columbia's brief love affair with Earache Records), and many in the scene longed for the darker, more obscure vibe of the eighties.

What Euronymous arguably did was help resurrect the term "black metal" before bringing it into wider use, using his own ideals to redefine it, taking qualities selectively from eighties bands he admired while adding a few of his own. The most notable of these was a level of seriousness certainly not present in the early bands; he would famously claim in *Kerrang!* magazine (along with a certain Count Grishnackh of Burzum) that although he *was* aware that Venom and Bathory were not practicing Satanists, he "chose to believe otherwise."

Today the term "black metal" is frequently used to describe extreme metal with certain musical characteristics: high-paced percussion, high-pitched "screamed" vocals, fast tremolo picking on the guitars, an emphasis on atmosphere and feeling, and an unholy aesthetic. Indeed, this is the definition many black metal musicians seem most comfortable with and it's one used (if only for the sake of clarity) at times in this book. Likewise, "death metal" is now generally used to describe bands that emphasize brutality or technicality above atmosphere and use deeper "growling" vocals and frequent riff changes.

For Euronymous however, "black metal" described bands celebrating "real" Satanism (and by this he meant a genuine theistic approach, literal devil worship, as opposed to the approach of organizations such as the Church of Satan), while death metal meant "real" death worship, the actual musical characteristics of the metal played by either party being wholly irrelevant.

"There exist no death metal bands today," he claimed in *Orcustus* magazine. "There are only a handful of (mostly great) bands (in case someone hasn't got it right—black metal has nothing to do with the music itself, both Blasphemy and Mercyful Fate are black metal, it's the LYRICS, and they must be SATANIC. If not, it is NOT black metal) and what we choose to call LIFE METAL bands. Take a band like Therion. Their music is quite OK, it's actually one of the best Swedish bands (even though that doesn't say much), but their lyrics STINK. They are about society and pollution, what the fuck has that got to do with DEATH? If a band cultivates and worships death, then it's death metal, no matter what KIND of metal it is. If a band cultivates and worships Satan, it's black metal. And by saying 'cultivating death,' I don't think about thinking it's funny, or being into gore. I'm thinking about being able to KILL just because they HATE LIFE. It's people who enjoy to see wars because a lot of people get killed. How many bands think that way?"

Contrary to popular opinion, Euronymous was not against death metal per se—indeed he praised certain bands such as Carcass in interviews—but was opposed to what he considered to be "false death metal" or "life metal," which he characterized as the increasingly acceptable face of the genre. All the same, despite his own definitions it cannot be coincidence that the impressive collective of bands appearing in Norway at this time (including such well-regarded names as Burzum, Immortal, Darkthrone, Emperor, Enslaved, Hades, Gorgoroth, Satyricon, Arcturus, Carpathian Forest, and Mysticum) all utilized certain *musical* traits now associated with black metal.

Furthermore, many of these bands had converted to the black metal cause after previously playing in death metal acts, albeit often ones with an atmospheric edge. Immortal and Hades, for example, had formed from the ashes of the bands Old Funeral and Amputation, Burzum also sprang from Old Funeral, Enslaved from Phobia, Emperor from Embrionic and Thou Shalt Suffer, while Mortem contained future members of Mayhem, Arcturus, and Stigma Diabolicum/Thorns. Perhaps most notably, Darkthrone underwent a dramatic transformation from a successful technical death metal band to a full-blown black metal outfit. As it turned out, Euronymous didn't consider many of the bands that surrounded him to be black metal at all, even some bands that today are seen to *epitomize* the genre, such as Immortal. Again Euronymous emphasized lyrics and intent over musical characteristics and appearance.

"Firstly Immortal is NOT a black metal band, as they are not Satanists," he told *Orcustus* zine. "And this is something they say themselves. They are into the atmospheres and moods concerning Satanism. Their new look is just a way for them to go deeper into what they have always been into... And further, those who have cared to read the lyrics of Darkthrone's *Soulside Journey* will know that they are the same Satanic lyrics, which means that

Soulside Journey IS a black metal album."

Mayhem's lyrics of the time were certainly Satanic in nature, though Necrobutcher casts some doubt as to whether this was reflected in the member's lifestyles.

"That was to provoke," he states. "People misunderstood, they looked into our thing and made their own assumptions that we are Satanists and in that period of time when people asked us about that we said, 'Sure.' We just said yes to everything just because people are stupid enough to ask this sort of thing and we were just laughing. No, I don't think [Euronymous] 'believed.' I think he loved to talk about it but since he was not a religious person I don't think—or I *know*—that he was not. It was more like that was a bad thing, an evil thing in many people's eyes, and he was a supporter of bad things."

While Euronymous often presented black metal as merely a medium to manipulate, commenting that young musicians should become Satanic terrorists rather than form yet more new bands, there's no doubt that music was in fact his first love. Indeed, though he stated that Enslaved and Immortal should not be considered black metal because they veered away from Satanic subject matter, he nonetheless provided both with advice and support. After all, he was still a great fan of artists as diverse as Kraftwerk and Kiss and even admitted in *Slayer* zine, "I love Satanic bands, but I don't care if they sing about eating carrots, if the music is great," going on to state that he would even sign bands who wore "light clothes and jogging suits" if he admired their music.

"I never felt like there was pressure to conform," recalls Mortiis (Håvard Ellefsen), then bassist of Emperor. "Euro didn't dictate the sound, he was definitely a music fan at heart and could appreciate a lot of music for what it was, black metal or not. He released Merciless, they weren't black metal, and was planning releases with Masacre from Colombia, which was death metal."

Through such leadership, Euronymous quickly built a sense of unity, one that increased in mid-'91, when (with the help of a number of others, most prominently Stian "Occultus" Johansen of early Norwegian black metal acts Perdition Hearse and Abhorrent/Thyabhorrent) he opened a record store in Oslo. Named Helvete, the Norwegian word for hell, its primary role in many ways was as a focal point for the scene, providing a place to sleep for various young participants (including Vikernes) as well as a setting for the somewhat unhinged parties of the period.

"They were black metal parties, you know," recalls Mortiis. "The mood was okay, some people would be ass-drunk, others would sort of sulk in corners, everyone wanted to live up to something I suppose. I remember I drove a map needle into my arm until the bone stopped it and I heard Euro once drove a spike into his forehead. I also remember that I broke a beer bottle over my own head during one of those parties. A guy once came in waving a gun—he might have been a member of Abhorrent/Thyabhorrent—all kinds of shit could happen."

"Obviously we had some crazy ideas about this and that... some stupid or weird ideas about humanity," says Enslaved's Grutle Kjellson. "But generally we had beers and we

Front and back covers of a catalogue/newsletter for the Helvete store and the Deathlike Silence label, dated November 1992. On the cover is Morgan "Evil" Håkansson of Swedish acts Marduk and Abruptum, also interviewed within.

laughed... we didn't sit there like this," he frowns and crosses his arms, "all the time."

"For a little while I moved into the basement together with Varg [of Burzum]," recalls Tomas "Samoth" Haugen of Emperor. "It was a shithole of a basement and I can't believe we chose to take residence there looking back at it. We hardly stayed there though. It was very dark and gloomy... and moldy. I really dived deep into the darkness during that time of my life. There were a lot of parties in the shop with a lot of crazy shit going on. The shop wasn't very organized looking back at it. Sometimes it was total chaos. It was more run by idealism rather than good business sense. But it became a good meeting ground for people who shared interest in this music and the lifestyle that came with it back then. And it had an atmosphere. It was very different compared to how things are today. There were no 'black metal catalogue fans' back then. It was total underground and there was a more genuine feeling amongst the bands and people involved."

"The shop was a meeting ground for people socially and a place to pick up albums and get insights," concurs Kristoffer "Garm" Rygg of Ulver. "You can't really underestimate the influence of Helvete and Euronymous in the formative days of black metal in Norway."

"It was also fairly cheap," recalls Silenoz of Dimmu Borgir. "He didn't overprice the CDs and I doubt that he made any money from it really. He was all about getting this extreme underground stuff to the kids."

It's often imagined that the store was mainly selling black metal records, but at the time there simply weren't enough of such items in existence to keep a store afloat, and Helvete stocked a great deal of material by bands that Euronymous himself had voiced a distaste for, such as Deicide and Napalm Death. While these helped pay the rent, the store nonetheless was geared toward attracting and nurturing underground metal fans, and was suitably decorated, the black walls adorned with inverted crucifixes, weapons, and records, though in some cases the latter had to be provided—and sold—by the regular customers themselves.

"In Norway in the eighties it was dead scene-wise, and suddenly there was a shop fifteen minutes away from my work," reveals Darkthrone's Fenriz, a regular at the store. "Finally I could see and meet fellow maniacs. I was also one of the guys who donated vinyl so the shelves would look filled… I donated sixty vinyl and that would be mainly boring thrash metal stuff."

"Whoever was there worked behind the counter at some point," explains Enslaved's Grutle of the shop's communal atmosphere. "I mean *I* sold records myself."

"In the beginning it was hardly anything," Metalion remembers. "There was like a used section with a bunch of vinyls, nothing else. But people would go there to hang out, drink, smoke, whatever… Guys from Darkthrone were always there and Emperor… The socializing was the most important. We used to live in the basement of the store, and as you know the Inferno festival is now organizing tourist trips there… Oh well… "

"They had a horrible selection," laughs Apollyon, then of Lamented Souls and later a member of Aura Noir and Dødheimsgard. "They didn't really have any distribution. I remember when the first black metal thing came out, the *A Blaze in the Northern Sky* album [by Darkthrone], Helvete didn't get it. They didn't have the connections [with distributors]… it wasn't like a proper shop. There was another shop called Hot Records, and I was there the day it came out… one of these [Helvete] 'hangarounds' came into the shop when I was there and when the owner turned his back, or was on the phone or something, he just nicked all the *Ablaze* albums and ran down to Helvete!" He laughs. "Obviously [the owner] just went to Helvete with the police and retrieved them… that was the kind of things these silly 'hangarounds' would do."

The shop did indeed attract a lot of new fans, many of whom looked up to Euronymous. Respect undoubtedly crossed over into idolization for some who, having not known him in earlier, less "evil" times, had something of a one-sided impression. With his old friends Manheim and Necrobutcher gone, Euronymous was able to preach an increasingly extreme and rigid manifesto and present himself as he wished to be seen, free of the constraints older contacts might have placed on him.

"There would be *many* kids, and I think Euronymous loved it too," recalls Apollyon, "lots of followers who would do anything for him. There were lots of bands and guys who brought their lunchboxes just to sit there all day and be with Euronymous."

Says Necrobutcher, "When I was out of the picture nobody knew who he was. So he could put on this fake thing. Put on this robe, paint his face white and say stuff that had no truth in it."

Manheim agrees: "When you are close with people that have been living with you for many years and know what you really are, you just can't try to be something you are not—"

Necrobutcher interjects: "—'cos your mates would immediately pick up on it and say, 'What the fuck are you saying?'"

"Right," says Manheim, "you will be exposed. But at the time when Euronymous was very extreme we still had a lot of contact. He could call me, we were talking about music, and all kinds of things, he was normal. The day after he could give you a call and he'd have friends over at Helvete and he'd be talking about burning churches like a different person. He'd be playing a role and he could do that, as there was nobody to correct him."

"He was trying to convince himself and people around him that he was purest evil and Satanic and all that shit," says Snorre Ruch. "I don't know how many people fell for it, but the media liked it."

Outwardly, and most noticeably in interviews, Euronymous continued to propagate an extremely evil image, becoming increasingly cold and heartless in his statements.

"I have no friends, just the guys I'm allied with, if my girlfriend dies I won't cry, I will misuse the corpse," he told Norwegian publication *Beat*. When asked about the humorous elements within *Deathcrush*, he explained, "That was then. Now we mean partying is bad. It's better to sit and cut yourself, than to go out and have fun… It's many years since I managed to feel love. This is just the way it is. This is a main concept."

Despite such comments, Euronymous wasn't at all the type to sit at home cutting himself or living out an emotionless, friendless existence, even if his comments appear, sadly, to have inspired some fans to behave this way. The regular parties and frequent socializing inherent to the movement alone suggest that the slogan of his label Deathlike Silence Productions ("No Mosh, No Core, No Trend, No Fun") was at least twenty-five percent inaccurate. In fact, most who met him report that Euronymous was a generally social and friendly individual, an enthusiastic music fan who loved to talk about his passion and enjoyed dealing with others. He certainly had a lot of friends, to whom he reportedly acted with generosity and kindness. One example was Grutle Kjellson and Ivar Bjørnson, founders of Enslaved, whom he not only signed to his label Deathlike Silence but also mentored in their early years. Despite the fact that their interests openly lay with the traditional Nordic Gods rather than Satanism, both men say that Euronymous was only ever supportive and never attempted to preach any Satanic ideas to them.

Grutle Kjellson says: "We told him about our concept and he said, 'Yeah, someone should do that, that's cool, to preserve the culture. I'm not into those things, but go ahead.'"

Adds Ivar Bjørnson, "The thing we spent the most time talking about was musical the-

Euronymous depicted in the Helvete store, taken from an article in *Verdens Gang* newspaper, Norway, 1993, after the shop's closure.

ory. When he came to visit our hometown—which is a key moment in Enslaved history—he brought his guitar. We had been listening so much to [Mayhem's] *De Mysteriis Dom Sathanas* tapes, the rough mixes without vocals. He had his guitar, and I had my guitar, and I could just ask him, 'How do you do that riff?' and he would explain it. He would give me a call and tell me that him and the guy from Thorns [Snorre Ruch] had developed this theory on how to record, it was just about sharing that stuff. My guitar style is still seventy or eighty percent those moments, you know, being fourteen years old."

In this way Euronymous helped out many younger bands in the scene, especially Enslaved and Emperor, both of whom he personally recommended to Candlelight Records, the label that issued the split record of the two bands. Interestingly, even before meeting Emperor, he'd offered thoughts and advice to guitarist Samoth and bassist Mortiis, just two of many individuals communicating with him by mail at the time.

"I first got in contact with him by writing to him," Samoth recalls. "I sent him the *Embryonic* demo, and he gave us some honest feedback. He didn't like it all that much, but pointed out good things too, and gave info on Mayhem, upcoming gigs, bands to check out and so on."

For those of us who never met Euronymous, it's very hard to pin down who he was as a human being, perhaps because he was so keen to deny his humanity and was increasingly consumed by the black metal personality he presented to the world, as a now-infamous quote in *Orcustus* zine underlines:

"I don't think people should respect each other. I don't want to see trend people respecting me, I want them to HATE and FEAR. If people don't accept our ideas as their own, they can fuck off because then they belong to a musical scene which has NOTHING to do with ours. They could just as well be Madonna fans. There is an ABYSS between us and the rest…. The HC [hardcore] pigs have correctly made themselves guardians of morality, but we must kick them in the face and become guardians of anti-morality."

Even Manheim, who knew him better than most, finds it hard to separate Euronymous from the character he created.

"There was cynicism in it," he ponders thoughtfully, "how he handled the death of Pelle, that was really shocking, 'cos up to that point things were just image and philosophical discussions. That was probably the breaking point, where we understood that he wasn't handling this very well. Øystein never changed to me, but the image took more and more space, how far he was willing to take the image was expanding. We had an intellectual discussion once about how far you could take something, and how fun it was to take it far and he found joy in exploiting that. How far can you push people? How far can you push yourself? So in that context that *was* a part of him. But I'm convinced that the image Euronymous was building up was not Øystein. I don't think it was real, but I think he might have *thought* he would go into that level of cynicism.

"But he *was* a kind person, he *did* care about people around him. [But he also believed] that to really explore the extreme, you had to *live* the extreme and that's where he departed from other people. Artists will say, 'We must go into the extreme to see how people will react to it,' but to *live* the extreme, that's something different and he wanted to do that. He talked about sex and said the evil thing to do is to have anal sex. You shouldn't have regular, normal, natural sex, you should have anal, so he was very strict, he wanted to explore that, to be this kind of person. So, is this the image, or the personality? I would guess if you spoke to scholarly people they would say it was the image, a role you were playing. But of course it mirrors some of you, because you are not able to live it if you could not mirror some of it."

"Euronymous was probably the most extreme guy I ever met," says Grutle, "he hated Nazism, 'cos he thought communism was much worse. He watched weird movies, he was very misanthropic, but still, he was one of the most friendly people I ever met."

"What he was advocating very strongly was seriousness in the music," adds Ivar, "and I think that explains the contradiction with how he was when people met him, to how he was in the media. I think he believed in it on some level, but I think it's possible to want the world to burn and see everything stop, and then go home and wish the best for yourself, your family, your kids. I think it's possible to have those two thoughts in your head at the same time. A lot of writers are fascinated with the 'double life,' a lot of writers write very extreme books

A photo of the Helvete store, depicting some of the items (many donated by friends and comrades) that decorated the walls. The dagger on the right was given to Hellhammer by his grandfather when he was eight. Photo courtesy of Samoth, who lived at the shop for a time.

and the thoughts the main characters have, these thoughts have to come from somewhere. Are you a homicidal maniac or sexual deviant yourself? A lot of people claim that *everyone* has these secret double lives to some extent and I think the only difference in the black metal scene was that these people chose to *vocalize* that double life."

18

A FIST IN THE FACE OF CHRISTIANITY
NORWAY PART II

IT WAS IN 1992 that the events in Norway began to take a more sinister turn, and words began to be replaced by actions. Just as Euronymous appears to have gravitated toward more extreme tendencies after Dead entered the picture, so too did the introduction of another strong personality, Varg Vikernes, also known at that time as Count Grishnackh.

Born with the name Kristian (later changed due to its religious connotations), Vikernes hailed from the city of Bergen on Norway's west coast and was something of an outsider in the predominantly Oslo-based scene. Originally a member of death metal band Old Funeral, he had moved toward the black metal scene following the group's dissolution. Like so many others, he had made some contact with the members of Mayhem prior to Dead's death (in a bizarre twist, it was he who, as a Christmas gift, sent the shotgun shells Pelle would eventually use in his suicide), but it was only later that he really established himself among his peers.

From interviews at the time, it's clear that Euronymous was impressed by Vikernes, in whom he may have seen something of himself. Both men possessed a strong and individualistic musical vision, and Vikernes' one-man outfit Burzum impressed Euronymous enough for him to not only sign the project to Deathlike Silence Productions, but also invite him to temporarily take over Mayhem's bass duties in Necrobutcher's absence. Just as importantly, Vikernes' ambitions also went some way beyond music, and he seems to have been on a path similar to Euronymous' in terms of his thinking, echoing a familiar sense of nihilism and misanthropy in interviews such as the one with *Orcustus* in which he memorably stated, "I use all my wisdom to spread evil and sorrow and hopefully death."

"I can understand that Øystein saw a protégé in him," reflects Manheim. "He was very

Probably the two most important—but also highly volatile—figures in early nineties Norway: Euronymous and Varg Vikernes.

eager to play his music, was proud of finding him, was talking of this young guy who was a huge talent. I only met him a few times but I thought he was … just dumb. But he was young and I'm not sure if I mixed up 'young' and 'dumb.' He wanted to go into the image and did so with force—it looked real but this is a kid who really wanted to be a part of something, it wasn't coming from him, it was he who dressed up into *it*. He found that in this scene he could *be* someone and he certainly was, and still is, so full respect to that, but at that point I just found it ridiculous."

In March 1992 Burzum's debut was issued on Deathlike Silence, the second Norwegian black metal album to be released, after Darkthrone's *A Blaze in the Northern Sky*. But as the black metal scene in Norway began to explode musically, so did the criminal activity associated with the movement. On June 6, 1992, Bergen's Fantoft Stave Church, an impressive and historically significant twelfth-century building, was attacked by arsonists, the wooden structure soon giving way to the flames and burning to the ground. While Vikernes was never found guilty of the attack, his peers at the time have stated that he admitted to the arson, perhaps an unsurprising revelation given that a photo of the ruins were brazenly used on the cover of his second official release, *Aske* (meaning "Ashes").

The attack would be only one in a spate of church burnings throughout Norway, with around ten other churches targeted before the year was through. As it turned out, Vikernes would later be found guilty of playing a direct part in many of the attacks in 1992, including the one on Holmenkollen Chapel in Oslo (burned in August), Skjold Church in Vindafjord (burned in September), and Åsane Church in Bergen (burned on Christmas Eve).

"Actually we knew about this before it happened," explains Snorre Ruch of the church burnings, "because Varg does not hold back on his stories. He likes to promote everything and himself and he had boasted to Euronymous that he was going to burn churches and Øystein boasted to me that there was this guy who was going to burn churches and I was like, [adopts disinterested voice] '*Yeah, whatever.*' Then it happened and I was like 'Oof... *Yeah, whatever,*'" he laughs. "Marius [Thorns/Arcturus] and me took some distance from that, we thought it was too silly, for us it was rebellious criminal fascination, especially with Varg, Øystein, and Bård."

Indeed, Vikernes was far from the only black metal musician and Helvete regular involved in the spree, though for the most part Euronymous himself had little to do with the actual attacks, something he later openly admitted—and defended—in *Kerrang!*

"It would be very stupid if I did things myself—if I was caught the whole organization would collapse," he explained. "I look after the economic side of things, and my record label provides the foundations. We have a group of militant people, taking care of things that need to be taken care of."

While he was perhaps exaggerating his own importance for dramatic effect, there's no doubt that Euronymous played a major role in setting the scene for the culture of destruction taking place across Norway. The "militant people" he spoke of—along with some aware of but uninvolved in their activities—would become known as the Inner Circle, Black Circle, or Black Metal Mafia, though more recent statements from those involved highlight that this was not as formal or organized a group as such phrases might suggest. Nonetheless, black metal's anti-Christian/Satanic ethos had, for the first time, been turned into significant direct action, and activities such as grave desecrations and church arson became relatively common.

Pinning down exactly what inspired this situation isn't easy, and it's important to note that the majority of those involved came from untroubled middle-class backgrounds and weren't involved in other illegal activity. With a few exceptions, drugs were only notable in the scene by their absence, and though drinking was popular with some, it was not widespread at that time. Some members of the circle, such as Mortiis and Vikernes, didn't drink or use drugs, and the use of intoxicants was criticized by several bands in interviews. Though certainly not true today, the Norwegian scene of the period could actually be quite militant and even puritanical, especially compared to most other youth music cultures, not least within metal itself.

"We were pretty young and inexperienced at that stuff—drugs were totally alien to us and we drank only rarely," recalls Mortiis. "During Emperor I just thought drunk people behaved like idiots and I wanted no part of it. In that sense, I was a lot smarter then than I am now! It appears to me that it's harder to get hold of [drugs] in these parts than it would be in the U.S., the UK, or societies where drug use is more ingrained and maybe not quite as vilified as it is over here. I mean to us drugs was something you saw in movies, it was almost as if they didn't really exist."

Because most members of the scene were from atheist families, this also wasn't a case of oppressed youths rebelling against overly religious parents. That said, as previously noted, Christianity is a heavily integrated part of Norwegian society, and one has to opt *out* of the church, rather than choose to be a part of it—something that caused much resentment in the black metal community.

For some within Norway's black metal scene, anti-Christian sentiments were an expression of pagan or Viking ideals rather than (or sometimes *as well as*) Satanic ones. The not entirely inaccurate concept of Norway as a pagan land wrongly conquered by Christianity in centuries past became a popular one, and there's no doubt that many participants did indeed see themselves as fighting an ideological battle.

"We all hung out and talked about our hatred for Christianity and how to get the Viking religion back," Samoth of Emperor (and session bassist on Burzum's *Aske*) later commented in *Spin* while serving time for his part in the arson of the Skjold church.

"I have always been fascinated by the Viking culture and myths, and also consider it a part of my Norwegian heritage," explains Samoth today. "I'm however not [personally] connected to it in any 'religious' way, like some Asatru groups. It's just something that is naturally there, and I like the nature aspect of it. Norway used to be a pagan land, but has, as so many other countries, been corrupted by the Christian dogma. This feeling was very strong back in the nineties and there was an urge to make a strong statement about it."

"We have to remember that Christianity was a religion forced on the people of Norway," commented Kristoffer "Garm" Rygg of Ulver in the 1994 documentary *Det Svarte Alvor*. "And as the sons of Odin we see it as our duty to take back that which once was ours."

"The Church has behaved so disgracefully, basely, and cruelly in Norway, it's incredible," Vikernes also commented in another black metal documentary, 1998's *Satan Rir Media*. "When they talk about Satanism, when someone burns a church, they ought to look at themselves and all the sacred places they have burnt, and the ruins on top of which they have built their churches."

"As long as I can remember I have been well aware of my history, and been a critic of religion in general," explains Jørn Inge Tunsberg, who was jailed for his part in the attack on Åsane. A past member of both Old Funeral, Amputation, and Immortal, he formed Hades in 1993, a band heavily inspired by Viking themes. "Back then, those actions were a fist in the face of Christianity, carried out in free will by each and [every] one of us! I believe there

Aftenposten aften
Hatte-løp på Ø

Holmenkollen kapell i aske

Alt gikk tapt

"Holmenkollen Chapel in Ashes," *Aftenposten* **newspaper, Norway, 1992. The church was burnt by Varg, Faust and Euronymous the night following the murder in Lillehammer.**

are more correct ways these days to protest against the Christianity in this world. But then again, I am still certain that the power to protest and provoke is very much alive in many of us, and it is important to stand [up] and protect yourself and your opinions at all times."

"I was once asked how I could think it was okay to burn churches once, and I tried to answer intellectually," ponders Manheim, who, though not directly involved in the attacks, was certainly kept up to date with their progress. "You know, you destroy a public property, which was a symbol of power in society, and it's just a church, it's a building, so as a symbolic act I can understand it and even find reasons to *do* that. If a person asked would *I* do that, the answer is no, I wouldn't. I have other expressions to do that, but I can understand the symbolism involved in burning churches. But you can argue that a lot of people who did [burn churches] didn't *have* that intellectual interest in what they did, they just did it as being *fans*, they didn't put much intelligence into it.

"I would talk about these things with Øystein and we were totally aligned, it was a symbolic act. Okay, we could understand it, but then you went to prison. Why? It's pointless and you don't destroy an organization [that way] because what you burn is state property, so what you can be assured of is that it will be rebuilt. I remember one call when they were going to burn one of the Viking churches, Borgund stave church, which is, you know, a thousand years old. We had this discussion and I tried to explain this was stupid, this was culture, inheritance, why don't you just go and burn some modern church that doesn't mean anything to anyone? So I guess that's the only time I reacted to the plans. Otherwise it was just, 'Oh, okay do what you want, it's not my thing.'" [The Borgund church was ultimately not burnt.]

"We were never part of any criminal actions," explains Ivar, speaking of his band Enslaved, another group with strong Viking themes. "But I can see their perspectives. I think it became ridiculous when people talked about 'Satanic terrorism,' because every church burning, without exception, happened when there were no people inside them, whereas terrorism is about finding the point where you can strike as many innocent people as possible, so that's a major difference."

"I must admit I'm very happy I didn't participate in those actions," recalls Ivar's long-time bandmate Grutle. "I mean, I understand the hatred toward Christianity, *I* have a strong hatred, it's the most evil invention in the world. From a historical point of view I have no regrets about the church burnings, but you have to look a little further and think a little further. My family, even back to the Middle Ages, living in fear of the state and the state church, everyone had to work really hard, baptize their children, get married in the church ... I come from the small place, so when you burn down a church, it is so closely connected to your family and the people around you for five hundred years, so it is not about religion. And burning a church ... people get *closer* to the church."

Undoubtedly, there was more at work behind the arsons than simply an ideological opposition to the church. There was, for a start, a somewhat cultish atmosphere, wherein younger participants (most of those carrying out these activities were in their late teens) wished to be accepted within the scene by older members, such as Euronymous. And a culture had been created by charismatic individuals such as Dead, Euronymous, and Vikernes, that celebrated evil, hate, misanthropy, and Satanism.

Interviews of the time saw bands attempting to break every taboo still standing, glorifying murder, torture, suicide, arson, and more, often tying this to an overtly spiritual, even supernatural, theme, with frequent references to the devil, spirits, hell, and the like. At the same time, music and art were being created that far surpassed what had come before—recordings whose timelessness has been proved by their enduring popularity. For those swept up in all this, the lines between everyday reality, art, ideology, and the glorious melodrama of black metal were blurred in what must have been an intoxicating mix.

"All that stuff felt like a great backdrop for our music," agrees Mortiis. "I think we all had this extremity sort of saturated into us. We were part desensitized, part too young to understand the magnitude of what we were starting. Every time I think about it, I think we were a lot closer to a Charles Manson scenario than any of us realized ... a lot closer."

One of the most central characters in the development of this culture, and one of the few alive today, Vikernes himself has an interesting take on the situation, acknowledging how many were caught up in this culture but taking care to make a separation between the behavior and motives of those who initiated and those who followed. In a 2010 interview for *Metal Hammer* magazine, he explained this point to me in some detail:

"Euronymous in particular didn't want black metal to become a trend. When we saw—in 1992—that all the failures from the death metal scene all of a sudden wanted to play black metal instead, making black metal the new trend, we did everything we could to make black metal too extreme for everybody else. By doing so we imagined that we could scare large groups of posers away from black metal. So, we used imagery and a language so extreme no sensible human beings out there would in theory want anything to do with us. This worked fine, of course, only we didn't realize that there are so many insanely stupid human beings

Out from the dark: Øystein 'Euronymous' Aarseth, the man who arguably did more than anyone to resurrect black metal and spread its influence around the world.

out there, who still wanted to be 'evil,' and wanted to commit crimes to prove it to us, just to be accepted into our select group. Every time we saw that others still 'liked us' and wanted to become our 'friends,' we had to step up the madness, so to speak, and go even further to alienate ourselves from them.

"Because of this process, led by Euronymous from his shop, we ended up promoting pure insanity and stupidity, alias 'evil,' and those who wanted to join our select group burnt churches, desecrated graves and so forth, to be accepted. What you talk about is the followers' point of view. They certainly were 'caught up' in this subculture, but we—Mayhem, Darkthrone, and Burzum—weren't."

Whatever the motivations behind the acts, by 1992 the phenomenon of what was generally labeled "Satanic terrorism" was spreading through Norway like wildfire, often beyond any direct connection to Varg, Euronymous, or members of the "Inner Circle." This was evident even in the early days of the church burnings, since one of the first churches to suffer was the Revheim Church, in the relative isolation of the city of Stavanger. The attackers were unconnected to the Oslo or Bergen scenes, but were certainly a part of the black metal culture, and later formed another important band, Gehenna. Elsewhere on the south coast of Norway in Kristiansand, another faction of anti-Christian metallers was also in existence, a group who were later invited to visit Helvete and would become to some extent the "muscle" of some of the operations discussed in Oslo.

"There was no 'black metal' scene in the beginning," explains Terje Vik Schei, then a death metal musician, but one who would soon adopt the pseudonym Tchort (a Slavonic word for the devil) and join black metal acts Emperor, Satyricon, and Carpathian Forest. "We were a few kids who listened to alternative music and hated the Christians and had fights with them, we desecrated their churches and graves. The papers started to write about it and we were contacted by Euronymous, who wanted us to come to Oslo and meet with them. We learned that there were more people like us, that they labeled all of us 'black metal' and [thought we should] follow certain rules—no white sneakers," he laughs, "We didn't know or care about this when we first met, and their jaws dropped to the floor when they saw us arrive in sweat pants and white sneakers!"

As Terje confirms, the Kristiansand scene was notably extreme even by the standards of the time, with members attacking Christians in the street with knives in the middle of the day. Going some way beyond mere anti-Christian ideology or even straightforward antisocial behavior, these activities were entrenched in a destructive Satanic culture similar to the one that had grown up in Oslo. Like Mortiis (whom he would replace in Emperor), Terje admits a certain "saturation" of extreme ideas. Even for Terje himself—no longer a Satanist and now married with children—this period is quite surreal to look back upon.

"I have to force myself in order to recall these events," he admits. "The actions were extreme, but so were we at that time. Living off human blood, decorating your flat with tombstones, animal carcasses, digging up graves and shit, does something to you, and what is considered extreme didn't seem so extreme back then. Again, it was more about the atmosphere, the emotions and feelings and pushing our limits that led to stuff like animal sacrifice, drinking blood, etc. We didn't see this as part of the music scene we now 'belonged' to, but as a part of the life situation we were experimenting with. We had some books and ideas on how rituals were performed, but we followed our own instincts—or lack of them—more than anything else. I remember that I passed out on the street on one occasion as I had been living off animal blood solely for quite some time."

Events in the Norwegian scene were about to take an even more dramatic turn. On August 21, 1992, Bård "Faust" Eithun, an eighteen-year-old drummer known for his work in Thorns and Emperor, was walking in Lillehammer's newly finished Olympic Park, having traveled from Oslo where he had recently moved to visit his mother. In the park he met an inebriated stranger, one Magne Andreassen, an older homosexual man who reportedly approached Bård for sex and suggested they go to the woods together. Eithun agreed and walked a long way into the wood with Andreassen before attacking him with a penknife that he had in his back pocket, stabbing him several times in his stomach until he fell to his knees, then continuing to stab him in his face, neck, and back, a total of thirty-seven times in total, until he appeared dead. He left the scene, but on hearing sounds coming from the dying man he returned to kick him in the head to be sure he had been killed. He then departed and made his way to his mother's house, where he washed off the blood and went to sleep.

While he was accused of luring Andreassen into the woods in order to murder him—and indeed Eithun was quoted in several publications admitting that he had planned to kill the man from the point he agreed to enter the woods—the motivation for the killing is still somewhat unclear. In interviews given soon after his conviction, Eithun seemed to suggest that the murder was done more out of morbid curiosity than any personal reason. "It's the kind of thing I've always dreamt about doing," he commented in *Petrified*. In another zine, *Goats of Pandemonium*, he claimed, "I killed this man … just to see what it was like."

Similar comments suggested this was not a hate crime, though an interview in *Spin* indicated that Andreassen's homosexuality may have had some impact. "I just very calmly decided to end this man's life," Eithun remarked, "Maybe my subconscious was telling me that because he was gay I had that right." Though the courts would find him guilty of murder, in recent years some of his peers have suggested an alternative theory, arguing that Eithun may have considered himself under attack, his statements in the press about a cold slaying being motivated by a desire to keep in line with the scene's strict mentality.

"I have heard some explanations from Bård on what triggered it," ponders Necrobutcher, "and if those things are correct, this guy hassled him . . maybe tried to attack him sexually. Say you walk down the street and a homo tries to fuck you in your ass, what would you do if you had a knife in your pocket? Would you stab the guy? Probably, yes. Maybe, if you're just eighteen years old, would you stab him more than one time? Maybe you would panic and just stab him 'til the guy let go of your hair and fell down … the only thing I know is what he said, but maybe he followed the guy himself, wanted to kill him, planned it, he just didn't like his face and waited until he was in the park and attacked him. But knowing this guy I really doubt that. If it was self-defense, I think it was a good thing—if it was cold-blooded murder, that I don't like."

The following day, Eithun headed back to Oslo and went to Helvete to meet with Euronymous and Vikernes. Explaining that he planned to turn himself in to police, he was dissuaded by Euronymous and Vikernes. Instead, that night the three traveled to the city's Holmenkollen Chapel and burnt it to the ground, heading up a mountain to properly view the spectacle. News of the murder spread quickly within Norway's tight scene, and Manheim—who supports the self-defense theory—reveals that Euronymous called him to talk about it even before Holmenkollen was torched.

"I tried to say, Helvete is two hundred meters from the main police station, so the thing to do now if the story is correct, which I believe it is, is go over there and report yourself 'cos that's the sensible thing to do. But Øystein was excited, he found this [murder] very thrilling … So they went and burnt Holmenkollen Chapel and to me that was the most stupid thing to do… What I knew about the story it was a self-defense case, I talked to him about it later and he seems honest about it. How would you answer [in interviews] if you were constantly asked [about it] and were also a world-famous character in black metal history? … He didn't go to Oslo immediately, he was shaky if I was told the correct story from Øystein. It was a bad thing that he went down to Øystein, who laughed about it and thought it was fantastic. He should have gone to someone who could actually have sat down, thought about it and tried to find a good way to talk to the police about it. He probably would have spent less years in prison if that was the case."

While there were up to fifty people in the Norwegian black metal scene who knew exactly who was involved in the various crimes being committed, the police remained clueless for a time. Almost as soon as 1993 began, however, events occurred that would bring the house of cards built by the Inner Circle crashing down around them.

It began in January, when Vikernes gave an interview to two young writers who hoped to sell their story to the newspaper *Bergens Tidende*. While the story didn't make it into the newspaper, it caught the eye of Finn Bjørn Tønder, a crime journalist at the paper. Tønder's interest was piqued because Vikernes was quoted as saying he had been involved in the church burnings. Although the police didn't agree with him, Tønder had suspected the burnings were the work of Satanists ever since learning from police investigating the Fantoft church arson that a dead animal had been found on the church's steps. After contacting the two aspiring writers, Tønder arranged with Vikernes that he and a photographer would come along with them to the musician's flat in order to do a piece for the paper.

The resulting interview described a young man living in an apartment with covered windows and Nazi and Satanic-related decor, the photos at the time also showing a large amount of Dungeons and Dragons role-playing material. The overall impression was of a living space that would probably seem slightly less outlandish to anyone who'd seen a typical teenage metal fan's bedroom than it seems to have been to Tønder. Similarly, the interview itself was not unlike the interviews given to sympathetic fanzines, full of bold statements and dramatically callous boasts. However, Tønder urged the Burzum mainman to support his claims with details that could be verified with the police.

Some claim that in doing so, he provided specifics that linked the crimes directly to the Norwegian black metal scene. Firstly, Vikernes reportedly explained that, for symbolic reasons, a rabbit had been decapitated and left on the steps of the church at Fantoft, something only someone involved with the crime could know, as it had not been reported in the press. Secondly, he allegedly mentioned that a gay man had been knifed at the Lillehammer Olympic Park, a crime that until that point had not been linked to the black metal scene at all. The very afternoon the article was printed Vikernes was arrested, thanks to dialogue between Tønder and the police.

"That was the point where a lot of shit happened," reflects Necrobutcher, "'cos he cleaned up a lot of the loose ends that the cops had, and of course that was not cool. But it would have happened sooner or later. One [person] can keep a secret, maybe two, but [when] some more people find out who was responsible for killing those people, setting those fires or doing the vandalism or whatever ... it would have come to light, but of course not in that dramatic way. He was nineteen years old and thought it would be a good promotion for the album."

During his incarceration, Vikernes consistently denied his guilt and stated that the interview had been a hoax carried out for promotional purposes. By March, he had been released by police due to a lack of evidence. In fairness to Vikernes, it should be pointed out that he still vehemently denies that this interview had any impact on others within the scene. During the aforementioned 2010 *Metal Hammer* interview, he stated:

"This is what the rats want you to believe, in an attempt to make me look like the bad guy, but the truth is that not a single soul was convicted because of that interview. I had to spend six weeks in custody and the Old Funeral drummer had to spend a night [under] the police arrest, but nobody ratted anybody out at this point. The police had no success what-soever because everybody kept their mouth shut.... Further, it was actually Euronymous' idea, and we did it to promote his record shop and black metal—because he was in dire financial troubles. My motivation was the same; I wanted him (Euronymous) to afford printing more Burzum albums. The first print had long been sold out, and he [couldn't] afford printing more records. In this respect it would have been a huge success, if only Euronymous hadn't closed down his shop a week later, because his parents didn't appreciate the attention from the press. That's what I spent six weeks in prison for ... In the end I have to say that those who accuse me of lying can just go fuck themselves, because all the police interviews still exist. I have read them several times, and so have my many lawyers, and the rats can tell as many bullshit stories they want to, but these interviews don't go away, and they all confirm my story a hundred percent."

Almost immediately after Vikernes' release, *Kerrang!* ran a now-infamous exposé on black metal, interviewing both Euronymous and Vikernes. The latter was featured on the cover in an equally notorious picture, hair down over his face with two large knives crossed over his chest, above a headline that read "ARSON ... DEATH ... SATANIC RITUAL ... THE UGLY TRUTH ABOUT BLACK METAL," beside a smaller picture of a corpsepainted Emperor. The article included some basic errors, including the consistent misspelling of Varg's pseud-onym, but nonetheless proved to be nothing short of dynamite.

While the article was presented as a tabloid-style exposé and was heavily critical of the Norwegian scene, it also gave it a huge dose of publicity, pouring gas on an already steadily burning fire. Those within the movement were encouraged by the coverage they were receiving in what was then the world's biggest rock and metal magazine, since while the article focused on Mayhem, Burzum, and Emperor, it also mentioned a number of other acts including VON, Darkthrone, Master's Hammer, Impaled Nazarene, Rotting Christ, Beherit, and Profanatica.

Most importantly, the article provided an instant gateway and guide to the scene for many who would become fans and even practitioners themselves. It's not hard to see, particularly in a pre-Internet age, the magic that these mysterious, criminal, corpsepainted

"Arson…Death…Satanic Ritual…" *Kerrang's*
memorable Norwegian exposé in 1993, featuring
Varg and Emperor on its cover, introduced
a new legion of fans to the genre.

devil-worshippers held for some of those reading, many of whom were undoubtedly curious to discover exactly what this "new" music actually sounded like.

The interviews themselves were typical of the time in their callousness, boastfulness, and drama, particularly in the quotes from Vikernes, who described the *Aske* record as a "hymn to church burning," commenting, "It's saying, 'Do this. You can do this too.' And we convert the souls of kids with our music…"

Later, in a quote that Vikernes argues was taken out of context, he states: "We support Christianity because it oppresses people, and we burn churches to make it stronger. We can then eventually make war with it. Human beings are worthless and stupid … they're not supposed to think. They're supposed to follow a god or leader. I support all dictatorships. Stalin, Hitler, Ceaucescu … and I will become the dictator of Scandinavia myself. I'm a Viking and we're supposed to fight … The only negative thing about [murder] is that when you kill someone they can no longer suffer."

Euronymous was quoted somewhat less than Vikernes, but nonetheless made an impact with his words: "I don't care if people die, even within my own circle. I have no feelings left … We are but slaves of The One With Horns. We are a religious people, and total obedience is a fundamental concept for us. I'm a piece of dust in the whole cosmos, compared to Him. What happens to us doesn't matter. If I had great enough reason to kill, I'd gladly serve twenty years in jail."

As it turned out though, it would be Vikernes who would end up serving time for murder, not Euronymous.

19
DEATH OF A LEGEND
NORWAY PART III

ON THE NIGHT OF August 9, 1993, Varg Vikernes undertook the long drive from Bergen to Oslo with Snorre "Blackthorn" Ruch, a copy of his Deathlike Silence record contract, and a collection of weapons, including knives, axes, and a baseball bat. Arriving at Euronymous' apartment at around 3 a.m. on August 10, Varg rang his doorbell, and having woken Euronymous, persuaded him to open the door and let him in, using the contract he had brought as a pretext while Snorre remained outside.

Having gained access to the apartment, Varg attacked Euronymous (who was still in his underwear) with one of several knives he had strapped to his body, repeatedly stabbing him, mainly in the back, but also in the neck and head. At one point Euronymous ran out onto the stairwell, screaming for help, where he passed Snorre (who was apparently so shocked by the sight of his bleeding bandmate that he blacked out), but his cries were in vain and he would soon die of his injuries, his body abandoned and found on the stairs a couple of hours later.

In interviews, Varg has stated that he killed Euronymous at the scene; indeed, on his own website he states that Euronymous died instantly after a knife wound to the head. However, during the fracas a lamp was broken and Euronymous fell upon the shards, with this accounting for many of the twenty-four puncture wounds found on his body.

"I've read the scripts from the court," explains Manheim. "Øystein had scars all over his underarms, [a] lot of stabbing in his back, even if [Varg] had stopped there, he wouldn't have bled to death. But in the struggle, defending himself or running away—in his underwear, woken up in the middle of the night—what killed him was that one of the lamps broke, and the glass from that Øystein stepped on, and cut the main artery in the foot, and was lying there for several hours bleeding to death."

Vikernes claims that Euronymous was the first to attack, as he stated in an interview with *Metal Hammer* two years after being jailed: "I turned up at 3 a.m. and we started to talk angrily, and he panicked and tried to attack me. I just threw him on the floor, and he got up

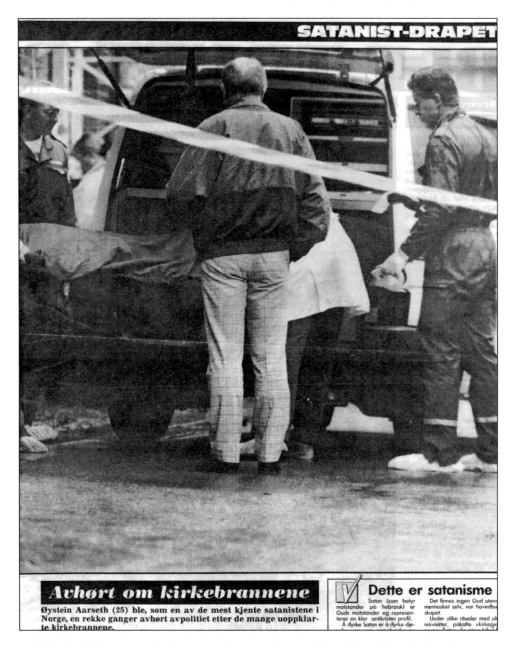

SATANIST-DRAPET

Avhørt om kirkebrannene

Øystein Aarseth (25) ble, som en av de mest kjente satanistene i Norge, en rekke ganger avhørt av politiet etter de mange uoppklarte kirkebrannene.

Dette er satanisme

Satan (som betyr motstander på hebraisk) er Guds motstander og representerer en klar antikristen profil. Å dyrke Satan er å dyrke dje-

Det finnes ingen Gud uten mennesket selv, var hovedbudskapet. Under ulike ritualer med ul rekvisitter, påkalte «kirkegje

The body of Euronymous is taken away, August 10th, 1993. Translation: "Øystein Aarseth was, as one of the most notorious/well-known satanists in Norway, questioned a number of times by police after the many unsolved cases of church fires." *Verdens Gang* newspaper, Norway.

and ran to the kitchen to get a knife. And I thought if he were going to have a knife so could I."

If the details surrounding the attack are hazy, so too are the motives for the murder. Vikernes has always maintained that Øystein was actually seeking to kill him and that the murder was a pre-emptive act of self-defense, as he revealed in the aforementioned *Metal Hammer* interview.

"Well the guy I murdered, he tried to kill me but obviously he didn't manage [laughs], so I killed him instead. It wasn't what I would call direct self-defense, because he was no real threat there and then. I could have beat him up and kicked him out in the street, but I killed him. If I didn't kill him then, he would have tried again. There was no point in giving him a second chance."

In our interview in 2010 for the same magazine he repeated this story. "I knew he planned (not just wanted) to kill me, and today I know that several others knew as well (because a few of Euronymous' former friends have told me they knew too), so I have no regrets. What goes around comes around. My plan was in fact to beat the shit out of him, so to speak, but when he tried to get hold of a knife things took a more dramatic turn. I know I could have done things differently, but I don't think the end result was too bad."

On his own official site (among other places), Varg explains that Euronymous had telephoned Snorre while Snorre was staying at Varg's flat and that he had listened in, hearing Euronymous explaining that he was planning to kill him.

"Maybe," says Snorre, "but in any case if Øystein said he wanted to kill Varg, it would be like he could say he wanted to kill anyone, without there being any pressure behind it. But then I think there might be some aspects of this conflict that I didn't catch before all this happened, there might have been other threats or incidents I don't know because I could care less what people say or think about each other."

Whatever the exact situation between the two parties, it was this one call that appears to have acted as a catalyst for the murder and dragged Snorre into the unhappy mess.

"It was mostly due to me being in Bergen and receiving the phone call that triggered the event," he confirms, "and that Varg didn't want to do the drive alone made me the natural person. There was a third person [who won't be named here; suffice to say that he was in the black metal scene but not a known musician]. At one point he was supposed to drive the car but then he came to his senses and said never. He provided an alibi for some time but later confessed that he knew what would happen ... that's the big thing that makes the whole case switch one way or the other; both me and the alibi knew what was going to happen, but still Varg tends to say that it was an impulsive act of self-defense."

Indeed, in court Snorre would condemn both Varg and himself to jail time by stating that the two were driving to Oslo specifically so that Varg could kill Euronymous, thus contradicting Varg's claims that the event was unplanned, which would have made Snorre a wholly innocent party. For his part, Snorre had lost his close friendship with Euronymous by the time of the killing, but certainly had no particular ill will against the man, and seems to have been drawn into the affair due to his somewhat fragile condition at the time. While his explanation below may read as an attempt at justification, it's worth pointing out just how open he is when talking about the matter, making no attempt to avoid blame for what happened.

"My story is that I'm already traumatized from before that," he sighs, referring to an incident in his childhood, "and I guess that's one of the reasons that I was going along with that at all... I was really stressed out at that time to say the least.... I hope no one thinks that I had an intention or anything to gain from killing Øystein. It was not my idea and it was not my intention but I got dragged in it 'cos I was in the apartment when Varg flipped. Me and this third person were trying to calm Varg down and get it under control and just say, 'Wait,' but he was so wound up and wanted to do this so we got dragged into it. Fortunately the third guy did not get any severe punishment."

Generally, those interviewed for this book believe that Euronymous was not, in fact, planning to kill the Burzum main man, but concede that Varg may well have believed this to be the case. Manheim comments, "We have no reason to believe that Kristian would not believe [any threats made], he was young, a loner, a strange guy with all these issues."

Euronymous had frequently made death threats in the past—once even telling the long-serving and highly respected metal journalist Malcolm Dome that he would not "live beyond the weekend"—and perhaps Varg was just the first to be aggressive or paranoid enough to take the threat at face value. Euronymous had already been before the courts for attacking a man at a bus stop with a broken bottle, and at the time many rumors still surrounded the deaths of Pelle and an attempt on another man's life, namely a Polish fanzine writer Euronymous claimed to have attempted to poison.

"We have just heard that he has moved to Chicago," he once told *Slayer Magazine*. "Unfortunately, the poison we gave him wasn't strong enough to kill him... But we also know that the poison caused him pain and that he suffers a lot from it, and in the end he'll also probably get cancer... if we don't kill him before that. He's going to die."

Whatever the truth about that story, there's no doubt that the relationship between Varg and Euronymous had soured dramatically as the year progressed. Varg was becoming increasingly interested in right-wing politics, while Euronymous had a history of involvement in communism. Varg was increasingly disillusioned with Euronymous for his lack of activism, and was also unhappy with his contract, believing that Euronymous owed him money—something his Mayhem bandmates say was very possibly true. Euronymous had never been particularly business-minded with either Deathlike Silence or the Helvete store, which had been closed at the start of the year following pressure from the police and, apparently, Euronymous' parents.

In fact, a major rift had opened up between the two musicians following the two Varg interviews, his arrest, and the subsequent media exposure in Norwegian's national press. Varg was now famous throughout the country and beyond, and many have suggested a growing rivalry between the two. Even Snorre, in his interview with *Slayer*, explained that there were many possible motivations for the murder, explaining that the two men shared many qualities and concluding that one of the reasons was simply that "murder is more extreme than arson," and that Varg had only "burned some churches while Bård had killed a man." In a recent interview, he told me:

"I think Euronymous and Varg found really good ways to manipulate each other. They both got really conspiratorial and started talking about surveillance and burning churches, and Euronymous was a very kind person but suddenly he started to act very [much] the opposite to compensate. So he became unpopular with everyone around him for some years and it of course escalated in the murder."

Certainly it's clear that Varg's dealings with the media and the authorities were something that Euronymous was becoming uncomfortable with, as were many others in the scene who were now under heavy police scrutiny. In the documentary *Pure Fucking Mayhem*, Anders "Neddo" Odden of death metallers Cadaver and later Satyricon and Celtic Frost explains: "[Øystein] Aarseth was fed up with all the pranks and the attention that Vikernes drew to black metal and Helvete. He thought Vikernes commercialized it. He didn't want any publicity. Øystein wanted it to be a closed cult system, unknown to outsiders. I met Aarseth in the summer of '93. He told me that he wanted to create a black metal movement that was based on the Hell's Angels. As such, Vikernes had to go because of the commercializing. Vikernes had good reason to take this seriously."

Ironically, any plans Euronymous might have had against Varg may have also sprung from fears for his own safety. Varg was certainly a man capable of direct action, having apparently led the church burning to a large extent. It's also interesting to note that in later years two Israeli metal acts, Salem and Orphaned Land, have claimed that Varg sent them mail bombs in the early nineties. Curiously, Euronymous' own fears appear to have been accentuated by a visit to a clairvoyant who predicted his death, seemingly at the hands of Varg. During Varg's trial, a Swedish woman named Ilsa Raluce Anghel, who had been in relationships with both Varg and then Euronymous (another apparently divisive point), described the following:

"On August 6, I got a call from Aarseth. He was furious about a letter Vikernes had written. He had had enough of Vikernes' shit-throwing and wanted to get rid of him. Aarseth asked me for advice: should he kill Vikernes or collect enough evidence to get Vikernes convicted for several church fires? He had closely evaluated both options. If Vikernes was to be killed, Aarseth would travel to Bergen and electrocute him with an electrogun. Some of the evidence of arson was to be gotten from Saida Anderson, a famous Swedish psychic. The fortune-teller said she had 'seen' several pieces of evidence which would convict Vikernes of up to four church fires, but she also said she could 'see' Vikernes getting twelve years in jail. Upon hearing this, Aarseth was scared stiff. He said Vikernes would never receive such a sentence for arson; to get twelve years he had to be convicted for murder! Aarseth contact[ed] me twice more in the last days before he was murdered. He gave the impression of being in a hurry. It was very important for him to do something before something was done to him."

"He wanted Ilsa's advice," Mortiis confirmed in a fanzine interview of the time. "Either he was going to go and get C.G. first, or to get technical evidence against him for burning four churches."

Regardless of where the blame falls, when the news about Euronymous' death was reported, it hit the scene hard. While some had become disillusioned with Euronymous,

"Murder victim threatened by Swedish Satanic Mafia," *Verdens Gang* **newspaper, Norway, 1993.**

particularly the members of Mayhem, a large number still considered him a close friend and mentor, an opinion many hold today. Paranoia also hit the Inner Circle, with fears that the attack had come from a rival scene, such as that within Sweden or Finland, with whom there had been some quarrels.

"How could I be comfortable with Euronymous being killed, reading about it in the newspaper and then not knowing who it was?" asks Darkthrone's Fenriz. "I would still go to work but I would have a knife, and on my headphones would be *Bonded by Blood* by Exodus, all of the fucking time, to be in 'attack mode.'... It was pretty unnerving. Then finding out it was Varg who did it ... well it was not a normal day at work. "

"His death was a surprise," comments Infernus of Gorgoroth. "I went [to his place] three weeks before the killing and Vikernes called up and was in a splendid mood, leaving Euronymous with quite a confused impression, so I knew there were ... issues. I was surprised [when I heard about the death] but I didn't automatically think of Varg. There could have been many others involved."

Many, however, already suspected Varg, due to the increasing hostility between the two men and his strange behavior in the days that followed. Varg had apparently set up an alibi—getting an associate to rent a video and use a particular bank card at a cash machine, to give the impression that Varg and Snorre were in Bergen that night—and also apparently taken gloves to the flat. However, he didn't wear gloves during the murder, and his fingerprints were found in Euronymous' blood on the stairwell. Not only that, but the Burzum contract with Deathlike Silence had been left signed and dated in the apartment, a smoking gun that was quickly traced back to Varg.

"I had to take a ferry back home from my work," recalls Grutle of Enslaved, a close friend. "On the bay I remember seeing my girlfriend, my parents, her parents, waiting for me and I thought, 'Oh, something is wrong, something is badly wrong.' Everyone gave me a hug and I said, 'Alright, what's up?' and my ex, I remember she was crying and she said, 'Øystein

A double-page spread in *Kerrang!* reports on Bård "Faust" Eithun's imprisonment on murder charges as well as Varg's impending sentence.

has been killed.' And I knew it was him, right away I knew it 'cos there was a rivalry in the last few weeks."

"I got a call from him the day after he killed Euronymous," explains Lee Barrett of Candlelight Records, a label that was considering signing Burzum for a time. "He phoned to tell me Euronymous was dead and by calling [me] he almost gave himself away. He definitely seemed eager to tell the news, he didn't admit anything in the slightest, he was trying to fob it off as Finnish black metal people, but by the time he'd phoned me the only people who would know about his death were the police and someone living in Euronymous' apartment block."

The resulting court case turned Varg into Norway's most famous criminal and brought chaos to the remains of the Inner Circle. As the police rounded up anyone with a connection to the movement—both inner members and those tenuously linked—for long interviews, the truth eventually began to come out, about the murders, church burnings, and desecrations. Many of the protagonists, who were mainly teenagers, found themselves pressured by the police to make statements about their peers, the result being that some confessed in order to reduce what by that point seemed to be inevitable jail sentences.

"After Euro was killed they bothered everybody," confirms Mortiis. "I was tricked into telling on people like Faust, which didn't make me very popular with him and a few others, which is understandable. When they pulled me in they told me they knew he'd killed that guy and they knew I knew and I was fucked if I didn't just verify, some bullshit like that… "

Prosecutions included Emperor's Samoth and Hades' Jørn Tunsberg, who would both be jailed for their parts in the church burnings. Bård "Faust" Eithun would be sentenced to fourteen years in prison for the Lillehammer murder, his part in the Holmenkollen arson, cemetery desecration, robbery (of material from churches) and possession of illegal weapons, videos, and explosives. Varg would receive a twenty-one-year sentence, the longest possible in Norway, for Øystein's murder, the attacks on Holmenkollen, Skjold, and Åsane and the possession of a large amount of explosives and ammunition. It is believed that these were to be used in an attack on Oslo's famous left-wing punk squat Blitz, though there was also a plan to blow up Nidaros Cathedral in Trondheim, the building featured on Mayhem's *De Mysteriis Dom Sathanas* album. Finally, Snorre Ruch was sentenced to eight years as an accomplice in Euronymous' murder.

Almost universally, those within the scene turned against Varg in support of Euronymous. A CD entitled *Nordic Metal: A Tribute To Euronymous*—incidentally perhaps the finest black metal compilation ever created—was later released featuring contributions from Norwegian acts Mayhem, Emperor, Mysticum, Enslaved, Mortiis (now working as a solo artist), Arcturus and—rather surprisingly—Thorns, as well as Swedes Abruptum, Marduk, and Dissection, three bands that strongly supported Euronymous in the feud. The booklet was full of quotes paying tribute to the deceased leader of the scene, and in some case even threatening Varg's life.

In contrast to Varg, Snorre seems to have escaped the scene's wrath simply because he was well-liked, as Necrobutcher explains, saying, "We weren't upset at Snorre at all 'cos everyone knew [him] and everyone that knew Snorre knew that he was a good guy. I don't know Varg Vikernes myself and I didn't know anybody he hung out with, he was a new kid on the block, nobody knew him."

"Maybe because I'm a decent guy?" Snorre laughs awkwardly when asked why he got such support from the Norwegian black metal community. "I think they understood that I didn't have any wish to kill Øystein and maybe they didn't like Øystein but they supported his views and thought that Varg had done a cowardly thing. Maybe they thought it was unfortunate I was there. I'm a very open person when I meet people, so I think people trust me. I think there grew a lot of hate against Varg—not everyone supported the church burnings, not many supported the killing, and not a lot of his verbal actions have been very popular either. I guess I have been very lucky and I have kept my head down during the case and not exposed myself in any way."

Other parties, such as Gorgoroth and Darkthrone—the latter having connections with both Varg and Euronymous—avoided becoming involved in the conflict altogether, choosing not to take sides.

"During the next two years a lot of people were angry and talking pro and against

Vikernes," explains Infernus. "That's rubbish, if people have a problem with Varg Vikernes they should go and tell him. I never met him and I don't think we would necessarily get along, but to the degree that I would have a problem with him, I would tell him."

Regardless of the differing opinions on the matter, Euronymous' passing and the trial that followed essentially marked the end of the Inner Circle and the peak of Satanic/anti-Christian activities within Norway, with the Kristiansand circle also disintegrating around this time.

"There was not a specific situation but many during a short period of time," explains Terje "Tchort" Vik Schei. "Attacking with knives some Christian preachers in the middle of the street, storming a church during a midnight mass and trying to slay the minister… when we attacked the Christians in the middle of the street people who knew us would recognize us and tell the police…some kids tried to make heroes of themselves by taking us down. I ended up almost killing

"Satanist revelations: 150 Kilo dynamite found at Count's [home]," *Verdens Gang* newspaper, Norway, 1993.

one of them, and it was for this I served time. We were hiding for some weeks, living only a day or two in each place. At one point we had to go to my friend's flat to collect clothes and money and the neighbors must have called the police because shortly after they busted the door and police with dogs busted our asses. They even came through the veranda windows in my mum's flat and she lives on the third floor so the police used the neighbors' apartments to lower themselves down, before bursting in through the windows looking for me.

"It's the same with the scene as it is with most of the other situations around the world," he continues. "Take down the leaders and the followers will spread for all winds. My friend and me who were behind all this that happened in Kristiansand were hiding from the police for some weeks and during this period there were some followers who offered themselves to the media and sold 'their' stories for money. Most of what they said was to-

"25 year-old found stabbed to death. Murder/
manhunt. Satanic circle to be turned upside down"
Dagbladet newspaper, Norway, 1993.

tal fiction but the media got their first interview and a face to put together with the headlines. It drew the attention away from us, but the local scene split because of this.

"I reduced my own sentence by giving the police access to things I had stolen from graveyards and giving myself away on various cases they had open. Looking back I have no regrets for my actions but I am mostly glad that I didn't turn anyone else in but myself. National police came to Kristiansand to interview us and we pretended to not know anything and that we didn't know the people they asked us about. They would show us photos of us entering Helvete, in talk with the people we just denied knowing—they knew everything already and just wanted us to confirm their knowledge. It was better for us just to shut up and say nothing."

"I felt the same way anyone would feel when your friends are convicted for murder and arson," reflects Necrobutcher of the whole period, "you feel sick to your stomach. I was hoping every day that there would be some fucking badass murders to take away the attention we had every fucking day, hoping the papers would get something else to write about, to take away the focus. Vandalism, to destroy someone's property, it doesn't have any meaning to me... and the churches were just built up again on taxpayers' money... All the people involved were under twenty and I think that speaks for itself."

While things appeared to have fallen apart within the Norwegian fraternity for a time, the explosion of criminal activity and media coverage had put black metal on the map, giving it a momentum that even today has yet to fade. While these sensational events inevitably overshadowed the amazing music coming from Norway, they also gave many of the bands involved a huge boost, bringing increased attention to both their works and those of the black metal scene as a whole.

20
THORNS

"Snorre has a very unique style of playing. I love the use of weird eerie chords and disharmonies, as well as the often very strict and dominant way of executing the riffs. Back in the day we used to play the so-called Grymyrk rehearsal tape a lot… it became an inspiration for many bands in the scene."

—Samoth (Emperor)

"I remember I got the Grymyrk tape when I was about fifteen from Frederik [Karlsson] of Funeral Dirge—before that had only heard "Ærie Descent" from Nordic Metal, a fucking brilliant compilation CD. Thorns always made a huge impact on me, for me it sounded like old, eerie fucking lullabies."

—Niklas Kvarforth (Shining)

SUITABLY DARK and obscure, the curious tale of Thorns illustrates how even the most arcane creation can have untold impact if discovered by the right people—in this case, impact that would far overshadow its creators' original intentions. Predating the Norwegian black metal revolution of the nineties, Thorns was the brainchild of guitarist Snorre Ruch, who formed the band while living in the Norwegian city of Trondheim. Musically he was primarily inspired by the thrash and first-generation black metal of the eighties, not that it would be particularly reflected in the highly distinctive playing style he developed between the years of fifteen and seventeen.

"I always liked fine arts and music," he explains today from his country home not far from Trondheim. "So it came naturally that when I was fifteen and was beginning to listen to metal, I bought a guitar to see what I could make out of it. I guess I was finishing with WASP, Twisted Sister, and Iron Maiden and going for the harder thrash stuff like Slayer and Metallica and then further to Venom and Bathory. It was in that spirit that I bought the guitar to try and make some hard music."

Like many metalheads in Norway at this time, he quickly made contact with national heroes Mayhem, who had recently released their *Deathcrush* mini-album. He would later visit the band in Oslo, becoming a close friend of several members.

"I made good friends with the Mayhem guys," Snorre confirms, "Euronymous, Nec-robutcher, Hellhammer, and Dead, and spent some weeks in Oslo. I used to hang around in Øystein's shop and met a lot of the new guys who were coming into the scene and knew the Darkthrone guys a bit, especially Fenriz, who was hanging out a lot in the shop. But I'm the kind of guy who keeps to himself a bit, not really that social and following what's happening all the time, so I can get a little isolated from that aspect of the metal scene. There's a big part of rock 'n' roll in it as well, people like to drink beer and go to concerts and party and all that, and I'm more like the Asperger kid who sits at home."

It was actually as an indirect result of Mayhem that Thorns—or rather "Stigma Diaboli-cum," as the outfit was originally known—was formed in 1989, Snorre finding a like-minded comrade in the form of Marius Vold, an Oslo-based vocalist who was also active in the band Mortem, later to evolve into Arcturus.

"I was in some smaller just-for-fun bands before that—and after as well—but that was my first personal musical project," Snorre explains. "I first got in contact with Mayhem hav-ing heard of them on a radio show and we started mailing back and forth. After some time being in Oslo visiting them I met Marius and he seemed very interested in things I played for him, like riffs and stuff. He was more into doing the vocals and being supportive around the things I wrote, because I was not certain that people would... " he pauses, "sometimes people think what I make is cool, sometimes I make stuff that is just *silly*," he finishes with a laugh. "Marius was also the main one writing the lyrics—or stealing them, or borrowing them from Shakespeare. I think the lyrics were secondary to the music... it was more impor-tant to have a cool song title than a lyric."

Working under the tasteful pseudonyms of Pedophagia (Snorre: guitar, bass, synth) and Coprophagia (Marius: vocals and drum programming), the pair crafted their first release, a three-track demo entitled *Luna De Nocturnus* that showcased an intense and challenging sound, the discordant guitars in particular communicating a heavy sense of creeping dread and often leading the music away from any sort of traditional song structure. Like most of their peers during this period, the darkness of the music was not yet totally mirrored by the band's aesthetic, and a close look at the tape's inlay reveals that the tongue-in-cheek pseud-onyms are echoed by the credits list, which thank Adolf Hitler, Stalin, Pol Pot... and Mayhem.

By 1990 the group had picked up a third member in the form of drummer Fetophagia (real name Bård Guldvik Eithun, soon to be known as "Faust"), and during that year the trio would record a rehearsal tape (playing original material alongside Metallica and Slayer covers) and a live tape, recorded when the band played a metal event in Stjørdal, appearing instead of Marius' other band Mortem, who were scheduled to play but had recently disbanded.

"When Bård joined us I don't know if he played in any metal band," comments Snorre. "I think he just played in a marching band or something like that. But he had a drum set and was very, very eager to play metal. Very, *very* eager."

While the group seems to have been regarded by many as a death metal band at the time, their music was nonetheless a far cry from the brutality of the Swedish and American camps or even the more atmospheric efforts of Norwegian death metal bands such as Old Funeral or Thou Shalt Suffer. Nor did it have a great deal in common with anything from the world of eighties black metal. Instead, the songwriting bore a distinctly experimental approach, with creepy and discordant riffs disrupting the flow of the more aggressive passages in a seemingly intentional and almost confrontational manner.

"I think it's mainly because I tend to see things in different ways," says Snorre with a nervous laugh. "I am a funny guy in some ways—I'm not your typical fellow, I'm afraid. I tend to twist things around a lot, it's just a part of my personality that things turn out the way they do. I try to challenge some of the basics of what is supposed to be musically correct or accepted to listen to. A lot of my music is dark and twisted and aggressive, but people that know me don't think I'm like that at all. It's like an outlet for my more frustrated side I guess."

In the latter half of 1990 the band expanded once more, thanks to the addition of a fellow Trondheim resident, bassist Harald Eilertsen. This evolution would coincide with a change of name, the band making the transition from Stigma Diabolicum to Thorns in a concerted attempt to distance themselves from a steadily expanding crowd of new bands.

"It was when a lot of bands started to call their bands Latin names, you remember that?" Snorre chuckles. "We decided we didn't want to do that and get lost in the 'Latin-name bunch' so we wanted something simple and different. 'Thorns' was something pointy and sounded cool I guess; it *hurts*—it's like that."

The following year would prove a significant one for the band, at least in retrospect. At the time, things were moving slowly due to the significant distances between the members—no small issue in the pre-Internet age. So it was that the most famous recording by the band was created with only half its members present, Snorre and Harald crafting a humble tape whose influence upon the Norwegian black metal scene would be nothing less than acute. Consisting of six numbers, it featured five tracks from the Stigma Diabolicum days ("Fall," "Thule," "Fairytales," "You That Mingle May," and "Into the Promised Land," curiously renamed "Lovely Children"), as well as a new number called "Home," a song that would later become known as "Ærie Descent," probably the band's most famous song to date. The recording was named the *Grymyrk* tape, "Grymyrk" being, as Snorre explained in a later webzine interview, "the grim world which all music and lyrics for the early material came from... a dead and silent world with its own strange logic. We even made a language for it... A thirty-word dictionary."

What's perhaps most strange—especially considering its influence—is that the tape features only guitar and bass, with no percussion or vocals whatsoever. Indeed, the recording was only ever intended as a working document to send the two non-Trondheim-based members so that they could work out their respective parts, and was never intended for any form of release, only attaining its later fame due to tape trading among close friends of the group.

"I think it's a little strange," admits Snorre of the tape's legendary status. "I don't really think it deserves so much credit, but in terms of melody and riffs it was innovative, so I see

Trøndertun folkehøgskole (Trøndertun Folk High School), where Snorre Ruch made the remarkably influential recordings known as the *Trøndertun* tape. Photo courtesy of Wikipedia.

what people saw in it at the time and why people still like it. But it's still strange because it's guitar and bass and nothing else. I guess a year after we made it people were really starting to say they liked it and were influenced by that, so we were very happy."

The absence of vocals and drums does little to dampen the spirit of the compositions; in fact, it only adds to their minimal and hypnotic quality, isolating the strange patterns that emerge from the songs. With its angular guitars, juxtaposing bass, and curious structures, the *Grymyrk* tape is a distinctly experimental take on the extreme metal template, and Snorre's unique riffing and creepy guitar work in particular would have significant impact upon the later work of other Norwegian bands, including Emperor, Satyricon and even Mayhem themselves. Truly groundbreaking, it remains difficult to pinpoint the musical influences that affected Snorre's composition style, the only clue coming from the man himself, who reveals that the epic bridge on the tape's one new number had a most unlikely source of inspiration.

"We have never accepted to be influenced by other metal 'cos we wanted to sound unique," he explains, "so we say we're influenced by children's music and classical music and computer game music and try to recode it into metal to get a new sound from it. I do remember that on 'Home' I had a lack of parts, so I took one of my favorite songs of [German synthpop act] Alphaville—'A Victory of Love' from the *Forever Young* album—and stole a part from that."

Aptly, the incomparable nature of the songs was mirrored by their highly unusual song titles. These proved so unlike the usual extreme metal fare—and of course were not clarified by any lyrical content—that Snorre even found his motives questioned in a rare interview in *Slayer*, editor Metalion suggesting that perhaps these titles were some sort of joke.

"I have a tendency to get ironic with things," he explains today. "I have since learnt that not all people understand it. ['Lovely Children'] was really a hate song against children, it's about an old folklore thing that says the trolls are changing their children with human children, and through that we get terrible children, 'cos they're really the trolls."

The following year would see vocals and drums finally recorded under the Thorns name, these appearing thanks to the *Trøndertun* tape, another highly significant release, though again one that was both unofficial and lacking the presence of most band members. Named after the college Snorre was attending at the time, the tape contained the aforementioned "Ærie Descent" (now missing the Alphaville bridge) and a new song entitled "Funeral Marches to the Grave." This time Snorre contributed both guitars and vocals, while assisted by fellow students Ronnie K. Prize (bass) and Terje M. Kråbøl (drums), the latter of whom later went on to work with metal bands such as Faustcoven and Antidepressive Delivery.

Proving that Snorre was a more than capable vocalist and also featuring a haunting use of synth, the recordings were somewhat less unorthodox in structure than their predecessors, but no less unique in nature. Indeed, the two songs remain largely unparalleled even today, the minimal but effective percussion and sparing use of bass capturing a truly gothic and archaic atmosphere, a tone mirrored by the occult and conspiratorial lyrics. Despite the creative success, there was no escaping the fact that the recordings featured only a quarter of the band's official lineup, and with the distances between the musicians making progress all but impossible, Snorre and his bandmates resolved to relocate in order to make a decent go of the band.

"I was kind of struggling to get a gang together who were interested in pulling in the same direction," Snorre sighs. "I thought, 'This has the right to live, I have to work harder and get a record together and start rehearsing with the guys,' so we decided to move to Oslo. So I, Marius, and Bård, we lived together—I don't remember if Harold was part of the band at that time, but at least the plan was to get a place and start writing an album."

Unfortunately, the whole endeavor proved something of a disaster. In fact, to this day the only recording under the Thorns name featuring either Marius or Bård is a 1992 rehearsal cassette known as *The Thule Tape*, which was actually recorded *before* the move.

"We never rehearsed!" laughs Snorre. "After half a year I moved back to Trondheim. Maybe I was never that ambitious, I was very happy making riffs and music but didn't necessarily need to complete things. I wanted to release a record though, but we never even got a place to rehearse, so you see it was a little difficult."

With Thorns seemingly a doomed project, Bård decided to concentrate on his other band, Emperor, while Snorre joined his old friends Mayhem, taking on the Blackthorn pseudonym and contributing to the content of the *De Mysteriis Dom Sathanas* album with some old Thorns riffs.

Of course, the events in the Norwegian black metal drama would soon drag both men into its chaotic and violent epicenter, the result being two lengthy sentences in connection to murder—in Snorre's case, of Euronymous himself. For Snorre it was particularly unfortunate, since he had done his best to avoid the social and criminal side of the Norwegian scene.

"Øystein talked to me a lot about this inner circle stuff," he recalls, "he wanted me to be part of this elite group of metal [in] Norway. I thought this was kind of silly and cute, 'cos I was reading some Conan and you have all these black circles and pompous bits and magic and yeah, it's not for me. He accepted it, he was sort of like, 'You are one of the closest guys here so whatever.'"

For several years the band lay dormant, the only reminder of their existence being (somewhat ironically) the *Nordic Metal: A Tribute To Euronymous* compilation, which featured a slightly different version of "Ærie Descent," recorded at Trøndertun college prior to the session that produced the two tracks included on the infamous rehearsal tape. The fact that Thorns now had two members in jail—including the group's central creative force—certainly didn't improve their prospects, and it began to look highly unlikely that the band would ever return to any significant activity. And indeed, that's probably how things would have remained if not for the support of Satyricon frontman and Moonfog Records owner Sigurd "Satyr" Wongraven.

"He called me in jail and asked if I was meddling with music of any sort and if I would be interested in releasing my old demos through his record label," recalls Snorre. "We talked and it ended up with him giving me an offer that if I wanted to make metal again he could hook me up with a computer and sound equipment so I could make music in [prison]. I was thinking about putting the metal on the shelf and just having fun with synthesizer and whatnot, but he was like, 'Give it another shot on metal and I will support you.' He has been very supportive and helped me with a lot of stuff. Without him there would not be Thorns today I think."

Though still in jail, Snorre was nonetheless able to progress fairly steadily due to Norway's comparatively relaxed approach to incarceration and rehabilitation, which allowed him to write and record in his cell using the equipment that Satyr had provided him.

"The first part of the sentences are high security," Snorre explains, "then after showing that you can be trusted, you are able to apply to more open forms of jails. There's a jail in Tønsberg, which is where Varg was later able to escape from. It's the sort of jail you are able to just walk out from, but no one wants to because you know you will have to serve your time anyway and there's not much better places to serve it than an old military camp with nice surroundings and schools. So it was very free; we could walk around as we wanted and meet each other and discuss and play music and," he pauses and laughs before adding with a hint of irony, "… yeah, have a *jolly good time.*"

Satyr's intervention had undoubtedly saved the group, and the first results of the band's resurrection would come about as a direct result of a meeting with another Thorns fan and central black metal figure, namely Samoth of Emperor. Serving time in the same Tønsberg prison as Snorre—having been incarcerated in 1995 for his part in the burning of Skjold Church—their conversations within the institution would help propel Snorre into action.

"I think we had met before on some rare occasions," explains Snorre, "but I don't think we had ever talked much. Samoth was like 'Silent Samoth' and I'm more like an easy person who jumps from subject to subject, playing a lot of jokes. So we weren't natural for each other, but when I met him in jail we had the time to sit down and talk. I was thinking about the old Thorns songs and I thought it would be a shame if they were never recorded and I thought, 'What if Emperor was playing the songs and recording them for me? Maybe I could even play guitar.'"

This initial thought would soon blossom into a collaboration between the two parties, Satyr suggesting that the two bands instead release a split record, covering one another's songs while introducing updates of earlier songs and new material. At first Snorre looked to Bård—with whom he actually served some of his sentence—but the drummer complained of being out of practice and was looking for something of a new start, not to mention the fact that he planned to remain in Oslo, whereas Snorre was determined to head back to Trondheim, presenting the same problem that had plagued the band before.

Thus Snorre began to work on the release alone, recording the guitars in his cell and creating all the percussion electronically, blending convincing metal drum patterns with more mechanical-sounding additions. Also appearing on the record were two session members, namely Satyr on vocals and another musician credited as S.A. Titan, who was persuaded to help with programming duties and orchestration.

"That's a guy who was also at the prison," Snorre reveals. "He was a classical composer dude, he went to a Wagner academy while he was there. He is like a total autist [sic] when it comes to making music—he has very high energy levels, a very special person, but he is very nice and I dragged him into it for fun, to see if we could spice up the music with some classical. And it worked—sort of. I really was never comfortable doing vocals, the reason I did the vocals on the Trøndertun tape was because there was no one around who could do it, and I was not really happy with it."

The Thorns half of the *Emperor vs. Thorns* album would feature four songs, lasting almost half an hour. These included an update of the signature song "Ærie Descent" (a track also covered by Emperor on the split), an update of the Trøndertun song "Funeral Marches to the Grave" (now renamed "Melas Khole"), a new song entitled "The Discipline of Earth" (written just prior to Snorre's incarceration and drawing once again on the Grymyrk mythology), and "Cosmic Keys," a cover of Emperor's "Cosmic Keys to My Creations and Times," with some new and rather thought-provoking lyrics. Retaining the slow pace and eerie, depressive leanings—mirrored by the bleak metaphysical and quasi-scientific lyrics—the recordings showcased a bigger and more symphonic sound, with the orchestral synth work added in Oslo following Snorre's release.

It was certainly a more than convincing return, and sharing a CD with the hugely popular Emperor meant that Thorns were introduced—or at least *reintroduced*—to a new generation of fans, the first three thousand of whom were treated to an eight-song bonus CD featuring both the *Grymyrk* and *Trøndertun* tapes (albeit with the earlier version of "Ærie Descent"). To support the release, Snorre was encouraged into giving a number of interviews, the guitarist now going under the pseudonym S.W. Krupp and sporting sunglasses and a shaved head, which initially caused some confusion among fans. One asked via the Moonfog website how the band functioned with both members in prison, to which Snorre memorably replied:

"Thorns function excellent whitout [*sic*] those two villains. They were up to no good anyways, and did not contribute to what Thorns is all about. Namely positive thinking, good attitude and politeness!"

Alongside the Emperor split was an equally high-profile appearance on Moonfog's tribute album *Darkthrone Holy Darkthrone*, where Thorns provided the standout track, namely a cover of the classic "The Pagan Winter." Inspired, curiously, by the Transformers animations, and in particular the most robotically voiced character, Soundwave, the song echoed futuristic concerns in both its rewritten lyrics ("The 666 machines are re-powered … ") and its electronically distorted vocals.

"I always was a fan of science fiction and stuff like that," explains Snorre. "I like playing around with vocoders and stuff like that and I guess the vocoder is the reason I made the song like that—to make it sound really cyber-sounding."

The content of Thorns' 2001 self-titled record would combine both sides of the group's musical personality. Lacking the grandiose overtones of S.A. Titan's orchestration, it is a record whose cold aggression and industrial overtones—evident in both the guitar sound and use of synths, samples, and programming—sit comfortably alongside other Moonfog releases of the period. At the same time, the angular immediacy of songs such as "Existence" and "Stellar Master Elite" is balanced by the more creeping malevolence of the two-part "Underneath the Universe" and "Shifting Channels," which give the slow, brooding feel of earlier material a more mechanized twist.

"I guess my personal taste at the time," Snorre comments when asked about the inspirations behind the record. "I go through phases, get new interests and lose other interests. [At that time it was] mainly Front 242, Nitzer Ebb—I thought that Front 242 was very hard in an electronic way and was inspired by that. I also listened a lot to [Klaus] Schulze and Tangerine Dream, I was always a fan of analog synth and music that's like … *unearthly*."

Despite the accolades the album received from the press—*Terrorizer* placed it at number two in its album of the year list and in the top forty of its album of the decade countdown—Snorre remains somewhat unhappy with the recording that would largely define him for over a decade afterward.

"I think that a lot of industrialized metal sounds crappy and I don't think the attempts we have made have been good enough to live on," he sighs. "I think metal [I make in the future] will always be more brutal and honest and to the core and as little produced as possible. I'm never happy with *anything*," he continues with a chuckle. "I like it, but I could wish for another production and other details, and the recording process was traumatizing as well." He laughs again, "It took *so* long. I had to do so many hours work on it alone and you get really, really, *really* fed up with it. I couldn't listen to it for a long time afterwards without feeling sick."

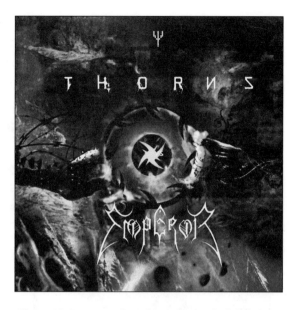

Thorns Vs Emperor, released in 1999, marked the return of this seminal outfit and saw old Thorns material given an updating by Snorre and a number of guest musicians.

As his words suggest, Snorre had once again handled the lion's share of the work, contributing guitars, bass, programming, keyboard, and even vocals on the closing electronic number, "Vortex." Alongside him was veteran drummer and longtime acquaintance Hellhammer, and the remainder of the vocals were shared by Satyr and Aldrahn of label mates Dødheimsgard, both of whom contributed lyrics alongside Snorre himself, who continued in the philosophical and scientific vein of the Emperor split.

"It was like a dystopian futuristic view, maybe some introspective stuff," Snorre said. "Aldrahn's lyrics are half-crazy and some are very negative. Actually the 'Stellar Master Elite' song was my attempt to twist the misanthropic thing in black metal into something positive, but it sounds only fascistic," he complains with a laugh. "Honestly, it was the first song written for that album and I was thinking, 'Fuck black metal, I want to make something really positive about humankind!'"

Despite the strong feedback the album received, it would sadly be the last Thorns release for some considerable time. In the year following its release, Snorre would instead collaborate with 3rd and the Mortal guitarist Finn Olav Holthe to create an aural accompaniment to an exhibition by renowned Norwegian artist Bjarne Melgaard (who has since angered members of the scene, notably Metalion, due to unauthorized use of images from *Slayer Magazine*), which included "modifications/mutilations" of text, images, and music from earlier Thorns releases. Thorns Ltd would be born from this venture, with Holthe and Snorre working alongside improvisational musician Jon T. Wesseltoft to create electronic ambient/ noise music and sound for artists such as Banks Violette, though Holthe would eventually leave the group in 2006.

Wesseltoft's continued work with Thorns Ltd, meanwhile, would coincide with him

Better late than never: The suitably otherworldly and science fiction-esque artwork of the long-delayed—and decidedly industrial-leaning—debut album.

joining Thorns itself, the two working with Aldrahn, Antidepressive Delivery guitarist Christian Broholt, and God Seed/Goat the Head drummer Kenneth Kapstad from around 2007 onward. The majority of recording would be completed a few years later, though a relocation on Snorre's part would delay him completing the finishing touches to the record. Keen to avoid the more processed leanings of the predecessor, the Thorns follow-up was consciously written as something of a return to the group's more earthy beginnings.

"No synths, no samples, we've been trying to work with just guitars, drums, and vocals to see how much we can get out of it," Snorre enthuses. "We wanted a more stripped-down sound, we like it that way, we are tired of this pompous overproduced stuff, we want it to sound a little old-school again. My nearest partner in writing the songs is Jon Wesseltoft, he lives in Oslo and is not a band guy, he's more in the noise/jazz scene, but he has a long history of listening to metal. He knows me and Thorns so well he can write Thorns riffs better than me almost, so I have utilized him and we have made a lot of music together."

As should be clear, Snorre has remained closely in touch with his musical roots, and in 2007 he gave permission for his early demo and rehearsal recordings with Stigma Diabolicum and Thorns to be released by Kyrck Productions, a Greek label specializing in special editions of early Nordic recordings. He has also kept close ties with Satyr over the years, providing guitars and songwriting to Satyricon on 1999's *Rebel Extravaganza* and again on *The Age of Nero* in 2008. Nonetheless, he has kept a certain

An 'album of the month' review in UK magazine *Terrorizer* in 2001 illustrated that Snorre had lost none of his power to impress.

distance from the rest of the scene and continues to work very much on his own schedule and on his own terms.

"It's not my major interest," he concludes when asked about the black metal scene today. "I've rather been following different things, I always thought a lot of the music made is ... well, *unnecessary* maybe." He laughs as his wife, also present in the room, begins to laugh at this comment. "My wife is laughing at me—she thinks I'm *cocky*. I want to continue making new music but always I was feeling a little not in the center of the black metal scene and I did not want to be either. I wanted to have my own expression and make something that had not been made before maybe, to *challenge* the listener a little."

21
DARKTHRONE

"It started with Darkthrone, especially the A Blaze in the Northern Sky album. I mean they were considered pretty dark and different to everyone else before that, but that's when I realized that black metal was more than just music. In the eighties you had bands like Sarcófago and Possessed which are now considered black metal, but then it wasn't, so Darkthrone really set the spark."

—Silenoz (Dimmu Borgir)

"Darkthrone is one of the most important bands for me. I was a big fan of their death metal-sounding output—Soulside Journey is still a favorite for that genre—but A Blaze in the Northern Sky is still the album that really struck me. They displayed a musical and aesthetic insight that ran infinite circles around the clumsy tough-guy acts that has led to the demise of black metal we are seeing these days. I'll never get into punk, but I admire them for the statement they've made with their development—they saw the ship sink long before many others. Ugh!"

—Ivar (Enslaved)

"They have got a good relationship to their music, they are not too serious or stiff, they can do different stuff and have a glint in the eye which is very good. Maybe this is a little Norwegian thing, this little irony where you are overdoing your badassness just for fun almost, and people misunderstand a little … "

—Snorre (Stigma Diabolicum/Thorns)

HIGHLY PROLIFIC, frequently controversial, intensely focused on the past yet forever pushing forward in their own musical evolution, Darkthrone long ago established themselves as a black metal institution. Consistently imitated but never replicated, they have played a massive hand in creating the blueprint for raw Norse black metal, their influence still audible in new bands around the globe today. In fact, excluding the "first wave" pioneers, the group are probably rivaled only by Burzum in terms of the sheer number of acts who have taken direct musical inspiration from their work. Yet despite all this, the band have refused to merely rest on their laurels and exploit their rich legacy. Instead they have carefully decon-

Darkthrone in their early death metal days. Ted Skjellum (later Nocturno Culto), Gylve Nagell (then Hank Amarillo, later Fenriz), Ivar Enger (later Zephyrous) and Dag Nilsen (later a session member).

structed a mythology that many bands would sell their souls for, and reinvented themselves with a sound and image that has challenged as many fans as it has enthralled.

For much of their existence—since 1993 in fact—the band has revolved around a partnership between guitarist, bassist, and vocalist Ted Skjellum, better known to the world as Nocturno Culto, and drummer and lyricist Gylve Nagell, otherwise known as Fenriz. Despite a much-voiced opposition to the mainstream and a general sense of misanthropy, the latter has become one of black metal's more recognizable faces, as famous for his unusual sense of humor, near-encyclopedic knowledge of metal, and eccentric manner as he is for his drumming.

Given the significant influence that Hellhammer and Celtic Frost have had upon him, it's interesting to note that Fenriz's route into music is not entirely dissimilar to Tom G. Warrior's. While thankfully he did not suffer the same trauma in his youth, like Tom he seems to have discovered his path in life at a very early stage, thanks to a combination of heavy exposure to music and isolation, in this case geographical in nature.

"It was *very* geographical!" he confirms, his voice characteristically expressive in tone. "We lived in the biggest crossroads in Norway and there were not any other kids living there, we were the only villa in a hill where there were only huts. This is a typical thing in Norway, everyone has a 'summer house,' and we were in a hill of summer houses, and we were the only villa. You can imagine, there were not so many children to play with, just the occasional visit from cousins. They also tried to put me in kindergarten, but I refused to go as the girls there wore pants!" He laughs, "I don't know where I got those ideas, I was probably intimidated 'cos there were so many children.

"I started [musically] with stuff like *Waiting for the Sun* by The Doors in '73. I was really young [he was born November 1971] but my uncle already understood that I wasn't cut out to listen to normal children's music at the age of two when he once played me some Pink Floyd, and so he started pushing other stuff on me, like Uriah Heep. We moved in '77 and so I didn't get any more help from him, and I kind of started from scratch with AC/DC and Kiss. That was a normal route, it was *inevitable* to get into Kiss and the Kiss trading cards 'cos they came in candy bags and everyone wanted those."

Strange as it may seem, these trading cards may be part of the reason so many of the central protagonists of nineties Norwegian black metal started creating music at such a young age. A huge number of Norwegian musicians interviewed for this book pinpointed Kiss, and specifically these Kiss cards, as their introduction to metal.

"It actually started with punk/new wave trading cards with English bands like The Clash, Sex Pistols, The Jam, bands like that—and *also* Kiss," Fenriz elaborates. "Then after a while they started coming *only* with Kiss, who were huge. But Kiss weren't any heavier than what I had listened to in Uriah Heep, so I was *searching* for that heaviness in the seventies, but I didn't have anyone showing me Black Sabbath. The first time I heard them was in '81, then it was like, 'Eureka!'"

Fast-forward five years from this pivotal moment, and in 1986 the young drummer formed a band of his own called Black Death, alongside local guitarist Anders Risberget. A five-track demo entitled *Trash Core '87* was issued the following year, before the band were joined by a second guitarist, Ivar Enger, and a second demo, *Black is Beautiful*, was released the same year. Featuring songs like "Nasty Sausage" and "Pizza Breath," it was a far cry from the band they would eventually become.

"At that time we had discovered punk, which was one of the reasons for do-it-yourself. Bands that were really shabby in playing style, like Cryptic Slaughter, could put out albums, so we felt we could at least *start* to have a band. I guess I was inspired by stuff like early Slayer, Cryptic Slaughter, and Celtic Frost. The cool thing about Tom G. Warrior was that the way he put the notes together was not like other riff-makers would make, but still he would make it very easy to play, that was the magic. And there was a lot of punk in early Celtic Frost too, there's no arguing about that. So we started up and called it 'trash core'—not like thrash, but *trash*, 'cos it was so bad—and there was punk with the metal from day one in the band."

"After two demos I understood instinctively that I would want to continue doing music more seriously than in Black Death, so in late '87 I changed the name to Darkthrone and we started writing a little bit more epic stuff. [The name was] inspired by the name of the Danish mag *Blackthorn*. From the get-go it was spelled in one word for me, later I would explain it more humorously by saying, 'Like Whitesnake.' The logo was in one word too, but when the new logo came [with help from Tomas Lindberg of Grotesque, and later refined by one Tassilo Förg]—the one everyone knows—there was confusion."

Fenriz now decided to, in his own words, "up the ante" and recruited a bass player

The band's original intended logo, drawn by Fenriz himself. Interestingly, the 'E' is based on that of the English Dogs logo and indeed, the original drawing resides in the sleeve of the drummer's copy of their Where Legend Began album today.

called Dag Nilsen, brought in via guitarist Ivar. A debut demo entitled *Land of Frost* was issued in 1988, before the introduction of a new guitarist Ted Skjellum, who replaced Anders. Ted had grown up close to the other members, but only met with them after witnessing the band's first performance (which included the one-off sight of Fenriz performing drums and vocals simultaneously) at Follorocken, the same annual "battle of the bands" Mayhem had participated in two years previously.

"We set up a meeting and decided that we would play our first gig in the spring of '88, and Ted was going to turn up and watch our live experience. Mind you, none of us had actually *seen* a gig except on TV—that was kind of a cool footnote; the first gig we went to was actually Darkthrone. So after the show Ted said, 'Yeah, it's hunky dory, I wanna join,' and the rest is history."

Hitting sixteen shortly afterward, Fenriz quit school and joined the post office, where he still works today, to help fund both his fervent music-collecting and Darkthrone itself. Doubling their efforts, the band rehearsed furiously in their cold-war bomb shelter rehearsal room (another interesting Hellhammer parallel) and released a promo tape in late 1988 entitled *A New Dimension*, featuring a song called "Snowfall" along with an introduction track.

"Most bands—people that are self-taught—they need to rehearse for at least two years before they can make a recording that can portray them in a way that is any good," says Fenriz. "So we didn't really have anything to show until late '88 with the 'Snowfall' track, which showed we could at least play a little bit and do a long and epic song. The title *A New Dimension* explains how much we rehearsed and that we took a tiny quantum leap from our first shitty demo."

Though Fenriz was personally keen to further explore the epic side of metal, the band found themselves instead evolving into a more aggressive death/thrash direction, quickly crafting another demo called *Thulcandra*, issued in early 1989. Following the tape, Nocturno would take over vocal duties within the band, due to Fenriz being unhappy with his own ef-

Photograph from the shoot for 1993's *Under A Funeral Moon* album, featuring Nocturno Culto.

forts. During 1989 the band played a number of shows, one of which was shown on TV and also became the fourth tape, *Cromlech*. This was then sent to a number of labels including UK label Peaceville, with whom the band were especially happy to get a contract, firstly because it was an English label, and secondly because it featured both Autopsy and Paradise Lost on its roster.

The first result of the deal with Peaceville was the debut album *Soulside Journey*, recorded in Stockholm's Sunlight studios in 1990 with owner and producer Tomas Skogsberg. During the recording the band stayed with Swedish death metallers Entombed, who were able to offer advice as they had recently recorded their debut album *Left Hand Path* at Sunlight (guitarist Uffe Cederlund was ultimately credited with co-producing the guitars on *Soulside*). Released in January 1991, the result was an effective death metal album that bore both a technical edge and a somewhat otherworldly atmosphere thanks to choice use of synth and an epic, slightly creepy approach to songwriting.

"We were influenced by American bands, but the key to our sound was that every riff on that album—except one, that's like a Celtic Frost riff—you could take and play on a synthesizer, and it would be horror movie music," explains Fenriz. "When people make horror movie music they don't use the blues scale, they use a certain scale and we made our riffs on this 'horror scale.' So we would call our music 'technical horror death metal,' inspired by maybe Necrophagia, Nocturnus, early Massacre and Death. I didn't actually watch almost any horror movies at all but that was the philosophy behind the riffs, to make it sound eerie, and we had some science fiction creep in there too. So if it's original that's the reason.

"We wanted to record the album where we did the [*Cromlech* demo] so we could use their board," he continues, "but it wasn't possible as we only had a thousand pounds to record the album with. He even didn't want me to bring any drums, he wanted me to play the stupid computer drums. I mean we were only seventeen, eighteen years old, we didn't have

A BLAZE IN THE NORTHERN SKY

Transiluanian Hunger

Left: Zephyrous on the cover of 1992's *A Blaze In The Northern Sky*. Right: Fenriz finally makes the cover on 1994's *Transilvanian Hunger*. Darkthrone originally intended these monochromatic portrait covers to be their visual trademark, but the approach quickly spread throughout the black metal scene.

much money, so that's why it sounds like it does, and that's why we never recorded with modern sound again and have been fighting modern sound since then. It should have had an Autopsy or Black Sabbath sound, that would be better."

Notably, it was to be the last time that the group would compromise their artistic vision, and while *Soulside Journey* was an effective and well-received album, its musical approach would soon be confined to the past as the group underwent a radical transformation in 1991. Though the band had already found success with death metal, three quarters of the lineup had come to the conclusion that it was time to add their voice to the Norwegian black metal movement—despite the fact that it barely existed at that point—due to a disillusionment with the genre they were playing. Thus, Darkthrone ceased work on the death metal follow-up album *Goatlord*, instead preparing *A Blaze In The Northern Sky*, an opus that would become known as the very first Norwegian black metal album.

"Definitely one major, major point was looking at my collection and [realizing] I had bought maybe five death metal releases from 1990," explains Fenriz of the stylistic shift. "I was so sick and tired of it, even though it was what we'd trained to play. I mean it was *okay* to play, but not to listen to other bands. And many other death metal bands came out with disappointing stuff after their promising demos ... it became apparent that what we got a kick out of was, to put it simply, Celtic Frost, Motörhead, and Bathory. Throughout 1990 it was more and more of this but the songs we made were still death metal—we had 13/16 beats and shit like that, it was almost jazz—and I was thinking in my head, 'This professionalism has to go, I want to *de-learn* playing drums, I want to play primitive and simple, I don't want to play like a drum solo all the time and make these complicated riffs.

"Ted and Ivar had also talked between them and said the same damn thing. Then one time they took the car and drove to my place, which was also the rehearsal place, without Dag 'cos he was really into the technical stuff, and said to me, 'What if we just skip playing all the intricate stuff and just play what we really care about, what we're listening to, what fires us up?' And I said, 'Oh yeah, let's go guys,' so we quickly stopped rehearsing the *Goatlord* material. But we had to use some of the material for the *A Blaze* album, 'cos we didn't want to make an EP with just three new total black metal songs. So we made three new black metal songs—'Kathaarian Life Code,' 'In the Shadow of the Horns,' and 'Where Cold Winds Blow,' and the rest would be *Goatlord*-ish material that was 'blackened' because of the studio sound we chose."

Even if some of the material on the album doesn't reflect it (at least to Fenriz's well-trained ear) the band's conversion to black metal felt like a total one. The group took a hefty dose of inspiration from the early pioneers, most notably Hellhammer and Celtic Frost, whose influence was evident in the key riffs of sublime songs such as "In the Shadow of the Horns." The band also completely reworked their aesthetic, adopting pseudonyms (Ted became Nocturno Culto, Gylve became Fenriz, and Ivar became Zephyrous) and wearing corpsepaint, becoming one of the most visible bands to do so thanks to the iconic sleeves of their next three albums, which each featured a band member in a stark, high-contrast, black-and-white photograph—intended at the time to be something of a visual trademark. Now so common in black metal sleeves that it sometimes seems obligatory, at the time it was a pretty revolutionary move.

"We saw early photos of Hellhammer, Sarcófago, and Dead from Mayhem and decided this was something that made sense for us. The first time I did it we were doing some sort of video shoot in early '90 for one of the death metal songs. I took a pencil and a pencil sharpener and on the side there's a thing [where] you can rub the pencil and get fragments and I rubbed this under my eyes" He laughs, "It's like *lead*, so I was pretty desperate. I mean that's a sign you're hungry, that you wanna rock, using lead from a pencil!"

Both Dead and Mayhem were already well known to the band, in Fenriz's case since 1987, when he had begun attending Mayhem rehearsals. Fenriz was some three years younger than both Euronymous and Necrobutcher, no small amount of time at that age, but not an unbridgeable gap, as it turned out. "They would just pick me up in the car," he explains. "I was already in Black Death then and they—like any sane person would do—hated the band, but they understood that I was a hungry kid that wanted to learn."

By 1991, Fenriz would be considered something of a fellow veteran and the two bands became closely associated, the members sharing many philosophical and musical ideas, and spending time together at Helvete, among other places. All the same, while Mayhem might have had a degree of influence, Fenriz is keen to correct the widely held perception that Darkthrone were somehow "converted" to the black metal cause by Euronymous.

"How would he do that?" he laughs. "We all have free wills. That's one of the most amusing rumors, but after a while it's repeated so much it's like a half-truth. The thing is that Mayhem were well into doing new stuff and we had on tape the *Live in Leipzig* show. It wasn't released until later but we had it on tape, that was one of the stuffs [*sic*] we listened to and it was very, very good. Top-notch black metal. But it was never like Euronymous would say, 'Hey, why don't you change to black metal?' That's ridiculous, we don't do it like that in the area that I'm from, it's just not done. We have very strong free wills."

Another opinion the two musicians shared was of the importance of Satanism within black metal. It is an attitude that Fenriz maintains today, and though he is not active in what might be thought of as a religious sense, he nonetheless argues that a belief in the Christian conception of Satan and hell was integral to the genre.

"That's a good part of black metal. If we didn't have *any* sort of belief in that, a lot of it would feel wasted. Certainly that belief in a *real* hell and a *real* devil would be one of the things that pushed black metal to become what it became, and make it worshipped. I think if everyone thought it was really cartoonish it would never even be… I mean it would have no one *worshipping*, say, a Bathory album. You get a good demonic feeling in a lot of this stuff. I don't think that, say, a really high-level *atheist* would start off something that would end up coming as black metal, there had to be *something* there."

Despite not taking part in the criminal aspect of the Inner Circle, Darkthrone were thus very much in alignment with many of its beliefs, and as a part of the scene Fenriz increasingly became friends with both Euronymous and Varg. However, he is again keen to put his relationships with both figures into perspective.

"I've never really been good friends with *anyone*," comes the surprising explanation. "I'm a loner basically, and that has to do with coincidences with living arrangements, where parents would move and not move. He was Euronymous, you know? He was the guy who had the best network in Norway together with Metalion so it would be very natural to hook up with those people as fast as humanly possible, and I already did that in '87, so by '91 I was already one of the old guys in their eyes I reckon. [Concerning Varg] again what I see of friendship is what you see on TV, you hang with persons for a lot of periods throughout your life. Well I never did that, so I think it's different. We were musical persons, we were strange and maybe the strangeness kept us together, the interest in what we knew was a deviant music style. Apart from that you'd say hello, say a few words and not so much more, go about what you were doing. It's typical Norwegian, we have a lot of space here and we keep to ourselves a lot."

Whatever the nature of their personal relationships with the band, both Euronymous and Varg were very supportive of Darkthrone. Period interviews see them frequently paying respect to the band, and there's no doubt that *A Blaze in the Northern Sky* did much to launch the Norwegian scene. However, it was, to put it mildly, somewhat less enthusiastically received by the band's label Peaceville, and specifically its owner Hammy. Not only was the album a far more primitive-sounding affair than the technical death metal album that was hoped for, swapping challenging time signatures and complex arrangements for simple, catchy riffs and a genuinely demonic atmosphere, but the production was now icy and lo-fi in the extreme.

"Hammy is from England, and most of the metal albums coming out of England in the eighties had really shabby sound," ponders Fenriz, "so I figured he would be used to shabby sound. But maybe he tried to move away from that, 'cos he was actually the producer for the first Paradise Lost album and they've said he tried to make it too clean. So we finally had an organic sound—we would bring Black Sabbath albums to the studio guy and say we didn't want modern sound, that we wanted sharp and cold guitars—and Hammy went totally ballistic, he wanted us to rerecord."

"We had done something fresh. I don't think *Soulside Journey* was that fresh and we can see which has stood the test of time. And it was a mistake that he couldn't see the fire in Darkthrone at that time. He only stuck by it 'cos I was like, 'Fuck the contract, we'll release it on Deathlike Silence Productions.' 'Cos it wasn't important for us at that point to have money, we had entered *the zone*, where nothing mattered but to make ugly black metal, primitive stuff. We weren't businessmen. What I remember is he said if a young band would just leave his label he would lose face, like some Japanese thing," he laughs and adopts a stern Japanese accent, "'No! We lose face, we cannot do it!' So he released it anyway, everyone's happy."

Like Hammy, bassist Dag Nilsen was also less than thrilled with the new direction the band had taken and departed after the recording of the album, having only stayed on as a session member for the band's convenience since he knew the bass lines. It was as a trio that the band recorded their third album, 1993's *Under A Funeral Moon*, the first Darkthrone album Fenriz considers entirely black metal, since all material had been written specifically for the record. The difference is clearly audible, and where the previous album had made use of chunky Frost-influenced riffs, the successor leaned more toward a Bathory/VON/Burzum approach, introducing a more minimal, dissonant style, fast tremolo melodies, droning, hypnotic song structures, and higher-pitched, raspy vocals.

Equally importantly, the album made use of a shockingly raw production. In itself that was nothing new within black metal, but here was a signed, established band choosing to go with the most primitive sound possible, and it was an important aesthetic decision that would prove hugely influential. Indeed, since that time there have appeared many new bands who place a high value on lo-fi production—despite the increased ease with which one can now attain a "professional" production—and argue, like Darkthrone, that this can be as integral to the aural experience as the composition of the songs themselves. It is a creative decision that is sadly much derided by those outside of the genre who fail to understand that what makes a production "good" or "bad" is entirely subjective, and that a clean, dynamic sound is not always the best medium for metal, nor the most effective way to achieve a powerful atmosphere.

Under a Funeral Moon would also mark the last appearance of Zephyrous, whose departure from the band coincided with his move away from Oslo, a relocation soon echoed by Ted, who was also tiring of life in the city.

"We started making songs for *Under a Funeral Moon* and everything went hunky dory until Ted decided that the whole Helvete scene was becoming a bit of a boy's club and moved pretty far away," recalls Fenriz. "I think Zephyrous was starting to think that too—these guys, especially Zephyrous, were the true misanthropes. They moved away and stopped rehearsing just 'cos they thought, 'Ah fuck, this is becoming stupid.' They were like the hummingbirds in the coal mine shafts—if the air got bad the hummingbird died and the people get the hell out. We should have got the hell out of the black metal party at that time, but no, people just kept coming."

"That's how I felt with the thrash metal party, I got into it a bit late then lots of idiots came and I thought, 'Fuck this, there must be something else.' Then I went to the death metal party, 'Yeah, this rocks,' then all the idiots started gate-crashing that. Anyway [their move] started to make it a bit difficult to hang out as a band and rehearse, but we finished the album, then we didn't do anything else. For the first time we didn't start rehearsing new material after coming out of the studio."

While his bandmates were deserting the Oslo social scene, Fenriz went the other way, finding an enthusiasm for alcohol and bar life in general for the first time. "As of 1991 I decided to quit the loner life," he explains. "I had been very involved in the tape-trading scene from '87 to '90 and I needed a break, I needed to have my first beer, 'cos I didn't have a normal youth period where I would hang round with the gang and drink beers underage. I would just be Fenriz in the underground and I needed a break and the break was fifteen years chugging beers and socializing."

Neither geographical challenges nor busy social lives could hamper Darkthrone's creative streak, and in early 1994 the band released their fourth album, the iconic and infamous *Transilvanian Hunger*. Though following a similarly hypnotic and discordant approach in terms of composition, it also employed a sound that—amazingly—proved even colder and more primitive than its predecessor. If the two previous albums had been lo-fi in comparison to *Soulside Journey*, this opus was lo-fi in comparison to just about *anything*, boasting a gloriously hideous non-production that would have seemed rudimentary even on a demo.

Still, if the sound qualities caused some controversy, it was nothing compared to the furor initiated by other aspects of the release. Within the black metal community itself the album caused no little antagonism, since the lyrics for the latter half of the record were penned by the recently jailed Varg Vikernes, not a popular figure in a community still reeling from the death of Euronymous. Particularly aggravated were sections of the Swedish scene, including Jon of Dissection and It of Abruptum, who had been particularly vocal in his support of Euronymous and his hatred for Vikernes, and a few thinly veiled threats were issued via *Slayer Magazine*.

"When Varg was jailed he had no means of communication," explains Fenriz. "And I would say, 'I have half the lyrics for my album, how about I give you the other half and you do what you want?' and he wrote back and said 'Yes, okay I'll do it.' And it came back without any message or anything like that, which was cool. Some people would say, 'Hey, you gotta be careful, some guys are pretty angry with you,' but nothing happened. Maybe I was just lucky, you know you always hear some rumor that some crazy guy has started on a journey from another country to get you, blah, blah, blah, but it never happens, just talk."

Far more problematic—at least to the wider metal world, now increasingly picking up on both Darkthrone and the Norwegian black metal scene—was a provocative statement that the band requested accompany the album, which read:

"We would like to state that *Transilvanian Hunger* stands beyond any criticism. If any man should attempt to criticize this LP, he should be thoroughly patronized for his obvious Jewish behavior."

Taken aback, label Peaceville made a public statement distancing themselves from the band and then refused to promote or advertise the album, while nonetheless refusing to censor the band or cancel the release.

"I regret it," admits Fenriz. "The statement actually meant: 'If you don't know where black metal comes from, why the hell would you try to review it in your magazine? Are you doing it because you need the money?' That is what I should have said. But I was young and my language was disgusting and flamboyant and very, very angry. As usual that [the word 'Jewish'] would be the prejudice you would use in jokes, but then it's quite okay for the press that some people aren't politically correct as long as they don't express it. After this we lost distribution in most parts of Europe, and we didn't have it back until many years later. They would boycott *Transilvanian Hunger*… now why is it not *still* boycotted do you think? Why would something be boycotted, and then not boycotted anymore? Again, the *money*, let's just leave it at that, again just seeing people running for the money."

Seemingly surprised by the storm surrounding them, the band released the album without the offending statement, and quickly issued a two-page press statement that seemed to dig them even deeper. The statement explained:

…Darkthrone can only apologize for this tragic choice of words, but PLEASE let us explain this. You see, in Norway the word 'Jew' is used all the time to mean something that's out of order. It's always been like this… WHY it is impossible to say, because Norwegians have always liked Jews and racism is not a big issue in Norway. You could actually ask the entire Norwegian nation for an apology, because the 'Jew' expression is used negatively everyday in Norway… Also it must be said that NONE of our albums have ever contained any racism/fascism or Nazi slant at all. Everyone can check this out by simply reading our lyrics… Darkthrone is absolutely not a political band and we never were. We ask everyone involved to look to our albums for the final proof that we are as innocent as humanly possible…

**Darkthrone play live (for what is likely to be the final time) in Oslo, 1996.
Pictured is Nocturno Culto. Picture: Nihil Archives.**

For his part Fenriz has since explained that he was going through a phase of being "angry at several races," after the left-wing phase of his early youth, which apparently once saw him arrested at an anti-apartheid march, and he has since lost interest in politics altogether. Rightly or wrongly, the apology failed to convince many of the band's intentions, especially since interviews with fanzines at the time had seen Fenriz claiming that the band were "fascist in outlook." The Varg connection also probably didn't help dispel the far-right accusations, and there was also the fact that the album sleeve carried the phrase "Norsk Arisk Black Metal," which translates to "Norwegian Aryan Black Metal."

"Again, it's the same youthful insanity," Fenriz comments of the sleeve design. "I had been protesting always against the major streams and this was a totally disgusting… a vulgar display of opinion, very vulgar. It's not something you bring up when you speak to your mother. But I think most people in their lives have been young and in an extremely fucked situation and said very bad things. For me it was unluckily an idea to put it on a record cover as it was the only means of communication I felt I had. I can also say maybe some of the statements were colored by the extreme situation we were in [following the death of Euronymous and the trials] and having your backs to the wall you end up lashing out against almost anything."

The band's next album, 1995's *Panzerfaust,* was free of political content but confirmed that the band were in no mood to play it safe, once again featuring lyrical contributions from Varg (this time on a single song entitled "Quintessence") and taking its name from an anti-tank weapon developed in Germany during World War II. Stylistically it followed neatly from the raw black metal sound of *Transilvanian Hunger,* perhaps not surprising since Fenriz wrote the entirety of both albums and, in the case of *Panzerfaust,* also handled all instruments. The album would be the first released on Moonfog Records, the band parting ways with Peaceville after their contract expired; not surprising, since things hadn't ended on a good note.

Fenriz also collaborated with Satyr in a project called Storm in 1995, blending black metal with traditional Norwegian folk music, something he would also do with the previously death metal-oriented solo project Isengard, which also released its second full-length album, *Høstmørke,* in 1995. As if that wasn't enough, in 1995 Fenriz also released *Transmissions From Empire Algol,* the second album of his ambient project Neptune Towers, played bass on *Kronet Til Konge* by Dødheimsgard, and played drums in *Moonstoned,* the debut album of Valhall, a Norwegian metal act he remains a member of.

Many of these efforts had been recorded in 1994, a year that Fenriz reports brought about both the end of his marriage and the beginning of the end of his love affair with black metal. Burnt out and disheartened by the direction the movement was taking, Fenriz found himself resentful of a scene that was suffering, as he saw it, from an influx of new bands and a move toward a more commercial sound.

"I think it got lost when too many people started becoming interested in the style. I mean all the bands that had something black metal in them up to '92/'93, all of them were great, then all the shit started to happen. But that happens to every scene, the poor guys who come along later, they can't see what's cool and what isn't. They were just there at the right time, which is not to be the creator of the scene but rather when it gets streamlined, that is where to be successful."

Perhaps unsurprisingly, 1996 heralded something of an end of an era for the band, seeing the release of sixth album *Total Death,* a record on which Fenriz relinquished all lyric writing, the void filled by Nocturno Culto and the vocalists of various Norwegian acts such as Emperor, Satyricon, Ulver, and Ved Buens Ende. The much-delayed *Goatlord*—the aborted second death metal album—was also released soon after. A hiatus then took place in the Darkthrone world, with Nocturno taking a break to spend time with his young family, and Fenriz hitting a period of depression which, combined with a general sense of disillusionment with the black metal scene, left him loath to continue with Darkthrone.

Darkthrone *would* continue, however, and in 1998 a resurrection of the group took place, primarily instigated by Nocturno Culto, who approached the band with a new drive, even taking over the non-musical responsibilities. For his part, Fenriz became far more vocal following the group's resurrection, giving more regular interviews, since by this point a great deal of myth and legend had built up around the band. This is perhaps unsurprising given that fans only had a few words and a few demonic-looking photos from which to draw their conclusions.

"Around 1994 the 'blackpackers' started coming from all over the world to Oslo, not even with an appointment, just coming to Elm Street [an Oslo bar frequented by musicians in the scene] to meet black metal people," he complains. "Then they would act all strange because you were not living like a caveman. They would be like, 'What, you're laughing?' Yeah. And you would hear a lot of strange rumors, so we started doing a lot of interviews in '98, '99, 'cos I wanted to set the record straight. The horrible thing about being in a band is it's like being in a house and you are trying to explain what's in there. People in bands aren't very good at communicating and when people aren't communicating *at all*, that's where the myths start. 'What do they have in the house? What are they building in there?'"

In addition to the relative silence of the band and the powerful aura created by their minimalist aesthetic, another factor that had made Darkthrone so mysterious and elusive was the fact that—aside from a one-off gig at Elm Street in 1996 organized by Satyr—Nocturno and Fenriz have not played live together as Darkthrone since way back in 1991.

"After our Finland mini-tour in spring '91 it was clear that we didn't want to play with [bassist] Dag on a steady basis anymore," Fenriz explains. "After that we went completely into *the zone* of black metal behavior. The 'fuck off' attitude and more-or-less necro lifestyle took a hold and we wanted to write more songs, not tour the album *at all*. It was fairly unanimous. Then Ted and Ivar moved away anyway. We actually played around twenty-plus gigs, including Blitz in Oslo and even Kafe Strofal, a squat, which *no* other metal band did as far as I know. I could write several books on why I don't wish to play live now. But for one, I dreamt as a child of *recording albums, not* being up on stage."

The albums that followed the band's return—1999's *Ravishing Grimness*, 2001's *Plaguewielder*, 2003's *Hate Them*, and 2004's *Sardonic Wrath*—took the mid-nineties Darkthrone template but broadened it, adding increasing inspiration from older thrash, punk, and crossover outfits. It would not be until 2006, however, that the band would really bite the bullet and fully commit to such influences, the result being *The Cult is Alive*, an album that shocked many of the band's followers thanks to catchy numbers such as "Graveyard Slut," "Whisky Funeral," and "Shut Up," whose titles alone suggested a significant shift.

"I had already been doing some more punk stuff," Fenriz considers. "I had done some crust riffs on *Hate Them* and punk vocals on *Sardonic Wrath*, and also in the beginning we had lots of punk influences. With *The Cult* we suddenly got our own studio. We should have got our own studio in '88—we really needed that to evolve our band and we didn't get it, so we evolved a different way. Once we had our own place we could rehearse together and it took off and there was Darkthrone in the direction we *could* have taken in '88… 'metal punk' is a style that is always shabby, always organic, it can *not* be modern studio-sounding at all."

Far from a one-off experiment, *The Cult is Alive* would herald a distinctly new era, the band delving intensely into what they refer to as "metal punk" over albums such as *F.O.A.D*, *Dark Thrones and Black Flags*, *Circle the Wagons* and *The Underground Resistance*, with more

The underground resistance: Fenriz and Nocturno Culto behind the counter of Oslo record store Neseblod Records.

emphasis on clear vocals, a gradual reduction of double bass drumming, and more punk and old-school metal overtones.

It's interesting to note that this new era of the band coincided with—and very probably helped trigger—the reunification of black metal with the hardcore and crust punk scenes. Having sprung from the same Motörhead-indebted roots, the two movements appeared to discover one another anew in the late noughties, having been culturally and musically separated in the nineties (a far cry from the early eighties, when the two were often distinguishable only by lyrical content). Just as earlier bands such as Venom, Bathory, Hellhammer, and Mayhem took inspiration from hardcore and crust punk alongside extreme metal, so have more contemporary groups such as Japan's Gallhammer, Canada's Iskra, and Sweden's Martyrdöd.

"Back in the day the difference was not so harsh," explains Darkthrone logo designer Tomas Lindberg—who began his career in black/death metal outfit Grotesque and went on to play in crust/hardcore acts such as Disfear and Skitsystem—in a *Metal Hammer* interview I conducted with him in 2012. "Even if my first band wore spikes and corpsepaint, we were still okay to say we listened to Heresy and Ripcord and whatever other hardcore bands … I'd say a major thing was when death metal became more common and was mentioned in the media, that generated a reaction in the underground and it was about being more evil and dark than anyone else… That was back to the roots, to the first Venom records, which had no politics whatsoever, but most of my crust friends, they all run round with Bathory patches on their jeans."

"Motörhead kind of created this sound with [the 1979 album] *Overkill*," considers Fenriz, "however they were the only band that ever got known for it, bands like Warfare and English Dogs didn't have many fans in the nineties I can tell you that, but their old albums are hot shit now. In the eighties all the bands mixed but the crowds didn't mix very well— it was the same in the nineties. What I didn't know was that there were punks listening to

The cover art to 2008's *Dark Thrones and Black Flags* hints at the band's change of tack since their early albums.

bands like Burzum 'cos it had this organic sound and not the disgusting modern sound, and they came through in the noughties; crust bands inspired by black metal. Crazy as it may seem, the two scenes had listened to each other a lot. It was damn funny when the bands had made lots of friends between black metal and crust and the crowds as usual were clueless… oh brother! People are really slow navigating round the underground."

While their earlier recordings may have offered some clues as to such inspirations, Darkthrone's more overt embrace of these punk elements proved genuinely shocking to many. Likewise, as one of the bands with the most otherworldly images in the second wave, it was very strange for many longtime fans to see the group deconstructing its carefully created aura with candid appearances in video interviews, a less straight-faced aesthetic, and more down-to-earth lyrics (for example the biographical numbers "Metal Hiking Punks" and "I Am the Working Class").

"I have always deconstructed the image since the 'blackpackers' came," Fenriz laughs, "and no one wanted that! Everyone wants the glamour and the glitz, no one wants to see Yul Brynner taking a shit in a cowboy movie. That's how it's always been, it's just natural."

Similarly, the indignant wrath within the group's music is now geared more toward elements of the metal scene as opposed to any god or religion (indeed, when your author visited Fenriz's home he was quick to point out that—despite his anti-religious stance—he had chosen his apartment in part because of its proximity to an interesting-looking church) as the chorus to "I Am the Graves of the '80s" from *Circle the Wagons* succinctly shows: "I am the graves of the '80s / I am the risen dead / Destroy their modern metal / and bang your fucking head!"

"If you see the anger I have, it's in the lyrics," explains Fenriz, "it's what drives me, it's total war against modern metal sounds, and that takes its toll. I'm on the barricades every day with this shit, having this constant war against the studio people, who are telling bands, 'Come on, take the easy way, take the click drums'... [Christianity and religion] that's like kid's stuff, that gets you angry as a kid, that's the ignition key. I mean those things were forced against you as a child and we thought it was super-daft and hated it to the bone. But just mulling about that when you're older, that wouldn't be very constructive. You can remove yourself from that so it doesn't bother me anymore. I would be really stupid to stick my head in that bee's nest, to seek out churches just to get annoyed," He laughs. "Actually that would be an original black metal idea, like, 'Say what can I do to really feel the hatred? Okay, I'll go to a sermon!'"

Despite these dramatic changes, Darkthrone have become such a familiar landmark in the extreme metal scene that it's hard to imagine them ever having not been there. And while the group may have left behind what many consider to be their "true black metal" sound and ideology, Fenriz remains no less vehement in his opinions on the genre and what he sees as its decline.

"The point is it takes a lot for me to get black metal feelings out of bands these days. Basically—and listen close, 'cos this is the most important thing—what did we do in '91? What did we have to listen to? What was the sound we liked? It was all the bands we talked about earlier, the bands that still rule are the ones that sound like those recordings, why would it be any different? People now are shocked that I don't want to listen to the thousandth clone band of Emperor or Darkthrone, but I was never into that, I was only into stuff from '91 and before that basically.

"So," he concludes, "if a band comes out nowadays they have to give me the black metal feeling and what gives me the black feeling? Something that sounds like it could have been released '81 to '91—so a Norwegian band that I like is Faustcoven, but does it have anything to do with what people now call 'Norwegian black metal'? I don't think so... sad story huh? But it makes total sense and is also damn true. When [new black metal bands] do it, how copied is it? How much did we copy? Are they keeping a tradition alive? I'm feeling that they are just taking snapshots of what we assembled. They can do *good* snapshots with the really organic sound, but we know if it stemmed from something real and we usually doubt, even if that's not fair, that there is the *realness*, the glint of the milkman's eyes that started it all."

22
BURZUM

"Filosofem is a perfect album, it doesn't even need any words as it's so perfect it's beyond belief. You can't believe that a human being has been capable of carving that out of nothing, it's amazing."

—Niklas Kvarforth (Shining)

AS A ONE-MAN PROJECT—perhaps the most famous within the metal world—the story of Burzum is intrinsically linked to that of its creator, Varg Vikernes. Since we have already examined the impact his presence and actions had upon the Norwegian black metal scene, there is probably no need to delve further into the events that led to his lengthy imprisonment. In fact, the point that needs to be highlighted is that while his crimes and controversial opinions are certainly responsible for a large part of his fame, on artistic merit alone he would be considered one of the genre's most significant and influential artists.

Born in Bergen under the name Kristian, Varg's early teens were characterized by a fascination with role-playing games, warfare, and metal music. Along with this came a focus on race and nationality, which began during his childhood in Iraq, where his father was working for Saddam Hussein—a figure he actually hails in early Burzum interviews (Hussein, that is; Varg's father seems to have become a somewhat distant figure after his parents divorced when he was twelve). According to Varg's homepage, he first began making music in a metal trio named Kalashnikov (after the Russian assault rifle) and later renamed Uruk-Hai, after the toughest orcs in J.R.R. Tolkein's *Lord of the Rings*.

No recordings appear to have been made by this outfit, and soon Varg became a part of Old Funeral (joining just before Olve "Abbath" Eikemo and Harald "Demonaz" Nævdal departed to form Immortal), playing guitar on the 1991 EP *Devoured Carcass*. As the black metal revolution overtook Norway, Old Funeral would gradually splinter into new groups, and in Varg's case this led to him working on his solo project Burzum, the name once again from *Lord of the Rings* (it means "darkness" in the Black Speech of Mordor).

Vikernes then underwent an almost unbelievably productive period of writing, crafting a huge library of songs that would furnish a spree of future releases. Writing alone, Varg's compositions were defined by his use of hypnotic repetition, catchy yet melancholic riffs,

An early Burzum promo photo of Varg Vikernes, captured in his Count Grishnackh persona.

simple yet perfectly suited drum and guitar work, and his uniquely tortured screams. With no input from other musicians, it was presumably his own listening tastes that dictated the Burzum sound: certainly Varg was always open in his passion for Bathory and VON, with early fanzine interviews also namechecking Mayhem and Thorns. Later autobiographical writings also cite the first Paradise Lost demo, Destruction and Celtic Frost, Dutch death metallers Pestilence, and some "underground house/techno" recordings. In an interview in 2010 for *Metal Hammer*, he also told me that he now believed Iron Maiden and the first two Kreator albums had the most impact on him, with Destruction's solos on *Infernal Overkill* specifically inspiring him to make his riffs "solo-like," and Bathory inspiring his drumming to be simple and "drum machine-like."

His entrance into the Oslo scene led to Euronymous signing Burzum after two 1991 demo tapes, releasing the self-titled debut album on Deathlike Silence in 1992, the first black metal release on the label. As with Old Funeral, Varg recorded in Bergen at Grieghallen with producer Eirik "Pytten" Hundvin (a relationship that would prove enduring), with his friends Demonaz and Euronymous present, the latter providing a guitar solo on the short and Bathory-esque "War." The album would prove as essential in cementing the second wave template as *Diabolical Fullmoon Mysticism* by Varg's friends and ex-bandmates Immortal, and Darkthrone's similarly monochromatic *A Blaze in the Northern Sky*. The epic yet bleak atmosphere was all-encompassing, the songs embodying a duality: a sense of calming catharsis alongside an oppressive, claustrophobic overtone.

For a time, Varg—now better known as Count Grishnackh (Grishnákh being a particu-

A cassette featuring early mixes of Burzum's debut album (minus the ambient tracks) sent to
Euronymous, who was releasing the record. Recorded over Metallica's *Kill 'Em All*, it features Varg's
handwriting and was rescued from Euronymous' apartment following his death.

larly malevolent orc from *Lord of the Rings*)—sought to turn Burzum into a full band, and
invited in drummer Erik Lancelot (later of Ulver) and Emperor's Tomas "Samoth" Haugen on
bass. The latter would appear on the iconic *Aske* EP (notoriously featuring the burnt remains
of Fantoft Church and packaged with a lighter featuring the same image), but Varg would
quickly return the band to a solo effort, having lost interest in the prospect of playing live.

    Aske would be released in 1993 on Varg's own Cymophane label, due to the collapse
of his friendship with Euronymous, as would the second full-length *Det Som Engang Var*
("What Once Was"), though both were actually recorded in 1992. Since this material was
written around the same time as the debut, it's unsurprising that it bears many similarities,
though the experience in the studio seems to have given the songs greater depth and more
intricate textures. The basic approach remained largely unchanged, however, and as before
Varg sought to distance himself from the precision playing and equipment he associated with
death metal, instead using whatever tools he happened to have access to. Tone and feel were
prioritized above technical details, an approach that served as a defining quality of black
metal in general.

    "We were searching around trying to find different sounds on different amps and
speakers to get this cold and narrow sound, which we have on at least the first three Burzum
albums," recalls Pytten. "We used very traditional drum recording techniques but if you want
to produce a good, traditional rock 'n' roll drum sound you would need a good rock 'n' roll

drum kit—and these guys never had a good drum kit. But if you take an unskilled musician and put them on a instrument or amp that they don't know, you won't get a better result... because if you don't know [an instrument] you can't express yourself on it... You also don't produce an [intentionally] ugly sound with really high-class equipment, you use a speaker which is not completely as it should be."

Initially distributed by Voices of Wonder, Varg was soon handed back their stock of records when the label decided they wished to cut ties with this increasingly contentious character as quickly as possible. Left without distribution and now in jail for a lengthy murder sentence, Varg initially sought help from Metalion, who sold some records as a favor but felt that Head Not Found was not properly equipped to handle Burzum. Earache Records had at one point courted Varg, but were put off by comments they felt were explicitly racist. For the same reason, Candlelight decided not to sign him, since they feared a boycott might lead to them losing distribution for *all* their artists.

The solution came from England and Tiziana Stupia, a Burzum fan who set up the Misanthropy Records label in order to give Varg the distribution he was unable to find elsewhere. Despite this, the label later voiced complaints (in particular via a compilation aptly titled *Presumed Guilty*) about artists on their label losing distribution from Rough Trade for this very reason—though there's little doubt that the notoriety and huge success of Burzum also helped the label expand their roster considerably.

1994's *Hvis Lyset Tar Oss* ("If the Light Takes Us") became the first album to be released through Cymophone and Misanthropy. Remarkably, this album had *also* been recorded in 1992, just a few short months after *Det Som* and a mere month after *Aske*. Despite this, a notable stylistic leap had taken place, the record boasting four lengthy numbers that resonate with a greater emotional scope than its predecessors, bearing a distinctly yearning atmosphere and an expansive, heavily synth-laden sound. Epic, bleak, and built around the huge trademark riffs, the album is again peaceful at times, while also presenting Burzum at its most discordant and abrasive; it is rightly considered a milestone in black metal.

The next release would be the final one in the first chapter of the project's history and arguably its finest effort, taking the genre to even more transcendental levels. Recorded back in 1993 but not released until three years later, *Filosofem* opens with the unbelievably atmospheric and immersive "Dunkelheit." With a title that translates as "darkness" (the song's "real name," Varg has explained, is "Burzum," but all titles were in German for the initial release), it was reportedly written back in 1991, and was apparently the first real song Varg wrote for Burzum. With a hypnotic riff, a ridiculously simple yet perfect synth accompaniment and mantra-like lyrics, the track is the closest Burzum have yet come to a single, and was even given its own promo video. The more ferocious and relentless "Jesu Død" is another highlight, as is a dark yet strangely soothing twenty-five-minute ambient number whose title translates as "Circumambulation of the Transcendental Pillar of Singularity."

Once imprisoned, Varg lost access to all instruments but a keyboard and so it was that

A flyer for 1993's *Aske* EP, featuring the burnt remains of Fantoft Stave Church, one of the few church arsons for which Varg was not found guilty.

his next release was an ambient album entitled *Dauði Baldrs*. Unveiled in 1997, it failed to impress, and while the follow-up, 1999's *Hliðskjálf*, was a marked improvement, it's interesting that these albums never reached the heights of the earlier ambient tracks that helped define the first four albums. Sadly, *Hliðskjálf* was the last release for over a decade, and during the rest of his incarceration Varg seemed keen to distance himself from Burzum, the black metal scene, and any Satanic associations that went with it.

Often using the Germanic pen name Hofding Warge, he instead concentrated on his ideological writings. The *Filosofem* CD had already included the postal address for the National Heathen Front, a group primarily concerned with race and ecology, and Varg was now increasingly outspoken about his Odinism and extreme right-wing/race-related views, which he not only espoused in his book *Vargsmål*, but in the journal *Filosofem*. Swastikas now appeared in the borders of his written correspondence, and he was famously quoted claiming that looking into brown eyes was like "looking up an arsehole." Misanthropy meanwhile released a Burzum shirt with a totenkopf (the SS skull and crossbones) urging the reader to support their local Einsatzkommando (a term used to describe the killing squads in occupied territories of Nazi Germany whose targets were Jews, communists, and other ideological enemies). Varg became something of a figurehead for the right-wing music scene, with leading far-right label Resistance Records even buying Cymophane. While some didn't care for the man's politics, many were disappointed by statements that suggested that any future recordings would remain clear of black metal due to Varg's disdain for the genre and "negro" instruments.

But when released from prison in 2009—after a highly publicized escape attempt in 2003 in which he was reportedly captured in a stolen car full of weapons and equipment from a military barracks (though he denies possession of any weapons)—Varg in fact quickly returned to making metal with Burzum, beginning with the 2010 *Belus* album. Originally given the delicate title "The White God," the statement that accompanied its release proved Varg was in no mood for diplomacy.

"I am no friend of the modern so-called Black Metal culture. It is a tasteless, lowbrow parody of Norwegian so-called Black Metal anno 1991–1992, and if it was up to me it would meet its dishonorable end as soon as possible. However, rather than abandon my own music, only because others have soiled its name by claiming to have something in common with it, I will stick to it. The 'black metallers' will probably continue to 'get loaded,' 'get high,' and in all other manners to behave like the stereotypical Negro; they will probably continue to get foreign tribal tattoos, dress, walk, talk, look, and act like homosexuals, and so forth. Some of the 'black metallers,' their fans and accomplices will probably even continue to pretend—and actually believe—they have something in common with Burzum, but let me assure you; they don't."

There's no doubt that Varg's statements in magazines (and on his website, which even relatively recently mentions "negroes and other inferior races") have long been politically charged, yet unlike most similarly minded artists his views have never found their way into his music. In fact, perhaps paradoxically, Burzum's huge popularity suggests that Varg has managed to tap into something truly universal. Though the post-prison albums (which include 2011's *Fallen* and 2012's *Umskiptar*) have not proven quite as significant as those recorded prior to his incarceration, Burzum remains hugely popular with a wide array of listeners, including those who completely disregard Varg's politics and worldview, which now seems to eschew the Odinist faith of his early prison years for what he calls a non-religious paganism.

"My guess would be a common feeling of despair," Varg explained in my 2010 *Metal Hammer* interview, when asked why he thought his music resonates with so many people. "And perhaps we also share the feeling of being alienated and even ostracized in a world that used to be ours, but isn't any more. Or perhaps it's simply because I am untrained and from a different musical background (classical), and because of that make music that is slightly different from the music made by those who are trained and hail from a traditional metal background. It might also be because I do everything myself, and therefore [the music] is less compromising. I really don't know. I am happy if others like my music, but I don't spend much time figuring out exactly why they do."

Whatever the reason, countless new black metal bands continue to appear with a clearly audible Burzum influence. In fact, along with Darkthrone, Burzum has proved arguably the most directly influential outfit in the genre and it's no exaggeration to say that a vast proportion of groups in today's scene simply would not sound the way they do if it were not for this eternally contentious outfit.

Mantas, Cronos and Abaddon of Venom enjoy the high life: *"Venom are rich—very rich"* lied the accompanying press statement—in fact, most of the band's income was spent on pyrotechnics. Photo courtesy of Spinefarm.

ABOVE: The circle is closed as Cronos and Venom perform at Norwegian black metal festival Hole In The Sky in 2010. Photo: Ester Segarra.

**ABOVE: Into the coven: King Diamond of Mercyful Fate live in New York, December 1984.
Photo: Frank White.**

ABOVE: A Swedish man in New York: Quorthon of Bathory visits America in 1987. Photo: Debra Trebitz/ Frank White Photo Agency.

ABOVE: Hellhammer's Steve Warrior shows off his punk roots with an Exploited T-shirt, January 1983. Photo: Martin Kyburz.

A phoenix from the ashes: Thomas Fischer/Tom G. Warrior in November 1984, not long after
Hellhammer had ceased to be and Celtic Frost had risen to take their place. Photo: Martin Kyburz.

TOP: Hellhammer in the Grave Hill bunker early 1984: Martin Eric Ain,
Bruce Day and Thomas Fischer/Satanic Slaughter. Photo: Martin Kyburz.
BOTTOM: Celtic Frost during the *To Mega Therion* era: Reed St. Mark, Thomas Fischer/
Tom G. Warrior and Dominic Steiner. Photo courtesy of Thomas Fischer.

**LEFT: Arguably Brazil's first extreme metal band, Vulcano, pictured in 1987.
Photo courtesy of Zhema Rodero.**

ABOVE: Blasphemy guitarist Caller of the Storms appearing in London on the Fuck Christ tour, 1993.
Photo: Nihil Archives.

TOP: Nocturnal Grave Desecrator and Black Winds, still smashing audiences today.
Photo courtesy of Ryan Förster.
BOTTOM: A flyer for Switzerland's Samael circa 1991's *Worship Him* album
with Masmiseîm, Xytras and Vorphalack.

ABOVE: Samael, older and wiser in 2011: Xytras, Mas, Vorph and Makro.
Photo courtesy of Century Media Records.

TOP: Rotting Christ during the *Non Serviam* sessions, 1994: Magus Wampyr Daoloth, Mutilator, Necromayhem and Themis Tolis. Photo courtesy of Sakis Tolis.
BOTTOM: Keeping the black flame alive: Sakis and Themis Tolis, founding members of Rotting Christ, pictured in 2013. Photo: Ester Segarra.

TOP: VON: Goat and Kill backstage in 1991. The elusive drummer Snake, as ever, sadly out of shot.
BOTTOM: VON's short-lived reunion lineup in London, 2010: Blood, Goat, Venien and J. Giblet G.
Photo: Dayal Patterson.

TOP: Master's Hammer in 2012 circa the *Vracejte konve na místo* album: Joe Harper, Jan Kapák, František "Franz" Štorm and Necrocock. Photo courtesy of František "Franz" Štorm.
BOTTOM: Funeral fog: Nuclear Holocausto performs at an early Beherit show.

ABOVE: The one and only Nuclear Holocausto strikes an iconic pose.

DAMAGE INC.

We're back again. Our first issue got off to a slow start, but in the end it sold pretty well — thanks to everyone for trying us! You've made it possible for us to carry on, and as you can see our second issue has been expanded to 32 BIG pages. We hope you'll enjoy it.

We've got more interviews this time, but we're still on the lookout for good punk bands to review. Drop us a line if you've got any good tips. We've also included a few record reviews this time, and we hope to have more in an even BIGGER issue next time. But that depends on how well this issue sells, which in turn depends on YOU.

To expand our readership, we hope to recruit distributors for Damage Inc. This is an opportunity for us to reach more readers, and an opportunity for you to make some money. You can find out details about distributing Damage Inc. elsewhere in this issue.

I'd also like to ask you to lend your support to the No More Censorship Defense Fund in their struggle against reactionary forces like the P.M.R.C. — you'll find the address in the article on the Dead Kennedys.

Well, that's enough from me. May you thrash unto death and enjoy the next 30 pages — and don't ever become a chickenshit comformist!

MANIAC

Damage Inc. is published quarterly by **Maniac Productions**, P.O. Box 62, N-3864 Rauland, Norway. Bands wishing to appear in this magazine can send demos/pix/bio/logo to the address above.

Damage Inc.'s unbelievable maniacs:
MANIAC Editor, stories, interviews.
KYORPÖN Pics, typesetting, layout.
NELLA Logos, artwork.

©**MANIAC PRODUCTIONS 1987.** The contents of Damage Inc. may not be reproduced without written permission from the publisher. All rights reserved.
Printed in Norway.

ABOVE: The second issue of *Damage Inc.* fanzine, 1987, created by a young Sven-Erik "Maniac" Kristiansen, pictured here. Image courtesy of Maniac.

TOP: A previously unpublished lineup photo circa *Deathcrush* recently discovered by Maniac:
Manheim, Maniac, Euronymous and Necrobutcher.
BOTTOM: Another previously unpublished photo from the *Deathcrush* recordings:
Maniac and Necrobutcher.

TOP: Previously unpublished photo from the *Deathcrush* recordings: Euronymous and Maniac.
Photo courtesy of Maniac.
BOTTOM: The 'classic' Mayhem lineup: Hellhammer, Dead, Euronymous and Necrobutcher.
Photo courtesy of Nihil Archives.

TOP: The man who introduced corpsepaint to black metal: Dead of Morbid/Mayhem poses for what has become one of black metal's best-known photos. Photo courtesy of Nihil Archives. BOTTOM: Another early-nineties Mayhem promo: Euronymous, Necrobutcher and Dead— again, at this time only Dead wore corpsepaint in the band.

ABOVE: *"We lit the fires"*—The infamous cover story in *Bergens Tidende* which saw Varg Vikernes talking about the church arsons and the unsolved Lillehammer murder.

TOP: In Memoriam: Dead and Euronymous, two of black metal's most significant figures, and ones whose influence still reverberates today. Photo courtesy of Nihil Archives.
BOTTOM: Inside the Helvete store: Euronymous with friends Jannicke Langård and Bård "Faust" Eithun, who also worked at the store. Photo courtesy of Jannicke Langård.

LEFT: Unholy allegiance: Varg and Euronymous in "happier" times. Photo courtesy of Nihil Archives.

RIGHT: One of the most timeless images taken of Euronymous which appeared in fanzines and, eventually, the *Nordic Metal: A Tribute to Euronymous* album.

ABOVE: One of the genre's most important musicians and a man whose distinctive guitar style spread like wildfire throughout the genre: Snorre Ruch of Stigma Diabolicum/Thorns. Photo: Peter Beste.

RIGHT: Darkthrone's Fenriz summons the spirit of black metal in an early nineties promo shot.

ABOVE: Varg Vikernes of Burzum in Norway, 2010, shortly after his release from prison. Photo: Ester Segarra.

ABOVE: Darkthrone circa the *Soulside Journey* era: Ted Skjellum (later Nocturno Culto), Ivar Enger (later Zephyrous), Dag Nilsen and Gylve Nagell (then Hank Amarillo, later Fenriz).

ABOVE: Pre-Emperor outfit Embryonic featuring (on the bottom row) a young Samoth and Ihsahn.

ABOVE: They were the black wizards—Emperor in 1993 with Samoth, Faust, Ihsahn and Tchort.
Photo: Nocturnal Art Productions.

TOP: Emperor play the UK in 1993: pictured are Ihsahn, Tchort and Samoth. Photo: Nihil Archives.
BOTTOM: An early promo photograph of Gehenna in the Norwegian countryside from 1993.
Photograph courtesy of Dolgar.

ABOVE: Last man standing: An archive shot of Ihsahn, who for a time was the only Emperor member
not to be incarcerated. Photo: Nocturnal Art Productions.

ABOVE: Gehenna in 1995: Dolgar, Sanrabb, Sarcana, E.N. Death and Dirge Rep. Photo: Nihil Archives.

ABOVE: Gorgoroth 1994: Hat, Frost, Infernus and Storm.

ABOVE: A live photo of Gorgoroth from 1994 featuring original vocalist Hat and drummer Frost. Photo: Nihil Archives.

ABOVE: Gaahl fronting Gorgoroth (or, retrospectively, God Seed) at Inferno festival, 2008.
Photo: Ester Segarra.

ABOVE: The past meets the present: Mayhem at Inferno festival in 2010 including a guest appearance by original vocalist Billy Messiah, performing alongside a crucified Attila Csihar. Photo: Ester Segarra.

ABOVE: A very early promo photo of Cradle of Filth: Paul Ryan, Ben Ryan, Daniel Davey, Robin Eaglestone and Paul Allender, with William "Was" Sarginson below. Photo courtesy of Nihil Archives.

ABOVE: A promo photograph of original Dimmu Borgir bassist Brynjard Tristan, taken to promote 1996's *Stormblåst*. Photo courtesy of Nihil Archives.

ABOVE: Masters of Disharmony: A backstage shot of Dimmu Borgir's Silenoz and Shagrath in 2003. Photo: Ester Segarra.

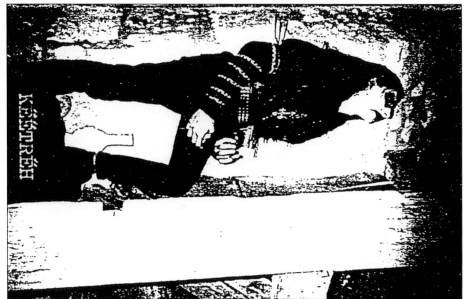

LEFT: Black Legions member Lord Aäkon Këëtrëh of Torgeist, Aäkon Këëtrëh and Belkètre in a typically murky portrait photo.
RIGHT: Lord Aäkon Këëtrëh and Vordb Dréagvor Uèzréévb pose for a Belketre promo photo somewhere in the French woodland where, legend has it, they lived for a time.

LEFT: *The Black Plague* fanzine, created in 1995 by the circle's co-founder Meyhna'ch of Mütiilatiɔn.
RIGHT: From *The Black Plague*: A suitably lo-fi reproduction of Black Legions co-founder Vordb Dréagvor Üezréévb
of Belkètre, Black Murder, Moëvöt and a multitude of other projects.

LEFT: The wraiths of Mütiilation: Mordred and Meyhna'ch lurk in the Black Legions castle, 1995.
RIGHT: Black Legions co-founder Meyhna'ch, performing with Hell Militia in 2010. Photo: Hervé Girod.

LEFT: Marduk live in Oslo, 1994.
RIGHT: B War of Marduk, live in France, 1994. Both photos: Nihil Archives.

LEFT: Jon Nödtveidt of Dissection conducts a pre-show ritual at Wacken, 2005. Photo: Ester Segarra.
RIGHT: Jon Nödtveidt of Dissection live in Oslo, 1994. Photo: Nihil Archives.

ABOVE: Watain recording the GG Allin song "Fuck Off, We Murder" with producer Tore "Necromorbus" Stjerna. Taken during the initial recording sessions for *The Wild Hunt* in Finland, 2013. Photo: Dayal Patterson.

LEFT: Lawless Darkness: Erik Danielsson of Watain, 2011.
RIGHT: *"I oppose life, everything that lives and breathes."* Niklas Kvarforth, 2011. Both photos: Ester Segarra.

LEFT: Controversial NSBM icon Capricornus of Graveland, Infernum and Thor's Hammer in the mid-nineties, some years before his apparent departure from the scene. Photo courtesy of Nihil Archives.

RIGHT: Do what thou wilt: Nergal of Behemoth in America, 2012. Photo: Ester Segarra.

TOP: Original Enslaved drummer Trym live in Oslo, 1994.
BOTTOM: Grutle of Enslaved live in Oslo, 1994. Both photos: Nihil Archives.

TOP: Erik Lancelot and Garm of Ulver in 1993. The Coil logo on the jacket
suggests the band were already taking inspiration from a wide array of sources
even at this early point in their career. Photo courtesy of Garm.
BOTTOM: The sadly departed Valfar of Windir, pictured in front of the thousand-
year-old Stedje Runestone, overlooking the band's hometown of Sogndal.

ABOVE: Norwegian Gothic: Garm of Ulver in London, 2011. Photo: Ester Segarra.

LEFT: Negură Bunget in Sarmizegetusa, Romania in 1999. Photo courtesy of Negru.
RIGHT: Negură Bunget in 2002, circa 'n Crugu Bradului: Sol Faur, Hupogrammos and Negru. Photo courtesy of Negru.

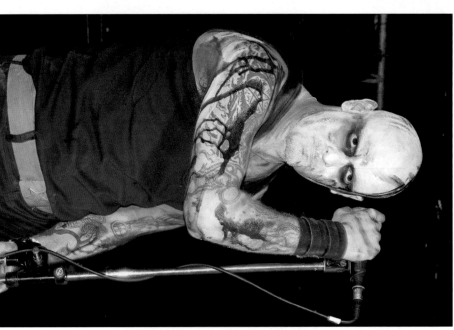

LEFT: Bearing the infernal flame: A.A. Nemtheanga of Primordial at a show in Dublin, 1994: Photo: Nihil Archives.
RIGHT: A.A. Nemtheanga of Primordial live in London some years later—2010 to be exact. Photo: Dayal Patterson

LEFT: Fleurety's Alexander Nordgaren (also ex-Mayhem).
RIGHT: Fleurety in 1996: Ayna B. Johansen, Svein Egil Hatlevik and Alexander Nordgaren. Courtesy of Svein Egil Hatlevik.

ABOVE: *"The corpsepaint came from Norway, that's a hundred percent for sure."* An unused image from Sigh's 1993 debut *Scorn Defeat* illustrated the band's new image. Photo courtesy of Nihil Archives.

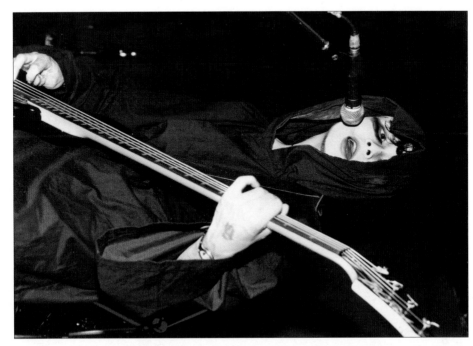

LEFT: Mirai Kawashima, co-founder of Sigh, live in London 1994. Photo: Nihil Archives.
RIGHT: Sax appeal: Dr. Mikannibal of Sigh at Inferno festival, 2007. Photo: Ester Segarra.

LEFT: Dødheimsgard: Malicious Records flyer for 1995's *Kronet til Konge* featuring Aldrahn, Vicotnik and Fenriz.
RIGHT: Clandestine of Dødheimsgard, live at Inferno festival, 2011. Photo: Ester Segarra.

ABOVE: Chemical imbalance: Cerastes of Mysticum in a derelict asylum, 1998. Photo: Nikolai Funke/Fotofunke.

ABOVE: *"Cumming all over Europe"*: The memorable poster for Mysticum's 1996 tour
with Gehenna and Marduk.

ABOVE: Dread of evil: Prime Evil of Mysticum live in London, 1996. Photo: Nihil Archives.

LEFT: UK post-black metal outfit Fen in late 2012: Derwydd, Grungyn and The Watcher. Photo: Tom Huskinson.
RIGHT: Jonas "B" Bergqvist of Lifelover, who unfortunately passed away during the making of this book. Photo courtesy of Prophecy Productions.

ABOVE: Fàbban of Aborym at the Slimelight club, London, following the band's show at the same venue.
Photo: Dayal Patterson.

ABOVE: Unused photo of AcidJess of Blacklodge in 2003 from the *Login:Satan* sessions. Photo: Matthieu Canaguier.

ABOVE: Underground black metal indeed: Saint Vincent of Blacklodge in an unused photo from 1999.
Photo courtesy of Saint Vincent.

ABOVE: Bloodied but unbowed: Kim "( )" Carlsson of Lifelover. Photo courtesy of Prophecy Productions.

ABOVE: *"The underground will remain as long as there are individuals sharing common views, spreading music without making it a commercial widespread cancer, cultivating the art of death in the shadows of this genre."* —Shatraug of Finland's Behexen.

ABOVE: Wolves In The Throne Room in Highgate Wood, London 2009: Will Lindsay, Nathan Weaver, Aaron Weaver. Photo: Dayal Patterson.

EMPEROR

"I remember being totally blown away by In the Nightside Eclipse, *which is still my favorite black metal album of all time. It was like the gates of hell opening."*

—Dani (Cradle of Filth)

IF BLACK METAL should ever get a hall of fame, there's a pretty good chance Emperor will be the first inducted. In their early days they carved a name for themselves as an act surrounded by an aura of danger, one that occasionally threatened to overshadow their musical achievements. Yet at the same time they were always an undeniable creative force, and quickly earned a place as one of the genre's early success stories. Indeed, they were one of the first Norwegian black metal bands to be signed by a foreign label, achieve significant album sales, and tour abroad. They also managed to survive as a band when three of their members were in jail. Most impressively, they managed the near-impossible feat of becoming one of the biggest bands in the genre while also being one of the most respected, ultimately winning over much of the metal mainstream as well as the black metal underground.

While the group's sound and lineup shifted continuously, it would always revolve around two key personalities, Samoth (Tomas Thormodsæter Haugen) and Ihsahn (Vegard Sverre Tveitan). Although both would be involved in numerous other projects over the years, it was Samoth who initially had the most band experience, and it was his invitation to Ihsahn to join an earlier group that ultimately led to the formation of Emperor. Like the majority of Norwegian black metallers, Samoth had entered the world of heavy metal through a childhood fascination with Kiss and then WASP, later developing a more serious interest in the thrash and death metal movements of the eighties.

"I was really into Metallica, Anthrax, Slayer, Testament, SOD, and Megadeth," he explains of his school days. "In ninth grade I had a practical placement once a week at a record store in the nearest town, Notodden [in the county of Telemark]. There was a metal guy working there and he lent me stuff like Sacrifice, Deathrow, Slaughter, Kreator, Possessed, DRI, Bathory, Cryptic Slaughter, etc., lots of really obscure stuff he had ordered by mail order from outside Norway. I became more hooked on extreme metal and started buying underground

A rare flyer for Zyltelab, a band featuring Samoth and Ildjarn of Thou Shalt Suffer (top row), and Thorbjørn Akkerhaugen, who would play a part in the history of both Thou Shalt Suffer and Emperor.

demos and fanzines, and writing to pen pals. I was really networking a lot and very active in the underground scene. I got in contact with Euronymous from Mayhem and that whole dark and extreme black metal feel attracted me."

Following in his family's bass-playing footsteps (his father, Jens Haugen, plays in respected blues act Spoonful of Blues), Samoth initially joined a local band playing covers of AC/DC, ZZ Top, Deep Purple, and Metallica alongside original songs, before forming a thrash side project called Conspiracy with some of the group's members. By this point he was exploring more extreme listening, and soon left both groups to form his own death metal band, initially called Dark Device, and then Xerasia. Working alongside two friends (Finn Arne Nielsen on vocals and bass and Ronny Johnsen on drums), Samoth moved from bass to guitar and set about writing original material, primarily inspired, he explains, by Brazilian thrash/death metal legends Sepultura.

1990 would witness both the band's first performance (at a "championship of rock" event) and a three-song rehearsal tape, but it was becoming clear that not only did the band's death metal sound require a second guitarist, but with Finn fast becoming bored, Samoth and Ronny would also need to find a new vocalist. Samoth had met Ihsahn the previous year at a blues/rock seminar (the two bonded immediately thanks to Ihsahn's Iron Maiden patch-covered jacket), and a short-lived metal project featuring the two had proved them musically compatible. Sensing a kindred spirit, Samoth invited him to join Xerasia, which promptly changed its name to Embryonic and soon released a twenty-minute demo entitled *The Land of the Lost Souls*.

Though Samoth was heavily enamored with death metal, he kept his options open and remained busy during this period, playing in a hardcore/grindcore band called Zyltelab (a play on the Norwegian word "syltelabb," meaning "pig's knuckle") and a drum machine-driven project called Spina Bifida, inspired by industrial bands such as Pitchshifter and Godflesh. Despite some live appearances in these groups, Embryonic was quickly becoming his focal point, and the group continued to evolve, changing their name to Thou Shalt Suffer in 1991 and moving into ever darker territories, adding eerie keyboards to the traditional death metal template.

If ever a promo photo captured a band headed in different directions... Thou Shalt Suffer—guess which two members would go on to form Emperor?

An EP (*Open the Mysteries of Your Creation*) and two demos (the four-track *Rehearsal* and *Into the Woods of Belial*) were issued that year, the trio assisted at various points by Thorbjørn Akkerhaugen (who would later record numerous black metal bands, including Emperor, at his studio Akkerhaugen Lydstudio) and Ildjarn (real name Vidar Våer). The latter was a musician Samoth had grown up with, and who had also played in Spina Bifida and Zyltelab. He would later become known for the unrivaled barbarism of his eponymous black metal project, which Samoth also briefly contributed vocals to.

By now Samoth (or Samot as he initially became, his pseudonym simply a reversal of his birth name Tomas) was engrossed in the black metal explosion consuming his country, and resolved to form a black metal band himself, a venture that Vegard (soon to be Ihsahn, but now going under the name of Ygg) was more than happy to be a part of. Ronny was less keen, however, and unable to find any other interested drummers, Samoth was forced to get behind the kit himself. Initially Thou Shalt Suffer remained the duo's main focus, but soon their energies were channeled exclusively into the new group Emperor and their former outfit was shelved, despite a rough recording of a half-hour-long track intended for the debut album.

Now in need of a bassist, the duo enlisted a local musician named Håvard "Mortiis" Ellefsen, who—like Samoth and so many of his countrymen—had initially discovered heavy metal as a child thanks to Kiss and their popular series of trading cards. Exploring thrash and first-generation black metal bands such as Sodom, Celtic Frost, and Bathory, Mortiis had made contact with Norwegian bands such as Amputation, Darkthrone, Old Funeral, and, of course, Mayhem. He also soon created his own publication, sensitively titled *Zombie Anal Sex Terror*, featuring international bands such as Bolt Thrower and Beherit. He and Ihsahn would first cross paths at school in 1988 when both boys were thirteen, Ihsahn quickly introducing him to Samoth and another metal-loving friend called Steinar Wahl, with whom Mortiis made his musical debut.

"Me and Steinar started our own death metal band in 1990 called Rupturence, that's where it started," explains Mortiis. "We were heavily into the early death metal/grindcore scene so we were into ripping off bands like Carcass, Xysma, and Funebre. I was singing and was total shit at it. We did a few rehearsal tapes, but I don't have copies and I lost contact with Steinar years ago. I know there's even video footage of a 'rock contest' we did—it was absolutely horrendous though, so nobody missed out!"

He laughs before continuing the story: "We did form another band right after, called Wilt of Belial, which was a bit more in the doom metal direction—we shared the drummer, Ronny Johnsen, with Embryonic—but we only lasted two months or so. I suggested we name the band Thou Shalt Suffer but that was rejected and Ihsahn later asked me if he could take it. After that I pretty much gave up music—I just wanted to keep doing my fanzine—but Ihsahn and Samoth asked me to join their new side project. At first I didn't want to, because I was sick of being in bands that would just split up [but] I did join after hearing two instrumental songs they'd put together. I brought some lyrics in and those songs became 'Moon over Kara-Shehr' and 'Forgotten Centuries' if I'm not mistaken, that was summer or fall of '91."

Indeed, Mortiis would end up penning the lyrics for all the band's early compositions, with Samoth and Ihsahn taking care of the songwriting. Together the trio would practice in the basement of a youth club in Akkerhaugen, the village where Samoth lived, rehearsing material and recording one-off rehearsal tapes unique to each fanzine/magazine lucky enough to be sent a copy.

"I remember we'd totally hate the kids on the top floor fucking dancing to Snap or Technotronix or whatever, and we'd be blasting through our songs in the cellar," recalls Mortiis of the rehearsals. "It was a culture shock for sure. The lyrics would deal with fairly dark and morbid issues… our interests were usually revolving around dark and occult themes [and] historic matters such as Elizabeth Báthory and Gilles de Rais. I remember I distinctly stayed away from Satanic themes because I found them redundant and I didn't consider myself a Satanist anyway. In terms of inverted crosses, 666, pentagrams… while I was in the band that stuff wasn't used, but I know pentagrams were used after I left."

In 1992 the band set about recording one of the most iconic demos of the era, a thirty-two-minute masterpiece of primal and malevolent-sounding noise entitled *Wrath of the Tyrant*. Unlike Thou Shalt Suffer—and partly due to the limitations of recording on a four-track recorder—the only appearance of keyboards was on the tape's introduction track, and the

The inlay for the original sleeve of the *Wrath of the Tyrant* demo, 1992. Note the pentagrams and inverted crosses that Mortiis states were not used during his time in the band! Image courtesy of Samoth.

eight tracks of raw and barbaric black metal instead focused on hateful yet catchy guitars and an aggressive battery, topped with a combination of piercing screams, growls, and disturbing chants. Cliché though it might be to label this ridiculously raw sound "evil," it's nonetheless an apt description; the recording sounds more like evidence of a case of demonic possession than a group of young musicians kicking out the jams.

"We were all listening to stuff like Venom, Bathory, Celtic Frost, and Sodom at the time—the darkest metal we could find," recalls Mortiis. "Tormentor, Master's Hammer, Immortal, Necrophagia… a lot of old-school stuff. And of course we were into Burzum, Mayhem, and Darkthrone, who were all coming out with music at the time too. I'd say that Burzum, Mayhem, and Darkthrone definitely inspired us in certain ways, I can't put my finger on it, but I suspect certain very distinct Mayhem riffs inspired the guitar work of Ihsahn and Samoth somewhat."

"We were very inspired by Bathory, Celtic Frost, Mayhem, Darkthrone, Tormentor, etc.," confirms Samoth. "At that time we weren't looking to do something original, but to capture that black metal feel that we had felt through some of these bands. We recorded it in our rehearsal room on a four-tracker, which didn't leave much room for editing and re-takes. It captured a very raw and primal attitude I think. There's a lot of feeling and youthful energy in that recording."

"The demo was very well-received," he adds, "and along with Enslaved's *Yggdrasil* demo, which came out about the same time, it became a demo bestseller at Euronymous' Helvete shop. We shipped tons of tapes out in the international underground network and later we also did a couple of official licenses of the demo, to Wild Rags in the U.S. and a Polish company." [The Wild Rags edition of *Wrath* is probably the best known, although it boasts a different introduction instrumental and, curiously, a cover featuring future bassist Tchort, who does not appear on the recording.]

To say that the demo impressed listeners in the underground would be an understatement. Having earned the respect of their peers, the band soon began to integrate more significantly into the Norwegian black metal scene, the members traveling about a hundred kilometers (sixty-two miles) from Notodden, Telemark, to spend time with Euronymous and the Oslo scene at Helvete, where Samoth even lived for a short time. It was around this period that another resident of the shop, Bård G. Eithun—or "Faust," a pseudonym he took from the German legend of a man who sells his soul to the devil—entered the Emperor fold. Bård was already a relatively established drummer who had played in the thrash act Decomposed Cunt and the influential Stigma Diabolicum/Thorns. Indeed, he had moved to Oslo to concentrate on that very group, but by now the outfit had all but ground to a halt. His entrance into Emperor—alongside Mortiis, his longtime pen pal—allowed Samoth to return to his instrument of choice and thus set up the dual guitars that would characterize Emperor from that point forward.

"I think the first time I actually met [Euronymous] was at a Darkthrone and Cadaver gig in Oslo," recalls Samoth. "I also met Dead at that show, and actually this was also the first time I met Bård Faust. Later I met Euronymous through the Helvete shop where we went to look for records or to hang around. I was never a close friend of his, but he was very support-ive of Emperor and wanted us to sign with his label Deathlike Silence. Bård Faust was more close to him as a friend. Bård joined Emperor in the fall of '92. He took over on the drums, and I went back to playing guitar, which made a lot more sense now that Emperor had started to become a priority for us."

In December 1992 Emperor made their first professional recording, heading to a cheap community studio outside of Oslo called Studio S, where the group recorded four old songs and two new numbers, "I Am the Black Wizards" and "Cosmic Keys to My Creations and Times." As epic as their titles suggest, both lyrically and musically the two songs marked the introduction of a more sophisticated and ambitious approach. This progression was echoed in the updated versions of the demo tracks: though still fiercely aggressive, mid-paced sec-tions now featured among the up-tempo blasting, and keyboards underpinned much of the music, a combination of haunting strings and catchy organ work contrasting with the buzz saw guitars and Ihsahn's possessed screams.

Though relatively simple in execution, the presence of synths on these recordings add-ed a new dimension of majesty and awe to the Norwegian black metal template, recalling the debut of Czech legends Master's Hammer and preceding the work of similarly minded outfits such as Gehenna and Dimmu Borgir by a good year or so.

"The writing process was quite quick, as the only new tracks for that session were 'I Am the Black Wizards' and 'Cosmic Keys,'" explains Samoth. "We had a really good flow and energy in the rehearsal room with Bård Faust on drums. We ended up recording at Studio S as it was affordable and Mortem and Arcturus had recorded there before with okay results. We had already used synth in a more obscure way in Thou Shalt Suffer, so it wasn't such a big step for us really; it added a lot of atmosphere, and we felt it suited our sound, especially the two new tracks. We also became more of a real band by this time, with some real possibilities in sight, so we got more focused on adding a bit more personality to our sound."

There's no doubt that the band succeeded in that aim, and four of the seven tracks (namely the two new numbers plus "Wrath of the Tyrant" and "Night of the Graveless Souls") found a home on the band's self-titled EP, the remainder later appearing on the *As the Shadows Rise* EP, released on Samoth's Nocturnal Art Productions. Appearing in mid-'93, the *Emperor* EP was initially released as a limited vinyl, then as a CD split with Enslaved, both released via Candlelight Records, a UK label founded by Lee Barrett, an employee of Plastic Head Distribution. It was the start of a working relationship that would last the band's entire career and one that owed much to Euronymous, who had initially intended to sign the band to his own label.

"Euronymous got contacted by Lee Barrett and he was curious about Norwegian black metal bands," Samoth recalls. "Euronymous suggested Emperor and Enslaved, and soon the offer came to do a split CD. We thought it was a cool idea, as we were good friends with

Enslaved and they were also supposed to do a full-length with Deathlike Silence. It worked out very well for us and we considered staying with Candlelight after that. We never actually signed any contract with Deathlike Silence, and then Euronymous got killed, so then that was no longer an option anyway. Luckily we hadn't already signed, as then we would have been stuck with Voices of Wonder, who had Deathlike Silence as a sort of imprint label at that point."

"Raw black metal with the majestic keyboards in the background—I felt it was a really nice touch," recalls Lee, who later sold Candlelight but continued to work for the company. "It reminded me of some of my favorite black metal albums, like *Under The Sign of the Black Mark* or *Blood Fire Death* by Bathory. A few bands had flirted with [keyboards], like Nocturnus, but I liked the way it was used tastefully and it gave it a bit of an otherworldly feel that set it apart.

"The first release I did was the Enslaved mini-LP [*Hordanes Land*] and that was a recommendation from Euronymous who I was tape-trading with," Lee clarifies. "He wanted to sign them to Deathlike Silence but he thought it would be a good idea if a smaller label did something with them first, to make them more popular for when the album came out. It was only going to be two mini-albums pressed to a thousand copies each. Back in '93 vinyl was still outselling CDs and it was decided to put both on one [CD], and luckily both bands were all right with that and that's when the label was born. I thought I'd just sell a thousand of each, I never had any intention of running a label. Next thing I know the furor around black metal kicked off and I sold ten thousand CDs in about a month and had a label on my hands by happy accident."

The band was undoubtedly on a roll—in fact, they were now probably the genre's leading band, at least in terms of popularity. In retrospect they were in a winning position, riding the back of two fantastic releases as well as the peak of the controversy exploding from Norway—controversy which they were a key part of, since the previous year had seen Samoth and Faust engaged in church-burning and, in the case of the latter, murder. Still, at this point those crimes remained unsolved, and with Candlelight's support the band made their way to the UK for their first tour.

This, however, would not take part before a lineup change that saw Mortiis replaced by Terje "Tchort" Vik Schei. Having lost his place in Emperor and become embroiled in the legal aftermath of the black metal crimes, Mortiis would later move to Sweden to concentrate on his highly successful solo ambient project, eventually expanding this into a full band and breaking into mainstream consciousness with more industrial metal-leaning efforts such as *The Grudge*.

"I was asked to leave Emperor on account of my verbal abuse and stupid temper at the time," recalls Mortiis. "I was getting to be a cocky fuck by that time so I was probably perceived [by outsiders] as an arrogant idiot in a great band. I did think it was rough for a while because I loved the band at the time. I wanted to live with my girlfriend who was living in Sweden so I figured move there instead. That of course triggered speculation among people that weren't even around, like I was running away, which certainly was not true ... I have always come clean about my past mistakes and would have come clean about this too if it was true, but it just wasn't. I was moving away from Norway, where I lived, because it sucked, and to my girlfriend in Sweden."

"I met with Samoth at Helvete and we visited a local pub and talked about music," remembers Tchort, then best known for his death metal band Green Carnation. "He was known as the Lord of Silence back then so it wasn't exactly a two-way communication—more of a monologue! He sent me a letter (before the a e-mail times!) and asked me if I was interested in playing bass with them and they sent me rehearsal tapes."

Amusingly, the two had first spoken when Tchort initially arrived on the Oslo scene, a meeting that proved somewhat more awkward, as the bassist explains: "Actually it was Samoth who asked about Green Carnation during one of the pub visits we had at Helvete," he

A flyer for 1993's *Fear of a Black Metal Planet* (a pun on the Public Enemy album of almost the same name) UK tour featuring Emperor and Cradle of Filth.

recalls dryly. "An ex-girlfriend of mine who lived near Samoth brought the demo tape with her and he somehow got his hands on it and made quite clear that he didn't like it. Just a couple of months before he had his own death metal band so I didn't see his point."

The original plan for the band's UK visit was for them to support Deicide at their London Astoria show, but that event was cancelled at the last minute due to death threats by animal rights activists aimed at Deicide vocalist Glen Benton. Looking to save this opportunity, Lee Barrett got together with a like-minded individual, Neil "Frater Nihil" Harding, who had recently reinvented the metal wing of Vinyl Solution under the name Cacophonous Records, and signed cult UK act Cradle of Filth. Together the two men created a tour that would showcase both bands, with Emperor headlining and Cradle of Filth supporting at a number of small venues during July 1993.

Though modest in scale, the tour was mutually beneficial to all parties, upping the profile of all the groups and labels involved. Fortunately, given the confined circumstances, the two parties ended up getting on famously.

"We loved them," recalls Cradle of Filth vocalist Dani. "Being down-to-earth English people we messed them around a bit, but they got used to our sense of humor. At that time Samoth was only called the Lord of Silence 'cos he couldn't really speak English… but he still understood our crude humor and sarcasm I think. They were nice, they weren't aloof … we talked about lots of things and then that deteriorated into drinking games. We partied pretty hard. I remember we stayed one night with Darren [White] from Anathema as his dad was away; there were people from Candlelight, Emperor, Cradle... we stayed up two nights, Nick Barker was trying to play Emperor songs on a harpsichord, we had a cake fight, it was proper young lads partying. "

"We were skeptical about [Cradle of Filth] and their music before we left for the tour, but they were very cool guys and we got on very well with them," confirms Tchort.

While partying may have been part of both band's agendas, darker interests were also at play, as both groups took an active interest in the occult—in fact, Samoth would later marry Cradle of Filth's backing vocalist/performance artist/Satanic priestess, Andrea Meyer. Of the two bands, however, Emperor were more extreme as characters, and Lee explains that he occasionally struggled in his role as tour manager. While a visit to the West Wycombe caves (former home of the notorious 1700s Hellfire Club) passed without incident, he found himself tested when the band ran amok in a local cemetery, particularly when one member appeared to become "possessed" and had to be restrained by his bandmates and dragged into the van kicking and screaming.

"They were hard work in some respects," Lee sighs. "You could never tell if they were happy or not, 'cos they didn't say much. Ihsahn was a really nice guy, Faust was a nice guy generally but... it's hard to be polite, but they were trying very hard to be as black metal as possible. Tchort would smoke a cigarette then stub it out on his arm—he had only just joined the band a few weeks before, so was making more of an effort in those terms I think."

"I'd heard from other sources that a murder had taken place but if you're living in the UK hearing all these rumors, you take them with a pinch of salt. Faust did actually get drunk one night and told me what he'd done and if I'm honest I didn't really believe him. I just thought of it as a bit of an adventure, I didn't think about it from a moral standpoint. It was all new to me, running a label, looking after a band—it was just a bit of fun, as strange as that may sound."

The tour was also stressful for Emperor due to its chaotic organization, and Ihsahn would end up suffering considerable burns to his face while preparing for the fire-breathing routine popular within the band at the time.

"We couldn't find any alcohol strong enough," recalls Lee, "we were buying standard vodka and it's just not strong enough, so I bought a tin of lighter fluid. It said 'non-toxic' on the back so I thought, 'This is probably gonna do the job.' He filled his mouth with it, we got the torch going then he blew the liquid out of his mouth and his whole head lit up on fire. Luckily I had a can of beer... he was just running 'round the garden like a headless chicken with us trying to chase him and put it out, he ended up with some quite nasty burns on his face. If you look at the pictures [of the shows] you can see he's not wearing the normal corpsepaint and he's got some quite nasty bubbles on his face. The fire-breathing was off the menu after that."

This was a busy and productive period for the band, who recorded their debut full-length, *In the Nightside Eclipse*, at Pytten's Grieghallen Studios shortly after their return. The

album would be praised almost unanimously by the black metal scene when
it was released the following February,
and remains at the top of countless
"best of" lists. An almost cinematic
affair, it's an intensely atmospheric
and majestic work. On tracks such as
"Into the Infinity of Thoughts" or "Towards the Pantheon"—even the short,
nameless intro track—the chilling aura
of the early/mid-nineties black metal
movement is almost tangible: the excitement, wonder, mystery, and sense
of communing with something greater
than oneself.

Emperor's *In the Nightside Eclipse*, an album whose
popularity has proved enduring.

The song structures, wall-of-
sound production, and performances
are notably refined from the earlier recordings, with greater technique allowing far greater
emotional scope. The percussion is organic and dynamic in both pitch and speed, alternating
between furious blasting and a steady, thunderous pace when the music slows. Fast, dissonant guitars build and fall endlessly, urgent-sounding riffs piling atop one another until the
tension is broken by a slower, soaring passage, the guitars dropping away (an element of the
production that seems to trouble the record's critics) to allow the synths to surge in what
almost feels almost like a moment of spiritual revelation. It is an album of great drama, at
turns terrifying and life-affirming—as complex and thrilling as black metal itself.

Though the influence of Master's Hammer has already been mentioned, it was undoubtedly this album more than any other that established the symphonic black metal sound,
one later picked up by numerous bands such as Dimmu Borgir, Diabolical Masquerade, and
Limbonic Art, to name but a few. Aptly, the lyrics written by Samoth and Ihsahn (along with
Mortiis, since rerecorded versions of two demo tracks also appear) mirrored the grandiosity
of the music, with wordy and poetic explorations of Scandinavia's nature (Norway is explicitly mentioned in the album's opening line) and Satanism. The fact that the album was the
product of four teenagers, one of whom had been turned away from UK pubs weeks before
for being underage, is hard to believe.

"We didn't really know that we had made a groundbreaking album," Samoth explains. "It's hard to know that while you are in the middle of the process of making it. We
knew it was a good album that had something personal and unique to it in our genre, but
we never really saw it becoming one of the classic black metal albums of all time. We were
definitely happy with it when we were done, and I must say I'm very proud of the album,

Probably the most memorable band logo in the genre, designed by Christophe Szpajdel who has gone to create logos for Horna, Graveland, Nargaroth and Wolves In The Throne Room.

even today. Now I see it almost in a historical sense … it had a great impact on how my life has become today actually.

"It was a fairly easy process as far as I remember," he continues. "By this time Mortiis was out of the band and for a while we [wrote] together as a three-piece with me, Ihsahn, and Faust. We also rerecorded 'My Empire's Doom' from the demo—but with new lyrics, it became 'Beyond the Great Vast Forest'—and 'I Am the Black Wizards' and 'Cosmic Keys' … so basically we wrote five new songs for that album. Ihsahn and I wrote both together and individually; we did a lot of jamming of ideas in the rehearsal room, and added on ideas we had been working on separately. All the song structures were done before entering the studio—many of them we played on our first UK tour in the summer of '93—however, a lot of the symphonic keyboard parts were actually made in the studio. We didn't have a keyboard player at the time, so we never rehearsed with keyboards prior to the recording."

"I don't remember much to be honest," admits Tchort of his sessions. "I remember that I played the bass in a huge hall but that's about it. Ihsahn was sick so he didn't do vocals or the vocals were not good enough—I don't remember which—and I remember the Count came down to the studio one time. He had this chain mail on his chest and was eating an ice cream. I think it's a great album with a great atmosphere and good songs. It was my first album [and] I wish that I had some more experience before I did that album as I am sure I could have done a lot better."

Despite Tchort's modesty, and the fact that technical ability is not always a must in extreme metal, there's little doubt that having four members who were all musically skilled, despite their young ages, was essential in realizing such an ambitious album, a point producer Eirik "Pytten" Hundvin expands upon.

"The guys were really dedicated and we were working bloody hard—and I mean *really* hard. The whole band was really competent … that kind of music, it's really, really difficult, drums and guitar, but also bass. The guys were better musicians so we had a really okay studio situation. But it was hard work, late-night, long sessions. We were using a lot of tracks too, up to thirty-two I think, we had to use different recording machines, 'cos I didn't have a thirty-two-track machine. I think we all felt we were creating something. Both Tomas and Vegard were perfectionists: I like people being serious about things, trying to get the best out of the situation and themselves, and they were absolutely having that attitude."

"In some ways it was a bit too much of a success in terms of running a business," laughs Lee. "I can't remember what the pre-sale was, but we had to press something like thirty thousand copies. My distribution deal meant I wasn't going to get paid for sixty to ninety days, but I had to pay for the pressing within *thirty days,* so I had all these releases lined up—like Monumentum—that I couldn't do. The bands ended up getting pissed off and jumping ship to a label called Misanthropy 'cos the owner was sort of hanging in the wings like a vulture, hoping to clean up basically."

The band now appeared to be in an unbelievably strong position, but any plans of touring the album were smashed when Faust was imprisoned, leaving the band without a drummer. Samoth was spending a lot of his time in Oslo at this point, where he was "basically living" in a rehearsal room used by many bands in the scene. So it was that he ended up contributing to several significant releases from 1994, namely Arcturus' *Constellation* EP (bass and guitar), Satyricon's *The Shadowthrone* (bass and guitar), and Gorgoroth's *Promo 94* and *Pentagram* albums (bass only). In early 1995, Samoth was also jailed for his part in the church burnings and with Tchort also imprisoned for his activities in Kristiansand, the band were put on an involuntary hiatus.

Things remained uncertain for some time, and even upon the release of Samoth and Tchort matters were far from resolved due to Faust's extensive sentence. Tchort soon departed (going on to resurrect Green Carnation and work with Blood Red Throne and Carpathian Forest, as well as Satyricon and Einherjer), leaving the band effectively a duo once more.

"When Samoth was released he and Ihsahn wanted to continue making music but they didn't think they would perform live again in the future with Faust being imprisoned for a long time," explains Tchort. "If they were going to record again in the future, they could handle the bass themselves. My firstborn had just died and I was emotionally fucked up and lost interest in music, so when they suggested my departure from the band, it totally made sense."

"Being incarcerated gives you a lot of time to think and you get to view life from a different perspective," considers Samoth philosophically. "I think I grew as a person in that period for sure, but I would have done so being free as well. I don't consider the incarceration as a hard part of my life. Actually, it was a very social part of my life, as I was forced to live around so many other people. I view it as a life experience. As far as the arson case goes, it's not something I think very much about at all. Basically, this whole ordeal is twenty years old, and I look back at it as a very different part of my life, [it] almost seems like a different life. There was a lot of youthful naivety back then, and I'm sure there are things that were said and done that could have been handled different by a lot of people involved in all the turbulence that went down. I try not to live too much in the past, and rather focus on where I am now and what lies ahead."

This would certainly prove to be true, and what appeared to be a badly damaged group would soon rise spectacularly from their own ashes.

During the first half of 1995 Emperor found themselves in the peculiar position of being on a career high, both in terms of sales and acclaim, but also having three-quarters of their lineup incarcerated. Despite this situation slowing the band's progress considerably, work was never allowed to grind to a halt completely. Prior to Samoth's imprisonment the guitarist had written three songs together with Ihsahn, and while serving his sentence he was able to write several more (the most notable being the ironically named "The Wanderer").

For his part, Ihsahn continued to rehearse with a new bassist called Jonas Alver, though finding a drummer proved an ongoing challenge after Faust's incarceration. Not that the band were short of interested and competent players—including Satyricon's Frost and Mayhem's Hellhammer—but in every case the candidates came with substantial commitments to other bands. The solution would eventually materialize in the shape of Kai Johnny Mosaker, otherwise known as Trym Torson, who had been playing with Bergen's Enslaved since their inception in 1991, but was now departing the group following a testing American tour and a shift in direction by the band.

"Right after I left Enslaved, Samoth called me and asked if I was interested in playing with them," Trym recalls. "Of course I said yes. I met Alver on the train and he told me they had tried different drummers like Hellhammer, Frost, Grim (ex-Immortal, R.I.P.), Erik Lancelot (Ulver), so then I was sure it would be very difficult for me to make a difference. I knew Ihsahn and Samoth from before and we were good friends, we had a good connection already and that probably was the edge I needed to be a member of the band."

Working as a four-piece, the rejuvenated outfit forged a new sound that retained the symphonic and orchestral overtones of the earlier material but channeled them in a distinctly different emotional direction. A definite statement of intent, the atmosphere that accompanied the new material was now focused less on awe, darkness, and mystery, and more on bombast, power, and grandeur. Confident with the quality of their writings, the group wasted no time, recording again with producer Pytten as soon as Samoth was available to do so.

"By the time that I was out on parole, in the summer of '96, we had quite a bit of material and a lot of willpower and energy to get going," remembers Samoth. "It was right into the rehearsal room, and by the end of the year we were already in Grieghallen recording and had our first music video that Fall."

This music video—which featured the group sans corpsepaint—would accompany the

A newly regenerated Emperor in 1996: Trym, Alver, Samoth and Ihsahn.
Photo: Runhild Gammelsæter

song "The Loss and Curse of Reverence," the title track of an EP released with much fanfare in the cold October of 1996. Issued both on CD and a limited run of seven and twelve-inch formats (incidentally the first vinyl this then CD-devouring writer ever bought), it further fueled the hunger for a follow-up to *Nightside*. Accompanied by a neo-classical synth reworking of "Inno A Satana" and a "new" song, "In Longing Spirit"—a memorable and dynamic effort that recalled the band's earlier efforts, perhaps unsurprisingly since it had been originally written in 1992—"Reverence" would set the tone for the second album, *Anthems to the Welkin at Dusk*. An aural hurricane, the album showcased an intense and high-paced musical assault that relied far more heavily on double bass blasting than before, complimenting these percussive bombardments with dreamy and almost whimsical synth-based passages and frantic solos.

"They already had several of the songs almost done when I joined," Trym remembers. "The basic ideas for the drums were made, but they also gave me the freedom to try different things. Fortunately *Anthems* fitted my style of drumming much better that *Nightside*, so it wasn't difficult for me to approach the new material."

"The change of drummer impacted the sound a bit," adds Samoth. "With Trym we incorporated some full-on blast beat parts to several of the songs, which created more contrasts in the structures."

Released in the summer of 1997, and featuring "The Loss and Curse ... " smack bang at

An unusually shaped flyer for Emperor's return to London in 1997, incidentally the first live show in the capital your author ever attended.

its center, *Anthems* certainly proved a very different record than its predecessor. Furiously high-tempo for the most part, the song structures were just as twisting, yet numbers such as "Ye Entrancemperium" (whose intro riff was written by none other than Euronymous) proved far less brooding than earlier efforts, instead propelling themselves forward with so much vigor that the whole thing feels like it might derail at any moment. Frantic yet carefully controlled, the album is almost a symphonic take on the spirit of *Wrath*, but with an added swagger, the synths now emulating horned instruments as well as strings, resulting in a knowingly pompous and ceremonial atmosphere that perfectly compliments the band's moniker.

"As with any Emperor release, it was an evolutionary step really," considers Samoth. "*Anthems* was possibly the first recording where we got a bit more progressive and took a real step further into the more complex Emperor soundscape. It was also the first album where we actually incorporated some death metal influences, something that was more noticeable on [follow-up] *IX Equilibrium*. Compared to *Nightside*, *Anthems* has more interesting things happening on the guitars I think, and it's not so layered by keyboard atmospheres at all times. Altogether a very strong album and it has a lot of fighting spirit, struggle, and emotion in it."

Though some listeners mourned the loss of the more mystical overtones of the debut album, the record was warmly received by much of the metal scene, and despite the progressive, classically leaning synth passages, its more aggressive sound made it more accessible to fans of other extreme metal genres such as death metal. Sales and reviews were positive, with the band picking up "album of the year" in *Terrorizer* alongside other accolades, and the group's tour of the album saw them visiting a number of respectably sizable venues.

Indeed, it seemed that the band were finally capitalizing on the creative achievements of the previous years, and the overall impression was one of confidence, the self-empowering lyrics mirrored by a record's sleeve that features the band members sitting upon thrones (the same throne actually) with the tagline 'Emperor performs Sophisticated Black Metal Art exclusively!'.

"The *Anthems* period was great for us," confirms Samoth. "We had really strong songs, we were very eager to build our band and we were finally heading back out on the road again as it had been around three or four years since our last show. As far as our musical direction, it was all a very natural evolution. We became better musicians and more confident songwriters, and really found something that was more unique as a sound."

The band's next release, issued two years later, would prove the most left-field of their career. Released on Thorn's label Moonfog, the *Emperor Vs. Thorns* split saw both bands offering a mixture of new and reworked songs as well as covers of one another's material, Emperor tackling Thorns' best-known number "Ærie Descent" while the Norwegian pioneers waded in with an inventive cover of "Cosmic Keys."

A strange and disjointed offering, the album is nonetheless not an entirely unrewarding one. The industrial bent of Thorns seems to have rubbed off on Emperor, and alongside the Thorns

Anthems To The Welkin At Dusk saw a shift in image, with the band abandoning corpsepaint and appearing as you see them here in the video for "The Loss and Curse of Reverence." Photo: Morten Andersen.

cover is "Exordium," a tense martial/industrial instrumental, as well as an electronic number entitled "I Am" that samples earlier songs by the group as well as "Fall" by Thorns. Also included is another classical synth reworking, this time a strangely jaunty rendition of "Thus Spake the Nightspirit" from *Anthems*, which like "Exordium" and "I Am" was predominantly created by Ihsahn in his Symphonique studio.

"I believe it was presented as an idea by Satyr," recalls Samoth, who met Thorns mainman Snorre Ruch while incarcerated. "We thought it could be a cool collaboration and decided to give it a go. I've always had a lot of respect for Thorns and Snorre's way of composing and playing. I do still count him as one of my musical inspirations. Anyway, the *Thorns Vs. Emperor* album wasn't such a big period for us, and not something we spent a lot of time on."

Only a few months later came the real follow-up to *Anthems*, namely third album *IX Equilibrium*. Like the band's "Ærie Descent" cover, it was recorded and mixed at Akkerhaugen Lydstudio (and co-produced by owner Thorbjørn Akkerhaugen, who had played alongside Ihsahn and Samoth in Thou Shalt Suffer). This time the band built upon the style showcased on *Anthems*, namely a fast-paced, dense, technical sound with orchestral flourishes and an indisputably in-your-face approach. Once again, much emphasis was put upon the conceptual content of the lyrics, which marked something of a turning point, as vocalist Ihsahn explains:

"Without suggesting any great philosophical weight to this album, the title *IX Equilibrium* touches on the alchemical concepts of aspiring and finding balance on a higher level. This is further expressed in 'An Elegy of Icaros,' idolizing a mythical figure who 'broke out' and fell, but where the will to aspire overshadows the outcome. However, looking back I also see how the album is not only taking opposition to 'normal society' (as is so often the case with metal), but also breaking away from the shallowness, hypocrisy, and conservative forces among the 'collective of outsiders' that every underground scene seems to acquire when they start setting the rules for their collective. This is clearly pointed out in 'Curse You all Men!,' which questions the genuine qualities beneath all the image. A third aspect of this album is also self-criticism, questioning one's own authority and motives, like in 'Of Blindness and Subsequent Seers,' though this comes forth more on [next album] *Prometheus*. All in all I think *IX* marks a turning point away from the more traditional black metal expression and points to the more introvert and experimental [fourth album] *Prometheus*."

Though the stylistic evolution was more gentle this time around, *IX* was a pivotal recording. The group largely discarded a sinister atmosphere to pursue more complex and progressive songwriting, while adding elements of heavy metal and death metal. The former was apparent in the more melodic and even anthemic moments on the album, such as the opener "Curse You All Men!" and hopelessly catchy "Warriors of Modern Death," not to mention the occasionally falsetto vocals, which took fans by surprise. The death metal elements were equally contentious, since the two scenes were still fairly divided, though in comparison to the late nineties shift of, say, countrymen Gehenna, these overtones were actually fairly subtle.

"By this time we had a lot more experience as a live band and that affected the way we wrote new songs," states Samoth. "With *IX Equilibrium* we yet again developed our sound and added both more death metal elements, as well as more progressive elements. Emperor was never a band that was afraid to add new elements, so we never thought of it being risky to add death metal elements, we already had some on *Anthems*, and we'd always been fans of Morbid Angel. We had also grown very tired of this separation issue between death and black metal." He adds, "I guess this is where it became clearer that Ihsahn and I had started to grow in different directions."

These diverging musical impulses would, in many respects, bring an end to the band. For his part, Ihsahn was now moving far more intensely toward the experimental and progressive end of the extreme metal spectrum, something that would become apparent with the self-titled solo albums that appeared from 2006 onward. The frontman was clearly already expanding his musical options from the end of the nineties onward, resurrecting Thou Shalt Suffer as a solo neoclassical project and performing in the experimental metal band Peccatum with his wife Ihriel and brother-in-law Lord PZ, vocalist of black metal outfit Source of Tide.

Samoth, on the other hand, increasingly focused upon the death metal roots that had surfaced within Emperor, leading him and Trym to form the band Zyklon with members of

**Men in black: promo photo circa *Prometheus: The Discipline of Fire & Demise* in 2001.
Photo: Sebastian Ludvigsen**

death metal outfit Myrkskog in 1998. Playing death metal with black metal and industrial overtones, the band's lyrics were contributed by ex-Emperor sticksman Faust, and they would issue their debut *World Ov Worms* in 2001, the same year as the final Emperor album, *Prometheus: The Discipline of Fire & Demise*. Written entirely by Ihsahn (who not only produced but also provided the majority of guitar, all the vocals, bass, synth, and programming), it unsurprisingly leans heavily toward a more progressive extreme metal sound.

**Emperor's first reunion tour in 2006. The second would take place some eight years later.
Photo: Shi Bradley/ Midnyte Photography.**

"At this point it was already clear to us that this would be our last album," explains Samoth. "Our last show was at the end of '99, and since then Emperor was never really a functional band anymore. I started to prepare what became Zyklon and put a lot of effort into getting that going. By the time we started recording *Prometheus* I was ready to hit the road with Zyklon, so *Prometheus* ended up being 'the Ihsahn album.' It was a different process than all the other albums, where it had been a strong group effort. On *Prometheus* there were no proper rehearsals, even Trym rehearsed most of the material on his own with click tracks, and the rest we all learned in the studio during the recording process really. I'm proud of that album too, no doubt, but it's the album that means the least to me as I was not so emotionally or creatively involved in it."

"I got a CD from Ihsahn with all the songs programmed with a click and a piano sound," recalls Trym, "so it was very difficult at that point for me to get a feeling of how this album would sound in the end. So I rehearsed on my own, trying to get the essence of every theme and do what I felt was the right way to go. Before we went in the studio, Ihsahn and I had one rehearsal where we went over most parts, to be on the same page. I also used the same click and piano track when I recorded this album, which made it more difficult to get in the 'zone.' I would do some parts quite differently today, when I have all the information of how the final results turned out."

Though unconventional, the album was both commercially successful and critically acclaimed, even earning the band a cover story in *Kerrang!*, something that seemed unimaginable even a few years before. Despite this, the record was never toured and the band split up the same year. This was not the end, however, as Emperor would reform in 2006 and 2014 to play a string of large and highly successful concerts, demonstrating just how wide the band's appeal had become, having traded their early danger for a surprising sense of respectability.

Emperor has continued to be a name held in the utmost regard, their unique and technical approach to composition proving somewhat unwieldy for the bands who followed (compared to Mayhem, Darkthrone, and Burzum, it's interesting to note how few groups have attempted to cover or take direct influence from their back catalogue) but no less popular. All the same, despite hopes that the group would record a new album, the members instead pressed on with their separate projects, Ihsahn continuing his solo work and playing with Ihriel in a folk/metal collaboration called Hardingrock, and Samoth pressing on with not only Zyklon, but also Scum (a "deathpunk" project featuring Faust, Happy Tom of Turbonegro, and Casey Chaos of Amen) and later The Wretched End. An extreme metal band taking inspirations from death, black, and thrash metal, this acclaimed outfit sees Samoth playing alongside Cosmocrator (Scum, Source of Tide, and Zyklon) and Swede Nils Fjellström, known for drumming in bands such as In Battle, Aeon, and Dark Funeral.

"I can't deny that I wish we could have kept Emperor going," concludes Samoth. "But at that time it felt like the right thing to split the band. We were sort of pulling in different directions and had different feelings and visions for what we wanted to do as a band, both musically and with touring. Rather than making too many compromises, we decided to end the band while the spirit was still there. Might sound like a hasty decision, but it was just one of those things. We knew we had built something strong with the Emperor name and wanted to keep that integrity and spirit intact. In retrospect we really did, as Emperor as an entity became even bigger after our split I think. I'm very grateful and proud for all the things we did accomplish with the band, especially when I think back to how we first started and how we built our entity from nothing in the middle of rural Norway, to becoming an international act and one of the key bands in the extreme metal movement. Emperor has been, and in a way still is, a big part of my life."

24
GEHENNA

"Back in the day when I was doing my label Head Not Found, Gehenna was one of the first bands I really dealt seriously with and I'm still very proud to have released the First Spell *mini-CD. Of course they progressed to what others say is greater things, and … I'm happy to see the band left a very interesting catalogue … Gehenna really didn't do any bad albums."*

—Jon "Metalion" Kristiansen (*Slayer Magazine*)

DESPITE HAILING FROM the black metal hotbed of early-nineties Norway, the appearance of Gehenna's 1993 demo *Black Seared Heart* took many by surprise. A remarkably impressive effort, the twenty-minute opus was the product of a group that had not only formed less than half a year before, but had very little connection with the rest of the country's burgeoning scene. However, despite the fact that the band had only begun in January 1993, the musicians within Gehenna had been playing extreme metal—and, in the case of some members, taking part in distinctly anti-Christian activities—for some time prior. Created by Steffen "Dolgar" Simenstad and Morten "Sanrabb" Furuly, both guitarists and vocalists, the initial lineup was completed thanks to Sir Vereda, who took on the role of drummer.

"Sanrabb and I have known each other since about the age of twelve, when my family moved from Oslo to Stavanger," explains Dolgar. "He actually started out in another band called Incarnator for a few months before me and him started our band, though this band became a one-man project before long. Not unlike other Norwegian bands, our first outfit Inanimate—the two of us and a bassist named Robert—had a more death-metal approach to the music but nothing was ever recorded, and we pretty soon parted ways with Robert. This was around '91–'92. We both wanted another musical direction, and we also started working with Sir Vereda—we knew him from school but had gotten to know him better by that time. Early 1993 we decided on the name Gehenna, and the music evolved into the direction you can hear on *Black Seared Heart*. We were only sixteen/seventeen years old at that time."

Dark and aggressive, but dripping with atmosphere and class, the recording steered away from the murky, violent, and fast-paced territories the band's peers were exploring at the time. Instead *Black Seared Heart* showcased a collection of melancholic and surprisingly considered compositions that highlighted melody above all, through a combination of memorable riffs, professional production, and some of the heaviest use of synths then seen in black metal.

The tape itself was limited to a mere hundred copies, but a seven-inch entitled *Ancestor of the Dark Sky*—the debut release of Dutch label Necromantic Gallery Productions—followed, showcasing four tracks from the demo.

"The demo was recorded during a hasty weekend in Soundsuite studio, which has later on become a much-used studio by metal bands—but prior to our

A fairly early shot of the band in *Kill Yourself* zine.

demo the only other extreme band that had recorded there was Incarnator. We had close to no money, and hence could not afford too many hours in the studio and simply did not have time for multiple takes and overdubs to make it flawless. I think it has stood the test of time quite well though."

All the more remarkable given the short time spent recording, the material's distinctive character may in part be put down to the band's isolation from the rest of the Norwegian scene. Much of this was due to geography: the band lived in the southwestern city of Stavanger, a location lacking the black metal community present in other cities like Oslo or Bergen.

"Isolated would be a good word for it," considers Dolgar. "We did not have any contact with any other bands at all until after the demo was released. And I am honestly very happy about that, because that kept us isolated from outside influences during that crucial time when we were forming the band. Sure other Norwegian bands probably had some influence, but Bathory no doubt was always the *main* influence. We just kept to ourselves in the beginning.

"That changed when we released the demo of course, and also when [bass player] Svartalv joined the band, because he was originally from Oslo. But still we did keep more to ourselves than people in Oslo or Bergen did I guess. I am not going to criticize, but looking at some of the other parts of Norway during the early nineties, I think perhaps there was a bit too much of that interchanging of band members going on. I mean, at the most extreme, you could see the same people in a handful of different bands, and that seems a bit unhealthy in my opinion."

Though all bass and keys on the recording session had been handled by Sanrabb and Dolgar, a photograph of bassist "Svartalv" (Kenneth Halvorsen) appeared on the *Ancestor* EP, since he had become a member by the time the photo shoot was taken. By the time the record sleeve was being put together, the band had taken on yet another member, and thus also to be spotted was the name of a new drummer, Dirge (or Dirge Rep, real name Per Husebø) who had recently replaced Sir Vereda. The latter's exit was largely due to his incarceration for the arson of Revheim Church in August 1992—one of the county's very first church attacks—as well as the arson of a Christian community center (an attack carried out with Sanrabb) and, allegedly, some drug-related charges.

The band would head into the studio in January of 1994 as a four-piece with the aim of recording a debut album, but the session would be quickly aborted due to a misunderstanding between the studio and prospective label No Fashion Records regarding budget. It was perhaps fateful, since prior to the next attempt to record, the band would be joined by a keyboardist named Sarcana. A talented player who was originally given the name Walpurgis before changing it for the pseudonym of her own choosing, she had approached the band after their live debut in Stavanger in February that year, a show heavily opposed by members of the church and other protestors.

"The 'church citycommision' [sic] protested our gig, but they lost," the band explained later in mid-nineties zine *Kill Yourself*. "The reason why they protested was because we were a death cult, and we were against all the good forces that protect life, etc., and because of our 'satanic' stage act as well as the contents of our lyrics. The ideological direction of the band was compared to fascism. And this, as you can imagine did not really charm these people. [But] politics have absolutely nothing to do with this kind of music."

Shortly after Sarcana joined the fold, the band headed back into the studio and recorded *First Spell*, released through Head Not Found, the label owned by *Slayer Magazine*'s Metalion. Only twenty-six minutes spread over five songs, it was originally intended as one half of a split album with labelmates Ulver, though it was later decided to release the recordings separately to allow each band greater control over the sleeve design. The *First Spell* cover has in fact proved iconic, its low-contrast, monochrome photograph of two figures (Dolgar and Dirge Rep, as it turns out) with horses, seemingly taken at night, proving just as mysterious as the music within. "Sanrabb and Garm argue to this every day [sic] over what the cover would have been," Dolgar later joked in the *Kill Yourself* interview.

Regardless of its brevity, *First Spell* proved a stunning and unparalleled work, one whose sound is as unique now as it was then, exhibiting a style rarely revisited by any band since. Slowing the pace even further—a point highlighted by a brooding rerecording of the song "Angelwings and Ravenclaws"—the record was saturated in synth, often in the form of an organ voice, resulting in a truly mysterious, almost mystical atmosphere. The five tracks also carried a funereal overtone, not least the closing number "Morningstar," which actually featured a riff adapted from Chopin's iconic "Marche Funebre."

"We spent a lot of time in the woods and in a local cave at night during those first years, trying to soak up the atmosphere, discussing our interests in the occult, talking about different ideas for the music and the band, so it all came from there. We lit a bonfire, watched the shadows play and listened to the sounds of nature. Perhaps that sounds like a black metal cliché, but that is actually the way it was. I know Sanrabb wrote the music for the song 'Morningstar' after attending a funeral, and that the lyrics for 'Unearthly Loose Palace' came

The *First Spell* mini-album, 1994.

from a dream, but I think those nights in nature's embrace were the biggest influence on what we wrote at that time."

First Spell brought the band to the attention of many new fans, and they soon joined the roster of Cacophonous Records, a UK label that had already signed many of the scene's hottest names, including England's Cradle of Filth, Japan's Sigh, and Ireland's Primordial. The first product of this union was the group's debut full-length, *Seen Through The Veils of Darkness (The Second Spell)*. Another striking opus, the record contrasted stylistically with its predecessor, and though it too utilized slow sections and sedate keyboard passages, the material was generally far busier, frequently shifting mood and tempo, unlike the more flowing songs of *First Spell*.

As with *First Spell*, the lead vocals and guitars were split between Dolgar and Sanrabb, with Ulver's Garm making a guest appearance, contributing his voice to "Vinterriket." Once again keys played a prominent role, frequently soaring alongside the other instruments in a symphonic manner very similar to Emperor's *In the Nightside Eclipse*, released the same year. Combined with surprisingly catchy riffs, the result was an epic and driving collection of songs, and arguably the most accessible chapter of their career.

"Close to all the basic song structures for our second album were already written when we recorded *First Spell*," explains Dolgar of the band's evolution, "so the development had already happened. The songs selected for *First Spell* were simply chosen because they had that common approach of being slower, mid-paced songs. We had actually recorded the *Seen Through* album before *First Spell* was finally released, which proves how slow things moved in the underground back then, mostly because of a lack of money."

1996's *Malice* (subtitled *Our Third Spell*) proved a natural successor, the symphonic black metal style refined with slightly more technical songs and a far less mystical atmosphere than *Second Spell*. The production was clearer, and though it did little with the bass (now played by newcomer Noctifer following Svartalv's return to Oslo) it ably separated the guitars, drums, vocals, and synths, the latter proving varied and adding a dreamy and carnivalesque vibe to the proceedings, a stark contrast with the nasty-sounding riffs. If the ethereal forest atmosphere of the past had been laid to rest, then the fourteen-minute-long "Ad Arma Ad Arma" was the nails in its coffin, the nuclear war-themed lyrics bringing a contemporary vibe as much as the industrial sounds utilized in its musical content.

"For this album we felt very strong as a unit, and it was sort of refreshing getting to start working on something new, considering that most of the previous albums were written simultaneously. It is perhaps our most complex album and again we experimented with one of the songs in the studio, 'Ad Arma,' based on a few existing riffs and a concept. At this time I guess we spent more time in the rehearsal room and less sucking up the atmosphere in the woods, which may or may not explain the different atmosphere on the album. In addition to this, Sanrabb and Sarcana wrote a lot of the music together, instead of her being presented mostly finished songs to write keyboards to."

The record received praise from fans and magazines alike and in the same year the band also set about a tour of Europe with Swedes Marduk and fellow Norwegians Mysticum, helping to raise their profile even further at a time when black metal—and keyboard-heavy exponents of the genre in particular—was beginning to break through to a much bigger audience.

With that in mind it's unsurprising that 1998 album *Adimiron Black*—which was preceded by a three-track single *Deadlights*—proved baffling for longtime fans. Now signed to Moonfog, the band had undergone a significant lineup shift, losing all members save for founders Dolgar and Sanrabb, and replacing them with newcomers E.N. Death on bass, Blod on drums, and Damien on keyboards. Stylistically, the band accentuated the nastier side of *Malice*, the synths taking a backseat on an album that introduced death metal influences at a time when it was still controversial to do so.

"We recorded a three-song demo just before Dirge Rep left the band, trying to see which direction we wanted to go musically," reveals Dolgar. "One of the songs, entitled 'Embryo,' sounded like a continuation from the *Malice* album, one—an untitled song—sounded more like a heavy metal song, and the last one was the song 'Adimiron Black,' which was the direction we eventually went in of course. After the demo was recorded, Dirge Rep left and soon after that Sarcana left. Eighty percent of the album was written after she left, so I do not think musical differences were part of her decision to leave. As you may know, she did not pursue any musical career after Gehenna, so I figure she was fed up with the whole thing. I also know she did not get along too well with Blod, who had replaced Dirge Rep on drums halfway through writing the album."

"We did want to go in a different direction after *Malice*, we wanted a crueler and less melodic style. We basically felt *Malice* was as far as we could go in that direction without it losing that sense of cruelty we feel black metal should have. Blod came in the band with a whole different background—from thrash and death metal—and Damien was more into electronic/ambient stuff, so we took advantage of their fresh (to us) approach to music."

Aesthetically, the band had also undergone a thorough reinvention. The cover for *Adimiron Black* was free of occult overtones and featured a gruesome scene of a dead, half-naked women and her gun-brandishing killer, while the record's lyrics delved into tales of war and murder, a far cry from the mystical-leaning, nature-inspired lyrics of old. To some extent this reflected the members' move away from the Satanic/occult mindset of their younger years toward the philosophies its members hold today.

"Being sixteen/seventeen years old, obviously we did not have a whole lot of life experience, and some of our thoughts from those days will seem a bit naïve looking back at them now. I guess everything was just more black-and-white, yes-or-no, back then. But reading some of our old lyrics, I still think there is a lot of great stuff there which I am not sure if we would have said or done very differently today. We are still very much the same people today; only like most other people (and a good bottle of wine) we mature with age."

"I do not read as much about the occult today as I did back then, but that interest is still a part of me. I never did consider myself a Satanist in the conservative, biblical definition of the term, but if you ask ten people what a Satanist is, you are very likely to get ten different answers. Science and philosophy are more important to me now, but keep in mind that some of what we call science today was considered occultism yesterday, and some of today's occultism/magic may be called science tomorrow. The borderlines between these are ever-changing. I do think most Christian believers interpret their Bible too literally, and it amazes me how little they question what is written."

In terms of musical output, *Adimiron Black* proved to be a mere sign of things to come. If that album had flirted with death metal, then the 2000 follow-up *Murder* was evidence of a full-on love affair, the band dispensing with a keyboard player and diving headlong into a world of chugging guitars, growled vocals, and even death metal-style guitar leads.

"On *Murder* Damien had left the band and we decided to just not use much keyboards when writing that album. Personally I feel *Murder* went a step too far into the realm of death metal, and I actually left the band before the recording of the album was completed. I think it is a fairly good album, I just don't think it is a very good *Gehenna* album."

With Dolgar gone the band soon ground to a halt. Despite their high profile in the early days and the gems within their discography, the band went out with more of a fizzle than a bang. Even today they have yet to earn the respect they deserve, especially given their pioneering role in creating black metal that celebrated atmosphere and melody without ever falling into overly commercial territories. Few bands have since touched upon such haunting territories and many, including Head Not Found's Metalion, have expressed surprise that Gehenna did not become as big as outfits such as Emperor. The reasons for

A Cacophonous Records advert for Gehenna around the time of 1996's *Malice* release.

this arguably illustrate the factors—aside from music *quality*—that can dictate a metal band's success.

"I think there are a number of reasons," reflects Dolgar. "I'm not sure if it was the best time for us to leave Cacophonous after *Malice*, because whatever else Cacophonous can, and have been, criticized for, at least they did get us out on tour. Sadly that never happened with Moonfog, although Moonfog certainly were a better label in many other aspects. If we had done more touring during the last half of the nineties—and further on of course—I think we would probably have been a better-known band.

"We get a lot of praise for that album now, and a lot of people think this is our strongest album, but it needed time to grow on people it seems. People expected a continuation of the melodic style from *Malice*, but when *Adimiron Black* was something very different, people did not know what to think at first, and so the album failed a bit commercially in the crucial short time period after its release. Artistically it was the right album at the right time, but commercially it was not. *Murder* probably just pushed things even further into the 'what-the-fuck' category. We were inactive as a band during the period of time when black metal went from the underground into the mainstream media with the focus on music instead of crime, which made it more acceptable as an art form and thus gave it better financial support."

Thankfully the story did not end there. In 2005 the band returned from the apparent dead with one of their most ferocious efforts yet, an album entitled *WW*. As the title makes clear, the work continues with the war themes explored since Malice, complimenting these with icy compositions, perhaps apt since Satyricon's Frost appears as a session musician on drums. With all symphonic elements gone, there are obvious similarities with *Adimiron Black*, and even more so with hypnotic early nineties Norwegian black metal such as Darkthrone, Burzum, and most specifically *De Mysteriis*-era Mayhem.

"*WW* is my favorite album of them all, no doubt," admits Dolgar. "The guitar sound alone on that album is enough to give me shivers down my spine, cold and harsh as the barbed-wire fences during the world wars. Probably our least accessible album; extremely raw and stripped down. I guess it does not appeal to everyone, even within those familiar with modern black metal, but the critics were much in praise."

While Gehenna is still certainly far from a full-time proposition—and indeed seems unlikely to ever become so again, due to other projects, work, and family life—the *WW* album marked a return of sorts, one eventually followed by 2013's *Unravel*. With its long, drawn out riffs and stripped down execution, it is perhaps the band's bleakest effort yet, and cements the band's reputation as a group unwilling to compromise their artistic vision. Meanwhile an almost entirely consistent and essential back catalogue remains available for exploration.

25
GORGOROTH

"For me Gorgoroth has always been one of the mainstays here in Norway as far as black metal goes. Through lineup changes and conflicts Infernus has led the horde of Gorgoroth through the ages, never lacking in quality. They are also one of the bands that has this element of unsafeness [sic] and you never really know what is going on. Norway needs bands like Gorgoroth."

—Jon "Metalion" Kristiansen (*Slayer Magazine*)

FROM THEIR CULT BEGINNINGS in the early nineties, through major-label tribulations, artistic reinventions, and periods of occasionally perplexing output, the career of Norway's Gorgoroth has been nothing if not varied. One of black metal's most recognized and notorious acts, Gorgoroth have made lifelong companions of both strife and controversy, becoming as well known for the strong personalities within the group and the events surrounding them as for the often brilliant music they have created.

Hailing from Sogn og Fjordane, some two hundred kilometers from Bergen, the band's lineup has always revolved around guitarist (and occasional drummer, bassist, and vocalist) Infernus, whose real name is Roger Tiegs. One of black metal's more memorable personalities, Infernus makes for agreeable but intense company, and even after several meetings with him, his sometimes unnervingly serious and carefully controlled manner remains striking. To this day he remains a contentious character, and readily admits that he is not an easy man to work with, a notion perhaps supported by the fact that around thirty musicians have passed through the group during its history.

That said, he is also disarmingly helpful and hospitable, and even though his sometimes evasive answers make it clear that interviews might not be his preferred activity, he is generous with both his time and space. Indeed, the majority of our interview took place at his home, in a meticulously neat living room that faces out onto a panoramic mountain view and hints at the personality of its owner due to the candles, guitars, weapons, and the numbers "666" mounted upon one wall.

"In the beginning when I was a kid I listened to all kinds of heavy metal bands without really having a direct, passionate approach to it," he begins, his voice so low that at times it's little more than a whisper. "Then around my early teenage years I started listening to early black metal bands and thrash metal bands like Destruction, Sodom, and Bathory. It was kind of an awakening, and brought with it something extra, which made me more devoted to the music and had an effect that would be life-lasting. It was a result of my passion for music and metal that I wanted to play and perform and create something myself. To the degree that it's possible to rationally explain why—whether there were other sources of inspiration, or voices telling [me] to do so—would be difficult to explain. I started rather late in time, playing guitar aged seventeen, I think. In retrospect I would have enjoyed having, say, piano lessons in childhood, but coming from a background like mine that was difficult. My parents enjoy music, but not as a passion I would dare to say."

Living in a thinly populated, predominantly agricultural area, like-minded musicians proved few and far between. Nonetheless, Infernus found two other suitable individuals, namely vocalist Jan Åge Solstad, who performed under the pseudonym Hat (meaning "hate" in Norwegian) and drummer Rune Thorsnes, otherwise known as Goat Pervertor. Thus in 1992 Gorgoroth was born, the trio taking their name from J.R.R. Tolkien's book *Lord of the Rings*, and more specifically a barren and lifeless location in Mordor, the land of darkness and fear. The following year saw the band debuting with an almost painfully raw three-track demo entitled *A Sorcery Written in Blood*, named from a line in the Bathory song "The Return of Darkness and Evil."

"They were from another village some twenty kilometers away," Infernus explains of his original bandmates, "so we didn't get to know each other before the age of sixteen. We were living in a small countryside area, located some three hours north of Bergen, and one had to be selective who one hangs around with. The ones you did tended to be the ones who were most similar in musical preferences and maybe their ideological views. It was an exciting time, spirits were very high—getting on with it, that is what mattered."

The unholy opus—which Infernus explains took four months to write and about four hours to record—would not only earn them a contract with France's Embassy Productions, but also land them on the front page of regional newspaper *Firda*, which took umbrage with the Satanic imagery of the band. Other than this burst of attention, however, the band kept largely to themselves during these early years, having limited dealings not only with those in their locality, but also with the rest of the Norwegian black metal scene, though they maintained sporadic contact with Euronymous and the Helvete circle thanks to occasional Oslo visits. It was in the capital that the band would eventually make their live debut, at a 1994 memorial event for Euronymous.

Infernus' dealings with the Oslo crowd also led him to meet Samoth of Emperor, who joined the band on bass for the debut album *Pentagram*, recorded in early 1994 at Bergen's much-favored Grieghallen studio. Opening with the utterly searing "Begravelsesnatt [Burial Night]," the half-hour recording proves a consistently ferocious listen thanks to memorable riffs, an almost constant percussive bombardment, an unfussy yet effective production, and

Antichrist, released 1996, showcased Gorgoroth's more atmospheric face.

Hat's utterly possessed, almost bird-like screeching. Despite its emphasis on speed and aggression, the album also includes brief nods toward atmosphere, most notably on the four songs written by Infernus, such as "Måneskyggens Slave [Moonshadow's Slave]," which contrast with the more driving approach of those written by drummer Goat Pervertor. Now widely regarded as a classic album, the ever-pragmatic Infernus is nonetheless not keen to give his own recollections or evaluations.

"You have a goal and the intention is clear, then you try and make it according to plan," he explains coldly. "To speculate to which degree everything turned out as planned or not is… it appears to me empty talk. Listening to a musician or painter talk about what he did at the time… I get a bad feeling when I listen to such talk. On the day of the release of an album, or the finishing of a painting, then the bonds should be cut off; to talk about how things *were* and how things *came* is not decent I think. I liked the album and when it was being released I was very happy with what we'd achieved, whether I like it today or not is not important."

Following the release of *Pentagram*, the band opted to sign with German label Malicious Records. Despite turning down an offer from Moonfog—the label of Satyricon's Satyr—the band did begin working with one half of the Satyricon duo, namely Frost (Kjetil Haraldstad), who joined as a session drummer following Goat Pervertor's decision to leave the band. Also exiting around this time was Samoth, leaving Infernus to handle all guitars and bass on second album *Antichrist*, recorded sporadically between December 1994 and January 1996. A twenty-five-minute gem, *Antichrist* saw a considerable expansion of the Gorgoroth sound, with sole composer Infernus developing the epic and melancholy atmosphere that he had touched upon in *Pentagram*. The slow and lurching "Sorg" introduces chanted vocals combined with surprisingly emotive guitar passages, while the despairing, self-titled number "Gorgoroth" utilizes fast, treble-heavy guitars and surprisingly expressive bass work to hypnotic effect.

While Infernus blames himself for what he believes was a step down in production values, the album's co-producer, Grieghallen resident Eirik "Pytten" Hundvin, who produced the first album alone, is positive in his recollections: "Gorgoroth developed from *Pentagram* to a colder, more hardcore black metal sound … Roger is a really hard-working musician. He's got really clear ideas about stuff and he was working hard both in keeping the sound as he wanted it and doing his own guitar parts."

Despite a short play length, *Antichrist* proved a varied work, with contrast provided by a number of more thrashy, straightforward songs such as the stomping and surprisingly catchy "Possessed (By Satan)." A similar swagger is evident in the sleeve notes where, after thanking the other "great and skilful [sic] musicians" who appear on the album, Infernus states that "He will also use this opportunity to congratulate, and say thanx to himself for doing his mesmerizing electric guitarsolos, hunting the Christians, writing his poetry of Darkness and Satan, for raping the nuns and kicking the lambs of Christ in the head... " Not far beneath this statement is a dedication to Euronymous (who Infernus explains was originally set to sign Gorgoroth on his Deathlike Silence label) and a large picture of the man himself.

"I met him some times and spent some time at his place but I would not say I knew him as a person," Infernus reflects. "He was charismatic and strong-willed I would say. Maybe one should in retrospect say *confused,* but he was an early part of the history, forming the direction of a scene, so if we should cut it down to the basics I would say he had a hard will and charisma. He was some years older and to the degree that I look up to *anyone* who has drive, who has ambitions, I would say, yes, I looked up to him. He made himself goals and did what it took to go there."

Half the vocals on *Antichrist* were performed by one Thomas Kronenes, otherwise known as Pest (Norwegian for pestilence or plague), who joined the band after Hat (who Infernus describes as "a good guy ... but tired of metal, and black metal in particular,") left the group during recording. Pest had been introduced to the band thanks to a drummer known as Grim (Erik Brødreskift), who had previously played with Immortal and would also appear on Gorgoroth's next album, 1997's *Under the Sign of Hell.*

"It was back in September 1995 as I remember," recalls Pest. "I was doing a show with my other band Obtained Enslavement and at that point I guess Hat had already left the band. Infernus and Grim came to the show to get a feel for me as a singer and came backstage after the show to ask me if I would be interested in joining them, at that point just for the London show with Cradle of Filth and Primordial ... but one thing led to another and I guess we were all satisfied with the way things worked out.

"I knew some of the vocals had already been recorded and it wasn't my album or even my songs, so it wasn't a big deal, it was just cool to finish it. I'd say that definitely Hat is a very, very extreme vocalist and at no point whatsoever can you really catch any lyrics. On songs like 'Possessed by Satan' I worked a bit more on the pronunciation of the lyrics. I think it was more appropriate for that song to do the vocals a little bit differently, the feel of the song is more like Bathory, so there's that half-screaming, half-singing where you can actually hear the words."

The next album (the third and final chapter in what is sometimes viewed as a classic trilogy) was released with the title *Under The Sign of Hell* (surely revealing another Bathory inspiration). It proved another storming record, combining the driving aggression of *Pentagram* with the melancholy and epic atmosphere found on *Antichrist.* The bluster in parts of that latter record is also present, as evident in the gloriously pompous "Profetens Åpenbaring [Prophet's Revelation]" and the irresistible black thrash of "The Rite of Infernal Invocation." Curiously, the band would eventually release a complete rerecording of the album entitled *Under the Sign of Hell 2011*, though predictably fans unanimously opt for the original, despite—or perhaps because of—its rougher sound.

"I still look at it—and I think a lot of our fans would agree—as some of the strongest material as far as Gorgoroth releases go," comments Pest. "For me *Under the Sign of Hell* is like Slayer's *Reign in Blood*, or [Metallica's] *Master of Puppets*, along those lines. I also thought it was important for *Under the Sign* to have some of that vocal extremity so you can't catch everything, although that was largely due to the production."

With three warmly received records behind them, the group set off on their first headlining tour, and while in Germany were approached by representatives of the native label Nuclear Blast, with whom they soon signed. This move would cause no small amount of controversy within the underground, since the label—who were in the process of signing several successful black metal bands including Dissection and Dimmu Borgir—were considered to be a major label and also had Christian connections.

Certainly, the first product of this surprise collaboration, the 1998 album *Destroyer* (or to give its full, Nietzsche-inspired title: *Destroyer, or About How to Philosophize With the Hammer*) did little to put fan's minds at rest. A combination of new and older, unreleased material, it was undoubtedly an incoherent experience, not helped by the fact that the album features no less than nine musicians, with a lineup variation on almost every song. Infernus handled, at various times, guitars, bass, vocals, and drums, with second guitarist Tormentor the only other real constant. *Under the Sign* drummer Grim had departed soon after that recording (sadly killing himself two years later), as had vocalist Pest.

"We did a support tour with Dissection and Satyricon in '96, then another tour that we headlined in '97 with Mystic Circle from Germany, then in between the two tours we recorded *Under the Sign of Hell*," Pest recalls. "It was during the second tour that made me decide to leave the band, it was nothing personal with the band or anything but I had Obtained Enslavement going and the plan was to concentrate on that, though it didn't exactly work out. A lot of *Destroyer* had been recorded ahead of time, because when we did the '97 tour and I decided to leave the band, there was an agreement between myself and Infernus that we would finish up a few tracks in the studio."

Predictably, the record felt more like a compilation than an album, not least due to the inconsistent production and the fact that no less than *four* vocalists appear over the course of eight songs. "*Destroyer* was recorded over a long time span and much of it... well, I would say it was the weakest album of the band," admits Infernus. "We were too much in a hurry and wanted to release something, and it was something which was not solid or mature enough."

The album is perhaps most notable for its introduction of Kristian "Gaahl" Espedal, a vocalist who would eventually play a large part in bringing the group to greater notoriety,

Raising Hell: The original lineup of Gorgoroth: Goat Pervertor, Infernus and Hat, in 1994.

both within the black metal movement and outside of it. "We come from more or less the same area and we went to the same schools at some time," explains Infernus. "I'm a bit older than him, and we didn't socialize as kids, but I was aware of him and chose him when we needed a vocalist due to his work in [his solo project] Trelldom."

Gaahl duly accepted the invitation but joined the group so near to the album's completion that he could only contribute to the opening title track, and indeed is scathing about the album, describing it to me today as "the worst album I know within black metal." It would not be until 2000's *Incipit Satan* that Gaahl would appear as the primary vocalist, recording in Sweden's Sunlight Studio with guitarists Infernus and Tormentor, new bassist King Ov Hell (Tom Cato Visnes), and drummer Sersjant (Erlend Erichsen), also known for his work in Bergen death metal act Molested.

Having a more traditional lineup certainly didn't make for a more traditional-sounding album however, and *Incipit Satan* proved an even more bewildering listen than its predecessor, due in large part to the industrial elements added by guest member Daimonion, better known as Ivar Bjørnson of Enslaved. First emerging during the opening title track—bringing things to a brief but jarring standstill only a minute into the song—the synths and electronics return sporadically throughout the record, most notably on the ambient number "Will To Power"—another Nietzsche phrase.

"We wanted to produce more sound effects on the album and I was hanging out with Ivar of Enslaved, so it was a natural thing to see if he could make his mark on the product," explains Infernus. "I was fond of the sound of the Sunlight Studios—I liked the production of [Darkthrone's] *Soulside Journey* and early Entombed—and wanted to try out something like that, that's why we recorded there. I was also tired of the process of making an album in Bergen—you can't separate work from slumber or socializing. At that point in time I wanted everyone to be prepared to go to the studio and stay in the studio until it was done."

If the electronic touches weren't enough to shock the longtime Gorgoroth fan base, then the final number surely was, thanks not only to its name—"When Love Rages Wild in My Heart"—but the crooning Elvis/Danzig-style vocals of Michael Krohn, well known within Norwegian rock circles for fronting the band Raga Rockers.

"I was from earlier in this band having two different vocalists on an album," Infernus comments, "and also after two weeks the vocalist we had on the album went home without finishing the product. I wanted something different and a friend of mine had some time available, and we'd been socializing somewhat before that and we needed a vocalist and I like his vocals—although in a different setting—so I said, 'Let's try it' and we enjoyed the result. If people want to cry about such things let them do so, it's not a concern. We don't feel a duty to please, the only thing that I should be able to feel is that it sounds right, that's the only thing that matters."

Incipit Satan is clearly something of an experiment, and it's notable that it was released at a time when many of the band's peers were also moving beyond their more conservative black metal beginnings. As to the surprisingly positive song titles, most notably "A World To Win," "Unchain My Heart!!!" and the final track, Infernus is unwilling to confirm whether these reflected a more positive attitude in the mind of their creator.

"I wouldn't go into discussing the lyrics in particular," he says, frowning. "I'm not a very... I would say that I don't have big shifts, my psychology is rather stable. It's not as if I am very much more affected by such issues as love—or am a happy guy—one year and not the next. I would say I am emotional, but I've never regarded myself as *exceptionally* so."

Whatever feelings Infernus was experiencing during the writing process, the atmosphere during the actual recording does not appear to have been a happy one. "It's an album that carries more anger in the studio than on the recording itself," explains Gaahl. "There were maybe too many egocentric persons, especially referring to my good friend Erlend Erichsen, the drummer. He's a character that works solely with his feelings, logic doesn't need to be present in his performing and I think that to find solutions to make that album was very interesting. It was extremely tense. *Insane* at times. We couldn't be in the studio at the same time, some of us. We knew what would happen if things didn't work a bit, so we were good at staying out of each other's way. A lot of artistic credibility in a way, especially with the drums... if [the drum parts] would have been changed or repaired it could easily have turned into a bloodbath." He laughs. "Of course, I stick to the side of the drummer in this situation ... He's probably more of an extreme than I am. I'm like… I won't do things if I can't put *myself* into it, but he will *force* himself into it, no matter what. That's also the reason I don't sing on the final track, it's not a song I want to touch. I've heard it through once and it's just bogus in a way, there's a lot of good melodies but it's been cut to pieces … I think the vocals are completely bullshit."

Stylistically *Incipit Satan* would prove something of a one-off, and following its release the band would undergo a period of significant reinvention, with Infernus taking a backseat in the creative process and Tormentor departing altogether, apparently due to a conflict of personalities with bassist King, among other things. It was King, in fact, who would now take over writing duties along with new drummer Einar "Kvitrafn" Selvik. Allowing two newer members to take the creative reins was a surprising move—and one that would have some implications in later years—but it is one that Infernus stands by today.

"It was because they were high on spirits [*sic*]," he explains. "They wrote music and so did I, but I did not feel comfortable delivering my material at that time. I think that it's the ultimate duty of someone writing music to know your limits. … So I didn't feel I could stand behind what I was writing at that time, and coincidentally that fell into a situation where those people *could* deliver. As it had been *before*, only this time I let others contribute *more* material, which again isn't a big deal as long as the albums can deliver. … It's never important to have complete control, as long as you know the result is going to be good."

King and Kvitrafn's compositions would see the light of day on 2003's *Twilight of the Idols (In Conspiracy with Satan)*, an album which (aside from the now-traditional nods to Nietzsche and Bathory in the title) bore little mark of Infernus, aside from his characteristic guitar playing. An extremely vicious-sounding record, *Twilight* practically tears from the speakers the second it starts, pushing everything into a wall of noise, before spreading its wings, retaining a single-minded approach while nonetheless gradually revealing the subtleties within the assault, thanks partly to its unusually clear production. The album also highlighted King's distinctive writing style, something which may owe much to his unusual musical background.

"Everyone was into metal when I was a kid," explains King, another generally polite but serious individual whose lightning-fast speech and high-strung manner set him apart from both Infernus and Gaahl. "When I got older I got tired of metal and started getting into jazz, but noisier stuff, like avant-garde jazz. When I was twenty-two, twenty-three I was offered to do my first Gorgoroth album and that's how I got into that sort of music. I already knew people in the scene, but I was not that interested … and I'm still not that interested actually. There are a few good bands around, but as a movement I don't see myself as part of it.

"*Twilight* was my first attempt to try and create an album and I'm still proud of it. I realized that because I had all this background in jazz and skills musically… I mean I liked the expression, the rawness, the atmosphere, but I also saw how many other directions it could take, that most of the musicians were not *able* to take. [I wouldn't say] it's a jazz influence, it's about how you are able to use harmonics and how you are able to create moves and I still think there's lots of unexplored fields and moves that can be put in this sort of music, to make things progress. Because you should never repeat yourself, it just gets boring for you. It's important to change, develop, and go somewhere. We had to take the band somewhere from the past though, so you also have these old Gorgoroth things in there too—I had to learn all the old songs to play live as well. But I never *think* when I make music, it's more about getting the album to work, it's not like a conscious choice, it happens by itself."

Twilight was well received by both press and fans, many of whom hailed it as a return to form, and the album put the band on the road to even greater success. As things transpired, however, a single show the following year would give an even bigger boost to the band's profile.

In February 2004 Gorgoroth traveled to Kraków in Poland for what is now an infamous performance, little knowing that it would boost the band's profile immeasurably. Taking place at a television studio known as Studio Krzemionki and recorded by national TV station TVP, the event was arranged by native label Metal Mind, who already had a history of filming extreme metal bands at the location for DVD release. An unusually elaborate production, the show made for an impressively morbid spectacle, featuring four naked and hooded mock-crucified models (two male, two female), burning torches, barbed wire, banners depicting the Sigil of Baphomet, and a large amount of animal blood and sheep heads.

The show would probably have made an impact on its own, but was quickly elevated into something more significant thanks to the massive furor it caused within Poland, with heavy press coverage in the days that followed. More pressing than the contrived shock of the mainstream media was the fact that the authorities were contacted even before the show came to a close. The result was the arrival of the police, who confiscated the tapes of the performance the very same night, leading to a full criminal investigation, with the band and promoters accused of causing religious offense as well as mistreating animals.

The latter charge had few legs to stand on—no pun intended—and the band quickly distanced themselves from claims of animal cruelty (particularly Gaahl, who later explained that he rarely eats meat for animal welfare reasons), explaining that the heads were bought from a butcher, and not the result of some unusually large ritual slaughter. The blasphemy charges were taken rather more seriously, however, with the heavily Roman Catholic population taking particular offense due to Kraków's status as the home city of then-Pope John Paul II. Incredibly, the band were ultimately forced to appear in court (not for the last time), though they escaped any punishment due to their ignorance of Polish law; the promoter was less lucky, receiving a heavy fine. On the plus side, the tapes would eventually be returned to Metal Mind, and ultimately released on DVD under the title *Black Mass Kraków 2004*.

"Basically I think it was just some woodworkers, carpenters working there who really had a relatively good day at work, putting together parts of wood for props," Infernus told me in an interview for my fanzine *Crypt* shortly after the trial. "One clever mind of them probably thought that this should be an opportunity to earn some easy cash, so found some antique paragraph of blasphemy law that you probably have in England and we have in Norway, that they actually don't use anymore, and referred to that law and called in the local police. So I think it was originally economically motivated ... by these fifty-year-old men, who felt that we were stepping upon their religious feelings. Which of course is nonsense. Then of course later on it became something which the public dived into, the local bishops made comments on it and so on. I think in the beginning we were not intending to make such a hassle about it, nor would the Catholic church, from their point of view, see any benefit in making so much hassle about it."

News of the incident spread worldwide and marked the beginning of a run of controversy that would ensure Gorgoroth's reputation as one of the most notorious metal bands on the planet. With the Kraków incident still fresh in people's minds, Gaahl found himself in court again, accused of assaulting and torturing a man in his house over a period of six hours. The trial received a great deal of attention, due both to Gaahl's near-celebrity status and the rather sensationalist nature of the case, which included, among other things, an allegation that Gaahl had given the man in question a cup to bleed into, so that the singer, or the victim (the story varies), could drink the blood, a charge Gaahl denied by explaining that he was merely wishing to keep blood off his carpet. Gaahl was sentenced to both a hefty fine and jail time, partly because—as the media soon discovered—this was not his first interaction with the penal system, the vocalist having served several previous sentences for similarly prolonged and extreme uses of violence, reportedly causing long-term injuries in at least one of those involved.

Like other controversial black metal figures before him, Gaahl began to attain something of a cult status, his seemingly mythic qualities reinforced by a brief but austere appearance in the widely viewed documentary film *Metal: A Headbanger's Journey* (2005). Another U.S. documentary, *True Norwegian Black Metal* (2007), added further fuel to the fire, playing heavily on Gaahl's intimidating interview manner, while also including an inaccurate narration that described him living in seclusion (when in fact he had a flat in Bergen), and saying that as a child he had only one classmate, who later killed himself (in fact he had attended a regular school, apparently the same one as bandmate Infernus). "The school story is completely out," Gaahl laughs. "They tied four stories into one, four different stories with four different people."

Gaahl's memorable appearances would paint him as a powerful and intense individual, boasting not only charisma but a dark and otherworldly personality. This is not an inaccurate portrayal, as Gaahl certainly is an unusual individual with a lot of presence. What such appearances don't convey is his surprising warmth and good humor; in fact, of all the people interviewed in this book, probably none laughed as frequently as Gaahl. Indeed, when speaking to the man himself it can be hard to picture the extreme and violent person described in these trials.

"I have extreme differences," he replies thoughtfully when I put this to him. "I despise violence. I can't even watch action films. But when it's needed, it's needed. Since I react and trust so much in my own feelings and emotions, I guess that's one of the reasons I can seem so different. I think that's the answer."

Gaahl maintains that far from being an aggressor, his acts of violence have only occurred where justified. As he told UK newspaper *The Observer*, "Everything deals with respect... The way I think of it is that you have to punish ... or teach... anyone that crosses your borders so that they won't do it again." He also asserted during our interview his belief that he (along with other members of the black metal scene) has been unfairly persecuted by the Norwegian authorities due to the nature of their beliefs and music.

"Varg would never have been sentenced to twenty-one years if not," he asserts calmly. "As a young man he would have received twelve or eight years. I don't think I would have been sentenced at all [for the assaults], I would have gone free, especially the last situation. When someone comes with a weapon to your door, it would be hard to persuade the police that, 'Oh, I didn't think of using the weapon!' [But] of course they played on all the clichés... If you saw his first explanation—which of course the police 'lost'—I apparently had a stone altar in my living room with twelve disciples in a circle, standing round, and we were going to sacrifice him. Of course this [statement] had to be destroyed as it would have killed the whole [case for the prosecution], but that was one of the first rumors that went round from the supposed witness. It was more of a charade than anything—my underground friends discovered before the trial who sent him."

As Gaahl explains, the incident was not an isolated event, but linked to his previous incarceration. "The two biggest sentences I received are linked to each other," he sighs, "but there's other ones that are separate and are just ordinary fights in a way. I've been to prison four times and I have been sentenced about fourteen times."

It seems safe to say that such a number would be considered fairly high by most people, even by Norwegian black metal standards. "Naaaaah," he laughs. "People run to the police whenever I do anything. I've always been under attack. The thing is, if you continue to win, people have a tendency to go to the police. I think it would be quite a normal amount in an area like this ... it probably deals with a lot of my friends in a way, and also the surroundings. There's this idea that people should not be different. [Though] it might be one of the reasons, I don't think black metal has so much to do with it. Maybe long hair."

As it turns out, much of Gaahl's conflicts seem to stem from his earlier years and his self-confessed involvement in gang activity, rather than any feuds relating to the black metal scene. Such personal conflicts also appear to have played a large role in the controversial views he held in his youth, views he expressed in a now-infamous 1995 interview in Polish zine *Holocaust* that has recently resurfaced. In this short but memorable feature, Gaahl expressed admiration for Hitler and the ancient Roman emperors, and stated, "There are always someone to kill or curse, especially subhumans (nigers, mulattoes, muslims and others!) [*sic*]."

In a 2008 interview with Götz Kühnemund of German *Rock Hard* magazine, Gaahl explained how such a mindset had been built up, and ultimately, it seems, destroyed: "In the early '90s, there were all these different youth gangs in Norway and one thing led to another. I was involved in gang fights and had false friends … there was no political disposition—not with me nor any of my friends. But you had to profess allegiance to a certain group if you wanted to defend yourself and not get your ass kicked … I've always had friends from different cultural backgrounds, hence I was exposed to different ways of thinking from the get-go. That's probably why I've never developed a deep set of political beliefs. But there have definitely been changes and an evolution in my thinking. I'm a different person today."

"I guess it had a lot to do with friends and surroundings," he explained in a more recent interview with me. "There were a lot of wars going on and it probably put more into it than was needed. Because it was not like one had this as a big agenda, but of course one speaks against the one that you confront, so it's easy to get into the topic in an interview. … I did have friends with different heritage, so it's not like it was one-dimensional in that sense, but there were different groups and you might focus more on what is your enemy at that point and that's the way things are easily put out into the world. That's maybe why I'm more known for Gorgoroth, because it is attacking someone, attacking a point of view. War gets attention."

Gaahl was not the only one whose appearances in court attached greater infamy to Gorgoroth. Sometime later Infernus and a friend were hit by rape allegations relating to an incident at his property in 2004, where a woman claimed to have been punched and raped by the two men. Both Infernus and his codefendant were found guilty in a 2005 trial, but proclaimed their innocence and appealed the sentence, claiming the sex was consensual, the result being that Infernus' conviction was changed to "gross negligent rape"—the judgment essentially being that he did not take part in any rape but should have been aware of it and prevented it. Ultimately he served 120 days for this and illegal possession of firearms.

By now the mounting notoriety of the group was proving too much for Nuclear Blast, and the label dropped the band in late 2004, something of a relief to both parties, it seems.

"I think both we, and Nuclear Blast, are celebrating every day we are not having to do anything together," Infernus told *Crypt* shortly after. "They basically gave us hassle all the time. They were standing in our way. It culminated in the last era, but it was more a mentality problem of some of the people working there. It wasn't any big thing they did, but the point is that they didn't do anything to support us, as they should have done. They also gave us some hassle due to some of the mongose [sic] moral views upon things which they, first of all, shouldn't have any views upon."

The stresses surrounding the unit appear to have had a far-from-detrimental effect on the band's creativity, with 2006 seeing the release, via Regain Records, of one of the group's finest efforts yet, an album entitled *Ad Majorem Sathanas Gloriam*, Latin for (with a slight translation error) "For the Greater Glory of Satan." Featuring Frost on session drums, with all music composed by King and all lyrics written by Gaahl, the album perfected the approach introduced on *Twilight*, retaining the wall-of-noise style while making a noticeably greater use of dynamics.

Ad Majorem was also notable for being the first Gorgoroth album sung entirely in English, although the contents of the songs have remained somewhat suppressed since Gorgoroth keep their lyrics unpublished, even going so far as to legally challenge fan sites that list them.

"In a way I think it was more of an ego trip 'cos I wanted to separate Trelldom and the other bands I work with," explains Gaahl of the choice to deviate from his mother tongue. "I think it is also to help me separate, since lyrically I have definitely made the Gorgoroth lyrics more into Trelldom lyrics, dealing with a lot of the same topics. It deals with a lot of runic and heathenistic topics, it deals with everything that can be … I probably should release these lyrics sometime, as I am very satisfied. Even 'Carving a Giant' … I would have to write a book if I were to describe all the connections in that song. It deals with the mystical and sacred realm of myself. I don't even know how to describe the [use of the word] 'giant' without feeling that I didn't succeed in putting the whole aspect of the 'giant' there."

Whether or not listeners were able to entirely comprehend the messages communicated by Gaahl, *Ad Majorem* was a hit with fans and critics, and the band established themselves as one of a very small number of black metal acts capable of achieving commercial success without watering down their sound or message. Indeed, all three members claimed to be dedicated Satanists, albeit with three very different interpretations of what that entailed.

Despite this common ground, all was not well within the group. Even in 2005, when I first met the band in person, the distance between the three men was striking, with Infernus at one point making the surprising admission that he had no idea of his bandmates' personal music tastes. Perhaps inevitably—given such strong, eccentric personalities—the cracks were beginning to form and the three soon found themselves embroiled in a lengthy internal battle, one sparked when Gaahl and King moved to "fire" Infernus from the band in late 2007. Citing his lack of creative input and a disrespectful manner toward session members and other creative partners, the band also stated in interviews that the move had been prompted by Infernus' support of the pro-hard-drugs "Never Stop the Madness" campaign and recent rape allegations. However, Gaahl confirms that such problems predated the release of *Ad Majorem* and indeed caused much deliberation regarding the release of that album.

"It was a really, really difficult decision to release it as a Gorgoroth album, but due to time and haste we decided to do it anyway," he explains. "We were actually in contact with the record label with the concerns around it. I regret more the mixing than the actual release though, because I definitely like Infernus' touch to the guitar, and if we had to use another guitarist it wouldn't have the same edge to it. Maybe it would be better … but it wouldn't be the same."

"We discussed it a lot, because we did think, 'Okay, he is the founder of the band,'" explains King of the split. "But even though it was a difficult choice, because of everything we knew behind the scenes, we thought this band will either fall apart and die, or go into two factions and see what happens. Actually me and Infernus are probably more on the same path, but when it came to running a band it didn't work with Infernus, at that point we simply didn't function as a band. To be honest it was Gaahl who thought of it. After some years he couldn't cope with being in a band with Infernus. For me it was then a simple choice, 'cos the only guy I had actually worked with in Gorgoroth was Gaahl, I never worked musically with Infernus. At that time, and in the end, he didn't pay much interest in the band, he was sort of in the background, so it was a natural choice to say, 'If this is going to break into two factions then I am going to continue working with Gaahl.'

"We don't work well together at all either," he admits of the singer, "but the result at the end turns out good. He's not taking part in the songwriting process, he never presents anything of his ideas, he just sits in the studio for hours and hours and hours staring at the wall. Then he goes home because he did not feel inspired that day. It's a very, very slow process to work with him [but] as long as you know the final result will be good, it's worth it."

Moving quickly following the split, Gaahl and King recruited various session musicians—including ex-Cradle of Filth/Dimmu Borgir drummer Nick Barker and Enslaved guitarist Ice Dale—and began touring using the Gorgoroth name and logo, playing some rather poorly received European club shows as well as a truly first-class performance at Germany's Wacken festival in 2008. Legally, however, there remained much debate about the status of the Gorgoroth name. Though Infernus continued to claim sole ownership, for all intents and purposes it appeared that the name was now the property of the Gaahl/King camp, not least since they had now been signed by a new label.

For that reason it was all the more surprising when Infernus was declared, over one year later, to have won the legal battle. As it transpired, King had in fact only filed an application for the trademark prior to the split with Infernus, as opposed to having been granted it through a court victory, as was generally understood (either through misrepresentation or misinterpretation) by the press and public. In fact the sole court case would not occur until 2008, with Infernus filing a lawsuit for misuse of the Gorgoroth name, a case that ended some six months later in his favor.

"This is just lies and misconception, being spread as part of a propaganda stunt," Infernus explained to me for an interview for *Metal Hammer*. "There was only one court case. One. It is always the case in Norway that you will get a trademark registered in your name when you apply for it, whether another party disagrees or not, it's just a formality. So they tried to present this as a court decision, which it was not. So we had to appeal the registration and, in theory, wait up to five years. As I didn't have five years I took them to court instead and that was the only court case which was held. The court then decided that King and Gaahl's trademark registration had to be deleted because it was invalid. They tried to register someone else's property as their own."

Gorgoroth in Bergen, late 2009, after their comeback performance at Hole In The Sky festival: Pest, Infernus and Bøddel. Photo: Ester Segarra.

More surprising than the verdict is Gaahl's reaction to the events. Far from being aggrieved, he appeared philosophical when we discussed the situation shortly after the ruling, even making some surprising revelations when asked if he had any regrets about the dispute.

"No I don't," came the quick reply. "It has gone the way I wanted it to. Well, I wanted to win the name, but I would have given it back to him. Yes, by all means, that was the plan all along. Why should I have the name? I would have given it back and I think Infernus knew this. In the trial he told me, 'I knew that I would get the true story from you, but I didn't expect you to speak so much for me.'

"We could have appealed and would probably have won then," he continued, "but it had already moved away to the extent that I wanted it to. It [the band] went in a way it shouldn't go, so that's why it had to be killed. It doesn't seem very logical but I don't necessarily work with logic. I [claimed the name] solely as an egocentric bit and even though I mean that everything is done right, Infernus needed a slap in the back of the head, and that goes for the other parties involved—one has to be harmful sometimes and it was time to burn Gorgoroth to the ground. I actually wanted to release an album in [the Gorgoroth] name—because there were only two albums under the name Gorgoroth that dealt with the topic I brought into it, and I like to work in threes—but my heart didn't come to do so—maybe the meaning was that this wasn't supposed to be released under this name."

Following the court case, Gaahl and King would adopt the name God Seed (taken from a song the two had penned on *Ad Majorem*), the plan being to release the material King had written for the next Gorgoroth album under this moniker. Ultimately, however, Gaahl would not record any vocals for the album and the material would be released on *The Underworld Re-*

gime in 2010 under the band name Ov Hell, with a lineup consisting of Dimmu Borgir vocalist Shagrath, Frost, Ice Dale, and ex-Gorgoroth live guitarist Teloch. Gaahl, meanwhile, would take a temporary hiatus to escape the circus that had built up around him following the court case and his announcement that he was gay, a rather unique event in the black metal sphere.

The God Seed name would resurface following this hiatus when Gaahl and King decided to collaborate once more in 2012, returning with a new lineup and a debut release—confusingly, a CD/DVD package of the 2008 "Gorgoroth" Wacken show, minus the Infernus-penned material. The band would then release an impressive album, *I Begin*, later the same year, featuring a new lineup that included the talented Stian "Sir" Kårstad of Trelldom and whose tracks (quite logically) alternate stylistically between King/Gaahl-era Gorgoroth and Trelldom.

Meanwhile, attention turned back to Infernus. Just as Gaahl and King had been busy following the split, so had the band's founder, who began working with Swedish drummer and producer Tomas Asklund, already well-known for his work in Dark Funeral and latter-day Dissection, as well as for being a committed Satanist. Together the two crafted the 2009 album *Quantos Possunt ad Satanitatem Trahunt* (which Infernus explains translates as "To Convert as Many as Possible Into Satanism") with the aid of returning guitarist Tormentor, returning vocalist Pest—now living in Tennessee—and, curiously, Frank Watkins of renowned death metal act Obituary, also a U.S. resident.

"There are practical problems obviously," Infernus told me in an interview for *Metal Hammer* UK, "but I chose people not according to practical reasons, but by what I deemed to be necessary. Above all it's nice to know that I have people around me which I can trust."

Though Pest would depart again in 2012, the album was a hard-hitting return to early Gorgoroth, combining aggressive, unfussy, and confident thrashy black metal with slower numbers that drew on the same epic melancholy and discordant territories as found on records such as *Antichrist*. Reviews generally proved favorable, and once again the lyrics (written by two friends of Infernus whom he describes as "not musicians, but devoted Satanists") were withheld.

"The one who has the sharpest ears and the dedication will be able to find their way into the material without any guiding from anyone of us," explains Infernus with a brief smile. "As a bonus, by not releasing the lyrics we make it more difficult for cover bands in the future. We recently had one cover band, and that was enough. They even called themselves Gorgoroth, I think… "

26
TRELLDOM

"Trelldom is a really strange band because not all the musicians are really into the [kind of] black metal music we did in the early nineties. Some of the guitar is really strange for that sort of music, very spacey, going places I never heard in black metal before. If you listen to the playing, especially the guitar and bass, it's not traditional black metal, but it's kept in a black metal tradition."
—Eirik "Pytten" Hundvin, renowned black metal producer

WHILE THEIR relatively high profile may be due in part to the notoriety of the group's central protagonist, Kristian "Gaahl" Espedal, Trelldom remain one of the more impressive and artistically driven acts from Norway. Formed in 1992 and named after the Norwegian word for slavery, the band initially saw guitarist Bjørn I, later known as Tyrant, writing the majority of the music, with Gaahl providing lyrics and vocals as well as overseeing the composition process, a role he had apparently adopted even before Trelldom's existence.

"Before I dared to place myself before a microphone I had helped other bands," he recalls. "There was a band called Helheim—not the same one that is in Bergen—one called Dies Irae … there were probably four bands I was helping out. I helped guide them as to what I saw was right and what I saw as wrong in their doings. I didn't start anything myself until '92. I met the one that later called himself Tyrant by accident and somehow we managed to work together and spoke the same language. He introduced me to some riffs, I had lyrics lying around, it was just an immediate connection. We basically formed that band having known each other for one week."

Trelldom would debut in 1994 with the *Disappearing of the Burning Moon* demo, also featuring bassist Børge "Taakeheim" Boge and drummer Rune "Goat Pervertor" Thorsnes, both also known for their work in Gorgoroth. A five-song, twenty-minute effort, the demo used rolling drums and long, relatively minimal riffs as weapons, although closing number "Til Evighet" deviated from the formula thanks to a crawling pace and bleaker vibe.

"We had great difficulties getting people that we wanted to work with," explains Gaahl. "Taakeheim was a friend of Tyrant who originally just played bass, but we used him as a drummer at rehearsal occasions, so we became a threesome in a way. Then I got in contact

One-man operation? The photo for the cover of *Til Evighet...* sees Bjørn and Ole Nic positioned behind main man Gaahl.

with Goat Pervertor and managed to hijack him and get him on drums and that's when we recorded *Disappearing of the Burning Moon*. Of course this was the first time in a studio, and it was not a *proper* studio either—there was a hole in the snare drum, so the sound of it is a bit strange. I stood for eight hours singing before we recorded because the band did not know the songs without the vocals, so I was kind of tired of them when I finally recorded them. It was not the *best* circumstances, but I have been to worse studios later on ... especially concerning Gorgoroth."

Whatever the technical hurdles, the resulting demo tape was enough to grab the attention of *Slayer Magazine*'s Metalion, who signed the band to his label Head Not Found and released their 1995 debut album *Til Evighet* ... ("To Eternity ..."), a nine-song effort that included rerecordings of four of the five demo songs. Though it was recorded by Eirik M. Husabø, the same producer as the demo, the opus was free from the murky sound of *Burning Moon*, and also lacked the deeper, growled vocals Gaahl employed during some parts of the tape. A notably crisper, icier-sounding effort overall, it also picked up the pace, and with the passionate and varied blasting of "Ole Nic" (a collaborator of Tyrant in the band Betrayer) it achieved a monochromatic take on black metal that resembled the sound of countrymen such as Gorgoroth, Burzum, and Darkthrone.

"I knew Metalion from exchanging letters, demo tapes, and music in general," says Gaahl of the record deal. "I didn't want to release anything but he managed to convince me to do so. It is still just a rough tape, I still have the proper recording myself—I just gave him the loose tracks, the unmixed release. I didn't want [the real version] to become public in a way, I wanted to keep it a bit closer. I don't know why, it was just a decision I made … since everything was beginning to lose [the] grip of its honesty around that time. Also before I recorded I had fired all of the other members so I just got in contact with Tyrant and asked him if we should record it and keep it safe in a way. So he found a new drummer [Ole Nic] and we rehearsed it two or three times and went into the studio and recorded it. Then I finished it off without them knowing, which is [the version] I have myself. It was basically to hold the creation. I don't know if it will be released, it probably *should* be, it's way better… it deserves the light of day."

The album packaging certainly made clear the temporary status of the lineup, stating, "Trelldom is: Gaahl, vocals, poetry and concept," and "This album is dedicated to Gaahl, and Gaahl only.—Await to behold the sinister words and divine poems of the philosopher Gaahl."

Not long after its release, however, the band did find a stable lineup, consisting of guitarist Ronny "Valgard" Stavestrand and bassist Stian "Sir Sick" Kårstad. Along with a drummer known as Mutt—who later played in two other projects with Gaahl, Gaahlskag and Sigfader—the group recorded at Grieghallen with producer Pytten in 1997 and 1998. A truly stellar effort, the resulting album *Til Et Annet…* ("To Another…") expanded the band's sound considerably, working from the same raw Norse black metal blueprint as its more generic pre-decessor, but adding numerous inventive songwriting touches along the way. These not only injected vital character but demonstrated a working band, despite Trelldom having earned a reputation as a solo project.

"I don't know how they work before they are in the studio," explains Pytten, "but when they're there I think they're each able to express themselves as musicians. They work as a team, with their own abilities, though I think [Gaahl] is the one who keeps it within the black metal frame."

While Pytten's able production highlighted the work of all musicians involved, the focal point for *Til Et Annet …* was undoubtedly Gaahl's impressive vocal performance.

"I'm really pleased with it," says Gaahl, "For my own sake I think there's *too much* vocals on it—now I find it a bit too extreme on the vocal part. But it's one of my favorite albums no matter what band. But still the singer could be a bit more…" he pauses, "well, he could *shut up* a bit more."

Gaahl's approach on the album sits in contrast to his calmer, more measured work with Gorgoroth, and at times the singer appears to push himself to his limits. "Slave Til En Kommende Natt" proves a good example of the man's range, complementing the pronounced bass lines with a combination of gravelly rasps and a distinctive, strangely slurred singing voice that drew comparisons to Public Image Ltd's John Lydon in its *Terrorizer* review. The slower title track also makes use of Gaahl's singing voice and features two of Gaahl's vocal lines running consecutively, a technique also used on the unforgettable final number "Sonar Dreyri," a testing and hypnotic eleven-minute epic centered around a single two-chord guitar riff.

"The last track ... Jesus man, that's some guitar playing," sighs Pytten. "A once-in-a-lifetime performance. Just doing two bloody chords, but keeping it going for over ten minutes—that's amazing. It was done in one take—I tell you one thing, it was really, *really* hard work doing that one take for the guitarist, but what he delivered was all he was able to and was amazing. He was very exhausted," he laughs, "and of course he hated the two chords when he came out of the recording room!"

Over these two chords Gaahl's vocals become increasingly tormented, culminating in some of the most extreme vocals yet contributed by a black metal band. "I did torment the rest of the band with having to play this song over and over again," laughs Gaahl. "I didn't reveal how I would do the vocals, I just did it mentally until I got in the studio. Due to the lyrics, it's a double vocal thing there, though it's in old Norse, so it wouldn't make sense to anyone now anyway. One of the vocal lines is the original, the other is put in later to make the conversation between the two ... well, not *characters*, it's a dialogue between one's self in a way. It's easier to see this kind of dialogue in the title track, which is the young, impatient one toward the old, patient one. That is a part of my own character, but also what I come from prior to birth. But then we are dealing with my hidden beliefs in a way, and I can't go into this without confusing people. I'm not a teacher in this form."

Lyrically speaking, the Trelldom albums—like his later work with Gorgoroth—deal primarily with Gaahl's spiritual beliefs, which primarily concern Norse shamanism and Odinism, along with beliefs concerning blood memory and ancestral knowledge, and the traveling back and forth within lives and time.

"I would say I am part of Odin," Gaahl explains today. "As I always try to explain, I use the word Satanist only because the world speaks with a Christian tongue and in their words I would be a Satanist—it is the opponent. I wouldn't say [I was] solely Odinist, [but] if I am Odin, then I am an Odinist."

While many black metal bands interested in the ancient Nordic religions either see Odin and the Norse gods as metaphorical archetypes, or instead real metaphysical beings, Gaahl's outlook is somewhat more complicated. "It's probably a bit of both in a way, it's difficult to explain because it deals with such a large sphere, but I think both of your suggestions would be correct in a way. Even though it might seem contradictory, neither excludes the other. I always try to put out information and I kind of feel that instead of seeing what I'm putting out there, that [people] narrow it down, they seem to put everything you say into a contradictive form, while I try to make people see that things *have* to be contradictory in a way, to tie everything together."

The superb follow-up album *Til Minne ...* ("In Memory...") would again feature Gaahl, Valgard, and Sir, along with session musicians Are (on drums) and Egil Furenes, who contributed traditional Norwegian Hardanger fiddle, primarily on "Eg Reiste I Minnet." As with *Til Et Annet ...* the album works with a fairly traditional Norse black metal formula while adding small but distinct touches, such as a brief yet surprisingly tranquil break on "From This Past"

Braving the Nordic winds: Sir, Gaahl and Valgard in 2007, circa the *Til Minne...* album.

and the spoken-word vocals of "Steg." Despite the continuity between the two records, they would be separated by a gap of almost a decade and it was not until 2007 that the album was released.

"We already recorded the album in 2001," Gaahl reveals. "Pytten the producer was busy, so were all persons involved ... During this space between [2001 and 2007] we always worked on the album, the guitarist never put it to rest, he added a lot to it, went in and out [of] the studio while I was in prison and did things. It is maybe my favorite album of all time."

Whereas at the time of the first two Trelldom albums Gaahl was known only among fans of the band, by the time *Til Minne* ... was released his work in Gorgoroth had made him one of the genre's best-known characters. Such notoriety would only be increased by the vocalist's legal battle with Gorgoroth founder Infernus and the news that he was gay, something of a shock for a scene which has a reputation, perhaps not entirely undeserved, for homophobia.

"Well it seems like humanity in general is this way," ponders Gaahl. "I don't know why sexuality should be seen so much as a danger for anyone. I don't think people should care what happens in a relationship between two people that they don't have anything to do with—why should they? It's really weird, but I don't think it's just black metal, I don't think it's just metal, I think humanity has always been this way. And especially after Semitic values entered the world. To be worried about what others think of you is a fault that humanity has brought along for a long time. I've never been worried about what people might think or feel about me."

All the same, an incident involving Gorgoroth/God Seed members and entourage, which apparently left a man hospitalized backstage at Wacken in 2008, was reportedly sparked by homophobic comments aimed at Gaahl. Elsewhere, modeling agent Dan De Vero, whom Gaahl was reported to have had a "close relationship" with, has also reported threats from the black metal community. Nonetheless, Gaahl reports that he has never encountered any hostility regarding his sexuality in person. Whether this comes down to the fact that Gaahl would be an unwise target for aggression, or a sign that the black metal scene is more tolerant than generally accepted, is unclear. Certainly his friendship with Bård "Faust" Eithun presents another level of complexity to an issue that is sometimes presented in black-and-white terms.

"It's been mainly positive I would say," Gaahl reflects. "I feel that there's a lot of people I have worked with that [are] a bit afraid to work with one's self and it's easy to blame one thing, so we'll see what we can do. I have to be a bit awake when it comes to this, it's not like there's a lack of friendship or disrespect when it comes to this, but there are elements that still worry me a bit, my earlier colleagues that have maybe the wrong reputation, are a bit worried about these things. But I've always seen it that way that if people don't dare to greet you no matter what, then you shouldn't waste too much time on them either.

"If the transformation had happened earlier in my life I probably would have told it then as well," he continues of his coming out. "So even if I may live in the past and the future at the same time, I still try to live in the present and what happened then was the case, and sadly I'm a bit too honest with what I am. I'm probably not good at being private, even though I'm a very private person. It was just about a period of one year that this would have been able to put out at a prior stage. I could have [done so then] but it was to protect the involved parties and also friends around me that were a bit worried about what people would think of them."

While Gaahl has sometimes expressed a wish to distance himself from black metal, he has always maintained a strong desire to continue with Trelldom—partly since he does not consider the project to *be* black metal—and despite its sporadic output, the project looks set to continue.

"There will be nine albums, even if the last one is released when I am ninety or something," he concludes. "The nine is the nine aspects of the soul or what we now use today as the word 'soul.' In the Norse speech we used nine different words for it, the psychology was highly developed, whereas with Christianity it has been reduced to two or three words. So I'm trying to explain and work on these different aspects with Trelldom. It's of course difficult as it has escaped our language nowadays. I'm trying to get in contact with it at least. I will probably add something like [the closing experimental tracks on previous albums] because

Vocalist, songwriter and actor Kristian Eivind Espedal, better known as Gaahl.

I want things to be connected, I want to put all the albums in one thread without going chronologically. It should be able to skip back and forth, it's in a way accidental as to what I pick out and what part of the soul I would work with. It needs to live on its own in a way. But definitely some of the aspects will have to be less wordy—I do see this happening because when I try to contact 'this,' there are some things which can *only* be sound."

THE OPUS MAGNUM

MAYHEM PART III

"I think it must be … Jesus, it's the opus magnum *of black metal, it's the opus magnum of* extreme metal, *it's a statement, it's a super-important record in the whole extreme metal genre. It's a great band and this album is unbelievable."*

—Nergal (Behemoth)

WHILE THE POTENTIAL of the early-nineties incarnation of Mayhem was cut short by Euronymous' murder in the summer of 1993, the crowning achievement of the man, the band, and in some people's opinion the *genre* was completed shortly before his death. Named *De Mysteriis Dom Sathanas* (or as the cover art confirms, "*Dom. Sathanas*," the "Dom" being short for "Domini"), the album's title translates as "Of Lord Satan's Mysteries/ Secret Rites" and was, according to Dead, named after an occult book he discovered.

That it was Dead who came up with the title highlights just how long the album had been in gestation. In fact, the legendary *Live In Leipzig* album—recorded in November 1990 but released almost three years later—had already captured Dead, Euronymous, Necro-butcher, and Hellhammer performing half the album's eight numbers, namely "Funeral Fog," "Pagan Fears," "Buried By Time and Dust," and "Freezing Moon." The latter track had also been recorded (along with demo number "Carnage") earlier that year by the same lineup for the *Projections of a Stained Mind* compilation on Sweden's CBR Records, and three of the remaining four new songs had also been in existence since Dead's time in the band.

But Dead was sadly no more, and due to the subsequent use of the photos of his body, Necrobutcher had also left the band. This left Euronymous and Hellhammer with a substantial void, one they initially filled with Euronymous' partner at the Helvete store, ex-Perdition Hearse and Abhorrent/Thyabhorrent frontman Stian "Occultus" Johansen. Providing bass and vocals, Occultus delivered the lyrics in a manner not dissimilar to Dead, both in terms of sound and delivery. "He's a total black metal head and very self-destructive," Euronymous

Euronymous playing his trademark Gibson Les Paul, still an unusual choice of axe in black metal circles.

told one zine, "which is very good regarding our stage show."

"At first it was only meant that I should play the bass but now I'm also doing the vocals," Occultus told Dutch zine *Masters of Brutality*. "[The album] will be even more delayed now… I have to learn all the trax for it and Euronymous is going to jail for 4 months because he cut a guy so he had to sew 38 stitches [*sic*] I don't have the slightest idea of when the *Mysteriis Dom Sathanas* will be released."

Occultus was right to have doubts over the album's release date and would also soon see for himself the more aggressive side of Euronymous' personality, the two falling out in a situation that, according to an interview of the time with Burzum's Varg Vikernes, led to a metal cross (stolen from a cemetery and apparently engraved with the words "my girl") burnt in his garden and used to smash his windows.

In fact, after Occultus' departure it was the Burzum mainman who played session bass while the group rehearsed without a singer, this lineup captured on the popular rehearsal bootleg *From the Darkest Past*. While Mayhem interviews at the time claimed Necrobutcher had departed due to the birth of his first child, the bassist is keen to make clear that this was not the case.

"I would say that [Euronymous] went behind my back and finished the recording," Necrobutcher clarifies. "He came to my place and borrowed the bass equipment I had, so I kind of knew what was going on, but at the same time I was in grief over Dead. I went over to Sweden to participate in his funeral and was kind of paralyzed over the loss of my friend. But I never left Mayhem, [they] carried on rehearsing in my absence. After it was recorded Euronymous invited me to his place and we were listening to it. Varg was playing only as a session musician to finish the album and we were talking about getting together again for the ten-year anniversary and doing a show in Oslo."

The band would also recruit Snorre "Blackthorne" Ruch, whose work in Thorns had proven massively influential upon many musicians within the Norwegian scene, not least Euronymous, who was hugely impressed with the guitarist's unique style of riffing. For his part, Snorre had joined due to the frustrating inactivity of his own group, the original agreement being that he would assist Euronymous with Mayhem in return for help with Thorns.

"I joined Mayhem when they had recorded most of the album," says Snorre. "I had a deal with Euronymous that, 'Okay, maybe you should play guitar in Mayhem and I will play guitar in Thorns and solve both our problems.' But then later I was thinking, [there's] hassle in both bands, maybe I should just join Mayhem and bring some of my songs over. But that happened after *De Mysteriis* was recorded. The Thorns riff on *De Mysteriis* [on 'From the Dark Past,' and taken from Thorn's 'Lovely Children'] was something he asked [for] and I said, 'Okay, of course, I have thrown this song away, do whatever you want with it.'"

Now all the band needed was a voice to finish the album. Ambitiously, Euronymous elected to contact Attila Csihar (best known for his work in the Hungarian band Tormentor and electronic project Plasma Pool) rather than induct one of the many vocalists in his home country. Yet having gone to the trouble of tracking down the vocalist and persuading him to travel to Norway, Euronymous' preparations for the recording of the vocals seem to have ceased, and arrangements for Attila's sessions were somewhat loose to say the least. In fact, it would be Snorre who ended up completing the lyrics, and though not contributing any recordings to the finished album, he would also spend time rehearsing with the band while the vocal parts were being worked out with the singer.

"When Attila arrived I was shocked that Euronymous hadn't prepared anything for him with lyrics," recalls Snorre. "I think Necrobutcher found a lot of Dead's drafts for [the remaining four tracks] and I had to rearrange them into songs so that Attila could sing them. I joined for rehearsals with Attila—I guess we rehearsed about fourteen days in Mayhem's rehearsal studio in Oslo. Then we went to Bergen [to record] at a later point and stayed a few days in Varg's apartment. [Attila] was a really nice chap, he came up here with his girlfriend and we hung out. He smoked a lot of pot during the recording sessions to get in the mood I remember, and that was kind of funny 'cos we were like, 'Is this good or is this bad?'"

"I didn't know about the scene," admits Attila. "I got in contact with [Euronymous] in '91 and he said they were working on the recording and when it's done they will invite me to sing, although there was a short period when they were talking that they might find another vocalist. I think it was that they both liked Tormentor, him and Dead, and I was told that I was Dead's favorite vocalist, which was an honor. I think we were talking about me joining the band, he wanted me to move to Norway but I said I had to finish my studies."

Though seemingly a long-running plan on the part of Euronymous, the decision to use Attila was certainly a surprise for many in the Norwegian scene. After all, not only was he surrounded by an abundance of local talent, but many of the vocalists in the country actually knew the songs on the forthcoming album inside out due to an instrumental tape that was making the rounds, a point Grutle of Enslaved recalls with a smile.

"I remember it was still not decided who should be the vocalist, so all of us were wondering who would get the phone call. Then suddenly we heard the guy from Tormentor was doing it! 'Tormentor, aren't they Hungarian?' and we thought, 'Yeah, that's going to be cool.'

So people were a little bit pissed that they didn't receive the phone call, but they thought, 'Well that's going to be interesting' and it was! Actually while [Attila was] doing the vocals Øystein went to the callbox and called me and said, 'He sings like a sick priest, he sings in Latin, with an accent, it's incredible!'"

There's no doubt that Attila's spirited performance has proven to be a defining factor of the record and in some quarters a controversial one. Deviating from the more traditional approach of his Tormentor days, the vocalist adopted a more demented and theatrical style, incorporating a noticeably drawling delivery and lurching creepily from screams and rasps to an almost operatic form of singing that made a feature of his distinctive Hungarian accent. It was a bold step that spoke of confidence on the part of the long-absent band, and one that stemmed directly from the freedom Euronymous had allowed the legendary vocalist in his performance.

"The way of singing it, we were talking about how to do it of course," recalls Attila. "I heard some demo recordings that had been done by Dead and Maniac before, but I like individualism… so when I talked to Euronymous in the studio I said, 'Why don't we try something else instead of making again the traditional screamed vocals?' The 'De Mysteriis Dom Sathanas' song, when I looked at the lyrics there was this Latin line so I thought, 'Let's do this voice there.' I came out with the low vocals with more melodies, and he liked it so much we did the whole recording that way."

While Euronymous' preparations for the vocals were minimal, his vision for the rest of the record was absolute and saw him leaving nothing to chance, particularly in terms of sound and acoustics. "Euronymous had specific ideas about each instrument and he had specific ideas about echoes," recalls Attila. "The drums were recorded in a huge concert hall, solos were recorded in a room and he was moving round all the time and saying, 'Okay, there we have it.' If you listen to records from the time and then *De Mysteriis* you hear the production is far and away better than anything else."

"The whole album was recorded in very spacious areas," confirms producer Pytten, who captured the opus in Grieghallen during 1992 and 1993. "Øystein, Hellhammer, and me were walking about talking about how to do it and I really wanted to use the stage for the drums. I really like big sounds—especially for the drums—and reverb on the leads. So the drums were done on stage and [in that hall] you have nine stories going up, so we closed the room side, but kept all the height. A lot of the guitars were done with closed miking, but all of the stuff with reverberation on the record was done with a Marshall stack and one microphone in a huge room, the main hall, and we were just moving about until we thought, 'Ah, this is it.' You find the sweet spots then you start working and you can't play that sort of loud music during daytime because the place is full of people, so we did that kind of stuff at night. You really needed thorough planning, you needed mixdowns—think about it, you only had sixteen tracks and at times you're using nine just on the drums."

It wasn't only the drums that would require large numbers of tracks. In fact, a crucial

Grieghallen (The Grieg Hall) in Bergen, Norway. Photo: Nina Aldin Thune, courtesy of Wikipedia.

ingredient in the creation of the album would be the repeatedly multi-tracked guitars, which create a huge (yet suitably icy and treble-heavy) wall of sound, a perfect backdrop for the dynamic percussion and the minimal approach of the bass lines. It's an approach that certainly separates the record from the thinner-sounding efforts of many other Norwegian acts during this period.

"He was very conscious about sound," continues Pytten, "Unlike a lot of people within Norwegian black metal he was using a Gibson Les Paul and a Marshall head and that's a very traditional rock sound. But he was really conscious about how it should sound, so he was telling me what he wanted and I was using my skills to produce it. Lots and lots of hard and serious work. Sometimes you were getting extremely tired and you wanted to go home, but when you looked at what you'd been doing you'd think, 'Okay, it was worth it."

And so it proved. Sadly Euronymous would never see the pressing of the finished masterpiece he had worked on for so many years, his murder occurring just prior to the original release date. It was in many ways the end of an era for the movement he had done so much to further, a genre that only continued to explode following his untimely death.

"I think that he would be working very hard with correspondence," comments Necrobutcher when asked what he thinks Euronymous would be doing if still alive today, "and distributing music. He would probably continue the work that we had already started with Deathlike Silence. He had signed all the good bands that Voices of Wonder stole before they went to separate places, so I think if he didn't die he would have all these great bands on this label. Before he died he saw all these bands popping up in Norway that came after us, so he saw the explosive development from day one, the feeling we had rehearsing in '84,'85 that just grew and grew. It's too bad he passed away and is not here to enjoy it."

"The worst thing with that was getting a letter from him in my mailbox the next day," sighs *Deathcrush* vocalist and longtime contact Maniac. "He sounded very determined about his future; unfortunately for him the future was terminated."

The record's release was ultimately postponed, as the parents of the guitarist had requested that Varg's bass lines be removed, a point that Hellhammer initially agreed to but ultimately decided against. To this day they remain, simply lowered in the mix and without credit to Vikernes. The distinctive cover art for the record was also kept as Euronymous intended: featuring Trondheim's massive Nidaros Cathedral bathed in an eerie blue, it is a perplexing image for a Satanically themed album but makes more sense when one learns that it was apparently Euronymous' plan—and one *Deathcrush* drummer Manheim suggests he would have attempted—to blow up the cathedral, reportedly with assistance from Varg, who was found to be in possession of a large amount of explosives at the time of his arrest.

Indeed, many facets of the finished album mirror the increased level of seriousness Euronymous had been injecting into the black metal scene, the whole presentation contrasting strongly with previous release *Deathcrush*. The album is generally considered one of the archetypal Satanic metal albums, though Necrobutcher—who was present for the writing of the lion's share of the material—is adamant that this isn't as clear-cut as it might seem.

"We were not practicing any religion, we made music," he explains simply. "The fact that the album is called *De Mysteriis Dom Sathanas* makes people think we are [a] Satanic band, but it's based on a book called that, which is about Satanism but is not about *worshipping* it. It was a book that inspired Dead to write the lyrics, but he is not around to answer that question and I never saw the book myself. If other people feel this is Satanic music, maybe it is. This is the great thing about art, you make it but other people can find other things in your art that you don't see yourself or that you don't think about yourself when you make it or perform it."

Finally issued in the middle of 1994, the album would be the final release on Euronymous' Deathlike Silence Productions. While the group's stellar reputation and macabre backstory would have been enough to guarantee attention, even objectively speaking it was a milestone in the black metal scene and hailed as a classic upon release. The long-delayed *Live in Leipzig* the previous year meant that four of the eight songs were already familiar to fans, not least "Freezing Moon," which arguably remains the most iconic song in Mayhem's back catalogue, its aura of despair still unparalleled in the band's catalogue or indeed anyone else's. Elsewhere Euronymous' own composition techniques were married to the snaking discordance of Snorre's writing style on newer songs such as "Cursed in Eternity" and "From the Dark Past." Masterminded by Euronymous, but with the close link to the Dead/Necrobutcher/Hellhammer lineup, the record is aggressive, cold, detailed and single-minded, and testament to both a new era of brilliance for the group but also the delayed realization of its previous lineup's work.

Several freezing moons later: *De Mysteriis Dom Sathanas* **is finally released in 1994.**

It was also the end of another incarnation of the band, and with half its participants either dead or incarcerated, the group once again ceased activity, destroying any plans Attila had to join the band permanently, at least for a time. In fact the singer would only learn of the band's fate some months later, and soon entered into a lengthy period of inactivity and depression.

"I read it in the papers," he sighs. "I only had the phone numbers for Varg and Eurony-mous and both the numbers didn't work, so I thought the guys were on holiday. Then I read [the news] in a Hungarian version of *Metal Hammer* and I thought, 'What the fuck is this?' I couldn't believe my eyes."

28
THE BEAST REAWAKENS
MAYHEM PART IV

EVEN AS EURONYMOUS was being laid to rest, the beast of Mayhem was once again stirring back into life. Meeting at the funeral of the guitarist, Necrobutcher and Hellhammer discussed the subject and agreed that they should rebuild the band, but recognized that this would be no easy task. With Dead and Euronymous gone, Occultus and Varg out of the picture, and Attila unreachable, the band looked to another ex-member, *Deathcrush* vocalist Sven-Erik "Maniac" Kristiansen, with whom Necrobutcher was still in close contact. No longer living in the mountains of Telemark, he had moved to the country's capital and was working on several musical projects, including one called Status Fatal, which he describes as "in the vein of a helpless Joy Division."

"I was in another band with Maniac called Fleshwounds," explains Necrobutcher. "It was a trio and a drum machine. He was in some kind of art school where you pay a fee and then you live there—they had a 'How to Be a Sound Engineer' course and Maniac had moved there from the mountain village where he lived. So when I talked to Hellhammer at the funeral I told him I was already in contact with Maniac and that he had improved his way of singing and was willing to step in."

The following year the lineup was completed thanks to teenage guitarist Rune "Blasphemer" Eriksen, who lived outside of Oslo and only had a marginal connection to the black metal scene. Originally discovering heavy metal via his older sister and her metal-loving boyfriends, he had developed a passion for the technical late-eighties thrash of outfits such as Slayer, Holy Moses, and Coroner. He was also a fan of death metal and had even started a band playing Obituary covers, releasing a demo in 1991 and playing a handful of shows the same year, including one with Kreator. Though not a particular fan of black metal (he explains that Rotting Christ's *Thy Mighty Contract* was one of the few examples he favored) he had gravitated to the Oslo scene out of a hunger for greater extremity. He eventually crossed paths with Hellhammer, who invited him to participate in another of his musical projects, a post-Mortem act called Descended, from which guitarist Steinar "Sverd" Johnsen had just been kicked out.

Maniac, Hellhammer, Necrobutcher and Blasphemer—the face of Mayhem from 1994 to 2004.

"I went to the same school as Hellhammer's girlfriend," recalls Blasphemer, "and he had heard some rumor that I was a very good guitar player. I bumped into him in Oslo and he had this side project thing with the guy from Arcturus and he asked if I would take part. That suited me very well as I was hanging around Oslo and wanted to do something in that scene. So I met up in the Mayhem rehearsal room. I think it was Mortem, we did a couple of tracks, but then a disaster happened so I kind of fled the city. It was me and the vocalist, we were drunk and somehow managed to trash the rehearsal room. I think someone had broken into his equipment box and we went totally nuts and started trashing stuff and that led to my departure from the scene for a few years. There was a lot of bad blood of course, and people were… not *threatening* but, like, Hellhammer said I managed to ruin his bicycle and was very pissed off. It's kind of funny and absurd now."

Fast forward to late 1994, and the talented guitarist would be offered the opportunity of a lifetime despite his earlier faux pas. "I kind of isolated myself and tried to start a black metal band with some childhood friends from school," he continues. "I was playing drums and we did that for a year and a half and were about to record a demo, but before we managed to do that Hellhammer got in touch with me again and said, 'Hey, long time no see, would you like to join Mayhem?' I thought, 'What the fuck is this?' but my heart was already there, I wanted to get more into this extreme stuff and really go for it. And at eighteen, you don't give a fuck about anything, you just go for it. So that's what I did."

"Hellhammer knew him, but since this episode that they vandalized our rehearsal space he was not the first on the list," explains Necrobutcher dryly. "But after a while we thought we would check him out. For one year we had been looking at different options… we were thinking to maybe wait until Snorre got out of jail, but that was still seven years ahead."

The move to resurrect the band initially proved universally unpopular, and fanzines bemoaned the decision to bring back the band in the absence of Dead and Euronymous, a point that Maniac admits made him hesitate. "I was very reluctant, but when I heard Blasphemer play all doubt was surgically removed. That's how I embarked on a roller coaster of cutting flesh, bloody pig heads, alcohol, misanthropy, and the guitar riffs of a genius. I think most people wanted Mayhem to remain buried. But Mayhem is still there. I am sure a lot of these people are not."

"There was a lot of crap actually," recalls Blasphemer. "I think Hellhammer got more shit than me. I mean, it was not like I forced my way into the band—I was asked and I accepted. I remember a couple of times when we were out he would end up in discussions, kind of defending why he did this. People were not that convinced and were certain that we would do this to go out and earn as much cash as possible. But with time it sort of bounced off because we did nothing. I mean, I joined in October '94 and we did not play until '97, we were just rehearsing all the time."

"We got no support at all basically," confirms Necrobutcher. "Nobody was excited. People asked how we could go on in Mayhem without Euronymous. A lot of people said that in the beginning. We felt that the only way to shut their face was to release good shit… That's why we rehearsed for four years."

"I think it was this common feeling that we should have material," Blasphemer confirms. "I was starting to compose, I had written 'Ancient Skin' and 'I Am Thy Labyrinth,' those two songs we were already starting to play at the end of '95 and every so often people would come by and like it and people started to get more belief. I'm not sure why it took so long, we were only doing weekend rehearsals and I was still living where I was raised, I was still at school so I was living partly at the rehearsal room and going back home sixty kilometers from Oslo. And weekend rehearsals meant beer of course… "

Just as *De Mysteriis* had endured an epic gestation period, so too did any evidence of the new lineup's existence. The first preview, rather appropriately, came via 1995's *Nordic Metal: A Tribute to Euronymous*, which featured a rerecording of the *De Mysteriis* track "Pagan Fears." It was not until the summer of 1997, however, that the band made their official return, thanks to a live show in Bischofswerda, Germany. Though hardly their finest performance, it marked their first appearance abroad since their eventful 1990 tour of East Germany and Turkey, during which they had not only recorded *Live in Leipzig* but played the first black metal show in Asia, in the Turkish city of Izmir, despite police interruption.

The first new Mayhem release was also issued in 1997, a two-track single making its way into the hands of attendees of the comeback show, as well as some of those at the London show later that year. Featuring a cover photo from 1987 that Euronymous and Necrobutcher had originally intended for the cover of *Deathcrush*, it was limited to five hundred copies and consisted of a rerecording of "Necrolust" and an exclusive version of the aforementioned new song "Ancient Skin." Now signed to UK's Misanthropy Records—a decision that raised eyebrows, since the label was most famous for having Burzum on their roster—Mayhem followed this a few months later with the EP *Wolf's Lair Abyss*.

Featuring four songs—"I Am Thy Labyrinth," "Fall of Seraphs," "Ancient Skin," and "Symbols of Bloodswords"—along with an electronic intro track, the opus remains one of the band's most intense recordings. Frequently high-paced, it is a mass of distorted bass, searing guitars, and blisteringly fast but detailed percussion, all topped off

A memorable *Terrorizer* cover captures the band's official return with *Wolf's Lair Abyss*, 1997.

by the inhuman screams of Maniac. Retaining the single-minded and often linear fury of *De Mysteriis*, the EP is nonetheless more technical and calculated, with unusually complicated drum patterns and guitar work breaking up the furious assaults.

"When you rehearse old songs as often as we did in those early years you begin to understand the patterns," reflects Blasphemer, "and I think subconsciously I wanted to have some of the similarities from [*De Mysteriis*]. But at the same time it has this weirdness, the weird timings, 'cos I was always into that technical side. It was a combination of what I did and the older Mayhem stuff."

"It was clearly aggressive people playing aggressive music," comments Necrobutcher. "Negativity, drinking a lot… a bunch of pissed-off guys you know? Hellhammer was the only one who had a job—he was working as night guard so it didn't collide with the rehearsals— so we were poor, *piss-poor* 'cos we didn't do anything else but the band."

Mixed by the band along with Knut and Garm of Arcturus, the *Wolf's Lair Abyss* tracks were consistent in style if not in sound. That's hardly surprising, as the recordings were carried out in two sessions after some of the initial results sounded *too* extreme, even for Mayhem's tastes.

"We actually recorded in a really good studio with a producer who was a member of TNT," laughs Necrobutcher. "We listened to it afterwards and realized we'd recorded it too fast, it was *too* aggressive, so we had to go back to Farout Studios in Oslo and record several of the songs again."

Despite these hiccups, the band did well to re-establish themselves within a scene that had been skeptical, earning magazine covers and healthy sales in the process. For most fans the tour that followed the release was also the first opportunity to see the group live and the band made sure to capitalize on their touring opportunities, decorating their stages with the pig's heads and animal skulls that had become their trademark. Maniac too proved a compelling and dramatic frontman, balancing a keen sense of showmanship with the same self-destructive streak that had characterized Dead's performances, this manifesting most obviously in his onstage self-mutilation.

"My approach was to enter another mindset and to get out of there alive," explains the vocalist. "During my best performances I think I managed to be in another world. I was not in the presence of an audience but a black vibrant light. My worst performances are best forgotten but unfortunately they are very vivid. Drunk beyond humanity. The cutting was directly inspired by Dead, especially after patching him up after the gig Mayhem played in Jessheim [Norway]. I realized back then that he actually went to other worlds, and years later I wanted to go there myself. But I think my worlds were different from his. An ecstasy hidden in a religious veil. And in general I hated religion. I still can't believe how I got there. I hated religion so much yet every time was like a revelation. Today I know how to get there perhaps because I might have achieved a spirituality lost to me in the past. Mainly thanks to Dissection and Watain. But anyway the cutting turned into a freak show where the audience wanted to see it more than they wanted to listen to the vocals or the lyrics. I don't think any of them understood *anything*, except maybe one percent of them."

The band would demonstrate their onstage proficiency on their next official album, a live opus recorded in Italy in late 1998 and released in 1999 under the title *Mediolanum Capta Est*, intended to mean "Milan is captured." Though it was never going to topple the raw brilliance of *Live in Leipzig*, the record nonetheless remains an intense and rewarding experience, particularly notable for its guest appearance by Attila.

Far more significant was the band's second full-length, which arrived midway during the following year. Titled *Grand Declaration of War*, it was divided into Parts II and III, and presented as the second and third chapters of a bigger work that had begun with *Wolf's Lair Abyss*, the opening track even beginning with the same riff that closed that EP. But it was there that any similarities ended, the music and lyrics taking a bold step away from conventional black metal. A complex concept album with a somewhat futuristic aesthetic, *Grand Declaration* saw the band taking the unusual step of entrusting all songwriting duties to their newest member, who went on to oversee every facet of the record's creation.

"Blasphemer basically had free hands writing all the music in Mayhem, we just tried to arrange our instruments," Necrobutcher explains. "Some parts I contributed a little bit, not much, Hellhammer contributed a lot of course—Blasphemer just told him when he didn't like it rather than telling him exactly what to play. We spent one year finding the right guy, then you have to build him up, psychologically and everything," he continues. "It was big shoes for him to fill and all these negative comments that we should quit and stuff like this all the time didn't help much, so we tried to build his confidence to release his potential—and then it did."

"*Wolf's Lair Abyss* was a bit more free," considers the guitarist. "I was pumping out the riffs that I had and people just hooked onto it and played along. After that I became more fussy with the drum patterns and had a lot of ideas that I would tell to Hellhammer. The other guys were very happy about it and who wouldn't be—one guy to sit at home and do all the work?" he laughs, before clarifying "I think they just realized I had a fucked up thing going. I didn't get any complaints so I just continued almost without any interference. That's how I write music—I am probably a demanding musician to work [with] and I guess will always be, 'cos I have very strong opinions: it's not just a riff, it's so much more, it's a very spiritual thing. That was a very *mental* album though… much more about thoughts than emotion."

Grand Declaration takes the listener on a journey through what appears to be a cataclysmic final conflict and its aftermath, and though it features much of the furious aggression of the band's earlier efforts, it is also far more dense, technical, and less straightforward than *De Mysteriis* or even *Wolf's Lair Abyss*, packing every song with angular guitar lines, heavy detail, and precise rhythm work. Even more notable is the use of programming and electronics, these coming to the fore following the nuclear Armageddon that segues Part Two into Part Three.

Making use of guest appearances by Ulver programmer Tore Ylwizaker, Øyvind Hægeland, the vocalist of progressive metal outfit Spiral Architect, and co-writer Anders Odden of Cadaver and Apoptygma Berzerk, it was these tracks in particular that polarized listeners. While many critics applauded the record for its forward-thinking nature, for other fans it was a vindication of earlier suspicions regarding the band's return, with some feeling that the band had moved too far from their core sound. Indeed, when asked in *Crypt* whether he felt he was being restricted creatively by the conservatism of certain Mayhem fans, Blasphemer replied, "Yes! Not many people ask me that but it's the fucking ugly truth. People still continue to surprise me in their pitifulness and absolute ignorance. I have felt the ties of the masses for sure but I can't allow myself to be tied."

"People fucking hated it, they said we had turned into a shit band," recalls Necrobutcher with a laugh. "They said, 'This doesn't sound like black metal should sound,' shit like that. But years later it seems people love that album and I really fucking appreciate it myself."

"It got 'album of the month' in *Terrorizer*, but the German press didn't really like it so much," recalls Blasphemer. "The more conservative [listeners] weren't that happy about it. But I never cared that much, you can't pay too much attention. You don't play in a band to please

FREE! DEICIDE POSTER! THE GORGOROTH SCANDAL IN FULL!

EXTREME MUSIC - NO BOUNDARIES

TERRORIZER

#118

CANNIBAL
CORPSE
TOP OF THE PILE

MONSTER
MAGNET
HIGH AND MIGHTY

DECAPITATED
SEVEN PUNISHMENT

AMEN
NO MERCY

SUICIDE, MURDER, HERESY - WHAT'S NEXT?

MAYHEM

PLUS: DEATH ANGEL I FROST I HYPOCRISY I SOULFLY I GOD
FORBID I THE END I EVERY TIME I DIE I PREMONITIONS OF WAR I
SCARVE I INSIDE CONFLICT I CYBER-FETISHISM AND MORE!

**Maniac on the cover of *Terrorizer* in 2004,
circa *Chimera*.**

people, you do what you do and you do
it all the way—if you have a vision see
it through, end of story.... But it was in
the air, there was so much experimentation going on so sooner or later I think
that had to happen. ... Actually later a
German guy wrote fifty or sixty pages
on one song ... it was [an academic
paper] teaching techniques and stuff. It
was heavy reading, I don't think I got all
the way to the end, but it was very cool,
like a recognition outside of what a black
metal album could do, a small victory."

While the impressive and complex
musicianship proved a defining factor of
the album, the songs also placed particular emphasis on Maniac, his distinctive screams now coupled with clearer
vocal declarations, which often acted to
push the heavily Nietzschean narrative
forward. Written entirely by the vocalist, the lyrics were as in-depth and uncompromising as
the music, the result of an intense partnership between the two men.

"It was an honor to work with him," says Blasphemer. "He is a tremendous artist with
some very clever ideas and it *was* mainly his ideas, but also something we shaped together to
a certain extent. If you pay attention to the album, it's very thorough and thought-through,
the music follows the lyrics and the lyrics follow the music very well on that album."

"That record was really hard to record as Blasphemer pushed me very hard in all kinds
of directions," recalls Maniac. "He knew exactly what he wanted and how to get it. It's part
of his genius I suppose. The album is like surgery both musically and lyrically. I would say that
there is not an ounce of spirituality; the lyrics deal with the end of this world and the beginning of another, but only through scientific destruction and harsh scientific reality. It is very
inspired by Nietzsche, although in retrospect I think that Nietzsche was rather spiritual, so
I think what I took from him was suited to my approach on how I perceived the world. I am
proud of this album but I could never repeat it and my worldview is very, very different now.
I have become a Satanist, but one far removed from the Church of Satan or the popular view
of Satanism. I am on my way home to the brilliant darkness."

The authoritarian nature of the record's lyrics, which frequently rallied against peace,
weakness, and stagnation, was mirrored by a wider exploration of totalitarian imagery and
themes during this period. Hellhammer had already raised eyebrows due to a number of

choice comments on the subject of race and an apparent fondness for swastikas, but the band as a whole had also been provoking the public's sensibilities since *Wolf's Lair Abyss* (the Wolf's Lair famously being Hitler's military headquarters), making use of the SS Totenkopf (skull and crossbones) and other historic Nazi imagery on merchandise.

"From the start when we called ourselves Mayhem it was about exploring the dark side of everything, negativity, developing into war, torture, crimes against humanity," explains Necrobutcher. "So when you put all these bad things together with bad psychological thinking and then you use symbols like the upside down crosses in the logo, to go a step further would be swastikas and stuff like that. Not swastikas, but stuff in that vein like the Totenkopf, a lot of bands used that. The path of exploring the darkness doesn't necessarily make us into Nazis. Or Satanists; none of us [current members] are interested in any type of religion."

"None of us is politically active at all," he continues, "except Euronymous who was a member of this Communist party—to support that would cost like ten pounds a year and you would get the magazine—but other than that we have never been interested in any political movement or party. [Maniac] was more interested in that way, but not active in any party or anything like that. Also Hellhammer had a fascination with old Nazi uniforms, stuff from the Second World War, this kind of stuff."

"I never had any say on those things, it was not my decision," says Blasphemer, whose provocative side project Mezzerschmitt—also featuring Hellhammer—would attract similar controversy. "The ideas usually came from one particular place and it was not something I endorsed I can say. I don't know if it was that serious even, or whether it was to pull someone's leg. But I don't recall being totally uncomfortable with anything; we always said the band was four different individuals with four totally different understandings of the world and politics. I've always been very lacking in politics, my interest was always the music so I guess you can draw your conclusions from that."

Despite the album's technological leanings, the band were happy to play the material live, and *Grand Declaration* was followed by a slew of live releases and a touring cycle that would push the band to the limits both as individuals and as a unit. In the midst of this came 2004's *Chimera*, whose title, Blasphemer explained to *Crypt*, was chosen to convey that "the world, its content and all common understanding is nothing but an illusion." Musically it was once again a change of tack, maintaining the complexities and stop/start structuring of its predecessor but proving a far more aggressive, traditional black metal record. Maniac's vocals also proved unusually guttural, a far cry from the spirited eloquence of the previous album.

"I kind of felt to take it further in that vein would be strange, perhaps *awkward*, and wanted to go more straightforward," explains Blasphemer, "so that was my attempt to write something straight ahead. I was also totally screwed up at that point, and I think that's why the album came out like that, I think every album sort of reflects the certain mental state you are in."

"Too much alcohol, too much drugs, fucked up at the rehearsals, the whole Mayhem machinery was going, it was crazy times," relates Necrobutcher of the period. "Today I would say some good songs came out of that album, like 'My Death.' But we should have worked completely differently. I wish that we could have lived in the rehearsal place for, like, half a year more before going into the studio, personally."

Narcotics were not entirely new to Mayhem—indeed, as Kvikksølvguttene the members had famously created a pentagram out of twelve grams of cocaine for their sleeve art—but by now drugs and general excess were threatening to pull the band apart, their live performances suffering as a result. Maniac was now visibly inebriated during many shows, something that caused arguments and even physical conflict between him and Blasphemer (who apparently kicked the singer down a flight of stairs), himself in the midst of something of a chemical haze.

"It was a pretty harsh period, but a necessary thing," reflects Blasphemer. "It was mostly me, but I wrote all the music anyway. I didn't use them as an inspiration really, just to get fucked up—if I had cash, it was constant. *Grand Declaration* was very well-received and I was feeling things were going very smooth and so it was very easy to go all the way. It prevents you from thinking, you just go for it. I remember I overdosed two times in the same day with amphetamines, so it was just a very unhealthy thing, always alcohol every occasion, every interview, all the time, even recording. I felt it was more important to be out partying and doing fucked up things, I could not focus. I was not happy with anything and I wanted to be numb. The band at this time also began to get a bit fractured and it was not the best relationship, at times it began to feel like a burden.... I wanted for us to be a really good live band but you know it was Maniac who was out at that time and that was his last tour. It was on the cards really, he didn't enjoy being on stage and it was obvious to everyone."

"Today I would say I was kicked out," clarifies Maniac, "and I understand why. [Blasphemer] is a musical genius whilst I am a mere musical laboratory accident. He knew where, and how, to guide me, but in the end my alcohol abuse was too much even for him. I think he was patient with me for much longer than…" he cuts off the sentence knowingly.

"It was too much of everything," admits Necrobutcher, "and you can't bring that on tour. We started to come out of the fog, the other people in the band, because we wanted to give the fans good shows and things like that and he just fucked up again and again and again. He was too drunk onstage all the time, forgot all the lyrics, sang in the wrong places. So after he fucked up the world tour we said, 'We can't carry on.'… From '97 to about 2006 I would say we were full-throttle, maximum liquor, drugs, craziness on tours; the last few years we kind of toned down this self-destructive thing. There's a progression when you wake up after being drunk for too many years, it's good to be awake."

After departing the band, Maniac would go on to form Skitliv, an impressive outfit blending doom and black metal with electronic elements. Mayhem meanwhile would once again look to their past in search of a replacement, just as they had done after the band's collapse in 1993. While Attila had been inactive for some years following the aftermath of *De Mysteriis*, he was now fronting Italian cyber black metal outfit Aborym, and having earned a reputation as something of a black metal legend, was also guesting with a wide range of bands such as Anaal Nathrakh, Keep of Kalessin, and drone act Sunn O))). It wasn't long before he was rejoining the group that had helped to make his name.

"First of all I'd like to say I appreciate what Maniac did for the band during the ten years he was on the job and I take my hat off for that," begins Necrobutcher, "but I can only speculate what would have happened if I called Attila in '93. It's a funny story; Euronymous, when he took Attila to Oslo to record, it was important to him that we didn't meet 'cos that would blow his plan to do this thing without me. Attila was look-

From the dark past: Attila returns to Mayhem.
Terrorizer, 2004

ing for something to smoke desperately and at that time basically you could call me about [obtaining] stuff like that. When we met in '98 we were brothers, you know, big-time—we hit it off 'cos we have a lot of similar ideas on big issues in life you might say—and I realized what happened, this scheme to control the product. I didn't have his telephone number, 'cos Øystein was in contact with the guy."

"I got in touch with the band again when I met them in Italy," explains Attila, speaking of their 1998 visit to Milan captured on *Mediolanum Capta Est*. "I spoke to Hellhammer even before that, there had been a blackout for a year or two, but after that we were in touch and there were some agreements that if they ever needed a vocalist they were going to ask me first. In 2004 Blasphemer called me finally. I had heard the last records and there was a musical progression and I must say Blasphemer is a really great composer and guitarist so it was cool to work together."

"I always got on well with the vocalists," says the guitarist, "both Maniac and Attila,

2007's Ordo ad Chao, one of the band's least compromising efforts.

though I didn't really know Atti-la then. He had a lot of ideas. By the end Maniac was not into it at all, so when you got a hungry vocalist back in, he gave a lot—you could really feel the difference in rehearsal and his voice had a lot of personality."

The results of this collaboration would surface on the 2007 album *Ordo Ad Chao*, a twist on the Freemason motto "Ordo Ab Chao" or "Order from Chaos." Like 2000's *Grand Declaration of War* it was conceived via intense collaboration between vocalist and guitarist, and based around a carefully conceived concept, with Attila handling all lyrics and Blasphemer writing all the music in the studio, even going so far as to record the basslines on all but one song.

"The composition was mainly between Blasphemer and myself but of course we shared ideas all the time, sending files back and forth," explains Attila. "In 2005 we laid down what the ideology should be for the next record, it was kind of a long process. That album went a little bit over the top, a lot of riffs and changes, there's a lot of details there that people don't see. Actually I don't think I ever worked as much on any lyrics, I tried to make it cryptic but every lyric had a meaning, I could talk for hours on the connections between songs and so on. The intro and the last song connected, it's like a frame, then the first three songs are more like an outer perspective and the next two an inner perspective. And it's on three levels; nature, society and religion. We took the slogan 'Ordo ab chao' and tried to turn it 'round, 'order *into* chaos' not 'order from the chaos.' There's a lot going on in the lyrics and the music; people would think it was very chaotic, but it's very organized. We like to challenge and the Ordo album was challenging for the fans."

That's something of an understatement. The polar opposite of *Grand Declaration of War*, *Ordo Ad Chao* was nonetheless just as daring a statement. Murky and bass-heavy, it is a swampy and inaccessible listen, revealing its mysteries and rewards only with considerable patience from the listener. Once again using unusual time signatures and song structures, the riffs and melodies are obscure even by Mayhem standards, and the production—courtesy of Attila and Blasphemer, the album being engineered and mixed by Arcturus' Knut Valle—saw the processed approach of earlier releases replaced by a sound as undeniably organic as a hunk of rotten meat. Even Hellhammer's percussion had undergone a radical transformation from its usually ultra-precise approach, having been recorded in just a few evenings, with only kicks being triggered and no equalizing whatsoever.

"I set it as my goal to make the most negative piece of shit ever," states Blasphemer. "We came up with this crazy concept that was perfect you know, it was all about questioning *everything*, basically what I wanted to do with the music was very on the border where people stop calling it music, everything was chaotic, hypnotic, acid-like. I think we managed something pretty unique on that album. It was more about exploring guitars and getting the ugliest possible riff out. Of course it had to be good, but it was more like a science of the music, trying to get it to absorb itself in terms of negativity."

While much of the band's fan base were excited to have Attila back in the fold, it was already clear that pleasing the tastes of Mayhem traditionalists was still a long way down the band's list of priorities. *Ordo Ad Chao*, though undeniably black metal, was nonetheless just as avant-garde and experimental as *Grand Declaration*, a point the band's live shows soon began to reflect. Central to this was Attila, who quickly turned the aesthetic of the genre on its head with a wide array of costumes that saw the frontman plastered in trash, singing from a sack, adorned as a tree, dressed as Bugs Bunny, appearing in a mock kitchen as a chef, and even wearing a dead pig's head, among other outfits. The pig's head drew some inevitable criticisms, though the singer was quick to point out that he himself was a vegetarian and very interested in nature (incidentally, if you ever want to talk with someone on the marvels of insect or deep sea life, Attila is your man).

"I think black metal is basically a multidimensional thing and it's not only about the human aspect," says Attila thoughtfully. "How can you manifest it? You use costumes, that was the idea with the makeup too I guess, the corpsepaint; not to hide yourself but represent something un-human in some way. It was also very challenging for me, I had to come up with a different costume for every show and so for a tour I really had to plan, it was a lot of extra work. I guess the bunny was one of the more challenging ones but also Hole In The Sky [festival] where they wanted to do an interview and I had this mummy costume, so I thought, 'Let's put it in a bizarre thing, make it the stage thing, the mummy gives an interview,' and we did it during the interview between two songs. To do this is extremely challenging and from challenges you learn, this is the way to step forward. *I* don't even understand always why we do it! For example, when we wrote [*Ordo Ad Chao*] we didn't know how it would come out. I don't have to do everything logically, but *afterwards* I always get the point."

Initially conceived by Attila and Blasphemer, the new stage show was very much in line with Attila's approach to art and life as a whole. In fact, where Maniac's lyrics had revealed a scientifically inclined, non-spiritual outlook, Attila's lyrics for *Ordo Ad Chao* drew upon a unique worldview and an interest in conspiracies and alternative views of the universe.

"I don't consider myself an artist in the traditional meaning, it's more like a channel," he explains, "these ideas are coming from somewhere and even I cannot say where. Of course there is me in there, but it's more about keeping the channel open and clean so that I can receive it. I always felt this channeling since the Tormentor times. I think our mind is working on so many levels that we're not aware of, not just the subconscious but the *supreme* consciousness. Where is an idea coming from? We don't know—people would say it's an electrochemical something in our brain, but I don't think it's just that, I think something is coming from outside, that there is knowledge *out there*. Like birds that have a map in their head or fishes, they don't get lost, and in a similar way I think we can connect to this knowledge. I think we have an ability to hook on this information and that's one of my goals in life; to understand that, and more and more I am looking to the ancients. People talk about the evolution of civilizations but if you look to the ancients they were able to make structures that we can't make today, such as Baalbek in Lebanon."

Though once again dividing opinion, the esoteric miasma that is *Ordo Ad Chao* also picked up heavy praise in many quarters, and it was partly its success—critically and artistically—that convinced Blasphemer he had said all he needed to within the group. Thus in late 2008 he quit the band primarily to concentrate on Ava Inferi (a gothic/doom metal band based in Portugal, where the guitarist had moved just before recording *Chimera*) and black thrash outfit Aura Noir.

"First of all it was like a swansong," he explains of *Ordo Ad Chao*, "everything was put into that and it was what I wanted *Chimera* to be. As soon as I did it I realized I wanted out and everything that could come up as a reason to leave the band suddenly was visible. It was something I'd probably blocked, 'cos I had made this 'armor' around me, I became very cold as a person, nothing really got to me. I didn't care, I was emotionless at certain points, then you crack the bubble and see what is really going on. Six or seven months without seeing the guys and it felt so right—I realized this is not me anymore, I cannot motivate myself to play fast music anymore. It was not overnight, it started with the drugs shit in 2003 and I think I reached a low period of my life in 2005 and 2006 and I put a lot of effort into making *Ordo Ad Chao* and all the things that had built up went into that."

The loss of the band's songwriter for the previous decade was no small blow, but Mayhem would once again survive and carry on, utilizing Limbonic Art's Krister "Morfeus" Dreyer and later Morten "Teloch" Iversen (Nidingr, ex-Gorgoroth/God Seed) and Charles Hedge (ex-Cradle of Filth) to take the band's live show to audiences across the world and craft new recordings. Since then the group has played countless territories in various continents, even returning to headline a festival in Turkey in 2011, a country the band once vowed never to return to. As always they work on their own timetable but given their illustrious and complicated past, it would be a confident man indeed who would dare predict what the future holds.

CRADLE OF FILTH
BLACK METAL ENTERS THE MAINSTREAM PART I

FEW THINGS provoke as much contempt within the underground of any subculture, musical or otherwise, as "selling out," but in black metal circles such disgust has been elevated to an art form. In fact, even in a book filled with Satanism, extreme politics, misanthropy, church burning, and murder, the inclusion of the following bands may well be the most controversial subject for black metal fans. Yet while some will lift their noses, the rise of bands such as England's Cradle of Filth and Norway's Dimmu Borgir—the two most successful acts to have emerged from the movement—is not only an important part of the genre's history, but has arguably provoked even greater extremity from the underground. Whether this success is for good or ill remains a matter of opinion, yet only the most stubborn of readers will deny that both groups touched upon brilliance at times, and were initially rooted in the black metal movement.

CRADLE OF FILTH

"Fucking Hell! I have no words… this is the ultimate! Brutal, Original, Melodic, Atmospheric… This is among the best Black Metal recordings ever!"
—Quote from Samoth of Emperor used on flyers for the band's debut album, *The Principle of Evil Made Flesh*

"I heard Cradle Of Filth for the first time in 1994 when Janto [Garmanslund, Hades] played their first album at his place and I was blown away! I must say that in my ears they almost invented theatrical-symphonic black metal, and demonstrated female vocals in a different way than I ever heard before!"

—Jørn (Hades/Hades Almighty)

Almost as soon as their debut album was released, Cradle of Filth became the most visible face of the black metal scene, a position they held for many years while nonetheless evolving toward a style that would be more accurately described as extreme symphonic, or extreme gothic, metal. Like their peers, the band's sales during the early nineties were dwarfed by the more successful death metal bands of the period, but when success did arrive, it did so dramatically. Indeed, the band have gone on to sell millions of albums, a feat that has made them arguably the biggest extreme metal band aside from Slayer (depending on your definition of "extreme metal"), and one of the more successful heavy metal bands generally.

Of course, back in 1991 when the band formed, there were few who would have believed that such good fortunes could await, including eighteen-year-old frontman Daniel Davey. Born and bred in Suffolk, England, the young vocalist had discovered metal some six years earlier when a friend gave him a mix tape featuring the likes of AC/DC, WASP, The Plasmatics, and Anvil, as well as Slayer, whose song "Evil Has No Boundaries" was by far the heaviest thing he had ever heard. Triggering something of an epiphany, Dani was soon exploring the darker side of the early/mid-eighties thrash scene, in the process developing a particular passion for the early albums of Celtic Frost, Venom, Bathory, Destruction, Sabbat, and Mercyful Fate, due to their combination of speed, aggression, and theatricality. This musical journey collided head-on with a long-running interest in the dark side that had begun as a child with John Landis' music video for Michael Jackson's "Thriller," and eventually evolved into a fascination with Wicca and the occult.

"My dad had a load of Denis Wheatley novels," Dani recalls, "and Suffolk, the environment I was brought up in, was kind of ingrained with myths and witches. When I was at school a couple of my girlfriends were practicing Wicca and witchcraft—it was just harmless fun, but it all rubbed off. A lot of people [into these things] are outsiders, sitting in the corner drawing pictures of their teacher being garroted, but it was nothing like that.... Having lived in a house that Matthew Hopkins [the] Witchfinder used to stay in… the essence of the place had that kind of vibe to it."

In fact, it was this very English take on the extreme metal experience that kick-started Cradle of Filth. Having already been in a number of bands spanning punk/hardcore, indie, and metal—with names such as PDA, Feast On Excrement, and The Lemon Grove Kids—Dani formed his new group with friend and guitarist Paul Ryan, whom he had met at college and who had initially got into heavy music via the punk and hardcore scene.

"We were very lucky having shows put on in our area that were benefit shows for the Hunt Saboteurs Association [an anti-hunting group]," recalls Paul. "An older brother of another friend was very much into this scene; everything from Subhumans and RDF from the dub crust side to Discharge and then Doom, Extreme Noise Terror, and Napalm Death on the extreme side. At first I was intrigued by what I was hearing but it didn't take long for me to totally love the extremity and freeness of it."

"The one thing I feel very blessed to have seen was the birth of extreme music genres," he continues. "Thrash metal had only just developed from metal, bands like Napalm and Carcass were viewed—and *were*—grindcore/crust punk bands. The term 'death metal' hadn't even been heard at that point. We had a friend that used to buy all sorts of records from [London store] Shades and he came back with Entombed's *Left Hand Path* and Cannibal Corpse's *Eaten Back to Life*. As soon as that Entombed record was put on we were all like, 'Foooooooook!' It blew our minds. Then Dani got *Deicide* by Deicide and we were completely in awe of it all. The whole death metal scene was starting to happen and Dani and I just knew we had to do something ourselves, hence the formation of the band."

An early promo shoot between the *Total Fucking Darkness* demo and the *Principle of Evil...* album: Dani Davey and Paul Ryan (top), Paul Allender, Robin Eaglestone and William "Was" Sarginson (bottom). Photo courtesy of Nihil Archives.

Originally called Burial, the group soon changed their name to Cradle of Filth, due to a UK death metal band of the same name. Initiating Dani's best friend John Pritchard on bass, and Darren Garden (a drummer found courtesy of an ad in a local music shop) into the fold, with Paul's keyboard-playing brother Benjamin added shortly after as a session player, the band set about working their collective backsides off during 1992. That year saw the creation of two demos (*Invoking the Unclean* and *Orgiastic Pleasures Foul*), a rehearsal tape (*The Black Goddess Rises*), a split with UK death/grindcore outfit Malediction (called *A Pungent and Sexual Mlasma* and featuring a mix of demo, rehearsal, and live tracks), as well as an aborted album entitled *Goetia* and finally the demo that clinched their signing, *Total Fucking Darkness*.

The band's sound proved as filthy as their name, the group playing a lo-fi and violent yet atmospheric form of death metal with hints of thrash and punk alongside a dose of primitive synth. At this point the sound certainly had very little to do with black metal, having more in common with the eerie early nineties death metal of Norwegian bands such as Darkthrone and Thou Shalt Suffer.

"The first demo was a lot like [seminal American death metal band] Master," Dani recalls, "but we were also a big fan of experimental death metal like Edge of Sanity."

"We recorded in a caravan in a muddy field on an eight-track in an afternoon each," says Paul. "Organic, literally, and sound-wise whatever we could get!"

"It was originally all about aggression," Dani explains. "We had very basic keys but with a thick pipe organ or a choir sample and 'cos it was with heavy death metal it would freak people out. It wouldn't be piled on, it would be just enough to send a chill down you. Later on we got more bombastic through listening to soundtracks."

Indeed, the atmospheric and orchestral side of the band would develop into a defining characteristic, the group taking influence from the epic melancholy and romance of the UK's death/doom scene that was exploding at the time with bands such as Paradise Lost, My Dying Bride, Decomposed, and Anathema.

"At the time we were still massive fans of Paradise Lost who summed it up best with [1991's] *Gothic*, and that whole great English thing comprised of Decomposed, Incarcerated, and My Dying Bride," explains Dani. "That kind of influence was what helped us change. We were almost part of that clique, that dark gothic movement in metal. It was a very dark atmosphere, a Charlotte Brontë atmosphere, almost aristocratic, what with Anathema harking on about 'lovelorn rhapsodies' and so on. We were really into the classical mythology of England and it felt very real. We were based in the spiritual homeland of witchcraft in England, so it had this pagan vibe attached to it which we just called 'graveyard music.' We were big literature heads, we were really into Bram Stoker, nineteenth-century authors, and penny dreadfuls. You also had movies like Coppola's *Dracula*, Shelley's *Frankenstein*, and *Interview with the Vampire*, there were a lot of things that were coming out that added to the overall influence."

Around the same time, of course, the black metal movement was reigniting around the planet following Norway's lighting of its once-damp fuse. As the band continued to tape-trade and make contact with the international underground, it was impossible not to feel those waves reverberating.

"We were in contact with Euronymous and bands like [Greece's] Necromantia, Impaled Nazarene, Moonspell," recalls Dani. "It wasn't just from Norway. There were bands like Blasphemy, Sarcófago, Master's Hammer and Root, Mortuary Drape from Italy. It was all very far-flung. It all just fell into place. We were making really dark music and were listening to really dark stuff, then Darkthrone came along and sort of revived all those memories of Bulldozer and Razor, those thrash bands that used to dress up with eyeliner and stuff, and it felt cool and right for us."

"The Deicide and Morbid Angel debuts had also swung it... I think that's where part of the direction of black metal came from. A lot of people will think it's bollocks, but I think the thing that started to divide black metal was Deicide. Even though it was Florida death metal, the aesthetics behind that release started the whole black metal thing again. It was a big influence. Everyone I was hanging around with at the time was listening to that and

[Morbid Angel's] *Altars of Madness*. The thing with Bathory is that suddenly everyone was like, 'What's your favorite Bathory album?' but there was a big gap between that [coming out] and the later stuff. If that was such a big influence then why did things not kick off *straightaway* rather than in 1991 when it all really began again?"

Soaking up this wealth of inspiration, Cradle of Filth slowly but inevitably began to move toward what was still a very loosely defined black metal scene, and one that left plenty of room for musical maneuver. "This is obviously the second wave of black metal at that point," Dani reflects, "but for us it was a revival of *old* ideals and imagery, and it picked up those themes from five or six years before. It didn't feel like a revival of those *sounds*, it had an artistic freedom to it. It was a good idea that came from a dying breed of bands who fizzled out, 'cos all these [first-generation] bands did one or two Satanic albums then went off and sang about the forthcoming nuclear holocaust or something. That's what I liked about the black metal movement, the experimentation which has now gone. I think it was more occult-based, and then it became colder and more necro later, and then everyone associated it with the icy north and the Nordic warrior and stuff like that, which I never considered. When I listen to *Don't Break the Oath* or *Infernal Overkill*, that's not what comes across."

The death/doom influences were already beginning to make their way into the band's sound by the second demo, *Orgiastic Pleasures Foul*, an opus that contains a significant synth interlude in the tellingly named "The Graveyard by Moonlight." By now the band had gained the attention of a London-based label called Tombstone Records and been offered a deal for a debut album. It was a venture, however, sadly fated for disaster, and soon the band found themselves without the means to pay the studio for their recordings, thus losing all the finished songs except two, "Spattered In Faeces" and "Devil Mayfair."

"The studio wiped the tapes," says Paul, "as once recorded, the label changed their minds and wouldn't pay! We had no money to pay for it ourselves so they binned it. A real tragedy that. From what I remember it was all in the death metal/grind vein. [Part of] 'Devil Mayfair' was actually played backwards on the third demo I believe."

"We were young and naïve," admits Dani. "Someone approached us and subsequently we couldn't finance what we'd recorded—which ran to the grand total of £2,000—so it was taped over, because back then tape was precious. It was a good amalgam of British mentality and that kind of dark edge from [third demo and next recording] *Total Fucking Darkness*. It was slightly heavier, faster, and more death metal-oriented, quite like Darkthone's debut. It was all part of destiny. I think things would have worked out differently, but that made us look at ourselves and decide to improve—get a second guitarist, get a full-time keyboard player, and be a bit darker with it all."

To that end the group did indeed expand, becoming a six-piece with the addition of Robin Eaglestone (wryly renamed Robin Graves), who replaced John on bass, as well as second guitarist Paul Allender and Benjamin Ryan, who was now very much a full-time member. The first result of this new lineup was the third demo, *Total Fucking Darkness*, an opus that in-

A range of flyers for the *Total Fucking Darkness* demo, 1993, featuring an earlier logo and a rather different aesthetic.

troduced the first glimpses of the sound the band would eventually become famous for. Though still including deep, growled vocals and fast, violent passages with frantic leads, the songs also incorporate far more prominent synths and slower and more melodic sections characterized by emotive chord progressions and steady percussion.

"I first auditioned as guitarist for the second demo but that didn't work out," Robin explains. "I didn't hear from them again until Jon left to go to college and they needed someone to play bass. It was a fairly low-tech, cheap, four-track studio session run by a friend of Paul and Dani's … these were bleak times in the middle of winter in a caravan somewhere out in the countryside. The *Goetia* album was sitting around on multi-track tape reel waiting to be paid for by the record company, so this new demo was a way forward for the band to get back on track with new things."

"Pure and simple, the influence of black metal with bands like Darkthrone and Burzum," opines Paul of the band's shift in sound. "As with death metal, as soon as we heard that we were totally in awe of the darkness of it."

As promising a listen as *Total Fucking Darkness* was, the official debut that emerged the following year, *The Principle of Evil Made Flesh*, more than overshadowed it. Maintaining the fast, aggressive passages and catchy riffs, the iconic full-length poured even more emotion into the atmospheric sections, the synths now far more central to the band's sound with several haunting instrumentals included. All the same, the synths are used in a more minimal fashion than on later records, rarely multi-tracked and mainly focusing around organ and piano parts, and this—combined with a clear but rather thin production—results in a uniquely esoteric feeling of mystery and depth, as if the recording had somehow been recovered from the dusty crypt of some ancient undiscovered temple. Such occult overtones were amplified by the eloquent blasphemies within the lyrics and the full-page adaption of the Church of

Satan baphomet (designed by Cacophonous Records' Frater Nihil), the overall feeling being one of devotion to some unholy yet righteous cause.

The dynamics of the band's sound also increased notably with this release, thanks to Dani's varied vocals, alternating between high-pitched screams and deep growls, and memorable spoken passages delivered by female vocalist Andrea Meyer, guest vocalist Darren White of Anathema, and Dani himself. The result was an album with a violent raw black metal feeling in parts, but one that also managed to further the evolution of symphonic black metal thanks to an air of genuine majesty and mystery. With its unusually sensual undercurrent and references to doomed romance, it also largely justified the tag of "gothic black metal," though Dani is understandably keen to qualify that categorization.

"[It's] gothic as in the melodrama, the architecture, the literature and the period," he clarifies, "rather than the music of the seventies and eighties, which I couldn't stand. I loved the look of the bands but the music was shit, without the drive of the guitars it sounded lackluster. There were exceptions like the Sisters [of Mercy, whom the band would later cover], but it was more the imagery."

With all music credited to Cradle of Filth, the making of the record seems to have proved inspiring for all members concerned, and saw the writing shift from the Dani/Paul powerhouse to something approaching a group dynamic.

"In those days everything was fresh, so writing was a really good experience with Cradle," explains Robin. "We were embracing everything going on in the UK as well as an uprising in darker styles from Norway. Though we never truly attempted to be a Norwegian-style band, it certainly lifted limitations on dark music in the UK and it all just started sounding more serious and atmospheric."

Remaining a six-piece, the album saw the introduction of Nick Barker on drums, replacing Darren Garden (who is not, as many fans believe, merely a pseudonym for Darren White), and short-lived second drummer William A. "Was" Sarginson. "Darren as far as I remember had a lot of pressure from his parents and I think just lost the will to keep doing it," Paul recalls. "We were sad to see him go, he was a great guy, younger than us and very, very funny... a great drummer too."

Despite the popularity of *Principle*, "commitment issues" would soon come to haunt the band. Propelled by their success, they headed to a Birmingham studio in January 1995 to record the follow-up. Entitled *Dusk... and Her Embrace*, it was a recording that, like *Goetia* before it, would not see the light of day in its original form, at least at time of writing. With much of the album recorded, the band was hit by a rift that literally split them in half, the Ryan brothers departing along with guitarist Paul Allender. The three would soon form The Blood Divine, a band that expanded on the gothic and atmospheric elements of Cradle but largely removed the more identifiable black metal traits. Also in the group was the aforementioned Darren White and drummer Was, briefly a member of Cradle and also of Solemn and December Moon, Robin Eaglestone's black metal side project.

"Speaking purely from my side," reflects Paul Ryan, who went on to work with the highly successful booking group The Agency, "by this point we were so stoned most of the time, and things were happening so quickly, we just got disillusioned with it all and people just started to fall out with each other. The Blood Divine was fun while it lasted, but you live and you learn."

Robin himself would also end up leaving Cradle for a spell during the creation of the original *Dusk*, temporarily replaced by one Jon Kennedy. Jon in turn would then return to Wales and his band Daemonum, who soon changed their name to Hecate Enthroned and for a time offered some competition to Cradle thanks to a similar sound and a high-selling debut. Complicated isn't the half of it.

"After we wrote most of the *Dusk* album with the *Principle* lineup I walked out," recalls Robin. "I remember we were halfway through the 'Queen of Winter, Throned' track so the rest of the band had to write one more song to have the album ready for the studio. This is where Jon Kennedy stepped in to do the album bass parts. Then the relationship between Cradle and [label] Cacophonous went all strange so that version of the *Dusk* album was never released and Jon Kennedy left. Ten months after I walked out, I rejoined the band and along with the newer members rerecorded lots of parts for *Dusk*."

"It was very Emperor-inspired I guess," ponders Dani of the original *Dusk*, which your author was lucky enough to hear and which unsurprisingly has more than a hint of *Principle* about its delivery and minimal synth work, "but because of the way it had been recorded we weren't totally happy with it and that was a bartering tool to then get us off Cacophonous—offer some new tracks from that. So they held on to those masters and we bastardized them and rerecorded them for the proper *Dusk* album which we won the right to release. All very incestuous!"

Recruiting guitarist Stuart Anstis and a keyboard player called Damien Gregori (real name Greg Moffitt), the band crafted their last Cacophonous offering, namely *Vempire … Or Dark Faerytales In Phallustein*. Technically an EP but totaling thirty-six minutes in length, *Vempire* immediately stands out as a much bigger and more symphonic experience. Both the female vocals and synths (primarily performed by Greg, with additional work by Academy Studios' Keith Appleton on the song "She Mourns A Lengthening Shadow") are more prominent, a point underlined by the anthem-like revisiting of *Principle* track "The Forest Whispers My Name."

"Without a doubt we were becoming more cinematic and very dramatic," Dani explains of *Vempire*. "It was very mythological, with mentions of past glories. It was meant to be a big-sounding album, very ornate-sounding, a *return*, whereas *Dusk* was a little more cultured and brooding. I think [it was due to] Greg and also partly us listening to more orchestral music. It was about that time that we got into that and movie soundtracks. That was the beginning of it and helped shape *Vempire*."

"Believe it or not, I answered a classified ad in *Metal Hammer*, something along the lines of 'name band with record deal require keyboard player, own gear essential, immediate

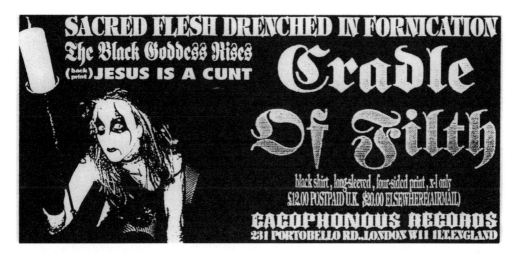

The Black Goddess Rises, Cradle of Filth's first, but not last, controversial T-shirt (see back print).

start,'" remembers Greg, now a prolific music journalist. "Coming into Cradle, I was not at all of that scene. I knew Mayhem through corresponding with Euronymous in the late eighties, but most of the early-nineties black metal movement passed me by as I was much too busy going to all-night Hawkwind concerts. Ultimately, I believe it was actually an advantage that I joined Cradle as an outsider. We had things in common—eighties thrash, Venom, Mercyful Fate, Sabbat, horror movie soundtracks—but I had no black metal axes to grind or points to prove. No one to impress.

"I'm not sure what Benjamin's setup was but my gear just seemed to sound bigger. It certainly wasn't the studio, as both *Principle* and *Vempire* were recorded at Academy and produced by Mags. But I loved vast-sounding synths and I composed my parts as I would for a cosmic symphony rather than for some Hammer Horror effect. Ironically, up to that point, I had little time for keyboards in metal and my move to playing keys stemmed from my burgeoning admiration for seventies synth music—Tangerine Dream, Klaus Schulze—which remains my significant other musical preoccupation to this day. When I joined Cradle I could barely play—it was one of those 'learn on the job' scenarios that you hear about but never believe actually happens."

Alongside new recruits Stuart and Damien, the EP also featured the talents of second guitarist and "December Moon member" Jared Demeter. Or rather, it didn't, since despite a credit and a photo comprised of a Photoshop merging of Stuart and Robin, he was merely a bizarre—and largely successful—invention to maintain the illusion of a six-piece lineup.

The follow-up, released later the same year on the much larger Music for Nations, was the long-delayed *Dusk ... and her Embrace*. Despite featuring pictures of new guitarist Gian Pyres within the sleeve, the album was created by the same key lineup as *Vempire*. The only notable change was that female vocals were now handled by "Lady Jezebel Deva," born Sarah Jane Ferridge, who would go on to become a fixture in the band, both live and on record. Despite challenges in the studio and tensions within the group, who were balancing work with an increasingly voracious appetite for hedonism, the album proved a highly successful venture.

"Compared to the sessions for *Vempire*, recording *Dusk* was a long, laborious, and extremely expensive process," recalls Greg, who was primarily listening to Greek composer and synth player Vangelis at the time. "It just seemed to take forever—about nine or ten weeks in the end. A version of the album recorded by the original lineup already existed in incomplete form and we used the drums from that version as the basis for the new recordings. To the original collection of songs we added 'Humana Inspired to Nightmare,' which I wrote in the studio, and 'Malice Through the Looking Glass' … to me, that song is that lineup of Cradle at its best, working together in at least some semblance of harmony. As for the other material written by the original lineup, well you can't argue with it can you? I think we did it immense justice and I'm incredibly proud to have been part of a truly great British metal album which I still think is the best thing Cradle have ever done. There's no doubt that the *Dusk* lineup which so many still speak fondly of could have lasted longer if we'd all just chilled the fuck out and acted like we were on the same team. We did have moments like that and they were truly amazing, but sadly they were rare."

Featuring a symphonic sound similar to *Vempire*, *Dusk* pushed the gothic side of the band even further, both in lyrics and aesthetic, which continued in earnest with a very English, vampire-inspired theme, dispensing with the overt Satanism of the past, in part perhaps due to the band no longer being directly involved with either their Satanic advisor Andrea Meyer or the explicitly occult-minded Nihil. Despite the more gothic air, however, the album's closing moments harked back to black metal's beginnings, thanks to a piece of spoken word from none other than Conrad of Venom.

"I'd already checked out the band so I knew what they were all about," recalls Cronos today. "The problem was I'd just had an operation to remove nodes from my throat, so I wasn't able to do any singing for a while and [Dani had] wanted me to come down and do a dual vocal. I said, 'I can do a spoken part similar to what I do on 'At War With Satan,' but I can't do any volume singing,' and they were happy with that. It was just good to go down and meet these young kids who had this great vibe about them and who were totally into what they were doing."

"It was kind of embarrassing," laughs Dani, who remains a huge Venom fan, and paid homage a few years later with a cover of the song "Black Metal." "We were crammed into this little house in suburban Birmingham and then Cronos appears and starts telling us all these great tour stories. He was the rabid captor of bestial malevolence that I had named my pet rabbit after and worshipped and we were sat there with some cheap wine! But it was cool and lent a magic to it and kind of tied what we were doing with what Venom and Angel Witch were doing, another massive strain of black metal."

In the intervening years, history has been rewritten by metal fans, to some extent at least, regarding *Dusk … And Her Embrace*'s association or disassociation with black metal, but it's worth remembering that the album was generally regarded at the time to be a part of the genre, albeit the more commercial end of it, a point highlighted by tours with other rising bands of the scene such as Dissection and Dimmu Borgir. That said, the band was now indisputably breaking away from their peers, and *Dusk* ended up with reported sales of around half a million records, about twenty times that of their debut and a truly astonishing feat.

"We knew *Dusk* was a great album and overall even better than *Vampire*, so we weren't surprised when it did well," recalls Greg. "We'd just been the subject of a record label bidding war and had top management vying for our contract, so smart people in the business also saw that we were really onto something. What was perhaps somewhat surprising was just how mainstream black metal suddenly became, and looking back I suppose we played a significant part in that."

"I think once we got past that original record company we spread our wings a lot more," Dani states. "We were offered bigger things and were playing with bands outside the black metal genre, playing huge festivals, appearing in big magazines, it was exciting at the time. There was a lot of opposition, I remember Dave Mustaine branding us a 'gay band' around *Dusk* but we knew what we wanted to do, and more money meant bigger budgets."

Like the band's album sales, shirt sales were also thriving, with a number of controversial designs increasingly visible—not least the iconic Vestal Masturbation shirt, which features a topless nun masturbating with a cross and a back print declaring "Jesus is a Cunt." Not one for first dates or job interviews then.

"It was one of those things we found hilarious at the time," laughs Dani. "People looked at us as being a bit gothic and sensuous, so we did something like that. My then-girlfriend—now wife—posed in a blacked-out room in my house, and then nowhere would print it. She was actually working at a T-shirt printing place but they were having none of it. In the end we had to go to a place in a tiny little village that was printing up like flags and stuff!"

Cradle of Filth would continue to grow as the years went by, retaining elements of their black metal past while exploring more symphonic, gothic, and heavy metal territories along the way. Likewise, their aesthetic would become somewhat more indebted to a Grimms fairy tale or a Clive Barker movie than second-generation black metal as the years went by, the band's use of face paints gradually moving away from what could be considered corpsepaint after *Vampire*. Nonetheless, Dani remains fond of the genre and proud of the band's early years, as he explained to me in 2007 in an interview for *Terrorizer*'s first black metal special.

"The thing that I remember was that mystery and that it was totally new, people combining music and ideas. People were younger and a bit more naïve and perhaps, dare I say, a bit more imaginative because of it. There was a sense back then of rallying toward a collective goal. It was all black and white, it was all bad photocopies. I think it was the first [Burzum] *Aske* T-shirt that had Grishnackh on the back and it was so badly taken it actually looked like

Two decades of *Terrorizer* covers highlight something of a shift in the band's image.

he was a towering Vampiric overlord, when in actual fact it was just a shit picture. It became mysterious because it was all rumor.

"A lot of bands now are trying to recreate a scene or keep it alive and it's born of nostalgia. There's a lot of people still wallowing in that whole 'We're here on a Nordic mountain waving our sticks around, painted like badgers' and it just isn't the same. The moment passed about eight or nine years ago, there are still good albums and good bands, some of the best albums have been released long after that date, Craft's last record for example, but I think the scene has burned itself out and maybe it's for the best. Maybe that nucleus has been demolished by a hammer blow and now all these little pieces are forming themselves again and have maybe spread further afield and become bigger and better, but I think that original feel has died. But maybe that's just me getting too old!"

30
DIMMU BORGIR
BLACK METAL ENTERS THE MAINSTREAM PART II

"Everyone raves on about 1996's Stormblast—*and it is a decent record—but it's with the follow-up that these guys really smashed onto the radar.* Enthroned Darkness Triumphant *stuck two fingers up at the traditional, lo-fi conventions of Scandinavian black metal by presenting a sound that was polished, professional, and powerful. They've since gone on to delight and annoy in equal measure ever since with their brand of unsubtle, bombastic metal. As far as I'm concerned, they long since left the domain of 'real' black metal but there's no arguing with a good hook or riff and Dimmu know how to pen plenty of these."*

—Frank "The Watcher" Allain (Fen, Skaldic Curse)

FORMED IN THE SUMMER of 1993 by a trio of seventeen-year-old musicians—Shagrath (Stian Tomt Thoresen), Silenoz (Sven Atle Kopperud), and Tjodalv (Ian Kenneth Åkesson)—Dimmu Borgir rose from the black metal scene that was by then well underway within Norway. Shagrath and Tjoldalv were old friends, having grown up as neighbors and schoolmates in the small town of Jessheim, and the two had met Silenoz around 1990/1991.

"Silenoz lived in a small place nearby called Nannestad and the first time I met him was at our local youth club," recalls Tjoldalv. "In this place we were allowed to rehearse, I had my band with Galder [Thomas Rune Andersen] called Requiem [which played death metal and became Old Man's Child in 1993], and Silenoz had his death metal band called Malefic and used to rehearse at this same youth club, so I believe this was the first time our ways were crossed."

Already heavily into thrash and death metal, the members were converted to the black metal cause by the Helvete scene and the wave of new music emerging from Norwegian acts such as Burzum, Immortal, Emperor, Satyricon, and Darkthrone.

Band contact:
Dimmu Borgir
c/o Stian Shagrath Thoresen
Klosterheimveien 9
0666 Oslo
Norway

No trend · No fashion · No peace · No fun · No life · No light

"No trend, no fashion, no peace, no fun, no life, no light": An early Dimmu Borgir flyer shows a young and unpainted Shagrath.

"I left quite a lot of money at Helvete," Silenoz recall with a laugh, "I can't remember who tipped us off about it, but it was like a fucking revelation—all these obscure albums and the mystique surrounding the shop made quite an impression on a fifteen-year-old kid. Oslo is like forty minutes from where I grew up, so it's like the 'big scary city.' We just went there to buy records and leave, we were too young to be taken seriously I guess at the time."

Taking their moniker from the dramatic volcanic formations in Iceland known as the *Dimmuborgir* (meaning "dark cities/forts"), the band can probably take some of the credit (or perhaps blame) for kicking off the trend of unwieldy black metal band names, a tradition still going strong today.

"It's pronounced '*Dim-moo-bor-geer*,'" explains Silenoz, "but it's an Icelandic word and the Icelandic would pronounce it differently to the way we do. We took the name because it was very different to other band names, then and even now, and we thought it was describing our music in a very good way, as our music was not so brutal at the time. There was more mystique surrounding the whole thing, so we felt that we were standing out compared to other bands and *should* therefore have a more peculiar name."

Indeed, though the trio had taken their first inspirations from eighties pioneers such as Celtic Frost and early Norwegian acts (as evident in recordings by Shagrath's first band Fimbulwinter), the trio soon found their music unconsciously echoing an influence from those Norwegian groups who had shifted toward a more mysterious, melancholy, and atmospheric approach through the use of keyboards.

"Fimbulwinter was more brutal, Dimmu Borgir is sad, it is made out of the deepest depression anyone can imagine," Shagrath explained in an early interview in *Thy Kingdom Come* zine. "Our mission is the deepest sorrow and total loss of happiness… We want to make people understand that it is best to put an end to their misery. We like to think that our music is the one little thing that can push them off the edge."

"We started jamming and practiced cover songs—Tormentor, Mayhem, Darkthrone, stuff like that," Silenoz recalls. "Then we started experimenting with our own stuff and saw that it was quite different to the covers we'd played. We figured out pretty early on that we would have a specific sound and expression. We saw other bands were experimenting with keyboards—Emperor, Enslaved, Gehenna—so it was kind of natural for us to pick up keyboards and try to incorporate that, as it was an element that was not heard much in that type of music. It was just done in the background, but once we started using keyboards we found we could incorporate them as a proper instrument and a tool for writing songs. I guess atmosphere was the main ingredient in everything we did, that's been the red thread throughout our career."

By early 1994 the band's lineup had expanded to a five-piece, with Tjodalv playing guitar, Silenoz contributing guitar and vocals, Shagrath playing drums, Brynjard Tristan (Ivar Tristan Lundsten) on bass, and on keyboards, one Stian Aarstad, a classically trained player whose role seems to have bordered on that of session member. Something of an enigma, as well as an outsider to the black metal scene, Stian stood out from the rest of his bandmates, using his birth name rather than a pseudonym, and exhibiting an idiosyncratic dress sense that not only included short hair and a limited use of face paint, but also a top hat and cape.

"He was living very close and was a childhood friend," Silenoz explains. "He had a little bit of training on keyboards and a weird style of playing which we felt fit. He wasn't really involved in any of the writing ever. He's got credit from fans saying he is such a great keyboard player—yeah, he might be a great keyboard player performing his instrument, but he was hardly ever present at rehearsals. When it came to studio work we would call him up and say, 'You need to play this and this part,' and he would come and then fuck off, he was not really part of anything, he was the obscure fifth member."

It was with this lineup that the band made their first recordings, and while they never released an official demo, they did issue a series of rehearsal tapes, with at least three appearing throughout 1994. Featuring a heavy use of synths and the atmospheric, mid-paced passages that would become the group's hallmark, these early tracks were soon laid down in a professional studio setting, leading to two separate releases; the *Inn I Evighetens Mørke* ("Into the Darkness of Eternity") seven-inch, released late 1994 on Dutch label Necromantic Gallery Productions, and the band's debut album *For All Tid* ("For All Time") issued early 1995 on controversial German label No Colours.

"It was actually recorded in two sessions," explains Silenoz of the first full-length. "We didn't have enough money so we had to stop recording and wait for some months—of course those songs have a different sound as we had to work with a different engineer. We never recorded any official demos so people didn't know what to expect from us ... and I guess we didn't either. We were pretty much clueless, it was a very juvenile, adolescent attitude—go in, hammer everything out, and get out of there. You were just driven by this feeling to get things done and finally get the album in your hands—you were just in ecstasy when that happened."

The album attracted the attention of UK label Cacophonous, who by now had signed a number of like-minded artists, in particular Cradle of Filth and Gehenna. Determined to build upon the warm reception their first album had received, the group began to craft a follow-up entitled *Stormblåst*, recording in two sessions in July and September of 1995. As before, the vocals were handled primarily by Silenoz, with lyrics—once again entirely in Norwegian—contributed by Shagrath, Silenoz, and Aldrahn of Dødheimsgard. This time round, however, there were also a few vocal contributions from Shagrath, who had swapped roles with Tjodalv, putting down his drumsticks in favor of the guitar.

Released in 1996, *Stormblåst* ("Stormblown") saw the band dramatically refining their use of synths, crafting an opus whose somber atmosphere and unhurried pace result in a immersive experience, a point evident from opening number "Alt Lys Er Svunnet Hen" ("All Light Has Faded Away"), which not only begins with a full minute-and-a-half of Stian's emotive piano work but waits for almost four minutes before introducing any real vocals. With drums and guitars taking a backseat—a point highlighted by six-minute instrumental "Sorgens Kammer" ("Chamber of Sorrow")—this is clearly not the album for anyone looking for a quick blast of Nordic fury, instead prioritizing atmosphere and a certain air of sophistication.

Despite the central role of the synths, Stian is the only member whose portrait does not appear in the album's booklet, though an unusually dapper Shagrath at least ensures the iconic top hat makes an appearance. But though groundbreaking within a black metal context, it later turned out that much of Stian's synth work was not quite as original as it appeared. In fact, it later transpired that "Sorgens Kammer" was an adaptation of a portion of the soundtrack to Amiga video game *Agony*, something the other band members maintain they only learned when its creator, renowned Welsh soundtrack composer Tim Wright, contacted the band in 2004.

As if that wasn't enough, around the same time the group discovered that the introduction to the opening track had also been "borrowed," from British prog rock act Magnum's "Sacred Hour." Indeed, in 2005 the band would completely rerecord the album (released as *Stormblåst MMV*), omitting the offending passages, boosting the production values, and upping the guitars, an element the band had long been unhappy with.

Having only signed to Cacophonous for one album, in late 1996 the band hooked up with Hot Records, an Oslo label that also released albums by Fimbulwinter and Old Man's Child. The sole result was the *Devil's Path* EP featuring the title track, a new song called "Master of Disharmony," and, somewhat unnecessarily, *two* cover versions of Celtic Frost's "Nocturnal Fear." Though not the most essential chapter in the band's catalogue, the EP introduced another important lineup shift, with bassist Brynjard Tristan replaced by Nagash (Stian Andrè Arnesen), a musician who already had experience with two other symphonic black metal bands, namely one-man outfit Troll and another rising group called Covenant. More significantly, Shagrath now took over the lead vocals (as well as keyboards, since Aarstad was away on national service), a role he would maintain in the years that followed. The decision suited Tjoldalv well, since he was—and is—primarily a drummer and had swapped roles with Shagrath in the early days of the band simply because both wanted to try out other instruments.

Dimmu Borgir in 1997: Tjodalv, Silenoz, Shagrath, Stian Aarstad, Nagash and Jens-Petter Sandvik, who "played the bass for the band for about two weeks," according to Silenoz. Photo courtesy of Nuclear Blast Records.

"On the second album I still did ninety percent of the vocals," says Silenoz. "It only happened later that I thought, 'Well you are a much better vocalist than me, so why don't you do all the vocals?' I think it was also a little bit about Shagrath wanting to be a frontman. I never wanted to be a frontman, I was always happier at the back."

By now the band had come to the attention of industry giants Nuclear Blast, who were beginning to add black metal bands to their roster. 1997 saw the first fruits of this union, namely a split VHS with Dissection and, more importantly, *Enthrone Darkness Triumphant*, the band's third album and the one that that would provide their breakthrough into the mainstream.

Featuring the same lineup as *Devil's Path* but with Stian Aarstad back behind the keyboards, the album saw a return to synth-heavy territories. Despite this, the music is markedly different from *Stormblåst*, exchanging the mournful, obscure vibes for a far more bombastic atmosphere. Though it retains classical overtones, the album also cuts back the solo piano-driven passages, pushing for a more orchestral approach, with guitars more frequent and far higher in the mix. Mirroring the songwriting shift was the sizable production, courtesy Sweden's Abyss Studios and Peter Tägtgren, fast becoming one of the scene's most popular producers.

"It was a step up in being professional," explains Silenoz of the move. "When we first went to Abyss Peter didn't know what to expect, I guess he had heard parts of the *Stormblåst* album and was like, 'Am I going to record this shit with this shit band?'" he laughs.

"They sent me stuff so I had some reference of what they were going to do," recalls Tägtgren, "and I was like, 'There's no way in hell it's going to sound like this and leave my studio.'" The end result was a far bigger and heavier-sounding album and therefore one that had a much wider appeal to metal fans outside the black metal genre. With warm reviews from the press and the support of a larger label, the album proved a huge success, eventually selling over 150,000 copies and putting openly Satanic songs such as "Spellbound by the Devil" and "Tormentor of Christian Souls" back into a mainstream metal scene that had largely moved away from such subject matter (and at that time, the band contained several members with an active interest/involvement in Satanism).

"When we were doing the album I thought, 'Okay this is pretty interesting,'" laughs Tägtgren, "I wasn't as impressed as the fans and media and I was really surprised how it blew up. It was a little too melodic for me at that time—I didn't really get it, but everyone else did!"

"We were absolutely ecstatic over creating such a great album and to be the first black metal band to do such a good production," says Tjoldalv. "It's a milestone, and is absolutely the breakthrough album for Dimmu Borgir. We felt that already then, that we had got the big breakthrough, a Norwegian black metal band signing with the biggest metal label."

Already a more widely palatable proposition musically speaking, the band's move to Nuclear Blast was accompanied by several amendments to the group's aesthetic. Most obviously, they were now singing entirely in English and had swapped the somewhat cryptic logo of old for a more legible option. Predictably, certain corners of the black metal scene began to call foul, though Silenoz is quick to defend the moves.

"It was a mutual decision, I think it was even the band's suggestion that we should have a logo that was more readable," he explains. "On *Devil's Path* we had changed to English so we were already starting to feel we had ambitions that were more than just being a garage band. We've always been accused of being a sellout, but we never changed the name of the band and there's still barely anyone who can pronounce it."

Setting off on a world tour in support of the album, Dimmu began to make more changes to their lineup during '97 and '98, taking on an Australian guitarist named Astennu (Jamie Stinson), who also played with Nagash in Covenant and another symphonic black metal outfit called Carpe Tenebrum. The ever unique Stian Aarsted was also replaced, initially by ex-Ancient member Kimberly Goss, and then a young synth player named Øyvind Johan Mustaparta, who became known as Mustis.

"We were supposed to do the Dynamo festival in 1997," Silenoz recalls of the event that led to Stian's departure. "We had the rehearsal the night before we were going to leave and everything was cool. Then the next day I was going to pick him up and he said, 'Oh sorry guys, I can't leave.' It was like, 'Why are you saying this one hour before we are supposed to go to Holland?!' He said, 'Sorry, I can't get off work,' you know, stupid reasons that he could have told us a week before. I think it was more that he wasn't allowed to go because his parents did not like it, they were afraid that being with us would be a catastrophe. Shaggy found Mustis at some bar in Oslo—he was not even old enough to be in the bar and did not have school or work or anything, so we asked him if he wanted to come down and try out."

With the band still touring heavily, 1998 saw the release of stopgap EP *Godless Savage Garden*, which featured four songs left over from the *Enthrone* sessions, a cover of Accept's "Metal Heart" and a smattering of live numbers. In 1999, they released *Spiritual Black Dimensions*, an album that built upon the foundations of its predecessor while developing the detail and depth of the songwriting and emphasizing the synth work of new player Mustis.

"Mustis was heavily influenced by soundtracks and was a much better keyboard player than Stian," states Silenoz simply. "He was never really heavily involved with the *arrangement* of the songs, as he was not skilled in that sense and I don't think he even cared, but he would come along with ideas for songs and riffs and he definitely left his touch on that album. That contributed to us opening up our sound to this huge cinematic feel, and of course Nagash and Shagrath were writing lots of keyboard stuff as well, and when you have *three* people writing keyboard stuff it's sure to be a big, symphonic-sounding album. Musically *Spiritual* is more advanced that *Enthrone* ever was; *Enthrone* has this innocent feeling whereas *Spiritual* has more finesse, and better songwriting and structures."

The band's fourth full-length is an undeniably more professional and dynamic effort, the symphonic, wall-of-sound approach boosted thanks in large part to the band's first use of clean vocals since Aldrahn's appearance on *For All Tid*. These were contributed by session singer ICS Vortex, also known as Simen Hestnæs, an ex-member of doom outfit Lamented Souls who had recently lent his soaring voice to avant-garde black metal outfits Arcturus and Borknagar. His stellar contribution to tracks like "The Insight and the Catharsis" add a truly rousing spirit to the record, which soon earned him a place as a full-time member of the group.

"We were actually in touch with Carl McCoy from Fields of the Nephilim," reveals Silenoz, "We always loved his vocals and had two parts we felt would just fit him perfectly. He was totally up for doing it but he couldn't travel to Sweden to the Abyss, he wanted to record in his own studio, he didn't want us present … I can't really remember the details, but we said, 'We are here and need to be in control of this and if it doesn't work out, it doesn't work out.' Then we were kind of stuck, we had a week left before we were going to mix and we didn't know who to turn to for clean vocals. So we called Vortex who came over and did some real killer vocals; in hindsight you can say this is a blessing in disguise, I'm sure it would have been killer too with Carl, but I guess there was a reason he wasn't supposed to sing on the album."

"Actually I was first asked to do session vocals on the *Devils Path* EP," admits Vortex, "but I overslept and nothing came of it. I think Brynjard was the first guy I met from Dimmu, I remember him being extremely evil at this black metal club," he laughs. "It was run in a kebab shop run by Pakistanis, all light green inside, a really horrible color. Frost had gotten permission to play black metal music every Wednesday so that's where we met, because no one else played black metal, at the time the Elm Street boys just played old rock, so we went there, and sat around drinking water and being extremely evil."

"A couple of years later they got back in touch when I was in Bergen," he continues "I was traveling straight from the studio where I was recording *The Archaic Course* with Borknagar and we did all the vocals in one night. I arrived in the evening and I remember it was a really good vibe in the studio, it was night, there were candles, it was full moon … it just clicked. Peter's studio is an old insane asylum, and it's a pretty good vibe, out in the forest, there's nobody around, it was pretty magical. Nothing was prepared—I hadn't heard the songs before or anything—but I did my stuff and it worked out pretty good. I got 10,000 Norwegian Kroner for the job and felt like a millionaire!"

Faster, darker, and more intense than *Enthrone*, the album was another huge success both creatively and commercially, but while the songwriting proved relatively problem-free thanks to the many talents involved, the same could not be said for the production and mastering process, which was wracked with headaches for all concerned.

"We wanted to do the same thing production-wise as on *Enthrone*, which is why we went back to Peter," explains Silenoz. "It was probably a bigger production but the end result did not really capture what we were looking for at the time. First of all, we ended up mastering the album twice; the first master that *we* really liked the label didn't like for some really strange reason, so there exist two masters of the album. When I want to listen to the album I put on the original master, I feel it was less chaotic and that's why we liked it, it was closer to the finished product of *Enthrone*."

"That was fucking chaos," groans Tägtgren, "because by then they became big and thought they knew everything! The recording was always good but mixing was fucking chaos, everyone was fighting with everyone else and in the end they went home with a shitty mix that *I knew* was a shitty mix, 'cos everyone was saying, 'I need to be louder!' All six of them, and I wanted to say, 'Shut the fuck up,' but in the end I was like, 'Okay, whatever you want to do,' and whoever had the loudest voice got their part louder. I mixed it and then Sven and Stian [Silenoz and Shagrath] came out alone and we remixed it and there was peace and quiet. I also wasn't happy with the mastering, I had nothing to do with it, they took away a lot of important frequencies and it just sounded totally bullshit, flattened, empty and [ironically!] with no dimensions."

Despite this, the album remains one of the high points of the band's career, though it's interesting to note that they opted to head for another Swedish studio, Studio Fredman, for their next album, 2001's somewhat transitional *Puritanical Euphoric Misanthropia*. The album, which saw the band abandoning corpsepaint in their photo shoots for the first time, also had them edging away from their established melodic black metal sound. By this time the band had undergone a major lineup shift, thanks to the departure of Astennu and Nagash, the two initially working together again on Carpe Tenebrum before Nagash left to concentrate on Covenant (now *The Kovenant*, after a dramatic gothic/industrial metal makeover). Nagash would be replaced by bassist ICS Vortex, while lead guitar duties would be taken over by Galder of Old Man's Child. In retrospect, Galder was an obvious choice; a longtime friend, his band had not only appeared on a split re-release with Dimmu but also shared several members over the years. Most obvious of these was the co-founder of both outfits, Tjoldalv, who now departed to play drums for newly formed melodic thrashers Susperia, ultimately replaced in both bands by Nick Barker, the British sticksman who had found fame with Cradle of Filth.

"I had first talked about leaving for some months after having my first child in '97," explains Tjoldalv. "You get other priorities when you become a father. But I changed my mind and was willing to sacrifice much and continue the hard work with Dimmu. I don't think the other guys were mature enough at that time to understand that I couldn't hang out partying every weekend anymore. I was twenty-one at this time and the oldest in the band. After they got kids themselves they started to understand the situation I had to deal with. We released *Spiritual Black Dimensions* in '99 and after doing some shows in U.S. and Canada, they unexpectedly told me that they had found a new drummer. They had talked to Nick Barker, who got sacked from Cradle of Filth, for a while behind my back. I had already started to put together a .new band the year before, so I went to fully concentrate on Susperia. Despite all this, me and the Dimmus have been friends all these years, and still are."

The lineup would remain in place for one more album, *Death Cult Armageddon*, another opus that proved pivotal in the band's career. With the writing predominantly split among Mustis, Shagrath, Silenoz, and Galder, the songs feature huge swaths of live orchestration courtesy of the Prague Philharmonic Orchestra, Norwegian arranger Gaute Storas, and Czech conductor Adam Klemens. Yet it remains a surprisingly heavy effort since the parts not featuring classical musicians are largely untouched by synths, creating an album of notable musical contrasts.

"We wrote the parts like we always do, with keyboards, then we had the conductor help transcribe that into notes because we're metal musicians and we don't know shit about notes," laughs Silenoz. "They were really professional and of course having a bigger budget helps you to spend more time on both mixing and recording, and that definitely helped that album to sound the way it sounds. It really has this huge apocalyptic, bombastic, and dramatic feeling to it. So everything just expanded and it was good to be able to—for maybe the first time—be totally completely happy with an album. Of course it wasn't perfect, because it it's perfect then you won't bother doing a new album, but it was damn close."

Despite its moments of brutality the album proved another huge seller, achieving 100,000 sales in the U.S. alone (making Dimmu the first Nuclear Blast signed act to do so). The relatively high-budget video for "Progenies of the Great Apocalypse" was given regular airplay on music channels, and other tracks appeared in a number of unlikely places, including the trailers for mainstream films such as *Hellboy* and *Stardust*.

Wisely, the band supported the record with a heavy touring schedule that would take up a good chunk of the next four years. This left the members burnt out, however, and

The star*everyone's talking about.

"The S1-200 amp is the very definition of guitar sound
and will break new ground - mark my words!"
Silenoz, Dimmu Borgir

Blackstar
AMPLIFICATION
the sound in your head

Find your nearest dealer at
www.blackstaramps.com

**Traditional endorsements, such as the one
here for Blackstar Amplification, illustrate
Dimmu Borgir's shift into the mainstream
metal scene in recent years.**

brought significant tension to the unit. An early casualty was drummer Nick Barker, who was let go in early 2004 and replaced onstage by Dane Reno Killreich and American Tony Laureano, of death metal acts Panzerchrist and Nile respectively.

"Well the thing with Nick was obviously not because he is a bad drummer," laughs Silenoz. "It was more on a personal level, there were personal clashes on tour and things we felt we could not get to the bottom of. Nick is a great guy and a great drummer and very talented, so from that point of view it was really fucked up and sad that it had to end that way."

"Definitely, looking back, things started to not be as fun as it used to," Vortex ponders. "I felt [Nick] was important within the band. But after *Death Cult* there was a lot of touring and it was a very good period for Dimmu commercially. There was the Ozzfest, and if Dimmu had continued doing concerts after *that* it would have been a *huge* step, but after so much touring the mood in the band was not the same. Actually when we were told we sold 100,000 copies I was like, 'Of course we have,' because we were working really, really hard and we were confident that it would just get bigger."

The band's next effort, *Sorte Diaboli* (released in 2007), saw a massive leap away from the industrial aesthetic of its predecessor. Instead, the band's first concept album tells the story of a medieval priest who begins doubting his faith and eventually becomes the Antichrist, the story explored in a number of high-budget and award-winning—but sometimes painfully hammy—promo videos. Musically, the album was a natural follow-up to its predecessor, perhaps the only surprising addition being Mayhem's legendary Hellhammer on drums.

"We've known Hellhammer for many years, he'd always liked the band and said, 'If you ever need my services I'm just a phone call away,'" explains Silenoz. "He's been playing all sorts of styles, from power metal to the most necro black metal, so for people here in Norway it was not a big surprise. Of course I can see why some people in, say, South America might think, 'What the fuck?,' their whole world is shattered because Mayhem is their biggest influence and they hate bands with keyboards, so I can see some people being offended."

Dimmu Borgir circa 2007's *In Sorte Diaboli* album with Silenoz in the forefront. Photo courtesy of Nuclear Blast Records.

Hellhammer would depart after the album's release, however, and more serious lineup chaos would follow, with both Simen and Mustis leaving under highly acrimonious circumstances, both publicly suggesting that Mustis had been cheated out of writing credits, while a statement issued by the band retaliated with claims of long-running unprofessional behavior and disinterest. Whatever the truth, the duo's departure did not have a major impact on the band's sound—though Simen's stunning clean vocals have been impossible to replace—and 2010's *Abrahadabra* saw the group continue in a vein similar to the two previous albums, utilizing both the Kringkastingsorkestret (the Norwegian Radio Orchestra) and Norway's Schola Cantorum choir, as well as clean vocals from Kristoffer "Garm" Rygg and Snowy Shaw, along with drums by Polish black metal veteran Dariusz Brzozowski.

Having moved away from their somber black metal beginnings over the years, Dimmu Borgir are now somewhat distanced from the genre, a point they readily admit. Unlike, say, Cradle of Filth, however, Dimmu are still generally seen as representing the genre by those outside the movement, a representation that manages to both infuriate hardliners in the scene and bring new listeners from mainstream metal into the thrall of black metal.

31
UNDERGROUND ETHICS

"I remember Euronymous and I were telling jokes back in the early nineties that everything would be ruined the day Nuclear Blast started to sign black metal bands, we used to have good laughs about that... I'm sure he would be very surprised to see what happened..."

—Metalion (*Slayer Magazine*)

TO THOSE who witnessed the birth of modern black metal during the late eighties and early nineties—a time when outfits such as Cradle of Filth and Satyricon were still releasing demo tapes with photocopied sleeves and hand-drawn covers—the idea that the genre would ever have a mainstream face must have seemed unimaginable. Not merely because of the extremity of the music, since death metal was already proving that extreme metal could attract large audiences and shift units, but because black metal—at least in its "second wave" form—had all but defined itself by an uncompromising code that required a Satanic (or at least anti-Christian or misanthropic) outlook and a strict adherence to a specific set of values.

As we've seen, many of these values were laid down by Euronymous of Mayhem and put into practice by the bands who surrounded him. Musicians rejected their death metal origins almost overnight and adopted a dress code of spikes, chains, and corpsepaint, in contrast to the casual street attire of the death metal scene. Lyrics became dominated by evil and Satanism as socially aware themes went out the window. Unashamedly reactionary, black metal positioned itself in opposition to a burgeoning "life metal" scene that had begun to gain acceptability by "normal" people. Black metal therefore became the most underground form of metal largely by nature of its extremity and closed-door approach to outsiders, and consequently, doing what was necessary to be considered credible within the scene almost *guaranteed* low sales and obscurity, because the genre's audience was initially so limited.

But somewhere along the way, against the odds, things changed. Very quickly certain bands began to find significant success, and in doing so had their underground status compromised. Even Euronymous himself, who along with the rest of Mayhem had consistently put dedication to the scene above making money, began to voice doubts about keeping the genre "underground." In many later interviews he explained why he considered it acceptable—

and perhaps even *necessary*—for bands to make money and achieve success as long as they stayed true to black metal values.

"There is obviously an antagonism between being 'underground' in the common sense of the word, and the original black metal ideas," he commented in *Isten* magazine. "If you start to look at how black metal bands were in the ancient days, such as Venom, Mercyful Fate, Hellhammer, Bathory, Destruction, Sodom, etc., you see that they had nothing to do with what is called 'underground.' They were signed to big labels, they earned well-deserved money and were NOT submitted to the hardcore laws which are ruling the 'underground' today... All these 'underground' rules look great at first sight— the music becomes a protest toward the commercial music industry. This is

Issue 3 of U.S. zine *Petrified*. Editor Jon "Thorns" Jamshid was also the owner of the Full Moon Productions record label.

good of course. But on the other hand—they KILL the bands. After eight years of being broke, I'm starting to become quite fed up. Why shouldn't I live on the music? Of course there are limits, I HATE to see Earache bands with videos on MTV, and I was DISGUSTED to see Entombed playing a playback show for discokids on a disco show on Swedish TV. These people shall FEAR this music. We must return to the old days of Venom and the other ancient ones. They were big, but they were NOT commercial!"

"Euronymous was an intelligent guy," comments Grutle of Enslaved. "A band has to survive. You have to sell records and bring the madness to the masses to live out your philosophy. He wasn't thinking underground and all that bullshit... he wanted to make something of it and after he died we did so. Selling a lot of records was a hundred percent Euronymous."

Ultimately, it is of course totally subjective as to which bands became "big" and which became "commercial," which stayed "true" and which "sold out." Even so, many acts once considered sacred have been seen, rightly or wrongly, to have betrayed their black metal roots: Cradle of Filth, Dimmu Borgir, and Satyricon—to pick the most obvious examples—were once an unquestionable part of the underground, but have been branded as traitors by some who say they compromised themselves in order to gain acceptability and/ or sign with major labels.

Other defining acts of the early days, such as Mayhem, Gorgoroth, and Dissection, also saw their audiences grow (the latter two even signing with major label Nuclear Blast Records), yet retained more of their "underground credibility," underlining that it's not high record sales that do the damage as much as the concessions bands are perceived to have made in order to achieve them. Similarly, it's interesting to note that in Norway Satyricon and Keep of Kalessin seem to attract more criticism than Dimmu Borgir (despite having smaller sales and a heavier sound), due to a heavier media presence—for example, frontman Satyr has appeared on pseudo-dating show *Dama til* ("Girlfriend"), Satyricon played a fashion show on national TV, and Keep of Kalessin have competed in Eurovision.

Erik Danielsson of Swedish black metal act Watain, one of the most successful and boundary-crossing acts in the genre today, is a man who has given a lot of thought to the various ways of bridging the gap between the underground and wider recognition, and has much to say on the subject.

"'Adapting' is what constitutes selling out," he explained to me in a largely unprinted interview for *Terrorizer* magazine in 2007. "Adapting to the preferences of the masses, ridding yourself of unwanted contents, washing your hands until they are clean and shiny, ready for mass production. The genius of black metal lies within its unbound chaotic essence, untamed artistry, and wild and evil creative thinking. This is why selling out is considered not so sexy within a black metal context. Both Gorgoroth and Dissection refused to adapt themselves to the will of others. Satyricon stands for rock 'n' roll entertainment, Dissection for Satanism. The former means showbiz, the latter means black metal. I see nothing wrong with being involved in showbiz—I like Frank Sinatra and stuff like that. But what I just don't understand is who these bands are trying to fool when they claim to still be bonded to the black metal legacy. They blindly follow rule number one in the book: 'How to lose one's credibility,' namely, 'Don't be credible.'"

"There are limits," opines Nergal of Behemoth, who like Watain have achieved a slow but impressive rise despite a fairly ferocious sound. "I'd hate to see Behemoth sell out, but then I know there is a bunch of people who probably think we sold out a decade ago. I know we can take this to the next level and make it *more* massive and *more* dangerous and crazy and still be on the covers of the magazines, have glamorous photo sessions and make fucking billion-dollar videos. One does not collide with another, that's how I see it and that's pretty much the attitude of the early black metal bands, they didn't care about these 'underground rules' and they are the originators of this whole genre, and if you spit at Venom you must be an idiot you know? They were very fucking glamorous, they were big, they wanted to be like Kiss but they were Satanic and dangerous and filthy and chaotic. You have to be smart and keep your eyes open and make sure you are not going to end up a clown in a circus someday. There's probably a very thin line between becoming really big and becoming very pathetic, so you have to be smart in how you promote your band, know what your foundation is, stick to your guns and just be honest. Then I'm pretty sure you can do whatever you want."

Perhaps unsurprisingly given its reactionary nature, as soon as black metal manifested a mainstream face in the mid-nineties the movement began to polarize, with underground black metal becoming more resolute and clearly defined in response to the increased commercialization of this once strictly subterranean movement. Where black metal as a whole had once shaped itself in opposition to a commercial death metal scene, underground black metal defined itself in opposition to that part of the black metal scene that was perceived as having betrayed itself or lost its original spirit. Taking inspiration from the movement's glory days, swaths of musicians have dedicated themselves to this cause in almost every country where metal exists.

Poland's *Holocaust* fanzine, issue VIII, created by eventual Pagan Records founder Tomasz Krajewski.

Perhaps ironically given the intolerance of the genre, a pretty universal set of values has formed, one that crosses international boundaries and frequently includes limited print runs, a lack of promotion, and stark, inaccessible imagery and sound. While many early bands utilized a basic aesthetic, poor productions, and limited releases—often on cassette format—due to a lack of resources (upgrading as soon as possible) many now employ such elements intentionally (right down to the use of cassette), despite design and recording software being far more widely available and CD and vinyl releases being much more affordable.

As we shall see in the next chapter, France's Black Legions played an early and important part in demonstrating how bands could adopt a strictly anti-commercial approach in an age where genuine success as a black metal band was becoming increasingly possible. Unlike the Norwegian scene that had inspired them, contact with the outside world was kept to a minimum and aside from a handful of "official" releases, most recordings were self-released and only distributed within the circle and to those considered worthy. American act Judas Iscariot were another band who proved a huge inspiration within this context, being somewhat less hardcore in their approach but sharing a taste for limited editions, tape-only releases and "anti-scene/anti-sellout" lamentations.

Further lessons in underground ethics would come from Germany via Moonblood and

---

Nargaroth, two acts whose influence remains as much about their aesthetic and conduct as their actual music. Moonblood followed a path similar to the Black Legions but impressively maintained the position for about ten years, refusing to release material on CD and instead releasing highly limited vinyl and a huge number of demo/rehearsal tapes. Though far less obscure, Nargaroth also stuck with the limited editions and demos, and their scene-referencing lyrics (reflected in song titles such as 'Black Metal ist Krieg,' 'The Day Burzum Killed Mayhem' and 'Erik May You Rape The Angels,' a composition dedicated to deceased drummer Erik 'Grim' Brødreskift) and statements addressing black metal as an ethos and faith in itself, seemingly above that of Satanism, an increasingly common phenomenon.

Such ultra-elitist approaches, which have been adopted (or at least admired) by many acts since, have been fueled, quite paradoxically, by the increased availability of once-obscure recordings, brought by downloading, online distros, re-releases, and auction sites. Where items were once limited to approximately the number they were expected to sell, the increased black metal audience of today means that limited items are often sought largely for their rarity. The result is a black metal scene where even fairly unimportant releases draw attention thanks to ridiculously limited runs of, say, sixty-six—or for the more right-wing, eighty-eight—and genuinely legendary material that was once almost impossible to attain is now easier to find on eBay in bootleg form or in official and limited special editions. Serious record collecting and even speculating have also come into play, meaning that records with limited or "die-hard" editions may in fact be picked up by less hardcore fans, who intend to sell at a later date.

"Things have changed," ponders Mikko Aspa of respected underground label Northern Heritage. "Limited items serve some function, but for bands who have reached a certain level, there are often more people waiting for the items than labels are pressing. I think in such cases it should be considered—do you want to release 'collector's items,' or spread music to those who want it?"

The Northern Heritage website actually puts its money where its mouth is, stating clearly its policy on release formats: "Northern Heritage does releases in all formats, aiming for decent yet traditional presentation and regular pricing. There are no special 'die-hard' collector's editions, nor unnecessary multi-format releases … All the vinyl are meant to be LISTENED. They are NOT status symbols, they are NOT collector's items of people who are afraid to listen the vinyls because its value could decrease from 'm' to 'vg' if they remove album from the plastic sleeve! Original idea of limited vinyls was to reach exclusively the true underground maniacs who listen this format with passion. Unfortunately too big part of records are nowadays ending into Internet auctions, sold to those who will pay hundreds of $$$ to obtain something they probably consider status symbol."

As mentioned, many (some without even realizing) present the black metal underground as a cause in itself, and thus place great value on elitism, obscurity, and inaccessibility, as opposed to bands such as Gorgoroth, Watain, or the late Dissection, who attempt to reach the largest audiences possible in order to spread specific spiritual messages, black metal being the *means* as opposed to the *end*.

"If I could sell in Justin Timberlake scales I obviously would," Gorgoroth's Infernus told me for *Crypt* in 2006, before commenting on bands who aim to maintain an underground status. "What is that for a self-handicapping way of perceiving the world? What is elite about limiting your own abilities of doing something properly? Of course, by those standards we are an overground band, we are contrary to that mongose-speaking [*sic*] of the 'underground.' I am a guy who is thirty-three years old and it made sense in the mid-eighties, when there were good bands who didn't have record deals, to talk about being 'underground,' but starting to idealize that situation today … I mean, how poor

The underground survives? Poland's Evilfeast and their excellent *Funeral Sorcery* album, originally released in 2005 on tape format in only 300 copies.

must a band be to not get a record deal these days? So what is the meaning? It is purely idiotic."

The position Infernus holds is shared by long-running Swedish band Marduk, who have seen the scene grow immeasurably since their inception in 1990, as guitarist and founding member Morgan Håkansson explains: "The scene was not so big at that time—there were a handful of people in each country, you more or less knew everybody involved in the scene. Euronymous had a vision first to make it very small and selective, then changed his mind to make it a big thing, which is very reasonable you know? You *should* make the most of everything you do. Some people that do recordings say they don't want anybody to hear them and that they want to keep it limited; it's a good idea but it doesn't work. Why not spread the word as far as possible? … It's a calling that you have obviously, you have a burning devotion to what you do, otherwise you shouldn't do it, otherwise I would do something completely different. I'm glad to have the opportunity and strength that I can march across the planet and spread my message in the most distant parts of the world."

"That's why I do these lyrics and that's why I don't want to stay underground," concurs Marduk (and Funeral Mist) vocalist Daniel "Mortuus" Rosten. "I want to spread light and darkness into the world. I still know there will always only be a small number of people who will fully understand it, so you can call that elitist, but it depends where you draw the line, I have a message with my lyrics and what do you do with a message? You want people to hear it."

It's a point upon which another Swede, ex-Marduk guitarist Peter Tagtgren, agrees, particularly in terms of his own production work (characterized by its clean, powerful, and accessible sound) on highly successful bands such as Immortal and Dimmu Borgir. "You lure people into something bad, you know what I mean?" he chuckles, "If you hear something [commercially successful and accessible] you want to hear what [that band] did in the past and it spreads like a virus... when you learn to listen to these more brutal albums *they* did, you can continue to bands that play even more brutal stuff. You can stand in the garage and record demos and never release them and do like this for the rest of your life—if you think that's underground then go ahead, I think you're an idiot if you do that. Spread the shit."

Despite the odd commercial success story, there are actually by definition more underground black metal bands now than ever before, simply because there are more black metal bands period. One need only look at the majority of the thousands, even *tens of thousands*, of black metal bands in existence now to see that few will achieve any real commercial success. Paradoxically, the underground has become quite a crowded place, far more so than the mainstream side of the genre, simply because most bands—even if they have no interest in underground values and harbor secret desires to be picked up by the masses—will never make it big due to black metal's inherent niche status.

The black metal underground is also no longer well-hidden from the outside world, due to the Internet and the loss of mystery that occurred in the genre as a whole when certain acts moved into the mainstream and people looked more closely at the scene that spawned them. For that reason it is not only Infernus who sees the concept of the black metal underground as losing relevance. Other musicians such as Watain's Erik Danielsson have distanced themselves from it altogether, as he made clear in the aforementioned 2007 *Terrorizer* interview:

"*First*, let me just make one thing clear; I piss on the underground! I piss on it as much as I piss on the rest of contemporary black and death metal," he spits. "We are on our own! People claim to be a part of something romantically elect, something dark and evil, something that is filled to the brim with creative art. Who the fuck are they trying to fool? ... a subculture in which there is no room at all for self-criticism or intolerance will never earn my respect... Even the demos of today's MySpace bands are released by labels. And re-released. And re-re-released. In die-hard versions... Now everyone is on their own. The artists will prevail and the Internet herd will fall into oblivion, painfully embarrassed for the rest of their lives when thinking back on their laughable attempts to make music in the name of the ancient ones, whose mere thought would—and will, one day—smother their greedy little underground forever.

"In the years when it served as the only source of information and availability for this kind of music, then it filled a purpose, and the restricted, esoteric feel to it was undeniable. Now, I don't know, although there are still many good bands on an underground level, the underground itself has become too repetitive, the spirit of revolution has been replaced by the spirit of the herd. Instead of taking things further people are trapped in patterns out of which most energy has already been drained. While one could speak of the entire black/death metal phenomenon as something interesting and filled with potential back in the days, now one can only make such reference to a handful of bands that can hardly be said to constitute the

Another seminal DIY offering: *Orcustus* **fanzine, created by Bård "Faust" Eithun in 1992.**

entire underground. They are more likely to alienate themselves from it intentionally, due to its mediocre and uninspiring nature."

While many will flinch at Erik's words, he is not alone. Many of those who were there in the early days argue that the underground only meant something when *all* black metal was "underground black metal," that the commercialization of certain elements of the genre have lifted the mystery and meaning from the beast as a whole. This is an opinion voiced by Metalion, editor of *Slayer*, and a man who has seen the genre develop from its humble beginnings.

"There is no way we can go back to how things once were. Black metal has been exploited and populated by the masses. And I'm sure there is still real black metal out there with people cutting themselves deeply with razor blades. But everything is so *big* and *normal* now, so everyone knows about it. For me, the magic is long gone though I certainly enjoy some current stuff as well. I really don't care anymore, what once was so unique and no one knew about is forever gone. It is very strange to see how public and normal everything is now."

Whether the magic of the movement has been lost is a matter of opinion, though there can be no doubt that many of today's bands are recycling musical and ideological ideas that are a decade or two old. That said, though there are more substandard bands than ever before, clinging onto the concept of the underground to disguise their own failures, there are also more underground black metal bands worthy of praise than ever before. Bands who are resolutely dedicated to creating black art without compromise still claim the underground as their own, and more importantly still believe that it has some meaning beyond a sales tactic. Shatraug of long-running Finnish underground institution Horna (and the newer but similarly minded Behexen) is one individual who still views the underground as a relevant concept, and speaks with some optimism on the future.

"I think Horna is still as much underground as when we released our first album. The name is known, we are touring and we've been around for a long time, but we are still doing this music from the depths of our souls, earning shit on the way. For me, selling out would be to try [to] please the commercial market, to do better and better productions, tons of merchandising, appearances on worthless events, making money as a top priority to gain. The underground will remain as long as there are individuals sharing common views, spreading music without making it a commercial widespread cancer, cultivating the art of death in the shadows of this genre…. What makes the underground is the aim to please and satisfy personal needs of worship and passion, not the needs of a commercial market or dictations of a record label."

One man who has experienced working both within the underground and outside it is Tom Warrior of Hellhammer and Celtic Frost. "Intuitively I've always been drawn to the underground," he says thoughtfully. "One of the few liberating things about losing Celtic Frost from my life was to make my music [in Trypticon] slightly more underground, that was something I missed in my life, especially after the *Monotheist* album came out. Of course I enjoyed touring at that level, but it isn't really what I'm all about. The underground has always been the birthplace of interesting stuff, so of course I like to see when a black metal band stays underground and as real as possible. But as I said, I enjoyed touring on a big level and I understand if other musicians want that too. And it's of course a legitimate argument if you want to spread a message. The question is whether these bands *really* have a message. Are they Satanists? Do they have a philosophy to spread? There's a lot of so-called black metal bands who simply project an image because they think it's cool, they are not practicing Satanists, and far from that, they don't even *relate* to any of the related philosophies, the hatred or the nihilism or anything like that. There's quite a number of bands who do it simply because they think it looks cool, and it's simply a cheap image tool.

"The funny thing is my many visits to Scandinavia, and Norway especially, have led me to come to the conclusion that many black metal bands have members who would like to be huge rock stars and I find that very surprising. When I looked at black metal from a distance in the 1990s and had not met any of these people I thought they were all practicing Satanists, and many, many years later I see that they're musicians, like any other musicians. Some of them are just wanting to be rock stars—they like the glamour of the music scene, they like the attention, the groupies, the drink, they do all the same rock star antics that many of the more decadent bands do. On the one hand I think that's very human, on the other it disappoints me deeply. Sometimes you see these very well-known black metal protagonists shirtless, bent back with their guitars in the air, and it could be someone from [eighties glam rockers] *Ratt*, it's almost pathetic. Those are people who have huge names within the history of black metal, the most radical form of metal and then you see them in poses and clothes like that and it just doesn't go together for me—but then what can I say? I sang on *Cold Lake*, who am I to speak? But we want to be realistic and honest here, right? I listen freely to music and of course will sometimes listen to something by Dimmu Borgir, even if it's just out of interest. I'm not envious or anything—I know how hard it is to be a musician and for them it's fantastic, they're probably living the same dream that I lived—but black metal is to me not just yet another form of heavy metal, black metal is something totally different. Black metal has an ideology, an agenda. It has a certain totally radical philosophy behind it and that combines much better with underground and meager possibilities than the glamour of showbiz. If you are going to play black metal you should stay true to these things, otherwise you shouldn't call yourself black metal anymore."

"In a way I feel like it's okay that bands have become mainstream as it's opened up new markets for us," counters Mayhem's Necrobutcher. "Another good thing is that when Dimmu are on tour they wear their Mayhem shirts and aren't afraid to say they were inspired by Mayhem when they started, same as all these other bands. We didn't have any plans to explore the commercial side of it ... but I would say all in all it's a good thing."

"I don't find it weird that Dimmu Borgir are so successful, what is weird is that Dimmu can actually *pass* as black metal and then people believe it," concludes Darkthrone's Fenriz, a man who has dedicated himself to a multitude of underground and non-commercial music forms. "That's kind of fantastic 'cos if that slab of music had entered Helvete in '91, everyone would die laughing, break it and throw it out. When you're in a band you have to take thousands of choices. You can make all good choices, or a lot of bad choices like a band like Cradle of Filth, it's not like you did one choice that was bad or good, it's thousands of decisions that result in a band with high sales and no credibility, or low sales and high credibility. Now choose, people."

32
LES LÉGIONS NOIRES

"I know it must be popular to say, 'I was into Black Legions bands when nobody cared,' but this is fact. I bought the stuff from Isengard distribution run by Darken of Graveland when these were seriously unwanted, some cash in mail and you got them without much competition. You could see almost everybody laughing at the low skills of musicianship and be[ing] annoyed about the hate mail some of these guys sent around, even to Finland. Distros would sell something like the first Mütiilation CD and the Vlad Tepes/Belkètre split CD for like five dollars because nobody wanted them ... yet all these officially published works are some of the most remarkable master-pieces recorded in [the] history of black metal."

—Mikko Aspa (Clandestine Blaze/Northern Heritage Records)

"To all those who could get a copy of this Dark Work, we did not in the least release this crime of Vlad Tepes and Belkètre to become popular or arouse any form of attention, for publicity or to earn money... This will be the first and last on a label. Later on, we will only release demos, without label, which will be duplicated only to an extremely limited number of people, those we will consider as worthy, and not sold, because such feelings as Solitude, Sorrow, Despair, and Hate mustn't be sold."

—An excerpt from a four-page manifesto included within the sleeve of the Vlad Tepes/ Belkètre split *March To The Black Holocaust*

WHILE BLACK METAL'S popularity would increase dramatically following the explosion of activity in Norway in the early nineties—to the extent that bands such as Emperor, Cradle of Filth, Dimmu Borgir, Satyricon, and even Burzum became familiar names in the mainstream metal scene—this was also responsible for a surge of activity in the opposite direction, with young practitioners around the world eager to enter the cult according to the original (second-wave) set of values.

France's contemporary black metal scene has earned a place as one of the most highly respected in the world, with bands such as Deathspell Omega and Blut Aus Nord providing a truly cutting-edge take on the genre, and others such as Arkon Infaustus and Antaeus dem-

onstrating uncompromising ferocity. However, it is the country's first contributions to
the movement that have arguably proven the
most significant, and specifically the releases
from a legendary collective known as Les Légions Noires (LLN) or "The Black Legions."

Alongside an admiration for early pioneers such as Bathory, this mysterious clique
took much of their inspiration from the Norwegian second wave—particularly bands
such as Darkthrone, Mayhem, and Emperor—
drawing on their fierce musical inaccessibility
while also adopting the ethos espoused by
such acts and expanding upon it considerably.
By retaining the Satanic and misanthropic ideals while taking the elitist, anti-commercial
stance to its logical conclusion, LLN not only
helped refine what could be described as an
underground black metal "code of conduct,"

The *Celtic Poetry* cassette by Vlad Tepes, 1994.

but stayed truer to such an ideology than the Norwegian scene that inspired them.

Whereas the attention brought by the activities of the Norwegian inner circle put its
participants in the spotlight, allowing many participants to find greater recognition, those
within LLN remained in the shadows. No compromises, musical or ideological, were ever
made, and the group retained the vital element of mystery and intrigue gradually lost over
the years as the corpsepainted wraiths of Scandinavia were revealed to be (in most cases at
least) normal human beings.

So effective was their wall of secrecy, in fact, that most of those involved in LLN have
now effectively disappeared entirely into black metal legend, leaving only their music, their
pseudonyms, and a few grainy photos behind. Even with the speculation of an army of enthusiasts on the Internet, solid information on the members is rare and rumor is rife. Outlandish
stories—many with a surprising element of truth—abound, with tales of castle and forest
dwellings, group suicides, and secret languages.

Even the music itself has become the subject of an unbelievable degree of debate due
to the fact that only a handful of recordings in the LLN discography were ever "officially"
released. While Euronymous had sometimes discussed the idea of only sending records to
those deemed worthy, the LLN made the notion reality by restricting practically all releases to
highly limited, home-recorded tapes, generally distributed only to close contacts and those
within the LLN circle itself. Now perhaps the most bootlegged bands in the entire black
metal scene, counterfeit copies of genuine Black Legion releases, bogus recordings, and even

Black Murder, primarily a project of Black Legions member Vorlok Drakkstein.

entirely fabricated bands are now commonplace on sites such as eBay, where genuine items and fake tapes alike go for ridiculous prices.

Careless labeling from the tape-trading days has caused further confusion, with the misspelling of band names leading to the accidental creation of "new" nonexistent projects, and other recordings surfacing as hoaxes recorded by imitators and traded under purposely deceptive titles. Similarly, many songs are often listed on the Internet and even physical re-presses as "Untitled" simply because the track names have been lost to the sands of time.

"The despicable behavior of Internet merchants and clueless fanboys have resulted in [people] digging up all the material that should have remained private," complains Mikko Aspa. "It's hard to think what would be the worst phenomenon in underground black metal, but I think the Black Legions fanboys, in all its laughable contradictory bullshit, probably belongs close to top. To respect Black Legions, to me, would be to create real black metal. Not make tributes to Black Legions, but worship Satan."

With so much intrigue around the music, it's not surprising that LLN are sometimes portrayed as an example of hype over substance, or a bunch of talentless musicians churning out poorly recorded rubbish under unpronounceable names. This is greatly misguided: though *some* of their output has proven far from essential, the circle did indeed produce some remarkable pieces of black metal art.

All the same, the group would only really achieve recognition in retrospect. Like so many pioneers in this book, their genius was almost completely overlooked at the time, and though fans now clamor for their releases, back in the late nineties your author was able to pick up key recordings such as the Vlad Tepes/Belkètre split for less than the price of a pint of beer—not a hypothetical equation incidentally, during those poor student days.

Like almost every aspect of their history, the beginnings of Les Légions Noires are shrouded in mystery. It is, however, widely agreed that the circle was formed by one Vordb Bathor Ecsed—an individual also known as Vordb Le Diable, Vordb Dréagvor Uèzréèvb, and Avaëthre. The exact year of LLN's formation is uncertain, but it would appear to be somewhere around 1991 that the idea actually came to fruition, having been conceived some years earlier.

Prior to the circle's creation, Vordb had played with another LLN musician seemingly called Laurent, but better known as The Lord Aäkon Këetreh, in Chapel Of Ghouls, a band formed in 1989 and whose only known release—a 1990 six-track tape entitled *Prays to Nothingness*—is one of the earliest examples of French black metal. For unknown reasons the duo changed their name to Zelda some time after, and recorded a four-track rehearsal in March 1991, featuring material that was more technically proficient and displayed a greater death metal influence. Later the band would change their name to Belkètre, and become one of the first official LLN bands.

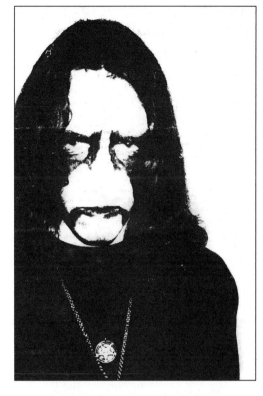

Satanicum Tenebrae, a solo project of Black Legions co-founder Meyhna'ch.

Another early member—probably a co-founder, and the man responsible for the term "Black Legions"—was one Meyhna'ch (real name Willy Roussel) who had recently formed Mütiilation. (The misspelling is intended; when asked about the peculiarity in *Northern Heritage* zine, Meyhna'ch replied, "we always make everything in 'wrong' way, Mütiilation is a 'wrong' project made for 'wrong' people in a 'wrong' world … happy?") Mütiilation was the longest visibly active group in the circle, and it would appear they were also the first to release any recordings, namely two tapes from 1992 (*Rehearsal 1992* and *Rites Through The Twilight Of Hell*), after which they issued the iconic seven-inch *Hail Satanas We Are The Black Legions*, from which the collective seems to have taken its name.

Another band joining the circle in its early days was Vlad Iepes, an act consisting of two musicians calling themselves Wlad Drakksteim and Vorlok Drakksteim (apparently not related, despite the choice of pseudonym), who entered the fold on the invitation of its founding members sometime after releasing their debut demo tape, *Rehearsal Winter '93*. Eventually becoming one of the best known of the Black Legions bands, these two members would lend their collective hand to a number of LLN acts.

By the year 1994 the collective had become well established, the trickle of releases that had begun the previous year (with *Despair*, Belkètre's debut tape, and *Abgzvoryathre* by Moëvöt, Vordb's solo project) now a veritable flood. The number of members in the circle isn't entirely clear, but appears to have included roughly ten to fifteen active musicians, with the five aforementioned individuals forming the nucleus. However, thanks to countless combinations of these members in projects and solo efforts, the number of "bands" recording music numbered somewhere between twenty and seventy, exact figures of *official* LLN acts being, of course, impossible to confirm.

LLN forged a hallmark sound, which was perhaps not surprising given the relatively small pool of musicians and their regular interactions. Taking the lo-fi approach to production to new extremes (Vlad Tepes memorably being described in one UK mail-order catalogue as making "Darkthrone sound like Rush"), LLN recordings can be split into two camps. On one side are aggressive, dirty-sounding black metal assaults, loosely played, with few—if any—overdubs, very little blasting in the percussion, and possessed-sounding vocals. At the other extreme sit somber and ritualistic black ambient pieces, generally without vocals but with enough depressive or disturbing overtones to equal their metal counterparts.

When not creating music, LLN followed in the footsteps of the Norwegian black circle and its creator Euronymous, issuing pledges of loyalty to the Satanic black metal cause and sending death threats and harassments to those considered traitorous, be it Christian metal bands or larger labels. Elsewhere the circle was more introspective and, as rumors contend, did indeed adopt their own language, usually referred to as "Gloatre." Never used in public statements, it seems highly doubtful that anyone ever *spoke* this language as such, but it might more accurately be described as a "code" used to disguise words in LLN music. The most obviously translatable word is "Vérmyapre" (vampire), and further examples are evident in unpronounceable band names such as Brenoritvrezorkre, Vagézaryavtre, and Vzaéurvbtre.

The rumor that members lived in a castle is also partly true, although this building, which appears in a number of photos of the period, was actually more of a manor or mansion that belonged to Meyhna'ch's family. A more unconfirmed story states that some members lived for a time in a forest, either in the very early days, as an attempt to distance themselves from society, or after they had departed the "castle" and had neither accommodation or income. The "Manson Family" comparisons made by Mortiis—who in fact has a curious link to the LLN story—earlier in this book seem particularly apt with regard to the circle, since references to "Helter Skelter" appear in at least one interview.

As should now be obvious, information on the circle is mainly second-hand at best, because interviews with the bands were rare. The members of Vlad Tepes were the most vocal, speaking in a number of fanzines, namely *Holocaust, Kill Yourself,* and *Petrified.* The latter was the work of Jon "Thorns" Jamshid of America's Full Moon Productions, a label that also released the band's five-track cassette *War Funeral March.* However, according to the Full Moon Productions webpage, after reviewing Belkètre and Vlad Tepes in *Petrified* and printing the band's contact addresses alongside the reviews, Thorns was promptly sent death threats by both bands, to which he responded in kind, stating that any attempts to enter his property would result in the bands' "leaving in body bags."

Elsewhere the circle's relationship with the international black metal scene was mixed. In the aforementioned interviews Wlad Drakksteim voices both an admiration and a distinct sense of disillusionment with the Scandinavian scene, heaping praise on acts such as Mayhem, Satyricon, Emperor, Bathory, and Burzum in his interview with *Petrified*, but later stating in *Kill Yourself* that the Scandinavian scenes had "…NOTHING IN COMMON WITH US! Norwegian bands made some great arts but unfortunately they are not as high as they let us to believe. Swedish ones just followed Norwegians … there is no single true black metal band in Finland."

Similarly, a Belkètre interview in Meyhna'ch's one-off zine *The Black Plague*, a tome essentially dedicated to LLN, has Vordb (under his Avaëthre pseudonym) asked what he thinks about "old, cult bands that seem to have nothing to do with Black Metal anymore," to which he responds, "Those bands have opened doors and now just slam them in our faces. They deny and destroy their own works and our legacy … May those dogs die like the rest, cult or not!"

Despite such hostilities, an interview with ex-Emperor bassist Mortiis—possibly seen as a like-minded soul due to his dark ambient works—was also included in *The Black Plague*, and it seems that at least one non-French act, Belgian stalwarts Enthroned, were invited to join the circle, though they declined, with frontman Nordagest apparently stating on an official forum that although Enthroned admired music by acts such as Belkètre they were put off by the behavior of certain members, which included sending either dead rats or rotten pizzas to Osmose Records.

Somewhere around 1996, the circle that had once burned so brightly began to implode. One issue was that material that had been shared only to trusted contacts was now becoming pirated and distributed against the wishes of its creators. However, the primary cause of the implosion seems to have come from Meyhna'ch's departure. There are many (unlikely) claims regarding the reasons for this, ranging from him being ejected for alleged drug addiction to the claim that he left of his own accord after taking offense at jokes regarding child abuse. For his part, Meyhna'ch has avoided mudslinging and remained diplomatic in interviews, stating, for example, in Spanish zine *Final Solution*:

"The Black Legions splitted [*sic*] in different parts around 1996 … I can't really tell why all ended, maybe because when too many dark souls stay together, there are tensions and feelings of competition about who will dominate the other ones."

"I created it with Vordb," explained Meyhna'ch in an interview with me following a performance with his current band Hell Militia. "I really don't miss it. I evolved and they did not. It's not that I don't want to speak of it, but I'm always asked about something that ended sixteen or seventeen years ago. The others they probably changed a lot more than I did, and finally I'm the one [who is] the fucking pariah. As well as the guy [Lord Beleth'Rim] from Vermeth and Torgeist—he's still active in a less public way—but him and me are probably the only ones who did not change, just [found a] different way of facing the truth. About the other ones I don't know, I don't keep in contact. People say a lot of things but it's dead for years now. I know some of them went in the woods to live like the Manson family, you know, without electricity and stuff like this, they chose their way I chose mine. Mine was to make music."

Whatever the reason for the schism, The Black Lord Beleth'Rim (who played with Vordb and Këetreh in a band called Torgeist and who still performs black metal today in Vermeth) was also set to depart. Spectators have tended to either put the blame for the circle's collapse on these two departing members, or instead point to the flaws of the remaining members. Either way, 1997 saw very little activity, with only a couple of releases, including the final solo tape of Aäkon Këetreh, who would himself also depart soon after. 1998 saw the final LLN release, a tape from Vlad Tepes, who finished their career, perhaps fittingly, with a compilation of cover material entitled simply *The Black Legions*, covering Brenoritvrezorkre, Belkètre, and Mütiilation.

And that, apparently, was the end of that. There are claims that The Black Legions still exist, hidden from the masses, distributing their music among themselves, but this seems unlikely. Others claim that the musicians have turned their backs on black metal altogether. As mentioned, Beleth'Rim is still active today, as is Meyhna'ch, who returned following a hiatus and greatly exaggerated rumors of his death. Vordb himself appears to have made a brief online presence in 2008, specifically to discredit a release claiming to contain new material from his Moëvöt project. Bootlegging and forgeries have only escalated since the downfall of the LLN, using material allegedly spread or sold by ex-members—a treachery perhaps, but one that many fans have to thank for the availability of the recordings.

MÜTIILATION

The majority of the Mütiilation discography was released in the years following the band's departure from LLN, though their early recordings are some of their most admired works. 1994's *Hail Satanas We Are The Black Legions* seven-inch remains iconic, but even more so is 1995's *Vampires of Black Imperial Blood*, which was not only Mütiilation's first full-length and Drakkar Production's first release, but also LLN's only full-length, non-split album released on a record label.

Though Mütiilation would be a solo project post-LLN (with Meyhna'ch programming drums and using a session drummer on 2007's *Sorrow Galaxies*), in the LLN days a number of other musicians appeared alongside Meyhna'ch, including bassist Mørdrëd and two drummers, Dark Wizzard of Silence and Krissagrazabeth (who also had an early LLN solo project entitled Belathuzur). The band would also use members of Celestia (a black metal band featuring Noktu of Drakkar Productions) for their rare live appearances.

Having engineered announcements of his own death—perhaps meant metaphorically but read literally by many—on 1999's *Remains of a Ruined, Dead, Cursed Soul* compilation,

Meyhna'ch re-emerged with new material on the aptly named *Black Millenium (Grimly Reborn)*, whose iconic cover features the protagonist in a wheelchair. He followed up with three more albums (2003's *Majestas Leprosus*, 2005's *Rattenkönig*, and 2007's *Sorrow Galaxies*) and several split/compilation records (including *From the Entrails to the Dirt*, which featured a cover of "My Way," a song first made famous by Frank Sinatra, but apparently covered here as a tribute to Sid Vicious) before the band officially split in 2009. On the band's official web space Meyhna'ch stated in typically bleak tones:

> "MÜTIILATION IS DEAD! No more hope, nothing more to say …
> Sorrow Galaxies was probably the consecration of Mütiilation's story. All I see is a empty grey horizon. I now just wait for Death. It was more than 15 years we spent … you and I. Now it's over … see you in Hell motherfuckers … "

The vocalist would contribute to a number of other projects however, including the short-lived Gestapo 666 (again featuring Noktu), Malicious Secrets (featuring Celestia bassist TND), Sektemtum, and perhaps most prominently, Hell Militia, an outfit featuring members of respected French outfits Vorkreist, Temple of Baal, and Arkhon Infaustus.

VLAD TEPES

One of the earliest LLN acts, Vlad Tepes were also one of the most visible and did much to fly the flag for the circle. As well as giving interviews in a number of fanzines and making three "official" releases, they were notably vocal about the circle itself. Their finale is named simply *The Black Legions*, and their second demo *Celtic Poetry* (1994) features the same words on the cover along with the goat skull and pentagram image that would become synonymous with LLN as a whole. In interviews, the group also revealed that many of their lyrics dealt directly with the LLN circle.

Frequently written off, like many LLN bands, as musically clueless, the works of the duo—Wlad (vocals, guitars, drums) and Vorlok (bass, vocals)—often showcase both impressive musicianship and songcraft, particularly on the part of main songwriter Wlad. Though they were undoubtedly "sloppy" players, the fact that most of their songs appear several times in different renditions (completists will find themselves with five or more versions of some key songs) reveals just how much spontaneity the band were capable of.

After releasing their debut cassette (*Rehearsal Winter '93*), the band would release three more demo tapes during 1994, the last of which, *War Funeral March*, was released by Full Moon Productions in a run of a thousand copies, but originally sold so badly that most copies ended up in storage, ultimately to be either binned due to damage or sold off in 2002.

Now much sought after, the opus was later released on CD by Embassy Productions, and despite the challenging discordance of the opening track—seemingly there to put off the weak of heart—the four remaining tracks are essential Vlad Tepes material.

Three more demos would follow before the band's split release with Belkètre, 1995's *March to the Black Holocaust* (released on CD by Embassy Productions in a thousand hand-numbered copies), one of the few official releases by the Black Legions and arguably one of the finest black metal splits of all time. Vlad Tepes' side proves to be raw as hell itself, with both thrash and punk overtones, yet also shows a surprising taste for melody, solos, and even groove during the eight contributions. Another split (*Black Legions Metal*) would follow in 1996, this time with Torgeist and released on Drakkar Productions, though this proved somewhat less essential and all but one of the songs would appear on the *Dans Notre Chute* tape a few months later.

1997's *Le Morte Lune* was an infinitely more significant effort. With ten tracks (nine previously unreleased), the tape is effectively an album and is well worthy of investigation despite the sound quality being enough to put off even hardened black metal fans. Crank up the stereo and immerse yourself, however, and this proves to be an atmospheric and varied listen, swinging from the melancholic, almost new wave vibe of "I Died From A Vampyric Grief" to the brief aural violence of "Dark War," seemingly inspired directly by *Deathcrush*-era Mayhem. A final covers tape (the aforementioned *The Black Legions*) would see the light of day in 1998 and mark the apparent end of both the band and the circle.

Wlad and Vorlok also played together (along with Vordb) in Black Murder, a band whose more chaotic and violent nature was perhaps not surprising given that sole songwriter Vorlok claimed he only composed "when I want to kill." Another seemingly short-lived project, in which Wlad dominated and Vorlok played only bass, was Vérmyapre Kommando, whose self-titled demo was based solely around war themes.

BELKÈTRE

Having released demos recorded as Chapel of Ghouls and Zelda, Vordb and Aäkon Këëtrëh settled on Belkètre (supposedly meaning "oath"), and issued three demos in 1993 and 1994 before release *March to the Black Holocaust* in 1995. Contributing eight tracks of pure malevolence recorded on a four-track recorder, the sound quality has an unusually icy, high-pitched rawness that slices straight into the unconscious. Opening number "Guilty" offers a momentary warning thanks to a combination of tape hiss and feedback, before erupting into some of the nastiest, most extreme black metal yet recorded. Genuinely unsettling in parts, the material includes unrelenting and uncompromising black metal tracks and crude, yet hellishly eerie, instrumentals such as "Hate."

Two years later a full-length album entitled *Ambre Zuerkl Vuordhre-
varhtre* (spelling varies) was recorded,
and, despite being supposedly shared
with only five people, soon spread outside of the circle. Notably different in
nature from the Vlad Tepes spilt, *Ambre* is a somewhat less searing listen,
boasting less rabidly aggressive material and with a production less harmful to the ears. The psychedelically
tinged album opens with a haunting
instrumental featuring multilayered
guitars that takes hold of the listener
and drags them—like a sleeping pill-
propelled suicide—into a melancholy,

The seminal *Hail Satanas We Are The Black Legions*
seven-inch by Mütiilation, 1994.

dreamy realm. The first proper song, "A Dark Promise," proves that the band had made
considerable steps in their songwriting, beginning with a swaggering riff and breaking into
well-considered leads, adopting something close to a traditional song structure as opposed
to a relentless assault.

For years a rumor persisted that the duo had committed group suicide (some versions
claiming that they'd committed several murders first), but there is no evidence of this and
the idea may even have stemmed from Vordb's words in *Black Plague* where he talks in somewhat fatalistic terms about his solo project Moëvöt: "Creation, more precisely the claim to
creation, is purely human and so undeniably illusive. Only destruction is Satanic and eternal.
I'm not a creator but a destructor. My works have no future in this world."

DARK AMBIENT PROJECTS

"Black ambient" projects were common in LLN and vary massively in nature and quality. Often ridiculously minimal, they have fueled LLN detractors; one notable example is
Mogovtre, whose demo, legend states, was recorded by members of Vlad Tepes by inserting a
microphone into the anus of either a rat or a Bichon dog. Despite such self-indulgence, some
Black Legions ambient projects are notable, perhaps the most acclaimed being the solo efforts
of the members of Belkètre—Vordb recording under the Moëvöt moniker and Aäkon Këëtrëh
recording under his own pseudonym.

In both cases the music is minimalist, melancholic, and frequently primitive. At times it

The magnificent *March to the Black Holocaust*, 1995. A split between two of the most celebrated (today at least) bands within the Black Legions, Vlad Tepes and Belkètre, and one of the few official releases to emerge from the circle.

appears purposely so, such as in the case of Aäkon Këëtrëh, where errors in simplistic linear material are so glaring that one can assume they were either intentional or kept for effect, a point also true of some of the creepy ambient tracks in Belkètre. Throughout the project's three demos—*Journey Into The Depths of Night* (1995), *Dans La Forêt* (1996), and *The Dark Winter* (1997)—Aäkon Këëtrëh retains a mournful atmosphere, while also advancing in terms of technicality, although don't go expecting Dream Theater—it's still pretty primal.

Also featuring a number of short keyboard and guitar tracks, Moëvöt takes a less fragmented approach and is more chilling in atmosphere, Vordb frequently making use of his vocal range and contributing genuinely impressive clean vocals in chants, often unaccompanied. Meyhna'ch's solo project, Satanicum Tenebrae, also dipped its toes into dark ambient territories and finally, though arguments over its LLN status continue, Beleth'Rim's project Amaka Hahina is also worth investigation.

> *"If we had to be something for 'Jesus Christ,' We would be its Last Breath. If We had to be something for 'mankind,' its shameful 'creation,' We wouldn't even accept to be its memory … If We had to be something for this 'world,' We would be its Last Twilight, an Irreversible Twilight … But all of them know the way of their own end and We are just here to prevent them straying from it."*
> —*March To The Black Holocaust* statement.

33
MARDUK
SWEDEN PART I

"When I think of black metal, I think of Marduk. With Marduk there is no compromise, and they keep on delivering one great album after the other. They are one of the most intense live bands that I know of, and there's no fucking bullshit with them. Marduk is krieg!"

—Hváll (Windir and Vreid)

FORMED WITH the ambitious goal of becoming "the most brutal and blasphemous metal act ever," Marduk have sweated for over two decades to bring blood, darkness, and an unrelentingly ferocious brand of metal to the world, rightfully earning a place as one of Sweden's most famous—or perhaps more accurately, *infamous*—black metal bands. Unleashed at the very birth of the nineties, they can be counted among the small number of bands who kept the unholy flame of black metal alive, just a few years before the genre exploded in a wave of church burnings, destruction, and notoriety. Against a tide of increasingly mainstream and inoffensive death and thrash metal, the Swedes brought life once more to the spirit of eighties pioneers such as Hellhammer, Celtic Frost, and particularly Bathory, whose work had profoundly impacted guitarist and founding member Morgan "Evil" Håkansson.

Despite this heritage, Marduk also illustrate the often blurred line between black and death metal (which was exploding in Sweden at the time), and initially leant unequivocally toward what is often referred to as the "Stockholm sound," popularized by Nihilist, Entombed, and Dismember. Favoring big doomy riffs, pounding, uncomplicated percussion, a sense of morbid groove and a downtuned, crunchy tone, the sub-genre took heavy inspiration from early American acts, a source that Marduk were also drawing upon directly in the forging of their uncompromising vision.

"For me black metal doesn't have a specific sound," spits Morgan, a man whose lighting-fast speech mirrors his well-publicized obsession with firepower and military history. "Today bands will say, 'Oh, we have black metal vocals,' but what *is* 'black metal vocals'? For me it can be any way you want. For me, black metal's definition is simply extreme music with

One of Marduk's earliest corpsepainted shoots, taken from debut album *Dark Endless*, 1992.

a Satanic philosophy and belief. We always had—and especially when we began—a lot of death metal influence from real death metal bands like Morbid Angel, early Deicide, Immolation, and Autopsy."

Another direct source of inspiration—not least in the band's adoption of corpsepaint—was Swedish vocalist Per "Dead" Ohlin of Morbid and Mayhem fame, with whom Morgan had become friends in the late eighties. Not surprisingly this also led to him becoming well acquainted with Dead's bandmate Euronymous, which led to visits to his Helvete store in Oslo and even attempts to arrange live shows for Mayhem in Sweden. When Dead died in April 1991, Morgan was one of a very small number of trusted contacts sent a piece of his skull by Euronymous.

"I still have it, it's like a holy relic you know?" Morgan confirms. "I started corresponding with Dead after he moved to Norway, early '89, and was in contact with him up until his death. I mean it's many years ago—and when I look upon it, he was only twenty-one, twen-

ty-two when he committed suicide
and how old was I—but I *was* impressed by him. He had a strong
personality and a strong belief. He
was an inspiring personality I would
say, very serious about what he was
doing, but still a very humorous guy.
It was probably the most bizarre humor somebody ever had, you know?
Very morbid, bad, typical Swedish
humor I would say. Euronymous I
considered to be a great friend and
comrade, we worked a lot together."

Marduk's own recording
career would begin shortly after
Dead's demise, with the band's sole
demo *Fuck Me Jesus*. Opening with
a sample from *The Exorcist*'s notori-

The infamous *Fuck Me Jesus* demo, originally
released on cassette in 1991, and rereleased with this
more well-known cover art in 1995.

ous "crucifix masturbation scene," the opus compounded its blasphemous content when
re-released on CD some years later thanks to a similarly themed cover illustration that led to
bans in at least seven countries. Recorded and produced by the talented Dan Swanö—then
known as vocalist of progressive death metal act Edge of Sanity, but soon to be famed for
production work at his studio Unisound—the demo proved a considerable hit, earning the
sort of impressive sales that are all but impossible in today's Internet age.

"We got in contact with a lot of bands and it was the days when you could sell *thousands* of copies of demos," Morgan explains. "Everything was exciting and there was a lot of
great music coming out. We formed a strong relationship with people all around the world,
with zines and printed magazines. It was a time when we had a strong vision to push the
boundaries beyond what had already been done, to go one step ahead. We had a very strong
devotion and concept and let that inspiration carry us wherever it might. Some people loved
it, some people hated it—that's the way it's always been. Dan Swanö had been a friend since
the early years, his studio was the focal point in this area… in the three or four years after
that bands were traveling from all over the world to record at his small studio."

The same year also saw the recording of a seven-inch entitled *Here's No Peace* (the title
came from a drawing Dead had sent Morgan), which would have been the band's first official
release had it not ultimately been shelved until 1997. The band also played their first live
shows, which also had a hint of Dead's destructive stage presence about them.

"We delivered bloodshed and violence," Morgan explains. "We mostly played in our
hometown and the area around, and it was very strange because people weren't used to what

we were doing at all. You know, we cut ourselves up and bled on the audience, it was quite intense and kind of a shock for a lot of people. But we got a really great following from the shows we did at that time."

Through a combination of explosive live shows and recorded material, Marduk steadily built a name for themselves and were soon signed by Swedish label No Fashion Records, who released their debut album, *Dark Endless*, in the closing weeks of 1992. Featuring a second guitarist in the form of one Magnus "Devo" Anderson, the recording proved even more death-ly than the demo, but though the band were satisfied with the finished product—despite having to record it in four days due to a limited budget—they were ultimately rather less than happy with their record deal. Following an alleged problem regarding payments, they decided to jump ship for the far more established French label Osmose Productions.

In September 1993, the band released their sophomore album, *Those Of The Unlight*, a record that saw a major lineup shift, with original bassist Richard Kaim and vocalist Andreas Axelsson departing, the former being replaced by B. War (Bogge Svensson) and the latter—more surprisingly—being replaced by Marduk's drummer Joakim Gøthberg.

"We had this lineup change right before the recording because we were not satisfied with the vocalist due to a general lack of interest—not turning up to rehearsals [for example] … So we decided to let him go and we hadn't even decided which vocalist to use when we began to record the album. In the end our drummer did a tryout for the vocals and it worked out very well. He actually put down three-quarters of the album the day he decided to become the vocalist. The whole album was recorded in three days and mixed on the fourth—working fast and furious you know?" Morgan laughs. "We didn't *know* another way to work, it wasn't like today when you spend ages in the studio, we just went in and did it."

Joakim's vocals proved far closer to the higher-pitched, "screeched" approach quickly becoming established within black metal, and the musical content of the album also largely mirrored such a transition. Gone were almost all "death metal" elements, the album dropping much of the raw brutality of its predecessor for a more ethereal atmosphere, greater melody, and the sort of urgent, treble-heavy riffing that was fast becoming the hallmark of Scandina-vian black metal. Perhaps most shocking of all was the inclusion of an emotive instrumental named "Echoes From The Past," which utilized not only clean guitars but also keyboards.

Remaining as productive as ever, the band released their third album, *Opus Nocturne*, at the end of 1994, a year that also saw them embark on their first international tour, along with labelmates Immortal. The album introduced another significant stylistic shift, the Swedes now presenting a far icier and more aggressive sound, characterized by thin, slicing guitars, an even more treble-heavy tone and insanely high-paced, blasting percussion. The reason for this shift was fairly straightforward, coinciding directly with the addition of new drummer Fredrik Andersson and the loss of second guitarist Devo.

"We decided to keep Joakim as the frontman and get a new drummer," explains Mor-gan. "Fredrik was an even more intense drummer and more hard-hitting, so we increased the speed, because we had already decided to become faster and go one step ahead from what we had done before. Joakim was really happy to just focus on vocals and it also meant we got a drummer who was really thrilled to be in the band and had that *hunger*."

The album was the last to be recorded with Dan Swanö and was also notable for the inclusion of the track "Materialized in Stone," a discarded Mayhem song title and the final direct tribute to fallen comrade Dead, following the aforementioned "Here's No Peace" and a song entitled "Burn My Coffin" on *Those of the Unlight*, taken from another unused song title that Dead had mentioned in correspondence with Morgan.

1995 brought a CD re-release of their demo, which caused a fair bit of controversy due to its title and artwork, with distributors refusing to handle the release in Germany, Austria, France, England, Holland, Belgium, and Switzerland. The band also gave a somewhat controversial interview featuring politically insensitive comments, which led to German magazines moving to boycott the band. More constructively, 1995 saw the band head to The Abyss studio—owned by Hypocrisy frontman Peter Tägtgren, with whom the group were already close—to re-mix *Those of the Unlight*. The band also recorded their next album there, namely 1996's *Heaven Shall Burn … When We Are Gathered*, whose title pays homage to Bathory's song "Dies Irae" and the line "Even the heavens shall burn when we are gathered."

Maintaining the high pace but boasting a far bigger, clearer sound, the album also introduced new gravel-throated vocalist Erik "Legion" Hagstedt, whom Morgan had first encountered while Legion was in a studio recording vocals for Ophthalamia, an act featuring members of black metal ambient act Abruptum, a project Morgan contributed to under his "Evil" pseudonym.

"I heard his voice and I really admired what he was doing," explains Morgan. "We got to know each other and became really good friends, we really had a connection. We actually fired [Joakim]. We were into doing more touring, we wanted to expand … People don't always want to focus, to work, to tour, and it's better then to be out of a band, out of the picture."

As well as cementing the band's musical style, the album also set another precedent thanks to the historical nature of its content, with "Glorification of the Black God" being a black metal adaptation of Russian composer Modest Mussorgsky's "Night on Bald Mountain" and the song "Dracul va Domni Din Nou in Transilvania" telling the story of Romania's Vlad Tepes, more commonly known as Vlad the Impaler. The story of the notoriously brutal and sadistic Wallachian ruler would continue on 1998's *Nightwing*, the band dedicating the second half of the album to telling the story of his life, a subject with which Morgan and Legion were both fascinated.

Nightwing and its follow-up *Panzer Division Marduk* both continued in a similar vein, focusing on high-speed brutality while boasting increasingly dynamic, clear, and punchy productions courtesy of The Abyss and Peter Tägtgren, who had now toured with the band as a second guitarist. Interestingly, 1999's *Panzer Division Marduk* is the second part of a loose "Blood, Fire, Death" trilogy concept—another crafty Bathory reference—and where *Nightwing* represented "blood," *Panzer* represented "fire" thanks to its focus on *firepower*, the record being saturated with military imagery, in the sleeve design, lyrics, title, and even music itself, thanks to the use of battlefield samples. It was a powerful aesthetic that recalled bands such as Bolt Thrower and one that would later be echoed by other black metal bands including Swedish supergroup War (again featuring members of Abruptum and Ophthalamia) and German band Endstille.

"I was reading a lot of history and some things inspire you so much you cannot let them go," Morgan remarks. "I was really inspired and was reading about it so much that I decided to incorporate these [themes] along with the other things we were doing, so some of the lyrics have a historical basis, some have not. I was interested in history since I was young and I have about four hundred books on World War II, along with books on Swedish and European history. I'm interested in lots of parts of history, but some creates music in my head and some doesn't. I tend not to be inspired by music, I tend to be inspired by *things*. When I watch a documentary about certain subjects it creates a soundtrack in my mind, that's the way it is with any historical happenings I use, [it's about] the picture it creates in my mind."

Strangely, while the cover to 1997 EP *Here's No Peace* had actually featured a German Panzer tank, the cover of the *Panzer Division Marduk* ended up featuring a non-German Centurion tank thanks to a decision by label Osmose, who perhaps foresaw the problematic nature of such imagery. The original image would eventually adorn the cover, however, on the 2008 reissue by Blooddawn Productions and Regain Records.

"It's a panzer but it's an English panzer," explains Morgan of the original release. "Actually it's a Swedish Centurion tank, made by the English, but that's the Swedish version. I wanted to use another photo, but the record label was a bit hesitant at that time to use things from World War II, so I found this picture taken [after the war] in Sweden. It really reflected the spirit of the album—aggressive and right in your face."

Perhaps predictably, given the Germanic-sounding title and the fact that the album was arriving on the back of speculation about the band's political affiliation, the subtle difference between a Swedish and German tank escaped most people. The band also hadn't done much to help the situation with the 1997 live album *Live in Germania*, whose title and eagle-adorned cover had caused many raised eyebrows. That being said, it's worth noting that the eagle design was the same one on all One Deutsche Mark coins at the time, a point the head of Osmose Records highlighted by changing some currency in France and sending the offended parties the coin in question.

"Yeah, it caused problems," recalls Morgan. "A lot of problems. But we overcame them all and I don't care. We're artists, we do what we do, if anyone wants to fuck with us, we'll fuck back. It's strange how people react to things. If you do a movie about a certain historical topic nobody would care, if you did a painting, nobody would care, but if you make music about it, it seems to be very annoying to people. But some people cannot see beyond certain things, because they are too politically correct to use their own heads. Magazines reacted very badly—they were faxing local promoters telling them to boycott us. But we only got stronger so it didn't really work. They wanted us to go out and say we're not this and we're not that, but I don't have an interest in saying 'I'm not this or that,' 'cos I didn't say I'm that in the beginning, you know? I'm not here to apologize for what we do … Even Slayer and Motörhead covered the same topics.… I don't care about politics, I read a lot about history and politics but I don't have a political view you know?"

All the same, the band did make an effort to explain in interviews that there was a clear difference between exploring real historical themes and advocating Nazi ideologies. This sated some critics, though the fact that Morgan had already said he was proud of his grandfather serving as a German officer in World War II somewhat undermined these statements.

Ironically, Marduk's attempt to distance themselves from extreme right-wing ideologies also ended up fuelling something of a backlash from certain elements in the extreme right of the black metal scene, who felt betrayed by such a move, the band even being attacked by name in the lyrics of Ukrainian act Aryan Terrorism, a side project of prominent NSBM band Nokturnal Mortum. Despite attacks from both sides, however, Marduk largely stuck to their guns, becoming one of the more successful bands in the international black metal scene and a regular and well-reputed touring act, a fact underlined by the release of another live album, *Infernal Eternal*, in 2000.

Indeed, by now the band had become a reliable fixture of the Swedish scene, to the extent that they were even at risk of becoming predictable, with 2001's *La Grande Danse Macabre* and 2003's *World Funeral* generally being received as solid but certainly not ground-breaking releases. It's telling that perhaps the biggest change from *Panzer Division Marduk* and the two albums that followed was the fact that the band were no longer signed to Osmose, instead releasing their works through their own record label, Blooddawn Productions, and distributing them via Swedish label Regain.

Stagnation was looming, but a significant turning point for the band was soon to occur following *World Funeral*, thanks to the departure of vocalist and frontman Legion. A somewhat acrimonious event at the time, one can't help but suspect that ultimately the split was beneficial to both parties, Legion going on to front the band Devian (also featuring Emil Dragutinovic, the drummer of Marduk from 2002 to 2006) and Marduk completely rejuvenating themselves with the addition of Daniel "Mortuus" Rosten, better known as Arioch, mainman of "Funeral Mist."

"Mortuus was the only one I wanted, so I set out to get him," Morgan states simply. "I contacted him and we spoke and we shared a lot of visions and ideas for what it could become. I wanted someone not only with focus, but a strong personality that would bring something new to the band. I didn't want a replacement that would sound exactly the same. I'd heard his voice and thought he used it in a very powerful way that would fit this band perfectly."

Frankly, it was a collaboration that surprised a lot of people. Funeral Mist represented a leading light in Sweden's "third generation" black metal underground, a slow-growing hotbed of revolutionary fanatics who were putting the country on the map with critically acclaimed

Vocalist since 2004, Mortuus surveys the battlefield. Photo: Ester Segarra.

and deeply religious (in the Satanic sense of course) efforts. In contrast, Marduk had become rather closer to the establishment, and were in danger of becoming viewed as safe by the scene. Yet the combination of the two forces would prove to be explosive, Marduk once again becoming a relevant, and even cutting-edge band, and Mortuus' talents reaching a far greater audience than before.

"Morgan called me and I thought about it for a few days," confirms Mortuus, a polite but extremely serious individual, whose sizable frame and guarded manner reflect his extensive training in martial arts. "After we discussed our goals, I realized we have lots in common about our opinion of black metal and our visions. One of the first things Morgan said was that I would have complete creative control of my work, which was essential."

"As far as a bigger audience goes: I am a musician, I want to spread my music. I have a message in my lyrics and I want as many as possible to hear it and I never try to have this underground, only-a-select-few-can-hear-it thing. I want as many as possible to hear my music, otherwise I wouldn't release it, I would just play for myself. It makes no sense—if you don't want people to hear your music, you should just record a demo and hand it to your friends that you trust. But why would you do that? I want everyone to get my albums, if they're not into what I'm doing, maybe they will be after they hear the album. *That's* more the point, rather than just keeping it away from everyone."

Vitally, Morgan and Mortuus also discovered common ground in their standpoint on Satanism, which plays a prominent role in both men's lives, and which both maintain is a mandatory element within both the genre and Marduk itself.

"*All* black metal is religious in my eyes," Morgan states. "All these different types of black metal ... to me it's black metal or it's not black metal. People ask me, 'Are you black metal?' Yes we are. We are one of probably only five bands who *are* black metal, 'cos no one wants to be black metal, they want to be 'neo-this' and 'experimental-that,' but we are proud to carry the banner of black metal."

"That's what black metal is," concurs Mortuus. "If it's not about devil worship or destructive Satanism, I couldn't call it black metal. It's not like black metal *has* to be Satanic—if it's not Satanic, it's not black metal, it's 'something else-metal'—there's a million labels, choose one of them. Black metal is Satanic metal. I really don't like to label myself, but if there *would* be a label for it, it would be devil worship. That's what it is, even if I don't like the term."

"It's something you discover in life and it's the call of your life, I would say, and it will always be," adds Morgan of his beliefs. "I think it's very clear with the lyrics and everything *why* we do it. For me it's a religion. I would say it's both metaphorical and literal, that's how I look upon it. [And] it's not that you have to have the *exact* same ideas to be in the band, but you have to have a certain shared ground in your philosophy or it wouldn't work. We share a lot of devotions and ideas and a burning desire for what we do. Otherwise I think it would be hard to work together on music and lyrics."

The first recorded result of this unholy union was 2004's *Plague Angel*, an album that proved to be a storming return to form. Alternating between high-tempo blasts (courtesy of drummer Emil Dragutinovic, who had replaced Fredrik Anderssonon on the previous album) and slower, moodier numbers such as "Perish In Flames" and "Seven Angels, Seven Trumpets," the album boasted both energy and dynamism, along with sharper riffs and a vocal performance that was both unconventional and memorable. Lyrically, the album continued in a familiar vein, exploring military and World War II themes in numbers such as "Steel Inferno," "The Hangman of Prague" (a reference to SS general Reinhard Heydrich) and "Warshau," while also tapping the Bible for inspiration in numbers such as "Everything Bleeds," based on Joan of Arc, and the Milton-esque "Life's Emblem."

"Religious fanaticism has always been a great inspiration, especially Christian fanaticism," replies Mortuus. "It highlights the darker sides of, for example, Christianity. I would say it's impossible *not* to discover that, if you study the Bible it is ten times as sick as any black metal band today."

"You have to know your enemy," smiles Morgan, "and there's also a lot of fascinating things to find there."

Such inspirations were more than clear in the 2007 follow-up *ROM 5:12*, named after the verse in the New Testament book of Romans that reads "Wherefore, as by one man sin entered into the world, and death by sin; and so death passed upon all men, for that all have sinned." It would prove an apt title for thve album, given the dominant themes involved, as Morgan related to me in somewhat bleak terms when we met in Stockholm for an interview for *Metal Hammer UK* a few months before its release.

"That chapter really reflects the spirit, the atmosphere and the lyrics of the album … There is a lot of thinking about death and how it is looked upon by humans, and how that perspective changes from time to time. We have taken a lot of influence from the German baroque writers for example, who looked at humans as merely a hopeless pile of bones, a hand full of nothing. 'Scepter and crown must tumble down … '" he quotes before pausing. "The word I would use to best describe the album is 'vanity.' The whole human race is vanity. All the humans here," he gestures at the other occupants in the bar, "are just ashes, bones. Nothing."

Including guest vocal appearances from Alan "Naihmass Nemtheanga" Averill of Ireland's Primordial and ex-Marduk member Joakim Gøthberg, the album also saw a far greater input from Mortuus, his personality shining through in the lyrics, which eschew war themes in favor of explorations of Christianity and mortality (familiar topics in Funeral Mist) as well as in the forty-four-page CD booklet of macabre medieval and religious imagery that he designed.

If anything, 2009's *Wormwood* was even closer to Funeral Mist territory, carrying with it the same raw, stark, and unsettlingly intimate vibe of Mist's *Marantha*, released earlier the same year. Representing something of a departure for Marduk—as well as a veritable sonic journey for the listener—the album reveals numerous surprising twists, from the rousing "Funeral Dawn" to the haunting details and emotive riffing of "Whorecrown," through to the minimalist "Unclosing the Curse." A startlingly bold move, the album was undoubtedly more challenging than its two predecessors, but perhaps all the more rewarding for it, and was widely praised by both critics and fans. In many respects Mortuus seems to have allowed the band to tap into something more personal and nightmarish, in contrast to the broader strokes of earlier material.

2012's *Serpent Sermon* did not move away entirely from such bleak pastures, a point highlighted by the creepy "Souls for Belial" and the brooding "Temple of Decay," which backs Mortuus' croaked utterances with atmospheric chanted vocals. Nonetheless, the album also saw the band utilizing a warmer production and coloring the riffing and song structures with a groove and epic overtone that hint at a similar accessibility and sense of stirring drama as the works of younger countrymen such as Watain.

A flyer for one of Marduk's regular live shows.

For a band often pigeonholed as somewhat one-dimensional, Marduk have exhibited a surprising amount of variation during their twenty-plus years. Whatever era one favors, the fact that they have been going so long, consistently recording and touring the world, remains impressive. In fact, playing live is still of utmost importance to the band, with Morgan's own ambitions for the future focusing largely touring new parts of the world, something that might suggest a shift in his attitude from earlier days.

"I believe in the power of our music, particularly live in front of an audience," he concludes. "I think it shows its most triumphant part when it gets right in your face. For me every country has its good and bad parts, but the opportunity to play many parts of the world for me has always been very fascinating, the true dedication of places like South America … We like to play the parts where not everybody plays. We were one of the first bands to play in Guatamala, Salvador, Venezuela—that was an amazing experience. People so dedicated there was fire in the air, you know? The feeling of playing in front of such a fanatic crowd is totally magic. There's a lot of parts we still haven't been … We're excited and thrilled at the opportunity to even play in Africa, places like that. I don't know if they have a scene, but later on for sure. I'd like to cover more of Asia as well. You still have the black-clad legions in the old Morbid shirts, you know? There always will be people in every country who are loyal and dedicated."

34
DISSECTION AND WATAIN
SWEDEN PART II

"When I was younger, I was obsessed with Dissection—the urgency and intensity of those classic first two albums was intoxicating to my teenage mind. Coupled with that classic Necrolord art-work, they presented the complete package, blending aggression and blistering speed with a sense of genuine melancholy. Okay, so the late Jon Nodtveidt was something of a maniac but there's few that can deny the man's prodigious talent and lasting legacy. That so many continue to ape his achievements speaks volumes."

—Frank "The Watcher" Allain (Fen, Skaldic Curse)

LIKE MARDUK, Dissection did much to blur the line between death and black metal, but ventured toward a far more melodic sound than their countrymen, the influence of classic heavy metal shining through despite the dark direction of the material. Founded in 1989, the band's roots lie in the short-lived thrash act Siren's Yell, formed by guitarist Jon Nödtveidt, bassist Peter Palmdahl, guitarist Mattias "Mäbe" Johansson, and drummer Ole Öhman in 1988. It was Nödtveidt and Palmdahl who would initially form the more death-metal-oriented Dissection, recruiting Öhman (who had played in the curiously named Rabbit's Carrot, another thrash outfit briefly featuring Nödtveidt) in 1990, and using Johansson as a live guitarist.

Following a demo tape entitled *The Grief Prophecy*, the group would take on a full-time second guitarist (John Zwetsloot) and craft the EP *Into Infinite Obscurity*, also released in 1991, which took its name from the short Zwetsloot-penned acoustic guitar piece that closed the record. Forming close links with Norway's emerging black metal scene during this period, Jon Nödtveidt—along with comrades from Abruptum/Marduk and Nifelheim—would spend time visiting Oslo, the group forging links between the Black Circle and Sweden's similarly minded True Satanist Horde, formed by Tony "It" Särkkä of Abruptum. A black/death metal project, Satanized, was also formed the same year with Nödtveidt providing guitars, but proved short-lived, playing a single live show and making some rehearsal recordings.

Necropolis Records promotional poster featuring a montage of early images, advertising Dissection's demo compilation *The Past Is Alive* (The Early Mischief), released 1997.

Dissection, meanwhile, were beginning to move away from their more atonal Swedeath roots and reveal a distinctive taste for haunting melody. The first real evidence was a 1992 cassette entitled *The Somberlain*, though it was the full-length album of the same name released the following year that really put the band on the map. A remarkable opus, it revealed a huge leap forward. Unlike many of their contemporaries, the band benefited from a bigger, slicker sound, this time thanks to the production skills of Dan Swanö (who, remarkably, recorded the album just before his twentieth birthday). Boasting stellar musicianship, the album blended an archaic and complex atmosphere—thanks to no less than three of Zwetsloot's classical guitar pieces and busy song structures overall—with the accessibility, riffs, harmonies and drive of heavy metal. The result was a melodic death metal template with an aesthetic and vocal approach more in line with black metal, an epic and melancholy combination. It was a style that would spread in Sweden during the mid-nineties, thanks to bands such as Sacramentum, Unanimated, Naglfar, and Vinterland.

Nödtveidt himself proved highly prolific during the early nineties and having worked with Satanized he joined a number of other projects, beginning with The Black, a band formed by drummer Make "The Black" Pesonen. Contributing his voice to a 1992 demo, *Black Blood*, he returned the following year to contribute vocals, guitars, and synth on a full-length entitled *Black Priest of Satan*, released in 1994. Boasting a primal, hateful, and genuinely sinister (especially on the demo) sound, the short songs showcased barbaric yet memorable riffs and catchy keyboard refrains, Nödtveidt delivering a far more extreme vocal style than in his main band.

In 1994 he would also provide vocals for *A Journey in Darkness*, the debut album of Ophthalamia, a group founded by It, which later featured both Öhman and Nödtveidt's brother Emil, with whom he also worked briefly on a project entitled Outbreak. The same year Nödtveidt would also guest—along with Zwetsloot—on Nifelheim's self-titled debut, repeating the favor for their 1997 follow-up *Devil's Force*. 1994, however, was also the year that Zwetsloot departed Dissection (forming an extremely short-lived project called Cardinal Sin, whose single EP release boasted definite *Somberlain*-isms, including an acoustic guitar instrumental) and was replaced by Johan Norman, a close friend of Nödtveidt who had played in Satanized.

With this lineup, and now signed to Nuclear Blast Records, Dissection returned to Unisound to record *Storm of the Light's Bane*. Maintaining the sophistication of its predecessor, the second album nevertheless streamlined the band's songwriting to some extent, opting for a bigger and slightly more straightforward sound while maintaining the technical flourishes. Dropping the acoustic numbers—likely due to Zwetsloot leaving—the album upped the Maiden-esque harmonies and thrash overtones, yet remains darkly epic, never more so than on the hugely powerful "Where Dead Angels Lie," later released as a single/EP.

1995 also was the year that Nödtveidt and Norman joined the Misanthropic Luciferian Order, a "Chaos-Gnostic" order founded by Nödtveidt's friend "Vlad," which the Dissection frontman would remain part of until his death eleven years later. On the official Dissection website, Nödtveidt described the MLO as a "'Luciferian' Order … for forbidden and hidden spiritual illumination and wisdom," and described his band as the "sonic propaganda unit" of the MLO. The group was also described as explicitly "anti-cosmic," essentially opposing the creator of the universe for imprisoning life within matter and order, and seeking instead a return to chaos. The move coincided with Nödtveidt departing The True Satanist Horde—who it was now felt were only dedicated to "pursuing a black metal lifestyle"—and the two camps fell out. It eventually departed Sweden and black metal altogether (reportedly after receiving threats) and leaving his band Abruptum in the hands of Morgan Håkansson, who had joined as a member in 1991.

While Nödtveidt entered an increasingly extreme lifestyle, Dissection were simultaneously rising to new heights, playing shows around the world, including a now-legendary appearance at Wacken in 1997 captured on *Live Legacy*. The old lineup had all but crumbled, Öhman leaving in 1995 (replaced by Tobias Kellgren, formerly of Satanized) to join Emil Nödtveidt's black thrash outfit Swordmaster, which soon evolved into glam/goth industrial metallers Deathstars. Palmdahl also departed to join Runemagick and then Deathwitch, replaced for a time by Emil. The same year also saw the release of a poorly received album by Nödtveidt's dark ambient/electronic project entitled De Infernali, though he would later explain that the project "was just something we made to get money for weapons."

1997 was probably Dissection's commercial peak, so for fans it was all the more shocking that it culminated in the frontman being arrested for his part in the murder of Josef Ben Maddaour, a gay Algerian man shot in the back of the head. The case shocked Sweden, even leading to a film based on the incident, *Keillers Park*, named after the location of the killing. Though details are unsurprisingly hazy, it appears that Nödtveidt and Vlad met the man after a night of clubbing and invited him to the park to drink, taking with them an electric shock gun and a pistol. Whether the intention was to kill or assault him is unclear, but either way he ended up being first attacked with the shock gun and then shot twice, though in court the two defendants told differing stories as to who had fired the gun.

Both men were ultimately sentenced to ten years, of which Nödtveidt served seven. During his latter years in prison, he worked on writing new material and rebuilding the band from scratch, since 1997 had seen the departure of Norman (later of Soulreaper) after a dramatic falling out with both the frontman and the MLO. Nödtveidt first approached Emperor's Bård Eithun, but the drummer felt he could not represent the now-strict Satanic stance of the group, and the lineup was ultimately completed with guitarist Set Teitan (Aborym, later Watain), drummer Tomas Asklund (previously of Dark Funeral among others and later of Gorgoroth), and bassist Brice Leclercq.

On October 30, 2004, only six weeks after Nödtveidt's release from jail, Dissection headlined a concert at the Stockholm Arena that included Nifelheim and Deathstars. Two weeks later saw the release of the single *Maha Kali*, recorded at Asklund's own Monolith studios. As he later explained to Denmark's *Evilution* zine, Nödtveidt had been working on the song in his mind since his arrest, and the final product certainly surprised fans who were expecting a continuation from the band's second album. Instead, the hymn to Mahakali (Hindu goddess of time and death, whom Nödtveidt described in an interview as "the wrathful one who devours the entire cosmic creation in the time of the complete dissolution, Kali Yuga, the ending times,") proved to be something new, the catchy riffs complimented by Indian-style female vocals.

The band's third and final album, *Reinkaos*, released mid-2006, was no less controversial and has divided fans ever since. Recorded in Deathstar's own Black Syndicate Studios—and engineered by Emil and Jonas "Skinny Disco" Kangur from the band—the album's crisp, clear sound was something of a shift from earlier efforts. Tight and minimal in form, the songs are notably upbeat and midpaced throughout, utilizing emotive and catchy riffs and leaning closer than ever to a heavy metal-inspired melodic death metal sound, leading to comparisons with the likes of In Flames. Unlike such bands however, the complex lyrics are entirely dedicated to the anti-cosmic beliefs of the MLO, with Frater Nemidial (Vlad) even contributing "esoteric formulae,' providing a fascinating glimpse into the spiritual framework that Jon and the band were now dedicated to." The result is a remarkably stirring and victorious-sounding record that is hard not to be caught up in, the depth and darkness of the concept contrasting with the accessibility and strict streamlining of the tunes, the only virtuosity now surfacing in the well-delivered leads.

Only three months later, having dissolved the band not long before, Nödtveidt died aged thirty-one from a single self-inflicted bullet wound to the head. Three years earlier, in Norway's legendary *Slayer* zine, he had stated "The Satanist decides over his own life and death and prefers to go with a smile on his lips when he has reached his peak in life, when he has accomplished everything, and aim[s] to transcend this earthly existence." Having released an opus he was supremely happy with, he may well have felt this was such a time. Whatever the exact reason for ending both Dissection and his own life, there can be little doubt that Nödtveidt remained dedicated to his religious beliefs, his suicide reportedly carried out in ritualistic fashion within a circle of lighted candles and accompanied by an MLO text.

In his final lengthy press interview given to the zine *Evilution*, Nödtveidt described his anti-cosmic beliefs at length. "I do not think the Christian devil has been that interesting," he explained. "For me Satan represents something so much bigger than this world, than this universe, than the creator of this universe. It is a force that is constantly counteracting the creation and breaking it down until everything has returned to its totally unlimited primal state of chaos." He also stated, "I see life as a path I'm walking on at the moment but ... I strive toward the peak where I can transcend this limited state." Such comments may offer some insight into Nödtveidt's decision, and though his beliefs, actions, and even music may split opinion, he has left an unarguably significant mark on the history, and perhaps psyche, of extreme metal.

While this was true within Sweden as much as anywhere else, by the time Dissection had reemerged from their forced hiatus, the character of Swedish black metal had changed considerably. In comparison to Norway whose protagonists have historically tended to lean toward isolation and individualism, often moving out into the countryside, particularly after their early twenties, Sweden's scene had always seemed to boast a far more violent and urban coloring, perhaps more comparible to biker gang culture. Now the contrasts were even more pronounced, and where the Norwegian movement had splintered into various different

Watain in 2010 circa the *Lawless Darkness* album. Photo: Ester Segarra.

musical and ideological directions, Sweden had become even more extreme, Satanic, and orthodox in its attitude. Musically speaking, a less polished, more monochromatic vision now dominated, the new millennium seeing a legion of fiercely committed acts such as Ondskapt, Funeral Mist, Ofermod, Craft, and Watain, appear alongside older groups such as Setherial, Arckanum and Dark Funeral.

Of these newer acts, it would be the latter that would most obviously pick up the burning torch of Dissection. Though their music and aesthetic are more categorically "black metal"—perhaps due to the genre having much clearer boundaries than when Dissection formed—they have nonetheless exhibited a similar ambition and a sound that frequently incorporates melody and groove. Formed in 1998, the band debuted with the *Go Fuck Your Jewish "God"* demo, an opus featuring the same core lineup (vocalist and bassist Erik Danielsson, guitarist Pelle Forsberg, and drummer Håkan Jonsson) that exists today. Showing their potential on their first two albums, *Rabid Death's Curse* (2000) and *Casus Luciferi* (2003), the band also made a name for themselves with their memorable live shows, with the Rebirth of Dissection tour of 2004 introducing many to their notoriously stench-ridden performances and their penchant for covering the stage (and occasionally the audience) in weeks-old blood.

In interviews the band also built a reputation for a distinctly confrontational stance, Erik frequently explaining his disdain for much of the black metal scene—bands and fans— and raising controversy by explaining how the band had killed wild birds and even attempted

Watain circa 2010, in their home city of Uppsala. Photo: Ester Segarra.

to buy pet dogs from the homeless in order to source blood for their shows. Indeed, as with Dissection, live shows have always been meant as a form of ritual/magickal experience, the band working with the same anti-cosmic framework as some of their countrymen.

"The first battle of the Satanist has to take place in the mind and in the soul," Erik explained to me in *Metal Hammer* in 2010, "because the human will and mind is meant to be restricted, it was created to be restrictive, it was not created to transcend itself. To transcend those barriers is my aim. Then you experience what has throughout history been known as enlightenment and take a step away from god, and that is the most important thing a human being can do in this life. To physically and mentally transcend the barriers that have been placed within."

Third album *Sworn to the Dark*, released in 2007, would prove to be something of a breakthrough and features guest contributions from Michayah Belfagor of Ofermod, as well as Set Teitan of Dissection, who became a live guitarist around the same time. Maintaining some of the *De Mysteriis* influence that had been evident on the first two albums, *Sworn* now saw the band shifting to incorporate attributes that drew increased comparison with Dissection—decipherable, religious lyrics, clearer production, an unashamed use of melody, and a similarly uplifting, victorious overtone.

Released via the sizable Season of Mist, the album launched Watain to a far wider audience, and follow-up *Lawless Darkness* did even more for the band's international profile. By far their most accessible album yet, *Lawless Darkness* drew in fans with its fist-in-the-air choruses, epic, melancholy passages, and even the occasional blues/rock-esque guitar lead—not to mention a guest appearance from Carl McCoy of Fields of the Nephilim. Combined with the band's regular touring and festival appearances, the opus quickly made them one of the genre's biggest names, the band following this up three years later with *The Wild Hunt.*

"Everything exists on smaller or larger scales," Erik explained in the aforementioned interview. "I know what black metal has done to me and *my* heart, and there's nothing that would prevent us from doing the same thing on a much larger scale affecting ten thousands of people in the same way. And if we can get thousands of people to turn their back toward god and start to walk the forbidden paths, be it that they become criminals, or do whatever it takes, whatever the devil wants from them, great. That's what rock 'n' roll has always been about, turning people away from god."

Indeed, despite the wide appeal of their music the band retain a destructive focus similar to their many religious countrymen, embracing an outlaw approach much like Dissection in their later years. And while they may now be accepted by the mainstream metal scene, Erik has always been quick to explain the group's explicitly antisocial worldview, memorably stating that he "totally encourage[s] any kind of terrorist acts committed in the name of Watain."

"One thing I would say, to make it plain and simple and erase possibilities of misunderstanding and the wrong kind of references, is that the Satanist is the *enemy of the world as we know it*. He is the enemy of order, the enemy of society, the enemy of the upholding of moral or ethical codes and he is the enemy because he has no other possibility, because the entrance of Satan into someone's heart means a transformation into someone who only feels for that. I am filled to the brim with *love* for my god and as a consequence of that love there is also a lot of hatred to the enemies of my god. Every upholder of law and order, every force that maintains the calm, nauseating *horror* of humanity, the sheep, the peasants… We will always be Watain, we will always be a pack of dirty wolves out for your daughters, we will always be the bad motherfuckers and if people want to bring us to another level, do it, but never forget that in our hearts we will always be the enemy."

35
SHINING
SWEDEN PART III

"In 1996 Shining and Kvarforth hit the black metal scene like an obscene obnoxious child gone wild. Their general attitude toward human life took everything a step further. And there was the music, which, from day one, was expanding the limits of black metal. Kvarforth is still obnoxious but more clever one might say. Two parallel straight lines enclose his space. An impossibility. The demons, I'm sure, know him by name, and Shining keeps creating great music."

—Maniac (Mayhem, Skitliv)

DESPITE PLENTY of personal connections to Sweden's contemporary black metal fraternity, Shining are not a band that fit easily within the scene there, or for that matter anywhere else. With an approach rather akin to a black metal Jim Morrison and a level of fame and notoriety mirrored only by such names as Euronymous, Gaahl, or Varg Vikernes, frontman and founder Niklas Kvarforth has proven himself not only one of the movement's most controversial individuals, but also one with considerable talent. And like Burzum, Shining is an outfit whose story is all but inseparable from its chief protagonist.

Remarkably, Niklas was only twelve when the band formed in 1996, and reports that it was actually his grandmother who introduced him to the movement by showing him her record collection and acts such as Burzum. Though not too interested at the time, by fourth grade his friend Alexander had brought bands such as Cannibal Corpse, Morbid Angel, and Deicide to his attention, and together the two boys soon formed a death metal band called Incinerate.

"Alex is partly English so was really good at the English language," Niklas recalls. "I still remember the first line of the song we wrote. It was called 'Necrophiliac Sarcasm' and the lyrics were 'Butchered by a maniac sixty years ago / sperms are flowing into the dead man's mouth / raping an old man while he was lifeless and helpless.' I wrote these lyrics down on my bench and that caused a big problem at school, I had to go to counselors and stuff."

By sixth grade Incinerate had become Tyrant, inspired by blacker bands such as Marduk, Dissection, Mayhem, and Thorns. Thorns would become a key musical influence alongside fellow Norwegians Manes, Strid, and Burzum, the latter reintroduced to Niklas by Andreas "Leere" Casado of the notoriously disturbing Swedish black metal outfit Silencer. Armed with these new inspirations, he soon formed a new band with drummer Ted Wedebrand called Voorhees (named after the villain from the *Friday the 13th* films), which in turn would become Shining.

"I was like, 'What other name can we use?,' maybe 'Krueger' but that didn't sound too good—'Hello we are Krueger from Sweden!' So we were talking about different movies and at the same time I said 'Shining'… I had a clear picture of what I wanted to do and I thought other people might not, so it became good to say, 'What shines for me might not shine for you.' So there were two meanings to it, the meaning it would have for me and it's a great mov-ie. Not a great book though—Stephen

Niklas Kvarforth of Shining performing live in Norway, 2008. Photo: Ester Segarra.

King hated the movie and said Kubrick had destroyed his vision. Fucking idiot. How the fuck can you hate anything by Stanley Kubrick, the misanthrope himself?"

Niklas was only thirteen when he recorded guitars and bass for Shining's debut release (the 1998 *Submit to Selfdestruction* seven-inch), an opus he unleashed via his own label, Selb-stmord (meaning "suicide") Services. As the name of both record and label suggest, Shining was from the start very much an exponent of what has become known as "depressive" or "suicidal black metal." This is perhaps unsurprising given the profound influence of Burzum and Strid and Niklas' personal connections with Silencer (these three acts, alongside bands such as Germany's Bethlehem, Australia's Abyssic Hate and Norway's Forgotten Woods, having had a large part in creating this particular sub-genre).

"I labeled Shining, unfortunately, as 'Swedish suicidal black metal' and from there this suicidal black metal genre was born in a way," Niklas explains. "But it was a huge mistake because I've never been good at explaining myself in the English language. The idea I had was something describing the melancholy and darkness and suicidal stuff in the human being and glorifying it. Not being like a kind of therapy but rather force-feeding people these ideals. Not a catharsis but to try to make them face the emptiness, the darkness, or whatever. Not just,

'Oh I feel so bad about myself because my girlfriend left me.' If I look at the bands that followed they have this self-pity which I was never interested in, even at thirteen."

One could probably accuse the young Niklas of precociousness, and his social group
was certainly somewhat unusual for a boy his age. "I was thirteen, but my friends were all
like twenty-five years old," Niklas explains. "I actually celebrated my thirteenth birthday at
a twenty-three-year-old's bar and got my first tattoos as a birthday present. It was pretty
strange. I guess looking back it seems fucking hilarious, because I wouldn't hang out with
a thirteen-year-old today. I went to school until I was sixteen—I remember because when I
was in eighth grade I gave the whole class *Submit to Selfdestruction* and they were like, 'Hey,
Niklas became a rock star.'" He laughs. "That's pretty fucked up considering it's worth one
hundred euro now. Then I started working at a kiosk where I sold candy and listened to Strid
and Thorns on headphones all day, reading porn magazines. I started my own label when I
released the first Shining and got some money from this and I went to college for about three
months, then worked full-time with the label and the band."

Despite his youth, Niklas' label would release some significant records, including the
first two Shining albums, 2000's *Within Deep Dark Chambers* and 2001's *Livets Ÿndhållplats*
("Life's Endingplace"), as well as releases by Craft, Ondskapt, Forgotten Tomb (an Italian act
following a similarly suicide-fixated path), and the aforementioned Bethlehem, who were
probably most famous for the outlandish and despairing screams of their first vocalist Andreas Classen. It was Classen whom Niklas recruited for Shining's debut full-length, and
along with Wedebrand and a bassist known only as Tusk, the four headed into Sweden's
famous Abyss Studios. Such a setting did not come cheap however, and financial hardship
faced the young musician, who reportedly paid about 20,000 Swedish kroner to record the
opus.

"We sent only to Misanthropy Records but they refused us and it was really hard,"
Niklas recalls. "I was sitting on five hundred copies of a Bethlehem LP and didn't sell them
until years later when I started doing it more seriously and got a proper distribution network.
[But there was] an old man that would pay me and my friend a lot of money to play poker
for clothes, so that you were naked. He wanted us to piss in his mouth when he was in the
bathtub and we got fifty euro, something like that. He always said we shouldn't piss in his
eyes but of course we did and we made swastikas on his wall in shit. He showed us child
pornography, stuff like that, he was a really twisted old man but he made a lot of money
selling moonshine to younger boys. We used to beat him up and steal his homemade liquor.
I was thirteen when I met him, I was introduced by Robert who sang on the first Shining
seven-inch."

Though his childhood was certainly dramatically different from that of many other
musicians, Niklas is quick to point out that he was happy during his youth, and doesn't see
it as the sole reason for the direction his life and art took. "We lived in a good house, I had
good food, went out with older friends, it was a pretty good experience… Actually I had a lot

of support from my grandmother, she loved what I was doing with the music and my mother was proud but very skeptical, she did not understand what I was doing. She didn't have a lot of time. My dad was okay, he was just a criminal, nothing special, an idiot. But I didn't have a bad upbringing at all, on the contrary I had a very good upbringing. I'm always hearing people complaining about their youth saying, 'Oh I got fucked in the ass and it made me into a psychopath,' but I don't buy that. I went through a lot of shit too and I'm more thankful for that, because it made me open my eyes and see the world through a more realistic perspective. For me it was definitely a good thing, otherwise I would be another blind idiot on the street. To some extent we have to experience negativity to experience the good in life."

While the events of his youth may not be entirely responsible for his character, they may partly explain why he seems to have been so ready for the darkness that the black metal scene offered. Another factor, however, was the onset of mental illnesses, and it is only recently that he has finally been diagnosed with bipolar disorder and schizophrenia.

"At fourteen I actually went berserk with nunchucks," he explains, "which ended up with me attacking and kicking my mother in the stomach so hard that she had to have an operation in her ovaries. My mother's husband I attacked with a chain and big ball with spikes on it and then I got locked up for the first time in my life. I had a lot of mental problems which I only found out about last year, though I knew I had some problems in my head. My mother was in denial, my father didn't know about it. It was when I moved at age nineteen that it really hit the fan and I had to go to emergency hospital because I attacked people with knives. I guess [my mother] didn't understand what mental illness does to you, she said, 'You have to look after yourself and live a better life.'" He continues thoughtfully, "I think there are two reasons for it, firstly the mental problems I had since my very birth but also because of the fact that I was so into negativity, darkness, evil, and all this shit that in the end it swallowed me. Back then I was constantly glorifying madness and all these things [and] I think they grew onto me in a way. I think it's a pretty common thing, people who are into this darker aspect of life get fucked over and become what they preach."

Such themes dominated the band from the start, yet musically Shining were initially relatively conservative, utilizing a distinctly Burzum-esque template for the first two albums. 2002's *III—Angst—Självdestruktivitetens Emissarie* ("Self-destruction's Emissary") saw the band edging away from their early sound however, the lineup also shifting, with Tusk replaced by his younger brother Alex, the aforementioned co-founder of Incinerate who now went by the name Phil A. Cirone. On drums was none other than Mayhem's Hellhammer, while second guitars were handled by Håkan "Inisis" Ollars.

It was the follow-up, 2005's *IV—The Eerie Cold*, that really saw the band refine their sound, introducing the style they are now known for, a compelling blend of black metal and doom, rock, blues, and classical. Though replacing Inisis with John Doe of Craft, Niklas still wrote all lyrics, and almost all the music. Seeking to break with the past somewhat, he now colored the songwriting with a much greater dynamic range and a far stronger emotional charge, utilizing a more intricate approach that included acoustic guitars, piano passages, film samples, and a definite sense of groove despite the more pronounced atmosphere of despair.

"For the first time I think we saw it as a full band and it was the first time we worked with a proper producer [Rickard Bengtsson]," Niklas reflects. "It was a strange time, I had a fiancée and we had a child and I tried to live my life with that. But I failed miserably."

Trouble was indeed brewing. While the album no doubt expanded the fan base, it was the events of the following year that really put Shining—and Niklas himself—in the spotlight. In August 2006, a statement was posted online by the band stating that the frontman had been missing for four weeks and was feared to have killed himself. Furthermore, it explained, instructions had been left with the band that the forthcoming launch show would feature a new vocalist known as Ghoul, a stranger to the band chosen by Niklas as a replacement. Further rumors suggested that a friend of Niklas' had been with him when he leapt off a bridge, apparently to his death in the waters below. In fact, Niklas simply relocated to Oslo during this time, working in a rock bar/club in town, while indulging himself, he explains, in sex, alcohol, cocaine, and heroin.

The launch gig did go ahead however, in none other than the band's hometown of Halmstad. Ghoul turned out to be Niklas wearing a zombie outfit, though he maintains that the band only became aware of this on the night itself. During the performance he was sporadically joined by three of the individuals he'd spent time with in Oslo, namely Attila Csihar, Roger "Nattefrost" Rasmussen of Carpathian Forest, and ex-Mayhem frontman Maniac, who appeared with a swastika carved into his forehead and spent much of the show assaulting Niklas, even smashing a chair onto his back. For his part, Niklas handed out razors to the audience and even kicked a fan who dared touch him. Causing outrage in the Swedish media, the whole incident is believed by some to have been a publicity stunt (an accusation the vocalist denies) but whatever the truth, it gave the band a massive boost in attention.

"We had a pretty violent breakup, me and my fiancée, and I felt I had to leave Halmsted," Niklas explains, "so I went to Norway and didn't tell anyone. People thought I was dead. Then I wanted to play a trick on the other members by reappearing at the show when they thought it was Attila that was going to do the whole thing. It is true I jumped off a bridge into the water—I was walking with a really stupid guy and jumped off as a prank and he thought that I drowned, but obviously I didn't, I just swam away. I went to Norway that night... We could have done the gig ten thousand times better of course and we got into huge fights after the show because the guitarists were very angry that I had not told them I was still alive. [The violence] wasn't planned at all, I just told Maniac to do what he wanted to do ... I told him that what we do on stage is not going to affect us—if he wants to beat me up, he can, I don't care that much."

Maniac had become a close friend by this point, Niklas not only staying with him in Oslo, but also joining his band Skitliv ("shit life"), an early demo of which was memorably titled *Kristiansen and Kvarforth Swim in the Sea of Equilibrium While Waiting*. Combining elements of black and especially doom metal with industrial touches, Skitliv has proved to be an engaging project and continues to feature both musicians, though Maniac undoubtedly remains the central figure.

"Mayhem were supposed to play in Stockholm when I was seventeen, it was the first time I was meant to meet Hellhammer," recalls Niklas of his first meeting with Maniac. "I was just out of a mental facility so I was pretty shook up and on meds. I went backstage and then I started to cry, then I started to laugh, then I started to cry and then I started to laugh again. Hellhammer thought it was hilarious but Maniac hated me and I wanted to beat him up and he wanted to beat me up... Later when I moved to Norway I was working at Rock In, clearing up the dishes from out-

Some girls gonna get hurt: A typically tasteful Shining promo shoot. Photo courtesy of Spinefarm.

side and I saw Attila and he was like, 'Hey man, what's happening? I heard you were dead, I'm so glad to see you.' We sat down and had a drink and he said Maniac is coming by and I was like, 'Oh my god, I don't want to meet that fucking doofus,' but then he came and told Attila he was starting a band called Skitliv. Attila said, 'Oh you should talk to Niklas,' 'cos I had that tattoo which is where they took the logo from, and I became the guitarist of Skitliv and moved in with him."

While Halmstad was surely the most noteworthy show, Niklas began to make a name for himself generally with performances that included self-mutilation and both sexual and violent engagements with attendees, the vocalist taunting and caressing audience and band members alike. It was around this time, in fact, that Niklas famously kissed Maniac on stage in London and Oslo, a move that genuinely horrified the more conservative elements of the black metal fanbase—a fact both participants were well aware of. However, provoking black metal fans is something Niklas clearly revels in.

"I am heterosexual and one of the most disgusting things is kissing a man," Niklas clarifies. "But then if people think I like to have a big cock in my mouth it doesn't really matter to me, 'cos I know what I like. [In the Bible] it says 'If a man lies with a man as one

It's pretty hard to shock or offend a black metal audience these days, but Shining still seem to manage it: Photo: Ester Segarra.

lies with a woman, both of them have done what is detestable,' so if all these people with their inverted crosses talk about evil and Satan then they should glorify homosexuality and not whine like children who don't get their toys for Christmas. What can I say? I think black metal in general is pretty weak. The only thing they do is talk, it's very easy to sit behind a computer and talk about what is 'true' and what is not. Put these people in the Central Park in New York and see what happens after fifteen minutes, see how cool their studs and inverted crosses are then. They should try experiencing real life— if you want to experience real evil it's not in the forest, it's on every fucking street corner."

While these years saw the band establish their reputation as one of black metal's more confrontational acts, it also saw them back up their actions with their art. In fact, 2007's *V—Halmstad* proved arguably the strongest record to date. By this point the lineup had changed completely, Hellhammer fired due to conflicting schedules and replaced by Ludwig Witt of stoner rockers Spiritual Beggars. A musician named Johan Hallander now handled bass, while Fredric "Wredhe" Gråby of Ondskapt and Peter Huss were on guitars. Huss proved a particularly significant choice, being a highly talented player who favors the technically accomplished compositions of bands such as Megadeth and Guns N' Roses, an act Niklas also favors.

V—Halmstad would clearly reflect such interests, maintaining the melancholy groove and black doom of its predecessor while adding plenty of intricacies, as well as the melody and accessibility of more commercial rock/metal music. It's interesting to note that Huss is the only member on the album still with the band today and certainly the albums that have followed—2009's *VI—Klagopsalmer* ("Hymns of Lament"), 2011's *VII: Född Förlorare* ("Born Loser"), and 2012's *Redefining Darkness*—have continued to hone the approach of *Halmstad*, combining aggressive and catchy black metal with elements of prog, doom, rock, and even pop. For Niklas, mainstream success is most certainly the goal of the group.

"I want Shining to be black metal's version of [German pop rock act] Tokyo Hotel—or a black metal version of Opeth for that matter," Niklas explains earnestly. "I want it to be big. I've always been inspired by [Swedish pop/rock outfit] Kent for example, who have been a huge inspiration since the second album, but I guess with the fourth album I felt now is time to leave the black metal scene and I wanted to distance myself from it as much as possible."

While the 2012 covers EP *Lots of Girls Gonna Get Hurt* saw the band at their most commercial-sounding yet, with Niklas doing his

2007's *V - Halmstad*, which takes its name from the band's home city.

best pop singer impression over the course of the four songs, Shining still maintain numerous black metal sections in their own songs, despite an apparent wish to leave the genre behind to an extent. Perhaps more of a barrier to any commercial success, however, is the explicitly negative direction of the band. While Niklas has steered away from his Satanic beliefs with Shining, instead painting from more earthly and often biographical truths regarding depression, hatred, relationships, and self-destruction, the explicitly pro-suicide message of the band seems something of a barrier to commercial audiences.

"That has been what is dazzling my mind the whole time," Niklas admits, "but whatever I do I can't change my opinion or my goal. But I can tone it down, and when it comes to normal media I will try and tone down the whole propaganda bit. But it is by far the most important thing in the band. It's really hard to explain why, but I am a misanthrope. I don't oppose god for example, god is not my enemy, but I oppose life, everything that lives and breathes. For me it's a personal pleasure to see people suffer. It gives me more than coming out of the studio knowing I have made an excellent album, if I find out, yeah this guy he killed himself and he had this big Shining altar at home, that really motivates me… so Shining is an anti-humanitarian band or has anti-humanitarian motives. The other guys in the band except for the guitarist, they don't support these kind of things, they are quite normal people and it would be horrible [for them] if something like that happened … but I feel that our music has the capacity to manipulate, if you will, the youth."

Despite the overwhelmingly malevolent motive apparently at work, Niklas is far from a one-dimensional character, and seems to have a capacity not only for extreme hostility, but also

VII: Född förlorare, **2011, which is—as you might have guessed—the band's seventh album.**

huge hospitality and affection. It is these wildly differing impulses that seem to leave him torn much of the time. "It's been really, really hard the last years to try to cope with this and get it to work with this life," he says. "Now I have a fiancée, we have a cat, and it's changed my perspective on how I experience love for example. At the same time I wouldn't hesitate one second to end their lives if that was the need, so to say, if that was my agenda. You need a positive thing in your life. It makes me wonder you know, it shows me I would have had the possibility to create something much better than what I have now. It shows me what I lost over the years, and that hurts a lot I can tell you. It gives me some hope that maybe I can still do this and lead a life where I can see a positivity, a life that could be considered as 'normal' or whatever. I battle with the question everyday because I know I can never lead a completely normal life because of the life I chose some years ago. So there's a duality. I'm fully aware of that."

Indeed, Niklas appears to view Shining as something of a *curse* in his life, a creative impulse that he must follow to its (and possibly his own) end. While some artists create during extreme highs or lows, he explains that he only writes during the times in his life and mental rollercoaster when he is completely emotionally numb. Thus, it seems that while being a reflection of his depression, Shining is also born out of a need to feel something, perhaps explaining the often painfully raw feelings of lament, sadness, and hate within the songs.

"Here we have another cliché—all great art is built upon suffering—but I think that's true," he concludes. "If the question is whether I would have chosen to live a normal life or suffered to create, I think I would have chosen a normal life actually. If I didn't know the pleasures of darkness and wasn't initiated in this as much as I am then, yeah, definitely I would rather have my eyes closed. It's the same with my mental condition, now that I'm aware I can't get well in my head I instead understand that I have to cope with it and that's the same with Shining. I understand I *have* to do it even if I don't want to, and believe me I really don't want to do it ninety-nine percent of the time."

POLITICS, POLAND, AND THE RISE OF NSBM

DESPITE ITS largely apolitical status during the eighties—and the fact that seminal acts such as Brazil's Mystifier and Canada's Blasphemy had featured non-Caucasian members—since the early nineties black metal has often been associated with racism, nationalism, and right-wing extremism. Such connotations undoubtedly stem from the genre's re-emergence via the early Norwegian scene and, perhaps more specifically, Jason Arnopp's 1993 *Kerrang!* cover feature, which explicitly described the protagonists as "Neo-Fascist Devil Worshippers."

Though somewhat misleading, the headline was not completely out of context—it was informed by quotes from both Varg Vikernes and Darkthrone, whom the article explained "describe themselves as fascist in outlook." In the years since, many acts have attempted to distance themselves from such associations, while on the other side of the coin, many acts have arisen who *are* explicitly neo-fascist and have pushed such an ideology into the music itself. With so many conflicting attitudes, it's little surprise that there's frequent discussion over the role of far-right politics in the black metal scene.

While it was no more mandatory to be a neo-fascist within the early Norwegian scene than it was to be a devil worshipper, it's true that the extremism that defined Norway's underground scene at the time frequently crossed into explicitly political ground. While Euronymous was a highly vocal supporter of communism, his peers were generally heading toward the opposite end of the political spectrum. On reflection, this isn't entirely surprising. Immigration within Norway and Scandinavia has traditionally been a fairly touchy subject; add to this the growing sense of Nordic/Viking pride that was being explored by bands at the time, along with the fact that the elitist concepts within Satanism can easily be interpreted/ misinterpreted within a racist context, and it's little surprise that a scene actively exploring misanthropy latched onto more specific forms of intolerance. Today Burzum remains the most influential act in this sense, since its mainman Varg Vikernes has always been happy to give race-related quotes in interviews, whether to sympathetic parties or mainstream magazines. Yet while Varg's openly racist statements famously caused distribution problems for the entire Misanthropy Records label, and Darkthrone's "Norwegian Aryan Black Metal" episode was undoubtedly the most spectacularly public fallout of the era, these were certainly not isolated incidents.

Indeed, a general flirtation with the extreme right was evident throughout the scene in the early to mid-nineties. Both Euronymous and Ihsahn were quoted questioning the value of the lives of starving African children, Hellhammer famously asserted that "black metal was for white people," and artists from such high-profile acts as Mayhem, Trelldom, and Dimmu Borgir utilized swastikas and/or racist language in interviews and correspondence. Elsewhere, the potent but short-lived project Zyklon B (featuring members of Emperor, Satyricon, and Dødheimsgard) raised eyebrows due both to its name—taken from the chemical used in the gas chambers in Nazi Germany—and the overtones of social Darwinism within the music itself.

In neighboring Sweden, many bands offered similarly controversial political positions, notably Marduk, who found themselves boycotted in magazines *Rock Hard* and *Metal Hammer* after an interview in which founder Morgan stated a wish to prevent immigration into Sweden and pride in the fact that his grandfather was an officer in World War II, a situation he didn't exactly ease when he told Norway's *Nordic Vision* zine that same year: "The main city is mainly occupied by immigrants—who poison our environment. Sometimes you wonder if you are in Sweden or in Somalia!" Even the usually introspective Katatonia were found giving some choice remarks on the subject of immigrants in the third issue of the *Petrified* zine.

To what extent all this reflected heartfelt political conviction as opposed to attempts at provocation is still a matter of debate. It's worth bearing in mind, after all, that in their early interviews many bands were advocating acts that were about as extreme as one could imagine ("Of course I'd enjoy to torture some fuckin' innocent children," explained the usually thoughtful Vorph, for example, in issue nine of *Slayer Magazine*), so whether one should read such provocative racist language literally is perhaps another matter for debate.

"It was part and parcel of the whole attitude," explains ex-Emperor frontman Mortiis, who used swastikas and racist language in his early days. "We were searching for the most extreme attitudes and ideologies we could find, and needless to say, once you get onto that path, right-wing ideas aren't that far away. To be honest I was part of that whole attitude at the beginning, we all felt pretty distrusting and non-caring toward normal society, always looking for the next extreme idea, record, piece of art, or whatever. I wasn't a politically aware person although I made statements, but they were rash, illogical, and nowhere near researched. I certainly did [use this imagery] myself for some of the original art for the [Mortiis] demo. Naturally I don't think any of us are very proud of those mementos today. But hey, if the New York Dolls can do it, why not a few silly teens from Norway?"

Two issues of the *Filosofem* journal. Featuring Varg Vikernes and named after the fourth Burzum album, it focused largely on racial and political subject matter.

While acts such as Mayhem would continue to provoke with right-wing imagery, pretty much without exception Scandinavian black metal bands began to drop their political preoccupations as the nineties progressed. Two factors are likely to have played a role: firstly the increase in the average age of the protagonists, but also the fact that black metal records were now selling in far more substantial amounts, meaning bands had more to lose by offending outsiders and the press.

Thus, while the activities of Scandinavian bands were undoubtedly a major catalyst, they were not, on their own, enough to give the genre a significantly political direction. But just as bands with a more hard-line Satanic agenda would appear in the years that followed—initially inspired by the fragmented exploration of Satanism taking part in early-nineties Norway—so too would Norway's flirtations with the extreme right be taken in a more organized direction over time by other individuals, this time within Eastern Europe, and primarily Poland, which took its leads straight from the Scandinavian pioneers.

"The Norwegian scene had a huge impact on the metal scene in Poland," recalls Graveland's Rob "Darken" Fudali, a key player in the Eastern European scene and perhaps the most outspoken black metal musician regarding race and politics after Vikernes. "Watching their actions and statements, we felt free to talk and act. But I think we owe it more to Euronymous than to Varg; Euronymous talked about politics and Varg learnt from him. At that time

Euronymous was like a father to the whole black metal generation, he created the Black Circle and released wolves… for me Euronymous was an authority, the most important person in the black metal underground. I did not mind his left-wing convictions. [My bandmates] Karcharoth and Capricornus were fascinated by Burzum. We read interviews with people connected with the Black Circle and we took it very seriously. Burning churches made a huge impression on us. We hated Christianity and such a sign of resistance against it was a revelation for us. We were as happy as kids, and we supported not only [the] Norwegian scene, but also the true Swedish black metal scene with bands such as Azahub Hani, The Black, and Pagan Rites."

Founded on the Scandinavian black metal scene's Satanic and anti-Christian building blocks, and bearing a similarly antisocial streak that frequently crossed into criminality, Poland's scene mirrored Norway's and Sweden's, but was colored by racial motives in a far more pronounced manner. Where Scandinavian bands—Burzum included—had predominantly left matters of politics to interviews, Polish bands were far more overt in their use of racial topics. This is evident in songs such as "A Dark Dream" by Veles ("Dream about power of the white race"), "Don't Let Your Folk Forget" by Thor's Hammer ("You are the only heir of this land / Your duty is eternal fight / In self-defense of Aryankind"), and "White Hand's Power" by Graveland (self-explanatory). Likewise, record sleeves were often explicitly nationalist or Nazi-oriented, as evident in the liner notes for albums such as Infernum's… *Taur-Nu-Fuin*… and Veles' *Night on the Bare Mountain* as well as the design for releases such as Fullmoon's *United Aryan Evil* demo or Thor's Hammer's *The Fate Worse Than Death*, whose various covers featured either a black/white handshake, or one of two photos of interracial romance, one placed subtly in front of a large explosion.

"The Norwegian black metal scene originated some customs that were not popular at that time," explains Darken, who has played with Veles, Thor's Hammer, Fullmoon, and Infernum, as well as his main band Graveland, "e.g. expressing ideological and political right-wing and racial convictions. In Poland people were prepared for this situation, because such values were in accordance with the warrior's instincts that were inside us. Norwegian black metal customs harmonized with our legacy, the pride of [the] white man."

For many, the fact that Poland was the source of such ideals was something of a surprise. Indeed, the use of Nazi German imagery and ideals by Polish bands *is* somewhat perplexing given Poland's treatment during WWII and fact that prominent Nazis in Germany viewed Slavic people as racially inferior, most obviously Hitler, who proposed in *Mein Kampf* that lands east of Germany be conquered and that the Slavic peoples (whom he described as "subhuman") be eliminated or enslaved. Perhaps with that in mind, bands such as Graveland made clear in interviews with zines such as Switzerland's *Skogen* that they distanced themselves from the Slavonic tag altogether, viewing themselves rather as Celts or Aryan.

However, understanding why the more casual racism found in some quarters of the Scandinavian scene should become a defining factor in Poland may require little more than a brief examination of the racial attitudes within Polish society generally. Norway may not be the most welcoming country in the world with regard to immigrants, but Jews, blacks, and other minorities certainly do not face the same level of economic discrimination, police harassment, and severe violence by skinhead gangs as in much of Eastern Europe. Thus it was that in Poland, Satanism soon began to take a back seat to political and racial motivations.

The movement in Poland was also characterized by the same attempts to organize that occurred in the Helvete circle, and was followed by the scene-related hostilities that came with such a move. "There were many bands supporting [the] Norwegian black metal scene [that] identified themselves with the 'true unholy black metal' ideology," recalls Darken. "These bands were young and inexperienced. At that time Behemoth was one of the strongest pillars of the movements, next to bands [such] as Xantotol, Veles, Fullmoon, Infernum, and Mysteries. In 1993 Nergal of Behemoth, Venom of Xantotol, and Blasphemous of Veles created The Temple of Infernal Fire. Other organizations such as the Black Circle were an example for The Temple of Infernal Fire; we wanted to have our own secret organization."

While the Temple's character was initially occult in nature (like the exclusively Satanic organization Fullmoon, a precursor formed by Venom of Xantotal) it quickly took on a more political edge, particularly after the departure of founding member Nergal.

"Originally it was a Satanist lodge opposing LaVey philosophy and many people from the Polish underground were members," Darken explains. "Later Capricornus, Karcharoth, and I changed the character of The Temple, placing emphasis on political issues. New people joined us. New people with new plans. The Polish scene radicalized and isolated itself from others—the 'not true' ones. We created our own underground by rejecting everything that was not black metal. Everyone wanted to be 'true,' no one wanted to be called 'poser'.... Lists of black metal enemies appeared and posers from these lists did not have easy life. When the situation was getting out of control and everything was more serious, Behemoth decided to back out from the underground and Nergal became an object of many attacks."

Indeed, many of these came via Darken himself—who had contributed keyboard compositions to Behemoth in the band's early days—and a series of insulting flyers was soon issued by the "Anti-Behemoth Front."

"I was very angry at Nergal at that time, he was one of the founders and I felt he betrayed our ideas," continues Darken, who eventually made his peace with Nergal some fifteen years later. "When Nergal left the underground and The Temple of Infernal, we changed name for The Temple of Fullmoon. At its best times almost all people from [Polish] black metal underground were members of The Temple of Fullmoon. We organized some meetings and conventions and the holy black metal war, the time of fire and blood, started. There are many wooden churches in Poland and many of them were burnt, [though] many were [actually] burnt because of the left-wing anarchist movement that started to use this method in their fight against Christian church."

Meanwhile, Nergal explains his departure from the Temple and the scene itself in the following terms. "The whole black metal thing in Poland … things were just getting uglier and uglier," he recalls. "It was aggressive, it was violent, and you know there's nothing wrong with being violent if it's done in the right way, but these guys were [entering] racial and political territories and I was not into this at all. I just wanted to make music, I wasn't into politics and the majority of black metal bands started going toward these political tendencies, which is how NSBM started, Poland was one of the originators, the country that started this ugly direction. I thought, 'I'm out of it,' it was nothing to keep me interested in this genre. When I quit people suddenly turned out to be enemies for obvious reasons, but I had no regrets. I didn't give a fuck, I'm going to keep doing what I do to the best of my abilities and I just kept on developing focus in the music."

Just as in Norway, the Polish underground black metal community caused no small amount of chaos, leaving behind a long trail of church burnings and desecrations. However, just as the criminal elements of Norway's inner circle were eventually brought to a standstill by police after its protagonists crossed from arson into murder, the more active elements of The Temple of Fullmoon eventually fell victim to the authorities for similar reasons.

"Followers and friends of Karcharoth [mainman of Infernum] and people from Thunderbolt were involved in murder," explains Darken. "One friend of Paimon from Thunderbolt murdered a homeless man. Then police arrested many people and started investigations about the church burnings. Paimon had to participate in visits to the scene of the crime. Once police took him to a small town with a wooden church, which actually Paimon did not [manage to] burn, but he had to explain to the police all his actions step by step. Angry inhabitants watched everything behind [the] church fence and they really badly wanted to lynch Paimon. As a result of this investigation three people were sentenced: Cezar, as a main murderer, to twenty-five years imprisonment, Uldor [Thunderbolt drummer] for four years, and Paimon was on probation [for attempted church burning]."

"Some [activities] were pacified by the police and finally The Temple of Fullmoon was dissolved," Darken explains. "These years had both good and bad sides. True unholy black metal ideology left a mark on the Polish underground. In Poland we do not have hundreds of black metal bands as it happens in Sweden. Trend did not kill the Polish scene and it did not disgrace its name. But at the same time this kind of extreme black metal is a weapon that turns against those who hold it. Hatred born in a group of people with psychopathic minds turns into fire that no one can predict and control. Those who kindle this fire are very soon ravaged in its flames. True darkness devours its children."

While things had spiraled somewhat out of control for those involved, the Polish scene had nonetheless put itself squarely on the map thanks to bands such as Graveland, Infernum, Veles, Gontyna Kry, Thor's Hammer, and Kataxu, all of whom pushed a far-right agenda within their music and interviews. With only a few bands in the country steering away from the direct influence of the radical right—predominantly Christ Agony, Holy Death, Mastiphal, Pandemonium, Behemoth, and Xantotol (and later newer bands such as Arkona, Kriegsma-

chine, Furia, and Evilfeast)—the rise of the Polish scene went hand-in-hand with the establishment of an extreme-right black metal subgenre, now known as NSBM—National Socialist
Black Metal.

Thanks in part to activity from neighboring countries such as Ukraine and Russia,
NSBM has become a movement in its own right, reaching territories such as Western Europe
and the Americas, with a degree of overlap occurring between fans of the genre and more traditional right-wing music such as Oi!, RAC (Rock Against Communism), and other far-right
branches of punk and rock.

Perhaps most famously, Resistance Records (a label closely tied to the white national-
ist/supremacist organization National Alliance and primarily known for the punk/"hatecore"
acts on their roster such as Angry Aryans) purchased Varg's Cymophane Records and also
began to release new black metal recordings, some under the sub-label Unholy Records. Perhaps the most iconic such release by Resistance was the 2000 split between Graveland and
Polish skinhead band Honor, called *Raiders of Revenge*.

"Honor was a very popular band on RAC/Oi!/skinhead scene in Poland at that time,"
Darken explains. "Honor's lyrics were very good. They rejected Christianity and Catholic
church and they referred to pagan native beliefs. One of my old friends who knew Olaf and
Szczery of Honor gave me an idea of recording a split. He knew that we would perfectly understand one another. So we met and we knew that we had to record this split for the people
and for the country… Honor wanted to find new audience among metal fans. I, in Graveland
with strong right-wing convictions, wanted to meet radical right-wing patriots. [The] split
was released by Resistance Records and caused some confusion among those who were occupied with restricting our freedom."

While the crossover between black metal and far-right genres has occurred to some
extent (particularly in Poland, where far-right organizations such as Niklot seem to be predominantly made up of black metal skinheads), many of the trappings of black metal—the
corpsepaint, Satanism, and general interest in darkness and depravity—have proven alienating for many in the skinhead scene, who perhaps would rather not see their activities and
ideologies depicted as evil or unholy. The harsh quality of the music has been another barrier,
and indeed many NSBM bands such as Germany's Absurd and Ukraine's Aryan Terrorism
[another Resistance-signed band] have channeled a lot of the upbeat, catchy punk influences
of RAC/hatecore music, though this in turn has made the music too happy or melodic for
many black metal listeners.

"There are many common factors in these two scenes," ponders Darken, who views
such merging as part of a larger picture, one naturally informed by his own worldview. "It is
not only about black metal or RAC/Oi!/skinheads, but about an outbreak of liberation ideologies strengthened by a mutual cooperation of people of different religions, political convictions, right-wing ideologies, left-wing ideologies. Today, skinheads read leftist articles about
banks and corporations. Leftist young are inspired by paganism. I think that contemporary

One of several notorious covers of *The Fate Worse Than Death* album by Poland's Thor's Hammer.

world with all its problems is a new place where many people have their own convictions and very often right-wing convictions."

The NSBM and far-right black metal scene grew slowly, like black metal itself, eventually reaching a wide array of territories, its peak thus far occurring around the mid- to late 2000s. Eastern Europe—a stronghold for the far right generally—would remain at the center of this rise, with Ukraine contributing a number of successful bands, such as Kroda, Hate Forest, and Nokturnal Mortum, whose symphonic folk black metal includes the use of traditional Ukrainian woodwind instrumentation. Russia meanwhile contributed bands such as the folk-leaning NSBM act Temnozor and an underground circle called Blazebirth Hall, a sort of far-right version of France's Black Legions, home to bands such as Forest and Nitberg.

While NSBM is an explicitly political beast, other bands with far-right ideals have chosen to explore more esoteric, and often nature-inspired territories. Indeed, it's interesting to note that the most successful far-right black metal bands rarely add political content to their music or art. First on the list must be Burzum, and second Ukrainian outfit Drudkh, which rose from the ashes of Hate Forest and managed to break into the black metal mainstream thanks to their emotive compositions and the fact that they refuse to print lyrics or give interviews, despite describing themselves as "Conservative Revolutionary" and having shirts emblazoned with the slogan "Art for White Intellectual Elite."

Ultimately, it seems that bands pushing a political agenda of any sort are likely to have only a limited overlap with the rest of the black metal scene, presumably to the disappointment of those who hoped to see the genre become a genuinely political movement. This is perhaps unlikely, since the nihilism and misanthropy often at the heart of black metal—as well as the shrouded nature of its aesthetic and vocal techniques that frequently render lyrics indecipherable—make it not particularly well-suited to expressing political opinion. In fact, for many within black metal the NSBM movement remains of little interest, partly for musical reasons and partly due to a distaste for the politics involved. Indeed, it's worth noting that the majority of bands and fans, even those who are actually sympathetic to the ideologies involved, feel that black metal should not be tainted with *any* politics, regardless of their nature.

"I ascribe as much raison d'être to NS Black Metal as to Christian 'Black' Metal, in other words: NAUGHT," explained Watain's Erik Danielsson in an online interview with *Beyond the Dark Horizon*. "Black Metal is a cult of Satan, its foundation is the cultivation of Chaos and Darkness, and no little pimple-ridden Internet-nazi movement can change that. Stick to your loathsome punk-music instead, it suits the greatness of your ideals much better... "

Euronymous explained his stance in one 1992 interview, saying, "As Mayhem is NOT a political band, I don't really like to mix topics like this into band interviews, but anyway I'm still keeping the faith. I openly admit that I am a Stalinist and I'm very fascinated by extreme countries like Albania and Rumania in the good old days." He also said in *Slayer Magazine* issue 8, "Even though I'm active in the most extreme communist party here (Albania inspirations) I leave to the Punks to write about that in the lyrics."

It's interesting to note that both Metalion and Euronymous were friends with the left-wing grind legends Napalm Death and loved their early work, *Slayer*'s editor explaining that it was only their continued use of socially aware lyrics *once they had been labeled as death metal* that the Mayhem mainman disliked. Indeed, Euronymous himself appears to have shared some of the band's values.

"He was a communist at one point," confirms Necrobutcher, "he liked the fact that [the Communist party] was a revolutionary party in Norway. In their party program it said they supported armed revolt against the government, he just supported evil things so he supported that as it was considered a terrorist organization here in Norway. But his girlfriend was an old communist back in the day. The idea that everyone was equal and everyone did their share and was treated equal, you know, it's good thoughts, that you can ride the public transport for free, it's a taxpayer thing, so he probably liked the general idea but when he got older he understood it was not working, he saw the Berlin Wall come down and the Soviet state collapse."

Whether Euronymous' own passion for communism (his signature was still including Communist iconography in letters written not long before his passing) was ideologically driven or inspired by its worst excesses, it was certainly a major interest, and the fact that it wasn't integrated in any way into his art—just as Varg's interest in the far-right was kept separate from Burzum—speaks volumes.

That said, black metal fans and musicians are not, for the most part, overly *sensitive* when it comes to the politically incorrect. For better or worse, most black metal listeners make a distinction between art and artist, something that is easier to do when politics are left at the door and not forced into the art itself. For instance, acclaimed American act Wolves in the Throne Room, who can probably be considered the genre's most high-profile left-leaning outfit (though their art is again apolitical), have never shied away from acknowledging the influence of Burzum. Black metal fans, unlike those of other many other genres, are rarely *offended* by the politics of an artist in a way that would stop them engaging with the artist's work, a point highlighted by Darken's admiration for Euronymous.

It's therefore not surprising that a degree of crossover between race-focused/nationalist bands and the non-political black metal scene is found completely acceptable, even if the ideologies in question are seen as bogus or at least irrelevant by some. For example, a number of musicians from the Polish NSBM scene have gone on to feature in secular bands without any significant backlash. Some of the biggest and most commercially successful black metal bands in the scene today, in fact, curiously feature ex-members of Polish NS band Swastyka (later renamed Sunwheel). The aforementioned Paimon, himself once a member of Swastyka as well as Veles, has gone as far as to publicly distance himself and his band Thunderbolt from their NSBM past in favor of a Satanic ideology, and has since lent his talents to a number of Norwegian apolitical acts including Dead To This World, Aeturnus, and Gorgoroth.

Likewise, black metal supergroup War caused some outrage due to their song "I am Elite," (which featured explicitly racist lyrics regarding "niggers and kikes," courtesy of vocalist All of Abruptum and Ophthalamia), yet both Peter Tägtgren (who played drums and produced the record) and Paul "Typhon" Thind (who released the record on his label Necropolis) are opposed to racism and politics within black metal.

"My biggest thing is censorship and freedom of speech," Typhon told the Metallian website. "Apparently that was All screaming the line and it wasn't planned. Peter Tägtgren called me up immediately and said he didn't want anything to be affiliated with him. I am not a big fan of racism. In fact I can't stand it. My parents are northern Indian and they moved to England. They experienced racism and I experienced racism… That said, I don't believe in that stuff but… to each his own."

"For sure it did [cause problems], 'cos there were lines in there that I didn't know," Tägtgren recalls, shaking his head. "It was not supposed to be like that, it was not racial shit, it was about hating everything except yourself, *you're* the elite. I didn't give a shit, and I still *don't* give a shit, as long as I know what *I* stand for. When Pain got big in 1999 people started digging and found stuff like War [but] I don't associate with the political speech that they have. It's the same as with those bands that I recorded who had a more right-wing thing; if they didn't go to me, they went to someone else and I'd rather have the money, no big deal. I felt the music was good and I really don't give a shit what they sing."

Necropolis were not alone, and other apolitical labels in the underground, such as Drakkar, have also published music by extreme right bands such as Grand Belial's Key and Arghoslent, alongside releases by non-political bands such as Watain, Tsjuder, and Mütiilation.

NS-oriented labels are also often happy to deal with apolitical bands and fans: Supernal Music, for example, was the home of non-NS bands such as Fleurety, Deinonychus, and The Meads of Asphodel, but increasingly promoted race-focused bands, signing acts such as Hate Forest/Drudkh, Sunwheel, and Capricornus. (Just as notable were the monthly newsletters of its highly successful mail order department, where owner Alex Kurtagi —now a writer for publications such as American Renaissance and Alternative Right—promoted far-right musings alongside the primarily apolitical releases on sale.) Similarly, No Colours Records, while primarily an NSBM label, released efforts by non-political bands such as Suicidal Winds, Falkenbach, Urgehal, and Inquisition.

However one chooses to view the bands themselves, there is little doubt that the label "NSBM"—now an umbrella term for any act displaying right-wing tendencies—is somewhat misleading and awkward. For a start, many of the bands in question are *Nationalist* rather than *National Socialist*. The number of bands dealing with specifically "National Socialist" ideas and themes is actually somewhat small, since that entails rather more than merely a pride in one's country of origin and a racist outlook. Indeed the pigeonholing nature of the label means that even many of the most openly race-conscious bands are hesitant to accept it.

"NSBM has never been an appropriate description of Graveland's music and activity," explains Darken. "First of all, we should ask: is black metal a wrong place for political convictions? If you think about a little bit longer, you will understand that this is an opinion spread and supported by governmental vipers and censors who work for them. Of course not each black metal band has to be politically committed—black metal is not hardcore! However, if a black metal musician has a need to express his political convictions and opinions he has a right to do it. No one has a right to censor him. True black metal is uncompromising, unpredictable, unyielding… a dangerous element! Black metal is fire! At the moment NSBM is popular in the underground as it is much more extreme and uncompromising than ordinary commercial black metal. Many black metal bands betrayed black metal ideas and became dull and unremarkable. In [the] underground NSBM fires anger and provokes radical actions. Government departments and other institutions restricting our freedom regard NSBM as a threat for public order! Although I do not identify with NSBM, I am glad that true black metal fights for survival and authenticity!"

At the same time, while NSBM and Nazi-related black metal undoubtedly attracts some listeners thanks to this perceived sense of uncompromising intolerance and misanthropy, there are some who see Nationalism, National Socialism, and racism in general as being incompatible with the sort of elitism at work in both black metal and Satanism. It's a point recognized by those within both the Satanic and far-right camps:

"Just belonging to a certain nationality will never make you superhuman," Dissection's Jon Nödtveidt, a prominent Satanist, explained to Metalcentre.com in 2003. "Simple racism or nationalism is nothing but just another herd mentality for feeble-minded humans to, without logical reason, make themselves feel superior to each other in all their confusion, without having to accomplish anything at all but just being the mentally passive, easily guided apathetic flocks of cattle that they are... The true elite is self-made!"

"I think that white supremacy is just as dumb it gets," explained Ritual Butcherer, guitarist for Finnish legends Archgoat, to *Crypt* in 2006. "The world is full of white trash without any kind of ideology, living their ordinary lives as valuable as dog's crap on your shoe. I see the [black metal] ideology as individualism, not as a race thing. If the only value you find in yourself is your race, rather than your achievements or beliefs, then you are standing on nothing. The whole black metal scene is full of true death and Satanism-oriented, non-Caucasian individuals from Greece, South America and more, who have been pioneers of this music. Now some lowlife who is just following the path these guys made over a decade ago, thinks he can question them by their origin. I have had the pleasure of being in contact with many band members from those mentioned countries and you could not even compare them to these modern black metal scum."

"Satanism is based on lies and egoism," argues Darken, who once told *Decibel Magazine* that "In the Third Reich, Satanists would end in [the] gas chamber." "There is no brotherhood and friendship—the basic elements ensuring the survival of people as a group for many years. Very often worshipers of Satanism fight against one another... Lies, betrayal, egoism—these are the values characteristic for worshipers of darkness and Satanism... Heathen religions have only one aim: to make a man a strong individual capable of surviving and ensuring future for his children. Then you are ready to live your life. You have strength to fight. You do not need to hide yourself in basements or cemeteries worshiping [a] demon who wants to possess your mind and soul."

While the far right certainly has more than its share of infighting, more pressingly there is also undoubtedly something of a paradox at work, in that far-right bands who believe strongly in the importance of their ideologies often (understandably) attempt to promote the far right as something more than merely a destructive force. Thus they often present ideals that are actually too *tolerant* for many in the black metal scene, since they promote unity and comradeship with the fellow members of your race and society, a far cry from the elitist, misanthropic, and society-destroying aspirations black metal has long carried.

It's a point that Mikko Aspa of Clandestine Blaze and Northern Heritage—another respected label working with both political and non-political bands and whose own band has been mistakenly labeled NSBM due to criticisms of Israel—raised in 2001 in an interview with the Chronicles of Chaos website.

"Nazi = national socialist. First of all: I'm not socialist of any kind, and I don't think any black metal should be. Nationalists think that their country or people in it are somewhat special, but I tend to think most people are just meat. Useless flesh, often stupid and unimportant… How could I be nationalist in a state which is against many things I stand for? Nazism is about conservative values, family values, endless and unquestionable love for white race and your country brothers… since when was this socialist garbage classified as black metal?! Ten years ago every black metaller from Norway to Poland remembered to tell how LaVey sucked because of his humane and life-loving ideology. Now the same people are making '14/88' slogans—which simply means 'save the kids, make good future for our kids.'"

"At some point I felt it was insult to call Clandestine Blaze NSBM, since it was not accurate," Aspa comments today. "But now, I don't know if I care. There are no songs that advocate or promote National Socialism. However, I know plenty of NSBM guys, skinheads, etc. and I have always distributed the stuff with my label. I feel, that as long as black metal remains credible, it's good. Some of NSBM does, some of it doesn't. A lot of anti-NSBM arguments is based on building straw-man accusations. And I can confess having been there myself too… I have no problem with any ethnic group, unless their actions and their intentions are clearly in conflict of mine. I have nothing against some people living in other side of world, minding their own business."

Ultimately, the role of politics in black metal is shifting and complicated, but it's important to remember that politics aren't something that play a big part in the lives of the average black metal fan. Even many (but not all) of those who passionately support NSBM are not politically active outside of their support for NSBM itself, in much the same way that the cause of Underground Black Metal sometimes overshadows actual Satanic practice for some, as seen earlier in this book.

Equally, many bands who are opposed or indifferent to NSBM do not see any need to divorce themselves on a personal level from friends or comrades in those sections of the scene. The sight of non-Caucasian fans and musicians wearing merchandise of outspoken right-wing bands and sharing beers, festival bills, and even the stage with swastika-wearing far-right supporters may seem a contradiction on paper, but then the real world is a complicated place, and the black metal scene no less so.

37
GRAVELAND
AND INFERNUM
POLISH BLACK METAL
PART I

"From the first time of hearing this band I was captured. With all the primitive clumsiness of handling their instruments, they stood out from a lot of 'talented musicians' who were doing releases at the same time leaving no memories or raising any emotion. Graveland managed to create their own sound, their own spirit and timeless classics of the genre. Still today when I listen to Graveland I feel they are one of the most important black metal bands overall. Their attitudes and approach seemed much more uncompromising."

—Mikko Aspa (Clandestine Blaze)

WHILE THE PROLIFIC multi-instrumentalist Rob "Darken" Fudali was—like the rest of his peers in Poland—inspired into action by the early-nineties black metal scene in Scandinavia, his initial passion for metal was ignited many years earlier while he was still in school. Indeed, it's interesting to note that the trigger for his musical conversion was the same larger-than-life American group that drew so many of the Scandinavian protagonists into the metal scene.

"When I was in an elementary school one of my colleagues gave me some materials of Kiss and I remember I was highly impressed by the way they looked," he laughs. "It was the Communist time in Poland and we did not have an access to metal music, only those who had families abroad in Western Europe countries had access to Western culture and they were able to 'smuggle' it to Poland. My colleague who gave me materials of Kiss had such a possibility, and thanks to him I found bands such as Nazareth, Budgie, Uriah Heep, UK Subs… and this is how it started. Later—before I spent two years in the navy, 1988 to 1990—I started to listen to Celtic Frost, Venom, Mercyful Fate, and Bathory. Slowly Communist censorship started to let Western music appear in Polish mass media and you could listen to entire albums in some radio programs! I was waiting all week long to listen to a new album and record it on my reel-to-reel recorder. I heard music of Sodom, Kreator, Celtic Frost, Possessed, Destruction, it was an unforgettable adventure. I remember the clothes, images, entire atmosphere of black metal impressed me and had a huge impact on my imagination. I remember fantastic photo stories from *Kerrang!* mag, [like the] duel of Cronos and Thor!"

Curiously, *Kerrang!*'s hammy, humor-filled photo stories were not the only examples of English drama that would provide inspiration for Darken in the early days of his main project Graveland. Officially formed in 1992 in Wrocław, the largest city

Graveland as a trio before the departure of Karcharoth and Capricornus. Picture courtesy of Nihil Archives.

in western Poland, the outfit would tie together various strands of musical, thematic, and ideological influence, some from very unexpected sources.

"When I decided to form Graveland, I was under a strong influence of black and doom metal. I wanted to play slow, gloomy, and dark music. At that time, I listened to Winter—very slow and dark doom metal. However, I also listened to Dead Can Dance and you can hear the influence of these bands in my early recordings. Pagan dark beliefs in my early recordings came from [the] BBC TV series *Robin Hood*, Aryanhood, Crom Cruach [Irish pagan deity], Hern [ghost from English folklore]. Satanist motives present in this series were also a strong inspiration for my imagination. Celtic beliefs fascinated me. Graveland name is Tir-Na-Nog—Celtic land of the dead. I approved Satan in all his personifications because I believed so-called Satan [was] in fact pagan entities that got evil names from Christians who stigmatized them and made them Christian enemies."

Graveland would be, from the start, a highly active project, releasing no less than six demos, three in 1992 (*Necromanteion, Promo June '92*, and *Drunemeton*), two in 1993 (*Epilogue* and *In the Glare of Burning Churches*), and one in 1994 (*The Celtic Winter*). A far cry from the band's later works, the first four of these are heavy on both electronic percussion and synths, blending atmospheric instrumentals with heavily mechanized industrial death/doom-oriented numbers. In fact, despite the screamed vocals, it was really only with the fifth and sixth demos that Graveland began to follow the black metal blueprint of Darken's Nordic peers, combining influences from early Emperor with older outfits like Bathory.

"I recorded these demos during Communism in Poland," explains Darken. "Sound is horrible because we recorded it in basements on very bad equipment, which was very often worn-out. We were very poor at that time, our families did not support us, they did not understand us and criticized us all the time. But despite strong opposition of our families and lack of proper equipment we did not surrender. We will remember those times forever… we were able to produce such amounts of energy which gave meaning to all our deeds. Our music was rather simple and primitive but it had power to shape us. We forged our thoughts and desires into melodies that healed our wounded souls… I like *In the Glare of Burning Churches* demo the most…. *Celtic Winter* was inspired by the Norwegian scene and it was the first step on Graveland's path toward war and hatred in the name of true unholy black metal."

The latter two demos saw Graveland expand from a solo project into a full band, with Darken joined by two new members, both of whom proved even more radical in character. First into the fold was bassist and guitarist Grzegorz "Karcharoth" Jurgielewicz, a firebrand and semi-established musician who had already recorded one demo, *The Dawn Will Never Come*, with his own outfit Infernum. It was through Karcharoth that Darken would meet drummer Maciej "Capricornus" Dąbrowski. A skinhead dedicated to the extreme right, the sticksman would become as famous for his politics as for his strong work ethic during the nineties, playing with several bands in the scene as well as keeping busy with his fanzine and later a solo project.

"Karcharoth played in Graveland before Capricornus joined us," recalls Darken. "They had known each other a long time—even when Capricornus had long hair! I [originally] met Karcharoth when I recorded *Necromanteion*, he wrote me and we met. Together we practiced and shared our ideas. At that time Karcharoth was known as Anextiomarus and had his own project Infernum with his friend [and drummer] Balrog. They both came to my house and we talked about black metal, criticized some poseurs, discussed occultism and Satanism, traded tapes and zines. I was a photographer during [the] first Infernum photo session. For the first time, I saw people painting faces in black metal war colors. I wanted to have such image in Graveland, too. I remember this Infernum photo session took place in an old Jewish cemetery. There was a man walking with his dog. We scared him because he did not expect to meet such painted demonic creatures like ourselves!

"When Anextiomarus officially joined Graveland, he changed his name for Karcharoth," Darken continues. "It was a perfect name for him because he was evil and unpredictable in his behavior, radical and psychopathic in his convictions. Evil attracted him. Rarely did I hear him speak well about other people. I saw his psychopathic nature, but I accepted him because I believe that people like him were the true core of unholy black metal. Moreover, I

was very glad to have him in Graveland! Karcharoth had a plan to live together with Capricornus, to sleep in coffins and to paint walls in his house in black. In his imagination women
existed only as an object of physical violence. Aleister Crowley was his master and mentor
until the last days of Karcharoth's life. He suggested to extend [the] Graveland lineup with
a percussionist and proposed Capricornus… At that time, Capricornus was in contact with
Euronymous, Grishnackh, Samoth. He published his zine *Into the Pentagram*, therefore his
knowledge about the black metal underground and musical novelties was very wide… [he]
was a great support for me. I saw the meaning of all our actions and I knew how to use this
knowledge to make Graveland other than thousands of other metal bands."

United by their shared political and musical goals, the three musicians set about organizing the Polish black metal underground, transforming The Temple of Infernal Fire—Poland's
answer to the Norwegian Inner Circle—into The Temple of Fullmoon, a collective whose
pursuit of "evil" involved explicitly far-right activities and attitudes.

"At that time each of us had some political convictions but the new wave of underground black metal allowed us to use our right-wing convictions in music," he continues.
"True unholy black metal was to be uncompromising and rebellious… to cross the lines and
get closer and closer to the core of the evil, to approve all its manifestations to release young
wolves free. You just could not be an evil black metal supporter hailing dark powers and condemn Nazism at the same time. Most people condemn Nazism as evil so [we] approved Nazism. It was natural and perfectly understandable. When I met Capricornus, he was already
part of that world. Burzum marked him to be a warrior. And together we were on the warpath
against everybody and everything."

As well as their interests in Nazism, together the three would start working on various
musical manifestations of this "true unholy black metal" ideology. Darken was the most prolific of the trio, contributing session keyboards to many bands in the early nineties, including
Infernum, Oppressor, Behemoth, Mysteries, Wolfkhan, and Veles. Together with Capricornus
he would also unite with Leinad of the band Mysteries for a short-lived project called Legion,
and the pair would also join Infernum. Karcharoth's main band had already gained some
momentum with a sound akin to a more atmospheric Graveland, complete with heavy use
of keys, simple, epic passages, and a distinctive vocal performance from Karcharoth himself.

"We helped one another in our musical projects. Graveland, Infernum, and Capricornus' Thor's Hammer," Darken explains. "Our strong cooperation was a result of our beliefs
and convictions. Together we supported black metal ideology and it motivated us and made
us soldiers of one army. Our art was our fight. We were at war against Christianity. Each
new album was like another battle we had to win. This war made us feel special under gods'
protection. Playing in other black metal bands was a sign of your commitment to the underground and black metal ideology. Supporting Karcharoth in Infernum was our duty, especially
when his percussionist Balrog left for the death metal band Oppressor. Karcharoth hated
death metal. He had always had sharp, accurate arguments against it. Karcharoth found a

musical label [Polish label Astral Wings] to release the debut, which paid for the recording session. Everything was fine until the album [...Taur-Nu-Fuin...] was released. Karcharoth and Capricornus worked on the ideological part of the album and prepared radical text which was printed on the booklet. It was the cause of our first confrontation with UOP—Urzad Ochrony Panstwa (Polish special police forces). The times of repressions and responsibility for one's words and actions had started."

Indeed, the Polish secret service were now taking a particular interest in members of the country's homegrown black metal scene, both due to the extremist politics brewing within it and the crimes (such as church burning) perpetrated by its members.

"After the release of ... *Taur-Nu-Fuin* ... Karcharoth started to have problems," Darken recounts. "As he was the youngest of the three of us, the police decided to [make] him [a target] of their repressions. For some reason the UOP found the ideology of the album highly dangerous and harmful for democracy and the state. To some degree we were prepared for this attack. We had information about what happened in Norway—how the police broke up the Black Circle—therefore, we knew what we should not do. We tried to avoid their mistakes. We were ready for the battle. However, Karcharoth had one weak spot—he was a schizophrenic. His illness was waiting for a stimulus to [activate] it. This way Karcharoth was the weakest of us and police agents decided to intimidate him and cause his mental breakdown. These times were hard for us."

A few months after the Infernum debut came the first Graveland full-length, *Carpathian Wolves*, which featured the same lineup as... *Taur-Nu-Fuin...* , but saw Karcharoth handling bass (rather than guitars and vocals), Rob handling guitars, keys, and vocals, and Capricornus providing drums. Drenched in Satanic and folklore references, it continued in a similar vein to the later demos, lending even more emphasis to the slow and doomy passages and eerie organ accompaniment.

"This album was inspired by Dracula, werewolves, and all these stories connected with vampirism," Darken explains. "Part of the Carpathian Mountains is located in the southeast of Poland. Even before World War II inhabitants were afraid of vampires, ghosts, etc. When someone committed suicide, before he was buried, his head was cut off and heart punctured with a stake. It was very popular, especially in the countryside. Vampirism perfectly fit [the] black metal image ... Dracula's famous war cruelty or the bloody reign of Elisabeth Bathory. I created specific vampiric melodies under the influence of one song of Blue Öyster Cult."

Wasting no time, the band soon began to work on a follow-up in the shape of 1995's *Thousand Swords*. Released on the Austrian label Lethal Records, this breakthrough album saw something of a stylistic shift, with Darken introducing a pronounced folk influence, resulting in a more rousing sound that hinted at the heroics of Bathory's Viking metal period. The iconic cover captured Darken wearing both corpsepaint and medieval clothing, the latter later becoming a familiar sight as the founding member embraced the medieval reenactment scene.

"I was under a strong influence of folk medieval music," Darken recalls. "I was inspired by one of my favorite soundtracks—*Conan the Barbarian* movie. I found out that [composer] Basil Poledouris took inspirations from medieval folk and songs from *Carmina Burana* [a medieval manuscript] performed by [Austrian composer] René Clemencic. I bought these recordings and it was a great discovery for me, a huge source of inspiration. Also Karcharoth started to listen to these recordings—I am sure you can hear these inspirations in Infernum's music. Karcharoth also liked modern Celtic folk and music of Enya and Loreena McKennitt. Bathory was a great source of inspiration through music, epic image, paganism. I really liked the style of swords and ancient garments. The first time [I saw] these things [was] in Venom and Manowar. I have always thought [of the] cult of [the] warrior as a true essence of metal music."

The now-deceased Karcharoth of Graveland and Infernum.

As triumphant as it was, both Infernum and Graveland were entering difficult times, and *Thousand Swords* would mark Karcharoth's final appearance within Graveland, his troubled mental state severely hampering the trio's attempts to record a follow-up to ... *Taur-Nu-Fuin...* in 1996. In fact, it would be a decade before the group's next release, with Karcharoth parting ways with his bandmates around this time.

"As keyboard player, I was to appear in a studio at the end of the recording session," Darken recalls. "Unfortunately, it did not happen. Karcharoth and Capricornus recorded guitars and drums but it was a very hard time for Karcharoth. He was angry and nervous. He argued with Capricornus over everything during recording drums. During the recording session at six in the morning, the UOP police agents came to Karcharoth's house and took him to an empty flat where he was beaten. After some hours, they let him go but made him promise to stop the recording session and dissolve the band. When the police let him go, he came to me. He was scared and shocked. He told me what had happened and started to convince me that we should stop our activities. Otherwise, the police agents would kill us all. Then he went to Capricornus to warn him.

"The same day I met Capricornus and the two of us decided to do our job and walk [our] once-chosen path," he continues. "As Capricornus and I did not follow his warning,

Graveland's Rob Darken has gradually moved away from the more overt trappings of black metal, while retaining a keen interest in re-enacting.

a few days later Karcharoth started to isolate himself from us. He spent time only with his friends from Thunderbolt and Fullmoon. From them we found out that Karcharoth started to call us 'Nazi' and blame us for all his problems. It was a clear beginning of his schizophrenia. He started to tell stories that were very hard to believe. When he found out that people from Thunderbolt and Fullmoon did not trust him anymore, Karcharoth decided to go to Norway. He took a ferry to Sweden where the police stopped him for twenty-four hours and sent him back to Poland. As the time passed, it was getting worse with him. Schizophrenia reduced him to a poor substitute of the person he had been in the past. He started to support left-wing ideology and became a member of communist party in Poland. In [2004], he committed suicide, jumping off the roof of a tenth-floor apartment building. Before he killed himself, he tried to reactivate Satanist black metal [band] Infernum with new people but they had to finish the recording session without him."

The resulting situation for Infernum was unusual and somewhat undignified. The original 1996 sessions for the second album were completed by Capricornus and Darken and released in 2005 as an album entitled *Farewell* on No Colours. At around the same time the remaining members of the second incarnation of Infernum set about completing the album they had begun with the now-deceased frontman, releasing this as *The Curse* in 2006 on the Sound Riot label. In addition, UK-based label Supernal Music re-released the debut album following the suicide, replacing the controversial political messages of the original, rather disrespectfully, with a piece of writing by an anonymous source who branded the album's mastermind Karcharoth a traitor and portrayed his death as "the ultimate act of penance."

Back in 1996, the remaining duo within Graveland found themselves without a label, Lethal Records dropping the band following the release of *Thousand Swords* supposedly due to their outspoken NS beliefs. However, it's interesting to note that Graveland's releases were fairly restrained, politically speaking, in comparison to most of their peers, and Darken is adamant that the label simply did not wish to pay them for their work.

"NSBM has never been an appropriate description of Graveland music and activity," he states. "Determined and uncompromising attitudes of Capricornus and Karcharoth who supported NSBM in Thor's Hammer and Infernum were responsible for associating Graveland with NSBM. I had my own vision of playing black metal and I stopped some ideas brought by Capricornus and Karcharoth. Maybe it caused their radicalization in their own projects."

All the same, the band's political stance (or perhaps, the political stance of the band's members) was now becoming well-known within the underground, and freed from their contract with Lethal, the group soon began their long relationship with Germany's right-leaning No Colours Records, with whom they released *Following the Voice of Blood* in 1997.

"Capricornus and I recorded this album under strong pressure," Darken recalls. "We had a feeling that it could have been our last album. We were surrounded by the police and rats. Our friends were intimidated by the police. A helping hand came from Germany—true German black metal underground supported us and encouraged us. *Following the Voice of Blood* is a still a black metal album but one can hear the time of paganism and a cult of warrior is coming. Capricornus decided to be a session player in Graveland. He wanted to concentrate on his solo project Thor's Hammer. After some interviews in U.S. musical magazines Graveland became a target of some Jewish organizations that fought against anti-Semitism."

Indeed, the group's notoriety would see them receiving an unexpected cameo on television show *The West Wing*, with art imitating life thanks to an investigation by U.S. secret service agents.

"The album was mentioned as an inspiration for a terrorist who wanted to murder the president of the United States," he explains somewhat incredulously. "In this episode, a terrorist writes a letter with death threats to the president and signs it 'Following the Voice of Blood.' [A] secret agent explains that it is a title of an album of a Nazi band! Typical Zionist method of fight[ing] against its opponents! Recently the album was banned by German BPjM [Federal Department for Media Harmful to Young Persons]. The police confiscated all albums stored in No Colours distro. There is no anti-Semitic or Nazi propaganda on this album. But there is something else there: a spirit of a white man. True nature of white nations. A spirit of resistance against all those who want to enslave us!"

Though the album did not turn out to be the band's final effort, it did signal an exit of sorts from the black metal scene. Following the release, Darken would reinvent the project by promoting the epic, Bathory-inspired undertones of the previous two albums, the first result being 1998's *Immortal Pride*. Along with this musical change came a dramatic transition of image and ideology, Darken turning his back on many of the non-musical trappings of the black metal scene.

"*Following the Voice of Blood* was the last black metal album," confirms Darken. "On *Immortal Pride* I changed Graveland's image and referred to neo-pagan tradition. At that time

I was deeply disappointed by the attitude of Norwegian black metal leaders after the dissolution of the Black Circle and the commercialization of true black metal and the Scandinavian scene. I wanted to cut Graveland off from black metal when it became a commercial trend. Actions [such] as the activation of Mayhem were just business and I despised it. My convictions and views matured, I gained some experience … and decided to leave black metal to angry young men, to new generations [and] walk a way more appropriate to my nature."

"I saw a chance for me as epic pagan metal was not quite as popular and there were only few pagan metal bands," he continues. "So I started to work on new ideas inspired by Bathory—especially by *Hammerheart* and *Twilight of the Gods*—and Manilla Road. I took inspiration from folk music, some specific melodies and rhythms. Today Graveland should not be identified with black metal or NS black metal. Some metal fans listen to Graveland albums only from times before *Immortal Pride*. I understand them. These older albums are much easier to listen to and not everyone likes the epic style which is much more difficult to understand in the contemporary world of corporation slavery. It is not a problem for me. I am a warrior protecting traditional white man values. Fidelity is my honor. Even if I have to go alone against mainstream, I will not turn aside."

These epic musical ambitions were more than evident on *Immortal Pride*, an opus comprised of two lengthy tracks—twenty-three and sixteen minutes long—bookended by a pair of instrumentals. Still vehemently anti-Christian, the album reflected Darken's passion for paganism and its connection with national identity, a focus that apparently went hand-in-hand with his renouncement of Satanism and the pursuit of darkness and evil. This pivotal album would mark the final appearance of Capricornus, who instead continued with the more explicitly political music of his self-titled project and Thor's Hammer until the mid-2000s, after which he all but disappeared from view (though many online sources suggest he has departed the scene for a more hedonistic lifestyle, even posting a photo of him apparently partying with a black friend as evidence). Darken, on the other hand, has continued to be highly prolific in his two main outfits Lord Wind and Graveland, both of which have continued with the themes of battle, paganism, and Slavic national identity.

"At that time I was involved in the activity of neo-pagan movements in Poland," he explains. "Pagan spirit appeared in my music and it is present there till today. I still hated Christianity and church but I understood that violence and hatred were not the only possible weapon. Hatred and violence were part of black metal underground but I saw that our actions made Christianity stronger. So I was faced with a choice: destruction or creation? And I chose creation. Culture and true native beliefs of our forefathers became my new weapon. Finally," he concludes, "I dissociated myself from Satanism when I understood that as a heathen I should not identify myself with Judeo-Christian religion and culture and Satan and Satanism are part of Judeo-Christian tradition… Approving the idea of existence of Satan implicates approving the Christian vision of world. And these are the things I do not believe in."

38
BEHEMOTH
POLISH BLACK METAL
PART II

"We've been friends with Nergal and Behemoth since the tape-trading days and we pretty much share the same background in terms of musical and artistic inspiration, obviously with two different expressions. Behemoth has always been a force of its own ever since their conception and has ploughed the way for themselves without hesitation and without asking anybody for permission. Their records speak volumes in terms of great musical craftmanship and their live rituals [express] such power and conviction you'd have to be both blind and deaf not to take notice. Their success is earned the hard way—the only true way!"

—Silenoz (Dimmu Borgir)

THE EXPLOSION of far-right black metal bands in Poland from 1992 onward would define the country's scene for the rest of the decade, but its first few years were surprisingly apolitical. Formed in Gdańsk on the Baltic coast in 1991, Behemoth was an early presence within Polish black metal, appearing at a time when only a handful of other outfits (notably Xanatol, Christ Agony, Pandemonium, Mastomah, and Mastiphal) were active. Originally a trio, the group's first incarnation brought together three young musicians, curiously all named Adam: vocalist and guitarist Adam Darski (Nergal, initially known as Holocausto), second guitarist Adam Malinowski (Desecrator), and drummer Adam Muraszko (Baal, originally known as Sodomizer). All still attending school, Nergal and Desecrator were only fourteen when the band began, with the band's oldest member, Baal, being only one year older.

"While I was in secondary school I discovered Venom and Bathory and just fell in love, you know?" recalls Nergal, the band's only remaining founding member. "I developed an interest in the more underground and independent scene, like Morbid Angel, Blasphemy, Beherit, Samael, Rotting Christ—the Greek school, the Norwegian school, I just got hooked. The energy was undeniable and the whole anti-religious aspect and rebellious factor was essen-

One of several Behemoth logos that was used briefly
in the beginning of the band's career.

tial. Punk had some of this 'fuck everything' vibe, but black metal was more spiritual. I was in garage bands before [Behemoth], kid's bands I would say. I was the only person who owned a professional instrument, so we just beat the shit out of it and made tapes, so-called albums, drawing covers ourselves and coming up with different titles. Every few months we'd come up with a tape with a bunch of shitty songs. Eventually I decided I wanted to form a band that was... well, we were not *professional*, but we were aiming to be professional one day."

The first evidence of the group's activities surfaced in the middle of 1992 in the form of their first demo, *Endless Damnation*, a highly primitive slab of doomy black metal that, though undeniably amateurish, drew on some of the primeval spirit of early Samael, Hellhammer, and Beherit. 1993's *The Return of the Northern Moon* proved rather more professional in terms of both production and songwriting, offering a definite nod toward the more modern sound emanating from Scandinavia, while keeping one foot planted firmly in the eighties, a point underlined by the cover of Hellhammer's "Aggressor." Released in early 1994, the third and final demo, ...*From the Pagan Vastlands*, would complete this evolution, maintaining the slower tempos of the band's first-generation influences while nonetheless leaning toward a second-generation blueprint, with Nergal even adopting the rasping vocals that had by then become uniform within the movement.

The shifts in the band's sound were echoed by those within the lineup itself, the group losing second guitarist Desecrator after the first demo, and gaining another on the third in the shape of Rafał Brauer, otherwise known as Frost. Throughout these tapes the band also broke up the metal tracks with keyboard instrumentals, contributed by session musicians Czarek Morawski and Darken. The latter would fall out spectacularly with Behemoth just a few years later when the band distanced itself from the increasingly politicized Polish scene and departed the Temple of Infernal Fire.

"I never met the guy personally [at the time]," explains Nergal of Darken, "the way it worked back then was that I would get a tape from him with intros or outros and he would allow us to use it. We've never been in the same studio working on the same songs, [but] he was a friend of the band in the very early stages."

Even as a demo band, Behemoth had become one of the biggest names in the still-growing Polish scene, the latter two demos receiving semi-professional tape releases by Pagan Records, a relatively new label founded by Tomasz Krajewski of *Holocaust* zine. The licensing for the recordings was also picked up by foreign labels—namely America's Wild Rags and Germany's Nazgul's Eyrie and Last Epitaph Production—further spreading Behemoth's name in the international underground.

"I would say the first demo tape with a proper cover and proper glossy paper was the first step up," Nergal considers, "I was like, '*Wow.*' I was blown away. ....*From the Pagan Vastlands* was a huge step up again, it sold four thousand or five thousand copies worldwide on cassette which is massive, I mean there's bands that release *albums* these days that sell five hundred copies. Tomasz was a great buddy, he was ten years older and he'd be like a good uncle or something—thanks to him I discovered many new titles and bands. It was a very inspiring relationship."

Despite their popularity however, these early years were a far from easy time for the band's members, due predominantly to the circumstances in their homeland at the time. "It was very hard," explains Nergal, "we did what we could to realize our dreams, to keep going. These days it's easy—when you are ten you get Rock Band or Guitar Hero, then you ask your dad and he buys you a guitar. Everything is available. Back then it was the late eighties, Poland was still a Communist country and even in the nineties when we became a democratic country and our economy opened up to the European market it was still so poor, there were hardly any professional instruments available, just shitty brands. Even in 1995 you couldn't go into a store and buy a Jackson or BC Rich, no way. I remember when I bought my first Jackson it was 1999 or 2000, before I had this guitar I didn't have a killer instrument at all. Same goes for CDs. I remember in the early nineties the average monthly salary would be equal to like two or three CDs at the store. I remember I got the Emperor/Enslaved split and I was *worshipping* it! I was worshipping this piece of plastic! Obviously it's different now, but in the nineties it was pretty fucking tough."

1994 would also see the band's first "official" release, namely a mini-album entitled *And The Forests Dream Eternally*, issued on short-lived Italian label Entropy. Still a favorite of Nergal today, its five songs granted the band a decent production for the first time and took the songwriting into more memorable territories, its updated take on the early Bathory template resulting in a sound with clear parallels to Nordic peers such as Gorgoroth. Even the bold declaration on the sleeve ("NO TRENDS! FUCK WEAKNESS! NO MORE 'FUN' STUFF! KILL TRENDY IDIOTS!") seems to have its roots in the Norwegian school of communication.

While the demos had included explicit praise of Satan/Lucifer alongside pagan subject matter, the band's lyrics were now intently focused on paganism and nature itself—in fact, the opening words of the release are "Pure Paganism I worship in the woods." And while early demo tracks such as "From Hornedlands to Lindisfarne" had tackled the rather Nordic topic of Viking invaders, the third number of the EP, "Sventevith (Storming Near the Baltic)," now revealed distinctly homegrown inspirations, referring directly to the Slavic god of war.

1993 demo *Return of the Northern Moon*, originally a cassette but re-released over the years on vinyl and CD.

Indeed, interviews of the time illustrate just how intensely focused the band were on their country's pagan roots, Baal telling the zine *Kill Yourself*:

"I hail Poland as the land of the Slavs, as the territory of pagan culture and the sanctuary of the nature [*sic*] ... our lyrics are filled with the Slavonic pagan mythology, our hatred against those who destroyed paganism, the personal emotions/metaphysical relationships, about the night and the nature of the universe ... I hate Christianity, as the religion which is directly responsible for the obliteration of the pagan Slavonic culture."

The following year the group returned to (the aptly named) Pagan Records to release their debut album *Sventevith (Storming Near The Baltic)*, reusing the song title from the previous year's release though not the song itself. Recorded in December 1994, the album saw Behemoth reduced to the core duo of Nergal and Baal thanks to a falling-out with Frost, though once again, the group employed a guest synth player to create instrumentals, this time Sascha "Demonious" Falquet, the young but talented writer behind Swiss black metal fanzine *Skogen*.

While the lyrics continued where the mini-album left off (once again the opening lines refer directly to the forest, the sleeve declaring the opus to be a "rebirth of our old pagan traditions") musically a massive leap had occurred, with the songs now complementing the nature-worshipping lyrics with emotive and epic folk ingredients. The heavy use of both synths and acoustic guitars gave the numbers a rich texturing and once again suggested a Norwegian influence, this time from Emperor, Dimmu Borgir, and, perhaps most of all, Ulver.

"I listened to a lot of Norwegian music, we were huge fans of that whole scene," Nergal confirms. "We recorded in like two weeks, it was in our home town and it was pretty amateurish. We used an eight- or twelve-track recorder, all analog—back then there were no computers, so the mix was happening on the [desk's] controls and you had to do it all at once. Sometimes there were three or four people doing certain things at once; one would go for delay, the other guy would be in charge of the fade-out ... it looked funny but of course it was also very, very stressful. [Demonious] was a friend of mine," he continues, "he was actually a kid, I was seventeen, he was fourteen or something. He came up with a primitive tune on his keyboard and sent it to me, I mean it wasn't anything spectacular but I just liked

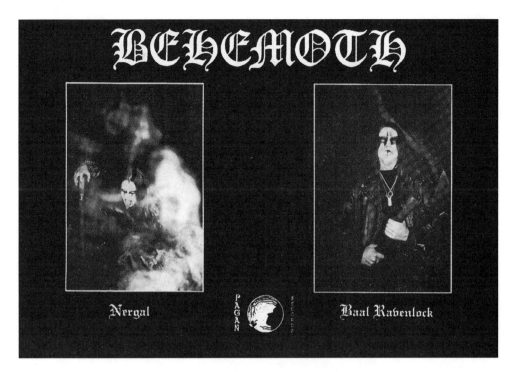

A Pagan Records flyer featuring both Nergal and Baal.

the vibe of it and asked him about using it on our record."

Around this time the band were actively distancing themselves from the increasingly right-wing Polish scene, Nergal departing The Temple of Infernal Fire circle that he had co-founded, which in turn reinvented itself as the more politically charged Temple of Fullmoon. He thus found himself criticized and confronted by members of acts from the rising NSBM scene, who berated him in interviews for his perceived acceptance of death metal, his association with supposedly "untrue" bands such as Christ Agony or Vader, for Behemoth's decision to sign to Pagan Records, and also for his use of Slavic themes, since they chose to identify instead with an Aryan identity. The sleeve of the debut full-length more than echoed this conflict and though the thank-you list included Graveland, soon to become one of the band's most vocal critics, it also stated in defiant form:

"BEHEMOTH sends pure hate and disgust to: all of the kids who disgrace the Polish scene, trying to be fascists without having any knowledge … This 'scene' is dead and BEHE-MOTH sits on the highest throne of the true one! If someone wants to beat us up or kill us, you are invited! Welcome to HELL!!!"

Behemoth would certainly continue drawing upon Slavic culture on their second full-length *Grom* ("Thunder"), released on German label Solistitium in early 1996 and featuring new bassist Leszek Dziegielewski of death metal act Damnation. A heavier and less straightforward listen than its predecessor, *Grom* is an occasionally chaotic album of strong contrasts that throws a wide array of musical ingredients into the mix, including female vocals, expressive half-sung, half-rasped vocals from Nergal (sometimes bringing to mind the work of Attila Csihar), time changes, folky acoustic guitar breaks and some punishing death metal elements.

"*Grom* was pretty much like a new band doing new music," explains Nergal. "We just wanted to develop a different sound, and went more into the pagan orientation, adding some extra elements, some female vocals—which wasn't very fortunate. I mean I know a lot of peo-ple *love* this album, but in my opinion I think there's a lot of crap on it. But then again it's a Behemoth album, it's not something I'm ever going to say, 'It wasn't me' or 'I had a blackout,' you know, I knew what I was doing. I was so much into these Slavic stories and I wanted to bring this into the music to make it more heathenish, more *pagan*, than regular black metal I would say. We were really into the Nordic thing and then after a while we decided we have our own culture, an ancient pre-Christian culture, which we found very inspirational and cre-ated something which was more original in a way."

Following the album's release, the band made a significant change in personnel, with Baal replaced by percussionist Inferno (Zbigniew Robert Promiński), a bandmate of Leszek Dziegielewski's (Les) in Damnation. Indeed, 1997 saw not only the release of Behemoth's *Bewitching the Pomerania* EP, but also Damnation's *Coronation* EP, featuring none other than Nergal on bass. Interestingly, Damnation's next official release—2000's full-length *Resist*—would feature neither Nergal or Inferno, but *would* include Baal on vocals, who had played with Les in blackened death metal outfit Hell-Born since 1996, and indeed, does so today, handling bass and vocals.

"[Baal] was in all the teenage bands I was in," explains Nergal. "I met him when I was a kid and lived just next door pretty much. We shared the same interest and we loved the same music and when I decided to form a professional band, I thought, 'Okay, he's in.' He wasn't really the greatest drummer, he was a bit like Abaddon, he had the passion and spirit for what we did and that's how we became companions. After a while, when Behemoth evolved in a more technical direction, he couldn't continue as it was just too complex."

Indeed, while the addition of Les and Inferno might not have had a direct impact on the songwriting—which Nergal apparently handled alone until around 2000—their abilities, particularly in the case of the latter, certainly allowed Behemoth to move toward the more precise death metal sound that the frontman desired.

"With Inferno in the band you can play pretty much any sort of music you want," continues Nergal. "He's not just a great technical drummer, he's a drummer who plays with heart—like a mix of Dave Lombardo—probably one of the greatest extreme metal drummers out there—and the spirit of Abaddon of Venom. But don't mix it up with abilities, 'cos Abad-don was a poor drummer, I just mean he's just a spiritually driven drummer, he's down for the genre and this band."

The group's resulting musical transition would be captured on the 1998 album *Pan-demonic Incantations*, before being cemented on the 1999 follow-up *Satanica*. "[*Pandemonic*

Incantations] was a bridge between the old and the new I would say," states the frontman. "We started playing music that was very fresh and different and defined that style with *Satanica*, so it was like a bridge between two different worlds. We just didn't want to stay in one place, we wanted to become *more* technical, *more* ambitious, and move in different directions. Stagnating is pretty much dying and not just in an artistic sense ... but we're talking about music, and playing the same music is pretty much standing in one place and dying."

Indeed, Behemoth would leave behind their early folk-influenced Nordic black metal sound entirely, increasingly honing what is generally described as a "blackened death metal" sound. Still, though albums such as *Thelema.6*, *Demigod*, and *Evangelion* employ the deep vocals and precise, technical brutality of death metal bands such as Vader or Nile, Behemoth nonetheless retain many links to their black metal past. Most obvious is their continued use of corpsepaint, the atmospheric overtones of old, and their distinctly anti-Christian stance.

The latter has seen Nergal come under fire in the band's heavily Catholic home, in particular with regard to a show the band played in the country in 2007, where frontman Nergal destroyed a Bible on stage and described the Catholic Church as "the most murderous cult on the planet." The incident would be brought to the courts on no less than three separate occasions, the final time by political party Prawo i Sprawiedliwosc ("Law and Justice"). The other two cases involved Ryszard Nowak, head of the "All-Polish Committee for Defense Against Sects," who lost his case against Nergal and then lost another case *brought* by Nergal after he continued to slander the frontman in the media.

"Even though he failed he was calling me a criminal in interviews so I decided to bring him to the court," Nergal explained to me in an interview for *Metal Hammer*. "I'm everything but a criminal, I pay big taxes and consider myself a pretty fucking good citizen. And actually I won the case, so the guy had to cover the cost of the trial, apologize in the biggest Polish newspaper, and on top of that I requested that he pay a thousand U.S. dollars to a homeless dog's asylum. Why? Firstly, I thought it would be funny as fuck, secondly I thought it would be the only positive thing this person does in their life and thirdly, I thought it might change the perception of metal for some people in Poland."

Going some way beyond simple anti-Christian sentiment, Nergal's philosophic and occult interests remain a central focus of Behemoth's work. Over the years the group have expanded from an exclusively pagan worldview (albeit with Satanic overtones) to encompass a wide range of left-hand-path thinkers including Aleister Crowley—whose own philosophy "Thelema" obviously inspired 2000's *Thelema.6*—and fellow Englishman Austin Osman Spare, whose form of magick, Zos Kia Cultus, inspired the 2002 album of the same name.

"The whole liberating aspect is just groundbreaking," he says of Crowley, "when you realize it's all about you and your decisions it gives your life a different quality. That's why I got 'Do what thou wilt shall be the whole of the law' on my back, because it's something you carry with you through life, it's fucking crucial and should tell you how serious I am about his words."

Never back down: Nergal today. Photo: Ester Segarra.

For Nergal, lyrical depth is essential within black and death metal, these being genres where many outfits utilize occult themes without any real understanding of what they are singing about. "We are really into the things that are definitely lacking in the extreme metal scene these days," he reflects. "There are millions of bands singing about different things but they don't mean it. When I hear a new band singing about something I don't trust it, I have the feeling that they don't stand behind what they say. When I listen to [Morbid Angel's] *Blessed is the Sick* or Samael's *Worship Him* I know that these guys meant what they say, but I don't get that impression any more. There is this wave of black metal from France that brings some freshness into the genre, the danger factor in the music is back and that's awesome—with Watain or Deathspell Omega for example, I get those goosebumps—but other than that there's very little inspiring happening."

Now into their third decade, Behemoth have achieved a huge amount of success, steadily breaking into the metal mainstream, signing to Nuclear Blast and touring alongside acts such as Slayer and even Marilyn Manson. Despite this they have maintained both their esoteric subject matter and a punishing and uncompromising sound, something Nergal is determined not to lose as the band continue to grow in popularity.

"I do care about other people's opinions but the opinion I care about the most is my own," he concludes. "I'm my own hardest critic. I'm a good enough musician that I can make music to please the masses—if I wanted to I would make more money and sell more records. But at the end of the day you don't want to look in the mirror and see a slut or a whore. You want to see an honest musician and artist."

39
ENSLAVED
FOLK AND FOLKLORE IN BLACK METAL PART I

GIVEN THAT black metal has positioned itself in opposition to the status quo, it's unsurprising that its practitioners have often looked to other periods of history for inspiration—particularly those that precede the domination of Christianity and other Abrahamic religions. While the artists who have chosen to explore the themes of historical, national, and cultural identity in the greatest detail have generally tended to sidestep the topic of Satanism, they have almost always maintained the firm anti-Christian stance inherent to the genre, alongside a focus on spirituality. With ancient folklore, beliefs, and mythology common subject matter alongside the wonders and mysteries of nature, it's unsurprising that both "folk black metal" and "Viking black metal" have proven largely synonymous with "pagan black metal."

However one chooses to label it, there's no doubt black metal has integrated folk themes and traditional forms of music to a far greater extent than any other form of metal before it. Indeed, it was black metal that played a key role in reigniting the wider "folk metal" explosion, a genre initially sparked by bands such as England's Golgotha and Skyclad, but which lay dormant until the late nineties and the rise of bands such as Finntroll, Falkenbach, and Moonsorrow, all spawned from the fringes of the black metal scene. For this reason, folk and Viking black metal has remained an often transitory movement, with many of the key albums either being sidesteps or starting points for the bands concerned, who have generally tended to become notably less "black" and rather more "Viking" or "folk" as time goes on.

An early case in point is the very godfathers of Viking metal, Bathory, whose Viking elements only began to surface on their fourth album, 1988's *Blood Fire Death*. Though heavy metal bands had hinted at pre-monotheistic themes of paganism and witchcraft before, this was the first point at which ancient historical and folk influences really began to really filter into extreme metal consciousness. In fact, the compositions themselves owe more to Wagnerian classical influences than actual folk music (acoustic guitars in the classic "A Fine Day To Die" aside) but the album nonetheless marks the introduction of localized folklore (in this case Northern European mythology) into a culture which until then had been largely preoccupied with inversions of Christian mythology.

In a move that would be imitated by many later bands, Bathory would leave black metal behind altogether on the next two Viking-themed albums, *Hammerheart* and *Twilight of the Gods*, but by then younger bands were present to fill the void and expand on these themes in a black metal context, most notably within the burgeoning scene in Norway. First and foremost were Enslaved, who adopted and pushed the concept into the second-generational black metal sound, becoming what many considered to be the archetypal Viking black metal band in the process.

ENSLAVED

"This is a band that always goes their own way, and has done so since their debut album. They never repeat themselves, and always explore new musical landscapes. I have nothing but the greatest respect for their musicianship and live performances. I think that they will be paving the way for other bands for many years to come."

—Hváll (Windir and Vreid)

Like many of Norway's black metal pioneers, Enslaved's origins lie within the death metal genre, in this case a short-lived demo outfit called Phobia. Formed by vocalist and bassist Grutle Kjellson and drummer Hein Frode Hansen (who later formed gothic metal band Theatre of Tragedy) when they were sixteen and seventeen respectively, the group soon expanded into a five-piece, making the somewhat unlikely move of recruiting a local twelve-year-old guitar player named Ivar Bjørnson in the process.

"We heard rumor of a little guy who enjoyed thrash metal," recalls Grutle with a smile. "There were no people playing metal where we lived, so we thought, 'Why don't we get hold of this little guy?' I remember the first rehearsal he was looking at me saying [adopts a high-pitched voice] 'How can you sing like that?' He already had this way of playing the guitar though, no one taught him how to play, he had his own way—he actually taught *me* and I was a few years older."

Despite the age gap, Ivar's and Grutle's backgrounds were not entirely dissimilar, with both being lured into metal via Kiss' seemingly ubiquitous promotional campaign in Norway.

"I was really into the Kiss thing without hearing any of the music," laughs Ivar. "In Norway every Saturday the kids would get these bags of goodies and the coolest bag was the Star Bag, where you would get these nice treats and Kiss pictures that you would trade at school. Also the most popular show at the time was about this family, and the girl would always have this dream where she would be onstage with Kiss, so it became a big thing for me, and my grandfather bought me a cassette and that's when I started to collect cassettes."

Moving onto WASP, then thrash, and eventually death metal, Ivar was certainly well-primed for a position in Phobia. However, with their use of synths, crawlingly slow passages and clean guitars, Phobia were far from a typical death metal band. In retrospect their atmospheric compositions showcase a short-lived sound that existed—particularly in Norway—around 1990/1991, one that provides something of a "missing link" between the death and black metal scenes. It's no surprise then that their *Feverish Convulsions* demo, released in mid-1991, shares many qualities with Darkthrone, Thou Shalt Suffer, and even Cradle of Filth output during the same period. Lyrically too, the band were looking beyond the typical gore themes of death metal and instead drawing upon some of the Viking themes that Enslaved would later become famous for.

"One of the songs on the demo is called 'The Last Settlement of Ragnarok,'" Grutle explains. "Ragnarok is obviously part of the [Norse] mythology—the Christians have rewritten things so it sounds like Armageddon, the end of the world, but to me it's always been like phases … you go as far as you can with something and it slips away or becomes a success. In Norse mythology you take the nine steps, then you can't go any further—that's Ragnarok. You date a girl for a few years, for example, and you can't go any further, that's Ragnarok."

Phobia would split up soon after the demo's release, playing their final show in Bergen's waterside USF Verftet (later home of Hole in the Sky festival and also the venue where the majority of this interview took place) shortly after their official disbandment. Grutle and Ivar weren't overly concerned, however, since before the demo had even been issued, Enslaved had already been formed, the two men joining forces with a local drummer named Kai Johnny Mosaker. A childhood friend of Ivar's, he initially went under the name K Johnny (for the first demo, entitled *Nema/Promo Tape 1991*) but would later become known as Trym Torson.

Working as a trio, the group decided from the start to focus their lyrics and concepts around Northern mythology, its members unwilling to be tied to the Satanic/occult concerns that were prevalent among their peers, but sharing the same strong anti-religious sentiments nonetheless.

"We were definitely linked to the black metal scene," ponders Ivar, who became known as H.M. Daimonion around this time. "Norway was pretty small, the inner circle was really no bigger than fifty people and these bands all had a profound orientation toward the occult and we didn't connect with that—simple as that. For us to start singing about that would be the most horrible betrayal toward the movement, so we needed to find our own conceptual expression, and that was the common ground we had."

"I remember seeing a play on TV about the Norse mythology," recalls Grutle of the event that sparked his interest in the subject. "I asked my mother, 'What is this?' and she said, 'Ah,

Enslaved's early promo photographs and live shows were far heavier on the Viking imagery. Photo courtesy of Ivar Bjørnson.

it's about the Northern gods' and went to get this book she wrote before she became a teacher. I was fascinated, 'cos you don't learn anything about it at all at school, the Norwegian school system had a subject called 'Christianity' when I grew up—now it's called 'Religion' which is better, you learn about other religions—and you heard about Norse mythology as some sort of burlesque, childish thing. Like, 'Oh, they used to think that Thor was running through the skies cracking the hammer and then you got thunder and lighting, ho, ho, ho.'"

"I was taken out of those classes myself," interjects Ivar, "and I think more parents should do it, it's not really healthy. I think there should be a separation between monotheism and religion, or turn it round and have 'religion' with the monotheistic religions—Christianity, Islam, Judaism—then 'belief systems,' 'cos it's *so* different. It's like classifying psychosis along with normal mental health. There's such a difference between Buddhism, Northern mythology, all these pantheistic religions on the one side who are saying, 'This could be the truth, we have a bunch of different gods representing things,' and monotheism on the other side. The finality of monotheism is so different to the ever-turning wheel of all the others."

As extreme metal musicians with an interest in Viking culture, it was inevitable that the members of the group would be influenced by the works of the mighty Bathory, and the Swedish legend's mid-period releases seem to have partly guided the group's incorporation of such themes into their own music.

"*Hammerheart* and *Twilight of the Gods* were the most important to me," Ivar explained to me in an interview at Wacken festival in 2008. "Bathory was an inspirational source because Quorthon used the ancestry and history in a very tasteful manner, using it philosophically, rather than just aggressively or in a politically tainted way. I've always been fascinated with nature and harsh weather, that's the stuff I grew up with, so mythology dealing with those topics just resonated naturally. I think the main factors are recognition and identification, this gives a sort of backbone, an identity, with the important distinction that though it's something you think is beautiful and are proud of, you don't start comparing it with other people's cultures. That's where problems start, when it turns to politics."

The band's interests in the ancient gods of their homeland was already evident on their second tape, 1992's *Yggdrasill*, its opening number "Helmdalir" containing the rather unambiguous lyrics: "Heimdall is the name of an Old Norse God … He is great and holy." Musically speaking, however, things were notably rougher around the edges than the likes of Bathory, with the furious, high-energy songs leaving little space for the epic and instead concentrating on rolling drums, chainsaw guitars, and eardrum-tearing screeches.

The follow-up—the iconic EP *Hordanes Land*, released by Candlelight as a limited vinyl and one-half of the legendary Emperor/Enslaved split CD—hinted at things to come, however, with slower, moodier passages and lengthy songs (three tracks in a half-hour), although the musical content remained pretty raw.

"Usually me and Ivar tried to rehearse during the week," recalls Trym, "and then we all rehearsed in the weekends, so we were all involved in the creation of the songs. The hardest part back then was the arrangements, we did struggle to make all the different parts flow together and, as you can hear, try not to make very long songs!"

One hugely supportive fan of the group was Euronymous, who heard the band around the time of *Nema* and told them to stay in touch, explaining that he might well be interested in signing the group to his label. While he would live up to his word, he nonetheless encouraged Candlelight to release *Hordanes Land* first in order to spread the name and drum up further interest in the group. In early 1994 the band's debut album *Vikingligr Veldi* was indeed released on Deathlike Silence, though by this point Euronymous was no longer alive to see it. He would surely have been proud, however, as the record proved a massive leap forward for the trio and one that remains a compelling listen today. Boasting a large but relatively raw production courtesy of Grieghallen and Pytten, its busy song structures, strong melodies, mysterious atmosphere, and orchestral, synth-heavy approach sit comfortably alongside other early symphonic-leaning efforts of the day such as those by Emperor or Gehenna.

"This was the first album we made," explains Trym, "and that made us more focused about the songs and how they connected to each other. It was also recorded in Grieghallen with the famous producer Pytten and we all were a bit star-struck to be in this situation … he was also more open to new things, and pushed us to perform the best we could at that time. Not everything was planned before we went in the studio, so a lot of the atmospheric and symphonic parts were things Ivar played with in the studio. We liked these new elements and how they added a new dimension to the songs."

"In those days everything was just done from a sincere personal wish to make some kind of audial [*sic*] expression," explains Ivar, who had handled synths as well as guitar within the band since its formation. "It was the same feeling as in May '91, everything was so intense and *physical* almost, you played the song in the rehearsal room and it felt like the most important thing ever. The idea to use symphonic elements and synthesizers was inspired by both the pomp of classical music as well as contemporaries: particularly Czech pioneers Master's Hammer. It was a way to add even more drama and intensity to the music—there could never be enough majesty and dramatic chord shifts."

"Ivar was really a young guy, a kid," laughs Pytten, who would continue working with the band for much of their career, "but he was a very focused person. Not just about the music, but about the whole situation. He was being the accountant, keeping track of hours, keeping the books, which was a new situation for me in the studio! But as a band they have always been really conscious and focused … they ended up being good friends of mine."

With Deathlike Silence effectively finished following Euronymous' death, the band signed to France's Osmose, releasing their second album, *Frost*, in late 1994, less than half a year after *Vikingligr Veldi*. Given this short gap it's surprising just how different the album is from its predecessor and stylistically it's a definite step back from that album's symphonic overtones. Despite retaining the use of synths, clean vocals, and clean guitars, the trio nonetheless forged a notably more traditional-sounding metal album, with a far rawer, guitar-focused sound.

"On this one we wanted to push the limits further and add more aggression and speed in particular," Trym states. "We felt more comfortable in the studio with Pytten and knew he could add the sound and atmosphere we wanted for this album. As the album was called *Frost*, we wanted to have a 'cold' sound, and I think we managed this very well. And as we had become better musicians, we could work on more advanced parts and at the same time make the arrangements better for each song."

Alongside the coldness remains a definite sense of atmosphere, and the minimal but ever-twisting sound aptly hints at harsh northern winters and terrible battles in the snow. Indeed, the band proved more engrossed in Norse lyrical preoccupations than ever, as evidenced by song titles that included "Yggdrasil" (the "world tree" in Norse cosmology), "Wotan" (or Odin, the leading player in the Norse pantheon), "Loke" (better known as Loki, the trickster god), and "Fenris" (Loki's ferocious wolf son). There is even a track called "Gylfaginning," which is named after the first part of the *Edda*, the book written some eight hundred years ago by Icelandic historian Snorri Sturluson and from which we take much of our understanding of the Norse gods.

By now there was certainly no questioning Enslaved's Viking credentials, a point cemented by the release of *Eld* in 1997, a record whose cover featured the blonde-haired Grutle seated on a wooden throne, goblet in hand, wearing a large Hammer of Thor and chain mail. If ever there was a poster band for the Viking metal scene—which now included countrymen such as Einherjer and Helheim—here they were, with an album that more than matched its cover in terms of content. Opening with "793 (Slaget Om Lindisfarne)," a sixteen-minute saga that more than matched Bathory for stirring and melodic majesty, it was an album that leaned closer toward the Viking metal template than ever before, making use of slower, more heroic passages and rousing, cleanly sung vocals.

Viking black metal's most iconic cover? *Eld*, 1997.

"*Eld* is an extremely important album in our discography—and I dare say that it is a very important album for the extreme metal genre," comments Ivar, "but it was comically underrated at the time of its release. In some circuits it was even ridiculed for the organic and rock-like production, clean vocals, and prog-influenced riffs. Those were the days when Abyss Studios was the shit, where every sound—including the silence between the songs—was the result of sound replacement and triggering. We were like the old geezers still using letters when the kids were using e-mail. Then in the 2000s when other people were also getting gagging reflexes from the silly plastic sound prevailing in metal, *Eld* came into fashion. Trends are silly, and can't be trusted either way."

Nonetheless, a clear black metal spirit still abounded, which the band drew on heavily for the following year's *Blodhemn*, a far more violent record that relied more heavily upon catchy, aggressive riffs, despite folk touches and a hint at the progressive direction to come.

Despite featuring new members—guitarist Roy Kronheim and recently departed Gehenna drummer Dirge Rep—the record marked something of a return to the band's musical past, though the cover image of the four members in period dress, standing on the shore with a longboat moored nearby, suggests the group's heart was in much the same place.

This two-pronged fork of lyrical consistency and an ever-shifting sound would become a hallmark of the group. *Blodhemn* itself marked the end of an era in many regards for the band, who introduced a pronounced progressive streak with 2000's *Mardraum: Beyond the Within*, then expanded on it considerably as time went on. Today the group are widely regarded as one of the most essential prog metal outfits going, and their Viking and folklore themes continue to take center stage lyrically, while the band shift sonically from record to record. Yet while their artistic devotion to the subject might suggest a literal praise of the mythology in question, the band are keen to distance themselves from later groups who adopted neo-paganism (or Ásatrú, the "faith of the gods") in a more religious sense.

"'Religious' is a Christian term, just like 'king'—there were no 'kings' in Norway or Sweden at that time," Grutle explains. "We're not religious, to be religious is to follow a god. In Norse mythology they didn't follow the gods, they had each god representing a certain feeling or force. Advising, rather than giving rules. You get some New Age people who say, 'I believe in Odin, I believe in Thor, I'm so religious.' Well if you're religious you're no better than the Christians."

Just as the band distance themselves from those who follow the Viking mythology as a faith, so too are they quick to play down the notion that there has been any integration of traditional Viking *music* into their sound. Indeed, as Ivar points out, such a feat is probably not even possible.

"We did a lot of research in the early days and were a bit surprised to find there *was* no musical tradition from that era," Ivar concludes. "There was only the vocal chants—storytelling in a melodic sense, remembering things through rhyme—and the pounding of the Viking ships, which resembles the heartbeat. Then we looked at these bands claiming to be Viking-sounding and traced *their* roots, which were actually from Christian medieval Europe—not very good if you want to be a pagan band."

In that sense, Viking metal (black or otherwise) differs most obviously from folk metal in that it opts to suggest the *mood* of its chosen subject matter, rather than integrate actual elements of the period. All the same, as we shall see, many bands within black metal would prove that the influence of medieval Europe—and even more recent decades—could provide just as valuable a source of inspiration.

40

MOONFOG AND ULVER
FOLK AND FOLKLORE
IN BLACK METAL
PART II

"In an over-populated Europe old Norway remains to this day nature's unspoilt realm: in the depth of her great forests stillness reigns as it did a thousand years ago. Here the modern world seems strangely unreal and irrelevant."

—Text from the sleeve of the Ulver/Mysticum EP, a telling insight into the psyche of the Norwegian scene in the early to mid-nineties

THE MOONFOG YEARS

A RESPECTED BAND in nineties Norway, Satyricon proudly drew direct inspiration from medieval Europe, even going so far as to dub themselves "medieval metal" in their early days. Unlike bands such as Enslaved, this fascination manifested itself most obviously through the incorporation of actual passages of folk music, as seen on their aptly named 1994 debut *Dark Medieval Times*, which makes extremely effective use of acoustic guitars, folk riffs, and even flutes, most notably on the album's lengthy title track. These influences would slowly disappear over the course of the band's next two albums, *The Shadowthrone* and *Nemesis Divina*, before being done away with in dramatic fashion on 1999's industrial-black makeover album *Rebel Extravaganza*, which concerned itself with an explicitly urban aesthetic.

Such historic folk interests were explored with some intensity around this time in Norway, particularly by the band's frontman Satyr, who indulged his interests both in Satyricon and medieval ambient solo project Wongraven, as well as with his label Moonfog, which included two folk black metal acts, both featuring Fenriz. First was Fenriz's solo project Isengard, a heavily Tolkien-inspired proposition which took its name from *Lord of the Rings* and its

**An advert for *Vinterskugge*, 1994, the debut
full-length of Fenriz's black/folk metal solo
project Isengard.**

logo from a role-playing game based on the same book. The project had actually begun in 1989 as a death metal entity, but increasingly integrated clean vocals and stirring folk traits into an otherwise Darkthrone-like template, culminating in full-lengths *Vinterskugge* (1994) and *Høstmørke* (1995). The result proved something of an acquired taste, particularly the latter album's loose compositions and "hey nonny" vocals.

The same year saw the marginally more polished *Nordavind* album released by Storm, a one-album project in which Fenriz collaborated with Satyr himself, the duo giving traditional folk a black metal overhaul. Unsurprisingly, the album bore heavy similarities to Isengard, Darkthrone, and early Satyricon, though the inclusion of female vocals alongside those of Satyr and Fenriz set it apart somewhat. Curiously, these were contributed by Kari Rueslåtten of The 3rd and The Mortal, who later claimed in the national press that she had been deceived regarding the true nature of the album, unaware of its anti-Christian and nationalistic overtones.

Fenriz's folk dabblings ended in 1995, and today he is at pains to distance himself from folk metal in general, including his own contributions to the genre. Interestingly, his inspirations during this period turn out not to have been the ancient folk music of his homeland that one might imagine, but an outfit from a much more recent period of history.

"In 1994 I was into the Norwegian seventies folk rock band called Folque," he explained to me during an interview on the subject of folk black metal in *Terrorizer*. "I was into pulling old, sad, shepherd's songs and Norwegian/Swedish traditional music into the metal scene. I wish I never did. Folk metal should be deleted. Luckily I was also into the Viking albums Bathory did so masterly some years before—*Hammerheart* and *Twilight of the Gods*—so many okay songs came out of the Isengard project."

Making it clear that he prefers the "death metal ordeal" of Isengard's early works to the "folk shit most people seem to prefer," Fenriz is even more damning of Storm and the prevalence of folk influences in Norway at the time.

"We were idiots and didn't understand that folk and metal should never mix," he laughs. "I thought Skyclad was amusing and my own fling with folk metal too, but after it was done … oh brother. Folk is good. Metal is good. But together? No. It sounds too merry for phat fuzz, and those of you who can't hear that must be lacking a chromosome or something. Isengard had at least something else to offer than pure folk metal, but Storm? I ain't touching that with a 666-foot pole."

Still, Fenriz's final contribution to the folk black metal canon would actually come in 1998, courtesy of one of the genre's most influential acts, Ulver.

ULVER

"The first I heard of Ulver was back in 1994–1995, when we were going to play a tribute concert for Euronymous and I spoke with Garm and got a flyer for his band. Ulver really influenced me in the process of making Hades' second album and I must agree with many fans, that the man has an awesome range both in music and vocals. Ulver is not music, but art!"

—Jørn (Hades)

Formed in late 1992, Ulver were one of a number of highly significant Norwegian groups that appeared in the aftermath of the country's initial black metal explosion. Somewhat younger than the musicians within already-established bands such as Mayhem, Darkthrone, and even Emperor, the outfit's founding member, Kristoffer "Garm" Rygg, was, like many of his peers, greatly inspired by the thriving Oslo scene he had discovered through visits to the Helvete store, a location and clique that provided the catalyst for his conversion to the genre.

"We were almost considered 'prospects' to use biker lingo," Kristoffer reflects today. "I think it's safe to say that when I was a teenager, visiting Helvete the first times, during the summer of '91, the whole shift was about to happen. It was quite clear from all the occult props and the highlighted records as to what you *should* be into, as opposed to the stuff on Roadrunner and Earache, so I'd say that shop was quite imperative in me getting into black metal. First and foremost the music felt more interesting; it was wrapped up in a more explicit aura of darkness and danger than death metal, so we quickly took to those rules like 'you shouldn't wear colorful clothes when playing extreme metal.' It was a sort of mass suggestion, or hypnosis going on, really. And there was a sense of almost patriotic pride that these first demos and albums were all Norwegian bands, a sense of *knowing* that this was the real deal."

Being sixteen, Kristoffer was too young to drink at either the city's now-famous Elm Street bar or the most popular venue of the era, Lusa Lottes pub, where legal drinkers such as Euronymous, Hellhammer, Faust, and members of Arcturus regularly sank beers. Kristoffer's situation was not unique however, and he soon found himself drinking alongside many of the younger black metal fans in Oslo at a bar called Møllers, a venue that employed a decidedly relaxed approach to age verification at the time.

Unsurprisingly, when Ulver formed the lineup incorporated many of Kristoffer's drinking partners, and the new band quickly grew into a six-piece as 1993 progressed. Taking care of the vocals himself, Kristoffer was joined by Sabazios/Mysticum bassist Robin Malmberg, guitarists Grellmund and Ali Reza (a Møllers regular of Iranian descent), and two slightly older and more experienced musicians, Håvard Jørgensen and Carl-Michael Eide, who both formed and played in Satyricon (as guitarist and drummer respectively) in its original, pre-Satyr/Frost incarnation. Taking their name from the Norwegian word for "wolves," the group began to craft a sound that drew heavily upon the prevailing spirit of the time, though their enthusiasm initially outweighed their ability, as Kristoffer explains.

"We wanted to be a part of things somewhat more actively than just being consumers, to be a creative force, and the only way to do that was to play in a band. The whole philosophy was that black metal was about *more* than music, but of course it was primarily about musical enthusiasm ... Carl-Michael was in Satyricon and had some musical skills, but the rest of us didn't."

Though generally working around the black metal blueprint, it's interesting to note that many of the musicians in the band's social circle would go on to make a name for themselves in bands with a distinctly innovative touch, such as doom outfit Lamented Souls, whose members would go on to such pioneering groups as Virus, Arcturus, Dødheimsgard, and Ved Buens Ende. Ulver would prove to be just as cutting-edge, adding their own distinctive take on the Nordic metal template almost immediately, perhaps paradoxically through the incorporation of inspirations from the past.

While a lo-fi and relatively generic rehearsal recording was leaked and later made available via trading circles, the band's only sanctioned tape was issued later in 1993 and revealed the pronounced folk and prog influences within the band's songwriting. Titled *Vargnatt* ("Wolf's Night"), and with half of its lyrics written by Jørn H. Sværen of *Orcustus* fanzine, who became a member of Ulver some seven years later, the half-hour-long opus showcased the work of all three guitarists—Reza, Grellmund, and Haavard playing lead, rhythm, and acoustic guitars respectively—contrasting tranquil guitar parts alongside the more aggressive and familiar black metal elements.

"I was really into bands that sounded *different*," comments Kristoffer on the integration of such elements, "and I think in those days that was a major criterion; to be a force to be counted on in the scene you had to create your *own* thing. This latter-day perception that true black metal only sounds like Darkthrone is just fucking silly, it's a lot of distortion on the original idea which included stuff like Mercyful Fate, for crying out loud. The *charisma* of the music was really paramount. I fondly remember the first Samael and Master's Hammer albums or more obscure releases such as the Rotting Christ/Monumentum split single, they all sounded very different to one another, but we loved it all the same."

The young wolves: Ulver in their demo era circa 1993, Mean and Haavard not pictured.

While the musical content may have tempered its assault with more reflective passages, the tape's sleeve revealed that the group were nonetheless in tune with the militant mindset of the era, memorably attacking two other new bands with the words: "We do not salute... Fleurety & Wind of Centuries... Guess you've not got to the point of understanding... you will remain nothing until the day you are nothing ... "

"It didn't take much to fall out with someone," he admits, "in a weird way it was almost like we were striving for enemies in addition to the obvious common enemy we had in Christianity or society. I have to laugh thinking about all this... it really defied logic, the mindset that most of us adhered to. It was outlined by some sort of *feeling* or *consensus* that was absolutely ludicrous, but made perfect sense at the time; the *evil* thing. There were times when it was uncomfortable and it was also hard to live up to the ideals we set for ourselves. We were young and living at home with our folks so you had this sort of double life, this world with these people on one hand, then going to school and chasing Christian skirt on the other—not so pure in retrospect. I guess 'theatrical' is a key word, *staging* yourself to a big respect."

The demo's sleeve also featured an early appearance of the popular Never Stop the Madness logo, a parody of Roadrunner Records' anti-drugs campaign, which suggests a certain affinity for narcotics within the group at the time.

"We were out every weekend, or going to the cottage, getting stoned and invoking the trolls," Kristoffer recalls with a laugh. "There were quite a few people who endorsed drugs—we expanded upon reality and challenged it, in true occult tradition … I remember a lot of people taking the stance that drugs could fuck up your mind and that's why you should take them, that you shouldn't fear that in a way. Of course, some people got severe problems because of that, I know musicians who had some hard years and still struggle with it … ending as acid casualties or junkies."

It was with fellow drug enthusiasts Mysticum that the band's first official offering would surface the following year, the two groups collaborating on a split seven-inch. Ulver's contribution to the release came courtesy of the song "Ulverytternes Kamp," a heavily acoustic number from the Vargnatt demo that contrasted sharply with the more futuristic sounds on the other side of the record.

"That was definitely something we thought about at the time," explains Kristoffer, "to present different faces of this new take on metal that was influenced by a lot of different things but was also shaping its own world and curious confines in a way. It was quite a magical time of revolting youth, quite creative, despite the outward appearance of it being destructive."

There was certainly an element of the destructive around Ulver by this point, with a significant lineup shift taking place that not only saw Robin leaving to concentrate on Mysticum, but, more acrimoniously, the departure of Carl-Michael, A.Reza, and Grellmund, the latter sadly committing suicide a few years later. The band shifted into a five-piece with the addition of three new members: guitarist/keyboard player Torbjørn "Aismal" Pedersen, bassist Hugh "Skoll" Mingay (previously of Fimbulwinter and later of Ved Buens Ende and Arcturus), and drummer AiwarikiaR, better known as Erik Lancelot.

"Erik was suggested by me by someone … might actually have been Euronymous," Kristoffer recalls. "He'd had a couple of rehearsals with Burzum when Varg wanted to have an actual band, while Samoth was playing with him, but that didn't work out, so I called him and we established a curious relationship which was very on and off. It was a mercurial relationship, us having strong similarities in certain areas and being complete opposites in others. I actually met our first guitarist [A. Reza] like a month ago and it was still weird, I think he still feels a bit disgruntled that we fired him back then. It *was* a stupid reason I'm sure, but that's what it was like back then, we could be quite ruthless with each other."

He continues: "Actually Shagrath [Skoll's bandmate in Fimbulwinter, now frontman of Dimmu Borgir] was supposed to be the guitarist on the first album, and rehearsed with us for six months or so, but then Dimmu formed and I didn't particularly dig that at the time. I have absolutely no problem with it now, but at the time I found it difficult, so I guess I gave him an ultimatum and he chose to go with them, which is how we got in touch with Aismal. He had just moved to Oslo from the northern city of Hammerfest and was an acquaintance of Tania 'Nacht' Stene [Ulver's cover artist for their first three albums], who introduced me to him. Carl-Michael left partly in sympathy to the other two guys I fired, but he also wanted to make a different kind of music to me and formed Ved Buens Ende which was really oddball stuff. Now I listen and think it's one of the coolest albums that came out of those times, but at the time we wanted to do different things basically."

Signing to Head Not Found, the label of *Slayer Magazine*'s Metalion, the band's next recording, 1995's *Bergtatt—Et Eeventyr I 5 Capitler* ("Taken by the Mountains—A Fairy Tale in 5 Chapters"), was initially drafted for a second split-release—with Gehenna, a band Kristoffer had introduced to Metalion—but was ultimately released as a standalone album.

"When we made the album it seemed too much of its own piece to amalgamate with someone else's vision," reveals Kristoffer. "It was in accordance with the elitist vibe that was going on at the time, though we were buddies with Gehenna ... I was even on their first album. We started rehearsing the album with the demo lineup, but that disintegrated in '93, so we recruited some other guys and rehearsed across the hall from Mayhem's rehearsal space and recorded in 1994 in a loft in the old town of Oslo."

As its title suggests, *Bergtatt* draws heavily upon Norwegian folklore, specifically popular legends based around the idea of people being lured into the mountains by trolls or spirits, the album's narrative being written from the perspective of a woman who suffers just such a fate. Inspired by Baroque poetry, such as that of eighteenth-century writer Ludvig Holberg, the lyrics were written by Kristoffer—now employing the pseudonym Garm—and translated into archaic Dano-Norwegian by new drummer Erik.

The music draws just as heavily upon folk influences as the lyrics, the first number (whose title translates to "Led Astray in a Forest of Trolls") dominated by Kris' clean, multi-layered, and surprisingly tranquil vocals, a definite eyebrow-raiser at a time when screamed vocals were the norm. The fourth number ("A Voice Beckons") goes a step further, featuring no metal elements at all, and throughout the remaining three songs there is a frequent use of clean-sung vocals (male and female), acoustic guitars, and flute accompanying the emotive and occasionally embittered black metal sections.

"We used to sit around and listen to traditional folk recordings, like for instance *Draum-kvedet* [a late medieval Norwegian poem]," explains Kristoffer when asked about the source of this musical influence. "We were quite into that at the time and it also synchronized with Norwegian history lessons at school, we picked up on a lot of National Romantic poetry and literature as well as painters like Lars Hertervig, J.C. Dahl, Thomas Fearnley, and the likes. It was a real interest and it felt natural to integrate all of that into Ulver. We felt no one had really done it that way; sure, you had the whole Viking thing, but what we were doing wasn't really anything to do with what, for example, the Enslaved guys were doing. We were almost trying to *reinterpret* the medieval and baroque perception of Norwegian culture—Christianity had long since established itself, so it was important for us to show it from a 'Satanic' angle and turn things round a bit. There's never been any shortage of megalomania in this band."

If *Bergtatt* had hinted at such preoccupations, its 1996 follow-up *Kveldssanger* ("Twilight Songs") completely cemented the vision. Entirely made up of short acoustic folk numbers and largely instrumental, this thirteen-song opus is a deeply emotional and atmospheric journey, infused with inspirations from romanticism, nature, and the night. Largely removed from black metal—or indeed metal of any sort—it nonetheless bears a melancholy and depth that seems to resonate among a certain type of metal listener, and the album would prove hugely influential in its own right, informing not only the black metal scene but directly inspiring the loose musical scene that continues to grow today around acts such as Empyrium, Tenhi, Nest, and Ainulindalë.

"Doing that album kind of signified that we were bound to go other places," the vocalist considers, "but we didn't imagine the album would get the recognition that it has now. It was more meant to give emphasis to the original idea that you didn't have to amp up, speed up, and scream in order to be 'black.' Some of our contemporaries hated it and others thought it was great, so it kind of went down as it always has ... reverence or revulsion. It was quite uncompromising so was bound to have an adverse effect on some people."

By this point, Kristoffer had joined the progressive symphonic black metal outfit Arcturus, as well as Borknagar, a Viking/folk metal supergroup that included members of Enslaved, Gorgoroth, and Immortal. Despite this, Ulver maintained their album-a-year release rate thanks to 1997's *Nattens Madrigal—Aatte Hymne til Ulven i Manden* ("The Madrigal Of The Night—Eight Hymns To The Wolf In Man"), an album that saw the band depart Head Not Found for the much larger Century Media Records. If anyone was expecting the band to temper their sound for a more commercial audience, however, they would be shocked, and the group once again surprised followers, this time by abandoning most of the folk touches that had become their hallmark in exchange for a stripped-down, Darkthrone-esque assault. Featuring the same lineup as *Bergtatt* (the acoustic songs of the second album had not required the talents of either bassist Skoll or second guitarist Aismal), the recording signaled a clear return to black metal territories, at least temporarily.

"These first three albums were already mapped out in '94," Kristoffer explains, "but we also felt a slight change of heart after the second album, that we came across as too soft or something. It was a matter of proving we could be damn well ferocious if we wanted to, but it also tied in with the lyrics and how we wanted to present the beast."

Indeed, with its screamed vocals, pounding percussion, and high-paced tremolos, the album is almost a textbook example of high-quality nineties Norwegian black metal—a strangely conservative move from a band as envelope-pushing as Ulver. Such convention even included a heavily caustic production, one so lo-fi it led to rumors that the album had been recorded in the forest on a simple analog recorder.

"It was actually the same studio [Bondi] that Mysticum used to record their album," reveals Kristoffer, "only twelve tracks, an early digital studio, basically a small desk with digital recorders. I think we amped up and played straight in and really made no effort in beautifying the product at all—much inspired by Darkthrone, I'll admit to that. Around 1999/2000 we recorded that album again with a string quartet—we'll probably never release that, but we did at one point want to reinterpret the album. We always had a very strong focus on and interest in the *sound* of things, because it does quite radically change what you're hearing. Melody is given far too much credit I think sometimes."

Having just delivered such a quintessential slice of black metal, the band's next move was to turn away from the genre altogether. Indeed, today Ulver have very little—if anything—to do with their black metal past, their live shows featuring no evidence of these early albums and their music exploring a wide range of styles from electronica to industrial to film scores and much more. Indeed, around this time the band would distance themselves quite publicly from the genre, most memorably in an interview for *Slayer Magazine*, where Erik stated:

"ULVER was born out of the Black Metal scene … However, bearing in mind the way ULVER has developed over the years both musically, lyrically, and philosophically, the label is becoming too limiting … The essence of Black Metal is Heavy Metal culture, not Satanic philosophy … the average Black Metal record buyer is a stereotypical loser—a good-for-nothing who was teased as a child, got bad grades at school, lives on social welfare and seeks compensation for his inferiority complexes and lack of identity by feeling part of an exclusive gang of outcasts uniting against a society which has turned them down."

Kristoffer was somewhat less harsh during the interview, but his criticisms were no less biting, stating, "[I] find it difficult to see myself as a part of this movement because a lot of Black Metal people follow very fallacious and narrow concepts of life. I seek to be impeccable, and this can only be achieved through open-mindedness. This implies interests outside what is common in the above circles … Black Metal now makes ignorant and unconfident young people feel warm and cozy, and functions more as a crutch for individual weakness than anything else. Now isn't that cute!"

The band would, however, release one last album that drew upon the genre—even if only in a small way—namely the expansive two-disc opus *Themes from William Blake's The Marriage of Heaven and Hell*, a highly progressive and experimental release which, as the name suggests, takes all its lyrics from *The Marriage of Heaven and Hell* by Romantic poet and artist William Blake. While fans were by now used to radical shifts from the band, today the album stands as a clearly transitional work, pre-empting the band's shift toward more mechanical territories.

Now going by the name Trickster G. (a pseudonym whose urban overtones neatly complemented the vinyl scratching and drum & bass touches on the record), Kristoffer shared vocal duties with a number of guests, including Fenriz, and Ihsahn and Samoth of Emperor. Aismal had departed by this point, but the group had been joined by keyboard player and programmer Tore Ylwizaker, a musician who would play a significant role in the group's future and its shift toward electronic territories. This shift would be more than evident on both 1999's aptly named *Metamorphosis* EP and 2000's *Perdition City—Music to an Interior Film*, an album on which Tore was the sole full member aside from Kristoffer himself.

Kristoffer "Garm" Rygg of Ulver in 1995,
circa *Bergtatt—Et Eeventyr I 5 Capitler.*

"We had [the first three albums] created in the mind from the start," Kristoffer explains, "we never saw beyond the third one, so when I started the 'black hybrid' the lineup sort of disintegrated, primarily because Tore came in and could expand the vision in a way the others couldn't. They sort of fell off as we did things they couldn't really add much to. Also, in '97, '98 I just didn't find metal very interesting any more, simple as that. I was being swayed by so many things from other places. The Blake album was a rite of passage of sorts, but it still had in its heart a lot of that [black metal] stuff. And that is why it was natural to get Ihsahn and Fenriz to read on top of it, because we were still *there*, in our hearts I suppose."

The band has only increased in stature as the years have gone by, Kristoffer himself going on to work with numerous artists, both as a musician and owner of Jester Records, a label whose first release was Ulver's aforementioned fourth album. While the majority of his output sits well outside the genre that originally made his name, Kristoffer's relationship to black metal is perhaps not quite as hostile as one might imagine considering some of the statements made in the late nineties. Indeed, since that time he not only signed Norwegian act Nidingr to his label, but has also provided some surprising guest appearances with the likes of Dimmu Borgir, Borknagar (who he left as a member in 1997), and most surprisingly, Fleurety, whose Department of Apocalyptic Affairs album he not only sang on, but also co-produced, contributions that provide some (admittedly loose) links back to the black metal and even folk black metal genres.

41
THE PROLIFERATION OF BLACK FOLK METAL
FOLK AND FOLKLORE IN BLACK METAL PART III

FOLK AND VIKING black metal continued to reign in Norway throughout the nineties, the country giving birth to Einherjer, Kampfar, and Hades, the outfit formed by Jørn Inge Tunsberg following his departure from Immortal. Incorporating both folk and Viking influences in their epic demo *Alone Walkying*, Hades were soon signed by Full Moon Productions for their debut album, the equally well-regarded ... *Again Shall Be*.

Combining raw and searing black metal with some of the most rousing guitar work of the period, the heroic overtones and catchy riffs on ... *Again Shall Be* echoed the work of many later Viking black metal bands. Lyrically, the combination of anti-Christian sentiment, heathen spirit, and national romanticism reflect the motivations behind Tunsberg's physical attacks upon the church, though Hades' members, like those of Enslaved, were careful not to commit to any pre-Christian faiths in a religious sense.

"The interest hailed from our national history, but it was Bathory who inspired me to use pagan terms in Hades' music," Tunsberg explains. "I guess the inspiration had been there for a long time. I was fascinated by myths, ancient religions, [the] Middle Ages, and so on since my early school days, and enjoyed the stories told through movies, books, music and so on. We did a lot of research for our topics, but I never considered myself 'religious' at all. I believe I am *anti-religious*. You can say that I accept that religion is among us, but I don't approve it to be sane!"

The band's next album (and in the opinion of many, including the band themselves, their best) was 1997's *The Dawn of the Dying Sun*, written predominantly in prison while Jørn served his sentence for the 1992 Åsane Church arson. Songs such as "Pagan Prayer" betray the familiar lyrical fascinations, though the band would soon shift tack somewhat, with a more futuristic aesthetic and a progressive sound with industrial overtones accompanying a forced name change (to Hades Almighty, due to an American thrash band named Hades).

While they came to the fore later, during the mid- to late nineties when folk's influence upon black metal was beginning to wane, arguably the most enduring folk black metal band from Norway was Windir, an outfit founded by Terje "Valfar" Bakken. Though Windir's two demos—*Sogneriket* and *Det Gamle Riket*, released in 1994 and 1995 respectively—revealed few folk inspirations, 1997 debut album *Sóknardalr* and its follow-up, 1999's *Arntor*, drew upon folk influence almost as overtly as earlier Norwegian groups like Storm. At the same time, Windir offered a rather more accomplished and fluid experience than the groups that preceded them, eschewing rawness for melody and combining black metal and folk elements with apparent ease. The result was hopelessly catchy, upbeat anthems that were simultaneously undeniably epic and earnest.

Though initially Valfar only used session musicians sparingly (impressively performing vocals, guitars, bass, synth and, unusually, accordion himself), after two albums he made the decision to expand the project into a full-fledged band. To do so he incorporated all five members of Ulcus (previously Ulcus Molle), the band of childhood friend Jarle "Hváll" and Jørn "Steingrim" Holen (the latter already an occasional drummer for Windir), who had already recorded an EP and full-length album of symphonic black metal.

"We grew up as next-door neighbors so we met long before I can even remember—he and his brother Vegard were my main buddies alongside Steingrim who lived five hundred meters from us," explains Hváll, whose hallway features many photos of the four men during their childhood years. "He felt like a brother to me, and I didn't view him as a bandmate, but as a family member. We all got into Kiss through Valfar's older brother when we were like five/six and from there it just evolved. Valfar was the first of us to get into black metal in 1992.

"Valfar kinda felt [the project] was stagnating after the *Arntor* album," he continues, "he wanted some new inputs and to get a live band up and running. I also felt that I was lacking something with Ulcus, and Valfar and me had talked about making music together. At first we considered making a new project, but we decided to continue under the Windir name, to develop what Valfar had started there. I love *Sóknardalr*, and thought it was fantastic when he released it, and *Arntor* is an absolute classic, with some of the most unique music ever made. A stroke of genius."

Working as a six-piece, the band would craft two more albums—*1184* and *Likferd* (released in 2001 and 2003 respectively)—Valfar and Hváll each writing the lyrics and music to half the songs on each opus, Hváll bringing in unused ideas from Ulcus while Valfar made sure the individual songs sat within the Windir sound. Both superb efforts, the two albums saw the band's songwriting expand considerably (perhaps their most famous number, "Journey to the End," is actually dominated by an almost dance-like electronic closing passage), yet the folk black metal tag remained apt, even if it's not one the members favored.

"Folk music is something that we grew up with," states Hváll. "When Valfar started to play accordion at a young age he became fascinated with old Norwegian melodies that had been used as hymns. The folk influence in Windir was mainly inspired by these hymns and the somber and depressing atmosphere found within them. He started to experiment with these dark, melancholic pieces of music, and gave them brand new life through his metal wrapping. It is at the backbone of most of the Windir music, and definitively gave Windir a unique sound. That said, I don't see any connection to what people call folk metal these days. Most of it is totally useless crap, I can't bear to even listen through a whole song. I hate the term folk metal, and so did Valfar. He

Viking days: Hades (now Hades Almighty); Jørn Tunsberg, Remi Anderson, Stig Hagenes, Janto Garmanslund.

did not want to be labeled as folk or black metal, so he named Windir's music Sognametal, mainly to distance himself from any scene out there."

Distance, in fact, would play a significant part in shaping Windir, the group's relative isolation and fascination with local heritage running deep throughout their work, "Sognametal" being a reference to the band's home village of Sogndal. Lyrics and sleeve artwork drew heavily from the band's locality, *Arntor* even featuring the unlikely sight of a tractor, highlighting Valfar's rural inspirations.

"The lyrics were based on the local history of Sogndal," explains Hváll, who for a time worked teaching history. "To narrow it down, it was based around the ancient legend of the farmer Arntor from Sogndal. Valfar, Steingrim, and I all grew up within a three-hundred-meter distance, with all of our houses situated on what was once was the farm of Arntor. Arntor unleashed the greatest sea battle in Norway (the battle of Fimreite in 1184) when he stood up for the farmers and chopped off the head of the King's taxman with an axe. The lyrics of Windir are a tribute to Sogndal and Norway, our nature, history and legends, with *Arntor* as the icon of all this."

Tragically, the lyrics of "Journey to the End" ("I embraced my vision, as it was common for me / A fate, a destiny, an inevitable early death") would prove prophetic, and both Windir and Valfar were cut short in their prime when the band's founder was caught in a snowstorm and died from hypothermia while traveling to his family's cabin. He was twenty-five. The remaining members of Windir/Ulcus would continue making music, however, primarily through the prolific and equally historically inspired black- and folk-tinged thrash of Vreid, as well as melodic black metallers Cor Scorpii.

Though Norway dominated folk black metal during the nineties, Ireland, another country with a rich history of folklore and folk music, also made something of a name for itself during this decade. Primordial, Cruachan, and Waylander are three respected Irish acts offering folk-influenced metal compositions, though it is undoubtedly Primordial who have maintained the closest relationship to black metal, to the extent that 1995 debut *Imrama* had only a few musical and thematic hints toward folk content.

"Quite early on we realized we didn't have much in common with early-nineties death metal," explains vocalist Alan "A.A. Nemtheanga" Averill, who joined Primordial in 1991 and has fronted the band since then. "Unlike our peers we were more interested in Bathory, Celtic Frost, Sabbat and we basically wanted to make something that had some sort of resonance with our history and culture and had some sort of Irish feeling, this earthly melancholy, this mixture of blood and tragedy. We weren't sure how to do it in the beginning as we were only sixteen but we sort of took a bit of Bathory, took a bit of the timing structures from Irish music, and just sort of merged them together."

The band's debut was probably their weakest moment, but from 1998—and the release of *A Journey's End*—onward the group would maintain an impressively consistent level of quality, merging folk and black metal with increasing ambition, forging tragic and melancholy epics while maintaining what could be described as a pagan/heathen outlook, a stance present even in *Imrama*.

"I think within the band back then I think I would have been more interested in pan-European history and the occult," Averill ponders, "and the other guys were pulling toward the druidic or shamanistic… 'Celtic mysticism' to get all airy fairy. We were pushing in different directions, which is why [*Imrama*'s] 'Awaiting Dawn' has reference to Lucifer, while the first song is written in Irish and is sort of a hymn to pre-Christian Ireland. I'm actually careful about using the word 'pagan'—because what does it mean beyond being a Roman insult of a word for someone that dwells on the land?—and I use the term 'pagan metal' very loosely—only two or three songs on the last current albums have anything to do with that, the rest is based in the here and now. I'm not really interested in writing fantastical hymns to mythological warriors doing heroic deeds who never really existed when there are far more relevant things to write about."

As the singer suggests, the history of Ireland has become much more of a focal point for Primordial than any particular theological position. Songs such as "The Coffin Ships" on 2005's *The Gathering Wilderness* album highlight this, remembering the disease-ridden ships that carried immigrants escaping the Great Irish Famine, ships that on average claimed a third of the passenger's lives. A similar direction was maintained on the critically acclaimed follow-up *To the Nameless Dead* (2007) and the equally impressive *Redemption at the Puritan's Hand* (2011), which both helped break the band to a wider audience via the sizable Metal Blade Records.

Still, while Primordial may certainly draw heavily from their country of origin, Averill is keen to highlight the broad scope of his lyrics and their wider relevance to the human condition. "Primordial was never exclusively about being Irish," he assures. "There should be universal themes that you can tap into no matter where you're from which maybe makes us more of an everyman band, people from anywhere can see themselves in the themes. There are plenty of [non-Irish] bands I feel a common bond with—Enslaved, Negură Bunget,' Drudkh, Ancient Rites—bands who have tried to sidestep the clichés and bring in an element of their relationship with their culture and history. That's what we always wanted to do, and we generally dwelt on the dark aspects of it. There's a lot of bloody passages of Irish history to draw on but I never wanted to say, 'This song is singularly about being Irish.' These are songs about sacrifice, redemption, alienation, martyrdom—things you should be able to feel wherever you're from."

As the years have gone by, the musical hybrid that is folk black metal has spread worldwide, finding particular resonance in Eastern European territories. This isn't entirely surprising, of course: not only is folk music still very popular generally within these territories, but there is also something of a political dynamic in place. The contemporary utilization of traditional folk music often implies a longing for the past, a romanticizing of times gone by, something nationalist movements tend to favor. As we have seen, Eastern Europe is home to many bands from NSBM and surrounding scenes and many draw heavily upon folk influences, most notably Poland's Graveland, Russia's Temnozor, and Ukraine's Drudkh, Kroda, and Nocturnal Mortem.

Of course folk influences and an Eastern European background certainly don't necessitate political views, as bands like Latvia's Skyforger and Romania's Negură Bunget highlight. The latter—alongside Dordeduh, the outfit formed when the band split into two camps in 2009—have proven a particularly fascinating entity whose folk leanings are unusually forward-thinking. Indeed, both Negură Bunget and Dordeduhs' use of traditional ethnic instruments has been as much a subversion of traditional musical values as an homage to them.

"Musical instruments can transcend the concreteness of physical space," explained Edmond "Hupogrammos" Karban (then frontman of Negura, now Dordeduh) told me in an interview for *Terrorizer* in 2008. "The traditional instruments we use—panpipes, flutes, a wood percussion instrument called 'toaca, xylophone, pipes known as 'tulnic' in Romanian, a large drum called 'duba,' timbales, various woodwind instruments—were born from a need to express vibes emanating from this land. Negură Bunget uses these folk instruments more like an experiment. We are definitely not a band interested in using them in a traditional way. From the perspective of a musician, every instrument has its own emanation, its own vibe

**Negură Bunget in 1995, back when they were still called Wiccan Rede
and wore corpsepaint. Photo courtesy of Negru.**

and its own way to express the vibes of the land that it is coming from. Some instruments can provide an intense traditional touch, others are more applicable in non-traditional contexts. I always felt that the full potentiality of the traditional instruments from my country had not been explored."

Within these groups then, the use of ethnic instrumentation is not a reference to the past but an attempt at breaking away from tradition and pre-established musical patterns. "In Romanian traditional music these instruments are used in a very strict and conservative way. There is not too much diversity in their use and many of these instruments are unable to provide many technical possibilities to the musician, so the potential for expression is limited. But the biggest disadvantage is that these instruments have been used in the same context for decades, which is becoming boring already. There are not too many things left to express in this field. This is why we are not really trying to use these instruments in their known contexts. Personally speaking, I was never really a big fan of traditional music. I think to a certain extent this could be seen as an advantage because one could have the opportunity to use all these traditional instruments in an unconventional way."

Outside of Eastern Europe, it is arguably Finland that has dominated the pagan/folk black metal scene—perhaps inevitable given the massive popularity of folk music in the country and the fact that the highly successful folk metal revival has been dominated by Finnish bands. A somewhat polarizing affair, this success has pushed bands like Finntroll out of the black metal scene altogether, while leaving less accessible acts deep within the underground.

Such largely undiscovered groups include the prolific Wyrd, Draugnim, and Häive (who—like Nokturnal Mortum and Negură Bunget—incorporate myriad traditional instruments, including "self-made kantele, mouth harps, glass bottles and straw").

Indeed, Finnish folk black metal tends to include a considerable number of acoustic instruments and be very much nature-inspired, the songs far earthier and less bouncy than the straight "folk metal" bands in Finland. All the same, it's interesting to note that like early black folk pioneer Fenriz, the source of these band's folk influences does not necessarily come directly from traditional folk music itself, but instead often arrives secondhand from older rock/metal bands who utilized aspects of traditional folk.

"The biggest single release that has influenced me both musically and lyrically is, without a doubt, *Tales from the Thousand Lakes* by Amorphis," vocalist and multi-instrumentalist Narqath of Wyrd explained to me in *Terrorizer*. "It got me interested in folklore and mythology and incorporating folk elements to metal. Traditional folk has never been a conscious influence for Wyrd, because I've never listened to it. But I suppose it's something that's in your blood, and has an unintentional influence through all the old Finnish pop stuff, which has a very strong Slavonic melancholy in its spirit."

Ultimately, where folk and Viking black metal goes from here is unclear. Given black metal's frequent preoccupation with the past, it seems likely that such historical, cultural, and musical inspirations will continue to be drawn upon to varying degrees, perhaps expanding due to a trickle-down effect from mainstream folk metal. All the same, given its transitory nature, folk and Viking black metal seem to be sub-genres destined to remain relatively sparsely populated; given the context it is actually apt that as listeners we are frequently forced into the past for lessons on the effectiveness of folk within black metal.

Speaking more widely, at this point black metal as a whole has arguably managed to become a form of folk music in itself. It has proved itself to be a seemingly universal voice with reoccurring key values, found in every continent on Earth and frequently incorporating distinct localizations in the many territories where it raises its head. With black metal's influence still spreading, this pattern only looks set to continue, and what musical combinations this will bring, only time will tell.

42

A TURN FOR THE WEIRD
PART I

GIVEN THE SPARSE and fragmented collection of bands that made up the black metal scene in its early days, diversity unavoidably became a defining characteristic of the genre. What is interesting, however, is that this diversity survived the intense process of unification that happened in Norway in the early nineties. Euronymous may have urged uniformity of appearance and belief, but his eclectic musical taste meant the same attempts were never made to streamline black metal's sound—indeed, by defining the genre solely by its Satanic ethos, Euronymous freed many musicians creatively.

Many key acts of the nineties would unwittingly create entire sub-genres through their innovation: symphonic black metal would come about thanks to the work of bands such as Emperor, Cradle of Filth, Dimmu Borgir, and Gehenna; the electronic dabblings of Beherit and Mysticum would help create industrial black metal; Abruptum would pioneer ambient black metal; Ulver and Isengard folk black metal, and so on. As Kristoffer Rygg has already suggested, before the genre became so narrowly defined musically—primarily due to Burzum and Darkthrone (much to their chagrin)—it was seen as *imperative* for bands to be unique. Along with the artistic and intellectual ambitions in the genre, it was probably inevitable that black metal would soon immerse itself in an unambiguously progressive and experimental period that still influences the genre today.

For whatever reason—perhaps because it had the largest pool of musicians at the time—the majority of explicitly experimental acts initially hailed from Norway. Three notable bands were Ved Buens Ende, In the Woods… , and Fleurety, all of whom dared to tread highly individual paths, their works ultimately met by a polarizing mixture of acclaim, indifference, and even contempt.

Debuting with the 1994 demo *Those Who Caress the Pale* (many of whose numbers would be released in a more refined state the following year on the full-length *Written in Waters*), Ved Buens Ende was comprised of three forward-thinking musicians, Carl-Michael Eide and Skoll (both already mentioned due to their role in Ulver) and Yusaf Parvez. Together these young men forged some of the most avant-garde black metal created to date, introducing a sound that would only be hinted at a decade later via acts such as Deathspell Omega. Drawing on influences as diverse as jazz, folk, and prog rock—as well as second-wave black metal—the wonderfully bleak compositions still sound fresh today, the (mostly clean) vocals, dissonant riffing, angular percussion, and challenging time signatures combining to offer a level of complexity all but unexplored at that time.

Sadly, VBE would split in 1997 due to differing musical visions, reuniting ten years later only to discover the same problem was now even more pronounced. Carl-Michael then formed the similarly experimental Virus with Einar Sjursø, while Yusef concentrated on the band Dødheimsgard.

In the Woods … would survive somewhat longer, though their time within the black metal sphere would be limited. Debuting in 1993 with the *Isle of Men* demo, and building upon this two years later with debut album *Heart of the Ages*, the outfit formed after the split of Green Carnation—a progressive metal project formed by Tchort of Emperor in 1990—of whom drummer Anders Kobro and brothers Christopher (bass) and Christian Botteri (guitars) had been a part. Bringing a hugely expansive approach to a folky Norse template, the group contrasted increasingly prominent prog and psychedelic overtones (later the band would tellingly release covers of Jefferson Airplane, Pink Floyd, and King Crimson) with harsh, high-pitched vocals and traditional second-wave riffing.

With obvious heathen overtones, the band initially shared parallels with acts such as Ulver or Primordial, but upon the release of 1997's excellent *Omnio* it was clear the band had left behind any black metal elements to instead pursue a more progressive rock/metal direction. 1999's *Strange in Stereo* would be the group's swan song, the band's split neatly coinciding with the reformation of Green Carnation, who quickly forged a successful career a considerable way from the black metal scene.

FLEURETY

"Fleurety has always been about creativity, and daring to tread outside the familiar paths. Alexander and Svein-Egil are both nonconformists in the truest sense of the word, refusing to release albums, or live on the same continent for that matter."

—Einar Sjursø (Virus)

Given that heavy metal is often considered a form of "outsider art," and black metal even more so, it's little surprise that explicitly experimental black metal bands tend to condemn themselves to a fairly limited audience. As a movement black metal is both fearlessly pioneering and fiercely conservative: on the one hand it rewards progression and artistic endeavor, but the flipside is that bands who completely disregard genre convention still risk alienating an already niche audience. It's a lesson Norway's Fleurety learned first-hand, yet emerged all the stronger for it, going on to find critical acclaim despite initially being misunderstood—and even reviled—within their home country.

Formed in December 1991 and named after an entity found in an encyclopedia of demons, Fleurety was created by Alexander Nordgaren and Svein Egil Hatlevik (or Varg and Nebiros, as they were initially known), two musicians from the village of Ytre Enebakk, some thirty kilometers south of Oslo. While the story of the duo's move from death metal to black metal closely mirrors that of many of their countrymen, their youth and relative isolation from the scene resulted in them joining the party later than many of the key Norwegian black metal bands.

"I got into black metal during the golden years," confirms Svein, who has at various time contributed vocals, guitars, bass, and synths. "Me and Alexander were in a band at the time called Transmogrification which was more influenced by American death metal and bands like Metallica. We were very fascinated by a flyer we got from the record shop Helvete but the first black metal album I bought was an album by Samael called *Worship Him* and I just thought, 'Hmmm, what's all the fuss about?' The first time I started liking black metal was when I heard Darkthrone's *A Blaze in the Northern Sky*, in the spring of '92. Transmog-rification lasted a couple of months, then we were sucked into this whirling vortex of black metal. We wanted to be demonic as well, like the other people." He laughs before adding, "That was kind of the only choice you had, everything else seemed dull and boring."

For the duo—as for so many other musicians in the underground metal scene—the transformation proved to be a total one. "I usually compare it to a sect," Svein laughs. "You become a young, adolescent man and you're looking for something interesting, when everything else seems boring and dull, and black metal seems so different. It was very all-consuming and I think that's very typical of people back then as it seemed so radiant and attractive. It was more than death metal or hardcore, more than any other subculture. It was taking shape in front of your eyes, whereas if you're a punk or a skateboard kid it's something that's already been established. But this was very fresh and diverse and no one really knew what this new thing was all about, you got the sense that something was happening that hadn't happened before.

"We were a couple of years younger, so it was kind of frightening to meet these people, that was also part of the fascination. Most of the time you were feeling alone and apart from this black metal thing, because I come from a small village and no one really knew what this new thing was until the paper started writing about church burnings and murders. It was like you had this secret and that was something strong, and it felt very special, being the only two black metal kids. It was you versus everybody."

This sense of excitement and esotericism shines through on *Black Snow*, the band's first and only demo, released in spring 1993. Produced by Carl August Tidemann—later of

A flyer for Fleurety's *Black Snow* demo, 1993.

Arcturus—the tape bore a clear yet distinctly lo-fi and scratchy sound that only added to its wonderfully obscure atmosphere. Utilizing relatively simple guitar passages and an often crawling pace, the songs hint slightly at the more avant-garde direction the band would make their name with—not least second track "Mortuus Est Dei Filius," which begins with Svein apparently assaulting his keyboard.

However, what really sets the demo apart from pretty much anything is the insanely shrill, piercing vocals produced by Alexander. Unsettling, even painful, they make the demo very much an acquired taste. This, coupled with the duo's distance from the rest of the Norwegian black metal scene, provoked a level of hostility usually reserved for death metal or Christian bands, with criticisms thrown by both Mysticum and fellow envelope-pushers Ulver. As if that wasn't enough, Svein even ended up being attacked at his home by some disgruntled members of another local black metal band.

"There was one time when people came to my place but it was a small incident," Svein recalls with a chuckle of bemusement. "It was an adolescent thing; you have to take into consideration that most of the people at this time were in high school or younger. It was mostly a war of words. It's not like drive-by shootings or people trying to control the drug market in one area of town, nothing like that."

While the band might have been making some unwelcome waves locally, their demo was already turning heads in the international underground, and the English label Aesthetic Death soon signed the band for a seven-inch release.

**Alexander Nordgaren and Svein Egil Hatlevik of Fleurety in 1994.
Photo courtesy of Svein Egil Hatlevik.**

"It was more popular outside of Norway than inside Norway because the general climate at that time was that every new band was a 'trendy band' unless you met them and
they were already your pals. We didn't know that many people in the scene and their attitude
was, 'Oh, we don't know these people so they have to be trendy,' it was a very simple logic.
But we had our own project and our own goals and we were very confident with our music at
that time and eventually got the record deal. Then we had a feeling that things were happening, this kind of teenage confidence when you think you're king of the world."

Following in a similar vein to *Black Snow*—even opening with a rerecording of the demo's
closing number, "Profanations Beneath the Bleeding Stars"—*A Darker Shade of Evil* was nonetheless a rather more formidable listen, benefiting from a meatier production, and a greater level
of ambition and musical ability, introducing clean melodic leads, acoustic guitars, and more
adventurous drum patterns. The inhuman screams remained, although this would be their final
airing, due to Alexander apparently damaging his vocal cords during the recording, not entirely
surprising to anyone who's heard the record. Svein, however, has another theory...

"I know that he felt a very strong pain in his throat after the recording," he explains,
"but I don't think that he'd be able to sing in that voice as a grown-up man. I think he was
fifteen or sixteen when we recorded that, and then you are still in the process of the voice
breaking. A change in vocal style would have been inevitable anyway."

The duo soon found a suitable home at the UK-based Misanthropy Records (a label whose roster was largely made up of bands from the more progressive and experimental side of extreme metal, such as In The Woods... , Ved Buens Ende, and Beyond Dawn) and unleashed their debut full-length, *Min Tid Skal Komme*, in the summer of 1995. A huge leap forward musically, it accomplished the seemingly impossible task of being genuinely innovative while still sitting comfortably in the black metal genre.

While the long, tranquil, folk-inspired acoustic guitar passages, expressive leads, desolate

***Min Tid Skal Komme*, 1995, arguably showcased the current post-black metal sound a decade before it became popular.**

riffing, blasting drums, melancholy atmosphere, and occasional use of synths meant that the album shared much with records like Satyricon's *Dark Medieval Times*, there was also clearly a more progressive edge that revealed itself in unconventional song structures, psychedelic guitar work, unusual time changes, and busy, almost funk-like bass work. Now featuring more traditional black metal vocals alongside the soaring and haunting voice of Marian Aas Hansen—who attended the same school as Svein and Alexander and would go on to achieve some success as a pop singer—the album married technical and emotive aspirations with ease, and arguably predated the post-black metal sound of bands such as Agalloch or Alcest by a decade.

"I think there was a rather upfront psychedelic prog seventies influence, a certain jazz influence, a certain folk music influence... and of course black metal!" says Svein. "We were listening to Pink Floyd and King Crimson and got the jazz influence indirectly from that sort of music. The folk influences were more from the kind of music that you have been hearing ever since childhood in Norway."

"It might have something to do with the general isolation we were in," ponders Svein of the band's consistently innovative approach. "We had our own perception of what kind of music we wanted to make. When we came to buy records at the Helvete shop we would buy all kinds of strange stuff, not just metal but prog or strange electronic stuff, a lot of diverse kinds of music. That was one of the rules or guidelines that you could get from the first years of black metal, that if your music or band sounded like some other band you were worthless

The eclectic *Department of Apocalyptic Affairs*, 2000.

and there was no reason why you should release records. So we were very deliberate that we wanted to make a contribution to broaden the spectrum of what this new style of music could be. We were breastfed that this was how it was supposed to be, so for me it was very natural that black metal would be a very experimental form of music. You had bands like Ved Buens Ende, Arcturus, to a certain extent Mayhem, Dødheimsgard, In the Woods..., Sole-fald—there were a lot of bands who had the same, or similar, mentality. One reason why you can say [the movement] did stagnate was you had certain benchmark releases, milestones, a lot of the albums by Darkthrone [for example] and people thought, 'Ah, this is how black metal is supposed to be.' The music people made became more streamlined."

Fleurety's next effort, the EP *Last-Minute Lies*, demonstrated a band that was certainly in no danger of becoming streamlined in any way, shape, or form. The record saw the band shedding the extreme vocals and many other black metal traits, though the beautiful melancholy of the debut remains. Misanthropy were unimpressed, however, after hearing the song "Vortex," as they felt it too experimental and too similar to Ved Buens Ende ("could be a point," admits Svein, "since that is the only song that we wrote inspired by Ved Buens Ende"), and let the band go. Recorded between June 1996 and September 1997, the record would not be released until 1999, due to a delay finding another label, the band ultimately settling on Supernal Records after meeting its owner at Mayhem's 1997 London show, where Alexander was performing second guitar duties.

As it turned out, *Last-Minute Lies* was pretty reflective of the band's new approach. Their second full-length, *Department of Apocalyptic Affairs* (released in 2000 but recorded in 1998), proved an even more varied work, with each song seemingly unconnected to the rest, not least because of the fourteen guest musicians who appear on the album. Given the band's unpopularity in Norway in the early days, there was no small irony in the fact that so many musicians from the country's black metal community—including members of Arcturus, Ved Buens Ende, and Mayhem—appeared. In an even more bizarre twist, the album not only featured guest appearances by the once-critical Kristoffer "Garm" Rygg, but was also co-produced by the now good friend of the band.

"You meet people, you have a similar interest and you find out you weren't that different anymore," explains Svein. "Suddenly you're not seventeen anymore, you're twenty-two, and generally the atmosphere of the music scene is different. You didn't have this same general climate of people being skeptical. People were more interested in meeting each other and talking to each other and during the course of this time we became friends with a lot of these people. Since you had all these different musicians within one arm's length we thought, 'Okay, we can have this guy on this song and this guy on that song,' and it just started snowballing."

By now the creative process within Fleurety was largely defined by an atmosphere of spontaneity, experimentation, and collaboration, which goes some way to explaining the record's diversity and lack of continuity. "The main difference [between the albums] is that one of them was rehearsed and we had specific plans about how it was going to be. There was some experimenting and some spontaneity going on, but it was more pre-rehearsed, whereas the second album was much more spontaneous. It was like, 'Okay we have a studio for a month, let's try to see what works and use whatever idea pops up in your head.' So the first album is more coherent and probably easier for people to listen to and it sounds like it's the same band playing from the beginning of the first song to the end of the last song, whereas the second album sounds like a combination of a lot of strange bands."

The fragmented nature of the recording reflected the group's lineup, and the band soon split as Alexander's work saw him leaving Norway to live in a variety of locations, including England, India, Romania, and Canada. Despite this, the band continues to show signs of life, with occasional releases since 2009, and while their experimental ways are probably less capable of shock now that black metal has broadened its perimeters so drastically, they nonetheless retain their potential as a force to be reckoned with.

43

A TURN FOR THE WEIRD
PART II

WHILE MOST OF NORWAY'S experimental bands rose from the aftermath of the initial black metal explosion, Arcturus actually preceded it. In fact, their roots lie in the 1987 formation of Mortem, a death metal band comprised of guitarist Steiner Johnsen ("Sverd"), vocalist and bassist Marius Void (of Stigma Diabolicum/Thorns), and drummer Jan Axel Blomberg (a.k.a. Hellhammer). Arcturus was formed as a side project in 1990, but soon took priority, releasing the *My Angel* seven-inch in 1991. A strange, gothic, keyboard-dominated affair with death metal vocals and very little guitar, the single was actually a love song to Marius' departed Hawaiian girlfriend. It wasn't long before Marius himself departed, replaced by Kristoffer "Garm" Rygg of Ulver, with Emperor's Samoth also recruited on guitar and bass, moving Sverd onto the keyboards. Three years after their first release came the *Constellation* mini-album, a release that ably reintroduced—and reinvented—the group.

"I remember thinking *My Angel* was one of the greatest things ever," explains Kristoffer, "at that time the synth element in metal still wasn't too established. Steiner was a connoisseur of classical music. He was at home with his Bach CDs on full blast, he was walking around different churches playing organs and could read notes like a motherfucker. He was a very musically minded guy who was playing all day, and when he wasn't playing he was chasing skirt. He wasn't really into the underlying philosophy of [black metal] and never really took an interest in the fraternity aspect of it. But Mortem released the *Slow Death* EP in '87, around Mayhem's formative years, so he had some respect due to that long-standing presence."

Originally, *Constellation* had only been recorded as preproduction for a debut full-length, and two years later came *Aspera Hiems Symfonia* ("Harsh Winter Symphony"), featuring rerecordings of the four songs on *Constellation* alongside four new numbers. With a lineup that saw Samoth replaced on bass by Ulver's Skoll and on guitar by Carl August Tidemann, *Aspera* presented symphonic black metal in an aggressive and catchy vein, yet with obvious progressive aspirations. Displaying sophisticated, twisting songwriting, remarkable performances, and a sense of gothic theatricality that had rarely been explored before in extreme metal, it

ventured into territories of both epic majesty and carnivalesque whimsy.

Such qualities would be more deeply
realized on the 1997 follow-up *La Masquerade Infernale*, an album that brought
the fringes of the avant-garde black metal
movement to much wider attention. Originally due to be called *The Satanist*, the album bore heavy occult overtones, as well
as a real sense of musical and intellectual
depth, offering what felt like an authentic
foray into sophisticated diabolical knowledge. While black metal had already boasted of its classical aspirations, the sublime
track "Ad Astra" seemed to offer the most
credible example yet, utilizing six classical
performers (including Ulver's Erik Lancelot
on flute!) in a highly emotive manner. Yet
offsetting accusations of pretension was
an inherent eccentricity and playfulness
that distanced the band from their more
po-faced peers, the record blending Edgar
Allan Poe-derived lyrics, live strings, electronic break beats (still a shocking inclu-

**The *Slow Death* cassette. Though now best
known as the band that became Arcturus,
Mortem made a name as one of Norway's first
extreme metal bands during the eighties.**

sion for many at the time), and a touch of Kurt Weill/Tim Burton-esque atmosphere.

"The aesthetic of that record was a deliberate focus on very small elements of *Aspera*,
especially 'Raudt Og Svart,' that circus-like… " Kristoffer pauses looking for the words,
"dancing… dead… doll aesthetic. We kind of decided that that was something we wanted
to expand upon. Black metal was extremely theatrical so it was a natural consequence of that
and being a bit more playful with it, adding some humor. Taking in that whole literary aspect
and things like Faust, it was kind of natural I think to make a devilish symphonic piece with
a sort of humpty dumpty devil."

There was certainly a glorious mix of pomp and bombast on much of the record, the album largely doing away with the rasped vocals of old in favor of clean, almost operatic vocals
from Kristoffer and Simen Hestnæs, who had entered the band (albeit as a guest) alongside
guitarist and producer Knut M. Valle.

"Knut and Steiner were thinking to do a side project and I was going to do vocals—the
first song was 'The Chaos Path'—but later it became part of Arcturus," reveals Hestnæs.
"Knut wasn't very black metal at all, he was a formidable guitar player who had come to town

Spaced out: Simen Hestnæs of Arcturus, live in 2012. Photo: Ester Segarra.

and wanted to jam with everybody. There was talk that Garm might not be interested in Arcturus anymore and that I might take over. But I guess when he heard the first songs he became very interested and for the album I'm sure that was a good thing."

Knut would actually play a key role in the record's realization, and while the bones of the songs were written by Sverd (who apparently only listened to Dream Theater and classical at this time, explaining the heavy progressive and classical leanings) it was left to Kristoffer and Knut—aided by various psychedelic substances—to build up the final tracks.

The 1999 darkwave/trip hop remix record *Disguised Masters* reflected the self-conscious attempts at genre cross-pollination going on at the time, and it was not until 2002 that a proper third album, *The Sham Mirrors*, would surface. A genuinely stellar effort, it presented a more refined take on the band's snaking sound, the lyrics now looking less to the past and more to a space-traveling future, an aesthetic reflected in the music's use of effects and slick synth melodies.

Frontman Kristoffer would depart soon after, but the band would survive, replacing him first with Øyvind Hægeland of Spiral Architect and then installing Hestnæs as a full-time member. The space-themed concept would also last—logical since Arcturus is actually named after a star—as would the carnival atmosphere of the first two albums. The latter surfaced most explicitly onstage, the band finally able to play live regularly, having only done so once with Kristoffer ("It's no secret I really had bad stage fright," he admits, "but I also had a strong stance that it would take away the distance and myth to be out in the world playing.") A somewhat more lighthearted attitude was also reflected on the 2005 album *Sideshow Symphonies*, which saw the band forging ahead in an epic prog metal direction, with less obvious experimentation but a similarly flamboyant theatricality.

"The most important thing was to give the impression that we really don't give a fuck, this is not Satanic or evil or whatever it's something completely different," Hestnæs explains. "Musically I think it's pretty dark, but it's not as intense metal-wise maybe, lots of slow tunes."

"I think they sort of misinterpreted some of the things that I left unexplained," ponders

Kristoffer. "I think they just took the whole circus too literally, the show with people throwing balls in the air and bears and just being
silly, it had nothing to do with how I perceived
that stuff at the time."

The band would go on hiatus after the
tours for *Sideshow Symphonies*, finally reform-
ing in 2011. In terms of breaking new ground
La Masquerade must still be their high point,
and like a nineties *Into The Pandemonium*, it
explores various tangents without restraint,
incorporating foreign elements without ever
deviating entirely from its metal foundations.
"I hate to sound arrogant," concludes Kristoffer, "but I think it might have been the record
that coined a genre description that I don't like
too much—'avant-garde metal.' Not only this
carnivalesque thing but also incorporating electronic beats which no one was doing then."

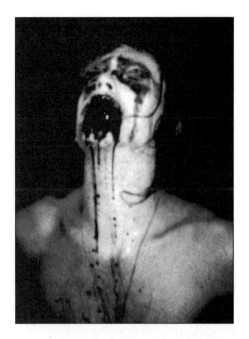

An early Manes promo, from the era
of their none-more-black demos.
Photo courtesy of Cernunnus.

1997 was a highly significant year in retrospect, since it also saw the release of the
genuinely eclectic *Hail Horror Hail* by Japanese act Sigh and *The Linear Scaffold*, the first album
of Oslo-based duo Solefald, a record that echoed the bombastic and ambitious nature of *La
Masquerade Infernale*. With similarly philosophical and intellectual aspirations—and shared
musical characteristics—Solefald's debut turned plenty of heads thanks to its bold lyrics and
aesthetic. Sure, the cover art and the use of a poem by Byron suggested a familiar reverence
for the past, but here too was talk of Sartre, urban architecture, modern transportation, and
television—elements purposely ignored by a scene that consciously rejected modern society
and its trappings. The aptly named *Neonism* released in 1999 would only build upon this
foundation, its unapologetically contemporary lyrics (still probably the only band in black
metal to mention a "broken public toilet") matching its equally incongruous (within a black
metal context) musical eccentricities.

As a result of this wave of experimentation, along with prevailing insecurities regarding
the stagnation of the genre, much of the wider black metal scene began to push their art into
uncharted waters. Established acts—Mayhem, Hades, Primordial, and Enslaved, to name a
few—began to offer increasingly forward-thinking works, in many cases ones that would be
indicative of their general trajectory as groups. In turn, as the new millennium progressed, a
new generation of bands surfaced who had grown up witnessing such experimentation and
felt it was natural to keep pushing at black metal's already loose boundaries.

The previously mentioned Negură Bunget would be one of several groups making use

**A more recent incarnation of Manes reflects the band's musical eclecticism with some suitably
unconventional press pictures. Photo courtesy of Cernunnus.**

of expansive ambient soundscapes, with America's Fauna, Ireland's Altar of Plagues, and
England's The Axis of Perdition all inspired musically and thematically by specific physical
landscapes. Debuting in 1995, France's Blut Aus Nord would begin life as an impressive but
far from groundbreaking project but would move toward similarly open-ended material, making a decisive impact with 2003's *The Work Which Transforms God*, its heavily instrumental
material drawing on both mystical and philosophical inspirations.

Their countrymen Deathspell Omega, meanwhile, have also drawn acclaim with similarly
inventive efforts, opting for a far denser and more intricate compositional style utilizing doom,
prog, death metal and jazz (among other elements) while maintaining an impressive level of
musicianship and a secretive but resolutely Satanic agenda. Elsewhere, America's Nachtmystium have won a considerable following, broadening their perspective by evolving from a traditional second-wave sound to encompass elements of psychedelic rock and even pop.

While the aforementioned groups would maintain their black metal identity despite
musical growth, others would evolve outside of the genre entirely. Two such examples are
Ulver and the group Manes, based in Trondheim, Norway. Comprising Cernunnus on guitars,
keyboard, and drum programming, and Sargatanas on vocals, the duo recorded some of the

most fearsome, lo-fi, and effective examples of black metal of the early nineties, releasing three demos before signing to Hammerheart and updating these songs on their haunting debut album *Under ein Blodraud Maane*.

The follow-up, 2002's *Vilosophe*, saw a massive shift however, throwing in elements of metal, jazz, post-rock, electronica, trip hop and more. It was too much for many fans, and indeed for Sargatanas, who departed when he heard the new material. Nonetheless the band, which now boasted a handful of new members, tapped even deeper into this vein with 2007's *How the World Came to an End*, a dark and resolutely urban opus, whose Massive Attack inspirations (including rapping) shine through what is left of the metal components.

"I never wanted to play by the established rules," says Cernunnus. "I really liked the idea of doing the totally opposite of what people want me/us to do. The reaction was surprise and shock, both positive and negative. Black metal people didn't know if they could like it because it had these techno things. There was one specific review, that I found really awesome, where we got a 'minus infinity' score! I think there are two almost separate sets of people [listening to Manes], with just a little overlap."

Despite such comments, there does remain a clear connection to the black metal community, since Manes not only played the Inferno festival after their transformation but have also revisited their old material on releases such as 2009's *Solve et Coagula*, which consisted of demo material recorded with Niklas Kvarforth of Shining and Malefic of Xasthur on vocals.

Indeed, while many in the black metal scene encourage an orthodox retention of particular sounds and aesthetics, it's also true that the genre's malicious tendrils have reached extensively into numerous other genres (prog, crust, folk, industrial, ambient, doom, classical, post-rock) in a manner other metal genres have not. The question must therefore be why so many key black metal musicians have been happy to delve into other forms of music in a manner their death or doom metal peers arguably haven't, and why black metal fans are so often happy to embrace this.

"Perhaps the earlier bands started with this kind of music because they liked the 'differentness' of it," suggests Cernunnus. "And so, when things became too popular, too commercialized, they looked for something new, the next step."

"You also have to take into account that when these first records were made these guys were in their pre-twenties and you're not in any sort of conclusive point in your creative life at that age," concludes Kristoffer. "I guess black metal, being more endorsing of the libertine lifestyle and chaos, is kind of open for more experimentation. Black metal has an extraordinary sway or depth to it aside from the actual music. It sounds fucking pompous but it has a *spirituality* to it. In a way it's *not* just music, that was the initial draw for me and one of the few things I still respect about it now."

44
SIGH

"Venom, Celtic Frost, Mercyful Fate, Black Sabbath, Iron Maiden, Frank Zappa, Franz Liszt, Schubert, Debussy, The Beatles."

—Mirai Kawashima, the main composer of Sigh, listing the ten acts that most influenced his band's music

SIGH are not only one of the longest-running Asian bands to come out of the black metal scene—as well as probably the most high-profile—but also almost certainly the most eclectic. In fact, they are one of the most eclectic bands related to metal *period*, their experimental approach and frequently off-the-wall compositions defying easy categorization. Yet while their albums have delved into numerous musical styles—from classical and jazz to reggae and even disco—the group still retain a recognizably black metal core.

Now one of Japan's most respected metal bands, the group's birth can be traced to a humble covers outfit called Ultra Death, formed by four university students, namely vocalist Mirai Kawashima, guitarist Kassy (short for Kashiwagura), bassist Satoshi Fujinami, and drummer Kazuki Ozeki. Formed in 1989, Ultra Death paid tribute to the likes of Venom, Slayer, Death, and Whiplash, bands that by the late eighties were increasingly popular in the Land of the Rising Sun, apparently even more so than in their countries of origin.

"Metal belonged to the mainstream when I was a teenager," explains Mirai. "Metallica's *Master of Puppets* was almost hitting the top 20 [on] *Billboard*, Venom came to Japan in 1987, and Slayer were popular. But after listening to those bands I started searching for more and more violent stuff and discovered underground thrash like Destruction, Kreator, Sodom, Deathrow, At War, and Post Mortem. I bought *Speed Kills*, a really great compilation with Slayer, Venom, Celtic Frost, Destruction and so on. I then bought their albums, looking at the thanks list, looking at the shirts they were wearing on the inner sleeve ... it was really difficult to get the info on this stuff in Japan, there was no Internet or anything then, so a thanks list was a real big information source."

In early 1990 Kassy was fired and the band became a trio, with bassist Satoshi taking over the role as guitarist, and Mirai taking up the bass. At this point the band adopted a new name, choosing the somewhat unusual moniker Sigh because, in their words, "a sigh can express a variety of emotions." It is a name that continues to be highly apt, defining the band's approach as much today as it did two decades ago. Committed to writing their own songs following this name change, the band nonetheless remained inspired by the eighties metal scene, a contrast to the many death metal acts springing up at the time.

Sigh live in London, 1993. Photo courtesy of Nihil Archives.

"I liked the early death metal stuff such as early Morbid Angel and early Deicide, they definitely had the thrash feeling and evil atmosphere, but it didn't take much time before I started thinking death metal was not something I wanted. Obviously it lacked something eighties thrash owned, probably the kind of 'fantasies' that bands such as Venom used to have. It was great fun to look at the photos of Venom. You know, bands like Celtic Frost, Venom, Bathory, early Destruction had an evil image, the lyrics were very evil, and that's what I wanted for heavy metal. But most of the death metal bands looked very normal. I didn't like the over-downtuned guitar sounds or growled vocals either and I was totally sick of the Morrisound sound, which sounded totally the same on every album. It's very hard to explain with words, but death metal missed some 'vibes' that I wanted."

The band's first demos, *Desolation* and *Tragedies*, both released in 1990, stood out a mile from this burgeoning death metal movement, instead recalling the dark and foreboding atmospheres of earlier acts such as Sodom, Hellhammer, and Samael, thanks to the often ritualistic approach, raw aggression, and unashamed primitivism. These were followed in 1992 by the band's first official release, a three-track EP entitled *Requiem for Fools* issued by Californian label Wild Rags. By now Kazuki had departed and Satoshi moved onto the drums (his third role in the band in as many years), while a new guitarist, Shinichi Ishikawa, also entered the scene.

"Still today, I don't know who was the influence on those demos," explains Mirai. "But with [*Requiem for Fools*] it was pretty obvious—Slayer. Slayer came to Japan for the first time in probably 1992, I went to see them, and it was one of the best shows ever and [the first track] 'The Knell' was written in the excitement after that. It doesn't sound like Slayer much, but I remember I thought we should take much a thrashier direction than those demos."

A participant in the international underground, Mirai sent a copy of the EP to Dead of Mayhem, but instead received a reply from Euronymous—due to the singer's demise—who was hugely enthusiastic, and soon signed the band to his Deathlike Silence label. Through this connection, Sigh discovered an entire community in Norway that was dedicated to the same metal values as they were, although the resurrection of the term "black metal" was something of a surprise to them.

"We sent out our demo to as many labels as possible but everybody else was enthusiastic about death metal from Florida. We missed the good old eighties days, but there was nobody we knew who had the same feelings, evil thrash metal was seen as completely outdated. Then all of a sudden, we started to know what was happening in Norway through Euronymous. He said eighties thrash was much better, and slagged trendy death metal, calling it 'life metal.' Through the mail exchanges, he introduced us to bands like Burzum, Emperor, Enslaved, and Darkthrone. [For me] black metal was born in the early nineties as a rebellion against the death metal and grindcore that was trendy back then. And obviously it had the perspective as a revival of eighties thrash metal, though I believe it was only in the nineties that people started calling bands like Sarcófago, Bathory, and Blasphemy black metal."

Characteristically exerting his influence, Euronymous convinced Sigh that they should utilize a darker image more in keeping with their music, and Mirai admits that the band did indeed adopt many of the traits of the Norwegian black metal scene ("the corpsepaint came from Norway, that's a hundred percent for sure") though he points out that very little influence was taken musically. 1993's debut full-length *Scorn Defeat* saw a band that had significantly refined their sound, introducing a far more dynamic approach, a heavier use of synth, radically improved production and an epic and theatrical atmosphere. Mirai's voice is more in keeping with the nineties "screamed" approach and is also notably clearer, all the better for communicating the wonderfully morbid lyrics of tracks like "At My Funeral." By today's standards the record might be considered a little clunky at times, but its ambition shines throughout, and it certainly broke new ground with its release.

"Now it takes half a year to finish up the recording of an album, but I remember we recorded and mixed *Scorn Defeat* in two or three days. The writing process was much simpler, we just showed the riffs to each other at the studio and started jamming. We didn't have the digital technology, so everything was so primitive compared to what we're doing today. But I can safely say that *Scorn Defeat* has a special vibe. Even if we rerecorded it with the technology and technique of today, we'd never reproduce it."

While *Scorn Defeat* was a unique listen, it was only with the 1995 follow-up *Infidel Art* that the band would really begin to really cut loose from the metal norm. Sometimes seen as a transitional album, it was this opus that would first demonstrate the band's taste for juxtaposing seemingly incongruous elements, with an almost cut-and-paste blending of differing musical styles, and sudden jarring swings between different moods. This was most noticeable on the ten-minute epic "The Last Elegy," which begins with a cheerful, major- key, waltz-like

Alternative shot from the *Infidel Art* photo session: Shinichi Ishikawa, Mirai Kawashima and Satoshi Fujinami. Photo courtesy of Nihil Archives.

classical passage before heading into far more despairing metal territories. Equally morbid and even darker than its predecessor, the album would nonetheless take listeners by surprise, not merely by the heavy use of synth and classical elements—which by themselves would have been enough to raise eyebrows—but the manner in which such ingredients were employed.

"I bought an expensive synthesizer called the Ensonique TS-12 after *Scorn Defeat*, which sounded brilliant back then," explains Mirai. "The orchestra sounds seemed to sound very real—not now though—so I abused it. But to be honest, I was not sure if it was too much for metal. Now you can find many albums with lots of keyboards in extreme metal, but in 1994, I didn't know any albums with as many keyboards as *Infidel Art*, so I was not sure if we were taking the right direction. Then I went to Norway to see my friends, like the Enslaved and Ulver guys, and somebody played me Satyricon's second album, which hadn't been released yet, and I was kind of relieved because it had lots of keyboard. I went to the rehearsal place in Oslo and found the keyboard they used which was also an Ensonique."

While it revealed an eclectic edge, *Infidel Art* merely hinted at what was to follow. In 1997 the band demonstrated that they had now immersed themselves completely in this approach to songwriting, thanks to the release of mini-album *Ghastly Funeral Theatre* and *Hail Horror Hail*, a full-length so bewildering that their label Cacophonous Records felt the need to add a warning to the sleeve.

"This album is way beyond the conceived notion of how metal, or music, should be," it reads. "In essence it is a movie without pictures; a celluloid phantasmagoria. Accordingly, the film jumps, and another scene, seemingly unconnected with the previous context, is suddenly inserted in between frames. Every sound on this album is deliberate, and if you find that some parts of this album are strange, it isn't because the music is in itself strange, but because your conscious self is ill-equipped to comprehend the sounds produced on this recording."

"Strange" was something of an understatement, the album taking "episodic" song-writing to new extremes. The opening title track was a perfect example, exploding in a frenzy of upbeat, blues rock leads and deliciously catchy riffing, making Mirai's frenzied screaming and sadistic slasher-esque lyrics ("Beyond all morality into insanity / I plunge my knife in you again and again") all the more disturbing. After two adrenaline-pumping minutes the song lurches into a serene orchestral piece, before collapsing into cacophony and finally returning to the opening riff.

"I got the idea from movies," reveals Mirai. "That [juxtaposition] often happens for the scene changes, and it's very effective, especially in horror movies. You know the happy song can sound scary in horror movies, it's a counterpoint technique. I have a lot on my music palette, so I always choose the best music to express our feeling. Classical stuff can express something that the heavy guitar can't and vice versa. Some people want to 'understand' music—'why jazz in metal?,' 'why this sound?' but it's ridiculous. If you listen to *Hail Horror Hail* and feel it's something scary, that's enough, you do not have to 'understand' it."

This use of contrast continues throughout the album, with another striking example coming courtesy of "Invitation To Die," a song that mixes electronic music, Spanish guitar, tambourine sounds, and soothing orchestration, overlaying this with unsettling lyrics that returned to the doomy, mortality-oriented territories of the debut: "We think it's always someone else / But what if no one else was sacrificed / What if the victim was yourself? / Contemplate your own mortality / The curse that marks all of humanity / You can never know your final moment / But worse, you can never avoid it / We all are born just to perish / To lose all that we truly cherish."

Optimism is not a big part of this haunting and often testing masterpiece, or indeed any Sigh release. Darkest of all is the third track "12 Souls," a genuinely chilling listen due—aside from its murderous lyrical content—to its discordant choir-like synths and confusing moments of psychedelic, nightmarish sound collage. But then, as mentioned, with this opus fear was the emotion the band were primarily aiming for.

"My purpose was actually to create something scary, not to create something experimental. Twentieth-century classical music was used in horror movies like *The Shining* and *The Exorcist*, so I started going through twentieth-century classical music, and found other experimental stuff like John Zorn and Frank Zappa. John Zorn explains his juxtaposition as a parallel to the scene changes in movies. It was a big revelation for me, I thought then we could do that in the sense of horror movies, so we used Zorn and Zappa's techniques and made them scary. To be honest, we were not sure at all how the album would be taken, even by the fans, so I understood that the label was totally scared of what we were doing. I was expecting that all the press would slag it off, saying, 'This is not metal' or something. But somehow, it got more good reviews than bad ones."

Indeed, reception to the work was almost overwhelmingly positive, with strong reviews in magazines such *Kerrang!* and *Terrorizer*, the latter including the album in their top ten of the year and later their top one hundred of the decade. Now recognized internationally, the band signed a deal with Century Media records, which came as a relief as they were somewhat unhappy with the promotion, distribution, touring, and creative interferences they were receiving with Cacophonous. Nonetheless, the label insisted they fulfill their four-album contract and the next release, 1999's *Scenario IV: Dread Dreams*, was duly released through them.

With the encouraging reactions to *Hail Horror Hail*, one might have expected an even more challenging follow-up, yet *Scenario IV* actually turned out to be a more accessible album than expected. Sure, there were still the frequent sudden shifts, the doomy Sabbath-esque parts, thrashy riffing, orchestral passages, and playful moments spliced together with wild abandon. All the same, there was a flow to the songs and the album as a whole that had not been present on previous records, with an abundance of strong melodies and catchy metal riffs distributed throughout the nine songs.

"*Scenario IV* has a huge influence from Zappa and The Beatles," reveals Mirai. "Being artistic and easy to approach at the same time, it is very important to us. Being artistic is easy. Being accessible is easy. But achieving both at the same time is very difficult— The Beatles and Zappa managed it."

Another factor that made the album more accessible was that, musically at least, this was a far less dark affair than previous releases. Similarly, the explicitly occult themes of the songs from *Ghastly Funeral Theatre* and *Hail Horror Hail* were no longer present, something which coincided with Mirai's apparent departure from such interests in his personal life.

"*Ghastly Funeral Theatre* was the peak of it," he admits. "I was into all kinds of occultism since I was a little kid. I think the albums from *Scorn Defeat* to *Hail Horror Hail* have an occult feeling, from the songwriting to the artwork to the lyrics, it reflected my interest and practice (like chanting mantra) of occultism. The artwork of *Ghastly Funeral Theatre* shows how to curse somebody. But to be honest, none of [it] seemed to work [for me]. Actually in 2007, we rerecorded 'The Curse of Izanagi' which was originally on *Hail Horror Hail*. The lyrics contain a lot of a spell from an occult book I have, it contains the words to curse a person to death. At first it was recorded for a compilation CD in Japan, but the plan fell through. Then it was supposed to be released on seven-inch EP, but all of a sudden the guy who was supposed to release this died of disease. Then we were planning to use it as a bonus track for the Japanese pressing of *Scenes from Hell*. However, the CEO of the label releasing this all of a sudden killed himself. I can't prove the connection of this song and the two persons' deaths—to be honest, I don't believe in these things at all—but it's too sinister you know?"

Having moved away from occult lyric matter, 2001's *Imaginary Soundscape* saw a dramatic shift away from black metal territory, retaining Mirai's black metal vocal style but minimizing most of the other extreme metal elements, instead blending heavy metal, psychedelic rock, and other more unlikely elements such as disco in an impressively incongruous manner. 2005's *Gallows Gallery* abandoned even the harsh voice, instead utilizing clean-sung vocals, something of a bridge too far for Century Media, who refused to release the work. In an effort to explain the delay caused by this, the band fabricated a story claiming that the label had become concerned because the album had been recorded using Japanese World War II sonic weaponry techniques ("I never thought people would believe that people could get harmed by the songs on CD!" laughs Mirai), a tale they later admitted was false. Though of less relevance to this book, these two albums were received with enthusiasm by the press and listeners, though by this time their fan base had unsurprisingly shifted.

However, despite appearances to the contrary the band had not discarded their black metal/thrash roots and 2007's *Hangman's Hymn* saw a swift return to violent extreme metal, complete with screamed vocals, aggressive guitars, and punishing drums. Like other works by the band, the album also included many non-metal ingredients, but unlike previous albums, the opus demonstrated a more homogenous approach to their integration. Soon after the release of the album, the band took on their first female member, Dr. Mikannibal, bringing them to a five-piece, since they had also taken on a new drummer, Junichi Harashima, in 2004, moving the multi-talented Satoshi back to bass duties.

Dr. Mikannibal—who is an actual doctor of science—would contribute vocals and saxophone, not to mention a strong element of sexuality thanks to her scantily clad live performances. The band had discovered Mika when looking for a model for the inner sleeve of *Hangman's Hymn*, at which point she handed Mirai (who would later become her partner) a sample of her previous work with a melodic death metal band called 29Jaguar. Appearing live with the band from 2007, her recorded debut occurred in late 2008, thanks to mini-album *A Tribute To Venom*—the band's second homage to the Newcastle legends, following 1995's live tape *To Hell and Back*.

Mika's role in the band has generated a good deal of interest in the group both from fans and the media, which is perhaps unsurprising given her eccentric character—eating insects, drinking cow's blood, and recording naked for example—and past exploits, as an extract from my 2009 interview with her in *Metal Hammer* confirms:

"After [I] graduated from high school in California I lived in Tokyo for a year selling drugs," she explains. "I lost everything, so I went back to my home town and started living with my family. Japan is a very difficult country for foreigners to live in because of the closed community and the extreme politeness. Even though I was born and raised in Japan, after spending almost four years in U.S. it was very difficult to understand what people were thinking. I couldn't adjust to fit in Japanese society and I think that was the reason I got into drugs so badly. I got totally paranoid and almost wanted to kill myself, my mental problem

Dr. Mikannibal and Mirai in 2010. Photo: David Hall.

was just getting worse and worse. My grandma used to be a teacher and because of her strict personality, I just knew she hated me so much. There was something she said that triggered me and I almost pushed her and hit her with something until her death... "

"...And you had some knives ready," added Mirai, "and were even planning to blow up your whole house with dynamite or something? She was really good at science, even back then, so she could build a bomb if she wanted ... "

"I could," she replies, "a simple one is not very difficult. But anyway I was totally paranoid, feeling that everybody in the world was trying to kill me. It wasn't just the house, I wanted to burn the whole world."

January 2010 saw the release of *Scenes From Hell*, which incorporated real orchestral instruments for the first time, including a heavy brass presence, with instruments such as trombone, tuba, trumpet, oboe, clarinet, and flute included alongside a string quartet. Interestingly it was actually Mikannibal's saxophone playing that initially inspired Mirai to incorporate so much brass into the album, giving it a military atmosphere, which in turn inspired the lyrics.

"These days I deal more with reality," explains Mirai. "People are scared of the haunted house where the whole family was slaughtered. But we live in the city where a hundred thousand people were burnt to death in one night during World War II! I can't even imagine how it was to see so many people dying around you."

Like its predecessor, *Scenes of Hell* contained songs that were far less episodic than earlier works, integrating the two main elements—in this case orchestral parts and metal—in a more cohesive manner. Nonetheless, the album demonstrated the same juxtaposition of moods, the triumphant and often jolly sounding brass riding across the more hellish metal parts, almost like the contrast of a military band and the suffering victims of an aerial assault. Such juxtaposition continued in 2012's supercharged opus *In Somniphobia*, and it seems safe to say it is set to remain central to the group's approach to composition.

Indeed, juxtaposition is one of the factors that has always made Sigh so fascinating and effective; not only the manner in which they mix "inappropriate" moods to great effect, but the very fact that they introduce emotions such as cheer or whimsy into extreme metal in the first place. How much of this is the result of an intellectual decision and how much is down to the composer's instincts is hard to say, even after numerous interviews with Mirai. For many Westerners, the appeal of Japanese bands is the fact that they interpret Western genres in a manner that throws up surprising results, and, as Mirai concedes, this may be one of several factors that give this great band their unique aura.

"I took classical piano lessons for twenty years, so I have a huge classical music background and I am a pianist/keyboardist, not a guitarist," he considers, "so the way of composition should be pretty much different from usual metal musicians. Also I'm a Japanese; I use [a] hundred percent different language and eat something different than Western bands, so it's very natural that the music I create is different from the metal bands from U.S. or Europe, even if it's not intentional. I believe the language has a big influence on music. The Japanese language is totally different from English—English is a very rhythmic language, but Japanese is much more melodic. We do not emphasize the accent at all, but instead tell the words by intonation, so obviously my perception on rhythm and melodies should be different from English speakers. Thus, it's inevitable that the Japanese bands sound different. But, I often see Japanese bands that sound exactly like Western bands! I truly admire them," he smiles. "They should have made a huge effort to be so unoriginal."

DØDHEIMSGARD

"I really like Dødheimsgard, both because of the obvious issues of the people in the band (and I think particularly Carl-Michael and Yusaf inspired each other a lot) and the sheer genius of the music. In fact, I think 'Shiva-Interfere' from 666 International *is actually the coolest song that ever came out of the entire scene … "*

—Simen Hestnæs, (Arcturus, Borknagar, Dimmu Borgir)

THE LAST TWO DECADES have been quite a journey for the evolving beast that is Dødheimsgard, who have made a dramatic transition from a conventional—even vaguely nostalgic—Norwegian black metal band to one of the major players in the industrial black metal scene. With a name that translates as "kingdom of death" or "death's realm/home" (they would later come to be known as simply DHG), the outfit formed in 1994 as a side project for Vicotnik—a.k.a. Yusaf Parvez of Ved Buens Ende—and Aldrahn/Bjørn Dencker Gjerde, then playing in Haerfaerd and later a contributor to myriad Norwegian acts including Thorns, Old Man's Child, and even (along with Vicotnik) Dimmu Borgir and Isengard.

"We were both pretty defiant creatures in very different ways and found each other to be quite funny individuals," recalls Vicotnik. "As common in those days, there was a lot of male bonding over fluids with high alcohol content, and this, more often than not, resulted in new bands forming. At the same time, Fenriz and myself were having pool competitions every time we went out to wet our palates—which was more or less two times a day—and Fenriz was kicking my ass so badly that the competition would potentially drag on forever if I was to ever regain any advantage. So we needed something else to occupy our evenings with, and Fenriz suggested making some music together. In the back of my head I thought that this would work well with what Aldrahn and I was doing, so I suggested it. Fenriz was very hesitant, but after twisting his arm a bit, he agreed to have a rehearsal with us. The rehearsal *killed*, [but] Fenriz was quick to point out that he was not joining. Aldrahn and I said, 'Okay, no big deal'—we were happy just to have had a rehearsal with the guy, somebody we admired as a musician and individual."

Despite their later avant-garde direction, Dødheimsgard were originally a very traditional Norwegian black metal band in sound and appearance.

In another time or setting, that could easily have been the end of the story, but thanks to the fertile ground of the nineties Norwegian scene, the project had already managed to put down the roots necessary for its survival.

"As time went on, Fenriz pointed out now and again that he was not joining the band, always out of the blue," Vicotnik explains. "I guess Fenriz just wanted us to nag him and really *want* him to join, and of course we did, we just respected his choice and left the question. One day Aldrahn and I were having a beer or twenty at Elm Street bar and suddenly Fenriz stormed in with really heavy, determined footsteps, his suitcase flapping around the whole room (he always walked around with business suitcase in those days) and went up to me, pulled out his arm in a handshake and asked, 'So, am I in?' That was it, DHG was a trio. We had already a bunch of songs ready, so all we had to do was start practicing."

The first fruits of the trio's labor was a three-song demo released the same year, quickly followed by full-length debut *Kronet Til Konge*, released in January 1995 on Malicious Records. With an apparent thrash influence and less-than-obvious melodies, it nonetheless proved a relatively familiar slice of Norwegian black metal, especially in the context of the band's later works. Featuring Vicotnik on drums, Aldrahn on guitars and lead vocals, and Fenriz on bass (unusually audible by the standards of the day), its sound is both mid-paced and considered, but also, perhaps unsurprisingly, a pretty stripped-down and raw affair.

"The aim musically speaking was to start off with the most primal form of black metal art and develop from there," explains Vicotnik. "To start with what was our generation's beginnings, and let things develop naturally. The material we wanted for *KTK* was very specific, and since it was very primal it did not take a very long time. We also wanted it to be a little flawed, so we did not spend years rehearsing it—when something was written, we stuck with it, there were no discussions about this or that riff, we made a song and moved on. We got instant interest from a label, which was kind of expected since we had Ferico [Fenriz] in our midst and the [general] reception to *Kronet Til Konge* was okay."

Remaining on Malicious, Dødheimsgard's next effort, 1996's much-hailed *Monumental Possession*, saw a lineup shift with the addition of guitarist Ole Jørgen Moe a.k.a. Apollyon of Aura Noir, Cadaver Inc., and Lamented Souls, and the departure of Fenriz. A second new member also entered the fold at this time, namely future Emperor bassist Jonas Alver.

"I always wanted Apollyon to join," explains Vicotnik. "I had played around with him on a few occasions before, and really liked the guy and felt a musical kinship to him. He is a very pleasant person to be around—of course he has an ego as well, but he does not wear it on his sleeves. We really wanted a second guitarist to fill out the sound a little and also to add more impulses to the outfit and let it develop. I guess we decided that he was the obvious choice for us, especially as our material progressed in a slightly more thrashy manner. My time as a drummer was drawing to an end as well. Since we knew that the era after *Monumental Possession* would become a lot faster and Apollyon was a little more accomplished as a drummer and I was slightly better

1995: A Malicious Records flyer featuring Fenriz advertises the *Kronet Til Konge* album.

than him on guitars, we saw that we could also do the good old switch as the material grew faster and more technical. With Alver, it was an obvious choice; our paths were crossing more and more as time went along, and simultaneously Fenriz was not sure if he was joining for the second album—the tedious part of this breakup was that Fenriz went forth and back on whether he was going to stay or not. I think maybe Fenriz was just sick of it all back then and wanted to unwind and do other things than metal for a while, and in retrospective I truly understand that."

The second album bears a notably more aggressive and straightforward vibe, thanks to a punchy production and caustic vocals, which were split between all the members except for Alver. Despite Fenriz's departure there is an undeniably Darkthrone-esque, eighties-inspired atmosphere to the thrashy, catchy numbers, and the fact that Apollyon's Aura Noir were working on the similarly minded debut album *Black Thrash Attack* around this time seems to have left its mark on *Monumental Possession*.

"We wanted to dig a little further down into our roots," explains Vicotnik. "All the guys in this era were really into thrash metal, so we wanted to mix this with a straightforward style of black metal. I also started opening my mind a little and began reading a lot of psychology, philosophy, religion and classic literature. I think this is more evident in Ved Buens Ende's music, but for example the outro on *Monumental Possession* shows that we are moving in on uncharted territory, a style of music that contains a blend of layers that was unfamiliar to us. Nevertheless, our main aim was to make a musical blend that had meant the world to us for years, to have a really warm and analog sound—we recorded two of the guitars through a bass amp—and tons of primal aggression. I am very happy with *Monumental Possession*, it is very straight to the point. [And] the drumming is more than half decent—I knew that this was the last one for me, so I wanted it to be solid."

Despite the efficiency of its actual creation, Vicotnik compares the atmosphere within the band following its completion to that of an abandoned ship, with the finished album gathering dust while the artwork and layout remained uncompleted. The experience appears to have been pivotal for Vicotnik, and from this point forward he would become the central figure within the group, the shift coinciding closely with a move into more avant-garde territories. "Even if the composing and the rehearsing went flawlessly, there were other issues that were just put to the side and expected to resolve themselves," he recalls. "This grew more and more frustrating to me as the months went on and on, and I took it upon myself to just finish it by myself."

The first evidence of the band's new direction was 1998's *Satanic Art*—released on Satyr's Moonfog Records after Malicious Records' collapse—an EP whose sound was several worlds away from the previous recordings. With a running time of sixteen minutes, the release served as a gentle introduction to the band's new incarnation (now a six-piece featuring the addition of Cerberus on bass, Galder of Old Man's Child on guitars, and Zweiss/Svein Egil Hatlevik of Fleurety on keyboards and piano), though there were also other motivations behind the record.

"This was what it all was building up to," explains Vicotnik. "I could not wait, I had had this style of track since '94–'95 and did not want to wait rehearsing and preparing a whole new album, so to speed things ahead a mini-album seemed like the clever thing to do. The contact with the label was also dwindling, so doing a mini felt a lot more secure, in case you got stuck with the costs."

Reflecting the taste for experimentation and sophistication prevalent at the time, the quarter-hour effort stands today as something of a stepping stone toward the more experimental and often mechanized style of the band's later works. Though more organic than later efforts, the material nonetheless blends clear industrial leanings with a cold and concentrated black metal assault, as well as including a good dose of diabolically tinged piano and violin work. Lyrically too, it served to challenge, flipping the ubiquitous ego-oriented lyrics of black metal on their head.

"Musically speaking it is a stepping stone most definitely," agrees Vicotnik. "But inside the band we had seen this period coming for a long time. I had songs like 'The Paramount Empire' and 'The Black Treasure' ready since before *Kronet Til Konge* was released, but it did not make sense to play at bpm levels I was not comfortable with as a drummer and we needed to kind of stick to the plan; to start off with the basic forms of extreme metal and step by step take it beyond. This is kind of what I had been gunning for all along: speed, aggression, originality, insanity. To make music that challenged the mind. I planned it all out in detail; the design, the way to record, how to mix other more organic stuff in the contents rather than the black-and-white, 'I am so powerful' lyrics or the 'I am a really evil guy in a really dark forest' concepts. Catering to more frail parts of the human mind and body like disease, mental illness, and mix it up with stuff like parapsychology, meta-physics, surrealism and spice it up a bit with duality thinking. From the weakest to the strongest animal, from wheel-chairs to flying capes, god and the devil, order and chaos etc. I wanted the music to almost feel like you were looking at it, as much as hearing it."

1999's challenging *666 International.*

"That's probably the best we did," considers Apollyon, who had moved from guitar to playing drums within the band. "It's maybe more Thorns-inspired. I think the last song is from an earlier recording session because the drums are sped up on the song, we recorded it slow and sped it up to the tempo we wanted it ultimately. You can hear that on a lot of releases [by bands] of that time, because of the drum pitch. *Satanic Art* was very much Vicot-nik, very much his band … from *Satanic Art* on he was starting to take over [the writing]."

In 1999 the monumental *666 International* was unleashed. Continuing directly from where *Satanic Art* had left off—to the extent that the album began with exactly the same piece of music the mini-album ended with—the record took the experimental attitude of its predecessor and ran with it. As part of another lineup shift, which saw Galder and Cerberus depart, *666 International* included a significant addition in the form of Vicotnik's close friend Carl-Michael Eide (Czral), who performed drums on the album as well as some guitar parts. No stranger to the musicians within DHG, he had, like Apollyon, already contributed to both Aura Noir and Cadaver Inc. and also played with Vicotnik in Ved Buens Ende, as well as in notable acts such as Ulver, Dimmu Borgir, and Satyricon. Thus the album would mark a period dominated by the Vicotnik/Czral partnership.

"I knew what I wanted," Vicotnik explains. "I gathered up every guitar riff I had, every piece of music I had written but not used. I took a portable bed and moved into the studio. I had riffs in bundles and together with Czral, we made drum patterns for every part we had. We added more and more layers on the parts and in the end we assembled the parts into songs. This way of working was totally new to me, but nevertheless, very interesting. The product almost had its own life and evolved all the time, it was almost like designing music. I am also glad it was done in the final era of hundred-percent analog production. We did not do this watching a computer screen, the whole thing was done working with the ears and with sounds. Almost three months later I moved out of the studio with an album I always wanted to make."

Though synth player Svein Egil Hatlevi wrote most of his parts in relative isolation, he is quick to admit that he didn't play an "essential role" in the album's creation, and his recollections of the period give some idea as to the unusual dynamics within DHG during this period.

"It was a much more chaotic band [than Fleurety]—there were more people involved, all wanting to do different things," he ponders. "But it was a good thing for the music. There was *some* discussions going on, but basically it was fragmented, everyone had a responsibility for their own instrument even though Vicotnik was … well, there was never a doubt that he was the owner of the band. I would make my intros and keyboard lines and see if he liked it, if he didn't I would do something else, I was very independent in terms of what I did with my own music. That felt natural, there were a lot of big egos in the band, so there wasn't much room for discussion as discussions could easily turn into arguments."

The record would be Svein's last appearance with the band, as upon attending rehearsals for the follow-up he found that there wasn't much space in the songs for his piano skills, not to mention that the three-day-a-week rehearsals required by Vicotnik were incompatible with his lifestyle at the time. *666* would also mark the last contribution to DHG from Apollyon, who was now playing bass, his third role within the band in as many recordings.

"*666 International* was really not my style," Apollyon admits today. "Carl-Michael was in the band too, so I only play bass on about sixty percent of the album or something. They recorded riff by riff, then in mastering put it all together, and they would call me up and say, 'Do you want to come down and record one riff?' and I would say, 'No, do it yourself,' so I play on about half of that album. I didn't like the album, I felt it was too chaotic. We had rehearsed some of the songs a couple of years before with me on drums and it was interesting, but then they decided to do this one-riff-at-a-time thing and process the drums. There are always good riffs and interesting parts, but I think it was also a drug problem back then on that album, some of the guys were really out on stuff. I never wanted it to be very experimental, [when I joined] I was probably looking to do Darkthrone-ish stuff, that kind of punkish black metal. I always liked simple stuff, 4/4. The later stuff was getting into 16/38 or something, fucking hell—crazy!"

The album was a indeed a twisting and angular beast of a record, one that required no little investment from the listener in order to unlock its true rewards. "I thought it had the potential to sell but also to destroy a band," says Vicotnik. "Some people got it the wrong way around though—they said that we were going commercial, but in my opinion this is one of the least commercial albums I have ever heard in my life. No real song structures, mixing two elements that really are at odds with each other, twelve-minute songs … If we ever thought about sales, we would have been most well off sticking to the *KTK* sound. Where reactions for *Satanic Art* were ninety-eight percent good, with both journalists and the public loving it, 666 was a harder sell. Our genre is very conservative and there's not really any way to avoid massive critique as well as massive praise when you do an album like 666. But I was very happy with the reactions. Means no difference to me if you get slaughtered or worshipped, as long as it is not indifference. Indifferent art has no function."

While some prefer the older recordings, the increased use of electronics on both *Satanic Art* and especially *666 International* was one element that undoubtedly had a profound impact on the scene, and its groundbreaking nature certainly raised the profile of the band. Where the stunning efforts of Mysticum had essentially been furious and primitive black metal songs with the addition of a dis-

Kvohst live in Oslo, 2007. Photo: Ester Segarra.

tinct drum machine sound, this was an altogether more carefully constructed proposition, the industrial and non-metal elements being closely integrated into the overall sound.

In fact, such was the apparent influence of this move that many have attributed the increased use of electronics within black metal to this one album. Interestingly, this cold and mechanized approach was also echoing within the roster of Moonfog Records, as evident in surprisingly industrial-tinged releases by Thorns (now featuring Aldrahn on additional vocals), Emperor, and Satyricon.

"When I was about ten to twelve years old, I really loved Depeche Mode so I guess in a way it started there," Vicotnik explains of the influences he was bringing to the band. "Many years later, in the prime of my black metal years so to speak, I on one hand listened to Celtic Frost, Bathory, Darkthrone, Mayhem, etc., and on the other hand I was an equally big fan of electronic music like Coil, Depeche Mode, Vangelis, NIN, Squarepusher. On the third there was also acoustic music like Leonard Cohen, Nick Drake, Chopin, Erik Satie, and Devil Doll. At some point I just felt compelled to be inspired by music in general, instead of just working within a small space of what was established and accepted."

A period of no less than eight years would pass before the release of the band's next album, namely 2007's *Supervillain Outcast*. Taking a more focused and streamlined approach, with an even more pronounced electronic edge, the album was a forward-thinking and often punishing example of experimental and industrial-leaning black metal, yet also showed an ear for melody, traditional song structures, and catchy riffs in tracks such as the irrepressible "Apocalypticism." The release would be the first without co-founding member Aldrahn (who had moved out of Oslo since *666 International* and was working with Snorre Ruch on Thorns), the lineup now featuring Czral on drums, Vicotnik on guitar, programming, samples, and additional vocals, Thrawn (Tom Kvålsvoll) on guitar and additional vocals, an individual known as Mort providing additional samples/programming, and a new vocalist, Kvohst, otherwise known as Mat McNerney, an English musician who had played in industrial black metal act Void with Czral and the equally progressive black metal-related band Code with Vicotnik. With Aldrahn gone, the writing process now centered almost exclusively around Vicotnik and Czral.

"The release for *Supervillain* was scheduled for 2003–2004, and even that would not [have] been a swift release in relation to *666*," says Vikotnik. "The biggest issue for the delay though was that it all went to pieces in the recording process; the budget was not big enough and none of us did a good enough job. I sat doing post-production work for years. Czral was instrumental… by that time, we had such intuition that we could just play without having anything prepared. He literally set the aim for *Supervillain*, he always said, 'Let's make the best black metal album of all time,' and even if we did or did not, that kind of became the slogan of the era. We started working a lot more professionally this time around: we made a surplus of songs, we got in a rehearsal coach, we practiced three times a week. It's the hardest I have ever spent working on a piece of music and the blood, sweat, and tears made the album as personal as it can get, there is not a second on that album I don't connect to. The reception was overwhelming … I never dreamt about as many top scores. Usually one would not care about this shit, but it was just overwhelming, you just could not stay totally indifferent to it."

The success of the album would prompt numerous tours for several years to follow, the lineup once again shifting continuously, leaving Vicotnik the only constant. With him at the helm of Dødheimsgard, however, it seems that the world can continue to expect music that steers far away from the generic, a point that harks back to one of the group's aims at their time of formation:

"Another aim was [always] to not make indifferent music," concludes Vicotnik, "I have always had a strong interest for art that stirs great emotions. It would not have mattered if people hated it, as long as the hate was real, strong, and had its reasons. Then, at least, that individual's reasoning has partly been awoken because of your music."

46
MYSTICUM
INDUSTRIAL BLACK METAL
PART I

"I got a tape with a few songs of Mysticum as they were signed on the same label as us. It was the first time I ever heard black metal with industrial and computer drums—I started to laugh at once because I thought it was so fuckin' mind-blowing and original! I listened to it for weeks without any pause, I fuckin' loved it! To me, Mysticum is a legendary band, and stand as one of the most original black metal bands hailing from the mighty North!"

—Jørn (Hades/Hades Almighty)

GIVEN THE BLEAKLY MODERN aesthetic that has surfaced within the work of bands such as Shining, Anaal Nathrakh and The Axis of Perdition, it's easy to forget that prior to Satyricon and Moonfog Productions' urbanization of the genre in the late nineties, black metal was almost exclusively obsessed with the ancient past. Seemingly denying the entire industrial revolution conceptually speaking, the movement was dominated by Old English fonts, primitive analog productions, old superstitions, folklore, references to folk and classical music, and numerous paeans to the glories of untainted nature and pagan religions.

Entirely alone stood Mysticum, an outfit who appeared from within the Satanically inclined Norwegian scene with a sound and aesthetic that combined industrial imagery, modern narcotics, and a passion for electronic percussion. The latter would prove particularly significant, and despite the band's bright flame burning comparatively briefly, their impact and influence would be huge, their use of samplers and mechanical beats a revolutionary touch that would accidentally kick-start the entire industrial black metal subgenre.

Formed in Asker, a municipality some twenty kilometers east of Oslo, the band saw the union of two parties: on the one side two longtime friends, bassist Mean Malmberg (often listed by his real name Robin Malmberg or simply Dr. Best) and vocalist/guitarist Prime Evil (also known as Ravn, Svatravn, and occasionally his real name Preben), and on the other side

**The master artwork for the Sabazios demo *Wintermass*, 1993,
later reissued as a Mysticum release.**

a vocalist/guitarist known as Cerastes (or Herr General). As a trio the group initially went under the name Sabazios, a reference to the ancient Indo-European god whose worshippers utilized the symbol of the snake.

"Prime Evil was a neighbor," explains Mean of his bandmate, "and he asked me if I wanted to play with him and his friend Marius. Prime Evil was five years older and Marius a year younger than me. We started a punk/grind band in my parents' house. I started with punk, but I also listened to Iron Maiden, Halloween, Anthrax, Testament, and some more."

Like Mean, Prime Evil was listening to a range of metal, punk, and grind bands (specifically "Uncle Slam, DRI, Gwar, Slayer, MOD, SOD, Carcass, Death, Cannibal Corpse, Nausea, Autopsy, Entombed, Rövarna, Dismember, Napalm Death, Scorn, Naked City, Exploited, Bolt Thrower, and Darkthrone") and together with Marius the three would create music in the short-lived group Sewer Disgust, releasing a self-titled demo in 1991.

"It was terrible music," reflects Mean. "But we played a festival for the youth called Asker Festival, [and] met Cerastes who was playing in another hardcore/punk band. He was a cool guy, we shared the same backstage room, had the same music interest and friends and we started to play together [in 1992] under the name Sabazios. At that time we also had a drummer, we went to the same school and he taught me to use the computer. [Later] I did layout for Enslaved, Ulver, Emperor, Mayhem and some others as I was the only one who could use a computer! Then we got a drum machine from a friend to test and Prime Evil bought it [in the end] because the drummer refused to play black metal and of course, he

Cerastes, Prime Evil and Mean Malmberg in a derelict asylum, 1998.
Photo: Nikolai Funke/Fotofunke.

loved the sound of the drum machine and it made the drummer's escape 'comfortable'!"

Prime Evil: "The drummer we had was not really interested, and we tested [the drum machine] and fell for the industrial sound and punctuality. We did try some good drummers, but we wanted the drum machine style."

"When we started using the drum machine, I've got to say I was a bit skeptical," admits Cerastes, who was listening to punk and grind such as PiL, The Exploited, Dead Kennedys, Napalm Death, Bolt Thrower, and interestingly industrial outfit Godflesh. "But after a few rehearsals the skepticism soon disappeared. The impersonal sound and military precision really appealed to me/us, and fitted our musically direction perfectly. The use of the death metal, I think, also shaped our composing and use of riffs from that point on. A genuine style which we identified with was created. At some point in time we gave Hellhammer a shot at playing drums. He played extremely well and tight, but the sound was just very wrong for us. So it's unthinkable for us to use something else but 0/1 drums."

The duty of programming the Roland TR-505, a cheap and rather primitive drum machine and MIDI sequencer, would fall to Mean, who was helped to a large extent in the early days by Einar Sjursø, drummer of Beyond Dawn and later Virus. Einar had studied at art school with Prime Evil and it was he—along with the Helvete store in Oslo—that Mean credits with introducing the group to the black metal phenomenon, though as Prime Evil explains, this was not an immediate transition.

"No clear decision was really made," he recalls. "We created our own style and sound which just very natural at that time. Sabazios was black metal, but we did not change overnight. We did not have any rules about how the music should be or about being 'anti-mosh,' it just changed by itself after listening more and more to black metal. Mourning, Diamanda Galás, Grotesque, Dissection, *Ola De Violencia* by Masacre, Samael, Beherit, Blasphemy, etc. And drugs, drugs, and *drugs!*"

Indeed, the band would soon acquire a reputation as the biggest drug worshippers in black metal, quite a revolutionary stance as the movement had essentially distanced itself from such activities, although a number of key figures in the Norwegian scene (who will remain unnamed) did in fact take their first trips thanks to the band. As it turns out Cerastes was the catalyst within the group itself, the wild-eyed guitarist enjoying an impressively wide range of illicit substances at the time.

"Amphetamines, LSD, psilocybin [mushrooms], MDMA, THC, PCP ... " he laughs. "Happy days!"

"Cerastes was deeply into it," explains Prime Evil, "so it naturally infected the rest of the band."

"In the black metal scene there was no drug use at all at that time," reflects Mean with a laugh. "Most bands avoided it and were beer drinkers. We poisoned the scene!"

Later graphic designs by the band would also memorably include images of syringes, the band suggesting in interviews that heroin was something that they might experiment with in the future. Though that is met by a "no comment" by the band today, there's no doubt that the drug-heavy—and heavily drugged—lifestyle of the band had a considerable impact on their creative process over the years, both in terms of musical inspiration and mentality.

"[We were] going to loads of underground techno parties in the early nineties, listening to hardcore techno, being drugged to the sky," recalls Cerastes. "Most of my musical creations have come out of a seriously fucked-up brain. At that time I was more or less marinated in amphetamines and acid and under the influence all the time. Being pretty disturbed, depressed, and quite crazy, due to the constant intake and lack of sleep, this surely had a major impact on my composing. Many times I've have had extremely long guitar sessions, which many of my riffs have emerged out of. Also my lyrics mostly came after being awake for many days. Our songs were written mostly together at rehearsals, where we exchanged ideas and riffs."

Though the drum machine was already in use by this point, Cerastes admits that the club music the band surrounded themselves with in their recreation time certainly encouraged their continued use of mechanical percussion. By 1993/1994 Mean's programming would be directly influenced by these dance beats, giving the band a truly unique rhythmic backbone and one that shocked more than a few of their peers. Indeed, despite effectively creating industrial black metal, the band's use of electronics was definitely inspired more by hard techno than industrial music per se.

"We all like Kraftwerk, Laibach, and Front 242," Mean ponders. "But our music is probably not influenced by this too much. But the differences from all other black metal bands in sound and style made us see ourselves as industrial black metal. There were maybe skeptics, but we couldn't care less. And there were many drummers that liked it, especially Einar (Beyond Dawn) and Hellhammer. But some fans of the scene were probably not developed enough at that time, so yes, some missed the point. We think we were before our time, no doubt."

By December 1992, however, these influences had yet to really surface in the group's songwriting, and the band headed into "Rolf's Cellar" studio to record Sabazios' sole demo, *Wintermass*. The original version, released in January 1993, memorably featured a piece of snakeskin on one panel.

"The name Sabazios came from Prime Evil who loved his snakes," explains Mean. "It was snake-worshipping—*Wintermasssssss*, like the snake."

"We used to put pressure on the 's' in the vocals, sounding like a snake," confirms Prime Evil, "this had a lot to do with the band's old name 'Sabazios,' which were snake-worshippers in old Greece."

Soon the band would change their name to Mysticum—a moniker that gave a crafty nod to two-thirds of their "sex, drugs, and Satan" motto—a move that followed discussions with Euronymous, who had floated the idea of signing the band to his label Deathlike Silence. The initial bond between the two parties actually came through their shared interest in snakes, with Prime Evil—who then had over ten species of snakes—selling the Mayhem mainman food for his own pets.

In June the band headed back to the same studio to record a new demo entitled *Medusa's Tears*, a four-song opus that saw their sound grow toward the fast-flowing and denser style they would soon become known for. The demo sleeve would once again be of note, featuring what may be the first appearance of the Never Stop the Madness logo, a parody of Roadrunner Records' anti-drugs campaign "Stop the Madness," which adorned all its releases for many years. Originally floated as an idea by Euronymous, the logo (essentially a modified version of the original slogan, replacing the broken syringe with a intact version) would be used the same year by Ulver and would later appear on Malicious Records releases by bands such as Zyklon-B and Gorgoroth, before being resurrected a decade later by U.S. bands such as Nachtmystium and Krieg.

Cannily, the following month Mean gave both of the band's demos to Hellhammer and Euronymous before they set off on their long drive to Bergen to record the *De Mysteriis Dom Sathanas* album. Listening to the material in the car, Euronymous was hugely impressed by its originality and contacted Prime Evil the next day, signing the band and beginning plans to release an album entitled *Where the Raven Flies*. The following month, however, Euronymous was murdered and the album plans put on hold.

It was during this period that Hellhammer became a member of the group for a time, though as mentioned the band felt an integral part of the group had been lost and the union was brief. Robin meanwhile kept himself busy by joining Ulver, contributing to both a rehearsal tape and the *Vargnatt* demo. It makes sense then that the first "official" release by both groups was a split seven-inch on Necromantic Gallery Productions, a Dutch label specializing in debut EP releases by Norwegian bands including Gehenna, Einherher, and Dimmu Borgir. Rarely has such a short release showcased the artistic possibilities of the black metal movement, with Ulver's "Ulverytternes Kamp"—a folky piece dominated by acoustic guitars—contrasting dramatically with Mysticum's "Mourning," a rerecording of a song from *Wintermass* captured during the *Medusa's Tears* sessions.

"It was Kris from Ulver's idea, he was really the one who wanted this song to be rerecorded since he liked it so much," explains Mean, who remains somewhat unsatisfied with the recording. "I can't really remember where we did the recording for this song, I think it was on the same studio as the album was recorded [Bondi Lydstudio]. I don't understand why we removed the cymbal/hi-hat sound with a lot of reverb on it—earlier fans said they missed that, and I could not agree more. It's also recorded with a pitch[shift] to the voice and the switch is really bad, you can hear it turned on and off."

The group would return to Bondi in February of the following year to record two new tracks for the compilation *Nordic Metal: A Tribute to Euronymous*, namely "In Your Grave" and "Kingdom Comes." Featuring a searing and icy production, the songs were nothing less than a revelation, even on a compilation of unparalleled high standards. The songwriting was now on another level, the highly memorable and relatively simple melodies combined with various bridges and twists, perhaps most memorably the eerie organ break in "Kingdom Comes" that creepily builds the tension before breaking into a truly epic and haunting pay-off. Synths and electronics now played a far greater role generally, the drum machine playing to its strengths by utilizing the sort of ultra-fast hi-hats and thumping bass hits simply not possible from a human drummer. Just as memorable were the sublime vocal performances of Prime Evil and Cerastes, which combined to hypnotic effect.

The compilation was released on American label Necropolis Records, and coincidentally Mysticum now looked to the U.S. for a record deal due to intense dissatisfaction with Deathlike Silence. In Euronymous' absence, the label had been taken over by the more mainstream Voices of Wonder, who had previously handled distribution for Deathlike. Like labelmates Enslaved, Mysticum wanted off the label and in April 1995 they broke contract and signed to Full Moon Productions, a Florida label run by Jon "Thorns" Jamshid, previously editor of *Petrified* and a longtime contact of Euronymous. A few months later, the group returned to Bondi to record their debut full-length.

"This was the most disruptive time in my life, total chaos," recalls Prime Evil, "so it's very hard to remember. The recording of *In the Streams of Inferno* album was done in couple of weeks; since we programmed our drum machine [beforehand, we were] only working with the sounds of it. I guess it was pretty normal studio work—with a lot of red wine for the vocals. One thing I remember well is different people showing up in the studio, and one of them was 'Saiithem' [Mathias Løken, who would later become the band's manager, a role he holds today] who [arrived] with another close friend of ours. We didn't really know him at that time, but he started to interfere when recording and mastering. He complained about our guitar sound, telling us it was too unclear etc. This started to piss us off," he laughs, "we just ignored him totally, which we shouldn't have done!"

Indeed, as Prime Evil suggests, the album would feature a far more compressed and less dynamic sound than the *Nordic Metal* tracks, particularly noticeable since the record features rerecorded versions of the two numbers originally on the compilation. A number of other old songs were also rerecorded—this time improving the sound including updated versions of "The Rest" and "Wintermass" from the first demo and a reworked version of "Crypt of Fear" from Medusa's Tears. The latter would prove to be one of the most impressive recordings on the album, its near two-minute synth buildup breaking into one of the band's most furious and possessed performances to date. Two ambient/industrial instrumentals bookended the album while at its center lay a song with the familiar title "Where The Raven Flies."

Though the sound certainly leaves room for improvement (though this was improved considerably for the 2013 re-release), the album's visceral power remains undeniable, harnessing a unique combination of chaos and focus, the linear but multilayered compositions encapsulating a demonic and otherworldly mass of guitar, bass, eerie keyboards, and utterly incomparable vocals, kept in line and driven ever forward by the industrial pummeling. Aptly, given that the members' main influences were apparently Satanism and hard drugs, the result is an intense assault on the senses that is as utterly dark, furious, and unbalanced as it is euphoric and transcendental. Unfortunately fans would have to wait over a year to actually *hear* it, the group sitting on the recordings until autumn 1996, instead releasing a promo tape entitled *Piss Off!!!* featuring a number of rough unmixed versions.

"Why we were so delayed sending the masters has no other reason than we had a little too much left from our celebration after finishing the recording," laughs Prime Evil. "It takes time to make all those smoke signals visible all the way over to Florida … "

The band would follow the release with a tour of Europe with Marduk and Gehenna that saw them playing twenty-four shows in twenty-five days, posters famously declaring the band to be "cumming all over Europe."

"That was a very fun experience—Gehenna were just sleep, sleep, sleep but Marduk became our best friends that time," recalls Mean, whose highlight was being given a huge box of marijuana in Switzerland. "Yes, they gave us five hundred grams of weed. Then we were so drunk we ate all their plants—fresh. Not a good thing to do. But we lost everything before the day was over as the bus driver took it away!"

"They were extreme," recalls Peter Tägtgren, who was playing guitar in Marduk at the time, "just really fucking extreme guys in their way of living. We were sitting in the lounge in the bus listening to techno and taking acid *every fucking day*, it was madness … one of the most fucked-up tours I did so far."

In November the band headed out for what was supposed to be a three-week tour with Cannibal Corpse, Angelcorpse, and Immolation in the U.S. and Mexico, though due to "complications" the band would ultimately play only two dates. A few months later the group recorded a song for Full Moon's *Tribute to Hell* compilation, namely "Eriaminell" (a play on the words "here I am in hell"), another stunning number defined by slow and memorable riffs, high-paced percussion, and an unforgettable bridge, this time featuring an otherworldly use of string effects.

Despite the sleeve of the first album mentioning the band's proposed second album *Planet Satan*, there followed a silence of four years broken only when the band headed into the studios to record a new number called "Black Magic Mushrooms." Another intense and truly outstanding number, it saw the band integrating their dance and industrial influences to a far greater extent than ever before. So were rumors true that the band had also recorded much of the long-awaited *Planet Satan* album?

"No, the only thing we recorded was 'Black Magic Mushrooms,'" explains Mean, "And I think that was the best song we ever made. But we never met in the studio. I had forgotten the riffs which I had made and the studio guy had to teach me the song again," he laughs. "What a fucked-up picture you are getting of me now!"

The song would see release as a split with Norwegian thrashers Audiopain (whose guitarist had produced the track), and the following year would see manager Mathias Løken release a compilation on his label Planet Satan Revolution, featuring most of their non-*Streams* material, including the demos, the two splits, "Eriaminell," and material from both *Piss Off!!!* and *Nordic Metal*. The CD's title, *Lost Masters of the Universe*, turned out to be accurate as the masters for the recordings had indeed been lost ("My father had used the master to record a stupid movie or something," explains Mean), meaning that everything had to be re-mastered from the tapes and EPs. If all this "activity" had raised any hopes of a resurgence of the group, they were dashed as the group remained dormant for another eight years. So what happened?

"Children, time, money, too much party for some," ponders Cerastes. "A few years after Euronymous' death, the scene had become very commercial, suddenly everyone played in a fucking black metal band. Black metal stuff in newspapers, national music awards given to bands, it all seemed very 'house-trained' and weak, we think that black metal lost its magic, originality, and pride. This made us lose interest in staying in the scene. Also lots of drugs were used at this time, therefore *Planet Satan* was put on hold."

Prime Evil would resurface as a vocalist in Norwegian deathrashers Amok and Italian industrial metal outfit Aborym, before departing and taking a hiatus from the scene, while both Cerastes and Mean seemed to have lost interest in making music. It seemed a situation that was unlikely to resolve itself and Mean admits that the three can be willfully stubborn and slow when they want to be. Indeed, it's worth mentioning that almost two years would pass between first speaking to Mean and the interviews appearing here finally taking place. It was all the more remarkable then when the guitarist one day mentioned in e-mail that

Mean, Cerastes and Prime Evil seem to have returned to their urban exploring roots following their reunion in 2013.

there were chances of a forthcoming reunion. A year later and the band announced a new deal with Peaceville Records, and began working on the re-release of their two previous CDs, re-mastering both and adding to the contents. Jump forward again to summer 2013 and your author was finally able to finally hear work-in-progress versions of new material destined for the now almost mythical *Planet Satan,* thanks to a short but memorable visit to Asker. Against the odds Mysticum, one of black metal's most lamented losses, had returned.

"Prime Evil had an enlightenment in summer 2011 and produced loads of riffs," Mean recalls. "He contacted us and we felt that the time was right for all to get back together. That was that. Cerates was always in a different world, I had to work hard to get him into the playing. But one rule we had—if one stops playing, Mysticum stops. Brothers forever."

It would be unwise at this point to take anything for granted with regard to this inimitable trio, with uncertainty apparently the only certainty in the Mysticum story. Still it seems fair to predict that this seminal group will continue playing only by their own rules, testing the sanity of fans, press, labels, and (perhaps most of all) their manager in the process.

47
ABORYM
INDUSTRIAL BLACK METAL
PART II

"I saw and heard Aborym for the first time at the Inferno Festival in Oslo the year they played and I was overwhelmed at how great they were. M: Fabban is a very accomplished musician and like a brother to me. I don't know why they wanted me to be part of the band but it is truly an honor."
—Prime Evil (Mysticum)

WITH AN EVER-EVOLVING SOUND and lineup, Italian veterans Aborym have both bewildered and rewarded listeners for over two decades, becoming one of the best-known bands to adopt the "industrial black metal" label in the process. Taking their moniker from a demon named Haborym Sadek Aym, discussed in the infamous book of demonology *The Lesser Key of Solomon the King*, the group would first find acclaim in the late nineties, though its original incarnation was in 1992 and was formed by the prolific musician known as Malfeitor Fàbban, who contributes bass, synth, and occasionally vocals to this day.

"I originally got into metal after listening to *Kill 'Em All* by Metallica in 1989," he explains. "Before that I used to listen to softer music, like Alice Cooper, Faster Pussycat, Pink Floyd, Led Zeppelin, AC/DC, Aerosmith, and Kiss, all bands that I listen to nowadays as well. The first time I ever listened to a death metal band was when a really weird lad at the bus stop asked me what kind of music I liked. He gave me then a demo of an unknown band … I think they were called Mortmain. After months of healthy tape-trading I fell in love with *Beneath the Remains* by Sepultura, then I discovered Carcass, Morbid Angel, and all the rest. At that time a friend of mine, Nicola Curri, who later on became the singer of Funeral Oration, was working on the artwork of the vinyl for *Live in Leipzig*, trying to emulate Dead's writing through some of his letters. That's how I discovered Mayhem and then a whole bunch of black metal bands.

"Aborym itself formed in 1992–'93," he continues. "At that time I used to live in the south, in a really tough city, where playing was basically impossible. There weren't any kind of rehearsal rooms, so if you didn't own a basement or a garage, you just couldn't play at all. In my city there was just delinquency, criminality, and poverty, try to figure out how impossible it would have been finding rehearsal rooms. However, my wish was huge, so I spent all the summer looking for a basement to equip, and once I found it I started to look for people to play with. We started like a sort of cover band: we only had couple of songs written and a Rotting Christ cover ("The Old Coffin Spirit") and *Beneath the Remains* by Sepultura."

Working as a trio—Fàbban appearing alongside guitarist Alex Noia and drummer D. Belvedere—the band's early recordings were captured on two tapes; a rehearsal, *Live in Studio* (1993), and a debut demo entitled *Worshipping Damned Souls* (1994). With a dark and obscure sound based around an early black/thrash metal template, the tapes unsurprisingly reflect the bands covered in the group's formative months, adding some solemn and minimalist organ passages into the bargain. Fàbban, however, would soon split the band up due to personnel issues, before working with other projects including the aforementioned Funeral Oration and (perhaps more significantly, giving Aborym's future recordings) M.E.M.O.R.Y Lab, an outfit that combined industrial music with metal.

In 1997 Fàbban reformed Aborym, this time determined to integrate electronics into a contemporary black metal formula. In 1998, having joined forces with guitarist Davide "Set Teitan" Totaro and a vocalist/guitarist/synth player known as Yorga SM, he recorded a five-song rehearsal demo entitled *Antichristian Nuclear Sabbath*, and the following year the band's debut album *Kali Yuga Bizarre* was released, featuring four of the songs from the *Antichristian* demo alongside five new numbers.

The result was a powerful, epic, and highly varied opus, one of the band's finest albums and one that, in retrospect, also reflects the grandiose and determinedly avant-garde direction black metal was taking at the time, its dramatic synths and soaring, clean vocals providing a nod to progressive Norwegian acts such as Emperor and Arcturus. Certainly the drum & bass break on third track "Horrenda Peccata Christi" could well have come off the latter act's *La Masquerade Infernale* album, while "Tantra Bizarre" saw the band move into even more experimental territory, blending traditional Eastern music with disorienting beats and bizarre vocals. The following track, "Come Thou Long Expected Jesus," proves even stranger, blending a choir recording with a rather rabid vocal declaration by guest vocalist A.G. Volgar of Italian goth rock group Deviate Ladies.

"The desire of creating something new and extremely violent at the same time, something that somehow could reflect the time we are living, the Kali Yuga," explains Fàbban of the inspirations behind the band's varied take on black metal. "I don't believe in bullshits like 'the true spirit of black metal,' I don't believe in 'this is true, this is not.' The essence of music is the expression of the essence and spirituality of the artist. All the rest is bullshit, stereotypes invented to diversify musical genres, trends, different ways of appearing. Experimentation—to my advice—is something inner in some men and artists: it's like a sort of overcoming, or self-overcoming. *Kali Yuga Bizarre* is the first album we recorded and it has

Aborym's core lineup during their *Kali Yuga Bizarre* era: Nysrok, Yorga, Seth Teitan, Fàbban.

to be taken as it is. It's a great album to my advice. I literally adore it. It's terribly honest and spontaneous."

The "Kali Yuga" that Fàbban refers to, according to Indian scriptures, is the final epoch of the world, the "end times" where strife and conflict are common, a period generally considered by believers to be the era that we live in today. These apocalyptic themes would become a defining theme in the years that followed, though on the debut album the lyrics were primarily in Italian, making the album's concepts largely impenetrable for those who didn't speak the language. This didn't stop a degree of controversy arising, thanks in part to the speech on "Come Thou … " which, among other things, poured scorn on "collective mediocrity" and declared that if the Chilean dictator Pinochet was to be punished for his crimes, so too should Fidel Castro. More pressingly, although Yorga SM's vocal abilities were undoubtedly magnificent, he was beginning to voice controversial opinions elsewhere that would tar the band's reputation for some years to come. In any case, he would be kicked out of the band some way prior to the album's completion, due to a conflict of personalities.

"A couple of dickheads who were part of the group have declared things that weren't on the same line as the philosophy of the band," Fàbban explains dryly. "Yorga upon all; such a mommy's boy. Since then, people started to point at us as a right-wing group, which we are *not*. Aborym are not a right-wing band, Aborym don't do politics. In fairness, Aborym are against *all* of those dorks who want to make politics through music."

As a result of Yorga SM's departure the group sought a new vocalist to complete the last few tracks of the album, soon finding a replacement in ex-Tormentor/Mayhem vocalist Attila Csihar, who by this point had returned to Budapest and was inactive within music, having entered a period of depression and self-destruction following Euronymous' murder.

"He was a man reduced to bits," claims Fàbban. "I called him to have a chat and to ask him something about [his band] Plasma Pool. I sent him the prerecording of *Kali Yuga Bizarre* and he made me understand he was really interested in that kind of music. He wanted to be back in the game somehow and I gave him that chance through Aborym. Attila Csihar should be very grateful to Aborym. Without us he would have never been back to the scene and he would have never been out of the tunnel [he was in]."

Whatever his state at the time, there's no doubt that Attila was as beneficial to the band as they were to him, and ultimately his joining brought a major boost in attention for the band. The ex-Tormentor and Mayhem vocalist initially appeared on *Kali Yuga Bizarre* as a guest—filling in for Yorga—only becoming the sole vocalist on the follow-up, 2001's *Fire Walk With Us*. Indeed writer Nathan T. Birk's *Terrorizer* review for the latter focused heavily on the Hungarian's presence, opening with the words: "Attila. Not the Hun, mind you, but the vocalist … man behind The Voice. The Voice that laid down the most haunting, tortured, just plain disturbing larynx contortions known to a piece of plastic with Mayhem's *De Mysteriis Dom Sathanas*. The man who commandeered the sporadic Tormentor (Hungary) from cult icons to carnival bizarre."

Of course, with "album of the month" status and a 10/10 mark in said review, the record clearly had more to offer than just great vocals, Birk concluding his write-up by stating, "Most black-heads will hate it, others will be curiously offended by it, and a fearless few will call it their own and use it as their very lifeblood," before ending with the bold words, "Thorns step aside."

Now featuring guitarist Nysrok Infernalien Sathanas (who had joined the band during the *Kali Yuga* sessions), *Fire …* was a far darker and more punishing effort than its predecessor. Moving away from the clean vocals and grandeur of old, it instead explored more extreme "industrial black metal" territories, the colder, more mechanized qualities being particularly noticeable on the cover of Burzum's "Det Som Engang Var," a track Attila apparently chose not to contribute to due to his friendship with Euronymous.

"I have vague, ethereal memories around [the whole recording]," ponders Fàbban of the band's harshest album. "It was a tough period. We weren't doing so well and that album explains a dark moment that pretty much everyone in the band has been through. Probably it's the most obscure album by Aborym. Listening to it nowadays, after so many years, makes me feel really proud of it. I think it's an amazing album."

It was an opinion shared by many fans and critics, and the band's next album, 2003's *With No Human Intervention*, met with a similarly overwhelming response, making *Terrorizer* "album of the month" status for the second time in a row and earning a swath of positive reviews. As with its predecessor, the album was built around a decidedly metal infrastructure, the electronic beats and samples adding a cold ruthlessness to the atmosphere without significantly altering the core sound. Increasingly, Aborym were integrating elements of goth, industrial, and EBM culture (reflected in the band's UV "corpsepaint" and club gear aesthetic, as well as in their choice of intoxicants), but without softening the ferocity of the assault, arguably the reason the band still appealed to many longtime black metal fans. The "club" overtones did not sit easily with everyone however, and live shows—such as their memorable London performance the same year—provoked plenty of horrified faces, specifically during the techno break within the set.

"During the years we've always shocked, we've always caused confusion and contradictions," comments Fàbban. "We have 'played' with our listeners, generating chaos, both in sound and in a conceptual way. And, well, this has always been really entertaining … I don't play a music genre like pop or rock, I don't play a genre which represents for me a sort of job or economical reliance, so I feel free to play whatever I like, without facing any kind of paranoia or issues. If someone turns his nose, my life doesn't change at all. If *Fire Walk with Us* is the darkest album by Aborym, *With No Human Intervention* is—without any doubts—the most psychopathic and experimental album of our whole discography. This LP is strongly related to chemical drugs and to a very long period of chaos, disorder, and intemperance."

Both the London show and the band's appearance in Oslo's Inferno festival the following year were notable for featuring a brief guest appearance by ex-Emperor drummer Bård G. "Faust" Eithun, his first live performances since leaving prison. Faust also contributed lyrics, spoken word, and even the album title for *With No Human Intervention*, and was one of a number of guests on the album, joining Nattefrost (Carpathian Forest), Mick "Irrumator" Kenney (Anaal Nathrakh), and Matt Jerman of UK band Void. Faust would soon become a full-time member of Aborym, the band's first human drummer since their reformation in 1997.

"I called [Faust] on the phone as I wanted to ask him if he would be joining Dissection again, at that time they were planning their return to the scene," recalls Fàbban. "He made me understand that ideologically speaking he didn't have anything to share with Dissection anymore and that he wouldn't [be] back with them. So I asked him to join Aborym. The answer was immediate. I wanted to give Aborym a more rock imprint … more 'metal' let's say, more acoustic, so that the acoustic and electronic could melt together, generating something completely new but classic at the same time."

Fàbban, Prime Evil, Nysrok, Faust: The short-lived *Generator* lineup which saw the band featuring as many Norwegian members within Aborym's ranks as Italian.

Further lineup shifts would occur in 2005, with Set exiting the band in somewhat acrimonious circumstances, the talented guitarist coincidentally joining the aforementioned Dissection (and later Watain) in Sweden. Also departing (though on better terms) was Attila, who had been invited to rejoin Mayhem. His role in Aborym was soon filled by a member of industrial black legends Mysticum, namely vocalist "Prime Evil."

"I was incredibly honored to be asked," the vocalist recalls, "I was also very nervous—to be the one to take over for this great singer was a bit scary at that time, but I practiced the lyrics and went to Rome to meet the band. My main influence for the vocals during the recording for Aborym was actually the Ilsa movies."

"He was the first person I called after Attila was back with Mayhem," says Fàbban. "I've always been a huge fan of Mysticum and having one of them in Aborym was a sort of a dream for me. And so it happened. We became great friends. In the past, Mysticum had been very important for our personal growth, but Aborym reached a point far beyond them. It was and it will always be a goal for us: to go over every single thing that has already been conceived. Overtake ourselves as we always did, without any rules but the ones we state."

The product of this new lineup was 2006's *Generator*, released by Season of Mist, the biggest label the band had worked with, highlighting the good standing the previous two albums had given them. The addition of a live drummer reverberates through the recording, the album adopting a more traditional second-wave black metal sound and putting less focus on the band's industrial influences, the presence of electronics predominantly surfacing in the synth work, providing an epic and symphonic (rather than aggressively techno) backdrop.

Sadly, Prime Evil would soon leave the band (and temporarily the scene) without recording any more vocals. *Generator* was also the last album to feature the band's longtime guitarist Nysrok, who Fàbban considered to have gone from an enthusiastic and vital member to a somewhat burnt-out individual with an overbearing reliance on intoxicants. In fact, Nysrok continues to create music in the successful electro/industrial band Alien Vampires, a group whose very raison d'etre appears to be such indulgences.

Now a trio, Fàbban and Faust are joined by guitarist, keyboard player and backing vocalist Paolo "Hell:IO:Kabbalus" Pieri.

As with many key industrial black metal bands, intoxication, specifically hard drugs, was one of the many trappings of industrial and club culture Aborym had embraced over the years, something that became public knowledge following Attila's arrest for possession of a large quantity of pills in 2002. Today however, Fàbban has largely moved away from drugs, and though his works in Aborym (such as 2010's *Psychogrotesque*, a concept album based around a nightmarish scenario in a mental institution and 2013's double album *Dirty*) suggest that his tastes remain as dark as ever, it seems he is intent on embracing a rather cleaner lifestyle.

"I quit with that shit," he states simply. "In fairness, I had fun at that time. Now I am in my mid-thirties and I'm not really interested anymore in those kind of things. I don't want to appear as a redeemed moralist—everyone is free to do whatever he wants—but I am a fanatic of nature, open air, mountains, and I really care about my life and health. I don't go to clubs and my circle of friends is really small as I care a lot about my privacy. ... Whenever it's possible I like to trek and hike up the Alps together with some close buddies. Reaching peaks at three or four thousand meters high is much more extreme than any club full of psychos and drugs, you can bet on it!"

48
BLACKLODGE
INDUSTRIAL BLACK METAL
PART III

DESPITE HAILING FROM the rather warmer climates of southern France, Blacklodge are in many ways obvious spiritual successors to Norway's Mysticum, thanks to their combination of black metal, industrial, hard drugs, and Satanism. Formed in 1998 as a solo act by one Saint Vincent, the project not only immediately embraced the musical possibilities that electronics offered, but also set out to explore the possible relationship between advancing technology and the realms of spirituality and the occult in its lyrics.

"The 'black' stands for the dark side of magic and the 'lodge' stands for esoteric secrets and initiation," begins founder and songwriter Vincent, who also took inspiration from the extra-dimensional "Black Lodge" on the *Twin Peaks* TV show. "The strong core of the band is to link our material, technical, and industrial world with religious feeling, mystical revelations, and magic, two topics that are usually considered paradoxical. The band sees religious experience through the infernal influence of the machine. Technology is widely thought of as a move away from spirituality, but I say something different. This *is* a move away from human equilibrium and harmonious consciousness, but it's not about leaving spirituality, but rather about imposing a massive black 'evil' spirituality. Difficult to explain in English maybe, but there is a spirit in the machine. There is a spirit in iron. And this spirit is acting, fighting against the harmony of humanity."

Unusually for a practitioner of industrial black metal, Vincent embraced electronic music prior to metal, as opposed to the other way around, though he explains that the music he was originally exposed to was predominantly "those electronic songs supported by the media, the beginning of techno, house music and so." While Vincent attributes his acceptance of electronic music to this early exposure, he was eventually moved to leave the electronic scene behind upon the rediscovery of an Iron Maiden record, a trophy from his childhood years.

Blacklodge circa 2010: Acid Jess, Saint Vincent and Narcotic. Photo courtesy of Saint Vincent.

"When I was a kid, I was hanging out in the forest with two other guys," he recalls. "We were young boy scouts having an adventurous trip in the unknown with small axes, wandering around the camp. It was very exciting and we were telling frightening stories while getting deeper and deeper into the forest. The day was fading and the dusk was turning the silent forest to a scary and weird place. Just before we set off to walk back, we noticed a small wooden house in the middle of a clearing. We were very young, but I was the oldest, and I challenged them to come with me inside the cabin. They were too scared, and me too, but I managed to push the door. I remember very well the fainting sun, getting weaker and weaker. We had to go back, but something inside of me, despite the fear, told me to bring something back from this house, like a symbol of the adventure I was living. There was lots of chaos everywhere there, and my eyes couldn't really see what was in there. My heart was beating hard, so I decided to take one of the first things I could find in the first box close to me on the ground. … It was Iron Maiden's *Killers*. I got fucking scared and then I screamed and started to run. The other kids did the same, screaming, like we found the house of the devil in the middle of the forest. We were cursed. I ran to the camp and kept preciously this vinyl, as a black magic book. Then I put it aside for years.

"When I became a teen, I found it again and listened to it. Then I understood what the curse was that hit me in this cabin, it was the curse of metal. I started to be totally addicted to Iron Maiden, then thrash and death metal progressively, and I was following this aside my interests in black magic. I was not satisfied with the lack of darkness and Satanism in metal music. And one day my best friend came with the album *In The Nightside Eclipse*, and my life took a new turn again and I got totally into black metal."

In 1994 Vincent formed his first band, Faust, a melodic black metal act in the vein of Swedish acts Dissection and Sacramentum. The band lasted for four years but achieved very little due to its various members' other preoccupations: namely alcohol, drugs, and women. In 1998, frustrated at the lack of opportunity to create what he describes as "serious and deep art," Vincent formed Blacklodge, an act that would allow him to rely solely on his own abilities. The following year saw the first Blacklodge recordings in the shape of the eight-song, album-length demo *InnerCells*, and a three-track CD EP entitled *Prince of Dark Cellars*, which also included multimedia material relating to the band. Something of a chaotic and noisy listen, the songs at this time were anything but refined, yet already bore the fast and mechanical percussion that would become the group's hallmark.

"I began to be obsessed by one thing: control," Vincent explains. "And at the same time I had my first PC, so I naturally started to write music on it. And I discovered a very satisfying thing—the control I was searching for. I started to write songs with an electronic basis and the first demo of Blacklodge appeared. I was alone at the beginning, and controlling all—the writing, the recording, the visuals, and so on, all the humans were replaced by the machine. And I liked the different sound of the result. *InnerCells* was recorded on a cheap computer with one gigabyte of hard drive and we quickly stopped using the keyboards, but it shows the will we had to use electronics. Some musicians joined me later on to create a real band and play live, but the spiritual basis of the band comes from here: the Machine controls the human. And we are still slaves of the beat when playing live."

The following year saw the release of the *Login:SataN Demo 2000*, which featured new material, a remix, an Impaled Nazarene cover, and a strange video clip featuring, among other things, a naked Saint Vincent. A two-year hiatus followed, during which the future of the band looked increasingly in doubt, largely as a result of the scorn they were receiving at the time from more conservative elements of the black metal scene.

"I didn't want to write more material," Vincent admits. "Many years had passed without a deal, and with very few live opportunities. We were very unpopular, except for a very few dedicated fans. The demos had been poorly distributed, as many people didn't understand why we were not playing typical black metal, and got quite lost with our sound and approach. Labels and people we were in touch with were very pessimistic about the band's future. People were telling us 'Hey, [you have] some nice tunes but you need to find a drummer.' I would tell them, 'We don't *want* a drummer, that's the spirit of the band, to mix human with machines through black metal,' and then they were kinda like, 'What the fuck?' The most silly reaction I heard was like, 'black metal is about nature and forests, not about cities and machines.' Well, then I knew that I was going to be lonely on this path. That created the spirit of the band, to continue our own way whatever the fuck people can say about us."

Login:SataN was the first release for Netherlands-based Blazing Productions and is, in hindsight, a pretty curious one given that the label is now known for its interest in paganism, "the preservation and celebration of our Indo-European Spirituality and Culture," and its focus on nationalist-related music releases. Far from promoting any sense of virtue, strength, or supremacy, Blacklodge's debut full-length exhibited extremely self-destructive tendencies and a passion for hedonism and debauchery, immediately noticeable thanks to a sponsorship statement from hardcore fetish website Redway.org and even a song named after the site.

More significantly, the album was littered with explicit drug references, songs such as "Need A Needle to Tap the Vein" and "Whiten Your Nose For Satan," dealing with the group's "extreme tragic experiences with hard drugs." The narcotic, industrial, and technological themes were aptly reflected in the cover art, which featured a male shooting up alongside circuit boards and concrete towers, not to mention a new syringe-decorated band logo. The sleeve art also featured a full-page photograph of Vincent wired up in a Los Angeles hospital bed following a heroin overdose.

"During the mid-nineties, while getting high on morbid trips with the black metal new wave, I got naturally interested in more 'dangerous' substances than the usual pot and alcohol. Cemeteries, knives, and extreme art started to get slightly boring. Then we were introduced to various kinds of drugs by a couple of friends, and started a kind of race to experience everything we could. This was a poor period for music, because we were too wasted to have a proper working band, but a fucking great trip where all seemed possible. After years being attracted by Satanism and occult stuff, I had finally the real possibility to do black magic and feel the presence of demons through psychoactive chemistry. The black metal concepts dealing with paganism, or nature, or old Middle Age powers then sounded terribly wrong to me. Satan was not there, he was breathing upon his throne during those evenings of decay and excess. I took some distance then from the typical black metal ideology, and took interest in more modern, contemporary concepts, that led me obviously to electronic music and industrial imagery. Mysticum was by then far more exciting than Emperor, even if I was a huge fan of *In the Nightside Eclipse*. My drug race crashed in summer 1999 where I did a heroin overdose in Los Angeles, after a 'Fear and Loathing in Las Vegas' trip where I was banned from most of the casinos after attacking a sheriff while being very drunk. This traumatizing event clearly then founded the real basis of Blacklodge and led to the second demo and first album *Login:SataN*."

While drugs remain a key part in Vincent's musical and spiritual journey, he is keen to point out that today he remains very much the pilot in his chemical journeys. "Without any doubt Blacklodge's music is 'under the influence' of drugs. But it is certainly not enslaved by drugs, rather it is *revealed*. Drugs don't write the music, but just clean my mind. With time I realized I didn't want to play punk/junk music influenced by wasted states, but I want to play the magic revealed through this Luciferian chemistry and open the gates that they opened to me."

While *Login:SataN* bore promise and set the foundations for the group, it was also the product of a chaotic recording period interrupted by personal problems. It therefore proved a mixed and sometimes unfocused effort, with certain numbers such as "The Empress" sounding particularly rough around the edges. Though the guitars were notably chuggier and the song structures less straightforward, the nature of the opus led to inevitable comparisons—and largely unfavorable ones—with Mysticum.

Login:SataN, 2003. The band's explicitly pro-drug position is evident from the cover art.

"It may sound surprising, but it's not that much of a main influence. I mean, the mixing of drugs, electronics, and black metal doesn't come from them, even if they were the very first to do this. When I heard Mysticum the first time, I thought, 'Fuck, that's great,' but I have to say, the connection with drugs appeared naturally because of the people we were hanging out with, not because we were listening to Mysticum, and, as they said, drugs were/are used by many other black metal artists, but only they spoke openly about it. And for the music, I've been more influenced by Traumatic Voyage, a German band [through whom] I discovered all the possibilities and depth of mixing psychedelic visions, black metal, and being totally free from scenes and so to achieve the purest music vibrating with your own souls.

"At the very beginning, extremely few people accepted our music and our artistic direction," he continues. "That was even more absurd: Mysticum was highly praised and worshipped, and at the same time people considered our musical direction to be totally nonsensical, and that it was highly irritating to speak about drugs. At this time I learned that fans and listeners can be very stupid, and that often it is more important to appear 'true' and 'dedicated' than to really have a balanced opinion. But I didn't care, the most important thing was to make my own thing, and not try to please people or so-called 'true black metallers.' Now, years after, it seems things are moving a bit and more and more bands are mixing electronics and black metal, which is a great thing. So we still feel like pioneers."

That claim would be substantiated by the mind-blowing follow-up album *SolarKult*, released in 2006, an opus that saw the band perfect the vision touched upon in the debut. Where *InnerCells* and *Login:SataN* are often chaotic, oddly produced and in places even seemingly out-of-time, *SolarKult* is breathtakingly precise, focused, and methodical, its pounding

Saint Vincent circa 2003.
Photo: Matthieu Canaguier.

beats, sound effects, live drums, and processed guitars twisting effortlessly around intricate compositions. On top of these sit the emotional and unhinged vocal performance, the most notably human element present in the machine-like odes. The result is a work that bridged the gap between the colder, more calculated sounds that came from the Moonfog label around the turn of the millennium and the possessed fury of bands like Mysticum. *SolarKult* also marked a conceptual evolution, moving away from the hedonism of the first album with notably more thoughtful lyrics that delved into more esoteric philosophical concerns.

"But at the same time, it's the same," counters Vincent. "Philosophically alchemical, like lead turning into gold, hard drugs turning into revelations, it's the same thing. The process of the band is clearly alchemical—alchemy links infernal matter, metals, and earthly things, with spiritual and higher conceptions and meaning. We do the same, pointing at the demonic forces. Religiously speaking I'm more alone, on my side, in my corner, watching and trying to understand the insane process that we are going through. I'm celebrating the downfall of humanity through technological apocalypse, because it's the greatest of all art being accomplished."

Vincent's heavily conceptual journey would continue in 2010 with *T/ME*, an opus released simultaneously with *Time Is the Sulphur in the Veins of the Saint...* by Austrian black metallers Abigor, the two albums made available separately on CD and released together on vinyl. Both were based around conceptions of time in relation to Satanism, though Blacklodge also explored wider subject matter, drawing upon the fascinating religious visions of nineteenth-century doctor and theosophist Anna Kingsford while painting from a wide musical and lyrical palette that directly referenced compositions by artists such Celtic Frost, Bach, and Nick Cave. The result was an album that saw the band relinquishing the precise and angular approach of *SolarKult* to explore a more despairing and psychedelic direction.

"It's surprising," Vincent ponders. "If time is the concept it should have been more ordered, more angular. But no, because this album, as downfall, is putting forward the human reaction to facing the angular pressure of time, which results in anguish, despair, and panic, which makes the music and the sound paradoxically more chaotic. The album is kind of a deception from previous illumination. *SolarKult* had the power of a clear vision, strength and clarity, and this one is falling into the chaos of doubt, despair, and uncertainty. *SolarKult* is like taking acid, but revelatory, a prophetic trip and *T/ME* is the bad trip flashback. The first album/level [was] the chamber of darkness, then in the extreme depths of darkness, the void, the Light of Truth appears—this is the SolarKult, the Chamber of Illumination. The next step is incarnation, for infinity falls into matter and limits, ruled by time."

Two years later the band would return with *MachinatioN*, an album that revisited the more ordered assault found on *SolarKult*, Vincent explaining that this was largely due to Blacklodge and Abigor agreeing to experiment more on their joint release, hence *T/ME*'s sidestep in direction. As intense and unrelenting as the band's second album, *MachinatioN* boasts similarly in-depth thematic content "This one is the Chamber of Control. This unveils the infernal process Satan put in shape to enslave humanity and establish the last ultimate empire on Earth ruled by him. A machination fueled by his trident, the three prongs of Satan: Medusa, the void of destruction and dissolution, swallowing souls and crumbling the deeds of men. Caesar, the claws of oppression compressing and ordering the men into systems that have more importance than the man's life itself. And the prong of Lucifer, revealing forbidden knowledge to daring wills, infusing the fire of rebellious visions to humanity. Those three prongs are three sides of modern Satanism, preparing the ultimate reign of the beast on Earth. Each song is related to one of the prongs."

Clearly going several thousand steps beyond the recycled hedonist and science fiction musings of so many industrially tinged metal bands, the thematic and lyrical content behind Blacklodge remains engaging and unique, perfectly complementing the musical vision and Vincent's own spiritual and philosophical explorations, which point to a pretty apocalyptic conclusion.

"[The way I see it] technology is neutral," he concludes. "I think there's more an evil root in the spiritual world incarnating down here through technology and fighting against the human core. Satan is the agent of incarnation, the guide from ideological, symbolical sphere into vile, corrupted, limited flesh. But technology itself is like an axe; you can cut a tree or kill people, it's not [inherently] evil. For me the solar kult is the religious/technological end, as for me the goal of humans is to master God's power, and that is symbolized by the sun, as the eye of Lucifer, shining with splendor as a calculated revenge unto God. So, the goal of all humans is to master nuclear power as the most powerful technological trophy and this race to power can just end in a global nuclear conflict. It sounds kinda old-fashioned and 'cold war' to say that, but I still believe as a real event to come. This is the solar kult, the worship of God's power, the ultimate fire, as worshipped by the Incas, and now all nations."

49
LIFELOVER
POST-BLACK METAL
PART I

GIVEN THE MYRIAD STYLES black metal explored in the nineties, it was perhaps inevitable that the bands that followed would go one step further and take core elements as their foundation while nonetheless moving into entirely new genres. If the years that preceded had seen acts going as far as they could from the core black metal sound while holding firmly onto the Satanic/occult/misanthropic ethos, now bands would rethink even that, taking elements of black metal's form but rebuilding them in an entirely new emotional, ideological, or spiritual direction. In a sense, it is less a change of form than of context. An early example is Solefald's *Neonism* as a contrast to Arcturus' *La Masquerade Infernale*; while both strayed from conventional black metal music considerably, it was Solefald who made a more obvious leap in terms of theme and aesthetic.

By the mid-2000s this phenomenon was surfacing with increasing regularity, Sweden's Lifelover being one such fascinating act. Spewed into existence in 2005, their conflicted relationship with the black metal scene located them comfortably within the "post-black metal" label. Like Solefald and Shining they bore a heavy urban overtone, and where other post-black bands such as Amesoeurs, Alcest, and Fen have tended to lean toward the romantic, pastoral, and uplifting, despite an inherent sense of melancholy, Lifelover's approach was as cynical as their name, their outlook unrelentingly bleak, urban, and fragmented. With elements of pop, shoegaze, depressive rock, and new wave, their sound was in many respects gloriously contradictory, but the black metal elements that swam within this strange brew are far less surprising when one considers the musical heritage of the band's founders.

Begun as a duo, the band was originally comprised of "B" (born Jonas Bergqvist, and otherwise known as Nattdal of orthodox black metal bands Ondskapt, Dimhymn, and IXXI) and the even more awkwardly named "( )", also known as Kim Carlsson of depressive black metal acts Hypothermia, Kyla, and Life is Pain. Speaking in 2010 to B—who sadly passed away the following year—it quickly became apparent that Lifelover's inception was just as chaotic as their music, born out of desperation and destructive actions.

"Lifelover was formed one morning in June 2005," he explained. "Me and ( ) had been awake for a pretty long time, drinking, and cutting ourselves, and the whole house we were in was full of vomit and blood. ( ) had laid some additional vocals for my black metal band Dimhymn for the recording of [second album] *Djävulens Tid Är Kommen*. For some reason the day after the 'blood massacre'— the first time we had ever met— we decided to sit down and play

Pulver, 2006.

some guitar together and just improvise with a lot of delay on it. We thought it sounded cool, demented, and urban, so we recorded the demo *Promo 2005* right there. Regarding the band's name, I had once been called a 'Lifelover' back in 2004 in an e-mail by a fucker that did not even know me, and he sent the same e-mail to a lot of people and labels. So we both thought it could be a fun thing to call the recording Lifelover."

"When me and B met for the first time, we took a ride into the countryside to record some music," recalled ( ) of the group's inception in a phone interview I conducted for *Metal Hammer* in 2011. "The first thing that happened was that we cut ourselves up. Then we took a walk in the woods until we were empty—you can probably imagine, the combination of blood loss and drinking alcohol, it makes you get into a bit of a different atmosphere. We began to make music and started turning the house we were in into something resembling a slaughterhouse, the walls being entirely covered in blood, each piece of furniture, each instrument, everything. In the end there was more blood than anything else and we were in a haze, but we simply felt we had to do something, so we started to play guitar together and that's when we recorded the first two songs that became Lifelover."

Sprawling and improvised, the band's promo would not prove reflective of the direction the band were ultimately to take, and it was not until the following year that the duo began to write new songs, in doing so forging the unique sound they are known for now. Expanding to a four-piece the group now saw B handling guitar, vocals and piano, ( ) responsible for lead vocals, with LR (Rickard Öström) providing lyrics for two songs and 1853 (Johan Gabrielson) contributing extra vocals and lyrics. Together the group worked to create their debut full-length, released in 2006 as *Pulver*, Swedish for "powder." With material written largely on an individual basis, the songwriting was dominated by B, with ( ), LR, and 1853 also contributing.

"The new sound really started when me and ( ) recorded the [*Pulver*] songs 'Nackskott' and 'Stockholm' together," B explained. "We both felt a big satisfaction with these songs, and when I continued to write I followed that direction but also found new directions at the same time, so the process of writing *Pulver* was very exciting indeed, and a new way of writing music for me. We recorded the songs over a period of two months and as you may hear, we did not lay much effort in making it a perfect record regarding the production. It was recorded during alcohol and drug abuse… ( ) recorded the vocals lying on the floor bleeding. It was two strange/sick months."

Strange and sick indeed: constructed in an often jarring cut-and-paste manner vaguely similar to that of Japan's Sigh, *Pulver*'s songs hinged on idiosyncratic juxtaposition, with strangely high energy passages and almost ska-like rhythms sitting alongside bleak and torturous sections, the programmed drums complimented by an array of often baffling samples. The resulting combination proved as striking and unusual as the photographs of the blood-soaked nude adorning the sleeve artwork, combining the founding member's black metal background with a clear influence from the likes of Joy Division and even The Cure.

"Dynamics is everything in music," considered ( ). "For us it's very easy to write something slow, cold, and bleak, but we want a challenge when we write music, and it's more interesting to write something different. I have no idea if it sounds happy, or strange, or crazy, or fucked up to people listening—just as long as the end result of the album is good, I'm satisfied. [The] samples we mostly pick from Swedish TV shows and old movies, things that we watched growing up. I don't really remember how the idea came up, but we did find that it made everything sound more demented and sick. We never reveal exactly what each sample comes from, we want people to wonder and try to find out for themselves, and to reveal such details destroys some of the mystic feeling they create.

"Regarding [influences] there are many bands that have given me that spark," B stated, "but it's really hard to name some of them, I don't know which to choose since I always have listened to so much different genres. I would not call us black metal, but of course both me and ( ) come from a black metal background, so it's not strange that we have elements of black metal in our sound."

Making the most of a highly productive inter-band chemistry, Lifelover quickly followed up *Pulver* with a superb album entitled *Erotik*, released in 2007. Despite still sounding like it could all fall apart at any moment, *Erotik* was nonetheless a notably more rounded and complete album, retaining the fragmented, pulsing sound but striking home with more emotive, even *harrowing*, compositions. This time the band were joined by guitarist H. ("Henrik"), with LR contributing some vocals as well as lyrics.

"With *Erotik* we in some way wanted to reflect the life and urban environments of

Stockholm," B explains. "We definitely wanted to do something different from *Pulver*, but still have some of that element left. We wanted it to have a 'narcotic' feel to it as well, and release all the madness inside of us. The sound became much darker in many ways."

Thematically the album proved almost painfully honest, giving an insight into the heart of the beast with an abundance of bleak urban booklet imagery and English-language songs— often with clean-sung vocals— painting a picture of depression and substance abuse. With the Swedish song titles translating to "A Man in the Worst Days of His Life," "The Road of Death," "Welcome to Powder City," and "Autumn Depressions," to name a few, it was certainly no walk in

Lifelover's brief deviation from the drum machine led to addition of Non into the ranks, the drummer appearing on 2009's *Dekadens* EP.

the park for either the listener or the creative forces within the band.

"It's quite simple; the lyrics reflect our lives and our lives consist mostly of a great amount of agony and angst," admits B. "And to reduce our angst we take those drugs necessary. And that's mostly it, but we have also touched subjects like love—or broken/lost love to be exact—hatred for mankind and suicidal thoughts. We also write about urban surroundings and miserable city life. It's not exactly positive lyrics but they probably are more honest than most bands out there. Lifelover totally reflects me as a person; when you have heard all of the music we have done and read all the lyrics, you know a bit of me, in one sense you can get to know me in that way. I think it's the same with the other guys as well to some extent."

In that sense Lifelover reflected an almost schizophrenic character, with upbeat, seemingly joyous passages sitting alongside moments of abject misery. It is these "happy" parts that feel most out of place within a black metal context but unlike, for example, Alcest, even the most cheerful of passages tend to drip with a hyperactive and manic, Prozac-fueled atmosphere.

"You can't honestly say that life is just misery all the way through," explained B of the

The Lifelover collective in 2011: H, Fix, ( ), 1853, B, Kral and LR.
Photo courtesy of Prophecy Productions.

choice to include these (seemingly) positive emotions in the music. "For some people it might be, but we reflect all feelings in our lives—even if I mostly feel like shit, my life has its bright moments as well. And I think that is the case with most people feeling down.

"We have never recorded anything sober, nor played live sober either for that sake, and I have written almost all the music and lyrics to Lifelover while being on different opioids or benzodiazepines. Thus I am an addict—they give me inspiration—it's tragic but what to do? Personally I take benzodiazepines (mostly clonazepam and diazepam) daily to survive my severe fucking agony and I used to take opioids daily as well, but I am through with taking them on a daily basis. I am diagnosed with 'generalized anxiety disorder' and have several different medications. On top of that I also do drugs like amphetamine, cannabis, and opioids now and then… but I do it only to be able to do anything at all. Otherwise I would be lying in bed all day, feeling like shit. I guess my life doesn't fit in the picture of the life of the ordinary Joe but I live as 'happily' as I possibly can and create music.

"I know the other guitarist H. and our bassist Fix is doing cocaine from time to time, they are also smoking cannabis daily as well as 1853 and LR and drummer Non. He is also stuck on benzodiazepines right now. ( ) is also smoking sometimes, but he is kind of an expert on beer, so I think alcohol is his kind of drug, but I know he enjoys pills and other stuff as well, all members do. Everything is a mirror of our lives."

It was a point that ( ) confirmed with me during our *Metal Hammer* interview in 2011. "I can't recall any song that we have recorded without being under the influence," admits ( ). "I am usually drunk, high, hungover or all of the above when I record my vocals and most of the others have their prescriptions. B as well, he makes most of the music, sitting in his haze with his guitar. None of us ever has an easy time, currently two of us are homeless and we have many people close to us being in bad situations, people in hospitals, people killing themselves, people trying to kill themselves. It's hard getting work here, it's hard getting apartments. I'm sure there are similar problems in your country but people from different countries deal with things in different ways."

The general themes of self-destruction were complemented in a more literal sense by the extreme self-mutilation of ( ), whose extensively scarred body is evident in sleeve art and promo shots. "I don't think we have written any lyrics that directly have reflected self-injury regarding cutting," explained B. "But of course most of the lyrics are rather self-destructive in a subliminal way. And what is self-harm really? Isn't a daily use of drugs pretty self-destructive? But for the cutting, yes it's merely ( ) who encourages this. I think every person in Lifelover at some point in their lives has cut themselves but except for in ( )'s case that lies behind us now."

The band's third album *Konkurs* (Swedish for "bankruptcy" or "insolvency") was issued in 2008, this time on Avantgarde Records. Now written and recorded as a five-piece without the contributions of LR, the album went for a more flowing sound, with mournfulness replacing the predecessor's jumpiness to a large degree. This reflected the long time spent writing and recording the record, and the aim of making a more dark, depressive, and professional album "with no happy parts," to quote B. Once again translated song titles support this claim, a few choice examples being "Time of Cancer," "My Hospital Wing," and "The Nail in the Coffin."

2009 would be the first year without an album for the band for three years, but was notable nonetheless, with mini-album *Dekadens* released on Osmose Records, who also set about re-releasing the band's first two albums, reflecting the growing fan base. A undeniably strong effort, *Dekadens* was dominated by B's writing and proved the band's most organic effort, even featuring live drummer Non ("Joel"). Having featured a previous drummer called S in live shows, the band's recorded material was now underpinned by live percussion for the first time, a move that heavily impacted the tone of the group.

The addition would be short-lived, however, and the band's final album, the fourteen-track *Sjukdom* (meaning "illness," "sickness," or "disease"), released in 2011, saw a return to programmed percussion. A somewhat divisive release, it polarized reviewers thanks to its often unforgiving and impenetrable nature, particularly at the start of the record. Now featuring a lineup stripped down to ( ), B, LR, and 1853, it also saw guest appearances by Gok and

P.G. of Swedish black metallers Ancient Death. Once again B wrote the lion's share of the music, though the lyrics were contributed by all members involved. The paraphernalia that accompanied the limited-edition version of the album (including a syringe and razorblade) proved the band had not strayed too far thematically, once again conveying a bleak and urban image of depression, alienation, and drug dependency.

The album would be the band's last, as on September 9, 2011, Jonas "B" Bergqvist sadly passed away. The remaining members of the band soon confirmed rumors of his death with a statement that explained: "On Friday morning, September 9th, B didn't wake up from his sleep. He didn't take his own life nor was he victim of any apparent action. The authorities in charge are still examining his body to find the exact cause of death... We, the remaining members of Lifelover have decided to lay the band to rest. This would be the only right thing to do considering B was the main composer of Lifelover."

Given the bleak tapestry the band drew upon, as well as the self-destructive lifestyles of its members, a death within the group was perhaps not entirely surprising. But as it turns out, B's death was, it seems, not self-inflicted or the result of any illegal substances. In fact, tragically, it seems to have stemmed from prescribed medication for the very anxiety disorder he had discussed in our interview. A family statement explained that the autopsy had shown an unknown poisoning and overdose and that B had been taking benzodiazepine since he was eighteen, increasing the medication as his body became used to each dose.

B's life was clearly a troubled one, but it's perhaps worth remembering that a surprising positivity surfaced in both Lifelover's music and B's own words and communications (he was one of the more enthusiastic of those involved with this book, for example), with Lifelover's many achievements (five essential releases in as many years, more than most bands achieve in decades of existence) providing obvious satisfaction.

"Our fan base is very diverse," he pondered. "We see as many black metal fans as we see 'normal' rock/pop fans... well, you name it, we see them all and that is a great pleasure to us. I see it as a sign that our music is so complex it appeals to so many different people. But yes, we have a lot of black metal fans, and that feels strange sometimes, but hey, to be honest, I don't care who listens to us—as long as our music depraves as many as possible, we are satisfied."

Always more than happy to polarize, Lifelover won over an impressive fan base, including both fans and critics within the black metal scene. Their legacy is a body of work that exhibits a wide emotional gamut rare in extreme metal. "There are a lot of [critics] out there," concluded B, "but I mostly just laugh against their ignorant Internet attacks. But we want to offend people too, not just 'charm' them. We have become that band that people love or hate, and I personally think that is great. If one looks back a bit in music history it is those bands that have become big and famous. But our goal is rather to become *infamous*!"

Mission accomplished, no doubt. Rest in peace B, and rest in peace Lifelover.

50
POST-BLACK METAL
PART II

BY ITS VERY NATURE, the term 'post-black metal' is a loose one—in fact, the term was first thrown around during black metal's experimental peak in the late nineties. In more recent years however, post-black metal has come to have a more specific meaning, one that embodies the ideological/aesthetic shifts mentioned in the last chapter as well as a particular sound, which tends to integrate musical forms and emotions that are (at first glance at least) seemingly incompatible with black metal's caustic spirit. Most notably, such music has made use of the introspection and emotional vulnerability found in post-punk, post-rock, and shoegaze, the latter resulting in the somewhat awkward term "blackgaze."

While Fleurety's debut album might have established the style, a major catalyst for the sub-genre was France's Amesoeurs, an outfit formed by two vocalists and multi-instrumentalists, namely Stéphane "Neige" Paut (then of radical French black metal act Peste Noir and Mortifera, an outfit formed by Noktu of Celestia) and Audrey Sylvain, a musician and dancer who would later join Peste Noir. Describing their efforts as a "kaleidoscopic soundtrack for the modern era," the group offered a mesmerizing blend of black metal, post-punk, and goth music, drawing influence from such diverse bands as Burzum, The Cure, Depeche Mode, Sonic Youth, Katatonia, New Order, and Joy Division, the latter having the biggest impact on the group's sound according to Neige. Bearing a melancholic beauty, the songs used piano, sparse gothic overtones, female vocals, and acoustic guitars alongside an occasional wall of black metal dissonance. While Amesoeurs left behind the Satanic and nationalist subject matter of Peste Noire, they nonetheless retained an overt sense of alienation from modern society, an element arguably fairly intrinsic to black metal. Explicitly urban, the band's releases (2006's *Ruines Humaines* EP, a 2007 split EP and the self-titled 2009 album) were both a celebration of city life as well as a clear rejection of it, the songs blending fascination with repulsion.

Though the band split after their first and only full-length, Neige would continue to follow a similar path musically with Alcest, which actually began life as a raw black metal solo project in 2000. Releasing a single demo, *Tristesse Hivernale* ("Winter Sadness") in 2001, Alcest took a hiatus before returning in 2005, reinventing itself in a fairly dramatically manner with the *Le Secret* EP, following this up two years later with debut album *Souvenirs d'un Autre Monde*

("Memories of Another World"). With Neige very much the central figure, the group (which has featured several members of both Peste Noir and Amesoeurs over the years) moved even further away from black metal (and even depressive rock) with *Souvenirs*, creating instead overwhelmingly uplifting and ethereal music dominated by clean vocals and equally clean guitars. Later releases such as the 2010 album *Écailles de Lune* ("Moonscales") and its follow-up *Les voyages de l'âme* ("The Journeys of the Soul") would see Neige returning to his roots somewhat, integrating fragments of black metal into the formula, this surfacing periodically in the guitar work and the occasional screamed vocals. Unsurprisingly, given their sound, Alcest have long found themselves labeled shoegaze/blackgaze, though as Neige explained to me in *Metal Hammer* in 2010, this actually came as something of a surprise to the band.

"At the *Le Secret/Souvenirs* period my musical inspirations were Yann Tiersen [a French musician whose work famously made up much of the soundtrack to the film *Amélie*], Ataraxia [an Italian neo-classical act], and Burzum, and for *Écailles De Lune* it was the fantastic and so underrated British post-punk band The Chameleons... As I said a lot of times in previous interviews, Alcest music never had any link with shoegaze for the simple reason that I discovered this style of music after having composed *Souvenirs*. Now I am listening to it a lot, it's great, especially bands like Slowdive, Pale Saints, Ride, etc."

While Amesoeurs' lyrics were bleak and drew heavily on exterior influences, Alcest's have, in contrast, been drawn exclusively from the intensely personal memories and inner reality of its central protagonist. In fact, the title of the first album is something of a key to the entire project, namely Neige's own childhood, in which he reportedly experienced overwhelming visions that he believes may have been of another reality.

"My aim with Alcest is to depict a dimension I used to see in visions when I was a child," he explained to me in our *Metal Hammer* interview. "It was like flashes, exactly like if you were reminding a nice moment of your life, with all the precise emotions you could feel with it but in my case these memories had nothing to do with what I was seeing around me in the real world. And this place was so indescribably beautiful and perfect, like an immense heavenly garden with pearly shiny streams and emerald green fields all around. Nobody can imagine the beauty and the serenity of it. Everything being static and moving at the same time, like water waves, all bathed in pearly colors and lived by kind of benevolent spirits. It was very strong, real, and had nothing to do with what we can see here, that's why I know it was not just my imagination. Well after a lot of research I guessed that it was memories of what could be 'afterlife' like you say, or 'before life' in my case because I've noticed that they are very similar elements with what describe people that had a near-death experience. It could be a place where the soul would rest between two earthly incarnations, a kind of peaceful haven of pure light and serenity. When I say 'memories from another world' this has to be taken literally."

While Neige maintains clear links to the black metal scene due to his membership in long-running Norwegian act Forgotten Woods (as well as working on a more explicitly post-rock/shoegaze project Old Silver Key with members of Drudkh), he has always been quick to highlight the overtly positive nature of Alcest. If Amesoeurs presented an emotional range and aesthetic apparently out of kilter with black metal, Alcest has marked an even greater leap, with both the emotional disparity and musical ingredients a point of departure, a point that Neige is very conscious of.

"I never consciously included happy parts in my music," Neige explained to me in the aforementioned articles, "they are here because I tried to make a musical interpretation of this otherworldly realm I was seeing as a child. And this realm was so beautiful and serene, I remember having an ecstatic feeling there, a feeling of pure and perfect joy. That's what I tried to reproduce in some passages of

**Urban alienation: The short-lived Amesoeurs.
Photo courtesy of Code666.**

my music… when I had a lot of projects, these were a way to express feelings that were out of the Alcest purpose. It allowed me to keep Alcest away from disturbing feelings… A lot of people don't like… the fact Alcest is very positive and luminous. This is a critic [*sic*] I totally understand. I am conscious that Alcest is very special in this way and that its 'positive' emotions can't be appreciated by everyone."

While they have certainly remained closer to the modern black metal template than both Amesoeurs and Alcest, England's Fen are another act whose work falls fairly undeniably under the post-black umbrella. Formed by Frank "The Watcher" Allain (vocals, guitar, keyboards) and his brother Adam ("Grungyn"), both of whom played—along with original drummer Daniel "Theutus" Spender—in black metal bands Antigone and Skaldic Curse, Fen have taken much of their inspiration from the territory in which the Allains spent their youth. Though a literal reference to the physical characteristics and bleak atmosphere of the marshy fenlands of eastern England, the significance of the name goes somewhat deeper, and like

Alcest, Fen draws heavily upon the youthful memories of its primary songwriter.

"We utilize landscape primarily as a metaphor," explains Frank. "Of course, there is a face-value element to this and much of the imagery described can be taken as read. Nonetheless, there is a deeper meaning to this—the external reflecting the internal—which has to be acknowledged. Heritage and the preservation of nature is important to me but every experience I undergo, every thought I have, is channeled through the prism of my own mind. It would be a fallacy to attempt to write objectively and as—for me—music is a very personal expression, this must also take shape within the lyrics as well. The name Fen refers to the area and landscape in which I grew up, but it also represents a mindset in which I felt trapped during this period. Bleak, desolate, solitary, and isolating."

Forming in 2006, the band released the *Ancient Sorrow* EP on Northern Silence Productions the following year, before signing to Italian label Code 666 and releasing their debut album *The Malediction Fields* in 2009. The album showcased a sound that balanced a significant black metal core with prog, shoegaze, folk and post-rock influences, the all-encompassing wall of dissonant, layered guitars, screamed vocals, and synth engulfing the listener before drawing back to allow the acoustic guitars to weave serene, even uplifting, textures.

"First and foremost, it is the originators of the second wave of black metal that are the main driving force behind my musical inspiration," states Frank. "The Scandinavian originators such as Ulver, Enslaved, Emperor and Dissection managed to invoke something at once otherworldly and evocative, yet simultaneously rooted within earthly landscapes… From outside the 'metal' spectrum, I personally draw a wide range of influences and guitar-led bands such as Slowdive, The Chameleons, Fields of the Nephilim, Sad Lovers and Giants, Sigur Rós, The Verve (first album and EP only) and My Bloody Valentine are just as important as the aforementioned black metal acts. Post-rock plays a part—Mono, Explosions in the Sky, Mogwai—as well as bands that essentially defy categorization like Godspeed You! Black Emperor and the mighty Swans. Neofolk and dark ambient are also relevant—Death in June, Sol Invictus, Of the Wand and Moon, Tenhi, Lustmord, Triari… some of the more ambient/less 'dancified' elements of the electronica spectrum resonate also. Boards of Canada, The Black Dog, Beaumont Hannant, B12 and others are all effective at weaving captivating atmospheres."

Atmosphere is an area in which Fen excel, the band continuing to utilize a sense of contrast within their compositions on 2011's *Epoch* album and 2013's *Dustwalker* (as well as *Towards the Shores of the End*, a split with like-minded project De Arma), running an emotional gamut that touches upon anger, frustration, and sadness, and at times even joy or hope. With an expansive yet introspective sound that explores both soil and soul, they share a certain resonance with acts such as Altar of Plagues, Negură Bunget, Agalloch, Drudkh, and Wolves in the Throne Room. Interestingly, while Fen retain a clear link to their black metal heritage, they do not shy away from the post-black label, even arguing its value as an extension of the movement that birthed them.

"I'd argue that the emotions and ideologies of the majority of the second wave are

**Alcest, with drummer Winterhalter pictured on the left and Neige on the right. Photo courtesy of
Prophecy Productions.**

simply being continued by the post-black metal movement," considers Frank. "Some of the
more obvious emotional outpourings are a little distanced from this but, by and large, a sense
of landscape, of poetry, of detachment from the herd and an empathy with something less
material and more spiritual is always there. In this, there is a direct kinship between bands
such as Ulver and Fleurety and the more recent bands. I'd argue the differences are slight. I
guess Satanism is the big differentiator but even the more Satanic second-wave bands only
ever really flirted with such concepts. Post-black metal for me identifies a sound and an outlook rooted in the second wave but divorced from some of the more cartoonish aspects of
traditional black metal.

"Is it perhaps that post-black metal is really a more acceptable synonym for 'grown-up
black metal,' pretentious as it sounds to dare voice that?" he continues. "Why not? Black
metal has always been pretentious and given that the members of the majority of the acts
thus far referenced are well into their thirties, who can honestly express surprise at such
thinking? A man in his mid-thirties with a wife, children, and stable job may feel deep unease
at screaming about Satan and bedecking himself in spikes, particularly if he does not 'feel' it.
We always talk of sincerity in music—perhaps post-black metal, for all the accusations of
'hipsterism' is in fact one of the most honest expressions of all?"

It's an interesting and undoubtedly divisive position, but it does raise an intriguing question—to what extent is Satanic ideology and a "traditional" aesthetic still a defining characteristic of black metal for its practitioners and followers? Obviously many will say— and have said in this very book—that these are essential, yet for some protagonists it clearly is not. Ultimately it's up to the reader, though it would seem odd to say that the post-prison Burzum metal albums, for example, weren't black metal. Or much of Mayhem's output. Or Thorns. Or Drudkh. Whatever perspective one takes, Fen are one act who highlight this transition and expansion of the genre.

"I personally am keen to ensure that there are no sonic limitations on what Fen is willing to incorporate from within black metal," Frank concludes. "The core aggression, the rolling sense of furious momentum, this is something that—as it currently stands—has to remain. Sonically, we will dip our toes in whichever soundscape is appropriate for the feeling we are trying to convey, though it must be said that some of the thrashier, deathier elements of the black metal spectrum are not really appropriate for us. What do we leave behind? Silliness, narrow-minded posturing, gang mentality, absurd rhetoric and taking pride in dedication to living life like a raging, disaffected teenager. I can see why some people revel in embracing the chaos but this is not for us… It's maybe an ideological thing more than anything else— Wolves in the Throne Room, sonically speaking, essentially sound like *Nightside*-era Emperor minus keyboards and with this in mind, the differences become even less pronounced. Is ideology *that* important? That is for the listener to decide."

Frank's mention of Wolves in the Throne Room is apt, since this American act are another band who feature a similar displacement of traditional ideological and cultural values but nonetheless retain the sound and spirit of the more transcendental end of the second wave. The band was formed in 2003 by Aaron Weaver (drums and synth) and Nathan Weaver (guitars and vocals), two brothers who grew up in the ecology-conscious DIY punk scene in Olympia in the American northwest, an area containing some of the last bastions of untouched nature and forest. Indeed the two actually formed the outfit at an "Earth First" gathering and Wolves' own eco-spiritual vision remains very much a lifestyle choice for the brothers, who both live and work on their own organic farm deep in the countryside. While their background was undoubtedly left-wing, the band itself is an apolitical entity, and actually taps into the same rejection of the modern world, reverence for nature, and spiritual overtones that characterized three of the band's biggest influences—Burzum, Emperor, and Ulver.

"I really hate to put ourselves in the category of left-wing actually 'cos that's not how we perceive ourselves at all," Aaron told me in a 2008 interview for *Metal Hammer*. "I don't think politics are an appropriate way to deal with the world's problems, or one's community. It's a lot more effective to define what your values are. I would say we value the earth, a simple 'country' lifestyle, we think that should be allowed to continue. I feel explicitly against racism, against fascism. I think that ideology comes from a place of fear and a fear of change, a place of hate and bitterness and these are negative emotions that one should overcome. I also think we're against modern civilization and the modern scientific-reductionist worldview."

"We always question the concept of civilization," Aaron also told me in a 2009 *Terrorizer* interview. "We look around and wonder if something went horribly wrong, maybe around four hundred years ago when the world began to change so rapidly, at the birth of modernity. There are perfectly fine things about the modern world, the modern way of looking at things, the scientific and mechanical way of understanding the universe. But I think it's also spiritually shallow, that's a big problem the human race needs to deal with."

Given such perspectives one might expect the band to incorporate folk overtones into their sound as many of their like-minded peers have, yet the ferocious wall of sound

**UK post black-metal outfit Fen, pictured in late 2012.
Photo: Tom Huskinson.**

on their first two albums—*Diadem of 12 Stars* (2006) and *Two Hunters* (2007)—proved to audiences that the Ulver influence was definitely secondary to that of Burzum. Varg Vikernes has long decried the modern world of course, and as Aaron explained to me in the aforementioned *Metal Hammer* interview, though Varg himself may not be seen as a particularly like-minded protagonist, within his records lies an expression the band can relate to wholeheartedly, what he described as a "cry for the utter destruction of the modern world, for wiping it out of your mind and wiping it off the face of the earth and replacing it with something ancient, simple and more primal." For Wolves the negativity and darkness of black metal is therefore not merely a means to an end, but a starting point for something broader.

"What I've always taken from occult study and spiritual practice is that one should attempt to transcend misery, hatred, and bitterness, the feelings black metal expresses so effectively and so purely," he explained. "That utter void, that hopeless morass of boundless sadness found in Burzum is something to be experienced and explored as the beginning of a path to transcendence and spiritual growth. I think it's really wrong to look at that as the end of a spiritual journey. I'm not trying to judge anyone—I have a lot of friends who are deeply

The forest whispers my name: Wolves In The Throne Room in their natural setting.

into left-hand-path magick and Satanic occult spiritual practice and I think it makes a lot of sense to them, it works for someone who wants to be alone, a hermit. But not for someone like me, who wants to build a life that reflects a spiritual set of values, things that I think are real and true."

Practicalities remain a focus for Wolves—as they once asked on their website, how does one go about raising Satanic children? What does a Satanic farm look like? Yet while they may not embrace the Satanic roots of the movement, by actually living off the land in relative isolation the group do take many of black metal's values to their logical conclusion, perhaps more so than those bands who claim to despise modern civilization and worship nature, then choose to live and work in a bustling metropolis.

Musically the group have continued to stay close to the Nordic black sound, and while 2009's *Malevolent Grain* EP saw the band showcasing a sound with more obvious post-black tendencies, the same year also saw the release of the *Black Cascade* album, perhaps their most single-minded release to date, with 2011 follow-up *Celestial Lineage* also maintaining the meditative ambient passages as well as clearly identifiable Burzum/Ulver traits. Like Fen, the band choose to deviate significantly from the traditional face of the genre, while holding onto what they consider its essential traits.

"Black metal is about a lot of things, on the surface it's very much about nihilism, despair, Satanism, left-hand path magic and all this sort of thing," Aaron told me in *Metal Hammer*, "but we were interested in something a little bit deeper in the music, which was an uncompromising call to destroy the modern world. We saw black metal as a cleansing fire, something to destroy everything you believe and that people have told you, something that would allow you to really gaze inwards and find some deeper, more ancient sense of truth.

AFTERWORD

THOUGH THE FINAL CHAPTERS of this book have sought to illustrate the concept of "post-black metal," it's extremely important to keep in mind that in the bigger picture there really is no post-black metal, no after the event, no building from the ashes, as much as some might wish to believe otherwise. There's no denying that black metal has always continued to evolve and take new shapes—that's a large part of what this book has been about after all. Thrash and death metal, as exciting as those genres can be, are now at a point where genuinely original acts have been a rarity for almost two decades, yet black metal's boundaries have continually expanded as new acts appear—who, after all, could have predicted the sound of bands such as Negură Bunget or Deathspell Omega back in the early nineties?

It would, however, be misguided to suggest that the history of black metal is some sort of linear timeline tending toward improvement. As reactionary as it might sound, it's also true that in recent times black metal has been appropriated by those who have little connection with its roots. Consequently, there are attempts to present black metal as having reinvented itself or transcended its beginnings, improving on what came before and leaving behind the efforts of the early pioneers. One example has been the attempt by some writers and musicians to present both post-black metal and the entire burgeoning USBM scene—which exploded in the mid-2000s after some years of relative silence, barring the efforts of bands such as VON, Profanatica, Demoncy, and Absu—as some sort of new beginning for the movement, or as the embodiment of the genre's most extreme, forward-thinking, or artistically relevant face.

Clearly this is nonsense. Ultimately, black metal is, and has always been, as much about revitalizing old inspirations as it is about innovation. While this book has tended to focus on the most influential or pioneering artists in order to track the development of both the music and culture (as well as the human stories behind it), there continue to appear equally worthy bands who instead tap into specific areas of the genre's past. Be it the South American legions who draw upon the first wave of the genre and breathe life into it, or the huge number of bands still creating masterpieces from the second-wave template (Behexen, Taake, Arckanum, the list goes on and on), the most memorable and well-crafted works have often been those working with familiar forms. Indeed, even in Norway, a territory now famous for its progressive undercurrents, a new underground has surfaced in the shape of the so-called Nidrosian black metal scene, with bands such Vemod and One Tail, One Head keeping the black flame of an earlier generation alive.

Black metal will surely continue to innovate and evolve, and this should be celebrated, but it should also be remembered that many of the most powerful efforts have come from bands utilizing conventional black metal frameworks and traditional ideologies, and this will likely continue, even if the spikes, Satanism, misanthropy, and other trappings are a barrier for some listeners outside the genre. And as fascinating and enjoyable as the last decade or so has been, have any bands really surpassed Emperor's *In the Nightside Eclipse*, Mayhem's *De Mysteriis Dom Sathanas*, or Burzum's *Filosofem*? Or, for that matter, *Welcome to Hell*?

ACKNOWLEDGEMENTS

Written between 2009 and 2013 in various parts of Norway, Brazil, Turkey and England.

Special thanks to Ester Segarra and to Adrian, Trisha, and Ian Hunt for their hospitality and for providing spaces where large portions of this book could be written. Huge thanks to Joel McIver for his patience and wisdom on the finer details of book writing and publishing. Thanks also to the members of Next Big Thing. And of course special thanks to Adam Parfrey, Bess Lovejoy, and Feral House for allowing this project to see the light of day.

Hails must also go out to the following people who—directly or indirectly—assisted in the making of this tome: Edward Ruff, Ilia Rodriguez, Jonathan Selzer, Sandra dos Santos, Ranth Patterson, Isabelle Uller, Vlad Spisak, Sinem and Kazım Uzunoglu, Marte Hennie, Jonathan Butlin, Alexander Milas, Niall Scott, Tommy Udo, Darrell Mayhew, Miranda Yardley, Louise Brown, Jonathan Horsley, Jill Liebisch, Adam Sagir, Dante Bonutto, Gareth Elliot, Matthew Vickerstaff, Jaap Wagemaker, Darren Toms, Lee Barrett, Dan Tobin, Jarne Brauns, Patricia Thomas, Andy Turner, Mathias Løken, Paul Groundwell, Sandra Hagblom, Michael S. Berberian, Gunnar Sauermann, Michelle Kerr, Gus Ratcliffe, Angela Davey, Dave Pybus, Guillaume Warren, Guro Juul Anderson, Eleanor Goodman, Ryan Förster, Talita Jenman, Martin Kvam, Yvette Uhlmann, Stefan Belda, Vanessa Thorpe, Mighell Necroriser, Duff Battye, Jon Luis Jon, Vincent (Black Metal Museum Germany), Martin Beerwölf (Black Death Nostalgia), Etienne Durth (Baron Von Durth), Christina Gajny, Jannicke Langård, Bill Connoly, Rodrigo Jimenez, Emily Power, Christian Misje, Neil Harding, Warren Schofield, Mikko Aspa, Ville Pystynen (Shatraug), Einar Einz Sjursø, Christophe Szpajdel, Jon Kristiansen (Metalion), Peter Tägtgren, Conrad Lant (Cronos), Jonas Åkerlund, Kim Petersen (King Diamond), Tom Gabriel Fischer, Ole Moe (Apollyon), Zhema Rodero, Gerry (Nocturnal Grave Desecrator and Black Winds), Michael Locher (Vorph), Sakis Tolis, George Zacharopoulos (Magus), Jason Ventura (Venien), Shawn Calizo (Goat), Attila Csihar, František Štorm, Marko Laiho (Nuclear Holocausto Vengeance), Jørn Stubberud (Necrobutcher), Kjetil Manheim, Sven Erik Kristiansen (Maniac), Rune Eriksen (Blasphemer), Gylve Nagell (Fenriz), Tomas Haugen (Samoth), Håvard Ellefsen (Mortiis), Terje Vik Schei (Tchort), Kai Johnny Mosaker (Trym), Vegard Tveitan (Ihsahn), Eirik Hundvin (Pytten), Steffen Simestad (Dolgar), Roger Tiegs (Infernus), Tom Cato Visnes (King), Kristian Espedal (Gaahl), Thomas Kronenes (Pest), Ivar Bjørnson, Grutle Kjellson, Daniel Davey, Paul Ryan, Gregory Moffitt, Robin Eaglestone, Sven Kopperud (Silenoz), Ian Kenneth Åkesson (Tjodalv), Simen Hestnæs (ICS Vortex), Willy Roussel (Meyhna'ch), Morgan Håkansson (Evil), Hans Rostén (Mortuus), Niklas Kvarforth, Robert Fudali (Darken), Adam Darski (Nergal), Kristoffer Rygg (Garm), Jørn Tunsberg, Jarle Kvåle (Hváll), Alan Averill (A.A. Nemtheanga), Tor-Helge Skei (Cernunnus), Svein Egil Hatlevik, Mirai Kawashima and Dr. Mikannibal, Yusaf Parvez (Vikotnik), Robin Malmberg (Mean), Preben (Prime Evil), Benny (Cerastes), Fabrizio Giannese (Malfeitor Fabban), Saint Vincent, Jonas Bergqvist (B), and Frank Allain (The Watcher). Thanks to the following for support: Metal Hammer, Record Collector, Decibel, The Quietus, Terrorizer, Thrash Hits, Zero Tolerance, Iron Fist, Revolver, Venia Mag, Metal Rules, Shu-izmz Radio, Lachryma Christi, Ave Noctum, Louder Than War, SoundShock, Rock Hard, Currentzz, Ruído Sonoro, Bizarre, Blunt, Norway Rock, Imperiumi, and of course anyone else who has helped in a personal or professional capacity since this list was written. Finally, respect goes to all those devoted souls who have helped keep this movement alive in one way or another since its inception.

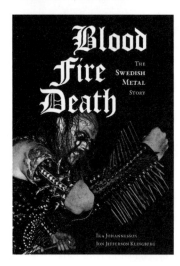
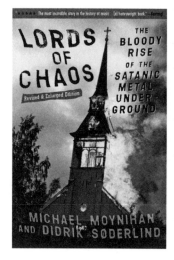
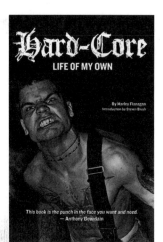
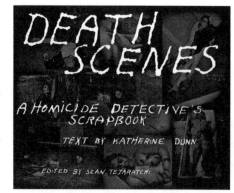